# Learning
# and
# Behavior

## *Fifth Edition*

## James E. Mazur

*Southern Connecticut State University*

Upper Saddle River, New Jersey 07458

**Library of Congress Cataloging-in-Publication Data**

Mazur, James E.,
    Learning and behavior / James E. Mazur.—5th ed.
      p. cm.
    Includes bibliographical references and index.
    ISBN 0-13-033715-3
      1. Learning, Psychology of. 2. Conditioned response. 3.
    Behavior modification. 4. Psychology, Comparative. I. Title.
BF318 .M38 2001
153.1'5—dc21
                           00-054719

VP, Editorial Director: Laura Pearson
Acquisitions Editor: Jayme Heffler
Editorial Assistant: April Dawn Klemm
Production Liaison: Fran Russello
Production Editor: Jessica Balch (Pine Tree Composition)
Prepress and Manufacturing Buyer: Tricia Kenny
Art Director: Jayne Conte
Cover Design: Bruce Kenselaar
Senior Marketing Manager: Sharon Cosgrove

Figure acknowledgments appear on pp. 419–422, which constitute an
extension of this copyright page.

This book was set in 10/11 Janson Text by Pine Tree Composition, Inc.
and was printed and bound by RR Donnelly & Sons Company. The
cover was printed by Phoenix Color Corp.

 © 2002, 1998, 1994, 1990, 1986 by Pearson Education, Inc.
Upper Saddle River, NJ 07458

Printed in the United States of America

10 9 8 7 6 5 4

**ISBN 0-13-033715-3**

Prentice-Hall International (UK) Limited, London
Prentice-Hall of Australia Pty. Limited, Sydney
Prentice-Hall Canada Inc., Toronto
Prentice-Hall Hispanoamericana, S.A., Mexico
Prentice-Hall of India Private Limited, New Delhi
Prentice-Hall of Japan, Inc., Tokyo
Pearson Education Asia Pte. Ltd., Singapore
Editora Prentice-Hall do Brasil, Ltda., Rio de Janeiro

*In memory of my parents, Ann and Lou Mazur, who responded to my early interests in science with encouragement, understanding, and patience.*

# Contents

**Preface**  xi

**1  THE PSYCHOLOGY OF LEARNING AND BEHAVIOR    1**

The Search for General Principles of Learning    2

The Nature of Scientific Theories    4

*An Example of a Theory about Behavior: Biorhythm Theory,  4  •  The Major
Components of Scientific Theories,  5  •  Judging Scientific Theories,  6
•  Issues and Techniques in Comparing Theory with Data,  7*

Behavioral and Cognitive Approaches to Learning    11

*The Use of Animal Subjects,  11  •  The Emphasis on External Events,  13*

On Free Will, Determinism, and Chaos Theory    16

**2  SIMPLE IDEAS, SIMPLE ASSOCIATIONS, AND SIMPLE CELLS    19**

Early Theories about the Association of Ideas    19

*Aristotle,  19  •  The British Associationists: Simple and Complex Ideas,  20
•  Thomas Brown's Secondary Principles of Association,  22*

Ebbinghaus's Experiments on Memory    23

*Ebbinghaus's Major Findings,  24  •  Ebbinghaus and the Associationists
Compared to Later Learning Theorists,  26*

Physiological Facts and Theories Related to Associationism    27

*The Basic Characteristics of Neurons,  27  •  Physiological Research on "Simple
Sensations,"  28  •  Physiological Research on "Complex Ideas,"  30
•  Physiological Research on Associative Learning,  32*

**3 INNATE BEHAVIOR PATTERNS AND HABITUATION 37**

Characteristics of Goal-Directed Systems 38

Reflexes 39

Tropisms and Orientation 40
*Kineses, 40 • Taxes, 41*

Sequences of Behavior 42
*Fixed Action Patterns, 42 • Reaction Chains, 44*

Habituation 45
*General Principles of Habituation, 47 • Physiological Mechanisms
of Habituation, 49 • Habituation in Emotional Responses:
The Opponent-Process Theory, 52*

**4 BASIC PRINCIPLES OF CLASSICAL CONDITIONING 58**

Pavlov's Discovery and Its Impact 58
*The Standard Paradigm of Classical Conditioning, 59 • The Variety of
Conditioned Responses, 60 • Pavlov's Stimulus Substitution Theory, 63
• S-S or S-R Connections?, 65 • Pavlov's Influence on Psychology, 66*

Basic Conditioning Phenomena 67
*Acquisition, 67 • Extinction, 68 • Spontaneous Recovery, 69 •
Disinhibition, 70 • Rapid Reacquisition, 70 • Conditioned Inhibition, 71
• Generalization and Discrimination, 72*

Temporal Relationships between CS and US 73
*CS-US Correlations, 75*

Other Conditioning Arrangements 76
*Higher-Order Conditioning, 76 • Sensory Preconditioning, 78*

Classical Conditioning Outside the Laboratory 78
*Classical Conditioning and Emotional Responses, 78 • Classical Conditioning
and the Immune System, 79 • Applications in Behavior Therapy, 80*

**5 THEORIES AND RESEARCH ON CLASSICAL CONDITIONING 87**

Theories of Associative Learning 88
*The Blocking Effect, 88 • The Rescorla-Wagner Model: Basic Concepts, 89
• The Rescorla-Wagner Model: Equations and Mathematical, Examples, 92
• Theories of CS Effectiveness, 96 • Comparator Theories
of Conditioning, 98 • Summary, 99*

Types of Associations 99
*Associations in First-Order Conditioning, 99 • Associations in Second-Order
Conditioning, 100 • Associations Involving Contextual Stimuli, 100
• CS-CS Associations, 101 • Occasion Setting, 102 • Summary, 103*

Biological Constraints on Classical Conditioning 103
*The Contiguity Principle and Taste-Aversion Learning, 104 • Biological
Preparedness in Taste-Aversion Learning, 105 • Biological Preparedness*

*in Human Learning, 107 • Biological Constraints and the General-Principle Approach, 108*

## The Form of the Conditioned Response    110
*Drug Tolerance as a Conditioned Response, 110 • Conditioned Opponent Theories, 112*

## Physiological Research on Classical Conditioning    114
*Research With Primitive Creatures, 114 • Research With Mammals and Other Vertebrates, 116 • Research With Human Subjects, 117*

## 6    BASIC PRINCIPLES OF OPERANT CONDITIONING    121

### The Law of Effect    121
*Thorndike's Experiments, 121 • Guthrie and Horton: Evidence for a Mechanical Strengthening Process, 123 • Superstitious Behaviors, 124 • Problems With the "Stop-Action Principle," 128*

### The Procedure of Shaping, or Successive Approximations    129
*Shaping Lever Pressing in a Rat, 129 • Shaping Behaviors in the Classroom, 131 • Shaping as a Tool in Behavior Modification, 131 • Making Shaping More Precise: Percentile Schedules, 132 • Versatility of the Shaping Process, 133*

### The Research of B. F. Skinner    134
*The Free Operant, 134 • The Three-Term Contingency, 135 • Other Basic Principles: Acquisition, Extinction, Spontaneous Recovery, Generalization, and Conditioned Reinforcement, 136 • Response Chains, 137*

### Biological Constraints on Operant Conditioning    139
*Instinctive Drift, 139 • Autoshaping, 141 • Reconciling Reinforcement Theory and Biological Constraints, 145*

## 7    REINFORCEMENT SCHEDULES: EXPERIMENTAL ANALYSES AND APPLICATIONS    148

### Plotting Moment-to-Moment Behavior: The Cumulative Recorder    148

### The Four Simple Reinforcement Schedules    149
*Fixed Ratio, 149 • Variable Ratio, 150 • Fixed Interval, 152 • Variable Interval, 153 • Extinction and the Four Simple Schedules, 154 • Other Reinforcement Schedules, 155*

### Factors Affecting Performance on Reinforcement Schedules    156
*Behavioral Momentum, 157 • Contingency-Shaped versus Rule-Governed Behaviors, 157 • Reinforcement History, 159 • Summary, 159*

### The Experimental Analysis of Reinforcement Schedules    160
*The Cause of the FR Postreinforcement Pause, 160 • Comparisons of VR and VI Response Rates, 161*

Applications of Operant Conditioning    165
*Teaching Language to Autistic Children, 165  •  The Token Economy, 167
•  Reinforcing Employee Performance, 168  •  Behavioral Marital
Therapy, 170  •  Summary, 171*

**8    AVOIDANCE AND PUNISHMENT    173**

Avoidance    174
*A Representative Experiment, 174  •  Two-Factor Theory, 175  •  Evidence
Supporting Two-Factor Theory, 176  •  Problems With Two-Factor
Theory, 176  •  One-Factor Theory, 177  •  Cognitive Theory, 179  •
Biological Constraints in Avoidance Learning, 181  •  Conclusions about the
Theories of Avoidance, 182  •  Flooding as Behavior Therapy, 183*

Learned Helplessness    184

Punishment    186
*Is Punishment the Opposite of Reinforcement?, 187  •  Factors Influencing
the Effectiveness of Punishment, 188  •  Disadvantages of Using
Punishment, 190  •  Negative Punishment, 192*

Behavior Decelerators in Behavior Therapy    192
*Positive Punishment, 192  •  Negative Punishment: Response Cost and
Time-Out, 194  •  Other Techniques for Behavior Deceleration, 196
•  The Aversives Controversy, 199*

**9    THEORIES AND RESEARCH ON OPERANT CONDITIONING    202**

The Role of the Response    202

The Role of the Reinforcer  203
*Is Reinforcement Necessary for Operant Conditioning?, 203  •  Expectations
About the Reinforcer, 205  •  Is Reinforcement at Work in Classical
Conditioning?, 206  •  Can Reinforcement Control Visceral Responses?, 208
•  Biofeedback, 209*

How Can We Predict What Will Be a Reinforcer?    212
*Need Reduction, 212  •  Drive Reduction, 213  •  Trans-Situationality, 214
•  Premack's Principle, 214  •  Response Deprivation Theory, 218
•  The Functional Analysis of Behaviors and Reinforcers, 219*

Behavioral Economics    221
*Optimization: Theory and Research, 221  •  Elasticity and Inelasticity
of Demand, 223  •  Behavioral Economics and Drug Abuse, 224*

**10    STIMULUS CONTROL AND CONCEPT FORMATION    227**

Generalization Gradients    227
*Measuring Generalization Gradients, 227  •  What Causes Generalization
Gradients?, 229*

Is Stimulus Control Absolute or Relational?    232
*Transposition and Peak Shift, 233 • Spence's Theory of Excitatory and Inhibitory Gradients, 234 • The Intermediate-Size Problem, 235 • Evaluating the Two Theories, 236*

Behavioral Contrast    238

"Errorless" Discrimination Learning    240

Transfer of Learning After Discrimination Training    242

Concept Formation    244
*The Structure of Natural Categories, 245 • Animal Studies on Natural Concept Formation, 246 • Developing Stimulus Equivalence, 248*

Stimulus Control in Behavior Modification    249
*Stimulus Equivalence Training, 250 • Study Behavior, 250 • Insomnia, 251*

**11    COMPARATIVE COGNITION    253**

Memory    253
*Short-Term Memory, or Working Memory, 254 • Rehearsal, 259 • Long-Term Memory, or Reference Memory, 263*

Time, Number, and Serial Patterns    265
*Experiments on an "Internal Clock," 265 • Counting, 268 • Serial Pattern Learning, 270 • Chunking, 270*

Language and Reasoning    273
*Teaching Language to Animals, 273 • Reasoning by Animals, 277*

**12    LEARNING BY OBSERVATION    282**

Theories of Imitation    283
*Imitation as an Instinct, 283 • Imitation as an Operant Response, 285 • Imitation as a Generalized Operant Response, 285 • Bandura's Theory of Imitation, 286 • Which Theory of Imitation is Best?, 288*

Factors That Affect the Likelihood of Imitation    290

Interactions Between Observational Learning and Operant Conditioning    291
*Achievement Motivation, 291 • Aggression, 292*

The Influence of Television    293

What Can Be Learned through Observation?    295
*Phobias, 295 • Drug Use and Addictions, 295 • Cognitive Development, 296 • Moral Standards and Behavior, 297*

Modeling in Behavior Therapy    297
*Facilitation of Low-Probability Behaviors, 298 • Acquisition of New
Behaviors, 298 • Elimination of Fears and Unwanted Behaviors,
299 • Videotape Self-Modeling, 301*

Conclusions: The Sophisticated Skill of Learning
by Observation    307

**13   LEARNING MOTOR SKILLS    304**

The Variety of Motor Skills    304

Variables Affecting Motor Learning and Performance    306
*Reinforcement and Knowledge of Results, 306 • Knowledge of
Performance, 309 • Distribution of Practice, 311 • Observational Learning
of Motor Skills, 312 • Transfer from Previous Training, 312 • Ironic
Errors in Movement, 314*

Theories of Motor-Skill Learning    314
*Adams's Two-Stage Theory, 314 • Schmidt's Schema Theory, 317*

Learning Movement Sequences    320
*The Response Chain Approach, 320 • Motor Programs, 321*

**14   CHOICE    327**

The Matching Law    328
*Herrnstein's (1961) Experiment, 328 • Other Experiments on Matching,
329 • Deviations from Matching, 330 • Varying the Quality and Amount
of Reinforcement, 331 • An Application to Single Schedules, 332*

Theories of Choice Behavior    335
*Matching as an Explanatory Theory, 336 • Melioration Theory, 336
• Optimization Theory as an Explanation of Matching, 337 • Momentary
Maximization Theory, 341 • Other Theories of Choice, 343*

Self-Control Choices    344
*The Ainslie-Rachlin Theory, 345 • Animal Studies on Self-Control, 346
• Factors Affecting Self-Control in Children, 349 • Techniques for
Improving Self-Control, 350*

Other Choice Situations    351
*Preference for Variability, 352 • Risk Taking, 353 • The Tragedy
of the Commons, 354*

**Glossary    358**
**References    373**
**Acknowledgments    419**
**Author Index    423**
**Subject Index    435**

# Preface

The purpose of this book is to introduce the reader to the branch of psychology that deals with how people and animals learn and how their behaviors are later changed as a result of this learning. This is a broad topic, for nearly all of our behaviors are influenced by prior learning experiences in some way. Because examples of learning and learned behaviors are so numerous, the goal of most psychologists in this field has been to discover general principles that are applicable to many different species and many different learning situations. What continues to impress and inspire me after many years in this field is that it is indeed possible to make such general statements about learning and behavior. This book describes some of the most important principles, theories, controversies, and experiments that have been produced by this branch of psychology in its first century.

This text is designed to be suitable for introductory or intermediate level courses in learning, conditioning, or the experimental analysis of behavior. No prior knowledge of psychology is assumed, but the reading may be a bit easier for those who have had a course in introductory psychology. Many of the concepts and theories in this field are fairly abstract, and to make them more concrete (and more relevant), I have included many real-world examples and analogies. In addition, most of the chapters include sections that describe how the theories and principles have been used in the applied field of behavior modification.

Roughly speaking, the book proceeds from the simple to the complex, both with respect to the difficulty of the material and the types of learning that are discussed. Chapter 1 discusses the nature of scientific theories and experiments, and it outlines the behavioral approach to learning and contrasts it with the cognitive approach. Chapter 2 first describes some of the earliest theories about the learning process, and then presents some basic findings about the physiological mechanisms of learning. Chapter 3 discusses innate behaviors and the simplest type of learning, habituation. Many of the terms and ideas introduced here reappear in later chapters on classical conditioning, operant conditioning, and motor skills learning.

The next two chapters deal with classical conditioning. Chapter 4 begins with basic principles and ends with some therapeutic applications. Chapter 5 describes more recent theoretical developments and experimental findings in this area. The next three chapters discuss the various facets of operant conditioning: Chapter 6 covers the basic principles and terminology of positive reinforcement, Chapter 7 covers schedules of reinforcement and applications, and Chapter 8 covers negative reinforcement and punishment. Chapters 9 and 10 have a more theoretical orientation (although many empirical findings are described here as well). Chapter 9 presents differing views on such fundamental questions as what constitutes a reinforcer and what conditions are necessary for learning to occur. Chapter 10 takes a more thorough look at generalization and discrimination than was possible in earlier chapters, and it also examines research on concept formation.

Chapter 11 surveys a wide range of findings in the rapidly growing area of comparative cognition. Chapters 12 and 13 discuss two types of learning that are given little or no emphasis in many texts on learning—observational learning and motor-skills learning. These chapters were included because a substantial portion of human learning involves either observation or the development of new motor skills. Readers might well be puzzled or disappointed (with some justification) with a text on learning that included no mention of these topics. Finally, Chapter 14 presents an overview of behavioral research on choice.

This fifth edition includes a number of changes, both to help students learn the material and to keep the information up to date. A glossary has been added so that readers can quickly find the definitions of key terms. Each chapter now includes references to a few Internet sites that provide further information or demonstrations of the concepts presented in the chapter. Each chapter has also been updated with new studies that reflect recent developments in the field. One trend in the field of learning seems to be the increasing use of human subjects in research on basic behavioral processes. This edition reflects this trend by including recent research with human subjects in several different areas, including classical conditioning, physiological mechanisms, rule-governed behavior, biological preparedness, stimulus control, and others.

I owe thanks to many people for their help in different aspects of the preparation of this book. Many of my thoughts about learning and about psychology in general were shaped by my discussions with the late Richard Herrnstein, my teacher, advisor, and friend. I am also grateful to several others who read portions of the book and gave me valuable feedback: Mark Branch, University of Florida; Gary Brosvic, Rider University; Valerie Farmer-Dougan, Illinois State University; Adam Goodie, University of Georgia; Kenneth P. Hillner, South Dakota State University; Peter Holland, Duke University; Ann Kelley, Harvard University; Kathleen McCartney, University of New Hampshire; David Mostofsky, Boston University; Thomas Moye, Coe College; Jack Nation, Texas A & M University; David Schaal, West Virginia University; James R. Sutterer, Syracuse University; E. A. Wasserman, University of Iowa; and Joseph Wister, Chatham College. In addition, I thank Marge Averill, Stan Averill, John Bailey, Chris Berry, Paul Carroll, David Coe, David Cook, Susan Herrnstein, Margaret Makepeace, Margaret Nygren, Steven Pratt, and James Roach for their competent and cheerful help on different editions of this book. I am also grateful for the assistance and advice provided by Jayme Heffler of Prentice Hall. Finally, I thank my wife, Laurie Averill, for her help on this edition.

J. E. M.

## CHAPTER 1

# The Psychology of Learning and Behavior

If you know nothing about the branch of psychology called *learning*, you may have some misconceptions about the scope of this field. I can recall browsing through the course catalog as a college freshman and coming across a course offered by the Department of Psychology with the succinct title "Learning." Without bothering to read the course description, I wondered about the contents of this course. Learning, I reasoned, is primarily the occupation of students. Would this course teach students better study habits, better reading and note-taking skills? Or did the course examine learning in children, covering such topics as the best ways to teach a child to read, to write, to do arithmetic? Did it deal with children who have learning disabilities? It was difficult to imagine spending an entire semester on these topics, which sounded fairly narrow and specialized for an introductory level course.

My conception of the psychology of learning was wrong in several respects. First, a psychology course emphasizing learning in the classroom would probably have a title such as "Educational Psychology" rather than "Learning." My second error was the assumption that the psychology of learning is a narrow field. A moment's reflection reveals that students do not have a monopoly on learning. Children

learn a great deal before ever entering a classroom, and adults must continue to adapt to an ever-changing environment. Because learning occurs at all ages, the psychological discipline of learning places no special emphasis on the subset of learning that occurs in the classroom. Furthermore, since the human being is only one of thousands of species on this planet that have the capacity to learn, the psychological discipline of learning is by no means restricted to the study of human beings. For reasons to be explained, a large percentage of all psychological experiments on learning have used nonhuman subjects. Though they may have their faults, psychologists in the field of learning are not chauvinistic about the human species.

Although even specialists have difficulty defining the term **learning** precisely, most would agree that it is a process of change that occurs as a result of an individual's experience. Psychologists who study learning are interested in this process wherever it occurs—in adults, in school children, in other mammals, in reptiles, in insects. This may sound like a large subject matter, but the field of learning is even broader than this, because researchers in this area study not only the **process** of learning but also the **product** of learning—the long-term changes in an individual's behavior that result from a learning experience.

An example may help to clarify the distinction between process and product. Suppose you glance out the window and see a raccoon near some garbage cans in the backyard. As you watch, the raccoon gradually manages to knock over a garbage can, remove the lid, and tear open the garbage bag inside. Imagine that the smell of food attracted the raccoon to the garbage cans, but that it has never encountered such objects before. If we were interested in studying this particular type of behavior, many different questions would probably come to mind. Some questions might deal with the learning process itself: Did the animal open the can purely by accident, or was it guided by some "plan of action"? What factors determine how long the raccoon will persist in manipulating the garbage can if it is not immediately successful in obtaining something to eat? Such questions deal with what might be called the **acquisition** phase, or the period in which the animal is acquiring a new skill.

Once the raccoon has had considerable experience in dealing with garbage cans, it may encounter few surprises in its expeditions through the neighborhood. Although the acquisition process is essentially over as far as garbage cans are concerned, we can continue to examine the raccoon's behavior, asking somewhat different questions that deal with the **performance** of learned behaviors. The raccoon will have only intermittent success in obtaining food from garbage cans—sometimes a can will be empty and sometimes it will contain nothing edible. How frequently will the raccoon visit a given backyard, and how will the animal's success rate affect the frequency of its visits? The animal will probably be more successful at specific times of the day or week. Will its visits occur at the most advantageous times? Such questions concern the end product of the learning process, the raccoon's new behavior patterns. This text is entitled *Learning and Behavior*, rather than simply *Learning*, to reflect the fact that the psychology of learning encompasses both the acquisition process and the long-term behavior that results.

## THE SEARCH FOR GENERAL PRINCIPLES OF LEARNING

Because the psychology of learning deals with all types of learning and learned behaviors in all types of creatures, its scope is broad indeed. Think, for a moment, of the different behaviors you performed in the first hour or two after rising this morning. How many of them would not have been possible without prior learning? In most cases, the decision is easy to make. Getting dressed, washing your face, making your bed, and going to the dining room for breakfast are all examples of behaviors that depend mostly or entirely on previous learning experiences. The behavior of eating breakfast depends on several different types of learning, including the selection of appropriate types and quantities of food, the proper use of utensils, and the development of coordinated hand, eye, and mouth movements. Except for behaviors that must occur continuously for a person to survive, such as breathing and the beating of the heart, it is difficult to think of many human behaviors that do not depend on prior learning.

Considering all of the behaviors of humans and other creatures that involve learning, the scope of this branch of psychology may seem hopelessly broad. How can any single discipline hope to make any useful statements about all these different instances of learning? It should be clear that it would make no sense to study, one by one, every different example of learning that one might come across. This is not the approach of most researchers who study learning. Instead, their strategy has been to select, presumably on an arbitrary basis, a few learning situations that are studied in detail, and then to attempt to generalize from these situations to other instances of learning. Thus the goal of much of the research on learning has been to develop **general principles** that are applicable across a wide range of species and learning situations.

B. F. Skinner, one of the most influential figures in the history of psychology, made his belief in this strategy explicit in his first major work, *The Behavior of Organisms* (1938). In his initial studies, Skinner chose white rats as subjects and lever-pressing as a response. An individual rat would be placed in a small experimental chamber containing little more than a lever and a tray into which food was occasionally presented after the rat pressed the lever. A modern version of a chamber similar to the one Skinner used is shown in Figure 1-1. In studying the behavior of rats in such a sparse environment, Skinner felt that he could discover principles that govern the behavior of many animals, including human beings, in the more complex environments found outside the psychological laboratory. The work of Skinner and his students will be examined in depth beginning in Chapter 6, so you will have the opportunity to decide for yourself whether Skinner's strategy has proven to be successful.

This strategy of searching for general principles is certainly not unique to the psychology of learning. Attempts to discover principles or laws with wide applicability are a part of most scientific endeavors. For example, a general principle in physics is the law of gravity, which predicts, among other things, the distance a freely falling object will drop in a given period of time. If an object starts from a stationary position and falls for $t$ seconds, the equation $d = 16t^2$ predicts the distance (in feet) that the object will fall. The law of gravity is certainly a general principle, because in theory it applies to any falling object, whether a rock, a baseball, or a skydiver. According to the law of gravity, neither the weight, chemical composition, shape, temperature, political persuasion, nor any other characteristic of the object is relevant: Notice that the above equation contains no terms for any of these properties.

Nevertheless, the law of gravity has its limitations. As with most scientific principles, it is applicable only when certain criteria are met. Two restrictions on the above equation are that it applies (1) only to objects close to the earth's surface, and (2) only as long as no other force, such as air resistance, plays a role. If we chose to ignore these criteria, it would be easy to "disprove" the law of gravity. We could simply drop a rock and a leaf and show that the leaf falls much more slowly. But once the restrictions on the law of gravity are acknowledged, our experiment proves nothing, since we did not eliminate the influence of air resistance. This example shows why it is frequently necessary to retreat to the laboratory in order to perform a meaningful test of a scientific principle. In the laboratory, the role of air resistance can be minimized through the use of a vacuum chamber. The leaf and the rock will fall at the same rate in this artificial environment, thereby verifying the law of gravity. For similar reasons, orderly principles of learning and behavior that might be obscured by a multitude of extraneous factors in the natural environment may be uncovered in a laboratory environment.

Once the restrictions on the law of gravity are specified, a naive reader might conclude that the law has no practical utility, because the natural environment provides no vacuums near the earth's surface. However, this conclusion is correct only if extremely precise measurements are demanded, because for many solid objects with a roughly spherical shape, the role of air resistance is so negligible that the law of gravity makes reasonably accurate predictions. Similarly, it would be naive to

**FIGURE 1-1**   An experimental chamber in which a rat can receive food pellets by pressing a lever. The pellets are delivered into the square opening below the lever. This chamber is also equipped with lights and a speaker so that visual and auditory signals can be presented.

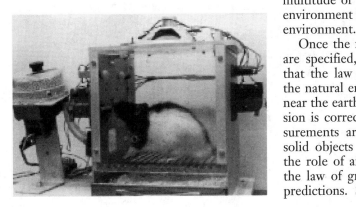

assume that a psychological principle has no relevance to the natural environment simply because that principle is most clearly demonstrated in the laboratory. Beginning with Chapter 2, every chapter in this text will introduce several new principles of learning and behavior, nearly all of which have been investigated in laboratory settings. To demonstrate that these principles have applicability to more natural settings, each chapter will also describe a number of real-world situations in which these principles play an important role. Many of the examples will come from the realm of behavior modification, a discipline that makes use of learning principles to help people cope with or cure a wide range of psychological problems.

## THE NATURE
## OF SCIENTIFIC THEORIES

Before beginning to examine any theories about learning, it is important to understand the major characteristics of scientific theories and the criteria frequently used to evaluate them. As with many abstract concepts, the characteristics of scientific theories may be best conveyed by considering a concrete example. Therefore, let us examine a specific theory of human behavior and evaluate its strengths and weaknesses as a scientific theory.

### An Example of a Theory
### about Behavior: Biorhythm Theory

Although it was probably most popular in the 1970s, biorhythm theory continues to have its advocates today. I first encountered this theory in a 1977 *New York Times* article, which reported that at least five National Football League teams were using information about the biorhythms of their players and those of their opponents to help them plan game strategies. Proponents of biorhythm theory claim that simply by knowing a player's date of birth, they can consult a chart that will predict how well the player is likely to perform on a given day. If these claims are true, the implications for a game strategy are obvious. If your opponent's dangerous wide receiver is due for

a poor performance, you can avoid using double coverage and make better use of your defensive players. If your running back will have a favorable biorhythm pattern on Sunday, you should plan to rely more heavily on your running game. A head coach would be foolish not to take biorhythms into account if they can actually affect a player's performance. But what are biorhythms, and how are they supposed to affect behavior?

According to Bernard Gittelson (1977, 1996), a proponent of biorhythm theory, the basic idea is that every person's behavior is influenced by three bodily cycles—a physical cycle lasting 23 days, an emotional cycle lasting 28 days, and an intellectual cycle lasting 33 days. Figure 1-2 shows an example of a person's biorhythm cycles over a two-month period. Each of the three cycles is in the positive range for half of a cycle and in the negative range for the other half. The positive range of a cycle is supposedly associated with good performance (for instance, smart decisions, creative ideas, above-average physical skills). On the other hand, if a person's cycle is low, he or she will tend to make mistakes, have accidents, and simply perform worse than average on most everyday tasks. Besides these high points and low points of the three bodily cycles, the times when a cycle crosses the zero mark (as shown by the horizontal line in Figure 1-2)

**FIGURE 1-2**   A typical pattern of a person's three bodily cycles over a two-month period, as hypothesized by biorhythm theory.

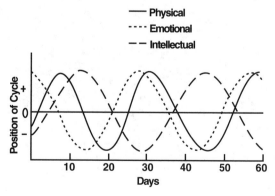

also play an important role in biorhythm theory. Days when a cycle crosses the zero point are called "critical days," and these are also times when a person's behavior is likely to be subpar.

The *Times* article described a number of cases that provide support for biorhythm theory. For instance, on November 19, 1977, when Ohio State football coach Woody Hayes punched a television cameraman on the sidelines as his team was losing, both his physical and intellectual cycles were low. On the following day, when Walter Payton of the Chicago Bears set a new NFL single-game rushing record, all three of his cycles were high. Biorhythm theorists suggest that examples such as these demonstrate how biorhythms can influence a person's performance.

How can the state of a person's biorhythms be determined simply by knowing the person's birthday? Biorhythm theory proposes that on the day a child is born, all three biorhythm cycles are at the zero position, and they begin by moving in the positive direction. Since the cycles are said to have periods of exactly 23, 28, and 33 days, the position of each cycle can be calculated for any future day. For instance, since the emotional cycle is said to have a period of 28 days, this cycle should reach a peak on the child's seventh day of life, return to zero on the fourteenth day, reach a low point on the twenty-first day, and so on.

If it is true that all people undergo such regular changes in their performance levels, and if a person's good and bad days can be predicted in advance, it should be obvious that biorhythms have implications that extend to many situations besides professional football. Gittelson (1977) described a number of examples of how biorhythm theory has been put into practice. At the time his book was written, over 5,000 Japanese companies were using biorhythm charts for all their employees in an attempt to reduce occupational accidents. A large Japanese bus company was sending each of its drivers a warning card whenever the driver had a critical day, urging extra caution. Swissair adopted a rule that no plane could be flown by a pilot and copilot who were both experiencing critical days.

Biorhythm theory is an example of a theory about behavior—it attempts to predict when a person's behavior during a variety of everyday tasks will be above average and when it will be below average. As a theory of behavior, biorhythm theory contains all the major components of the typical psychological theory. We can therefore use biorhythm theory as a means of examining the features that most psychological theories and most scientific theories have in common.

## The Major Components of Scientific Theories

Science is an enterprise concerned with gaining information about **causality,** or the relationship between cause and effect. A simple example of a cause is the movement of a paddle as it strikes a Ping-Pong ball; the effect is the movement of the ball through the air. In psychology and other sciences, the word **cause** is often replaced by the term **independent variable.** This term implies that the experimenter is often "free" to vary the independent variable as he or she desires (for example, the experimenter can control the speed of the paddle as it strikes the ball). The term **dependent variable** replaces the word **effect,** and this term is used because the effect *depends* on some characteristic of the independent variable (the flight of the ball depends on the speed of the paddle). The conventions of science demand that both the independent and dependent variables be observable events, as is the case in the Ping-Pong example. In the case of biorhythm theory, the independent variable is the number of days that have elapsed between a person's date of birth and some test day. The dependent variable is the person's level of performance on some specified task on the test day.

To predict the relationship between independent and dependent variables, many scientific theories make use of what are called **intervening variables.** Intervening variables are purely theoretical concepts that cannot be observed directly. To predict the flight of a Ping-Pong ball, Newtonian physics relies on a number of intervening variables, including *force,* *mass,* *air resistance,* and *gravity.* You can probably surmise that the intervening variables of biorhythm theory are the three bodily cycles with their specified time periods. It should be emphasized that not all psychological theories include intervening variables, and some psychologists object to their use precisely because they are not directly observable. Later in this chapter, the debate over the use of intervening variables will be examined.

The final major component of a scientific theory is its **syntax,** or the rules and definitions that state how the independent and dependent variables are to be measured and that specify the relationships among independent variables, intervening variables, and dependent variables. It is the syntax of biorhythm theory that describes how to use a person's birthday to calculate the current status of the three cycles. The syntax also relates the cycles to the dependent variable, namely performance, by stating that positive cycles should cause high levels of performance, whereas low or critical cycles should cause low performance levels. To summarize, the components of a scientific theory can be divided into four major categories: independent variables, dependent variables, intervening variables, and syntax.

## Judging Scientific Theories

When reading about biorhythm theory for the first time, most people will form some opinion about its validity. Some may be convinced by the examples of Woody Hayes and Walter Payton and conclude that the theory is correct; others may decide the examples are merely coincidences and remain skeptical. In this text, however, we will be less concerned with how the average person thinks about behavior and more concerned with how the scientist thinks about behavior. Let us therefore examine some of the major criteria used by scientists to evaluate a theory for its scientific merit, and we can try to determine how well biorhythm theory meets these criteria. Although there is no universally accepted list of standards for judging scientific theories, the following five criteria are generally thought to be among the most important.

1. *Testability (Falsifiability).* A theory should make unambiguous predictions that can be tested against the facts. This criterion is often called **falsifiability,** for it is generally agreed that a good theory is one that could, in principle, be proven wrong. One way a psychological theory might fail to meet this criterion is if it did not make any clear predictions about observable behavior. At first glance, it may seem that biorhythm theory makes very clear predictions: High biorhythm cycles predict good performance, and low or critical cycles predict poor performance. Unfortunately, the relationship between biorhythms and performance is not so straightforward, because on many days one or two cycles will be in a positive phase and the other one or two will be negative, and it will not be clear what prediction to make from such a mixed pattern.

These uncertainties in prediction make biorhythm theory more difficult to test than it might be. A scientific theory must make definite predictions, because if there is room for reinterpretation and modification of the predictions after the data are collected, any result can be explained by the theory. Suppose we want to predict the performance of a weightlifter for whom one cycle is low and the other two are high. If the weightlifter has a good performance, we could say that this was because of the two positive cycles (therefore, the theory is supported). If the weightlifter's performance is poor, we could attribute this to the one negative cycle (therefore, the theory is supported). This example shows how ambiguity about the relationship between intervening variables and observable behavior can make a theory unfalsifiable, and a theory that cannot be proven wrong has no predictive value.

2. *Simplicity.* If two theories are equal in their ability to account for a body of data, the theory that does so with the smaller number of hypothetical constructs and assumptions is to be preferred (Popper, 1959). Without a competing theory with which to compare biorhythm theory, it is not possible to make any meaningful judgment about its simplicity. However, the dimension of simplicity can be illustrated by considering two theories about the solar system. Ptolemy proposed that the

earth is at the center of the solar system. In order to account for the data (the motions of the sun, stars, and planets), he had to propose a cumbersome theoretical system involving numerous interconnected cycles and epicycles. By hypothesizing that the sun is at the center of the solar system, Copernicus was able to account for the same set of observations with many fewer theoretical assumptions. Although both theories can predict the motions of objects in the night sky, Copernicus's theory is scientifically preferable because of its comparative simplicity (even if we ignore other, more modern observations that support Copernicus's theory but not Ptolemy's theory).

3. *Generality.* Theories that deal with more phenomena, with a greater range of observations, are usually judged to be better than theories of more restricted scope. If biorhythm theory only applied to football, it would be a less impressive theory. If it applied to tennis players, pole vaulters, and all other athletes, it would be a more general theory of sports performance. Actually, biorhythm theory is even more general than this. We have seen that it has been applied to the performances of people in many different occupations, including airline pilots, bus drivers, and factory workers. This broad generality is a virtue of biorhythm theory.

4. *Fruitfulness.* An important property of a scientific theory is its ability to stimulate further research and further thinking about a particular topic. Part of the logic behind this criterion is that although a theory may eventually prove to be incorrect or of limited accuracy, it will have served a useful function if it provoked new studies that otherwise would not have been done. Often an experiment designed to test a particular theory will uncover a new phenomenon, one that the theory cannot explain. This can be a healthy state of affairs for a scientific discipline, because the new information can pave the way for the development of a more sophisticated theory. With respect to biorhythm theory, Gittelson (1996) described a large number of studies that have been conducted to test the theory. It is possible that research on the patterns of good and bad job performances, though stimulated by biorhythm theory, might lead to a bet-

ter understanding of occupational accidents, regardless of whether biorhythm theory is supported or refuted.

5. *Agreement with the Data.* This final criterion is the most obvious test of a theory—how well it coincides with the facts. If a theory makes predictions that clearly contradict some well-established facts, the theory must be either modified or discarded. On the other hand, if a theory accounts for some specified body of facts fairly well, it may be retained, at least temporarily. This criterion leads us to the complex topic of how research is conducted to test scientific hypotheses.

## Issues and Techniques in Comparing Theory with Data

The evidence for biorhythm theory exemplifies three different methods frequently used to collect psychological data, each of which will be encountered in later chapters of this book. For the purposes of this introduction, only the most fundamental characteristics of these research methods will be discussed. (Many texts have been written about the research strategies used in the behavioral sciences; for example, Bordens & Abbott, 1998; Cozby, 1997; Elmes, Kantowitz, & Roediger, 1999; McBurney, 2000.)

*Anecdotes or Case Histories.* Much of the evidence in support of biorhythm theory comes from anecdotes about famous people such as Walter Payton and Woody Hayes. Gittelson (1996) cited numerous examples about celebrities who suffered from accidents or tragedies on days when their biorhythms were particularly unfavorable. For example, he reported that on the day when President Gerald Ford decided to grant Richard Nixon an unconditional pardon for any possible crimes committed during the Watergate affair (a decision that many political analysts felt was a mistake), Ford's intellectual and emotional cycles were low. As another example, actress Marilyn Monroe died of an overdose of sleeping pills on August 5, 1962, when, according to Gittelson, her physical cycle was critical and her emotional cycle was low. Gittelson's book is filled with dozens of examples of this nature. Although such anecdotes certainly make interesting reading, from a scientific point of view this type of evidence has serious shortcomings. Can you see any problems with these types of data?

Gittelson's use of anecdotes is in some ways similar to the **case history** approach used in some branches of psychology, including behavior modification (particularly in reports about patients with rare psychological disorders, where a clinician may encounter only one or two cases of the disorder). A concern that is frequently raised about the use of case histories is that the cases reported may represent a **biased sample.** That is, perhaps the psychologist has reported only those cases where treatment of the disorder was successful, and not those where the treatment was ineffective. To avoid this type of criticism, clinical psychologists usually report such information as the number of cases of the disorder they have encountered, the number of patients selected for treatment, the criteria used to select these patients, and the number of cases in which treatment was judged to be successful. However, with the anecdotal evidence for biorhythm theory, we are given no such information. Although the cases of Gerald Ford, Marilyn Monroe, and others seem to support the theory, we do not know how many other cases Gittelson may have examined that did not support the theory. Perhaps Gittelson has reported 90 percent of the cases he has examined, or perhaps only 20 percent, with the remainder failing to support the theory. We have no way of knowing, and without this information the anecdotes are essentially worthless from a scientific standpoint.

*Observational Techniques.* This term will be used to denote a wide range of research techniques, including field observations (the simple observation of people or animals in natural environments), the use of surveys and questionnaires, and the use of archival data (the information contained in written documents and records). What these techniques have in common with the case history method is that the experimenter is a more or less passive observer, making no effort to manipulate the variables that control a subject's behavior. Unlike the case history approach, however, observational techniques always involve a systematic effort to obtain a representative sample from the population of interest.

Gittelson (1977) reported a number of studies that exemplify the observational method. In one case, a researcher named Newcomb took a random sample of 100 accident reports from the files of a utility company. Because the sample was chosen at random, we can assume that it was an unbiased sample of the entire population (that is, of all the accident reports on file for this company). Newcomb found that 53 of these accidents occurred on a worker's critical day. Unfortunately, we are not told what criteria Newcomb used to define a critical day. If he counted only those days on which a cycle crossed the zero point, then his findings are impressive, for only about 20 accidents would be expected on critical days by chance. However, in his work, Gittelson also treats the days before and after a cycle crosses the zero point as critical days. If Newcomb also used this three-day criterion for critical days, the results are not remarkable, since it can be shown that by chance alone 52 of the accidents should occur on such loosely defined critical days. The difference between the 52 accidents expected by chance and the 53 accidents actually counted could easily be the result of what statisticians call **sampling error.** That is, if several random samples of 100 accidents were drawn from the same files, there would almost certainly be differences in the number of critical-day accidents from sample to sample (perhaps 44 in the second sample, 58 in the third, 47 in the fourth, and so on).

The best solution to the problem of sampling error is to increase the amount of data in the sample, because with larger and larger samples, we can have increasing confidence that the sample is representative of the entire population. A number of observational studies on traffic accidents with larger sample sizes have found no correspondence between biorhythm cycles and the frequency of accidents (Pitariu, Bostenaru, Lucaciu, & Oachis, 1984; Trinkaus & Booke, 1982). Because of their larger sample sizes, we can have more confidence in these studies than in Newcomb's.

***Experimental Techniques.*** With observational methods, the researcher simply examines the independent and dependent variables as they already exist and tries to discern the relationship between them. In an experiment, the researcher actively manipulates the independent variable in some systematic way. The program of distributing warning cards to the drivers of a Japanese bus company on their critical days can therefore be called an experiment. The independent variable was whether or not the drivers were informed about their critical days. Accident rates from the year before the program began were compared with rates after the warning-card program was adopted. The logic of this experiment was that if drivers were aware of their critical days, they might use extra caution and thereby reduce their chances of an accident. In the first year of the warning cards, the accident rate for this company decreased by nearly 50 percent.

Although on the surface this result seems to support biorhythm theory, most psychologists would be very cautious about drawing any conclusions from this study. The problem is that besides the warning cards, many other variables that could affect the accident rate might have changed from one year to the next. Perhaps the decrease in accidents occurred because in the second year many of the drivers were more experienced. Perhaps the bus company replaced some of its unreliable drivers with new ones. Perhaps, on average, there were less severe weather conditions during the second year. This sort of variable—one that is not of interest to the researcher but can nevertheless affect the results of an experiment—is called a **confounding variable.** In any experiment where a single group of subjects experiences two or more conditions in succession, there is always the possibility that a confounding variable can affect the results.

One more explanation of the drop in accident rate deserves serious consideration. Whenever people realize they are participating in an experiment, there is the possibility of a **placebo effect.** In medical research, a **placebo** is a medically inactive pill that may be given to one group of patients while a second group receives an actual medication. If patients are not told whether the pills they are taking are the drug or the placebo, it is frequently found that patients from both groups will report the pills to be beneficial. Thus, although the placebo has no more curative powers than a spoonful of sugar, many patients report improvement simply because they expect the pill to help them. Placebo effects (also called **expectation effects**) can occur in behavioral research as well as in medicine. In the study of Japanese bus drivers, the drivers were certainly aware that the warning cards were designed to lower the accident rate, so it is possible that the decrease in accidents was merely a placebo effect. In this example, it is easy to speculate about the factors that could produce such an effect. When they received warning cards, the drivers probably devoted more thought to safety than usual. They may have considered how dangerous to their passengers and damaging to their careers an accident could be, and as a result they may have driven more carefully on those days.

The problems created by expectations do not necessarily disappear when subjects are not informed that they are participating in an experiment. Research by Rosenthal (1966) and others has shown that a sort of placebo effect can occur if only the person administering the experiment knows what sort of result is being sought. It is easy to imagine how the wishes of the experimenter can affect the outcome of an experiment. Suppose an experimenter is trying to prove that a particular type of training can help students solve simple geometry problems. One group, usually called the **experimental group,** receives the special training before taking the geometry test, whereas the second group, the **control group,** receives no initial training. If the experimenter who administers the test knows which subjects are experimental subjects and which are control subjects, the behavior of the experimenter (even one with the most honest intentions) may be slightly different for the two types of subjects. If an experimental subject rapidly solves a problem, the experimenter may say "correct" and have a hint of a smile. If a control subject gives a correct solution, the experimenter may again say "correct" but look worried or displeased. Such subtle differences in the experimenter's behavior can have large effects on a subject's performance.

To avoid placebo effects and experimenter effects, many studies employ a **double-blind** procedure, which means that neither the subject nor the person conducting the experiment knows whether that subject is in the control group or the experimental group. It often takes some ingenuity to devise a way of making the control subjects believe they are receiving some experimental treatment. Before reading further, can you think of a way to control for possible placebo effects in a study such as the one conducted with bus drivers in Japan?

If the accident rate of bus drivers decreases after they receive warning cards on critical days, this could be due to:

1. some confounding variable such as weather conditions,
2. a general increase in the drivers' concerns about safety,
3. a belief among drivers that they are receiving information that should help them avoid accidents, or
4. the opportunity to be more careful on critical days, when a driver might otherwise have an accident.

Gittelson proposed that the fourth possibility is correct, but to be convinced, we must control for the first three possibilities. One simple solution would be to place half of the drivers in an experimental group and half in a control group. Experimental subjects would receive warning cards on their critical days, as in the Japan study. Control subjects would receive just as many warning cards, but they would be distributed randomly, without consideration of the status of a driver's biorhythms. Neither the drivers nor their supervisors would know which drivers were receiving warning cards on critical days and which were receiving them randomly. You should return to the four possible explanations cited above to convince yourself that this procedure controls for the first three factors. If the experimental group had substantially fewer accidents than the control group, we would have to conclude that this was because they were given warning cards specifically on their critical days.

Hines (1998) conducted an extensive review of 134 studies that attempted to test biorhythm theory. Of these, 99 studies found no support for the theory. Of the 35 studies that claimed to show some support for the theory, Hines found that most suffered from flaws in design or data analysis. Some used periods of more than 24 hours as critical days, a problem discussed above in relation to Newcomb's study. Others had statistical errors or used questionable methods to analyze their data. Hines concluded that there is no good evidence for the validity of biorhythm theory.

***Statistics and Significance Tests.*** In the hypothetical experiment involving Japanese bus drivers, suppose the accident rate decreased 33 percent in the experimental group and 27 percent in the control group. This difference of 6 percent between groups might have resulted from the drivers' information about their biorhythms, or it could be simply the result of sampling error. How large a difference between two groups must we find before we can be confident that the result is due to our manipulation of the independent variable rather than to sampling error? In trying to answer this question, psychologists frequently rely on **inferential statistics** (so named because they assist the researcher in drawing inferences or theoretical conclusions from empirical results).

The use of statistics in behavioral research is a vast topic, and many texts describe the use of different statistical procedures and the logic behind them (for instance, Howell, 1999; Runyon, Coleman, & Pittenger, 2000; Thorne & Giesen, 2000). The most common question addressed by a statistical test is: What are the chances that an observed difference between two groups is simply due to sampling error? If the likelihood that the results are attributable to chance is low, then it is said that the difference between groups was **statistically signifi-**

**cant.** In statistical jargon, the term *significant* implies nothing about the importance of a finding; it simply means that it is unlikely that the result occurred by chance.

A result is usually called significant in psychological research if the probability that it occurred by chance is less than .05. We might read that a difference between an experimental group and a control group was "significant at the .05 level." This is another way of saying that so large a difference between groups would be expected only 5 times in 100 on the basis of chance alone. It is therefore highly probable that the difference was the result of the experimenter's manipulation of the independent variable.

## BEHAVIORAL AND COGNITIVE APPROACHES TO LEARNING

The field of learning is frequently associated with a general approach to psychology called **behaviorism,** which was the dominant approach to the investigation of learning for the first half of the twentieth century. During the 1960s, however, a new approach called **cognitive psychology** began to develop, and one of the reasons for its appearance was that its proponents were dissatisfied with the behavioral approach. This book considers both perspectives, but it places more emphasis on the behavioral approach, so it is important for you to understand what the behavioral approach is and why cognitive psychologists objected to it. Two of the most salient characteristics of the behavioral approach are (1) the heavy reliance on animal subjects, and (2) the emphasis on external events (environmental stimuli and overt behaviors) and a corresponding reluctance to speculate about processes inside the organism. Let us examine each of these characteristics in turn and see why cognitive psychologists objected to them.

### The Use of Animal Subjects

*Advantages and Disadvantages.* A large proportion of the studies described in this text used animals as subjects, especially pigeons, rats, and rabbits. Researchers in this field frequently choose to conduct their experiments with nonhuman subjects for a number of reasons. First, the possibility of a placebo effect or expectancy effect is minimized with animal subjects. Whereas a human subject's behavior may be drastically altered by the knowledge that he or she is being observed, this is unlikely with animal subjects. Most studies with animal subjects are conducted in such a way that the animal does not know its behavior is being monitored and recorded. Furthermore, it is unlikely that an animal subject will be motivated to either please or displease the experimenter, a motive that can ruin a study with human subjects. A second reason for using animal subjects is convenience. The species most commonly used are easy and inexpensive to care for, and animals of a specific age and sex can be obtained in the quantities the experimenter needs. Once animal subjects are obtained, their participation is as regular as the experimenter's—animal subjects never fail to show up for their appointments, which is unfortunately not the case with human subjects.

Probably the biggest advantage of domesticated animal subjects is that their environment can be controlled to a much greater extent than is possible with either wild animals or human subjects. This is especially important in experiments on learning, where previous experience can have a large effect on a subject's performance in a new learning situation. If a human subject tries to solve some brain teaser as part of a learning experiment, the experimenter cannot be sure how many similar problems the subject has encountered in his or her lifetime. When animals are bred and raised in the laboratory, however, their environments can be constructed to ensure they have no contact with objects or events similar to those they will encounter in the experiment.

A final reason for using animal subjects is that of comparative simplicity. Just as a child trying to learn about electricity is better off starting with a flashlight than a radio, researchers may have a better chance of discovering the basic principles of learning by examining creatures that are less intelligent and less complex than human beings. The assumption here is that although human beings differ from other animals in some respects, they are also similar in some respects, and it is these commonalities that can be investigated with animal subjects.

Criticisms of the use of animal subjects seem to boil down to three major arguments. First, it is argued that many important skills, such as the use of language, reading, and solving complex problems, cannot be studied with animals. Although cognitive skills such as language and problem solving have been studied with animal subjects (see Chapter 11), most behavioral psychologists would agree that some complex abilities are unique to human beings. The difference between behavioral psychologists and cognitive psychologists seems to be only that cognitive psychologists are especially interested in precisely those complex abilities that only human beings possess, whereas behavioral psychologists are typically more interested in learning abilities that are shared by many species. This is nothing more than a difference in interests, and it is pointless to argue about it.

The second argument against the use of animal subjects is that human beings are so different from all other animals that it is not possible to generalize from the behavior of animals to human behavior. This is not an issue that can be settled by debate; it can only be decided by collecting the appropriate data. As will be shown throughout this book, there is abundant evidence that research on learning with animal subjects produces findings that are also applicable to human behavior.

The third argument against the use of animals as research subjects involves ethical questions, as discussed in the next section.

***Ethical Issues and Animal Research.*** In recent years there has been considerable debate about the use of animals as research subjects. Viewpoints on this matter vary tremendously. At one extreme, some of the most radical animal rights advocates believe that animals should have the same rights as people, and that no animals should be used in any type of research whatsoever (Regan, 1983). For example, an organization called People for the Ethical Treatment of Animals (PETA) has as its slogan, "Animals are not ours to eat, wear or experiment on." Some members of this and similar organizations are trying to promote legislation that would ban all medical and scientific research with animals. Others, both animal welfare advocates and members of the general public, take less extreme positions, but believe that steps should be taken to minimize and eventually phase out the use of animals in research (see Bowd & Shapiro, 1993; Compton, Dietrich, & Johnson, 1995).

In response to such criticisms of animal research, some scientists have emphasized the many advances in medicine, including vaccines, surgical techniques, and prescription drugs, that would not have been possible without research on animals. They warn that if research with animals were to stop, it would severely impede progress in medical research and it would hamper efforts to improve the health of the world population (Biermann, 1990; Pardes, West, & Pincus, 1991).

In the realm of psychological research, one of the strongest advocates for animal research is Neal Miller. Miller has documented the many benefits that have resulted from psychological research with animals, including ". . . behavior therapy and behavior medicine; rehabilitation of neuromuscular disorders; understanding and alleviating effects of stress and pain; discovery and testing of drugs for treatment of anxiety, psychosis, and Parkinson's disease; new knowledge about the mechanisms of drug addiction, relapse, and damage to the fetus; . . . and understanding the mechanisms and probable future alleviation of some deficits of memory that occur with aging" (N. E. Miller, 1985, p. 423).

Others have agreed that the benefits of psychological research with animals have been substantial, and that progress in dealing with mental health problems would be jeopardized if animals were no longer used as subjects in psychological research (Baldwin, 1993). For those interested in learning more about the complex issues related to the use of animals in scientific research, a thought-provoking book by Petrinovich (1999) provides a comprehensive review of this topic from historical, legal, and ethical perspectives.

One trend that has resulted from the debate over animal research is the development of alternatives to the use of animals. For example, the cosmetics industry has made progress in devising methods to test the safety of its products that do not involve animals. However, such alternatives to animal experimentation are seldom possible in psychological research. If you want to study the behavior of an animal, you must observe the animal, not a culture in a test tube or a computer simulation.

Although it may be impossible to eliminate the use of animals in psychological and biomedical research, many new regulations have been put in place in an effort to improve the well-being of animal subjects. In the United States, most colleges, universities, and research centers that use animal subjects are required to have an Institutional Animal Care and Use Committee (IACUC) to oversee all research projects involving animals. The IACUC must review each project with animal subjects, before it begins, to ensure that all governmental regulations are met and that the animals are well cared for. Any pain or discomfort to the animals must be minimized to the extent possible. For example, if an animal undergoes surgery, appropriate anesthesia must be used. Regulations also require that all research animals have adequate food and water, a clean and well-maintained living environment with appropriate temperature, humidity, and lighting conditions, and the continual availability of veterinary care. (It is unfortunate that there are no similar regulations guaranteeing adequate food, a warm place to live, and health care for the human members of our society.)

For the animal experiments described in this book, the year of publication offers a good indication of what types of regulations governed the research. Studies conducted since about 1980 have been governed by increasingly strict regulations designed to ensure the humane treatment of animal subjects. Older studies were conducted during times when there were fewer regulations about animal research. However, it is probably safe to say that even before the advent of tighter regulations, the vast majority of the experiments were done by researchers who took very good care of

The American Psychological Association's "Guidelines for the care and use of animals" can be found at *http://www.apa.org/science/anguide.html.*

their animals, because they realized that one of the best ways to obtain good research results is to have subjects that are healthy and well treated.

## The Emphasis on External Events

The term *behaviorism* was coined by John B. Watson of Johns Hopkins University shortly after the turn of the twentieth century. Watson is usually called the first behaviorist, and his book *Psychology from the Standpoint of a Behaviorist* (1919) was very influential. In this book, Watson criticized the research techniques that prevailed in the field of psychology at that time. A popular research method was introspection, which involves reflecting upon, reporting, and analyzing one's own mental processes. Thus a psychologist might attempt to examine and describe his thoughts and emotions while looking at a picture or performing some other specific task. A problem with introspection was that it required considerable practice to master this skill, and even then, two experienced psychologists might report different thoughts and emotions when performing the same task. Watson (1919) recognized this weakness, and he argued that verbal reports of private events (such as sensations, feelings, states of consciousness) should have no place in the field of psychology.

Information about the APA's Committee on Animal Research and Ethics can be found at *http://www.apa.org/science/bsaweb-care.html.*

"States of consciousness," like the so-called phenomena of spiritualism, are not objectively verifiable and for that reason can never become data for science. In all other sciences the facts of observation are objective, verifiable, and can be reproduced and controlled by all trained observers. . . . (p. 1) . . . we may say that the goal of psychological study is the *ascertaining of such data and laws that, given the stimulus, psychology can predict what the response will be; or, on the other hand, given the response, it can specify the nature of the effective stimulus.* (p. 10, italics in original)

Watson's logic can be stated in the form of a syllogism:

| Given that: | 1. We want psychology to be a science. |
| And that: | 2. Sciences deal only with events everyone can observe. |
| It follows that: | 3. Psychology must deal only with observable events. |

According to Watson, the observable events in psychology are stimuli and responses; they are certainly not the subjective reports of trained introspectionists.

Whereas Watson argued against the use of unobservable events as psychological *data*, B. F. Skinner has repeatedly criticized the use of unobservable events in psychological *theories*. Skinner (1950, 1953, 1985) asserted that it is both dangerous and unnecessary to point to some unobservable event, or intervening variable, as the cause of behavior. Consider an experiment in which a rat is deprived of water for a certain number of hours and is then placed in a chamber where it can obtain water by pressing a lever. We would probably find an orderly relationship between the independent variable, the number of hours of water deprivation, and the dependent variable, the rate of lever pressing. The rule that described this relationship would be a part of the syntax of our theory, and this rule is represented by the arrow in Figure 1-3a.

Skinner has pointed out that many psychologists would prefer to go further, however, and postulate an intervening variable such as *thirst*, which is presumably controlled by the hours of deprivation and which in turn controls the rate of lever pressing (see Figure 1-3b). According to Skinner, this intervening variable is unnecessary because it does not improve our ability to predict the rat's behavior—we can do just as well simply by knowing the hours of deprivation. The addition of the intervening variable needlessly complicates our theory. Now our syntax must describe two relationships—the relationship between hours of deprivation and thirst, and that between thirst and lever pressing. Because both theories are equally predictive, by the criterion of simplicity, the theory without the intervening variable (Figure 1-3a) is preferable.

Skinner also argued that the use of an intervening variable such as thirst is dangerous because we can easily fool ourselves into thinking we have found the cause of a behavior when we are actually talking about a hypothetical and unobservable entity. Some other intervening variables that can find their way into a psychological theory are *anger, intelligence, stubbornness,* and *laziness.* To illustrate how an intervening variable can be treated as the cause of a behavior, suppose we ask a father why his 10-year-old son does not always do his homework. The father's answer might be, "Because he is lazy." In this case, laziness, an unobservable entity, is offered as an explanation, and accepting this explanation could prematurely curtail any efforts to improve the problem behavior. After all, if the cause of a behavior is

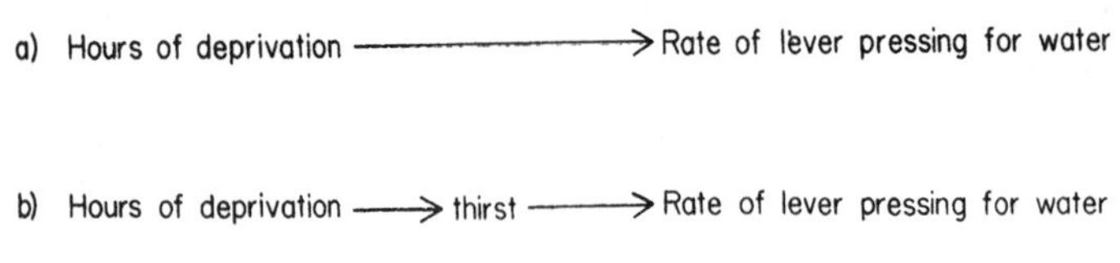

a)  Hours of deprivation ————————→ Rate of lever pressing for water

b)  Hours of deprivation ——→ thirst ——→ Rate of lever pressing for water

**FIGURE 1-3**    (a) A schematic diagram of a simple theory of behavior with no intervening variables. (b) The same theory with an intervening variable added. In this example, the intervening variable, thirst, is unnecessary, for it only complicates the theory.

a.

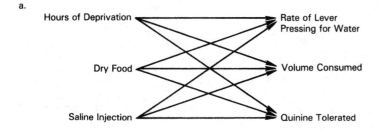

b.

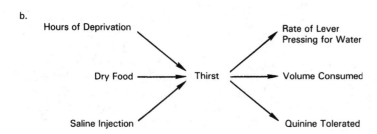

**FIGURE 1-4** (a) The arrows represent the nine relationships between independent and dependent variables that must be defined by a theory without intervening variables. (b) The arrows represent the six relationships the theory must define if it includes the intervening variable of thirst. Neal Miller argued that the second theory is superior because it is more parsimonious. (After N. E. Miller, 1959)

inside the person, how can we control it? However, Skinner proposes that the causes of many behaviors can be traced back to the external environment, and by changing the environment, we can change the behavior. Perhaps the youngster does not do his homework because he plays outside all afternoon, eats dinner with the family at a fairly late hour, and then is too tired to do his assignments. If so, a simple change in the boy's environment might improve his behavior. As just two possibilities, either the family dinner hour could be made earlier or the boy could be required to come home an hour or two before dinner to do his homework. In short, the potential for controlling a behavior may be recognized if an intervening variable such as laziness is rejected and an external cause of the behavior is sought.

Neal Miller (1959), another psychologist with a behavioral orientation, took issue with Skinner's position that intervening variables are always undesirable. Miller suggested that intervening variables are often useful when several independent and dependent variables are involved. Starting with the example shown in Figure 1-3, he noted that the number of

hours without water is only one factor that might influence a rat's rate of lever pressing for water. The rat's rate of pressing might also increase if it were fed dry food, or if it were given an injection of a saline solution. Furthermore, the rate of lever pressing is only one of many dependent variables that might be affected by hours of deprivation, dry food, or a saline injection. Two other dependent variables are the volume of water consumed and the amount of quinine (which would give the water a bitter taste) that would have to be added to make the rat stop drinking.

As shown in Figure 1-4a, Miller proposed that each of these three dependent variables would be influenced by each of the three independent variables. Once all of these variables are added, a theory without intervening variables would need to have a separate rule for describing each of the nine cause-and-effect relationships, as symbolized by the nine crossing arrows in Figure 1-4a. This fairly complicated theory could be simplified by including the intervening variable, thirst. We can assume that each of the three independent variables affects an animal's thirst, and thirst controls each of the three dependent variables. Figure 1-4b shows that once the intervening variable, thirst, is included in this way, only six cause-and-effect relationships have to be described— three to describe the relationship between each independent variable and thirst, and three more to describe the relationship between thirst and each dependent variable. In this case, the criterion of simplicity favors the theory with the intervening variable. Miller showed that the potential advantage of including intervening variables increases as a theory is expanded to deal with more and more independent variables.

As you might suspect, Miller's argument has not ended the debate over intervening variables. In reply to the sort of logic presented by Miller, Skinner's (1956a) position is that if so many variables affect thirst, and if thirst controls so many different behavior patterns, then whatever thirst is, it must be quite complicated, and the simpler theory depicted in Figure 1-4b does not do justice to this complexity. On the other side, those who favor the use of intervening variables also use another line of argument: They point out that intervening variables are commonplace in other, firmly established sciences. As already noted, many familiar concepts from physics (for instance, gravity) are intervening variables, since they are not directly observable. Some psychologists have therefore reasoned that progress in psychology would be needlessly restricted if the use of intervening variables were disallowed (Nicholas, 1984).

As the case of Neal Miller illustrates, it is not correct to say that all behaviorists avoid using intervening variables. As we will see, the theories of many psychologists of the behavioral tradition include them. The difference between theorists of the behavioral and cognitive approaches is only one of degree. As a general rule, cognitive psychologists tend to use intervening variables more freely and more prolifically than do behavioral psychologists. The theories of cognitive psychologists include a wide range of concepts that are not directly observable, such as short-term memory, long-term memory, sensory information storage, attention, rehearsal, and so on. Behavioral

For more information about the behavioral approach, there is an excellent tutorial on behaviorism by Dr. Jay Moore at *http://server.bmod.athabascau.ca/html/Behaviorism.*

psychologists tend to use intervening variables more sparingly and more cautiously.

The debate over the use of intervening variables has gone on for decades, and we will not settle it here. My own position (though hardly original) is that the ultimate test of a psychological theory is its ability to predict behavior. If a theory can make accurate predictions about behaviors that were previously unpredictable, then the theory is useful, regardless of whether or not it contains any intervening variables. In this text, we will encounter many useful theories of each type.

## ON FREE WILL, DETERMINISM, AND CHAOS THEORY

**Determinism** is a philosophical position that all the events of the world, including all human behaviors, are determined by physical causes that could, at least in principle, be discovered and analyzed with the techniques of science. A fair number of psychologists assume that this position is correct and use it as a starting point for their study of human behavior. On the other hand, many people find the determinist position unacceptable because it rules out the possibility of **free will**—the idea that some nonphysical entity, such as the will or the soul, can direct human behavior. For instance, many religions maintain that human beings are free to choose between good and evil. Those who believe in free will therefore claim that not all human behavior can be predicted or explained by a scientific analysis (which assumes there is a physical cause for every behavior).

The doctrine of determinism has been criticized, not only by philosophers and theologians, but by some scientists as well, partly because of the recent growth of interest in **chaos theory.** Chaos theory provides mathematical techniques for dealing with complex physical systems, and it has been applied to a great variety of scientific topics, ranging from the beating of the human heart to weather forecasting. One of the themes of chaos theory is that complex physical systems may be inherently unpredictable, at least in some ways.

One important principle of chaos theory is that physical systems have *extreme sensitivity to initial conditions* (Duke, 1994). Stated simply, this principle says that a tiny change in the current conditions can snowball into much larger changes as time passes. A hypothetical example of how this might happen is known as the *butterfly effect.* The small air movements that occur when a butterfly beats its wings could serve as a trigger for larger and larger changes in wind direction and velocity, and some time later, global weather patterns might be different from what they would have been if the butterfly had remained still. That such small events can sometimes have large consequences in the long run has been verified by computer simulations designed for weather forecasting. For example, changing the current temperature by one-thousandth of a degree might have no appreciable effect on the short-term weather forecast, but it could lead to a completely different long-term forecast. For this reason, some scientists believe that we will never be able to make accurate long-term weather forecasts for specific days (for example, predicting the weather for a particular location two weeks ahead of time). On the positive side, meteorologists should be able to make reasonably accurate short-term forecasts (a day or two ahead of time) as well as general predictions about weather trends (for example, that November will be colder and wetter than October).

Maybe you can already see how this principle from chaos theory has implications for our study of human behavior. Human beings are very complex, and so are their environments. If it is not possible to predict what the weather will be two weeks from now, what chance do we have of predicting exactly what a particular person will do or say at a specific moment two

weeks from now? Such accuracy in predicting the minute details of human behavior may never be possible (Guess & Sailor, 1993). However, it may be possible to make accurate predictions about short-term behavior patterns and about general long-term trends, just as it is possible (at least sometimes) in weather forecasting. As examples of short-term behaviors, you can probably make some fairly accurate predictions about what will happen if you walk toward a sparrow that is feeding in the grass, or what will happen to the flow of traffic as the light changes from green to yellow to red. As an example of a general long-term trend, you can probably predict how the number of students you see studying in the college library will change as final exam week approaches. However, you can probably not make accurate predictions about specific long-term events, such as exactly which students you will see in the library at a specific date and time several weeks from now.

It is not necessary to be a determinist to pursue the sort of scientific analysis of behavior that is described in this book. Regardless of your religious beliefs or your philosophical convictions, you can profit from reading this book as long as you are willing to observe that there is some regularity and predictability in the behaviors of both humans and animals. Science is not needed to point out the regularities in behavior, but by using the scientific method as it has been described in this chapter, we can gain a clearer understanding of these regularities and make more accurate predictions about future behavior. We can proceed in this fashion without taking any particular position on the free-will/determinism controversy.

## CHAPTER SUMMARY

Much research on learning and behavior is aimed at developing general principles that are applicable both to people and to other species in a wide variety of situations. All scientific theories must define their independent variables and their dependent variables. Many scientific theories also contain intervening variables, which cannot be directly observed. Five characteristics of good scientific theories are testability, simplicity, generality, fruitfulness, and agreement with the data. To test psychological theories, several different research methods can be used, including case histories, observational techniques, and experimental techniques.

Behavioral psychologists have often used animal subjects because they are interested in general principles of learning that are shared by many species, because animals are less complex than human subjects, and because their environments can be controlled to a greater degree. Critics of animal research have questioned whether we can generalize from animals to people, and they have raised ethical concerns about the use of animal subjects.

Behaviorists have argued that psychology should deal only with observable events, whereas cognitive psychologists regularly use intervening variables such as hunger, memory, attention, and so on. Skinner argued that intervening variables make scientific theories more complex than necessary. However, Neal Miller showed that if a theory includes many independent variables and many dependent variables, including intervening variables can actually simplify a theory.

Determinists believe that all human behavior is caused by physical factors that could, in principle, be discovered and predicted by the scientific method. Critics of determinism assert that human behavior is at least partly the result of free will or other factors that science can never uncover. The deterministic approach has also been challenged by chaos theory, which has shown that even inanimate objects such as weather systems are virtually impossible to predict in the long run.

## REVIEW QUESTIONS

1. What are the four main components of scientific theories? Illustrate each with a concrete example. What are five characteristics of a good scientific theory?

2. What are the main differences between case histories, observational techniques, and experimental techniques? What are some procedures that are often used in psychological experiments to try to eliminate confounding variables?

3. Why did B. F. Skinner believe that intervening variables should not be used in psychological theories? How did other psychologists respond to Skinner's position?

4. What is the debate over free will versus determinism about? How has scientific research on chaos theory raised new challenges for the determinist position?

## CHAPTER 2

# Simple Ideas, Simple Associations, and Simple Cells

The scientific investigation of learning did not begin until about the end of the nineteenth century. The first part of this chapter presents some historical developments, both theoretical and experimental, that preceded the beginnings of this field and that had a strong influence on it. Most of these developments also preceded the emergence of the field of psychology itself. Although no single event marks the beginning of psychology as a separate discipline, an event frequently cited is the founding of the world's first psychological laboratory in Leipzig, Germany, by Wilhelm Wundt in 1879. Prior to this time, the study of psychology was considered to be a part of the discipline of philosophy, and it was philosophers who most frequently lectured and wrote about psychological topics. The writings of a number of philosophers, who spanned several centuries but are now collectively called **Associationists,** constitute some of the earliest recorded thoughts about learning.

## EARLY THEORIES ABOUT THE ASSOCIATION OF IDEAS

### Aristotle

Aristotle (c. 350 B.C.) is generally acknowledged to be the first Associationist (although Aristotle did not use this term). He proposed three principles of association that can be viewed as an elementary theory of memory. Aristotle suggested that these principles describe how one thought leads to another. Before reading about Aristotle's principles, you have the opportunity to try something Aristotle never did—to conduct a simple experiment to test these principles. This experiment, which should take only a minute or two, might be called a study of **free association.** Get a piece of paper and a pencil, and write the numbers 1 through 12 in a column down the left side of the paper. Table 2-1 contains a list of words also numbered 1 through 12. Reading one word at a time, write down the first two or three words that come to mind. Do not spend much time on any one word—your first few responses will be the most informative.

Once you have your list of responses to the 12 words, look over your answers and try to formulate some rules that describe the types of responses you made. Can you guess any of Aristotle's three principles? Aristotle's first principle of association was **contiguity:** The more closely together (contiguous) in space or time two items occur, the more likely will the thought of one item lead to the thought of the other. For example, the response *chair* to the word *table* illustrates association by spatial contiguity, since the two items are often found close together. The

**TABLE 2-1   Words for the Free-Association Experiment**

1. apple
2. night
3. thunder
4. bread
5. chair
6. bat
7. girl
8. dentist
9. quiet
10. sunset
11. elephant
12. blue

response *lightning* to the word *thunder* is an example of association by temporal contiguity. Notice that an understanding of cause and effect is not necessary for such an association to develop. Although most adults understand that thunder and lightning are both products of the same electrical discharge, a young child or an uneducated adult might associate these two concepts without understanding the physical connection between them. Other examples of association by contiguity are *bread-butter* and *dentist-pain.*

Aristotle's other two principles of association were **similarity** and **contrast.** He stated that the thought of one concept often leads to the thought of similar concepts. Examples of association by similarity are the responses *orange* or *pear* to the prompt *apple*, or the responses *yellow* or *green* to the prompt *blue*. By *contrast*, Aristotle meant that an item often leads to the thought of its opposite (for instance, *night-day, girl-boy, sunset-sunrise*). Most people who try this simple free-association experiment conclude that Aristotle's principles of association have both strengths and weaknesses. On the negative side, the list of principles seems incomplete, and other factors that affect the train of thought may have already occurred to you. On the positive side, Aristotle's principles have some intuitive validity for most people, and they seem to be a reasonable first step in the development of a theory about the relationship between experience and memory.

## The British Associationists: Simple and Complex Ideas

For Aristotle, the principles of association were simply hypotheses about how one thought leads to another. For many of the philosophers who wrote about Associationism several centuries later, this topic assumed a much greater significance: Associationism was seen as a theory of all knowledge. The **British Associationists** included Thomas Hobbes (1651), John Locke (1690), James Mill (1829), John Stuart Mill (1843), and others. These writers are also called the **British Empiricists** because of their belief that every person acquires all knowledge empirically—that is, through experience. This viewpoint is typified by John Locke's statement that the mind of a newborn child is a *tabula rasa* (a blank slate) on which experience makes its mark. The Empiricists believed that every memory, every idea, and every concept a person has is based on one or more previous experiences.

The opposite of Empiricism is **Nativism,** or the position that some ideas are innate and do not depend on an individual's past experience. For instance, the Nativist Immanuel Kant (1781) believed that the concepts of space and time are inborn, and that through experience new concepts are built on the foundation of these original, innate concepts. The Empiricist position is the more extreme of the two because it allows for no counterexamples. That is, a demonstration that most concepts are learned through experience does no damage to the Nativist position, which acknowledges the role of experience. On the other hand, it takes only one example of an innate concept to refute the Empiricist position. As we shall see several times throughout the text, modern research has uncovered many examples that are at odds with the extreme Empiricist position.

Fortunately, Associationism is not logically tied to extreme Empiricism. We can grant that some concepts are innate, but that many concepts are developed through experience. The British Empiricists offered some hypotheses both about how old concepts become associated in memory and about how new concepts are formed. According to the Associationists, there is a direct correspondence between experience and memory. Experience consists of **sensations,** and memory consists of **ideas.** Furthermore, any sensory experience can be broken down into **simple sensations.** For instance, if a person observes a red box-shaped object, this sensation might be broken down into two simple sensations—*red* and *rectangular.* At some later time, the person's memory of this experience would consist of the two corresponding **simple ideas** of *red* and *rectangular.* Thus, as illustrated in Figure 2-1a, there

is a one-to-one correspondence between simple sensations and simple ideas. A simple idea was said to be a sort of faint replica of the simple sensation from which it arose.

Now suppose that the person repeatedly encounters such a red box-shaped object. Through the principles of contiguity, an association should develop between the ideas of *red* and *rectangle,* as shown in Figure 2-1b. Once such an association is formed, if the person experiences the color red, this will not only invoke the idea of *red,* but by virtue of the

**FIGURE 2-1**   Some principles of Associationism. (a) The one-to-one correspondence between simple sensations and simple ideas. (b) After repeated pairings of the two sensations, an association forms between their respective ideas. (c) Once an association is formed, presenting one stimulus will activate the ideas of both. (d) With enough pairings of two simple ideas, a complex idea encompassing both simple ideas is formed. The complex idea may now be evoked if either of the simple stimuli is presented.

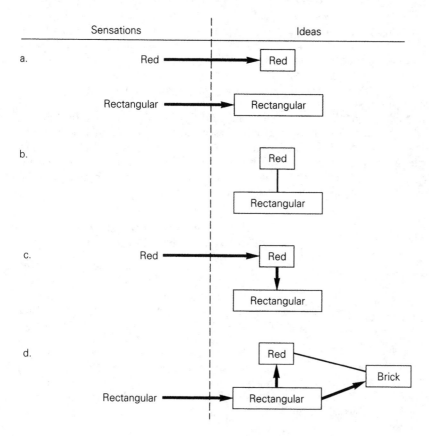

association the idea *rectangular* will be invoked as well (Figure 2-1c).

It should be obvious how this sort of hypothesis can explain at least some of the results of a free-association experiment. For instance, the idea of *thunder* will "excite" the idea of *lightning* because of the association between them, an association developed according to the principle of contiguity. But many of our concepts are more complex than the simple ideas of *red, rectangular, thunder,* and *lightning.* In an attempt to come to grips with the full range of memories and knowledge of the world that all people have, several Associationists speculated about the formation of complex ideas. James Mill (1829) proposed that if two or more simple sensations are repeatedly presented together, a product of their union may be a **complex idea.** For instance, if the sensations *red* and *rectangular* occur together repeatedly, a new, complex idea of *brick* may form. Mill did not have much to say about how this event takes place, but Figure 2-1d shows one way to depict Mill's hypothesis graphically. Once such a complex idea is formed, it can also be evoked by the process of association when the sensation of either red or rectangle occurs. Mill went on to say that complex ideas could themselves combine to form **duplex ideas.** In short, Mill suggested that all complex ideas (1) can be decomposed into two or more simple ideas, and (2) are always formed through the repeated pairing of these simple ideas. In the following passage, Mill (1829) describes the formation of a hierarchy of ideas of increasing complexity:

> Some of the most familiar objects with which we are acquainted furnish instances of these unions of complex and duplex ideas.
> Brick is one complex idea, mortar is another complex idea; these ideas, with ideas of position and quantity, compose my idea of a wall. . . . In the same manner my complex idea of glass, and wood, and others, compose my duplex idea of a window; and these duplex ideas, united together, compose my idea of a house, which is made up of various duplex ideas. (pp. 114–116)

This, then, was the view that all ideas, no matter how complex, are the product of simple ideas, which are in turn the product of simple sensations. As with Aristotle's principles of association, there are both strengths and weaknesses in this hypothesis. Some complex concepts are taught to children only after they have become familiar with the simpler ideas that compose them. For instance, it is only after a child understands the concepts of *addition* and *repetition* that the more complex concept of *multiplication* is presented, and it is often introduced as a procedure for performing repeated additions. For older students who know how to calculate the area of a rectangle, *integration* may be initially presented as a technique for calculating the total area of a series of very thin rectangles. In both of these examples, a complex idea is formed only after the mastery of simpler ideas, and it is difficult to imagine learning these concepts in the opposite order. However, other concepts do not seem to follow as nicely from Mill's theory, including his own example of the concept of *house.* A two-year-old may know the word *house* and use it appropriately without knowing the "simpler" concepts of *mortar, ceiling,* or *rafter.* With *house* and many other complex concepts, people seem to develop at least a crude idea of the entire concept before learning all of the components of the concept, although according to Mill's theory this should not be possible. Thus, although it appears to have validity in some cases, Mill's theory is at best incomplete. Some more recent theories about concepts and their formation will be presented in Chapter 10.

## Thomas Brown's Secondary Principles of Association

As mentioned above, Aristotle's list of principles of association seemed incomplete. Another Associationist, Thomas Brown (1820), tried to remedy this situation by proposing nine secondary principles of association to supplement Aristotle's list. These principles are of more than historical interest, because in one way or another each of these principles has been investigated by modern researchers. Briefly, Brown's secondary principles were (1) the *length of time* two sensations coexist determines the strength of the association, and (2) the *liveliness* or vividness of the sensations also affects the strength of the association. According to Brown, "brilliant objects" or "occasions of great joy or sorrow" will be more easily associated and better remembered. A stronger association will also occur (3) if the two sensations have been paired *frequently*, (4) if they have been paired *recently*, or (5) if both sensations are *free from strong associations* with other sensations. For instance, if you meet many new people at a party, you may find it easier to remember the name of someone who introduces himself as *Jeremiah* (a fairly unusual name) than someone called *John* (a name that you probably associate with quite a few people). Other factors that can affect the strength of an association are (6) *constitutional differences* among different individuals, (7) a person's current *emotional state*, (8) the momentary *state of the body* (healthy, ill, intoxicated), and (9) a person's *prior habits*.

The primary principles of Aristotle, the secondary principles of Thomas Brown, and James Mill's hypotheses about the development of complex ideas can be thought of as the earliest theories of learning, for they attempted to explain how people change as a result of their experiences. Yet although they had their theories, the Associationists conducted no experiments to test them. In retrospect, it is remarkable that despite an interest in principles of learning spanning some 2,000 years, no systematic experiments on learning were conducted until the end of the nineteenth century. This absence of research of learning was not a result of technological deficiencies—the first experiments on learning were so simple that they could have been performed centuries earlier.

## EBBINGHAUS'S EXPERIMENTS ON MEMORY

Hermann Ebbinghaus (1885) was the first to put the Associationists' principles to an experimental test. In his memory experiments, Ebbinghaus might have used lists of words as study materials, but he felt that words were not ideal because any subject will have many pre-existing associations between words (such as *coffee-hot*), and these previous associations will undoubtedly affect the subject's performance. To avoid this problem, Ebbinghaus invented the **nonsense syllable**—a meaningless syllable consisting of two consonants separated by a vowel (for instance, HAQ, PIF, ZOD). Ebbinghaus constructed a master list of some 2,300 nonsense syllables, and by drawing from this list at random he could construct a list for study of any desired length.

Ebbinghaus himself served as his only subject in all of his studies, which continued for several years. This arrangement is not acceptable by modern standards, because the likelihood of experimenter bias is high in such an arrangement. Furthermore, any single subject might be somehow atypical and unrepresentative of people in general. Despite these potential pitfalls, Ebbinghaus's results have withstood the test of time: All of his major findings have been replicated by later researchers using the multiple-subject procedures that are standard in modern research. The basic plan of most of his experiments was to read a list of nonsense syllables out loud at a steady pace, over and over, until he memorized it perfectly. Periodically, Ebbinghaus would test his memory by trying to recite the list by heart. By counting the number of repetitions needed for one perfect recitation, Ebbinghaus had an objective measure of the difficulty of memorizing a list. But how could he measure what was left of this learning at a later time (say, 24 hours later)? Ebbinghaus's solution was to learn the list to perfection, then allow some time to pass, and finally relearn the list to perfection, again counting how many repetitions were necessary. His measure of the strength of memory was what he called **savings,** or the decrease in the number of required repetitions during the second learning period. For example, if a list required 20 repetitions during the initial learning, but only 15 repetitions during the relearning phase, this constituted a savings of 5 repetitions, or 25 percent. As shown below, the measurement of savings proved to be a sensitive way to gauge how the effects of an initial learning experience persisted over time.

## Ebbinghaus's Major Findings

*List Length.* One of Ebbinghaus's simplest and least surprising results concerned the relationship between the length of a list and the number of repetitions needed to master it. Naturally, longer lists required more repetitions. Ebbinghaus found that he could learn a list of 12 nonsense syllables after about 17 repetitions. However, the number of necessary repetitions increased to 44 for a list of 24 items and to 55 for a list of 36 items. The general rule suggested by these results is that if the amount of material to be learned is doubled, the time needed to master the material is more than doubled. To put it another way, as list length increased, the study time required per item increased.

*The Effects of Repetition.* One of Thomas Brown's secondary principles of association states that the frequency of pairings directly affects the strength of an association. This principle is obviously supported by the simple fact that a list that is not memorized after a small number of repetitions will eventually be learned after more repetitions. However, one of Ebbinghaus's findings offers some additional support for the frequency principle. If

he continued to study a list beyond the point of one perfect recitation (for instance, for an additional 10 or 20 repetitions), his savings after 24 hours increased substantially. In other words, even after he appeared to have perfectly mastered a list, additional study produced improved performance in a delayed test. Continuing to practice after performance is apparently perfect is called **overlearning,** and Ebbinghaus demonstrated that Thomas Brown's principle of frequency applies to periods of overlearning as well as to periods in which there is visible improvement during practice.

*The Effects of Time.* Thomas Brown's principle of recency states that the more recently two items have been paired, the stronger will be the association between them. Ebbinghaus tested this principle by varying the length of time that elapsed between his study and test periods. As shown in Figure 2-2, he examined intervals as short as 20 minutes and as long as one month. The graph in Figure 2-2 is an example of a **forgetting curve,** for it shows how the passage of time has a detrimental effect on performance in a memory task. The curve shows that forgetting is rapid immediately after a study period, but the rate of

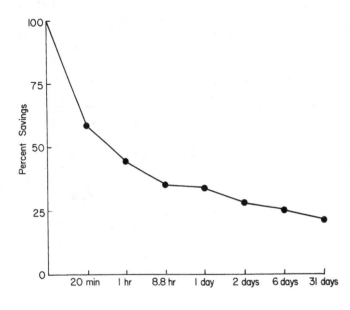

**FIGURE 2-2** Ebbinghaus's forgetting curve. The percentage savings is shown for various time intervals between his initial learning and relearning of lists of nonsense syllables. (After Ebbinghaus, 1885)

You can conduct an experiment that demonstrates your own rapid forgetting of new information at *http://coglab.psych.purdue.edu/coglab/Labs/BrownPeterson.html.*

**TABLE 2-2   Ebbinghaus's Rearranged List Experiment***

| List 0 (Original list) | List 1 (1 item skipped) | List 2 (2 items skipped) |
|:---:|:---:|:---:|
| I1 | I1 | I1 |
| I2 | I3 | I4 |
| I3 | I5 | I7 |
| I4 | I7 | I10 |
| I5 | I9 | I13 |
| I6 | I11 | I16 |
| I7 | I13 | I2 |
| I8 | I15 | I5 |
| I9 | I2 | I8 |
| I10 | I4 | I11 |
| I11 | I6 | I14 |
| I12 | I8 | I3 |
| I13 | I10 | I6 |
| I14 | I12 | I9 |
| I15 | I14 | I12 |
| I16 | I16 | I15 |

*Note: An original list of 16 syllables (represented here by the symbols I1 through I16) was rearranged to test for possible associations between items separated by one syllable (List 1) or associations between items separated by two syllables (List 2).

additional forgetting slows as more time passes. The shape of this curve is similar to the forgetting curves obtained by later researchers in numerous experiments with both human and animal subjects (Blough, 1959; Peterson & Peterson, 1959), although the time scale on the *x*-axis varies greatly, depending on the nature of the task and the species of the subjects. Forgetting curves of this type provide strong confirmation of Thomas Brown's principle of recency.

*The Role of Contiguity.*   The Associationists' principle of contiguity states that the more closely together two items are presented, the better will the thought of one item lead to the thought of the other. Ebbinghaus reasoned that if the contiguity principle is correct, the strongest associations in his lists should be between adjacent syllables, but there should also be measurable (though weaker) associations between nonadjacent items. He devised an ingenious method for testing this idea, which involved rearranging the items in a list after it was memorized, and then learning the rearranged list.

His technique for rearranging lists is illustrated in Table 2-2. The designations I1 through I16 refer to the 16 items as they were ordered in the original list (List 0). Once this list is memorized, there should be a strong association between I1 and I2, a somewhat weaker association between I1 and I3 (since these were separated by one item in the original list), a still weaker association between I1 and I4, and so on. There should be similar gradations in strength of association between every other item and its neighbors.

The rearranged list, called List 1 in Table 2-2, was used to test for associations between items one syllable apart. Observe that every adjacent item in List 1 was separated by one syllable in the original list. If there is any association between I1 and I3, between I3 and I5, and so on, then List 1 should be easier to learn than a totally new list (there should be some savings that are carried over from List 0 to List 1). In a similar fashion, List 2 tests for associations between items that were two syllables apart in the original list.

In this experiment, Ebbinghaus used a 24-hour forgetting period between his study of an original list and his test with a rearranged list. If List 0 was simply relearned after 24 hours, the savings amounted to about 33 percent. In comparison, Ebbinghaus found an average savings of 11 percent if List 1 was studied 24 hours after List 0, and a savings of 7 percent if List 2 was used. Although the amount of savings with these rearranged lists was not large, the pattern of results was orderly: As the number of skipped syllables increased in the rearranged lists, the amount of savings was diminished. These results are completely consistent with the principle of contiguity, because they imply that the strength of an association between two items depends on their proximity in the original list.

***Backward Associations.*** In one experiment, Ebbinghaus learned a list one day and then attempted to learn the list in the opposite order the following day. As the British Associationists described it, the contiguity principle makes a straightforward prediction for this experiment. Since simply reversing the order of the items does not change the contiguity of any two items, and since the strength of an association is a function of contiguity, it should be just as easy to learn the reversed list as to relearn the original list. Ebbinghaus's experiment did not confirm this prediction, however. He obtained a savings of only 13 percent with reversed lists, much less than the 33 percent savings obtained when simply relearning original lists. This study points out a limitation of the contiguity principle: If we wish to estimate the likelihood that presenting one item will lead to the recall of a second item, we must know not only how closely the items were paired in the period of study but also the order in which the items were presented. The backward-list experiment suggests that recall is better when items must be remembered in the same order in which they were originally studied.

## Ebbinghaus and the Associationists Compared to Later Learning Theorists

Although both Ebbinghaus and the British Associationists preceded the beginnings of behaviorism and cognitive psychology, there are a number of parallels between the early writers and these two modern approaches to learning. The Associationists did not conduct experiments, but in their theoretical approach they were similar to modern cognitive psychologists. Like cognitive psychologists, the Associationists were interested in thought processes and in the nature of human knowledge. They speculated about the relationship between unobservable simple ideas and complex ideas. They showed little interest in observable behavior, or in how experience with various stimuli might alter a person's later behavior.

Ebbinghaus, on the other hand, was more representative of the behavioral approach. His experiments dealt with observable stimuli (the lists of nonsense syllables) and overt behavior (his recitation of the lists). Ebbinghaus's presentation of his results would satisfy the strictest behaviorist: His book is filled with tables that show how some objective measure of behavior (usually savings) depended on some clearly defined independent variable (such as the number of repetitions, the amount of time since original learning, and list rearrangement). For instance, the forgetting curve in Figure 2-2 plots the dependent variable, percent savings, as a function of the independent variable, time since original learning. As a strict behaviorist would surely argue, we need no intervening variables, no hypotheses about thought processes, to see the systematic manner in which the passage of time affects the ability to recall.

A behaviorist might also argue that this example shows that we do not need a theory about thought processes in order to put findings such as Ebbinghaus's to practical use. Thus the forgetting curve might suggest that if you must take an examination in which a good deal of rote memorization is involved (such as a history exam in which the names, places, and dates have little more inherent meaning to you than nonsense syllables), you should do your final studying as close to the time of the exam as possible. Ebbinghaus's forgetting curve suggests that a substantial fraction of this type of material may be lost after only a few hours.

As another example, Ebbinghaus's experiment on overlearning suggests that you may be wise to continue to study even after you seem to have mastered the material to be remembered, because overlearning increased the amount of savings obtained at a later time. Finally, the experiment on backward lists indicates that the order in which you study the material can affect your ability to recall it. If you know that the exam will present you with a list of dates and require you to describe what events took place on those dates, you should study by using dates as stimuli and by responding with the appropriate event (rather than attempting to recall dates for various events). Notice that each of these conclusions can be reached simply by examining Ebbinghaus's results and generalizing to other situations where rote memorization is involved. They do not depend on a theory of knowledge, on an understanding of what ideas are or what associations are, or on a theory of what goes on in our brains when we learn. The point is that a strict behavioral approach, which emphasizes orderly relationships between stimuli and responses, can yield useful information about behavior without theorizing about internal events.

## PHYSIOLOGICAL FACTS AND THEORIES RELATED TO ASSOCIATIONISM

Having examined some of the earliest theories and experiments on learning, we can now turn to a different set of questions. What goes on in a creature's nervous system when it is presented with some fairly simple stimulus, such as the color red or a rectangular shape? What happens in the nervous system when the stimuli *red* and *rectangular* are repeatedly paired and the animal begins to associate the two? How does a creature's sensory systems allow it to recognize more complex stimuli, such as bricks, automobiles, or people's faces? Physiological psychologists have attempted to answer these questions, with varying degrees of

progress so far. This section provides a brief overview of some of this research. This material should give you a different way to think about sensations, ideas, and associations, and it will provide a useful foundation for topics discussed in later chapters. To understand this material, it is necessary to have some understanding of how nerve cells or neurons function. The next section provides a short summary, but for more information, you may want to read the section on neurons that can be found in nearly every textbook on introductory psychology.

### The Basic Characteristics of Neurons

Despite large differences in their overall structures, the nervous systems of all creatures are composed of specialized cells called neurons, whose major function is to transmit information. The human brain contains about 10 billion neurons, and there are many additional neurons throughout the rest of the body. Whereas neurons vary greatly in size and shape, the basic components of all neurons, and the functions of those components, are quite similar. Figure 2-3 shows the structure of a typical neuron.

The three major components of a neuron are the **cell body,** the **dendrites,** and the **axons.** The cell body contains the nucleus, which regulates the basic metabolic functions of the cell, such as the intake of oxygen and the release of carbon dioxide. In the transmission of information, the dendrites and the cell body are on the receptive side—they are sensitive to certain chemicals called **transmitters** that are

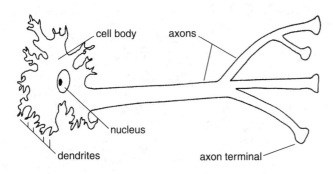

**FIGURE 2-3**   A schematic diagram of a neuron.

A short, interactive tutorial on neurons and transmitters can be found at *http://www.csuchico.edu/psy/BioPsych/neurotransmission.html.*

released by other neurons. When its dendrites and cell body receive sufficient stimulation, a neuron is said to "fire"—it exhibits a sudden change in electrical potential lasting only a few milliseconds (thousandths of a second). The more stimulation a neuron receives, the more rapidly it fires: It may fire only a few dozen times a second with low stimulation but several hundred times a second with high stimulation. The axons are involved on the transmission side. Each time a neuron fires, enlarged structures at the ends of the axons, the **axon terminals,** release a transmitter that may stimulate the dendrites of other neurons. Thus, within a single neuron, the flow of activity typically begins with the dendrites, travels down the axons, and ends with release of transmitter by the axon terminals.

The term **synapse** refers to a small gap between the axon terminal of one neuron (called the **presynaptic neuron**) and the dendrite of another neuron (called the **postsynaptic neuron**). As Figure 2-4 shows, the presynaptic neuron releases its transmitter into the synapse. This transmitter can affect the postsynaptic neuron in one of two ways. In an **excitatory synapse,** the release of transmitter makes the postsynaptic neuron more likely to fire. In an **inhibitory synapse,** the release of transmitter makes the postsynaptic neuron less likely to fire. A single neuron may receive inputs, some excitatory and some inhibitory, from thousands of other neurons. At any moment, a neuron's firing rate reflects the combined influence of all its excitatory and inhibitory inputs.

### Physiological Research on "Simple Sensations"

One theme of Associationism that has been uniformly supported by subsequent physiological findings is the hypothesis that our sensory systems analyze the complex stimulus environment that surrounds us by breaking it down into "simple sensations." Quite a bit is now known about the traditional "five senses"

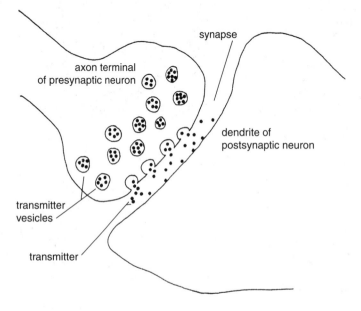

**FIGURE 2-4**   A schematic diagram of a synapse between two neurons. The chemical transmitter released by the axon terminal of the presynaptic neuron causes changes in the dendrite of the postsynaptic neuron that makes the neuron more likely to fire (in an excitatory synapse) or less likely to fire (in an inhibitory synapse).

(sight, hearing, touch, taste, and smell) and about several internal senses (which monitor the body's balance, muscle tensions, the position of the limbs, and so on). The evidence consistently shows that each of these sensory systems begins by detecting fairly basic characteristics of incoming stimuli. A few examples will help to illustrate how this is accomplished.

The nervous system's only contact with the stimuli of the external environment comes through a variety of specialized neurons called **receptors.** Instead of dendrites that are sensitive to the transmitters of other neurons, receptors have structures that are sensitive to specific types of external stimuli. In the visual system, for example, the effective stimulus modality is, of course, light, and receptors sensitive to light are located on the **retina.** As shown in Figure 2-5, light entering the eye is focused by the **cornea** and **lens,** passes through a gelatinous substance called the **vitreous humor,** and finally reaches the retina. If we make an analogy between the eye and a camera, then the retina is the counterpart of photographic film. It is on the retina, which lines the inside surface of the eyeball, that a miniature inverted image of the visual world is focused. Some of the receptors on the retina are called **cones** (because of their shape), and different cones are especially sensitive to different colors in the spectrum of visible light. In the normal human eye, there are three classes of cones, which are most effectively stimulated by light in the red, green, and blue regions of the spectrum, respectively. A red-sensitive cone, for example, is most responsive to red light, but it will also exhibit a weaker response when stimulated by other colors in the red re-

gion of the spectrum, such as orange, violet, and yellow. Similarly, a green-sensitive cone is most effectively stimulated by green light, but it is also stimulated to some extent by blue and yellow light. Although we have only three types of cones, our ability to distinguish among a large number of subtle differences in color stems from the fact that different colors will produce different patterns of activity in the three types of cones. A particular shade of yellow, for example, will produce a unique pattern of activity—the red and green cones may be activated to approximately the same extent, and the blue cones will exhibit very little activity. Since no other color will produce exactly the same pattern of activity in the cones, this pattern is the visual system's method of encoding the presence of a particular shade of yellow.

We can think of cones as neurons that decompose the complex visual world into what the Associationists called "simple sensations." Notice that no matter how intricate a visual stimulus may be, a single red-sensitive cone can communicate only two primitive pieces of information to the rest of the nervous system: its color, and its location in the visual field (which determines where the light hits the retina).

All the other sensory systems have specialized receptors that are activated by simple features of their respective sensory modalities. The skin contains a variety of tactile receptors, some sensitive to pressure, some to pain, some to warmth, and some to cold. In the auditory system, single neurons are tuned to particular sound frequencies, so that one neuron might be most sensitive to a tone with a frequency of 1,000 cycles/second. Such a neuron would be

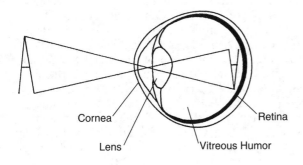

Cornea

Lens

Retina

Vitreous Humor

**FIGURE 2-5**  How light from an object in the environment enters the eye and is focused on the retina in an inverted image.

less sensitive to equally intense tones of higher or lower pitches. Regarding the sense of taste, most experts believe that all gustatory sensations can be decomposed into four simple tastes—sour, salty, bitter, and sweet. Some very exacting experiments by Bekesy (1964, 1966) have shown that individual taste receptors on the tongue are responsive to one and only one of these four simple tastes. In short, the evidence from sensory physiology is unambiguous: All sensory systems begin by breaking down incoming stimuli into simple sensations.

## Physiological Research on "Complex Ideas"

The essence of James Mill's theory of complex ideas is the notion of a hierarchy: At the bottom of the hierarchy are simple ideas, which can unite to produce complex ideas. Complex ideas can unite to form duplex ideas, and so on. Although Mill was concerned with the memories (ideas) of past sensations, his concept of a hierarchy of increasing complexity must certainly have some relevance to the processing of current sensations. After all, whereas our visual systems start by detecting the basic features of a stimulus—color, brightness, position, and so on—each of us can recognize complex visual patterns, such as the face of a friend or a written word. Somehow, the simple sensory attributes detected by the receptors on the retina must be combined to yield more "complex ideas," such as *my friend Paul* or the written word *music*.

Although the mechanisms of visual pattern recognition are still largely a mystery, some impressive research by Hubel and Wiesel (1965, 1979) offers a few clues about how neurons higher in the visual pathways respond to more complex stimulus features than do the cones on the retina. The general procedure used by Hubel and Wiesel can be summarized briefly. They would isolate a single neuron somewhere in the visual system of an anesthetized monkey (or cat) and record the electrical activity of that neuron while presenting a wide range of visual stimuli (varying in color, size, shape, and location in the visual field) to

the animal. The electrical activity of the neuron was recorded by piercing it with a **microelectrode** (a very thin wire), which was connected to suitable amplifying and recording equipment. The question Hubel and Wiesel wished to answer was simple: What type of "detector" is this neuron? That is, what type of visual stimuli would make the neuron fire most rapidly?

For our purposes, the neurons of greatest interest are those in the **visual cortex**, an area in the back of the head, just beneath the skull. Recall that on the retina, a receptor can be stimulated by a simple point of light: If the point of light is sufficiently bright and if it strikes the receptor, the receptor will respond. In the visual cortex, however, Hubel and Wiesel found individual neurons that responded to more complex shapes. One class of cells, which Hubel and Wiesel called **simple cells,** fired most rapidly when the visual stimulus was a line of a specific orientation, presented in a specific part of the visual field. For example, one simple cell might fire most rapidly in response to a line at a 45-degree angle from the horizontal, projected on a specific part of the retina. If the orientation of the line were changed to 30 degrees or 60 degrees, the cell would fire less rapidly, and with further deviations from 45 degrees the cell would respond less and less.

What sort of neural connections from the retina to the visual cortex might explain why a simple cell is most responsive to a line of a specific orientation? Imagine that a simple cell in the cortex receives (through a chain of intervening neurons) excitatory inputs from individual receptors that are positioned in a row on the surface of the retina, as diagrammed schematically in Figure 2-6. Furthermore, suppose that receptors on either side of this row have inhibitory connections to the simple cell (as represented by the minus signs in Figure 2-6). Since each of the rods becomes active when light falls on it, and since the simple cell's activity level is increased by excitatory inputs and decreased by inhibitory inputs, you should be able to see that this simple cell will be maximally excited by a line of 45 degrees. You should also see why lines

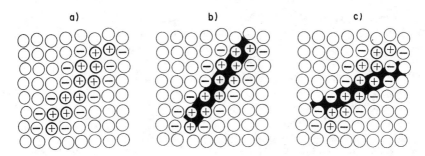

**FIGURE 2-6** (a) A schematic diagram of a portion of the retina illustrating the possible connections between receptors on the retina and a simple cell in the visual cortex. The plus signs mark receptors with excitatory inputs to the cortical cell, and the minus signs mark receptors with inhibitory inputs to the cortical cell. (b) If a line of 45 degrees is projected onto this portion of the retina, the cortical cell becomes highly active because of the many excitatory inputs. (c) A line of less than 45 degrees stimulates some receptors that inhibit the cortical cell and fewer receptors that excite the cortical cell, so as a result, the cortical cell fires less rapidly.

of somewhat different orientations will produce some lesser degrees of activity in the simple cell.

It should be emphasized that this discussion of the neural connections between the retina and the visual cortex is mere speculation—no one has yet managed to trace the "wiring diagram" for a simple cell. Nevertheless, since all receptors on the retina are responsive to single points of light, it seems logically inescapable that some such integration of information must occur between the retina and the line-detecting cells in the visual cortex. Therefore, it is probably not too great a distortion of James Mill's views to say that a visual receptor on the retina is the physical counterpart to a simple idea (a point of light), that a simple cell in the visual cortex is the physical counterpart

to a more complex idea (a line of a specific orientation), and that it is some sort of union of the information from several simple ideas that makes the more complex idea possible.

A line of a specific orientation is admittedly still quite simple compared to some of the complex ideas about which Mill wrote—bricks, mortar, walls, windows. Unfortunately, relatively little is known about how the visual system reacts to such complex stimuli. However, Hubel and Wiesel did find some cells a bit more sophisticated than their simple cells. Some cells in the visual cortex were maximally excited by stimuli with two edges intersecting at a specific angle. For instance, one cell might respond to the corner of a rectangle—two edges forming a 90-degree angle. Another cell might be most responsive to part of a triangle—two edges that formed an angle of, say, 45 degrees. Among the most complex visual detectors ever reported are cortical neurons in macaque monkeys that could be called "hand detectors" and "face detectors" (Desimone, Albright, Gross, & Bruce, 1984). For instance, the face detectors responded vigorously to human or monkey faces, whereas a variety of other stimuli (shapes, textures, pictures of other objects) evoked little or no response.

You can test your ability to discover the properties of simulated simple cells at *http://coglab.psych.purdue.edu/coglab/labs/ReceptiveField.html*.

This type of evidence for visual feature detectors has led some sensory psychologists to espouse the **single neuron doctrine** of perception (Barlow, 1972). According to this view, the visual system (and probably other sensory systems) is arranged in a hierarchy of increasing complexity, and at the highest levels are neurons that respond to very specific features. Are there single neurons that are activated by such complex stimuli as the face of a friend or a 1976 Pinto? Those who favor the single neuron doctrine believe that the brain may indeed contain such specialized neurons. But this is only one possibility. Another is that an entire cluster of neurons may be activated by a complex visual stimulus, and it is the activity of this entire group of cells that corresponds to a complex idea. Still another view is that a large portion of the neurons in the visual cortex are activated by a complex visual stimulus, and it is not which neurons are active so much as the specific pattern of activity that encodes the nature of the stimulus (Lashley, 1929, 1950; Pribram, 1966). At the present time, no one knows which one of these possibilities is most accurate.

As an empiricist, James Mill believed that experience is at the root of all simple and complex ideas. However, when Hubel and Wiesel (1963) examined cells in the visual cortex of newborn kittens with no previous visual experience, they found feature detectors similar to those found in adult cats (though the neurons of kittens were more sluggish in their responsiveness to visual stimuli). If we wish to call feature detectors the physiological counterparts to Mill's ideas (either simple or complex), then we must grant that, at least in cats, these ideas are innate: Individual cells in a kitten's visual cortex are prewired to respond to specific visual features (lines, angles) before the kitten has seen any visual patterns whatsoever. Yet although feature detectors are present at birth, experience plays an important role in two ways. First, visual experience keeps the feature detectors functioning well. Hubel and Wiesel (1970) found that if kittens were deprived of visual stimulation during certain **critical periods** of their young lives, the feature detectors of these kittens would deterio-

rate and become nonfunctional. Second, the response characteristics of such feature detectors can be modified depending upon the type of visual stimulation a kitten receives. Blakemore and Cooper (1970) raised some kittens in an environment with large vertical stripes on the walls and other kittens in an environment with horizontal stripes. The feature detectors of kittens raised with vertical stimuli responded primarily to edges of approximately vertical orientation, and few cells responded to horizontal lines. The opposite was found for kittens raised with horizontal stimulation. These studies with young kittens show that heredity and environment both contribute to the types of visual feature detectors found in the adult animal.

## Physiological Research on Associative Learning

For many decades, psychologists and physiologists have tried to discover the physiological changes that take place during learning. A survey of this research could fill many volumes, and this section can provide only a very brief summary of a few important theories and research findings. There are different theories about what takes place at the cellular level during learning. One possibility is that neurons may grow new axons and/or new dendrites as a result of a learning experience, so that completely new synapses are formed. A second possibility is that learning involves changes in already existing synapses. Let us examine each of these possibilities.

*Growth of New Synapses.* Some of the best evidence for the hypothesis that new synapses are developed as a result of experience comes from studies in which animals were exposed to enriched living environments. Rosenzweig and his colleagues (Rosenzweig, 1966; Rosenzweig, Mollgaard, Diamond, & Bennet, 1972) placed young rats in two different environments to determine how early experience influences the development of the brain. Some rats were placed in an environment rich in stimuli and in possible learning experiences. These animals lived in groups of

10 to 12, and their cage contained many objects to play with and explore—ladders, wheels, platforms, mazes, and the like. Other rats were raised in a much more impoverished environment. Each animal lived in a separate, empty cage, and it could not see or touch other rats. These rats certainly had far fewer sensory and learning experiences. After the rats spent 80 days in these environments, Rosenzweig and his colleagues found that the brains of the enriched subjects were significantly heavier than those of impoverished subjects. Differences in weight were especially pronounced in the cerebral cortex, which is thought to play an important role in the learning process. Other studies have shown that exposure to enriched environments can produce similar changes in adult animals, and that in some cases very brief exposure can have significant effects. For instance, Ferchmin and Eterovic (1980) found increased brain weights in young rats after the animals had spent only four 10-minute periods in an enriched environment.

What types of changes at the cellular level accompany these differences in overall brain size? Microscopic examinations have revealed a variety of changes in the brain tissue of rats exposed to enriched environments, including more branching of dendrites (indicative of more synaptic connections between axons and dendrites) and synapses with larger surface areas (Rosenzweig, 1984). Other studies have found that more structured types of learning experiences can produce cellular changes in more localized areas of the brain. Spinelli, Jensen, and DiPrisco (1980) trained young kittens on a task in which they had to flex one foreleg to avoid a shock to that leg. After a few brief sessions with this procedure, each kitten's cortex was examined. The experimenters found that (1) a larger region of the cortex was responsive to stimulation of the foreleg involved in the avoidance training (compared to the cortical region responsive to the other, untrained foreleg) and (2) there was a marked increase in the number of dendritic branches in this specific area of the cortex. These and other studies provide compelling evidence that relatively brief learning experiences can produce significant increases in the number, size,

and complexity of synaptic connections (Jones & Schallert, 1994).

There is an increasing belief among neuroscientists that the growth of new dendrites and synaptic connections underlies the formation of long-term memories (Kolb & Whishaw, 1998). In humans, studies have shown that dramatic **arborization,** or the branching of dendrites, occurs in the months before birth and in the first year of life. At the same time, other connections between neurons disappear. It is not clear how much of this change is due to maturation and how much to the infant's learning experiences (Casaer, 1993). However, it appears that as a child grows and learns, numerous new synaptic connections are formed and other, unneeded connections are eliminated. These neural changes continue at least until the adolescent years (Huttenlocher, 1990).

*Growth of New Neurons.* Until quite recently, the accepted theory of neural growth was that except before birth and possibly during early infancy, no new neurons can grow in the brains of animals. According to this view, all learning takes the form of changes in existing neurons (such as arborization), and that any neurons that are lost due to illness or injury cannot be replaced. However, there is now a growing body of evidence that this traditional view of neural growth is incorrect, and that new neurons continue to appear in the brains of adult mammals. For example, one study with adult macaque monkeys found new neurons developing in several areas of the cerebral cortex (Gould, Reeves, Graziano, & Gross, 1999). The growth of new neurons, called **neurogenesis,** has also been observed in other species, and in some cases this growth appears to be related to learning experiences. For instance, in one experiment, some rats learned tasks that are known to involve an area of the brain called the hippocampus, and other rats learned tasks that do not involve the hippocampus. For the first group of rats, after the learning period, new neurons were found in a nearby area of the brain that receives inputs from the hippocampus. For the second group of rats, no new neurons were found in this area. These results suggest that new neurons can grow during a learning experience, and that exactly where they grow may depend on the specific type of learning that is involved (Gould, Beylin, Tanapat, Reeves, & Shors, 1999).

Other research with rats has found evidence that new neurons may grow after a brain injury, and that these new neurons may help the animal recover some of the abilities that were lost as a result of the injury (Kolb, Gibb, Gorny, & Whishaw, 1998). Although most of the research so far has been with non-humans, there is some evidence for the growth of new neurons in adult humans. Further research on this topic should provide valuable information about the brain mechanisms of learning, and it may lead to new treatments for people who suffer strokes or other brain damage (Ogden, 2000).

***Changes in Existing Synapses.***   There is now plenty of evidence that some changes in neural connections do not depend on the growth of new synapses, but rather on chemical changes in old synapses. For example, if the neurons in a slice of rat brain tissue are given a brief burst of electrical stimulation, this can produce long-lasting increases in the strengths of existing connections between neurons. The increase in the strength of excitatory synapses as a result of electrical stimulation is called **long-term potentiation,** and the effect can last for weeks or months (Bliss & Lomo, 1973). Long-term potentiation has also been observed in human brain tissue removed during the course of surgical procedures (Chen, Lee, Kato, Spencer, Shepherd, & Williamson, 1996).

This phenomenon has been demonstrated in brain areas that are thought to be implicated in the storage of long-term memories, such as the hippocampus and the cerebral cortex. For this reason, some investigators believe that long-term potentiation may be a basic process through which the brain can change as a result of a learning experience (Maren & Baudry, 1995). However, the issue is controversial, and others believe that the potential importance of long-term potentiation to learning and mem-

ory processes has been overstated (Geinisman, 1999). In any case, this phenomenon is currently the focus of a good deal of research. Long-term potentiation has been demonstrated, not just in brain slices, but in the brains of living and behaving animals, and there are some tantalizing hints that it may play a role in the learning of new associations (Leung & Shen, 1995; Stefan, Kunesch, Cohen, Benecke, & Classen, 2000).

What type of chemical changes could cause an increase in the strength of a synaptic connection? One possibility is that as a result of a learning experience, the axon terminal of the presynaptic neuron acquires the capacity to release more transmitter. Another possibility is that the cell membrane of the postsynaptic neuron becomes more sensitive to the transmitter, so that although the amount of transmitter in the synapses may be the same, the response of the postsynaptic neuron will be greater. In experiments on long-term potentiation, researchers have found evidence that both presynaptic and postsynaptic changes may be involved (Davies, Lester, Reymann, & Collingridge, 1989). Recent studies suggest that the mammalian brain has at its disposal a number of different chemical mechanisms for altering the strengths of the connections between neurons (Madison, Malenka, & Nicoll, 1991). Some examples of how simple learning experiences can produce chemical changes in individual synapses will be presented in later chapters.

***Where Are "Complex Ideas" Stored in the Brain?***   Before concluding this brief survey of the physiological approach to learning, we should take one final look at James Mill's concept of complex ideas. What happens at the physiological level when a child learns the concept *house* or when a kitten learns to recognize and respond appropriately to a snake? Although the answer to this question is not yet known, a number of different possibilities have been proposed.

One hypothesis is that every learning experience produces neural changes that are distributed diffusely over many sections of the brain. That is, the physical or chemical changes described in the preceding sections do not occur in just a few neurons in one part of the brain, but in many neurons in many different brain areas. This hypothesis was supported by some classic experiments by Karl Lashley (1950). After training rats to run through a maze, Lashley removed sections of the cerebral cortex (different sections for different rats) to see whether he could remove the memories of the maze. If he could, this would show where the memories about the maze were stored. However, Lashley's efforts to find the location of these memories were unsuccessful. If a small section of cortex was removed, this had no effect on a rat's maze performance, no matter which section was removed. If a larger section of cortex was removed, this would cause a rat's performance in the maze to deteriorate, no matter which section was removed. Lashley therefore concluded that memories are stored diffusely throughout the brain, and removing small sections of the brain will not remove the memory. Other studies have also provided support for the view that large sections of the brain undergo change during simple learning experiences (John, 1967; John, Tang, Brill, Young, & Ono, 1986).

A very different hypothesis is that the information about individual concepts or ideas is **localized,** or stored in small, specific sections of the brain. For example, some writers (such as J. Konorski, 1967; Wickelgren, 1979) have suggested that, in addition to innate feature detectors like those found by Hubel and Wiesel, the cerebral cortex may contain many unused or dormant neurons, perhaps with weak inputs from various feature detectors. As a result of an animal's learning experiences, one (or a small set) of these dormant neurons might come to respond selectively to a particular complex object. To take a simple example, after an animal has had sufficient exposure to the complex object we call an *apple*, some cortical neuron might develop excitatory inputs from detectors responsive to the apple's red color, roughly spherical shape, specific odor, and other characteristics. In this way, an animal that at birth had no complex idea of an apple might develop the ability to recognize apples as a result of its experience.

The hypothesis that specific memories and ideas are stored in small sections of the brain also has evidence to support it. One type of evidence came from the research of Penfield (1959), who electrically stimulated areas of the cerebral cortex of human patients during brain surgery. When Penfield stimulated small areas of the cortex, his patients, who were anesthetized but awake, reported a variety of vivid sensations, such as hearing a specific piece of music, or experiencing the sights and sounds of a circus. Although it might be tempting to conclude that the electrical stimulation had triggered a site where specific memories of the past were stored, Penfield's findings can be interpreted in many ways, and their significance is not clear.

Better evidence for localized memories comes from reports of people who suffered damage to small sections of the brain as a result of an accident or stroke. Brain injury can, of course, produce a very wide range of psychological or physical problems, but in a few individuals the result was a loss of very specific information. For example, one man had difficulty naming any fruit or vegetables, whereas he had no trouble identifying any other types of objects (Hart, Berndt, & Caramazza, 1985). Another person could not name objects typically found in a room, such as furniture, walls, and so on (Yamadori & Albert, 1973). Another could no longer remember the names of well-known celebrities, but he had no problem with the names of other famous people, such as historical and literary figures (Lucchelli, Muggia, & Spinnler, 1997). These cases suggest that specific concepts are stored in specific areas of the brain, and that concepts belonging to a single category are stored close together.

The debate over whether the neural representation of complex ideas is localized or distributed has gone on for many years, and it has not yet been resolved. It is possible that both hypotheses are partially correct, with some types of learning producing changes in fairly specific parts of the brain, and others producing changes over large portions of the brain (Thompson, 1991). Modern-day neuroscientists continue to investigate the question asked by James Mill over a century and a half ago:

What are complex ideas, and how does the human brain acquire them and retain them? We still do not have a very good answer to this question, but we know much more than James Mill did, and we are learning more with each passing year. If and when neuroscientists eventually discover how the brain stores information about complex concepts and ideas, this will be a milestone in the psychology of learning.

## CHAPTER SUMMARY

Over the centuries, philosophers called Associationists proposed principles about how the brain forms associations between different thoughts and ideas. Aristotle proposed the principles of contiguity, similarity, and contrast. Thomas Brown added other principles to the list, such as frequency, duration, recency, and liveliness. James Mill developed a theory of how the repeated presentation of two or more simple ideas can lead to the formation of more complex ideas. Ebbinghaus conducted some of the first scientific research on learning and memory, using lists of nonsense syllables as his stimuli and repeating the lists to himself until he memorized them. By letting some time pass, relearning the list, and measuring his "savings," Ebbinghaus demonstrated several basic principles of learning, including contiguity, recency, and overlearning.

Specialized sensory neurons in the eyes, ears, and other sense organs respond to very simple sensory properties, much as the Associationists suggested. Neurons in the eye respond to specific colors, and neurons in the ear respond to specific pitches of sound. In the brain, the inputs from many sensory neurons are often combined, so that individual neurons may respond to more complex stimuli, such as edges, angles, and corners of a visual stimulus. In monkeys, individual neurons that respond to faces and hands have been found, but how animals or people are able to identify the many complex stimuli in our environments is still largely unknown.

Physiologists assume that whenever an individual learns something new, there is a physical change somewhere in the brain or nervous system. Some axon terminals may begin to produce neurotransmitters in greater quantities, or some dendrites may become more sensitive to existing neurotransmitters, or completely new synapses may grow between neurons. Brain researchers have obtained good evidence for each of these different types of changes. Lashley's research with rats suggested that many different sections of the brain are changed during a simple learning experience. However, research on humans with brain injuries suggests that some types of information may be stored in fairly small, specific areas of the brain.

## REVIEW QUESTIONS

1. Describe Aristotle's three principles of association, some additional principles proposed by Thomas Brown, and James Mill's theory of complex ideas. Give examples to illustrate these principles.
2. What procedure did Ebbinghaus use to study memory? How did his results offer evidence for the principles of frequency, recency, and contiguity?
3. Use the example of color vision to explain how our sensory systems begin by breaking down complex stimuli into "simple sensations." How did Hubel and Wiesel study the properties of individual neurons in the visual cortex of cats and monkeys, and what did they find?
4. Discuss some research findings about what changes take place in the brain during learning. What sorts of evidence have been used in the debate between those who believe that a simple learning experience produces changes in many different parts of the brain and those who believe that the changes occur in small, localized parts of the brain?

## CHAPTER 3

# Innate Behavior Patterns and Habituation

When any animal is born, it is already endowed with a variety of complex abilities. Its immediate survival depends on the ability to breathe and to pump blood through its veins. If it is a mammal, it has the ability to regulate its temperature within narrow limits. If its survival depends on the ability to flee from predators, it may start to walk and run within minutes after birth. Newborn animals are also equipped with a range of sensory capacities. As Hubel and Wiesel (1963) have shown, kittens have inborn visual cells responsive to colors, edges, and probably other aspects of the visual world. Such innate sensory structures are by no means limited to kittens, nor to the visual system.

One major purpose of this chapter is to provide examples of the types of behavioral abilities that an animal may already possess as it enters the world. There are good reasons for examining innate behavior patterns in a book about learning. First, many learned behaviors are derivatives, extensions, or variations of innate behaviors. Second, many of the features of learned behaviors (for example, their control by environmental stimuli, their mechanisms of temporal sequencing) have parallels in inborn behavior patterns. Another purpose of this chapter is to examine the phenomenon of habituation, which is often said to be the simplest type of learning.

Most of the examples of innate behavior patterns described in this chapter are based on the work of **ethologists**—scientists who study how animals behave in their natural environments. Although both ethologists and psychologists in the field of learning study animal behavior, their purposes and strategies are different. The testing environments of learning psychologists tend to be barren and artificial, for their goal is to discover general principles of learning that do not depend on specific types of stimuli. Ethologists usually conduct their experiments in the animal's natural habitat or in a seminaturalistic setting, because their purpose is to determine how an animal's behavior helps it to survive in its environment. Ethologists are interested in both learned and innate behaviors, and many of the behavior patterns they have studied in detail are **species-specific** (unique to a single species). In recent years, psychologists who study learning have shown increasing interest in innate behaviors and species-specific behaviors. As a result, the work of ethologists is having greater impact on both research and theory in the field of learning.

One characteristic that is common to many behaviors, both learned and unlearned, is that they appear to be purposive, or goal-directed. As we will see, this is true of some of our most primitive reflexes as well as our most complex skills. For this reason, it will be useful to begin this chapter with some concepts from **control systems theory,** a branch of science that deals with goal-directed behaviors in both living creatures and inanimate objects.

## CHARACTERISTICS OF GOAL-DIRECTED SYSTEMS

Control systems theory provides a general framework for analyzing a wide range of goal-directed systems. The terminology used here is based on the work of McFarland (1971). A relatively simple example of an inanimate goal-directed system is a house's heating system. The goal of the heating system is to keep the house temperature above some minimum level, say 65°F. If the house temperature drops below 65°F, the heating system "spontaneously" springs into action, starting the furnace. Once the temperature goal is reached, the activity of the heating system ceases. Of course, we know there is nothing magical about this process. The activity of the heating system is controlled by the thermostat, which relies on the fact that metals expand when heated and contract when cooled. The cooling of the metals in the thermostat causes them to bend and close an electrical switch, thus starting the furnace. Heating of the metals opens the switch and stops the furnace.

The thermostat is an example of a fundamental concept in control systems theory, the

**comparator.** As shown in Figure 3-1, a comparator receives two types of input, called the **reference input** and the **actual input.** The reference input is often not a physical entity but a conceptual one (the temperature that, when reached, will be just enough to open the switch and stop the furnace). On the other hand, the actual input measures some actual physical characteristic of the present environment—in this case, the air temperature in the vicinity of the thermostat.

Any comparator has rules that it follows to determine, based on the current actual input and reference input, what its output will be. In the case of a thermostat, the output is an on/off command to the furnace, which is an example of an **action system.** The rules that the thermostat follows might be: (1) if the furnace is off and the air temperature becomes one degree lower than the reference input, turn on the furnace, and (2) if the furnace is on and the air temperature becomes one degree higher than the reference input, turn off the furnace. With a setting of 65°F, these rules would keep the air temperature between 64°F and 66°F.

The product of the action system is simply called the **output**—the entry of warm air from the radiators in this example. As Figure 3-1 shows, the output of the action system feeds back and affects the actual input to the comparator. For this reason, such a goal-directed system is frequently called a **feedback system** or a **closed-loop system.** The output of the

**FIGURE 3-1**    The concepts of control systems theory as applied to a home's heating system.

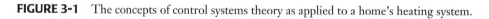
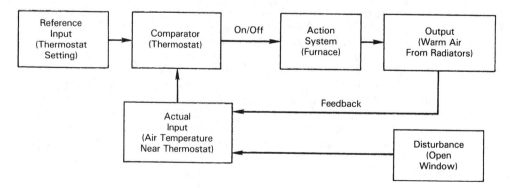

action system (warm air) and the actual input to the comparator (air temperature) seem closely related, and you may wonder why two separate terms are needed to describe them. The reason is that there is not always a close relationship between the output of the action system and the actual input, for other factors can affect the actual input. One example is the **disturbance** depicted in Figure 3-1. If a window is open on a cold day, this will also affect the air temperature near the thermostat, which may then be very different from the temperature of the air coming out of the radiators.

This example illustrates six of the most important concepts of control systems theory: comparator, reference input, actual input, action system, output, and disturbance. We will encounter many examples of goal-directed behaviors in this book, and it will often be useful to try to identify the different components of the feedback loop in these examples. The next section is the first of many in this text that will make use of the concepts of control systems theory.

## REFLEXES

A **reflex** is a stereotyped pattern of movement of a part of the body that can be reliably elicited by presenting the appropriate stimulus. You are probably familiar with the patellar (knee-jerk) reflex: If a person's leg is supported so that the foot is off the ground and the lower leg can swing freely, the light tap of a hammer just below the kneecap will evoke a small kicking motion from the leg. As with all reflexes, the patellar reflex involves an innate connection between a stimulus and a response. The stimulus in this example is the tapping of the tendon below the kneecap, and the response is of course the kicking motion.

A normal newborn child displays a variety of reflexes. A nipple placed in the child's mouth will elicit a sucking response. If the sole of the foot is pricked with a pin, the child's knees will flex, pulling the feet away from the painful stimulus. If an adult places a finger in the child's palm, the child's fingers will close around it in a grasping reflex. Some of the newborn's reflexes disappear with age. Others, such as the dilation of the pupils and the closing of the eyes in response to a bright light, or coughing in response to a throat irritation, persist throughout life.

If you ever accidentally placed your hand on a hot stove, you probably exhibited a flexion reflex—a rapid withdrawal of the hand caused by a bending of the arm at the elbow. The response is very rapid because the association between sensory and motor neurons occurs directly in the spinal cord. Figure 3-2 depicts a cross section of the spinal cord and some of the neural machinery involved in this reflex. The hand contains sensory neurons sensitive to pain, and their lengthy axons travel all the way into the spinal cord before synapsing with other neurons. In the flexion reflex, one or more small neurons, called **interneurons,** separate the sensory neurons from motor neurons. The motor neurons have cell bodies within the spinal cord, and their axons exit through the front of the spinal cord, travel back down the arm, and synapse with individual muscle fibers in the arm. When excited, the muscle fibers contract, thereby producing the response. The physiology of this reflex is sometimes called the **spinal reflex arc,** after the shape of the path of neural excitation

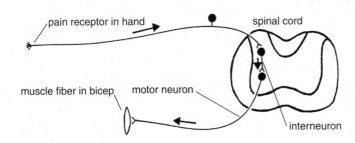

**FIGURE 3-2** A cross section of the spinal cord, along with the components of the spinal withdrawal reflex.

shown in Figure 3-2. Of course, not one but many of such sensory neurons, interneurons, and motor neurons are involved in producing the reflexive response.

Thus this description of the chain of connections in the spinal reflex arc is consistent with the standard definition of a reflex—a stimulus elicits a response. There is more to the story of the spinal reflex arc, however, so now let us see how this reflex can be viewed as a feedback system. Within the muscles of the arm are structures called **stretch receptors,** which serve as the comparators of the feedback system. We will not go into detail about how this happens, but the stretch receptors compare (1) the goal or reference input—the commands sent from the motor neurons to the muscle fibers telling them to contract, and (2) the actual amount that the muscles have contracted. Notice that the mere fact that some motor neurons have sent their commands to the muscle does not guarantee that the arm is safely withdrawn from the dangerous object. There might be a disturbance—an obstruction that impedes the movement of the arm. Or the muscles may be in a state of fatigue and therefore fail to respond sufficiently to the commands of the motor neurons. If the muscles have not contracted sufficiently for any such reason, the stretch receptors begin to stimulate the motor neurons (which in turn stimulate the muscle fibers more vigorously), and this stimulation continues until the contraction is completed. In short, the comparators (the stretch receptors) continue to stimulate the action system (the motor neurons and muscle fibers) until the goal (a successful muscle contraction) is achieved.

This analysis of the spinal reflex arc shows that feedback can play a crucial role in even the simplest reflexive behaviors. Stretch receptors and neurons with similar functions are found in many parts of the human body and in other animals. In all cases, the function of these cells is to determine whether or not the commands of the motor neurons have been carried out. As we turn to other classes of innate behaviors, we will find further examples of closed-loop movement systems.

## TROPISMS AND ORIENTATION

Whereas a reflex is the stereotyped movement of a part of the body, a **tropism** is a movement or change in orientation of the entire organism. The first to study tropisms was Jacques Loeb (1900), who called tropisms "forced movements," to suggest that no intelligence, will, or choice was involved. For example, a *geotropism* is an orienting movement that relies on a sensitivity to gravity. Loeb conducted a simple experiment in which a sea anemone was placed with its head down in a test tube. Within minutes the anemone had regained its normal head-up orientation. Loeb cautioned that this sort of purposeful movement does not mean that a creature has "a mind" or intelligence, because plants also exhibit geotropisms. Regardless of how a seed is oriented when planted in the ground, its roots will grow downward and its stalk upward, which shows that plants can also exhibit goal-directed "behavior." Later researchers (such as Fraenkel & Gunn, 1940) grouped tropisms into two major categories: **kineses** (plural of **kinesis**) and **taxes** (plural of **taxis**).

### Kineses

A frequently cited example of a kinesis is the humidity-seeking behavior of the wood louse. This creature, though actually a small crustacean, resembles an insect, and it spends most of its time under a rock or a log in the forest. The wood louse must remain in humid areas in order to survive—if the air is too dry, it will die of dehydration in a matter of hours. Fortunately for the wood louse, nature has provided it with a simple yet effective technique for finding and remaining in moist areas. To study the wood louse's strategy, Fraenkel and Gunn (1940) placed several wood lice in the center of a chamber in which the air was moist at one end and dry at the other. They found that the wood lice usually kept walking when they were in the dry end of the chamber, but they frequently stopped for long periods of time in the moist end. As a result, they tended to congregate in the moist end of the chamber.

What distinguishes a kinesis from a taxis is that the *direction* of the movement is random with respect to the direction of the humid areas. The wood louse does not head directly toward a moist area or away from a dry one because it has no means of sensing the humidity of a distant location—it can only sense the humidity of its present location. Nevertheless, its tendency to keep moving when in a dry area and stop when in a moist area is generally successful in keeping the creature alive.

The wood louse's humidity-seeking behavior is another example of a feedback system. Although we do not know exactly how the wood louse measures humidity, its behavior tells us that it must have a comparator that can detect the actual input (current humidity) and compare it to the reference input (the goal of high humidity). The action system in this case is the creature's locomotion system—the motor neurons, muscles, and legs that allow it to move about. Locomotion is, of course, the output of this action system, but there is no guarantee that locomotion will lead to the goal of high humidity. The wood louse may move about incessantly if it finds itself in a dry location, but if there are no humid areas nearby, the goal of high humidity will not be achieved as a result of this locomotion.

## Taxes

Unlike kineses, in a taxis the direction of movement bears some relationship to the location of the stimulus. One example of a taxis is a maggot's movement away from any bright light source. If a bright light is turned on to the maggot's right, it will promptly turn to the left and move in a fairly straight line away from the light. The maggot accomplishes this directional movement by using a light-sensitive receptor at its head end. As the maggot moves, its head repeatedly swings left and right, and this oscillating movement allows it to compare the brightness of light in various directions and to move toward the direction where the light is less intense.

The maggot's taxis is primitive, for it can only point the organism in a single direction—away from the light. A more sophisticated taxis is exhibited by the ant, which can use the sun as a navigational aid when traveling to or from its home. On a journey away from home, the ant travels in a straight path by keeping the sun at a constant angle to its direction of motion. To return home, the ant changes the angle by 180 degrees. The ant's reliance on the sun can be demonstrated by providing it with an artificial sun that the experimenter can control. If this light source is gradually moved, the ant's direction of travel will change to keep its orientation, with respect to the light, constant (Schneirla, 1933).

In some cases it can be shown that an organism's bodily orientation is controlled by more than one stimulus. For example, many fish remain in an upright position by using both gravity and a sensitivity to light (which is normally most intense directly overhead). Figure 3-3 illustrates the findings of von Holst (1935), who varied the direction from which light was projected into an aquarium in order to study the orienting mechanisms of a particular species of fish called *Crenilabrus*. On the left is a *Crenilabrus* whose gravity-sensing apparatus has been removed. This subject's orientation is totally controlled by the direction of the light. If the light is projected from the side, the fish continues to aim its back directly toward the light; if the light is projected from below, the fish swims upside down. On the right is a *Crenilabrus* whose gravity-sensing apparatus is intact. With light coming from the side, the visual and gravitational stimuli are placed in conflict, and the fish strikes a compromise between the two. However, when the light comes from below and is thus maximally discrepant from the gravitational stimulus, the fish apparently ignores the light and relies on the gravitational cues. This last result makes more sense once we understand that the fish's usual method of adjusting to the direction of the light is to equalize the intensity of the light striking its two eyes. With the light coming from below, the intact fish can both respond to the gravitational cues and equalize the light

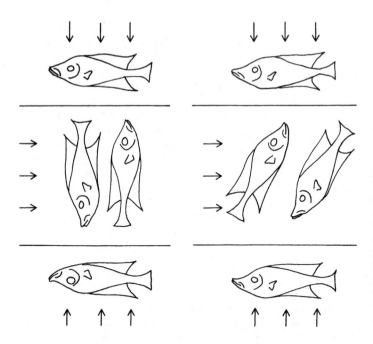

**FIGURE 3-3** On the left is a fish with its gravity-sensing mechanism removed. Regardless of the direction of incoming light (shown by arrows), this fish orients itself so that the light is directly overhead. On the right is a normal fish. When light comes from the side, the fish's orientation represents a compromise between the visual and gravitational cues. (After von Holst, 1935)

intensity (or lack of intensity) in its two eyes by remaining upright.

## SEQUENCES OF BEHAVIOR

So far we have considered innate behaviors consisting of either a brief movement or a continuous series of adjustments. The innate behavior patterns we will now examine are more complex, for they consist of a series of different movements performed in an orderly sequence.

### Fixed Action Patterns

The ethological term **fixed action pattern** has been used to describe some of these behavioral sequences. Although some ethologists (Eibl-Eibesfeldt, 1975) include simple reflexes in the broader category of fixed action patterns, this category also encompasses more elaborate sequences of behavior. A fixed action pattern has the following characteristics: (1) It is a part of the repertoire of all members of a species, and it may be unique to that species; (2) suitable experiments have confirmed that the animal's ability to perform the behavior is

not a result of prior learning experiences; and (3) if it consists of a sequence of behaviors, these behaviors occur in a rigid order regardless of whether they are appropriate in a particular context. That is, once a fixed action pattern is initiated, it will continue to completion without further support from environmental stimuli.

As an example of a fixed action pattern, Eibl-Eibesfeldt (1975) described the nut-burying behavior of a particular species of squirrel:

> The squirrel *Sciurus vulgaris L.* buries nuts in the ground each fall, employing a quite stereotyped sequence of movement. It picks a nut, climbs down to the ground, and searches for a place at the bottom of a tree trunk or a large boulder. At the base of such a conspicuous landmark it will scratch a hole by means of alternating movements of the forelimbs and place the nut in it. Then the nut is rammed into place with rapid thrusts of its snout, covered with dirt by sweeping motions and tamped down with the forepaws. (p. 23)

Although all members of the species exhibit this behavior pattern, this does not prove that the behavior is innate. Each squirrel may learn how to bury nuts by watching its parents early in life. To determine whether the behavior pattern is innate, Eibl-Eibesfeldt conducted a **deprivation experiment** in which all possible means of learning the behavior were removed. A squirrel was separated from its parents at birth and raised in isolation so that it had no opportunity to observe other squirrels burying nuts (or doing anything else, for that matter). In addition, the squirrel received only liquid food and it lived on a solid floor, so it had no experience in handling food or in digging or burying objects in the ground. The animal was kept well fed, so that it had little chance of discovering that storing away food for a time of need is a good strategy. When the squirrel was full-grown, Eibl-Eibesfeldt finally gave it some nuts, one at a time. At first the squirrel ate the nuts until apparently satiated. When given additional nuts, it did not drop them but carried them around in its mouth as it searched about the cage. It seemed to be attracted by vertical objects, such as a corner of the cage, where it might drop the nut. Obviously, it could not dig a hole in the floor, but it would scratch at the floor with its forepaws, push the nut into the corner with its snout, and make the same covering and tamping-down motions seen in the burying sequence of a wild squirrel. This careful experiment demonstrates conclusively that the squirrel's nut-burying repertoire is innate. The caged squirrel's scratching, covering, and tamping-down motions in the absence of dirt show how the components of a fixed action pattern will occur in their usual place in the sequence even when they serve no function.

As with simple reflexes, it usually takes a fairly specific stimulus, which ethologists call a **sign stimulus,** to initiate a fixed action pattern. In the case of the squirrel, the sign stimulus is clearly the nut, but without further experiments we cannot tell which features—its size, shape, color, and so on—are essential ingredients for eliciting the response. For other fixed action patterns, systematic investigation has revealed which features of a stimulus are important and which are irrelevant. In humans, Provine (1989) has found evidence that contagious yawning (the tendency to yawn when someone else yawns) is a fixed action pattern that may occur if we see the entire face of a yawning person. Seeing only the yawner's eyes or only the mouth is not enough to elicit contagious yawning.

Another example of a fixed action pattern is the innate begging response of newborn herring gulls. When a parent enters the nest, the young gulls beg for food by pecking at the parent's beak. This pecking acts as a sign stimulus for the parent, who responds by regurgitating food to feed the chicks. But what aspects of the parent's appearance elicit the chicks' begging responses in the first place? By presenting the chicks with a series of models that mimicked an adult gull to various degrees, Tinbergen and Perdeck (1950) determined that a red spot on the otherwise yellow beak of the parent is an important sign stimulus. A yellow beak with a blue spot elicited fewer pecks, and a solid yellow beak fewer still. But while the presence and color of this small red spot were quite important, other aspects of the model's appearance mattered very little. For instance, the young gulls would peck energetically at a hand-held yellow pencil-shaped rod, especially one with a red spot near the tip.

The tendency for fixed action patterns to be elicited by a seemingly poor imitation of the natural sign stimulus is prevalent in adult animals as well as in newborns. A classic example is the territorial defense response of the male three-spined stickleback (Tinbergen, 1951). During the mating season, this fish will fiercely defend its territory against intrusion by other male sticklebacks. (Female sticklebacks are allowed to enter.) The male's stereotyped threat behaviors are elicited by the sight of a red patch on the underside of the intruding male. If the intruding male stickleback does not have a red patch (which can only happen if the spot has been painted over by a devious experimenter), it will not be attacked. On the other hand, the defending male will attack pie-shaped or cigar-shaped pieces of wood that are placed in its territory if the objects have a red patch on the bottom.

A more surprising finding is that sometimes an unrealistic model can elicit a stronger response than the actual sign stimulus itself. One example is provided by the oyster catcher, a bird that lays white eggs with brown spots. If

**FIGURE 3-4**   An oyster catcher attempts to roll a supernormal egg back to its nest. (After Tinbergen, 1951)

one of its eggs rolls out of its nest, the bird will retrieve it with stereotyped head and neck movements. However, if given a choice between one of its own eggs and a replica that is four times as large, it prefers this **supernormal stimulus** to the normal one, and strains to bring this "egg" to its nest (Figure 3-4). In a similar way, Rowland (1989) found that female sticklebacks were strongly attracted to models of male sticklebacks that were larger than any males they had ever seen.

One conclusion to be drawn from this discussion of sign stimuli is that whereas it is fairly easy to determine what stimulus elicits a fixed action pattern, it requires systematic research to discover exactly which features of the stimulus actually control the animal's behavior. We might have expected the shape of an intruding fish to be a crucial variable in eliciting the defensive response of the male stickleback, but it turns out that shape is relatively unimportant. As we will see in later chapters, this same question can be asked about any learned behavior that occurs in the presence of a specific stimulus: Which characteristics of the stimulus are controlling the behavior, and which are irrelevant? In attempting to answer this question, researchers in the field of learning use techniques that are fundamentally the same as those used by ethologists.

## Reaction Chains

Ethologists distinguish between fixed action patterns and what are sometimes called **reaction chains.** The difference is that whereas fixed action patterns continue until completion once started, in a reaction chain the progression from one behavior to the next depends on the presence of the appropriate external stimulus. If the stimulus is not present, the chain of behaviors will be interrupted. On the other hand, if a stimulus for a behavior in the middle of a chain is presented at the outset, the earlier behaviors will be omitted.

An interesting example of such a sequence of behaviors, all innate, is provided by the hermit crab. The hermit crab has no shell of its own; instead, it lives in the empty shells of gastropods (mollusks). Frequently during its life, the hermit crab grows too large for its present shell and must find a larger one. Reese (1963) identified at least eight separate fixed action patterns that usually occur in a sequence as this creature searches for and selects a new shell. A crab with no shell or with an inadequate shell exhibits a high level of locomotion. Eventually during its travels, the crab spots a shell visually, at which point it approaches the shell and touches it. The crab grasps the shell with its two front legs, and then climbs on top of it. Its cheliped (claw) is used to feel the texture of the surface—a rough texture is preferred. The crab then climbs down and rotates the shell in its legs, exploring the external surface. When the aperture of the shell is located, this too is explored by inserting the cheliped as far as possible. If there is sand or other debris in the aperture, it is removed. Once the aperture is clear, the crab turns around and inserts its abdomen deeply into the shell, and then withdraws it, evidently to determine whether the size of the interior is acceptable. If the shell is suitable, the crab turns the shell upright, enters it once again, and then goes on its way.

The behaviors in this sequence and the stimuli that prompt them are diagrammed in Figure 3-5, which helps to emphasize the distinguishing characteristic of reaction chains—that the performance of one behavior usually produces the stimulus that elicits the next be-

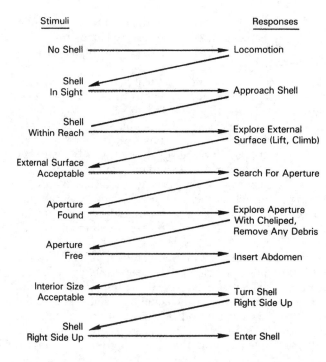

| Stimuli | Responses |
| --- | --- |
| No Shell | Locomotion |
| Shell In Sight | Approach Shell |
| Shell Within Reach | Explore External Surface (Lift, Climb) |
| External Surface Acceptable | Search For Aperture |
| Aperture Found | Explore Aperture With Cheliped, Remove Any Debris |
| Aperture Free | Insert Abdomen |
| Interior Size Acceptable | Turn Shell Right Side Up |
| Shell Right Side Up | Enter Shell |

**FIGURE 3-5**   The hermit crab's reaction chain of shell searching and selecting behaviors. The behaviors form a chain because each successive behavior usually leads to the stimulus for the next behavior in the chain.

havior in the chain. For instance, the first behavior of the chain, locomotion, eventually results in visual contact with a shell, which is the stimulus for the second response, approach. The response of approach brings the crab into close proximity with the shell, which is the stimulus for the third response, lifting, and so on. Unlike the behaviors of a fixed action pattern, those of a reaction chain do not always occur in this complete sequence. The sequence can stop at any point if the stimulus required for the next step is not forthcoming. For example, Reese (1963) found that shells filled with plastic were similar enough to usable shells to elicit the first six behaviors of Figure 3-5. However, since the aperture was not open, the seventh behavior did not occur, and the crab would eventually walk away. On the other hand, the initial steps of the sequence may be omitted if the stimulus for a behavior in the middle of the sequence occurs. When crabs were presented with a suitable shell with the aperture directly in front of them, they would often omit the first five behaviors and proceed with the last four behav-

iors of the sequence. This dependence on external stimulus support makes the behaviors of a reaction chain more variable, but at the same time more adaptable, than those of a fixed action pattern.

## HABITUATION

For his vacation, Dick has rented a cottage on a picturesque lake deep in the woods. The owner of the cottage has advised Dick that although the area is usually very quiet, members of the fish and game club just down the shore often engage in target practice for a few hours

The Web site of the Animal Behavior Society provides information about research in animal behavior, including career opportunities: *http://www.animalbehavior.org.*

You can read case studies about how animal behaviorists have contributed to species and habitat conservation at *http://spot.colorado .edu/~halloran/abscc/ccintro.html.*

during the evening. Despite this forewarning, the first loud rifle shot elicits a **startle reaction** from Dick—he practically jumps out of his chair, and then his heart beats rapidly and he breathes heavily for several seconds. After about half a minute, Dick has fully recovered and is just returning to his novel when he is again startled by a second gunshot. This time, the startle reaction is not as great—his body does not jerk quite as dramatically, and there is not so large an increase in heart rate. With additional gunshots, Dick's startle response decreases until it has disappeared completely— the noise no longer disrupts his concentration on his novel.

This example illustrates the phenomenon of **habituation,** which is a decrease in the strength of a response after repeated presentation of a stimulus that elicits the response. In principle, any elicited response can exhibit habituation, but in practice, habituation is most evident in the body's automatic responses to new and sudden stimuli. The startle reaction is one example of such a response. Another is the **orienting response:** If a new sight or sound is presented to a dog or other animal, the animal may stop its current activity, lift its ears and its head, and turn in the direction of the stimulus. If the stimulus is presented repeatedly but is of no consequence, the orienting response will disappear. Similarly, if an infant is played a tape recording of an adult's voice, the infant will turn its head in the direction of the sound. If, however, the same word is played over and over, the infant will soon stop turning toward the sound. Therefore, both animals and humans will typically exhibit an orienting response to a novel stimulus, and they will both

exhibit habituation of the orienting response if the same stimulus is presented many times.

An important characteristic of habituation (which distinguishes it from both sensory adaptation and muscular fatigue) is that it is **stimulus-specific.** Thus after Dick's startle reaction to the sound of gunfire has habituated, he should still exhibit such a reaction if the back door slams. An infant that has stopped turning its head toward a speaker playing the same word over and over will again turn toward the speaker if a different word is played. In this way, psychologists can tell that even infants just a few months old can distinguish subtle differences in human speech sounds (Polka & Werker, 1994).

The function that habituation serves for the individual should be clear. In its everyday activities a creature encounters many stimuli, some potentially beneficial, some potentially dangerous, and many neither helpful nor harmful. It is to the creature's advantage to be able to ignore the many insignificant stimuli it repeatedly encounters. To be continually startled or distracted by such stimuli would be a waste of the creature's time and energy. A study by Dielenberg and McGregor (1999) shows how animals can habituate to a fear-provoking stimulus if the stimulus repeatedly proves to be insignificant. Rats were presented with a cat collar that contained a cat's odor, and the response of the rats was to run into a hiding place and remain there for quite a while. However, Figure 3-6 shows that after several presentations of the cat collar, the rats' hiding times decreased and came close to those of the control group (rats that were exposed to a cat collar that had no cat odor on it).

A creature that was unable to habituate to insignificant stimuli would probably have a difficult time attending to more important stimuli. In fact, there is some evidence that the rate of habituation in human infants is correlated with mental abilities later in life. Laucht, Esser, and Schmidt (1994) found that infants who displayed faster habituation to repetitive stimuli at 3 months of age obtained, on average, slightly higher scores on intelligence tests when they were 4 1/2 years old. Another study found that adolescents who showed very slow

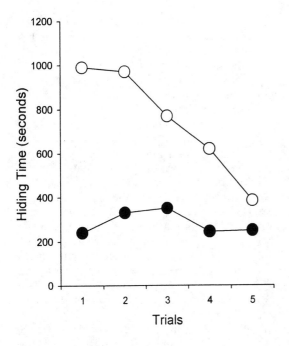

**FIGURE 3-6** The amount of time rats spent hiding when exposed to a cat collar with cat odor exhibits habituation over successive days of exposure. The filled circles are from a control group of rats exposed to a cat collar that had no cat odor. (From Dielenberg & McGregor, 1999)

habituation to repetitive stimuli had a higher risk of developing the severe psychiatric disorder schizophrenia later in life (Hollister, Mednick, Brennan, & Cannon, 1994). These are correlational studies, not experiments, so it would be a mistake to try to draw any conclusions about cause and effect from them. However, this research does suggest that the ability to habituate to repetitive, unimportant stimuli early in life may be one predictor of later mental abilities and mental health.

The usefulness of habituation is witnessed by its universality throughout the animal kingdom. Even before birth, the human fetus exhibits habituation to such stimuli as vibration or sounds (Groome, Watson, & Dykman, 1994). Habituation can also be seen in hydra, which have among the most primitive nervous systems found on our planet, consisting of diffuse networks of neurons (Rushford, Burnett, & Maynard, 1963). There have even been reports of habituation in protozoa (one-celled organisms). In one study, Wood (1973) found a decline in the contraction response of the protozoan *Stentor coeruleus* with repeated pre-

sentations of a tactile stimulus. At the same time, the *Stentor's* responsiveness to another stimulus, a light, was undiminished.

## General Principles of Habituation

Anyone who questions the feasibility of discovering general principles of learning applicable to a wide range of species should read the extensive literature on habituation. We have seen that habituation occurs in species as different as *Stentor coeruleus* and *Homo sapiens*. Furthermore, it is not just the existence of habituation that is shared by such diverse species. In a frequently cited article, Thompson and Spencer (1966) listed some of the most salient properties of habituation, properties that have been observed in human beings, other mammals, and invertebrates. Several of Thompson and Spencer's principles are described below.

1. *The Course of Habituation.* Habituation of a response occurs whenever a stimulus is repeatedly presented. The decrements in responding from trial to trial are large at first,

but get progressively smaller as habituation proceeds.

2. *The Effects of Time.* If after habituation the stimulus is withheld for some period of time, the response will recover. The amount of recovery depends on the amount of time that elapses. To draw a parallel to Ebbinghaus's findings, we might say that habituation is "forgotten" as time passes. Suppose that after Dick's startle response to the gunshots has habituated, there are no more gunshots for 30 minutes, but then they begin again. Dick is likely to exhibit a weak startle reaction to the first sound of gunshot after the break. (Thus there is some savings over time, but also some forgetting.) In comparison, if there were no further shooting until the following evening, Dick's startle reaction after this longer time interval would be larger.

3. *Relearning Effects.* Whereas habituation may disappear over a long time interval, it should proceed more rapidly in a second series of stimulus presentations. In further series of stimulus presentations, habituation should occur progressively more quickly. To use Ebbinghaus's term, there are savings from the previous periods of habituation. For example, although Dick's initial startle response to the sound of gunfire on the second evening of his vacation might be almost as large as on the first evening, the response should disappear more quickly the second time.

4. *The Effects of Stimulus Intensity.* We have already seen that a reflexive response is frequently stronger with a more intense stimulus. Such a response is also more resistant to habituation. Habituation proceeds more rapidly with weak stimuli, and if a stimulus is very intense, there may be no habituation at all.

5. *The Effects of Overlearning.* As in Ebbinghaus's experiments, further learning can occur at a time when there is no longer any change in observable behavior. Thompson and Spencer called this *below-zero* habituation because it occurs at a time when there is no observable response to the stimulus. Suppose that after 20 gunshots, Dick's startle response has completely disappeared. After a 24-hour interval, however, he might exhibit little savings from the previous day's experience. If there

were 100 gunshots on the first evening, Dick would probably show less of a startle response on the second evening. In other words, although the additional 80 gunshots produced no additional changes in Dick's behavior at the time, they did increase his long-term retention of the habituation.

6. *Stimulus Generalization.* The transfer of habituation from one stimulus to new but similar stimuli is called **generalization**. For example, if on the third evening the sounds of the gunshots are somewhat different (perhaps because different types of guns are being used), Dick may have little difficulty ignoring these sounds. The amount of generalization depends on the degree of similarity between the stimuli, and it is always the subject, not the experimenter, who is the ultimate judge of similarity. For this reason, psychologists can use habituation as a tool to determine exactly which stimuli an individual finds similar. For example, S. P. Johnson and Aslin (1995) presented 2-month-old infants with a display that featured a dark rod moving from side to side behind a white box (Figure 3-7). At first, the infants would look at this display for many seconds, but after repeated presentations, this orienting response habituated. Then, the infants were tested with two new stimuli—a solid rod moving back and forth with no box in front and a broken rod moving back and forth. Which new stimulus would the infants find more similar to the original display? Evidently, they found the solid rod more similar, because they spent less time looking at the solid rod than at the broken rod. In other words, the infants showed more generalization of habituation to the solid rod than to the broken rod. Based on this finding, Johnson and Aslin inferred that these young infants treated the original stimulus as a solid rod (not a broken rod) moving behind the box, even though the middle part of the rod could not be seen.

Many experiments have used similar procedures to examine a wide range of skills in human infants, including their ability to perceive faces (Easterbrook, Kisilevsky, Muir, & Laplante, 1999), to detect changes in the outline of an array of objects (Clearfield & Mix, 1999), and to analyze cause and effect in a

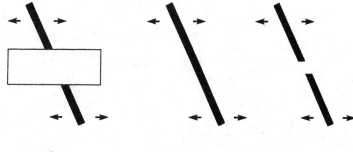

Habituation stimulus        Test stimuli

**FIGURE 3-7** In the study of Johnson and Aslin (1995), infants were repeatedly shown the stimulus on the left until their orienting responses to the stimulus habituated. They were then tested for generalization, using each of the two stimuli on the right.

chain of events (Cohen, Rundell, Spellman, & Cashon, 1999). This strategy of using habituation to measure surprise or changes in attention has proven to be a valuable technique for studying the perceptual and mental abilities of infants, even those less than one month old.

## Physiological Mechanisms of Habituation

***Research with a Simple Creature.*** Because the principles of habituation are common to a wide range of creatures, simple and complex, some psychologists have speculated that the physiological mechanisms of habituation may also be similar in different species. Of course, this speculation could be wrong—it is certainly conceivable that two species that exhibit similar patterns of habituation from a behavioral perspective might have very different physiological mechanisms producing this habituation. Nevertheless, this possibility has not deterred some researchers from investigating the physiological changes accompanying habituation in fairly primitive creatures. The strategy of studying fairly primitive creatures, which have nervous systems that are smaller and less complex, is known as the **simple systems approach.** It is best exemplified by the work of Eric Kandel.

Kandel and his colleagues (Antonov, Kandel, & Hawkins, 1999; Castellucci, Pinsker, Kupfermann, & Kandel, 1970; Kandel & Schwartz, 1982) have spent several decades studying both the behavior and the nervous system of *Aplysia,* a large marine snail (see Fig-

ure 3-8a). They chose to study this animal because its nervous system is relatively simple—it contains only a few thousand neurons, compared to the billions in a mammal's nervous system. Kandel and his coworkers investigated the process of habituation in one of *Aplysia's* reflexes, the gill-withdrawal reflex. If the creature's siphon (described as a "fleshy spout") is touched lightly, its gill contracts and is drawn inside the mantle for a few seconds. The neural mechanisms that control this reflex are well understood. The siphon contains 24 sensory neurons that respond to tactile stimulation. Six motor neurons control the gill-withdrawal response. Each of the 24 sensory neurons has a **monosynaptic** connection (that is, a direct connection that involves just one synapse) with each of the six motor neurons. In addition, other axons from the sensory neurons are involved in **polysynaptic** connections (indirect connections mediated by one or more interneurons) with these same motor neurons. Figure 3-8b depicts a small portion of this neural circuitry.

If the siphon is stimulated about once every minute for 10 or 15 trials, the gill-withdrawal reflex habituates. Complete habituation lasts for about an hour, and partial habituation may be observed for as long as 24 hours. If such trials are given on three or four successive days, long-term habituation (lasting several weeks) can be observed. What changes at the physiological level are responsible for this habituation? Through a series of elaborate tests, Kandel's group was able to determine that during habituation, a decrease in excitatory

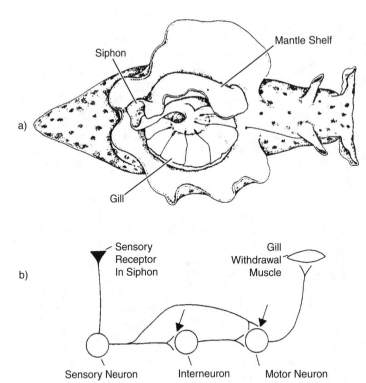

**FIGURE 3-8** (a) The marine snail *Aplysia*. (b) A small portion of the neural circuitry involved in the gill-withdrawal reflex. The sensory receptors in the siphon synapse either directly with a gill motor neuron or with an interneuron. In either case, Kandel and his associates found that habituation occurs in the first synapse of the chain, as indicated by the arrows. (From Kandel, 1979)

conduction always occurred at the synapses involving the axons of the sensory neurons (the points marked by arrows in Figure 3-8b). These researchers also found that there was no change in the postsynaptic neuron's sensitivity to the transmitter. What had changed was the amount of transmitter released by the presynaptic (sensory) neurons—with repeated stimulus presentations less transmitter was released into the synapse. Kandel (1979) noted that this mechanism of habituation is not unique to *Aplysia*. Physiological investigations of habituation in two other species (the crayfish and the cat) also found decreases in the amount of transmitter released by the sensory neurons.

Having determined exactly which neurons underwent changes during the habituation of the gill-withdrawal reflex, Kandel proceeded to ask questions at a deeper level: What chemical mechanisms are responsible for the depressed transmitter release of the sensory neurons? Each time a neuron fires, there is an influx of calcium ions into the axon terminals, and this calcium current is thought to cause the release of transmitter into the synapse. Perhaps this calcium current into the axon terminals becomes progressively weaker with repeated stimulation of the sensory neuron. The appropriate studies supported this hunch: the calcium current grew weaker during habituation, and in the recovery period after habituation, both the calcium current and the response of the postsynaptic (motor) neuron increased at the same rate (Klein, Shapiro, & Kandel, 1980). The experimenters concluded that a decrease in the calcium current causes a decrease in the amount of transmitter released into the synapse, which in turn decreases the excitation of the motor neuron, producing a weakened gill-withdrawal response.

The work of Kandel and associates nicely illustrates the potential advantages of the simple systems strategy in physiological research on learning. Because of the comparative simplicity of *Aplysia*'s neural networks, researchers have been able to pinpoint the neural changes responsible for habituation and to begin examining the chemical processes involved as well. This research shows that, at least in some cases, learning depends on changes at very specific neural locations, not on widespread changes in many parts of the nervous system. Furthermore, this learning involved no anatomical changes, such as the growth of new axons, but merely changes in the effectiveness of already established connections between neurons.

### Research with Mammals, Including Humans.

Because the nervous system of a typical mammal is so much more complex than that of *Aplysia*, it is much more difficult to identify the individual neurons that undergo change during habituation to a stimulus. Nevertheless, substantial progress has been made in locating the brain locations involved in habituation, at least in certain specific cases. Michael Davis (1989) has conducted extensive research on one such specific case—a rat's startle response to a sudden loud noise. The startle response is measured by testing a rat in a chamber that sits on springs, so that the rat's movement when it is startled shakes the chamber slightly, and this movement is measured by a sensor. As with humans, the rat's startle reaction will habituate if the same loud noise is presented many times. Davis wanted to know what parts of the rat's nervous system were responsible for this habituation.

To begin, Davis had to determine which parts of the nervous system were involved in the startle reaction in the first place. Through many careful studies, Davis and his colleagues were able to trace the entire circuit through the nervous system (Davis, Gendelman, Tischler, & Gendelman, 1982). The circuit began in the auditory nerve, then worked its way through auditory pathways to the brainstem, and then to motor pathways that controlled the muscles involved in the startle response. Further research indicated that the changes during habituation took place in the early portions of this circuit (that is, in the auditory pathways). Although the exact neurons

responsible for the habituation have not been identified, Davis's findings are similar to those from *Aplysia* in two respects. First, the neurons that undergo change during habituation are on the sensory side of the circuit. Second, the changes take place within the reflex circuit itself, rather than being the result of new inputs from neurons elsewhere in the nervous system.

Other studies with mammals extend but also complicate the physiological picture of habituation. In some cases of habituation, higher sections of the brain seem to be involved, including the auditory cortex, which is located on both sides of the brain, in the area of the temples. Using guinea pigs, Condon and Weinberger (1991) found that if the same tone was presented repeatedly, individual cells in the auditory cortex "habituated"—they decreased their sensitivity to this tone, but not to tones of higher or lower pitch.

With modern brain imaging techniques, such as positron emission tomography (PET) and magnetic resonance imaging (MRI), it has become possible to identify brain areas that are involved in habituation in humans. This research is still in its early stages, but so far the results suggest that many different areas of the human brain can show habituation in their responsiveness to repeatedly presented stimuli. For instance, MRIs have shown habituation in the visual cortex to visual stimuli (Condon, McFadzean, Hadley, Bradnam, & Shahani, 1997), and PET scans have displayed changes in the cerebellum as a person's startle response to a loud noise habituates (Timmann and others, 1998). Once again, we have evidence of changes in specific areas of the nervous system as a result of repeated presentations of a specific stimulus.

Neurophysiologists use the term **plasticity** to refer to the nervous system's ability to change as a result of experience or stimulation. All in all, the physiological studies of habituation demonstrate that plasticity is possible in many different levels of the nervous system, and that this plasticity sometimes results from chemical changes in existing synapses rather than from the growth of new synapses.

## Habituation in Emotional Responses: The Opponent-Process Theory

Richard Solomon and John Corbit (1974) proposed a theory of emotion that has attracted a good deal of attention. The theory is meant to apply to a wide range of emotional reactions. The type of learning they propose is quite similar to the examples of habituation we have already examined—in both, a subject's response to a stimulus changes simply as a result of repeated presentations of that stimulus. Opinions about their **opponent-process theory** differ greatly, and as you read this section you might want to form your own opinion about the theory's scientific merit, using the criteria for scientific theories discussed in Chapter 1.

*The Temporal Pattern of an Emotional Response.* Imagine that you are a premedical student taking a course in organic chemistry. You received a C+ on the midterm, and your performance in laboratory exercises was fair. You studied hard for the final exam, but there were some parts of the exam that you could not answer. While leaving the examination room, you overheard a number of students say that it was a difficult test. A few weeks later you receive your grades for the semester, and you learn to your surprise that your grade in organic chemistry was an A-! You are instantly ecstatic, and you tell the good news to everyone you see. You are too excited to do any serious work, but as you run some errands, none of the minor irritations of a typical day (long lines, impolite salespeople) bother you in the least. By evening, however, your excitement has settled down, and you experience a state of contentment. The next morning, you receive a call from the registrar's office. There has been a clerical error in reporting the grades, and it turns out that your actual grade in organic chemistry was B-. This news provokes immediate feelings of dejection and despair. You reevaluate your plans about where you will apply to medical school, and you wonder whether you will go at all. Over the course of a few hours, however, your emotional state gradually recovers and returns to normal.

This example illustrates all of the major features of a typical emotional episode as proposed by opponent-process theory. Figure 3-9 presents a graph of your emotional states during this imaginary episode. The solid bar at the bottom marks the time during which some emotion-eliciting stimulus is present. In our example, it refers to the time when you believed your grade was an A-. The $y$-axis depicts the strength of an individual's emotional reactions both while the stimulus is present and afterward. (Solomon and Corbit always plot the response to the stimulus itself in the positive direction, regardless of whether we would call the emotion "pleasant" or "unpleasant.") According to the theory, the onset of such a stimulus produces the sudden appearance of an emotional reaction, which quickly reaches a peak of intensity (the initial ecstasy in our example). This response then gradually declines to a somewhat lower level, or plateau (your contentment during the evening). With the offset of the stimulus (the telephone call), there is a sudden switch to an emotional after-reaction that is in some sense the opposite of the initial emotion (the dejection and despair). This after-reaction gradually declines, and the individual's emotional state returns to a neutral state.

To strengthen their arguments, Solomon and Corbit reviewed some experimental data from a situation where the initial emotional response was decidedly negative, but where heart rate was used as an objective measure of a subject's emotional reaction. In this experiment (Church, LoLordo, Overmier, Solomon, & Turner, 1966), dogs were restrained in harnesses and received a number of 10-second shocks. During the first few shocks, a dog's overt responses were typically those of terror—it might shriek, pull on the harness, urinate or defecate, and its hair might stand on end. At the termination of the shock, a typical dog's behavior was characterized as "stealthy, hesitant, and unfriendly." Intuitively, we might not feel that these after-reactions are the "opposite" of terror, but they are certainly different from the initial reaction. After a short

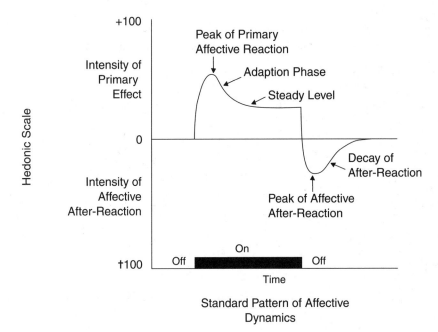

**FIGURE 3-9** The typical pattern of an emotional response according to the opponent-process theory. The solid bar shows the time during which an emotion-eliciting stimulus is present. (From Solomon & Corbit, 1974)

time, the stealthiness would disappear and the dog's disposition would return to normal—"active, alert, and socially responsive." Heart-rate measures provided more compelling support for the pattern in Figure 3-9: During the shock, heart rate rose rapidly from a resting state of about 120 beats/minute to a maximum of about 200 beats/minute, and then began to decline. At shock termination, there was a rebound effect in which heart rate dropped to about 90 beats/minute, then returned to normal after 30 or 60 seconds.

*The a-process and b-process.* Solomon and Corbit describe several other examples of emotional episodes, but let us now turn to the intervening variables of their theory—the internal processes that, they propose, underlie an individual's observable emotional responses. They hypothesize that the pattern shown in Figure 3-9 is the result of two antagonistic internal processes that they call the **a-process** and the

**b-process.** The a-process is largely responsible for the initial emotional response, and the b-process is totally responsible for the after-reaction. The left half of Figure 3-10 shows how these two processes supposedly combine to produce the pattern of Figure 3-9. Solomon and Corbit describe the a-process as a fast-acting response to a stimulus that rises to a maximum and remains there as long as the stimulus is present. When the stimulus ends, the a-process decays very quickly (see the middle left graph in Figure 3-10). In the heart-rate study, the a-process would be some hypothetical internal mechanism (perhaps the flow of adrenaline) that produces, among other responses, an increase in heart rate. The antagonistic b-process is supposedly activated only in response to the activity of the a-process, and it is supposedly more sluggish both to rise and to decay. The middle left graph in Figure 3-10 also shows the more gradual increase and decrease in the b-process. In the heart-rate example, the b-process would be

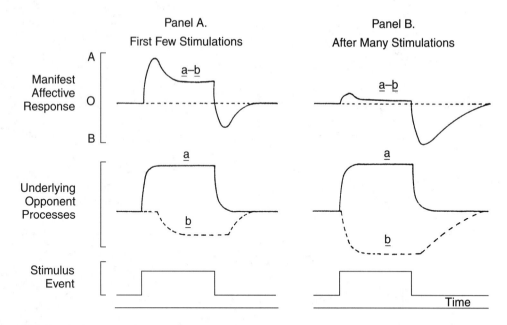

**FIGURE 3-10** According to opponent-process theory, a person's emotional reaction (or "manifest affective response") is jointly determined by the underlying a- and b-processes. The proposed time course of these processes during the first few presentations of an emotion-eliciting stimulus is shown on the left. The right side shows the predicted patterns after many repetitions of the same stimulus. (From Solomon & Corbit, 1974)

some internal mechanism causing a decrease in heart rate.

Note that in Figure 3-10, the b-process begins to rise while the stimulus (the shock) is still present. Solomon and Corbit propose that when both the a-process and the b-process are active to some degree, the resulting emotional response can be predicted by simple subtraction. That is, the action of the a-process will be countered to some extent by the action of the b-process, and the emotional response will be weaker. According to the theory, it is the rise in the b-process that causes the drop in the initial emotional reaction from the peak to the plateau. When the stimulus ends and the a-process quickly decays, all that remains is the b-process, which produces the emotional after-reaction. Before reading further, you should make sure you see how the two processes in the middle left graph of Figure 3-10 combine to produce the pattern in the upper-left graph.

***The Effects of Repeated Stimulation.*** Up to now the discussion has been restricted to an individual's first encounter with a new stimulus. However, a crucial feature of the opponent-process theory is its predictions about how the pattern of an emotional response changes with repeated presentations of the same stimulus. To put it simply, the theory states that with repeated exposures to a stimulus, the primary emotional response exhibits a sort of habituation—it becomes progressively smaller—while at the same time there is a marked increase in the size and duration of the after-reaction. The top right graph in Figure 3-10 shows the predicted pattern of an emotional response after many stimulations. The middle right graph shows that, according to the theory, this change is the result of an increase in the size of the b-process. Solomon and Corbit propose that whereas the a-process does not change, the b-process is strengthened with use and weakened with disuse. With repeated stimulations, the b-process rises more quickly, reaches a higher maximum, and is slower to decay after the stimulus is terminated.

Solomon and Corbit supported these predictions by describing the pattern of responding after dogs received a number of shocks in the study by Church and colleagues (1966). After several sessions, there was little if any heart-rate increase during the shock. However, after shock termination, heart rate decreased by as much as 60 beats/minute, and it took from two to five minutes (instead of a minute or less) for heart rate to return to normal. The dogs' overt behaviors also exhibited changes with experience:

> During shocks, the signs of terror disappeared. Instead, the dog appeared pained, annoyed, anxious, but not terrified. For example, it whined rather than shrieked, and showed no further urination, defecation, or struggling. Then, when released suddenly at the end of the session, the dog rushed about, jumped up on people, wagged its tail, in what we called at the time "a fit of joy." Finally, several minutes later, the dog was its normal self: friendly, but not racing about. (Solomon & Corbit, 1974, p. 122)

In short, with extended experience the dog's overt behaviors paralleled its heart-rate response: the reaction to the shock was smaller than before, but the after-reaction was larger and of longer duration.

***Other Examples.*** Solomon and Corbit claim that opponent-process theory describes the temporal dynamics of many different types of emotional experiences, and a few more of their examples will give some indication of the generality of the theory. They discuss the emotional responses of parachutists on their initial jumps and on later jumps, as reported by S. M. Epstein (1967). Overall, the emotional experiences of parachutists resemble those of the dogs in the heart-rate study. Novice parachutists appear terrified during a jump; after the jump, they look stunned for a few minutes, then return to normal. Experienced parachutists appear only moderately anxious during a jump, but afterward they report feelings of exhilaration and euphoria that can last for hours. They claim that this feeling of euphoria is one of the main reasons they continue to jump.

A graphic example involving a pleasurable initial reaction followed by an aversive after-reaction deals with the use of opiates. After a person's first opiate injection, an intense feeling of pleasure (a "rush") is experienced. This peak of emotion declines to a less intense state of pleasure. As the effect of the drug wears off, however, the aversive after-reactions set in—nausea, insomnia, irritability, anxiety, an inability to eat, and other physical problems, along with feelings of craving for the drug. The withdrawal symptoms can last for hours or a few days.

For an experienced opiate user, the pattern changes. The injection no longer brings an initial rush, but only mild feelings of pleasure, if any. This decrease in the effects of a drug with repeated use is called **tolerance,** and it is observed with many drugs besides opiates. Some theorists have suggested that drug tolerance is a good example of habituation (for example, Baker & Tiffany, 1985). According to the opponent-process theory, however, tolerance is the product of a strengthened b-process. The stronger b-process also explains why, with repeated opiate use, the withdrawal symptoms become more severe, and they may last for weeks or longer. At this stage, the individual does not take the opiate for pleasure but for temporary relief from the withdrawal symptoms. In terms of the opponent-process theory, each injection reinstates the a-process, which counteracts the withdrawal symptoms produced by the b-process. Unfortunately, each injection also further strengthens the b-process, so the individual is caught in a vicious cycle. Solomon and Corbit propose that their theory provides a framework for understanding not only opiate use, but all addictive behaviors (such as smoking, alcoholism, and the use of barbiturates and amphetamines). We will see in Chapter 5, however, that other researchers who study drug use disagree with the details of the opponent-process theory.

Why is it that many emotional reactions include both an a-process and an antagonistic b-process? Solomon and Corbit suggest that the b-process is the body's mechanism, albeit imperfect, of avoiding prolonged, intense emotions. Extremes of emotion, whether positive or negative, tax the body's resources, so when any a-process persists for some time, the corresponding b-process is evoked to counteract it, at least in part. If this is indeed the function of the b-process, then the examples of addictive behaviors clearly demonstrate that this mechanism is imperfect.

*A Brief Evaluation.* As discussed in Chapter 1, two characteristics of good scientific theories are that they make testable predictions and that these predictions are then found to be consistent with experimental results. Opponent-process theory does make specific predictions about the pattern of emotional responses that have been tested in quite a few experiments. In many cases, the theory's predictions have been supported (for example, Glover, 1992; R. L. Solomon, 1980), although in some cases they have not (Eiserer, 1990; Fanselow, DeCola, & Young, 1993). Another characteristic of good theories is fruitfulness—the ability to stimulate new ideas and new research. Opponent-process theory can definitely be classified as a fruitful theory. It has been followed by a number of related theories that use the basic opponent-process idea in somewhat different ways (some of which are discussed in Chapter 5). It has been applied to a diverse range of human behaviors, including food preferences (Zellner, 1991), the effects of exercise (Lochbaum, 1999), and the treatment of patients with anxiety disorders (Ley, 1994).

Despite its successes, a common criticism of opponent-process theory is that there is little concrete evidence about the actual physiological mechanisms that might correspond to the hypothetical a- and b-processes. Of course, this situation could be remedied if researchers find physiological processes that behave as the theory predicts. For example, one study with rats has found a section of the brain (known as the *nucleus accumbens*) that appears to be involved in both the initial positive reaction to opiates and the negative after-reactions (Koob, Caine, Parsons, Markou, & Weiss, 1997). Fur-

ther research on this or other brain areas might well unearth clues about why the positive reaction is weakened and the after-reaction is strengthened with repeated opiate use.

Critics also point out that the different examples used by Solomon and Corbit exhibit vastly different time courses. In the heart-rate studies with dogs, the b-process lasts only seconds or a few minutes. In an addiction, the b-process may continue for months. Is it likely that the same physiological mechanisms are involved in emotional events whose durations differ by a factor of 10,000 or more? Critics have argued that there may be nothing more than a superficial resemblance among the different examples Solomon and Corbit present.

In defense of opponent-process theory, we might assert that as long as emotional responses conform to the predictions of the theory, it does not matter whether these patterns are based on a single physiological mechanism or on a dozen different ones. On a strictly descriptive level, the major characteristics of emotional episodes emphasized by opponent-process theory (the peak, the plateau, the after-effect, the changes with repeated stimulation) appear to be fairly well documented by case histories, systematic observations, and experiments. Whether or not these patterns share a common physiological mechanism, the data suggest that the theory captures some characteristics of emotional responses that are quite general. Though it has been called a weakness, the theory's ambitious attempt to unite diverse emotional situations in a single framework may actually be its greatest virtue. The broad viewpoint provided by opponent-process theory allows us to see commonalities among our emotions that would probably go unnoticed in a more myopic analysis of individual emotional responses.

## CHAPTER SUMMARY

One of the simplest types of innate behaviors is the reflex, which is a simple response to a specific stimulus, such as blinking when a bright light is shined in the eye. Kineses are random movements in response to a specific stimulus, whereas taxes are directed movements (such as a fish using the brightness of the sky to keep its body upright). Fixed action patterns are sequences of behavior that always occur in a rigid order, whereas reaction chains are more flexible sequences that can be adapted to current circumstances. The concepts of control systems theory, which describe a comparison between the actual state of the world and a goal state, are helpful in analyzing these innate behavior patterns.

Habituation is the decline and eventual disappearance of a reflexive response when the same stimulus is repeatedly presented. Habituation gives a creature the ability to ignore unimportant, repetitive events. In both simple and complex creatures, habituation exhibits the same set of properties, such as forgetting, overlearning, and stimulus generalization. Research with simple creatures such as the snail *Aplysia*, as well as with mammals, has traced the physiological and chemical changes that occur in the brain during habituation and specific brain structures involved in habituation in a few cases.

The opponent-process theory of Solomon and Corbit states that many emotional reactions consist of an initial response called the a-process and a later, opposing response called the b-process. Repeated presentations of the same stimulus strengthen the b-process, so that the initial reaction grows weaker and the

after-reaction grows stronger and lasts longer. This theory has been applied to a wide variety of emotional reactions, including drug addiction, the emotions involved in parachute jumping, and responses to painful or aversive stimuli.

## REVIEW QUESTIONS

1. Describe an example of each of the following innate behavior patterns: reflex, kinesis, taxis, fixed action pattern, and reaction chain. Select one of these examples and show how it can be analyzed using the concepts of control systems theory.

2. List several of the general principles of habituation and give a concrete example to show how each principle works. Why is this simple type of learning useful? How can habituation be studied in human infants?

3. Why have researchers devoted so much study to habituation in the snail *Aplysia?* What has been learned about the neural and chemical mechanisms of habituation in the gill-withdrawal reflex in this creature?

4. Diagram the pattern of a typical emotional response to a new stimulus, according to opponent-process theory. Now diagram the changed pattern that occurs in response to a stimulus that has been frequently repeated. Use a specific example to explain the different parts of the emotional reaction in both cases.

## CHAPTER 4

# Basic Principles
# of Classical Conditioning

Part of the excitement of conducting scientific research arises from the ever-present possibility that a routine experiment, conducted with a fairly mundane objective in mind, can produce an unexpected finding of great importance. The history of science records many stories of such serendipitous discoveries, and in one such story the main character was the Russian scientist Ivan Pavlov.

## PAVLOV'S DISCOVERY
## AND ITS IMPACT

Although he eventually became one of the most famous figures in the history of psychology, Pavlov was trained as a physiologist, not as a psychologist. He conducted a substantial amount of research on the physiology of the digestive system, and in 1904 he was awarded the Nobel Prize in Medicine and Physiology for this work. Pavlov was interested in the various substances secreted by an animal's digestive system to break down the food eaten. He analyzed the chemical composition of the digestive juices, measured the times they were secreted during the course of a meal, and attempted to discover the neural mechanisms controlling these physiological responses. One of the digestive juices Pavlov studied was saliva, which is the first secretion to make con-

tact with any ingested food. The subjects in Pavlov's studies were dogs, and he developed a surgical technique that enabled him to redirect the saliva from one of the dog's salivary ducts through a tube and out of the mouth, so that it could be measured. Figure 4-1 pictures Pavlov's experimental apparatus, which included a harness to restrain the subject and the devices for recording each drop of saliva.

In Pavlov's research, a single dog might be subjected to several test sessions on successive days. In each session the animal would be given food, and its salivation would be recorded as it ate. Pavlov's important observation came when studying dogs that had been through the testing procedure several times. Unlike a new subject, an experienced dog would begin to salivate even before the food was presented. Pavlov reasoned that some stimuli that had regularly preceded the presentation of food in previous sessions, such as the sight of the experimenter, had now acquired the capacity to elicit the response of salivation. Pavlov recognized the significance of this unexpected result, and he spent the rest of his life studying this phenomenon, which is now known as **classical conditioning**. He concluded his subjects were exhibiting a simple type of learning: Salivation, which began as a reflexive response to the stimulus of food in

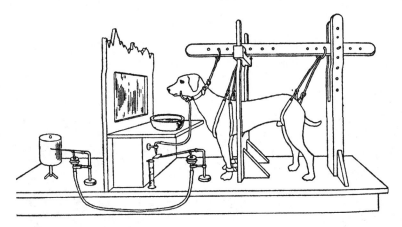

**FIGURE 4-1** Pavlov's salivary conditioning situation. A tube redirects drops of saliva out of the dog's mouth so they can be recorded automatically. (From Yerkes & Morgulis, 1909)

the dog's mouth, was now elicited by a new (and initially ineffective) stimulus. Pavlov speculated that many of an animal's learned behaviors might be traced back to its innate reflexes, just as a dog's learned behavior of salivating when the experimenter appeared developed from the initial food-salivation reflex. If so, then we might be able to discover a good deal about an animal's learning mechanisms by studying the development of learned reflexes, or **conditioned reflexes,** in the laboratory. With this goal in mind, Pavlov developed a set of procedures for studying classical conditioning that are still in use today.

### The Standard Paradigm of Classical Conditioning

To conduct a typical experiment in classical conditioning, an experimenter first selects some stimulus that reliably elicits a characteristic response. The stimulus of this pair is called the **unconditioned stimulus,** and the response is called the **unconditioned response.** The term unconditioned is used to signify that the connection between the stimulus and response is unlearned (innate). In Pavlov's experiments on the salivary response, the unconditioned stimulus (abbreviated US) was the presence of food in the dog's mouth,

and the unconditioned response (UR) was the secretion of saliva. The third element of the classical-conditioning paradigm is the **conditioned stimulus** (CS), which can be any stimulus that does not initially evoke the UR (for instance, a bell). The term conditioned stimulus indicates that it is only after conditioning has taken place that the bell will elicit the response of salivation.

Figure 4-2 is a diagram of the sequence of events of a single trial of classical conditioning. In its simplest form, a classical-conditioning trial involves the presentation of the CS (say, a bell) followed by the US (for instance, the food). On the initial trials, only the US will elicit the response of salivation. However, as the conditioning trials continue, the dog will begin to salivate as soon as the CS is presented. Any salivation that occurs during the CS but before the US is referred to as a **conditioned response** (CR), since it is only because of the conditioning procedure that the bell now elicits salivation.

The abbreviations for the four basic elements of the classical-conditioning paradigm will appear repeatedly in this and later chapters, so be sure that you have no confusion about what each term represents. The two components of the initial stimulus-response pair are the US and the UR. Through the

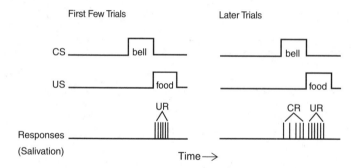

**FIGURE 4-2** The events of a classical-conditioning trial both before a conditioned response is established (left) and after (right).

procedures of classical conditioning, a new stimulus, the CS, begins to elicit responses of its own, and these responses to the CS are called CRs (since they are learned, or conditioned, responses).

## The Variety of Conditioned Responses

As Chapter 3 showed, the bodies of both humans and animals exhibit a large number of reflexive responses. Some of these reflexes involve overt muscular movements, and others involve the internal responses of various glands and organs. Classical conditioning has been observed in many of these reflexes, including the knee-jerk reflex, the eyeblink, and others (Hull, 1934; Schlosberg, 1928). It is also possible to classically condition various organs such as the heart, the stomach, the liver, and the kidneys. In fact, it is probably only a slight exaggeration to state that any reflexive response (that is, any response that is reliably elicited by some US) can be classically conditioned, given enough pairings between the US and some CS.

Over the years, researchers in classical conditioning have converged on a small number of conditioning **preparations** (that is, conditioning situations utilizing a particular US, UR, and species of subject) that can be studied easily and efficiently. As the number of studies involving a specific preparation grows, it gains the additional advantage of the accumulated technical knowledge surrounding that preparation. For these reasons, on subsequent pages we will repeatedly encounter studies employing the same conditioning preparations. The following conditioning situations, among others, have been used in a large number of experiments on classical conditioning.

*Eyeblink Conditioning.* Conditioning of the eyeblink reflex has been studied with both humans and rabbits as subjects. Figure 4-3 shows a typical procedure for eyeblink conditioning with rabbits. The subject is placed in a tight compartment to restrict its movement. The US in this case is a puff of air directed at the eye, and the UR is of course an eyeblink. Both the timing and the magnitude of an eyeblink are recorded by a potentiometer, which measures the movement of a thread attached to the rabbit's eyelid. In other eyelid-conditioning studies, the US is a mild electric shock delivered to the skin in the vicinity of the eye, a stimulus that also reliably elicits an eyeblink as a UR. In such studies, the CS may be a light, a tone, or some tactile stimulus such as a vibration of the experimental chamber, and the duration of the CS is typically about one second. Like the UR, the CR is an eyeblink, but its form may be different. Whereas the unconditioned eyeblink is a large and rapid eyelid closure, the conditioned response is often a smaller and more gradual eyelid movement. The most common measure of the strength of conditioning is the percentage of trials in which a CR is observed. Eyeblink conditioning often requires a large number of CS-US pairings. For example, it may take well over 100 pairings before a CR is observed on 50 percent of the trials.

For a long time, most of this research was conducted with rabbits, but in recent years

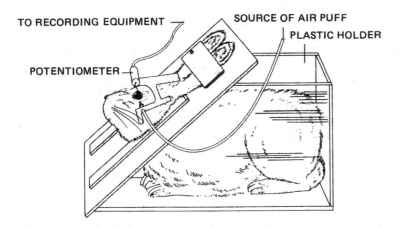

**FIGURE 4-3**  An eyeblink-conditioning arrangement. The potentiometer measures the movement of the rabbit's eyelid in response to either an air puff or some conditioned stimulus. (From Domjan & Burkhard, 1982)

there has been a revival of interest in human eyeblink conditioning. Research with humans has been used to map the brain areas involved in conditioning, to help diagnose psychological disorders, to study the effects of awareness on learning, and for other purposes (Steinmetz, 1999; Woodruff-Pak, 1999).

*Conditioned Suppression.*  In this procedure, which is also called the **conditioned emotional response** (CER) procedure, the subjects are usually rats, and the US is an aversive event such as a brief electric shock delivered through the metal bars that form the floor of the experimental chamber. The unconditioned response to shock may include several different behaviors—the animal may jump, squeal, and temporarily stop what it was doing before the shock occurred. The measure of conditioning in this situation is the suppression of ongoing behavior when the CS (which signals that a shock is forthcoming) is presented. So that "ongoing behavior" can be measured automatically and reliably, a separate task on which the subject will respond at a fairly steady rate is included in this procedure. Most frequently, hungry rats are given the opportunity to press a lever, and occasionally a lever press will result in the delivery of a food pellet. It is fairly easy to schedule the delivery

of food pellets in such a way that the animal will press the lever slowly but steadily for an hour or more, now and then earning a bit of food.

As in eyeblink conditioning, the CS may be visual, auditory, or tactile, but the duration of the CS is generally much longer in the conditioned suppression procedure—CSs of one minute or more are commonplace. When the CS is first presented, it may have little effect on the subject's lever-pressing behavior. The rat may pause for a few seconds to notice this novel stimulus (an orienting response), but it will soon resume its lever pressing. However, after a few pairings of the CS and shock (in which the shock arrives at the end of the 1-minute CS and lasts for perhaps 1 second), the subject's behavior is markedly different— its rate of lever pressing suddenly decreases as soon as the CS is presented, and the animal may make only a few lever presses during the minute that the CS is present. If you observed a rat in this situation, you might say that the rat looked "afraid" during the CS, which is why this is sometimes called a conditioned emotional response procedure or a conditioned fear procedure. We do not need to speculate about the rat's emotions, however, to make use of the objectively measurable change in the animal's behavior. The extent to which lever pressing is suppressed provides us with a measure of the strength of conditioning. To calculate the level of suppression, the rate of lever pressing during the CS is usually compared to the rate just prior to the onset of the CS. For example, if the rat was pressing the lever at a rate of 40 responses per minute before the CS and this rate dropped to 10 responses per minute in the presence of the CS, this would constitute a suppression of 75 percent.

Conditioning takes place in far fewer trials in the conditioned suppression procedure than in the eyeblink procedure, perhaps partly because the shock is more intense than the air puffs or mild shocks used in eyeblink conditioning. Whatever the reasons, strong conditioned suppression can often be observed in fewer than 10 trials, and in some cases significant suppression to the CS is found after just one CS–US pairing.

### The Skin Conductance Response (SCR).
This conditioning preparation is also called the **electrodermal response**, and in the past it was known as the **galvanic skin response**. In this preparation, the subjects are usually human. The SCR is a change in the electrical conductivity of the skin. To measure a person's SCR, two coin-shaped electrodes are attached to the palm and the electrodes are connected to a device that measures momentary fluctuations in the conductivity of the skin (caused by small changes in perspiration). The conductivity of the skin is altered by emotions such as fear or surprise, which is why the SCR is often one measure used in lie detector tests. One stimulus that reliably produces a large increase in skin conductivity is electric shock, and a similar increase in conductivity can be conditioned to any CS that is paired with shock. For instance, the CS might be a tone, the US a shock to the left wrist, and the response an increase in conductivity of the right palm. One reason for the interest in the SCR is that since it provides a response that can be quickly and reliably conditioned with human subjects, many complex stimuli (such as spoken or written words) can be examined as CSs.

### Taste-Aversion Learning.
This conditioning procedure has been extensively investigated since about the late 1960s. Rats are frequently the subjects in this research, but other species (pigeons, quail, guinea pigs) have also been used. By definition, the CS in this procedure is the taste of something the subject eats or drinks. In many cases, the food is one that the subject has never tasted before. After eating or drinking, the subject is given an injection of a poison (the US) that makes the animal ill. Several days later, after the subject has fully recovered from its illness, it is again given the opportunity to consume the substance that served as the CS. The usual result is that the animal consumes little or none of this food. Thus the measure of conditioning is the degree to which the subject avoids the food.

There are a number of reasons why taste-aversion learning has received so much attention in recent years. For one thing, as will be discussed in Chapter 5, some psychologists have suggested that taste-aversion learning is not an ordinary example of classical conditioning, but that it violates some of the general principles that apply to most examples of classical conditioning. Second, a taste aversion often develops after just one conditioning trial, and this rapidity of conditioning is advantageous for certain theoretical questions. Third, a taste aversion is something that many people experience at least once in their lives. Perhaps there is some type of food that you refuse to eat because you once became ill after eating it. You may find the very thought of eating this food a bit nauseating, although most people enjoy the food. If you have such a taste aversion, you are not unusual—one study found that over half of the college students surveyed had at least one taste aversion (Logue, Ophir, & Strauss, 1981). A taste aversion may develop even if the individual is certain that the food was not the cause of the subsequent illness. I once attended a large dinner party where the main course was chicken tarragon. Besides passing food around the table, we evidently passed around an intestinal virus, because many of the guests became quite ill that evening. For some, the illness lasted for over a week. The result of this accidental pairing of food and illness was that several years later, some of these guests still refused to eat chicken tarragon or any food with tarragon spicing. Taste aversion can be strong and long lasting!

## Pavlov's Stimulus Substitution Theory

*The Theory.* Pavlov was the first to propose the theory of classical conditioning that is now called the **stimulus substitution theory.** On a behavioral level, the theory simply predicts the changes that supposedly take place among the observable events of conditioning—the stimuli and responses. The theory states that by virtue of repeated pairings between CS and US, the CS becomes a substitute for the US, so that the response initially elicited only by the US is now also elicited by the CS. At first glance, this theory seems to provide a perfectly satisfactory description of what takes place in many common examples of classical conditioning. In salivary conditioning, initially only food elicits salivation, but later the CS also elicits salivation. In eyeblink conditioning, both the UR and the CR are eyelid closures. In SCR conditioning, an increase in skin conductance is first elicited by a shock, and after conditioning, a similar increase in skin conductance occurs in response to some initially neutral stimulus.

*Problems with the Theory.* Despite these apparent confirmations of the stimulus substitution theory, today very few conditioning researchers believe the theory to be correct. The theory has several problems. First of all, the CR is almost never an exact replica of the UR. For instance, it was already noted that whereas an eyeblink UR to an air puff is a large, rapid eyelid closure, the CR that develops is a smaller and more gradual eyelid closure. That is, both the size and the temporal pattern of the CR differ from those of the UR. This fact, however, only allows us to reject the strictest interpretation of stimulus substitution theory, one that states that the CR will be identical to the UR in all details. In defense of stimulus substitution theory, Hilgard (1936) argued that since the intensity and stimulus modality

of the CS and US may be different, such differences in response magnitude and timing are to be expected. After all, URs of different sizes can be obtained simply by changing the intensity of the US—a strong shock will produce a large eyeblink UR, and a weak shock will produce a smaller UR. Given such variability among URs themselves, it seems unrealistic to expect that the CR will be identical to the UR in all respects.

A somewhat larger problem for stimulus substitution theory is that whereas many USs elicit several different responses, as a general rule not all of these responses are later elicited by the CS. For example, Zener (1937) noted that when a dog is presented with food as a US, a number of responses, such as chewing and swallowing of the food, occur in addition to salivation. Yet although a well-trained CS such as a bell will elicit salivation, it will generally not elicit the chewing and swallowing responses. Thus not all of the components of the UR are present in the CR. Conversely, a CR may include some responses that are *not* part of the UR. For instance, using a bell as a CS, Zener found that many dogs would turn their heads and look at the bell when it was rung. Sometimes a dog would move its entire body closer to the ringing bell. Obviously, these behaviors were not a normal part of the dog's UR to food. Because of such results, it was clear that stimulus substitution theory had to be modified if it were to remain a viable theory of classical conditioning.

Hilgard (1936) suggested two ways in which the theory might be amended. First, it should be acknowledged that only some components of the UR are transferred to the CR. Hilgard noted that some components of the UR may depend on the physical characteristics of the US, and they will not be transferred to a CS with very different physical characteristics. Thus, although a dog will chew and swallow food when it is presented, it cannot chew and swallow food that is not there (when the bell is rung). Second, it should be recognized that a CS such as a bell frequently elicits unconditioned responses of its own, and these may become part of the CR. For instance, when it first hears a bell, a dog may exhibit an orienting response—it may raise its ears, look in the direction of the bell, and possibly approach the bell. Although such orienting responses usually habituate if the bell is inconsequential, they persist or increase if the bell is paired with food. A more recent theory of classical conditioning, called the **sign-tracking theory** (Hearst & Jenkins, 1974; Tomie, Brooks, & Zito, 1989), emphasizes precisely this aspect of an animal's response to a CS. It states that animals tend to orient themselves toward, approach, and explore any stimuli that are good predictors of important events, such as the delivery of food. It is not very surprising that some components of the orienting response to the CS are retained as part of the CR. In short, the form of the CR may reflect both the unconditioned response to the US and the unconditioned response to the CS itself.

Possibly the strongest argument against stimulus substitution theory arises from the finding that in some cases the direction of the CR is opposite that of the UR. For instance, one response to an electric shock is an increase in heart rate, but in studies with guinea pigs, Black (1965) observed conditioned heart rate decreases to a CS paired with shock. Another example involves studies in which animals (usually rats) are given a morphine injection as the US. One of the URs to morphine is hyperthermia, or an increase in body temperature. In experiments where some CS is repeatedly paired with morphine, two types of CRs have been observed. Sometimes the CR is an increase in body temperature, as predicted by stimulus substitution theory, but in other cases the CR is a decrease in body temperature. Conditioned responses that are the opposite of the UR have been called **conditioned compensatory responses** (Siegel, 1982).

Examples of conditioned compensatory responses seem to demonstrate that stimulus substitution theory is inadequate as a general theory of classical conditioning. Still, some theorists (such as Eikelboom & Stewart, 1982) have suggested that these examples are not as damaging to stimulus substitution theory as they appear on the surface. However, let us simply emphasize that one of the most widely held beliefs about classical conditioning—that it involves the simple transfer of a response from one stimulus to another—is not consistent with the following facts.

1. The sizes and temporal patterns of the CR and UR may differ.
2. Not all components of the UR become part of the CR.
3. The CR may include response components that are not part of the UR.
4. The CR is sometimes opposite in direction to the UR (or at least to the most obvious part of the UR).

For all of these reasons, it is often difficult to predict in advance what the CR will look like in a specific instance. It may resemble the UR, or it may be very different.

### What Is Learned in Classical Conditioning?

Having surveyed the arguments for and against stimulus substitution theory, let us now turn to Pavlov's speculations about what changes might take place in the brain during classical conditioning. Pavlov had limited information about the physiology of the brain, and the specific details of his theory have since been proven wrong. On a more general level, however, his speculations still constitute a viable physiological theory of conditioning.

Pavlov proposed that there is a specific part of the brain that becomes active whenever a US (such as food) is presented, and he called this part of the brain the **US center.** Similarly, for every different CS (a tone, a light), there is a separate **CS center,** which becomes active whenever that particular CS is presented. From what we know about the physiology of the sensory systems (Chapter 2), these assumptions seem quite reasonable, especially since the exact nature of CS centers and US centers is not important to Pavlov's theory. It does not matter, as far as this theory is concerned, whether a CS center or US center is a single neuron, a group of neurons with similar functions, or even a particular pattern of activity in a set of neurons. Pavlov also assumed that for every UR (say, salivation) there is part of the brain that can be called a **response center,** and it is the activation of this response center

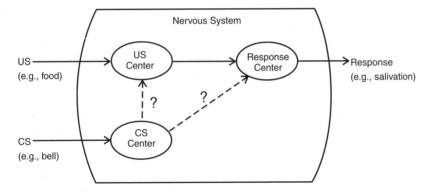

**FIGURE 4-4** Two possible versions of Pavlov's stimulus substitution theory. During classical conditioning, an association might develop from the CS center to the US center, or from the CS center directly to the response center.

that initiates the neural commands that ultimately produce the observed response. Furthermore, since the US elicits the UR without any prior training, Pavlov assumed that there is an innate connection between the US center and the response center (see Figure 4-4). Finally, Pavlov proposed that somehow an association develops during the course of classical conditioning, so that now the CS produces activity in the response center (and a CR is observed).

As Figure 4-4 suggests, there are at least two types of new associations that would give the CS the capacity to elicit a CR. On one hand, a direct association between the CS center and the response center might develop during conditioning. Since this association is between a stimulus and a response, it is sometimes called an **S-R association.** On the other hand, the connection between the CS and response centers might be less direct. Perhaps an association between the CS center and the US center is formed during conditioning. Later, when the CS is presented, the CS center is activated, which activates the US center (through the newly formed association), which in turn activates the response center (through the innate association). This hypothesis constitutes the position that an **S-S association** is formed during classical conditioning. Pavlov tended to favor the S-S position, but he had little empirical support for this view. More re-

cently, however, experimenters have devised a number of clever techniques to try to distinguish between these two alternatives. The next section describes one such procedure.

### S-S or S-R Connections?

In the absence of physiological information about what neural changes take place during classical conditioning, how can we distinguish between the S-S and S-R positions? Rescorla (1973) used the following reasoning. If the S-S position is correct, then after conditioning, the occurrence of a CR depends on the continued strength of two associations—the learned association between the CS center and the US center, and the innate association between the US center and the response center (see Figure 4-4). If the US-response connection is somehow weakened, this should cause a reduction in the strength of the CR, since the occurrence of the CR depends on this connection. On the other hand, if the S-R position is correct, the strength of the CR does not depend on the continued integrity of the US-response association, but only on the direct association between the CS center and the response center. But how can a reflexive US-response association be weakened? Rescorla's solution was to rely on habituation.

Rescorla used a conditioned suppression procedure with rats, but instead of the usual electric shock, a loud noise was used as the US. Rescorla's previous work had indicated that a conditioned suppression of lever pressing would develop to any CS paired with the noise, but also that the noise was susceptible to habituation if it was repeatedly presented. The design of the experiment is shown in Table 4-1. In Phase 1, two groups of rats received identical classical conditioning with a light as the CS and the noise as the US. In Phase 2, the habituation group received many presentations of the noise by itself, so as to habituate the subjects' fear of the noise. The control subjects spent equal amounts of time in the experimental chamber in Phase 2, but no stimuli were presented, so there was no opportunity for the noise to habituate in this group. In the test phase of the experiment, both groups were presented with the light by itself for a number of trials, and the subjects' levels of suppression of lever pressing were recorded. Rescorla found high levels of suppression to the light in the control group, but significantly lower levels of suppression in the habituation group. He therefore concluded that the strength of the CR is dependent on the continued strength of the US-response association, as predicted by the S-S position but not the S-R position.

The technique of decreasing the effectiveness of the US after an excitatory CS has been created is called **US devaluation.** In Rescorla's study, devaluation was accomplished by habituating fear of the noise, but other techniques have also been used. For instance, if the US is food, it can be devalued by satiating the subject (Holland & Rescorla, 1975). In a study with quail, the US was a sexual encounter, and satiation was achieved by allowing the birds to have repeated sexual intercourse (Hilliard & Domjan, 1995). The results of these studies also supported the S-S theory.

Somewhat related studies on **US revaluation** have been conducted with human subjects, and the results have been similar. For example, in experiments using the SCR, a CS (such as a picture of some common object) is paired with an aversive US (either shock or loud noise), and then the intensity of the US is changed. If the US intensity is decreased, skin conductance responses to the CS decrease as well, just as in Rescorla's experiment (Davey & McKenna, 1983). Conversely, the intensity of US can be increased. For example, K. White and Davey (1989) presented subjects with a picture of a triangle followed by a 65-decibel tone. Because this tone was not very loud, subjects showed little SCR to either the triangle or the tone. Then, the tone was presented by itself, but its intensity was increased to 115 decibels, which made it aversive. Finally, the triangle was again presented (without the tone), and subjects showed a large SCR to the triangle. Once again, these results suggest that subjects had formed an S-S association (between triangle and tone in this case) because the response to the triangle could be changed by changing the value of the tone without further presentations of the triangle.

Other research on the associations formed during classical conditioning will be described in Chapter 5. For now it is sufficient to understand how questions about the workings of the nervous system can be addressed in a meaningful way without actually tracing any specific neural connections.

## Pavlov's Influence on Psychology

It is difficult to overstate Pavlov's importance in the history of psychology. Pavlov continued to study classical conditioning for the first few decades of the twentieth century, and during that time he trained scores of stu-

**TABLE 4-1   Design of Rescorla's (1973) Experiment**

| Group | Phase 1 | Phase 2 | Test |
|-------|---------|---------|------|
| Habituation | Light→Noise | Noise (habituation) | Light |
| Control | Light→Noise | No stimuli | Light |

dents in his research techniques. Classical conditioning was vigorously studied in Russia, and Pavlov's ideas also influenced many learning theorists in America, including John B. Watson, Clark Hull, and Kenneth Spence. At present, investigation of the principles of classical conditioning continues at many universities in the United States, the former Soviet Union, Europe, and elsewhere. One measure of Pavlov's importance to the field of learning is the fact that nearly all of the terms and concepts discussed in this chapter (including nearly all of the phenomena described in the next section) were first identified by Pavlov.

## BASIC CONDITIONING PHENOMENA

### Acquisition

In most classical conditioning experiments, several pairings of the CS and the US are necessary before the CR becomes fully developed. On the first few trials, there may be little or no conditioned responding to the CS. With addi-

tional pairings, conditioned responding gradually increases in strength. The part of a conditioning experiment in which the subject first experiences a series of CS-US pairings, and during which the CR gradually appears and increases in strength, is called the **acquisition phase.** Figure 4-5 shows the results of an acquisition phase in an experiment on eyeblink conditioning with human subjects (Trapold & Spence, 1960). The measure of conditioning is the percentage of trials on which a conditioned eyeblink response was recorded. Subjects in Group A received 130 trials with a strong air puff as a US, and this group exhibited a typical acquisition curve. The likelihood of a CR gradually increased over the first 50 trials or so, and subsequently there was little or no additional increase in the percentage of CRs with additional conditioning. The pattern of results suggests that even if Group A received many more conditioning trials, the percentage of CRs would probably never rise above about 55 percent. This value—the stable maximum level of conditioned responding that is gradually approached as conditioning proceeds—is called the **asymptote.**

**FIGURE 4-5** The acquisition of eyeblink CRs of human subjects. Subjects in Group A received 130 trials with a strong air puff as the US. Subjects in Group B received 90 trials with a strong air puff followed by 40 trials with a weaker air puff. (After Trapold & Spence, 1960)

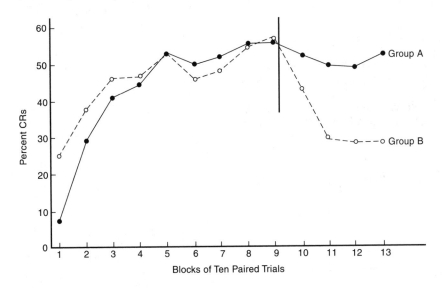

One factor that has a major influence on the asymptote of conditioning is the size or intensity of the US. In general, if a stronger stimulus is used as a US (a stronger puff of air, a larger amount of food), the asymptote of conditioning will be higher (a higher percentage of conditioned eyeblinks, more salivation). This point is demonstrated by the results from Group B in Figure 4-5. For the first 90 trials, these subjects experienced the same conditioning procedures as did Group A. However, beginning on trial 91, a weaker air puff was used as a US for Group B. You can see that shortly after this, the percentage of CRs in Group B decreased and approached a stable level of about 30 percent. Evidently, this was the asymptote, or the highest level of conditioned responding that could be maintained with the weak air puff.

Strong USs not only produce a higher asymptote, but they also usually result in faster conditioning. That is, it may take fewer trials for a conditioned response to appear with a strong US than with a weak one. The same is true about the intensity of the CS. Imagine one conditioning experiment in which a faint tone was used as a CS, and another with a very loud tone as a CS. It should come as no surprise that conditioning will occur more rapidly with the loud tone.

## Extinction

The mere passage of time has relatively little effect on the strength of a conditioned response. Suppose we conducted an experiment in salivary conditioning, repeatedly pairing a bell and food until our subject reliably salivated as soon as the bell was rung. We could then remove the animal from the experimental chamber and allow a week, a month, or even a year to pass before returning the subject to the chamber. At this later time, upon ringing the bell, we would most likely still observe a CR of salivation (though probably not as much salivation as on the last trial of the initial training session). The point is that the simple passage of time will not cause an animal to "forget" to produce the CR once the CS is again presented.

This does not mean, however, that a conditioned response, once acquired, is permanent. A simple technique for producing a reduction and eventual disappearance of the CR is the procedure of **extinction,** which involves repeatedly presenting the CS *without* the US. For example, suppose we followed the acquisition phase of our experiment on salivary conditioning with an extinction phase, in which the bell was presented for many trials but no food was delivered. The first two panels in Figure 4-6 show, in an idealized form, the likely results of our hypothetical experiment. Like the acquisition phase, the course of extinction is usually gradual. In the beginning of an extinction phase, there are large reductions in the amount of salivation from trial to trial. Toward the end of the extinction phase, the decreases in conditioned responding occur more slowly, but eventually the CR will disappear altogether.

When the extinction phase is completed, we have a dog that behaves like a dog that is just beginning the experiment—the bell is presented and no salivation occurs. On the basis of this observation alone, we might conclude that the procedure of extinction simply reverses the effects of the previous acquisition phase. That is, if the animal has formed an association between the CS and the US during

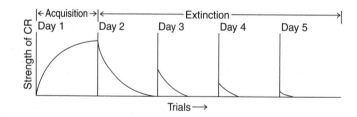

**FIGURE 4-6**  Idealized changes in the strength of a CR across one acquisition day followed by four days of extinction.

the acquisition phase, perhaps this association is gradually destroyed during the extinction phase. The simplicity of this hypothesis is appealing, but it is almost certainly wrong. At least three different phenomena show that whatever association was formed during acquisition is not erased during extinction. These phenomena are spontaneous recovery, disinhibition, and rapid reacquisition.

## Spontaneous Recovery

Suppose that after an acquisition phase on Day 1 and an extinction phase on Day 2, we return our subject to the experimental chamber on Day 3 and conduct another series of extinction trials with the bell. Figure 4-6 shows that on the first several trials of Day 3, we are likely to see some conditioned responding to the bell, even though no CRs were observed at the end of Day 2. Pavlov called this reappearance of conditioned responding **spontaneous recovery** and treated it as proof that the CS-US association is not permanently destroyed in an extinction procedure. Pavlov's conclusion was obviously correct: If extinction serves to undo or erase the learning that occurred in acquisition, why would CRs spontaneously reappear without further conditioning trials? Whatever happens during extinction, it is not a simple erasure of the previous learning, and the passage of time seems to be an important variable. If more time elapses between the first and second extinction sessions, more spontaneous recovery is observed (Brooks & Bouton, 1993).

Several different theories about spontaneous recovery have been developed. One popular theory, which we can call the **inhibition theory,** states that after extinction is complete, the subject is left with two counteracting associations (Konorski, 1948). The CS-US association formed during acquisition is called an **excitatory association** because through this association the CS now excites, or activates, the US center. According to this theory, a parallel but **inhibitory association** develops during extinction. When extinction is complete, the effects of the excitatory and inhibitory associations cancel out, so that the US

center is no longer activated by the presentation of the CS. However, inhibitory associations (or at least newly formed ones) are more fragile than excitatory associations, and they are therefore more severely weakened by the passage of time. With respect to Figure 4-6, this theory would say that at the end of Day 2, the inhibitory CS-US association is strong enough to counteract completely the excitatory association, so no CRs are observed. However, between Day 2 and Day 3 the inhibitory association is weakened, so at the beginning of Day 3 it can no longer fully counteract the excitatory association, and some CRs are therefore observed. Further extinction trials on Day 3 strengthen the inhibitory association (just as they did on Day 2), and so conditioned responding once again disappears.

If we were to conduct further extinction sessions on Days 4, 5, 6, and so on, we might again observe some spontaneous recovery, but typically the amount of spontaneous recovery would become smaller and smaller until it no longer occurred (see Figure 4-6). According to the inhibition theory, this happens because the inhibitory association becomes progressively less fragile with repeated extinction sessions, until it can withstand the passage of time as well as the excitatory association.

The existence of spontaneous recovery is firmly established, but the inhibition theory is just one of several theories about extinction and spontaneous recovery (Boakes & Halliday, 1975; Estes, 1955; Skinner, 1950). Some experiments by Robbins (1990) supported a theory that, during extinction, the subject stops "processing" or "paying attention to" the CS. Conditioned responses then disappear, because when the animal stops paying attention to the CS, it stops responding to the CS. Later, when the animal is brought back to the conditioning chamber after some time has passed (for example, at the start of Day 3 in Figure 4-6), the animal's attention to the CS is revived for a while, leading to a spontaneous recovery of CRs.

Another plausible theory of spontaneous recovery states that the CS becomes an ambiguous stimulus because it has been associated both with the US and then with the absence of the US (Capaldi, 1966). Referring again to Figure 4-6, after Day 2, the dog has experienced one session in which the bell was followed by food and one session in which it was not. At the start of Day 3, the dog cannot know whether this session will be like that of Day 1 or like that of Day 2, and its behavior (some weak CRs at the start of the session) may be a reflection of this uncertainty. As Bouton (2000) has put it, the CS "is ambiguous, and like an ambiguous word, its current meaning—or the behavior it currently evokes—is determined by the context. . . . Instability, lapse, and relapse are to be expected from a modern understanding of behavioral change" (pp. 57–58). Consistent with this theory, rats in one experiment displayed less spontaneous recovery of a taste aversion when a specific stimulus (a buzzer) was presented throughout every extinction session. The rats may have learned that the CS presented in a quiet environment was followed by the US, but the CS presented with the buzzer was not (Brooks, Palmatier, Garcia, & Johnson, 1999). In other words, the presence of the buzzer may have helped to reduce the ambiguity of the CS.

If the different theories of spontaneous recovery seem confusing to you, it may be reassuring to know that there is confusion and disagreement among the experts about this topic. Surprisingly, psychologists still do not fully understand the causes of extinction and spontaneous recovery, two of the most basic phenomena of classical conditioning.

### Disinhibition

Suppose that an extinction phase has progressed to the point where the CS (a bell) no longer evokes any salivation. Now, if a novel stimulus such as a buzzer is presented a few seconds before the bell, the bell may once again elicit a CR of salivation. Pavlov called this effect **disinhibition** because he believed that the presentation of a distracting stimulus (the buzzer in this example) disrupts the fragile inhibition that supposedly develops during extinction. According to the inhibition theory, the more stable excitatory association is less affected by the distracting stimulus than is the

inhibitory association. The net result is a slight excitatory tendency manifested in the reappearance of the conditioned salivary response.

As in the discussion of spontaneous recovery, let us be sure to separate data from theory. On one hand, we can be confident that disinhibition is a real phenomenon, because it has been observed a number of times in different experiments (Bottjer, 1982; Winnick & Hunt, 1951). On the other hand, the inhibition theory may or may not be the correct explanation of why disinhibition occurs.

### Rapid Reacquisition

This phenomenon is similar to the "savings" that are found in experiments on list learning (Chapter 2) or habituation (Chapter 3). In classical conditioning, if a subject receives an acquisition phase, an extinction phase, and then another acquisition phase with the same CS and the same US, the rate of learning is substantially faster in the second acquisition phase—the **reacquisition phase.** Furthermore, the rate of learning tends to get faster and faster if a subject is given repeated cycles of extinction followed by reacquisition (Hoehler, Kirschenbaum, & Leonard, 1973). The speed of reacquisition is probably due in part to the presence of spontaneous recovery, which gives the subject a head start at the beginning of the reacquisition phase. However, even if steps are taken to eradicate spontaneous recovery before the reacquisition phase begins, the rate of reacquisition can still be faster than original acquisition (Napier, Macrae, & Kehoe, 1992).

As with spontaneous recovery and disinhibition, we do not yet have a complete explanation for the phenomenon of rapid reacquisition. Nevertheless, these three phenomena make it abundantly clear that there is no simple way to get a subject to "unlearn" a conditioned response, and that no amount of extinction training can completely wipe out the effects of a classical conditioning experience. Extinction can cause a conditioned response to disappear, and after repeated extinction sessions, spontaneous recovery may disappear, but the subject will never be exactly the same as before the conditioning began.

## Conditioned Inhibition

Although disagreement still exists over whether inhibition plays an important role during extinction, there is general agreement that a CS can develop inhibitory properties as a result of certain conditioning procedures (see Miller & Spear, 1985). If it can be shown that a CS prevents the occurrence of a CR, or that it reduces the size of the CR from what it would otherwise be, then this CS is called an **inhibitory CS** or a **conditioned inhibitor** (sometimes designated as a CS–). Pavlov discovered what is probably the simplest and most effective procedure for changing a neutral stimulus into a conditioned inhibitor. This procedure involves the use of two different CSs, such as a metronome and a flashing light. Suppose that in the first phase of an experiment, we repeatedly pair the sound of the metronome with the presentation of food until the subject shows a stable salivary response to the metronome. The metronome can now be called an **excitatory CS** (or CS+), because it regularly elicits a CR. In the second phase of the experiment, the dog receives two types of trials. Some trials are exactly like those of phase one (metronome plus food). However, on occasional trials (selected at random), both the metronome and the flashing light are presented simultaneously, but no food is delivered. The term **compound CS** is sometimes used to describe the simultaneous presentation of two or more CSs, such as the metronome and the light. At first, the dog may salivate both on trials with the metronome and on trials with the compound CS. As phase two continues, however, the animal eventually learns that no food ever appears on trials with the compound CS. The result is that the dog continues to salivate on trials with the metronome alone, but little or no salivation occurs on trials with both the metronome and the flashing light.

There are two ways to interpret the results of such an experiment. One possibility is that the light has become a conditioned inhibitor.

On the surface it seems to satisfy the definition of a conditioned inhibitor—its presence causes a reduction in the size of the CR from what it would otherwise be. But notice that we have only tested the light in a single context (in compound with the metronome). Another possibility is that the animal has learned nothing about the light by itself, but only about the metronome-plus-light compound. In other words, perhaps the animal has learned something about the compound CS as a unit (that it is not followed by food), but if presented with the flashing light without the metronome, the animal may treat this as a totally new (and neutral) stimulus. To determine whether the light by itself has developed general inhibitory properties, some test of the light in a new context is needed.

Pavlov recognized this problem, and he developed a test that offers a much more convincing demonstration of the inhibitory properties of a stimulus such as the flashing light. Suppose that a third stimulus, a tactile stimulus applied to the animal's leg, is developed into an excitatory CS (that is, it reliably elicits salivation). Now suppose that, for the first time, the animal receives a trial with a compound CS consisting of the tactile stimulus and the flashing light. This procedure of testing the combined effects of a known excitatory CS and an expected inhibitory CS is called a **summation test.** If the flashing light is truly a conditioned inhibitor, it should have the capacity to reduce the CR produced by any CS, not simply that of the metronome with which it was originally presented. Based on the results of Pavlov and others, we would probably find that the flashing light reduced or eliminated the CR to the tactile stimulus, even though these two stimuli were never presented together before. This type of result indicates that the flashing light is a general conditioned inhibitor, because it evidently has the ability to block or diminish the conditioned salivary response elicited by any excitatory CS.

A second method for determining whether a stimulus is inhibitory is to measure how long it takes to turn the stimulus into an excitatory CS. Suppose that one group of dogs, the experimental group, has received the training with the metronome and flashing light described earlier, so we believe the flashing light is a conditioned inhibitor. A second group of dogs, the control group, has not been exposed to the flashing light before, so it is presumably a neutral stimulus for this group. Now suppose that both groups receive a series of trials with the flashing light paired with food. Since the flashing light is supposedly a conditioned inhibitor in the experimental group, the acquisition of conditioned responding should be slower in this group. This is because any excitatory conditioning that occurs must first offset the inhibitory properties of the CS before a CR is observed. This technique of testing for the inhibitory properties of a CS is called a **retardation test** (Rescorla, 1969) because the development of conditioned responding should be retarded with a CS that is initially inhibitory. The retardation test and the summation test are the two most common techniques for showing that a CS is a conditioned inhibitor.

Why did the flashing light become a conditioned inhibitor in Pavlov's experiment? The following rule of thumb may make this phenomenon easier to understand: A stimulus will become a conditioned inhibitor if it reliably signals the absence of the US in a context where the US would otherwise be expected to occur. In our example, the metronome provided the "context" in which food was normally presented. Because the flashing light signaled the absence of an otherwise imminent US, it became an inhibitory CS.

## Generalization and Discrimination

After classical conditioning with one CS, other, similar stimuli will also elicit CRs, although these other stimuli have never been paired with the US. This transfer of the effects of conditioning to similar stimuli is called **generalization,** which is illustrated in Figure 4-7. In this experiment on eyeblink conditioning, rabbits received a few hundred trials with a 1200-Hz tone as the CS and a shock near the eye as a US.

The data shown in Figure 4-7 were collected on a test day when tones of five different frequencies were repeatedly presented in a random sequence, but no US occurred on any trial. In other words, these tests were conducted under extinction conditions. As can be seen, the 1200-Hz tone elicited the highest percentage of CRs. The two tones closest in frequency to the 1200-Hz tone elicited an intermediate level of responding, and the more distant tones elicited the fewest responses. The function in Figure 4-7 is a typical **generalization gradient,** in which the *x*-axis plots some dimension along which the test stimuli are varied and the *y*-axis shows the strength of conditioned responding to the different stimuli. In general, the more similar a stimulus is to the training stimulus, the greater will be its capacity to elicit CRs.

In some cases it is much more difficult to predict which stimuli a subject will find most similar to the CS used in conditioning. Consider an experiment with human subjects that used printed words as CSs (Razran, 1949). After conditioning with a small set of words,

**FIGURE 4-7** A typical generalization gradient. Rabbits in an eyeblink conditioning experiment received several hundred pairings of a 1200-Hz tone and a shock. The graph shows the results from a subsequent generalization test in which the 1200-Hz tone and four others were presented but never followed by the US. (From J. W. Moore, 1972)

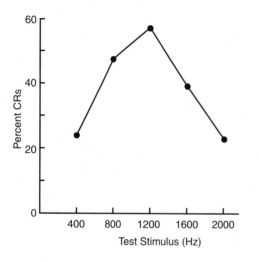

Razran looked for generalization to other words. One clear conclusion from this research was that generalization among words cannot be predicted merely on the basis of their physical similarity. For example, after conditioning to the word *day*, subjects showed generalization of 20 percent to the word *may* (which is similar in appearance and sound but not in meaning) and generalization of 40 percent to *week* (which is similar in meaning but not in appearance or sound). In this case and others, similarity of meaning was more important than physical similarity. The rules for generalization among linguistic stimuli may be similar to those that predict performance on a free-association task (see Chapter 2), for Razran also found evidence for the Associationists' principle of contrast (considerable generalization from *day* to *night* and from *dark* to *light*). Such patterns of generalization among semantically related words are obviously dependent upon a person's experience— a person who did not understand English would exhibit little generalization from *day* to *week* or *night*.

The opposite of generalization is **discrimination,** in which a subject learns to respond to one stimulus but not to a similar stimulus. We have seen that if a rabbit's eyeblink is conditioned to a 1200-Hz tone, there will be substantial generalization to an 800-Hz tone. However, if the 800-Hz tone is never followed by food, but the 1200-Hz tone is always followed by food, the animal will eventually learn a discrimination in which the 1200-Hz tone elicits an eyeblink and the 800-Hz tone does not. This type of discrimination learning is important in many real-world situations. For instance, impala and other species of prey on the African plains can learn to discriminate between wild dogs that have just eaten (and will not attack again) and wild dogs on the hunt (which are very dangerous). The latter will elicit an obvious fear reaction in the prey, whereas the former will not.

Although the concepts of generalization and discrimination are easy to describe, a number of theoretical problems have puzzled psychologists since the time of Pavlov. Why does conditioning with one stimulus cause a "spread

*The Encyclopedia of Psychology* has links to many articles on classical conditioning and other types of learning at *http://www. psychology.org/links/Environment_Behavior_ Relationships/Learning.*

of excitation" to similar stimuli? Can we predict, in advance, what stimuli a subject will treat as similar? How does experience affect the shape of a generalization gradient? What types of training will produce the most accurate levels of performance in a task where a difficult discrimination is required? These and other questions about generalization and discrimination will be examined in Chapter 10.

## TEMPORAL RELATIONSHIPS BETWEEN CS AND US

In any experiment on classical conditioning, the precise timing of the CS and the US can have a major effect on the results. All of the experiments discussed so far involved what is called **short-delay conditioning** (see Figure 4-8), in which the CS begins a second or so before the US. It is well established that this temporal arrangement produces the strongest and most rapid conditioning. The optimal delay depends on what conditioning preparation is used, who the subjects are, and other factors. For example, in human eyeblink conditioning, the fastest acquisition occurs with a delay of about 0.4 seconds if the subjects are young adults, but with older adults, conditioning is faster with a delay closer to 1 second (Solomon, Blanchard, Levine, Velazquez, & Groccia-Ellison, 1991).

Studies have shown that the early onset of the CS is important: In **simultaneous conditioning,** where the CS and US begin at the same moment (Figure 4-8), conditioned responding is much weaker than in short-delay conditioning (M. C. Smith & Gormezano, 1965). This may be so for a number of reasons.

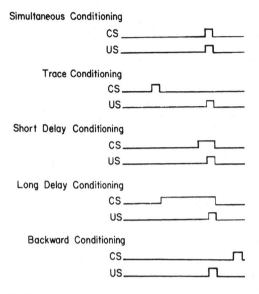

**FIGURE 4-8**   The temporal relationships between CS and US in five types of classical conditioning.

For one thing, if the US begins at the same moment as the CS, the subject may be so busy responding to the US that it fails to notice the CS. Furthermore, if the CS does not precede the US, it cannot serve to signal or predict the arrival of the US. As we will see again and again, the predictiveness of a CS is an important determinant of the degree of conditioning the CS undergoes and of whether this conditioning is excitatory or inhibitory. The following rules of thumb, though not perfect, are usually helpful in predicting the outcome of a conditioning arrangement:

- To the extent that a CS is a good predictor of the presence of the US, it will tend to become excitatory.
- To the extent that a CS is a good predictor of the absence of the US, it will tend to become inhibitory.

It should help to keep these rules in mind when examining the other conditioning arrangements discussed in this section.

As shown in Figure 4-8, **trace conditioning** refers to the case in which the CS and US are separated by some time interval in which

neither stimulus is present. The term trace conditioning is derived from the notion that since the CS is no longer physically present when the US occurs, the subject must rely on a "memory trace" of the CS if conditioning is to occur. In a number of studies, the amount of time elapsing between CS and US presentations, or the **CS-US interval,** was systematically varied. That is, one group of subjects might receive a series of conditioning trials with a 2-second CS-US interval, another group with a 5-second CS-US interval, and so on. The results of such studies showed that as the CS-US interval is increased, the level of conditioning declines systematically (Ellison, 1964; Lucas, Deich, & Wasserman, 1981). In some cases, the decreases in conditioning are quite dramatic. For instance, in eyeblink conditioning there is virtually no evidence of conditioned responding if the CS and US are separated by as little as 2 seconds (Schneiderman, 1966).

A similar pattern emerges in **long-delay conditioning,** where the onset of the CS precedes that of the US by at least several seconds, but the CS continues until the US is presented (see Figure 4-8). In long-delay conditioning, CS-US interval refers to the delay between the onsets of the CS and US. Here, too, the strength of the conditioned responding decreases as the CS-US interval increases, but the effects of delay are usually not as pronounced as in trace conditioning (which is understandable, since in long-delay conditioning, the subject does not have to rely on its memory of the CS). In both trace and delay conditioning, studies of the CS-US interval provide support for the Associationists' principle of contiguity. However, the results are also consistent with the predictiveness rule, because as the CS-US interval increases, it becomes increasingly difficult for the subject to predict the exact moment when the US will occur.

In long-delay conditioning, Pavlov noted that the temporal location of the CRs changed over trials. Early in training, a dog would salivate as soon as the CS was presented, although the CS-US interval might be 10 seconds. As conditioning trials continued, however, these early CRs would gradually disappear, and the dog would salivate shortly before the food was presented (8 or 9 seconds after CS onset). This pattern indicates, first of all, that the dog had learned to estimate the duration of the CS quite accurately. In addition, it is consistent with the rule that the stimulus that is the best predictor of the US will be the most strongly conditioned. In this example, what stimulus is a better predictor of the US than CS onset? Obviously, it is the compound stimulus—CS onset plus the passage of about 10 seconds. Consequently, it is this latter stimulus that ultimately elicits the most vigorous CRs.

The bottom of Figure 4-8 shows an example of **backward conditioning,** in which the CS is presented after the US. Even if the CS is presented immediately after the US, the level of conditioning is markedly lower than in simultaneous or short-delay conditioning. From the perspective of the contiguity principle, this does not make sense: If the CS and US are equally contiguous in short-delay conditioning and in backward conditioning, the contiguity principle predicts that equally strong CRs should develop. As with Ebbinghaus's backward-list experiment (Chapter 2), the weakness of backward conditioning points to a limitation of the contiguity principle—besides their temporal proximity, the order of the stimuli is important. Although backward conditioning may result in a weak excitatory association (Ayres, Haddad, & Albert, 1987; Champion & Jones, 1961), other studies have found that after a sufficient number of trials, a backward CS becomes inhibitory (Siegel & Domjan, 1971). The reasons for this inhibitory conditioning are quite complex (see Tait & Saladin, 1986; Wagner & Larew, 1985), but once again the predictiveness rule can serve as a useful guide: In backward conditioning, the onset of the CS signals a period of time in which the US will be absent. That is, as long as the backward CS is present, the subject can be certain that no US will occur.

## CS-US Correlations

In each of the conditioning arrangements discussed so far, the temporal pattern of stimulus presentations is exactly the same on every trial. For example, in long-delay conditioning

the onset of the US always follows the onset of the CS by the same amount of time, and the US never occurs at any other time. We can describe this perfect correlation between CS and US with two probabilities: The probability that the US will occur in the presence of the CS is 1 (that is, the US is certain to occur); the probability that the US will occur in the absence of the CS is 0. In the real world, however, the relationships between stimuli are seldom so regular. A rabbit in the forest must learn to recognize stimuli that could indicate that a predator is nearby. The rustling of leaves could be a predator, or it could be simply a breeze. On some occasions the sound of a snapped twig may mean a hunter is nearby; on other occasions it may not. There are also times when a predator's attack is not preceded by any perceptible stimulus.

These less-than-perfect correlations between signals and consequences can also be stated in probabilistic terms. Given a particular stimulus, the probability of an attack by a predator may be high (but not 1). In the absence of the stimulus, the probability of an attack may be lower (but not 0). Although the relationships among stimuli are variable and uncertain in the real world, the ability to detect those imperfect correlations that do exist between signals and consequences has obvious advantages. It is important for an animal to know which stimuli are the most dependable signals of possible danger. In the laboratory, classical conditioning procedures can be used to evaluate an animal's ability to detect imperfect correlations between stimuli.

A series of experiments by Rescorla (1966, 1968) showed how the probability of the US in the presence of the CS and in its absence combine to determine the size of the CR. In a conditioned suppression procedure with rats, the CS was a 2-minute tone that was presented at random intervals averaging 8 minutes. For one group of rats, there was a 40 percent chance that a shock would occur during a 2-minute CS presentation, and there was a 20 percent chance that a shock would occur in any 2-minute period when the CS was not present. The US might occur at any moment during the presence or absence of the CS. Notice that neither the presence nor the absence of a CS was a definite signal that a US would occur, and neither provided any information about the timing of a US (since a shock could occur at any time). The only information the CS provided was whether the probability of shock was high or low.

The results can be summarized as follows. Whenever the probability of shock was greater in the presence of the tone than in its absence, the tone became an excitatory CS (that is, response suppression occurred when the tone was presented). When the probability of shock was the same in the presence and absence of the tone (for instance, a 40 percent chance of shock in both the presence and absence of the tone), there was no suppression at all to the tone. In another experiment, Rescorla included a group in which the chance of shock was actually lower when the CS was present than when it was absent (so the CS signaled a relative level of safety from shock), and in this case the CS became inhibitory.

Based on these results, Rescorla concluded that the traditional view of classical conditioning, which states that the *contiguity* of CS and US is what causes an association to develop, is incorrect. Notice that in the groups with equal probabilities of shock in the presence and absence of the CS, there were many pairings of the CS and US, yet there was no conditioning to the CS. Rescorla therefore proposed that the important variable in classical conditioning is not the contiguity of CS and US but rather the *correlation* between CS and US. If the correlation is positive (that is, if the CS predicts a higher-than-normal probability of the US), the CS will become excitatory. If there is no correlation between CS and US (if the probability of the US is the same whether or not the CS is present), the CS will remain neutral. If the correlation between CS and US is negative (if the CS signals a lower-than-normal probability of the US), the CS will become inhibitory.

The correlational approach to classical conditioning is substantially different from an analysis based on contiguity, for it implies that an animal can learn about the long-term relationship between CS and US. (A short time sample from a conditioning session could give very inaccurate estimates of the probabilities of shock in the presence and absence of the US. Only with long time samples can accurate estimates of these probabilities be made.) Although exactly how animals can accomplish this feat is still a matter for debate, Rescorla's studies show that animals can learn about the correlation between CS and US even in the absence of a recurring and predictable temporal pattern. More importantly, these studies clearly demonstrate the weakness of another common belief about classical conditioning—that conditioning depends on a close pairing (contiguity) of CS and US. Instead of reciting the contiguity principle, students of classical conditioning would be much better off remembering the predictiveness rule: If a CS predicts that the US is likely to occur, the CS will become excitatory; if the CS predicts that the US is not likely to occur, the CS will become inhibitory. This rule is not perfect, but it works well in most cases.

## OTHER CONDITIONING ARRANGEMENTS

Thus far we have examined only procedures in which a CS is paired with (or correlated with) a US. However, other classical conditioning procedures involve the pairing of two CSs instead of a CS and a US. Two such conditioning arrangements are described next.

### Higher-Order Conditioning

In **second-order conditioning**, a CR is transferred from one CS to another. Pavlov described the following experiment to illustrate this process. First, the ticking of a metronome was firmly established as a CS in salivary conditioning by pairing the metronome with food. Because it was paired with the US, the metronome is called a **first-order CS**. Then another stimulus, a black square, was presented and immediately followed by the metronome on a number of occasions, but no food was presented on these trials. After a few trials of this type, the black square began to elicit salivation on its own, despite the fact that this stimulus was *never paired directly with the* *food* (but only with the metronome, a CS that was frequently paired with the food). In this example, the black square is called a **second-order CS** because it acquired its ability to elicit a CR by being paired with a first-order CS, the metronome.

Pavlov also reported that although it was quite difficult to obtain, he sometimes found evidence of **third-order conditioning** (the transfer of a CR from a second-order CS to yet another stimulus). He believed that these examples of second- and higher-order conditioning were important because they broadened the scope of classical conditioning. If there were no such thing as higher-order conditioning, then the only time an animal could learn through the process of classical conditioning would be when it encountered some US (food, water, a predator). But since higher-order conditioning is possible, new CRs may be acquired any time the animal encounters an already conditioned CS along with some new, neutral stimulus. As more and more stimuli become CSs as a result of an animal's everyday experiences, the opportunities for further learning through higher-order conditioning will expand at an increasing rate.

The following example illustrates how higher-order conditioning can play an important role in an animal's ability to avoid dangerous situations in its environment. Although wolves are among the major predators of deer, the sight of a wolf does not elicit an unconditioned fear reaction in a young whitetail deer. Instead, the sight of a wolf must become a CS for fear as a result of a young deer's experience. This conditioning might occur in at least two ways. The sight of a wolf might be followed by an attack and injury to the young deer. More likely, however, the sight of wolves is simply paired with visible signs of fear in other deer. (For simplicity, let us assume that the sight of fear reactions in other deer elicits an innate fear reaction in the young deer.) In either case, the sight of wolves eventually becomes a first-order CS for a fear response in the young deer. Once this happens, higher-order conditioning can occur whenever some initially neutral stimulus is paired with the sight of wolves. Perhaps certain sounds or

odors frequently precede the appearance of wolves, and through second-order conditioning, these may come to elicit fear. Or perhaps wolves are usually encountered in certain parts of the forest, and so the deer becomes fearful and cautious when traveling through these places. Although these examples are only speculative, they show how an initially neutral stimulus (the sight of wolves) can first develop the capacity to elicit a fear response and can then transfer this response to other stimuli.

Second-order conditioning has also been demonstrated with humans. For example, in what is called **evaluative conditioning**, subjects are asked to evaluate different stimuli—to rate how much they like them using a scale that ranges from "very disliked" to "very liked." The first-order CSs are typically words that people consistently rate as being positive (such as *honest* or *friendly*) or negative (*cruel, arrogant*). These words are first-order CSs, not unconditioned stimuli, because they would certainly have no value to someone who did not know the English language. For English speakers, these words presumably attained their positive or negative values because they have been associated with good or bad experiences in the past. In some studies, the second-order CSs are nonsense syllables, and if a nonsense syllable is repeatedly paired with a positive (or negative) word, subjects later give the nonsense syllable itself a positive (or negative) rating (Cicero & Tryon, 1989).

In one interesting study, pictures of people's faces were the second-order stimuli, and while looking at some of these faces, subjects heard either positive or negative adjectives. The subjects later rated the faces as being "liked" if they had been paired with positive adjectives and "unliked" if they had been paired with negative adjectives. These positive or negative ratings of the faces occurred even if the subjects could not remember the adjectives that had been paired with individual faces. In other words, subjects knew they liked some faces and disliked others, but they could not say exactly why (Baeyens, Eelen, Van den Bergh, & Crombez, 1992).

This type of evaluative conditioning has long been used in advertising. A commercial may present a certain brand of cola along with stimuli that most viewers will evaluate positively, such as young, attractive people having a good time. Advertisers hope that viewers will be attracted to the people and that this positive reaction will become conditioned to the product being sold. If the conditioning is successful, you may later have a positive reaction when you see the product in a store, regardless of whether or not you remember the commercial.

### Sensory Preconditioning

**Sensory preconditioning** is similar to second-order conditioning, except that the two CSs are repeatedly paired *before* the US is introduced. For example, let us return to Pavlov's experiment on second-order conditioning with the black square, metronome, and food. To conduct a parallel experiment on sensory preconditioning with these same stimuli, we would first expose a dog to many trials on which the black square was paired with the metronome. In the second phase of the experiment, the metronome would be paired with food, and of course the metronome would eventually elicit salivation. In the final phase of the experiment (the test phase), we would present the black square by itself to determine whether it would now also elicit a CR of salivation. If it did, this would be a successful demonstration of sensory preconditioning. Various studies with this type of design have demonstrated the existence of sensory preconditioning (Brogden, 1939; Pfautz, Donegan, & Wagner, 1978). Such results provide further evidence for the existence of S-S associations, and they show that these associations can form between two "neutral" stimuli as well as between a CS and a US.

## CLASSICAL CONDITIONING OUTSIDE THE LABORATORY

Few psychologists now believe that the bulk of our learned behaviors arise directly from the principles of classical conditioning. Whereas classical conditioning can explain how reflexive behaviors are transferred from a US to some

new stimulus, it cannot account for behaviors that have no obvious eliciting stimulus (such as walking, playing, or cooking a meal) or for totally novel behaviors (uttering a sentence never heard before, solving a problem in calculus). In later chapters we will examine other principles of learning that are more applicable to such "spontaneous" and "creative" behaviors. Yet although Pavlov probably overestimated the importance of classical conditioning for everyday human behaviors, we should be careful not to make the opposite mistake of underestimating its importance. Classical conditioning is relevant to behaviors outside the laboratory in at least two ways. First, it offers a means of understanding behaviors we usually call "involuntary"—behaviors that are automatically elicited by certain stimuli whether we want them to occur or not. As will be discussed, many emotional reactions seem to fall into this category. Second, research on classical conditioning has led to several major treatment procedures for behavior disorders. These procedures can be used to strengthen desired "involuntary" responses or to weaken undesired responses. The remainder of this chapter examines the role of classical conditioning in these nonlaboratory settings.

### Classical Conditioning and Emotional Responses

For the most part, emotional responses such as feelings of pleasure, happiness, anxiety, or excitement are difficult to measure in another person, and this makes them difficult to analyze scientifically. However, if we temporarily dispense with scientific rigor and examine our introspections, it should become clear that these sorts of emotional reactions are frequently triggered by specific stimuli. Furthermore, it is often obvious that the response-eliciting properties of the stimulus were acquired through experience. Suppose you open your mailbox and find a letter with the return address of a close friend. This stimulus may immediately evoke a pleasant and complex emotional reaction that you might loosely call affection, warmth, or fondness. Whatever you call the emotional reaction, there is no doubt that this particular stimulus—a person's handwritten address on an envelope—would not elicit the response from you shortly after your birth, nor would it elicit the response now if you did not know the person who sent you the letter. The envelope is a CS that elicits a pleasant emotional response only because the address has been associated with your friend. Other stimuli can elicit less pleasant emotional reactions. For many college students, examination period can be a time of high anxiety. This anxiety can be conditioned to stimuli associated with the examination process—the textbooks on one's desk, a calendar with the date of the exam circled, or the sight of the building where the exam will be held.

Classical conditioning can also affect our emotional reactions to other people. In one study using evaluative conditioning, subjects were asked to look at photographs of people's faces, and each photograph was paired with either a pleasant, neutral, or unpleasant odor. When subjects later had to evaluate their preferences for the people in the photographs (with no odors present), they gave the highest ratings to faces previously paired with pleasant odors and the lowest ratings to those paired with unpleasant odors (Todrank, Byrnes, Wrzesniewski, & Rozin, 1995). This research will surely give encouragement to companies that sell mouthwash, deodorant, and perfume.

It is instructive to look for examples of classical conditioning in your daily life. In the following example, many readers will probably understand the emotional reaction of my friend Phil. Like the video games that have largely replaced them, pinball games can evoke a high level of enjoyment and excitement in some people. I once watched as Phil took his turn on a pinball machine that awarded a free game for a high score. During the course of play, the winning of a free game was signaled by a loud clunk. As Phil reached the critical score and heard the loud clunk, he smiled with satisfaction and exclaimed, "That's the most beautiful sound in the world!" Of course, objectively speaking, the clunk was not a beautiful sound at all. What Phil probably meant was that for him, the sound evoked a pleasant emotional response. By being repeatedly paired with the winning of a free game, this ordinary sound gained the capacity to elicit the emotional response of excitement.

A final, personal example shows that conditioned emotional responses are not under voluntary control and that they are not necessarily guided by logic or by a knowledge of one's environment. Before my wife, Laurie, and I were married, our jobs required us to live over 200 miles apart. We visited each other on weekends, about twice a month. Laurie owns a very distinctive winter coat—a white coat with broad horizontal stripes of red, yellow, and green. It is easy to find her in a crowd when she is wearing that coat. One day when Laurie was at her job and I was at mine, I was walking across the campus when I saw, ahead of me, someone wearing a coat just like Laurie's. My immediate reaction was a good example of a conditioned response—my heart started pounding rapidly, as when a person is startled by a loud noise. This response persisted for 10 or 20 seconds. What is noteworthy about the response is that it did not make sense—I knew Laurie was several hundred miles away, and the person wearing the coat could not possibly be her. In addition, whereas Laurie has a full-length coat, the coat I saw was short, and the person wearing it was a man with a beard. Yet none of these discrepancies was enough to prevent my conditioned heart-rate response, and my skin conductance response undoubtedly exhibited a large increase as well.

## Classical Conditioning and the Immune System

As you probably know, the body's immune system is designed to fight off infections. Whenever bacteria, viruses, or foreign cells enter a person's body, the immune system produces antibodies that attack and kill these invaders. For a long time, scientists tended to think of the immune system as a fairly independent system that had little communication with other bodily functions. This viewpoint has changed, however, and there is now abundant evidence for complex interactions between the immune system and the nervous system. To put it another way, there is abundant evidence that psychological factors can affect the workings of the immune system (Ader & Cohen, 1993). For example, it is known that intense or prolonged psychological stress can weaken the immune system, making the individual more susceptible to illnesses ranging from the common cold to cancer.

There are also quite a few experiments showing that the immune system can be influenced by classical conditioning. Ader and Cohen (1975) conducted a landmark study in this area. They gave rats a single conditioning trial in which the CS was saccharin-flavored water and the US was an injection of **cyclophosphamide,** a drug that suppresses the activity of the immune system. A few days later, the rats were injected with a small quantity of foreign cells (red blood cells from sheep) that their immune systems would normally attack vigorously. One group of rats was then given saccharin-flavored water once again, whereas a control group received plain water. Ader and Cohen found that for rats in the saccharin group, the response of the immune system was weaker than for rats in the plain water group— fewer antibodies were produced by rats in the saccharin group. In other words, it appeared that the saccharin, which normally has no effect on the immune system, now produced a conditioned response, a weakening of the immune system. Later studies replicated this effect and, by ruling out other possible explanations, demonstrated that it is indeed due to classical conditioning (Ader, Felten, & Cohen, 1990).

In addition, there is now growing evidence that immune system activity can also be increased through classical conditioning (Alvarez-Borda, Ramiraez-Amaya, Perez-Montfort, & Bermudez-Rattoni, 1995). Solvason, Ghanata, and Hiramoto (1988) reported a particularly clear example of a conditioned increase in immune activity. Mice exposed to the odor of camphor as a CS were then injected with the drug **interferon** as the US. Interferon normally causes an increase in the activity of **natural killer cells** in the bloodstream—cells that are involved in combating viruses and the growth of tumors. After a few pairings of the

camphor odor and interferon, presenting the camphor odor by itself was enough to produce an increase in natural killer cell activity. A similar study with healthy human adults also obtained increases in natural killer cells through classical conditioning (Buske-Kirschbaum, Kirschbaum, Stierle, Jabaij, & Hellhammer, 1994).

Although much about the nature of classically conditioned immune responses remains a mystery, researchers have recognized the potential importance of this phenomenon. For people whose immune systems have been temporarily weakened through illness or fatigue, the development of psychological techniques to strengthen immune activity could be quite beneficial (Olness, 1999). In contrast, some medical treatments require a decrease in immune activity. For example, in operations where an organ is transplanted from one person to another, it is essential to suppress the activity of the immune system so that the body does not reject the transplanted organ. One study with mice demonstrated that using conditioned stimuli may help in such situations. First, saccharin was paired with cyclophosphamide to establish it as a CS for immune suppression. The mice then received small grafts of transplanted skin. After receiving the skin grafts, some of the mice were again exposed to saccharin, and these mice were slower to reject the transplanted skin than were mice not given any more saccharin (Gorczynski, 1990). No studies of this type have yet been conducted with human subjects, but this type of research may eventually produce ways to better control immune system activity for the benefit of the patient.

## Applications in Behavior Therapy

*Systematic Desensitization for Phobias.* One of the most widely used procedures of behavior therapy is **systematic desensitization,** a treatment for phobias that arose directly out of laboratory research on classical conditioning. A **phobia** is an excessive and irrational fear of an object, place, or situation. Phobias come in numerous forms—fear of closed spaces, of open spaces, of heights, of water, of crowds, of speaking before a group, of taking an examination, of insects, of snakes, of dogs, of birds. Some of these phobias may sound almost amusing, but they are no joke to those who suffer from them, and they are frequently quite debilitating. A fear of insects or snakes may preclude going to a picnic or taking a walk in the woods. A fear of crowds may make it impossible for a person to go to the supermarket, to a movie, or to ride on a bus or train. A fear of birds or of open spaces may literally make an individual a prisoner in his or her home.

How do phobias arise? After Pavlov's discovery, classical conditioning was seen as one possible source of irrational fears. This hypothesis was bolstered by a famous (or, more accurately, infamous) experiment by John B. Watson and Rosalie Rayner (1921). Watson and Rayner used classical conditioning to develop a phobia in a normal 11-month-old infant named Albert. Before the experiment, few things frightened Albert, but one that did was the loud noise of a hammer hitting a steel bar. Upon hearing the noise, Albert would start to cry. Since this stimulus elicited a reliable response from Albert, it was used as the US in a series of conditioning trials. The CS was a live white rat, which initially produced no signs of fear in Albert. On the first conditioning trial, the noise was presented just as Albert was reaching out to touch the rat, and as a result Albert began to cry. Albert subsequently received seven more conditioning trials of this type. After this experience, Albert's behavior indicated that he had been classically conditioned—he cried when he was presented with the white rat by itself. This experimentally induced fear also generalized to a white rabbit and to other white furry objects, including a ball of cotton and a Santa Claus mask. After a month had passed, these stimuli still elicited some fear in Albert, although his reactions to them were somewhat diminished.

If this experiment sounds cruel and unethical, rest assured that modern legal safeguards for the protection of human subjects would make it difficult or impossible for a psychologist to conduct such a study today. In any case, Watson and Rayner concluded that a long-

The full text of the Watson and Rayner article, as well as classic writings by Pavlov and others, are available at *http://www.yorku.ca/dept/psych/classics/topic.htm#behaviorism*.

lasting fear of an initially neutral stimulus can result from the pairing of that stimulus with some fearful event. Today, psychologists recognize that phobias are complex phenomena that can arise through means other than classical conditioning, such as through observational learning and verbal communication (Mineka, 1985; Rachman, 1991). Nevertheless, classical conditioning still seems to be an important component in the development of many phobias.

If this analysis is correct, then the principles of classical conditioning should also describe how a phobia can be cured. To be specific, if the CS (the phobic object or event) is repeatedly presented without the US, the phobia should extinguish. Yet numerous case histories indicate that phobias can be extremely persistent. Why is it that phobias do not gradually disappear on their own? For example, if a teenager's fear of crowds stems from a childhood experience in which he was lost in a crowd, why doesn't the phobia extinguish as a result of repeated exposures to crowds with no aversive consequences? One obvious explanation is simply that the individual carefully avoids the phobic object or event, and without exposure to the CS, extinction cannot occur. Another possible explanation is the self-sustaining nature of some phobias. Thus if a person is fearful of crowds, any attempt to attend a movie, a football game, or the like will result in fear, discomfort, and possibly embarrassment if the person becomes so anxious that he or she must leave abruptly. If this happens, the phobic stimulus has once again been paired with aversive consequences, and the phobia may be strengthened.

Systematic desensitization can be viewed as a procedure in which the patient is exposed to the phobic object in a gradual way, so that fear and discomfort are kept to a minimum and extinction is allowed to occur. The treatment has three parts—the construction of a fear hierarchy, training in relaxation, and the gradual presentation of items in the fear hierarchy to the patient. The **fear hierarchy** is a list of fearful situations of progressively increasing intensity. At the bottom of the list is an item that evokes only a very mild fear response in the patient, and at the top is the most highly feared situation.

After the fear hierarchy is constructed, the patient is given training in **progressive relaxation,** or **deep muscle relaxation.** This technique, developed by Wolpe (1958), is a means of inducing a state of bodily calm and relaxation by having the person alternately tense and relax specific groups of muscles. For instance, the patient is first instructed to make a fist and to tense all the muscles of the hand as tightly as possible. After holding this tension for 5 to 10 seconds, the patient is instructed to release the tension and to concentrate on making the muscles of the hand as relaxed and as limp as possible for 15 to 20 seconds. This same procedure is used for muscles in the arms, neck, head, trunk, and legs. The idea behind this procedure is that many people have a high level of muscle tension without being aware of it, and if simply told to "completely relax" a set of muscles, they will be unable to do so. However, by contrasting a high degree of muscle tension with subsequent relaxation, a person can learn to relax the muscles on cue. The progressive relaxation procedure takes about 20 minutes, and when it is completed patients usually report that they feel very relaxed. At this point the extinction of the phobia can begin.

The therapist begins with the weakest item in the hierarchy, describes the scene to the patient, and asks the patient to imagine this scene as vividly as possible. For example, in the treatment of a teenager who developed a fear of driving after an automobile accident, the first instruction was to imagine "looking at his car as it was before the accident" (Kushner, 1965). Because the patient is in a relaxed state, and because the lowest item did not evoke much fear to begin with, it usually can be imagined with little or no fear. The patient is instructed to continue to imagine the scene for about 20 seconds. After a short pause in which the patient is told to relax, the first item is again presented. If the patient reports that the item produces no fear, the therapist moves on to the second item on the list, and the procedure is repeated. The therapist slowly progresses up the list, being certain that the fear of one item is completely gone before going on to the next item. A typical fear hierarchy contains 10 or 15 items, but there have been cases in which lists of over 100 items were constructed. The hierarchy for the patient with a fear of driving included the following nine items:

1. Imagine looking at your car as it was prior to the accident.
2. Imagine leaning against your car.
3. Imagine sitting in your car with the ignition turned off.
4. Imagine sitting in your car and turning on the ignition, with the car stationary but the motor idling.
5. Imagine backing out of your driveway and turning the car so you are in a position to drive off.
6. Imagine driving the car around the block on which you live.
7. Imagine driving along a straight road with no intersections.
8. Imagine you are approaching an intersection with no traffic appearing.
9. Imagine approaching the same intersection with another car nearing the intersection to your right, where there is a stop sign. (This was the situation leading to the patient's accident.) (paraphrased from Kushner, 1965, pp. 194–195)

In this case, the patient made rapid progress, and after only six sessions, the young man could again drive his car without fear. A 3-month follow-up found no return of the phobic symptoms. This case history is a bit unusual in the brevity of therapy (10 to 20 sessions are more typical) but not in its final outcome. Paul (1969) reviewed about 75 published reports on the use of systematic desensitization that together involved thousands of patients. In most of these reports, about 80 to 90 percent of the patients were cured of their phobias—a very high success rate for any type of therapy in the realm of mental health. There were only a few reports of relapses, and no evidence of **symptom substitution** (the appearance of a new psychological disorder after the original problem disappears). This mass of evidence suggests that systematic desensitization is an effective and efficient treatment for phobias.

Some variations of systematic desensitization replace the patient's imagination with more realistic stimuli. Sturges and Sturges (1998) treated an 11-year-old girl with a fear of elevators by systematically exposing her to a real elevator (beginning by having her just stand near an elevator, and ending with her riding alone on the elevator). A variation that relies on modern computer technology is **virtual reality therapy,** in which the patient wears a headset that displays realistic visual images that change with every head movement, simulating a three-dimensional environment. For instance, a man with a fear of flying was exposed to more and more challenging simulations of riding in a helicopter, and eventually his fear of flying diminished. Virtual reality therapy has been successfully used for fears of animals, heights, public speaking, and so on (North, North, & Coble, 1998). This technique has several advantages over traditional systematic desensitization. The stimuli are very realistic, they can be controlled precisely, and they can be tailored to the needs of each individual patient. The procedure does not rely on the patient's ability to imagine the objects or situations (Finfgeld, 1999). Because of these advantages, it seems likely that the use of computer-generated stimuli will become more widespread in the future.

*Aversive Counterconditioning.* Although it may sound paradoxical, people are frequently very poor at controlling their own behaviors. Consider several classes of behavior that are all too common in our society— overeating, excessive drinking, smoking, drug abuse. Whereas many people who engage in these behaviors know they are potentially harmful and claim they would like to stop, they also claim that they are unable to do so. The problem is that although the behaviors are detrimental to one's health, there are strong sources of motivation for continuing the behaviors. The motives may be of different types: Performing the behavior may be highly enjoyable, or refraining from the behavior may be unpleasant, or both. To put it simply, these behaviors have short-term advantages and long-term disadvantages. We will examine such conflicting motives in more detail in Chapter 14, but for now let us consider one behavioral technique designed to combat these unwanted behaviors.

The goal of **aversive counterconditioning** is to develop an aversive CR to stimuli associated with the undesirable behavior. For instance, if the patient is an alcoholic, the procedure may involve conditioning the responses of nausea and queasiness of the stomach to the sight, smell, and taste of alcohol. The term counterconditioning is used because the technique is designed to replace a positive emotional response to certain stimuli (such as alcohol) with a negative one. In the 1940s, Voegtlin and his associates conducted extensive research on the use of aversive counterconditioning as a treatment for alcoholism (Voegtlin, 1940; Lemere, Voegtlin, Broz, O'Hallaren, & Tupper, 1942). Over the years, more than 4,000 alcoholics volunteered to participate in Voegtlin's distinctly unpleasant therapy. Over a 10-day period, a patient received about a half dozen treatment sessions in which alcoholic beverages were paired with an emetic—a drug that produces nausea. Conditioning sessions took place in a quiet, darkened room in which a collection of liquor bottles was illuminated to enhance their salience. First, the patient received an emetic, and soon the first signs of nausea would begin. The patient was then given a large glass of whiskey, and was instructed to look at, smell, taste, and swallow the whiskey until vomiting occurred (which was usually no more than a few minutes). In later conditioning sessions, the whiskey was replaced with a variety of other liquors to ensure that the aversion was not limited to one type of liquor. It is hard to imagine a more unpleasant therapy, and the patients' willingness to participate gives an indication both of their commitment to overcome their alcoholism and of their inability to do so on their own.

Because a number of different treatments for alcoholism are known to promote short-term abstinence, the real test of a treatment's effectiveness is its long-term success rate. Figure 4-9 shows the percentages of former patients who were totally abstinent for various lengths of time after the therapy. As can be seen, the percentage of individuals who were totally abstinent declined over time. The diminishing percentages may reflect the process of extinction: If over the years a person repeatedly encounters the sight or smell of alcohol (at weddings, at parties, on television) in the absence of the US (the emetic), the CR of nausea should eventually wear off. At least two types of evidence support the role of extinction. First, patients who received "booster sessions" (further conditioning sessions a few months after the original treatment) were, on the average, abstinent for longer periods of time. Such reconditioning sessions probably counteracted the effects of extinction. Second, those who continued to associate with old drinking friends (and were thereby exposed to alcohol) were the most likely to fail.

If the declining percentages in Figure 4-9 seem discouraging, several points should be made. First, a similar pattern of increasing relapses over time occurs with every known treatment for alcoholism, and in fact Voegtlin's success rates are quite high compared to those of other treatments. Furthermore, these percentages are extremely conservative estimates of the success of Voegtlin's procedures because he employed a very strict criterion for success—total abstinence. Individuals who drank with moderation after the treatment were counted as failures, as were those who suffered a relapse, received reconditioning sessions, and were once again abstinent. Figure 4-9 therefore presents the most pessimistic view possible regarding the effectiveness of this treatment. In the United States, the use of aversive counterconditioning as a treatment for alcoholism has increased substantially since the mid-1970s, with success rates remaining about the same as in Figure 4-9.

Aversive counterconditioning has also been used with reasonable success for other problems besides alcoholism, including drug use, cigarette smoking, and sexual deviations. It is often included as one component of multifaceted treatment programs that also involve family counseling, self-control training, and other techniques (Junginger, 1997; J. W. Smith & Frawley, 1990).

In a case study involving a sexual deviation, Marks and Gelder (1967) used electric shock as a US to eliminate a male client's fetish for female clothing. Before therapy, the client was aroused (as measured by penile erection) by a photograph of a nude female (which is consid-

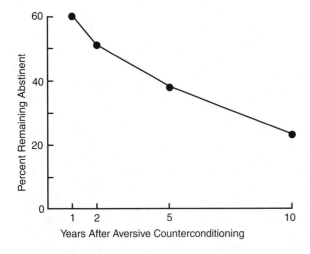

**FIGURE 4-9**   The percentages of Voegtlin's clients who remained completely abstinent for various amounts of time following aversive counterconditioning for alcoholism. (After Lemere & Voegtlin, 1950)

ered normal), but also by the sight of female panties, a slip, a skirt, and pajamas. The client then received 20 trials in which the panties were paired with shock, after which they no longer elicited arousal. The other items continued to produce arousal, however. Next, the other pieces of clothing were paired with shock, one at a time, until only the nude photograph (never paired with shock) elicited arousal. In this way, the man's abnormal sexual attraction to clothing was eliminated while leaving his sexual attraction to females intact.

In summary, aversive counterconditioning is a procedure that attempts to decrease unwanted behaviors by conditioning aversive reactions to stimuli associated with the behaviors. Its effectiveness is variable. It appears to be a useful procedure for eliminating certain sexual deviations. When used as a treatment for alcoholism or smoking, some clients have relapses, but others remain abstinent for years. The success rates are significantly higher than those found when individuals try to stop drinking or smoking without professional help. The effectiveness of aversive counterconditioning can be enhanced by offering periodic reconditioning sessions and by instructing clients to avoid stimuli associated with the problem behavior (bars, drinking companions, smoke-filled rooms, and the like).

*Treatment of Nocturnal Enuresis.* Children usually learn to use the toilet instead of wetting their pants by about age 3 or 4. For most children, the control of nighttime elimination occurs shortly afterward. However, a substantial portion of children continue to wet their beds at ages 5 and older, and this behavior becomes an increasing problem for both child and parents. The problem is aggravating for the parents, who must do all the extra laundry. Among the disadvantages for the child are the discomfort, the anger of one's parents, and often the reluctant declining of invitations to be an overnight guest with friends or relatives. Fortunately, most cases of nocturnal enuresis (bedwetting) can be cured by a straightforward procedure developed by Mowrer and Mowrer (1938), called the bell-and-pad method. The pad, a water-detecting device, is placed be-

neath the child's sheets, and a single drop of urine will activate the device and ring the bell to wake up the child. The child is instructed in advance to turn off the alarm, go to the toilet and urinate, and then go back to sleep. The bell and pad are used every night until the problem disappears.

In developing this procedure, the Mowrers were guided by an understanding of the principles of classical conditioning. The bell is a US that elicits two responses in the child: (1) awakening, and (2) the tightening of those muscles necessary to prevent further urination (responses that occur because the child has no difficulty retaining urine when awake). The goal of the procedure is to transfer either or both of these responses to an internal CS—the pattern of bodily sensations that accompany a full bladder. For simplicity, let us call the CS a full bladder. By repeatedly pairing a full bladder with the bell, the response of awakening and/or tightening the muscles so as to retain one's urine would eventually be elicited by the full bladder alone, before the bell sounds. Notice that either awakening and going to the bathroom or retaining one's urine is an appropriate response in this situation.

The classical conditioning explanation of the bell-and-pad method is not the only one; others have suggested that avoidance learning, as described in Chapter 8, is involved. Yet regardless of which is the most appropriate explanation, the procedure is largely successful. Various studies have found success rates of about 80 percent, and in some of the "unsuccessful" cases the symptoms, though not completely gone, were improved. Relapses are a frequent problem, however, with perhaps 25 percent of the children eventually experiencing a return of bedwetting (S. B. Johnson, 1981). These relapses can be readily treated with a period of reconditioning, but Young and Morgan (1972) tried a modified procedure in an effort to minimize relapses. With the alarm system active, children were given a type of overlearning in which they drank two pints of liquid just before going to bed (thus making the task of remaining dry more difficult). Only 10 percent of the children trained with this procedure had relapses, compared to 20 percent without the overlearning procedure. The bell-and-pad method is more effective than the medications that are commonly prescribed to treat enuresis (Rajigah, 1996), and more doctors are now recommending this treatment method to parents (Vogel, Young, & Primack, 1996).

***Summary of the Classical Conditioning Therapies.*** Behavior therapies based on principles of classical conditioning have been used to strengthen, eliminate, or replace behaviors. The Mowrers' treatment for nocturnal enuresis is an example of a procedure designed to strengthen a behavior—nighttime retention. Systematic desensitization is used to eliminate the emotional responses of fear and anxiety. Aversive counterconditioning is designed to replace pleasant emotional responses to such stimuli as alcohol and cigarette smoke with aversion. Each of these procedures has its share of failures and relapses, but each can also boast of long-term successes for a significant percentage of those who receive treatment.

## CHAPTER SUMMARY

In its simplest form, classical conditioning involves the repeated pairing of a conditioned stimulus (CS) with an unconditioned stimulus (US) that naturally elicits an unconditioned response (UR). After repeated pairings, the CS starts to elicit a conditioned response (CR). Pavlov used the salivation response of dogs to study classical conditioning, but in modern research some common preparations are eyeblink conditioning, conditioned suppression, the skin conductance response, and taste-aversion learning.

According to Pavlov's stimulus substitution theory, the CS should produce the same response that the US originally did. In reality, however, sometimes the CR is different in form, and sometimes it is actually the opposite of the UR. At the physiological level, stimulus substitution theory states that neural centers for the CS become connected to either the center for the US (an S-S connection) or directly to the center for the response (an S-R connection). Some experiments on US devaluation or revaluation favor the S-S view.

Throughout the animal kingdom, instances of classical conditioning exhibit the same basic principles, including acquisition, extinction, spontaneous recovery, disinhibition, conditioned inhibition, generalization, and discrimination. The most effective temporal arrangement for conditioning occurs in short-delay conditioning, and weaker conditioning usually occurs in simultaneous, long-delay, or trace conditioning. In backward conditioning, the CS may become a conditioned inhibitor. In other conditioning arrangements, such as second-order conditioning and sensory preconditioning, a CR is transferred, not from US to CS, but from one CS to another.

In everyday life, classically conditioned responses can be seen in our emotional reactions to many different stimuli. In behavior therapy, systematic desensitization is used to extinguish phobias by gradually presenting more and more intense fear-provoking stimuli while the patient is in a relaxed state. Aversive counterconditioning is used to replace positive responses to certain stimuli (alcohol, cigarettes) with negative responses. Alarm systems are used to train children to avoid bedwetting.

## REVIEW QUESTIONS

1. What is Pavlov's stimulus substitution theory? What are its strengths and weaknesses? How do experiments on US devaluation or revaluation help to decide whether S-S or S-R associations are formed during classical conditioning?

2. What three different types of evidence show that extinction does not simply erase the association that was formed during classical conditioning?

3. Describe one temporal arrangement between CS and US that produces strong excitatory conditioning, one that produces weak excitatory conditioning, and one that can produce inhibitory conditioning. Give a reasonable explanation of why each different procedure produces the results that it does.

4. What are two different types of behavior therapy that are based on classical conditioning? For each, describe the procedure and give an example. How successful is each treatment?

## CHAPTER 5

# Theories and Research on Classical Conditioning

Chapter 4 described some of the most basic terms and concepts of classical conditioning and some of the ways it can affect our daily lives. Most of the concepts presented in that chapter either were developed by Pavlov or can be traced back to some of his ideas. Pavlov saw classical conditioning as a simple, mechanical, rule-governed type of learning, yet one that might account for a good deal of our learned behaviors. The present chapter examines some of the ways in which psychologists' conceptions of classical conditioning have changed over the years. Perhaps the clearest theme emerging from modern research on classical conditioning is that although it is one of the simplest types of learning, it is more complicated than was once believed. This is not to say that modern conditioning experiments have obtained chaotic results that follow no rules; rather, it is simply that the modern rules (theories) of conditioning have become more complex and more sophisticated.

This chapter will survey some current themes and issues in the field of classical conditioning. The chapter is divided into five sections, each of which addresses different questions. The first section is concerned with the conditioning process and the question of *when* conditioning takes place: Under what conditions will a stimulus become an excitatory CS,

or become an inhibitory CS, or remain neutral? What factors determine whether the stimulus will become a strong CS or a weak CS? These are certainly very basic questions, and this section will describe a few well-known theories that attempt to answer them. The second section deals with the products of conditioning: *What types of associations* are developed in different conditioning situations? In Chapter 4, we examined some evidence that an S-S association between the CS center and the US center is developed during simple conditioning. We will see, however, that a CS-US association is only one of many possible associative products of the classical conditioning process. The third section, on biological constraints, examines *what types of stimuli* are easily associated in classical conditioning and what types are not. As this section will explain in detail, the answer to this question is not simple, and it depends on the specific CS/US combination used and on the species of the subject.

The fourth section of this chapter presents modern theories that try to predict *what form* a conditioned response will take. Will the CR be similar to the UR, the opposite of the UR, or something entirely different? We will see that besides its theoretical importance, this issue has significant practical consequences, as when a stimulus that has been associated with a drug might later elicit a response that either mimics or opposes the reaction to the drug itself. The final section of this chapter examines both the process and products of classical conditioning from a neurophysiological perspective. This section will describe research that examines how classical conditioning alters the functioning of individual neurons as well as studies that investigate what areas of the brain are involved.

## THEORIES OF ASSOCIATIVE LEARNING

One of the oldest principles of associative learning is the principle of frequency—the more frequently two stimuli are paired, the more strongly will an individual associate the two. Thomas Brown (1820) first proposed this principle, and we have seen data from Ebbinghaus and from classical conditioning experiments that support this principle. The principle was also the cornerstone of several influential mathematical theories of learning (Bush & Mosteller, 1955; Estes, 1950; Hull, 1943). Because of this widespread acceptance of the frequency principle, it is not surprising that an experiment by Kamin (1968) that contradicted this principle attracted considerable attention. We will examine Kamin's experiment in the next section. We will then go on to consider several different theories of classical conditioning that have been developed in an effort to avoid the limitations of the frequency principle and provide a more adequate analysis of the processes of associative learning.

### The Blocking Effect

To make the description of Kamin's experiment and others in this chapter easier to understand, some notational conventions will be adopted. Because these experiments included not one but several CSs, we will use capital letters to represent different CSs (for instance, T will represent a tone, and L will represent a light). Usually only one US is involved, but it may be present on some trials and absent on others, so the superscripts + and ° will represent, respectively, the presence and absence of

the US. For example, T+ will denote a trial on which one CS, a tone, was presented by itself and was followed by the US. The notation TL° will refer to a trial on which two CSs, the tone and the light, were presented simultaneously, but were not followed by the US. Nearly all of the experiments described below employed counterbalancing procedures in which the roles of L and T were reversed for half of the subjects in each group. The purpose of this counterbalancing was to ensure that the results of an experiment are not affected by some uninteresting differences between CSs of different modalities. To avoid unnecessary confusion, however, there will be no mention of this counterbalancing in the descriptions of the experiments.

Kamin's original experiment used rats in a conditioned suppression procedure. Table 5-1 outlines the design of the experiment. There were two groups of rats, a **blocking group** and a **control group.** In the first phase of the experiment, subjects in the blocking group received a series of L+ trials, and by the end of this phase, L elicited a strong CR. In Phase 2, the blocking group received a series of LT+ trials. These trials were exactly the same as Phase 1 trials except that a second CS, T, occurred along with L. In the test phase, T was presented by itself in extinction for several trials so as to measure the strength of conditioning to this CS.

Conditions for the control group were identical except for one important difference—in Phase 1 no stimuli were presented at all. Thus the first time these subjects were exposed to L, T, and the US was in Phase 2. It is important

**TABLE 5-1   Design of Kamin's (1968) Blocking Experiment**

| Group | Phase 1 | Phase 2 | Test Phase | Result |
|---|---|---|---|---|
| Blocking | L+ | LT+ | T | T elicits no CR |
| Control | — | LT+ | T | T elicits a CR |

to realize that both groups in this experiment received exactly the same number of pairings of T and shock. Because of the equal number of pairings, the frequency principle predicts that conditioning to T should be equally strong in the two groups. However, Kamin obtained a strikingly different result: Whereas he observed a strong CR to T in the control group, he recorded essentially no conditioned responding at all to T in the blocking group. Because the only difference between the two groups was that the blocking group received conditioning trials with L in Phase 1 but the control group did not, Kamin concluded that this prior conditioning with stimulus L somehow "blocked" the later conditioning of stimulus T. Since Kamin's pioneering work, the blocking effect has been demonstrated in numerous experiments using a variety of conditioning situations, with both animal and human subjects (for example, Goddard & Jenkins, 1988; Martin & Levey, 1991).

An intuitive explanation of the blocking effect is not difficult to construct: To put it simply, stimulus T was redundant in the blocking group; it supplied no new information. By the end of Phase 1, subjects in the blocking group had learned that stimulus L was a reliable predictor of the US—the US always occurred after L, and never at any other time. The addition of T to the situation in Phase 2 added nothing to the subject's ability to predict the US. This experiment suggests that conditioning will not occur if a CS adds no new information about the US.

This experiment demonstrates that conditioning is not an automatic result when a CS and a US are paired. Conditioning will occur only if the CS is informative, only if it is predictive of something important, such as an upcoming shock. This view seems to imply that the subject has a more active role in the conditioning process than was previously thought— the subject is a selective learner, learning about informative stimuli and ignoring uninformative ones. For two psychologists, Robert Rescorla and Allan Wagner (1972), the blocking effect and related findings underscored the need for a new theory of classical conditioning, one that could deal with these loose notions of

You can try an interactive simulation of salivary conditioning that demonstrates acquisition, extinction, and blocking at *http://www. uwm.edu/People/johnchay/cc.htm.*

informativeness and predictiveness in a more rigorous, objective way. The results of their collaborative efforts was the Rescorla-Wagner model, now one of the most famous theories of classical conditioning.

## The Rescorla-Wagner Model: Basic Concepts

The Rescorla-Wagner model is a mathematical model about classical conditioning, and because of its technical nature, it can be quite challenging to understand. The next section will present the quantitative details of the model. However, the basic ideas behind the theory are quite simple and reasonable, so let us begin by examining these ideas in an informal way. This section is designed to give you a good understanding of the concepts behind the model without using any equations.

Classical conditioning can be viewed as a means of learning about signals (CSs) for important events (USs). The Rescorla-Wagner model is designed to predict the outcome of classical conditioning procedures on a trial-by-trial basis. For any trial in which one or more CSs is presented, the model assumes that there can either be excitatory conditioning, inhibitory conditioning, or no conditioning at all. According to the model, two factors determine which of these three possibilities actually occurs: (1) the strength of the subject's expectation of what will occur, and (2) the strength of the US that is actually presented. The model is a mathematical expression of the concept of *surprise:* It states that learning will occur only when the subject is surprised—that is, when what actually happens is different from what the subject expected to happen.

You should be able to grasp the general idea of the model if you learn and understand the following six rules:

1. If the strength of the actual US is greater than the strength of the subject's expectation, all CSs that were paired with the US will receive excitatory conditioning.
2. If the strength of the actual US is less than the strength of the subject's expectation, all the CSs that were paired with the US will receive some inhibitory conditioning.
3. If the strength of the actual US is equal to the strength of the subject's expectation, there will be no conditioning.
4. The larger the discrepancy between the strength of the expectation and the strength of the US, the greater will be the conditioning (either excitatory or inhibitory) that occurs.
5. More salient (more noticeable) CSs will condition faster than less salient (less noticeable) CSs.
6. If two or more CSs are presented together, the subject's expectation will be equal to their total strength (with excitatory and inhibitory stimuli tending to cancel each other out).

We will now examine several different examples to illustrate how each of these six rules applies in specific cases. For all of the examples below, we will imagine that a rat receives a conditioning procedure in which a CS (light, tone, or similar stimulus) is paired with the presentation of food as a US. In this conditioning situation, the CR is activity, as measured by the rat's movement around the conditioning chamber (which can be automatically recorded by movement detectors). In actual experiments using this procedure, the typical result is that as conditioning proceeds, the rat becomes more and more active when the CS is presented, so its movement can be used as a measure of the amount of excitatory conditioning.

*Acquisition.* Consider a case in which a light (L) is paired with one food pellet. On the very first conditioning trial, the rat has no expectation of what will follow L, so the strength of the US (the food pellet) is much greater than the strength of the rat's expectation (which is zero). Therefore, this trial produces some excitatory conditioning (Rule 1). But conditioning is rarely complete after just one trial. The second time L is presented, it will elicit a weak expectation, but it is still not as strong as the actual US, so Rule 1 applies again, and more excitatory conditioning occurs. For the same reason, further excitatory conditioning should take place on trials 3, 4, and so on. However, with each conditioning trial, the rat's expectation of the food pellet should get stronger, and so the difference between the strength of the expectation and the strength of the US gets smaller. Therefore, the fastest growth in excitatory conditioning occurs on the first trial, and there is less and less additional conditioning as the trials proceed (see Rule 4). Eventually, when L elicits an expectation of food that is as strong as the actual food pellet itself, the asymptote of learning is reached, and no further excitatory conditioning will occur with any additional L-food pairings.

*Blocking.* Continuing with this same example, now suppose that after the asymptote of conditioning is reached, a compound CS of L and tone (T) are presented together and are followed by one food pellet. According to Rule 6, when two CSs are presented, the subject's expectation is based on the total expectations from the two. T is a new stimulus, so it has no expectations associated with it, but L produces an expectation of one food pellet. One food pellet is in fact what the animal receives, so the expectation matches the US, and no additional conditioning occurs (Rule 3). That is, L retains its excitatory strength, and T retains zero strength.

This, in short, is the model's explanation of the blocking effect: No conditioning occurs to the added CS because there is no surprise—the strength of the subject's expectation matches the strength of the US.

*Extinction and Conditioned Inhibition.* Let us now think about a slightly different example. Suppose that after conditioning with L has reached its asymptote, the rat receives trials in which L and T are presented together, but no food pellet is delivered on these trials.

This is an example in which Rule 2 applies: The strength of the rat's expectation will exceed the strength of the actual US. This is because the previous training with L will give the rat a strong expectation of food, yet the strength of the actual US is zero (since no US is presented on these extinction trials). According to Rule 2, both CSs, L and T, will acquire some inhibitory conditioning on these extinction trials.

Let us be clear about how this inhibitory conditioning will affect L and T. Because L starts with a strong excitatory strength, the trials without food (and the inhibitory conditioning they produce) will begin to counteract the excitatory strength. This is merely an example of extinction: Presenting an excitatory CS without the US will cause the strength of the CS to weaken. In contrast, T begins this phase with zero strength, because it has not been presented before. Therefore, the trials without food (and the inhibitory conditioning they produce) will cause T's strength to decrease below zero—it will become a conditioned inhibitor.

*Overshadowing.* In a conditioning experiment with a compound CS consisting of one intense stimulus and one weak one, Pavlov discovered a phenomenon he called **overshadowing**. After a number of conditioning trials, the intense CS would produce a strong CR if presented by itself, but the weak CS by itself would elicit little if any conditioned responding. It was not the case that the weak CS was simply too small to become an effective CS, because if it were paired with the US by itself, it would soon elicit CRs on its own. However, when presented in conjunction with a more intense CS, the latter seemed to mask, or overshadow, the former. Overshadowing has been observed in experiments with both animal and human subjects (Spetch, 1995).

The Rescorla-Wagner model's explanation of overshadowing is straightforward. According to Rule 5, more salient stimuli will condition faster than less salient stimuli. If, for example, a dim light and a loud noise are presented together and followed by a food pellet, the noise will acquire excitatory strength faster than the light. When the total expectation based on both the noise and the light equal the strength of the food pellet, excitatory conditioning will stop. Because the noise is more salient, it will have developed much more excitatory strength than the light. If the dim light is presented by itself, it should elicit only a weak CR.

*The Overexpectation Effect.* Besides being able to account for existing data, another characteristic of a good theory (called fruitfulness in Chapter 1) is the ability to stimulate new research by making novel predictions that have not been previously tested. The Rescorla-Wagner model deserves good grades on this count, because hundreds of experiments have been conducted to test the model's predictions. Its prediction of a phenomenon known as the **overexpectation effect** is a good case in point.

Table 5-2 presents the design of an experiment that tests the overexpectation effect. Two CSs, L and T, are involved. For Phase 1, the notation "L+, T+" is used to indicate that on some trials L is presented by itself and followed by a food pellet, whereas on other trials T is presented by itself and followed by a food pellet. The two types of trials, L+ and T+, are randomly intermixed in Phase 1. Consider what should happen on each type of trial. On L+ trials, the strength of the expectation based

**TABLE 5-2    Design of an Experiment on the Overexpectation Effect**

| Group | Phase 1 | Phase 2 | Test Phase | Result |
|---|---|---|---|---|
| Overexpectation | L+, T+ | LT+ | L, T | Moderate CRs |
| Control | L+, T+ | No stimuli | L, T | Strong CRs |

on L will continue to increase and eventually approach the strength of one food pellet. Similarly, on $T^+$ trials, the strength of the expectation based on T will grow and also approach the strength of one food pellet. Note that because L and T are never presented together, the conditioned strengths of both stimuli can individually approach the strength of one food pellet.

In Phase 2, rats in the control group receive no stimuli, so no expectations are changed. Therefore, in the test phase, these rats should exhibit a strong CR to both L and T on the first several test trials (which are extinction trials).

The results should be quite different for rats in the overexpectation group. In Phase 2, these rats receive a series of trials with the compound stimulus, LT, followed by one food pellet. On the first trial of Phase 2, a rat's total expectation, based on the sums of the strengths of L and T, should be roughly equal to the strength of two food pellets (because each stimulus has a strength of about one food pellet). Loosely speaking, we might say that the rat expects a larger US (two food pellets) on the compound trial because two strong CSs are presented, but all it gets is a single food pellet. Thus, compared to what it actually receives, the animal has an overexpectation about the size of the US, and Rule 2 states that under these conditions both CSs will experience some inhibitory conditioning (they will lose some of their associative strength).

With further trials in Phase 2 for the overexpectation group, the strengths of L and T should continue to decrease, as long as the total expectation from the two CSs is greater than the strength of one food pellet. When tested in the next phase, the individual stimuli L and T should exhibit weaker CRs in the overexpectation group because their strengths were weakened in Phase 2. Experiments have confirmed this prediction that CRs will be weaker in the overexpectation group than in the control group (Khallad & Moore, 1996; Kremer, 1978).

The model's accurate prediction of the overexpectation effect is especially impressive because the prediction is counterintuitive. If

Brief tutorials on blocking, overshadowing, and other topics of classical conditioning can be found at *http://brembs.net/classical*.

you knew nothing about the Rescorla-Wagner model when you examined Table 5-2, what result would you predict for this experiment? Notice that subjects in the overexpectation group actually receive more pairings of L and T with the US, so the frequency principle would predict stronger CRs in the overexpectation group. Based on the frequency principle, the last thing we would expect from more CS-US pairings is a weakening of the CS-US associations. Yet this result is predicted by the Rescorla-Wagner model, and the prediction turns out to be correct. The overexpectation effect is only one of several counterintuitive predictions of the Rescorla-Wagner model that have been supported by subsequent research.

## The Rescorla-Wagner Model: Equations and Mathematical Examples

Having examined the Rescorla-Wagner model in a nonmathematical way, we are now in a better position to tackle the more difficult task of learning the mathematical details.

*Notation.* In the model, the strength of a US is signified by A, and a subscript can be used to identify exactly what US is presented. For example, $A_1$ could represent the strength of one food pellet, $A_2$ could represent the strength of two food pellets, and $A_0$ could represent the strength of a trial with no food pellets. The letter V is used to represent the conditioned strength of a CS, and again subscripts are used to indicate which CS is being discussed. For example, $V_L$ could be the conditioned strength of a light, and $V_T$ the conditioned strength of a tone. V is positive if the CS is excitatory and negative if the CS is inhibitory. Because the subject's expectation is said to be based on the total strength of all CSs that are presented on a given trial, a special term, $V_{sum}$, is used to represent this total. The salience of each CS is designated by S. For example, $S_L$ could represent the salience of a light, and $S_T$ the salience of a tone. The salience of a CS must be a number between 0 and 1. Finally, the notation $\Delta V$ (pronounced "delta V") refers to the change in strength of a CS that occurs on a single conditioning trial. ($\Delta V_L$ is the change in strength of the light, and $\Delta V_T$ is the change in strength of a tone.)

According to the Rescorla-Wagner model, on any conditioning trial, the following equation can be used to describe the change in strength of a CS on a single trial:

$$\Delta V_i = S_i \times (A_j - V_{sum})$$

The subscript i refers to any single CS, and the subscript j refers to any single US. Notice that the quantity in parentheses, $(A_j - V_{sum})$, represents the difference between the strength of the US and the total strength of the subject's expectation (based on the sum of all the CSs presented on a given trial). $\Delta V$ will be positive whenever this quantity is positive, it will be negative when the quantity is negative, and it will be zero when the quantity is zero. This quantity in parentheses is simply multiplied by the salience parameter for the CS to determine how much excitatory or inhibitory conditioning is predicted for a single trial.

Although almost anyone could memorize this equation, for most people it will take more work to understand how the equation is actually applied to specific cases. The best way to gain such an understanding is to use the equation to make predictions for a variety of conditioning situations. We will now work through several such examples, using numerical and graphic aids to make the predictions concrete.

Because both A, the strength of a US, and V, the conditioned strength of a CS, are hypothetical quantities that cannot be directly observed, we can use any convenient scale of numbers to represent these quantities. To keep the calculations as simple as possible, we will arbitrarily assign a strength of 100 to one food pellet.

***Acquisition.*** Consider the first conditioning trial on which L is paired with one food pellet. If L is the only CS present, then $V_{sum} = V_L$, and $V_L = 0$ because there has been no prior conditioning with L. For the purposes of this example, we will set the salience value of the light, $S_L$, equal to .2. To calculate the amount of conditioning on this trial, we need to solve the following equation:

$$\Delta V_L = S_L \times (A_1 - V_{sum})$$

Inserting the values we have chosen, we get

$$\Delta V_L = .2 \times (100 - 0) = 20$$

Therefore, on this first trial, $V_L$ should grow by 20 units. This process of growth is depicted graphically in Figure 5-1.

On trial 2, $V_L$ (and therefore $V_{sum}$) begins at 20, so the equation becomes

$$\Delta V_L = .2 \times (100 - 20) = 16$$

This equation states that on trial 2, $V_L$ will increase by another 16 units, so after two trials, $V_L = 20 + 16 = 36$ (see Figure 5-1). Notice because of the smaller discrepancy between $A_1$ and $V_{sum}$ on trial 2, the amount of learning is smaller than on trial 1 (16 units instead of 20). Figure 5-1 shows that the increase in $V_L$ should be 12.8 on trial 3, but only 2.7 by trial 10. By the end of trial 10, $V_L$ has risen to 89.3, and with additional trials it would get closer and closer to the asymptote of 100. To summarize, the Rescorla-Wagner model predicts that in simple acquisition, the initial increases in $V_L$ will be the largest, and the increments will become smaller and smaller as the asymptote is approached.

***Overshadowing.*** It is easy to show how the Rescorla-Wagner model accounts for the phenomenon of overshadowing. Let us assume that we begin a new conditioning experiment with two CSs, the same light used in the previous example ($S_L = .2$) and a very loud noise (salience of the noise = $S_N = .5$). Figure 5-2 shows the results of several conditioning trials with this compound CS. On trial 1, $V_{sum} = V_L + V_N = 0$, so the discrepancy between $A_1$ and $V_{sum}$ is 100, as in the previous example. Unlike the previous example, however, there

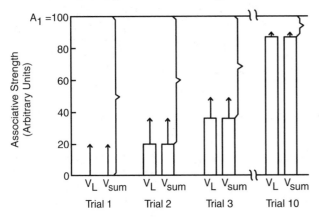

☐ Associative Strength Before Trial

} Discrepancy Between $A_1$ and $V_{sum}$

↑ Change in Associative Strength on Trial

**FIGURE 5-1**   Predictions of the Rescorla-Wagner model for simple acquisition with a single CS. Parameter values used were $A_1 = 100$, $S_L = .2$.

are two CSs whose associative strengths must be incremented, so we need to solve two equations:

$$\Delta V_L = .2 \times (100 - 0) = 20$$

$$\Delta V_N = .5 \times (100 - 0) = 50$$

Notice that $\Delta V_L$ is the same as in trial 1 of the first example. For the more salient noise, however, the increment in conditioned strength is 50 units. Thus, after trial 1, $V_{sum} = 20 + 50 = 70$. At the start of trial 2, therefore, the difference between $A_1$ and $V_{sum}$ has already been reduced to 30. The equations for trial 2 are

$$\Delta V_L = .2 \times (100 - 70) = 6$$

$$\Delta V_N = .5 \times (100 - 70) = 15$$

Therefore, total increment in $V_{sum}$ on trial 2 is 21, so that after two trials, $V_{sum} = 70 + 21 = 91$.

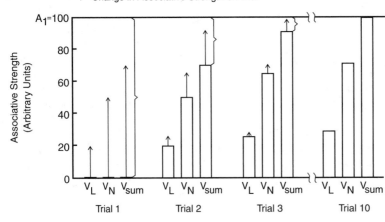

☐ Associative Strength Before Trial

⟩ Discrepancy Between $A_1$ and $V_{sum}$

↑ Change in Associative Strength on Trial

**FIGURE 5-2**   Predictions of the Rescorla-Wagner model for a case where an intense noise overshadows a light. Parameter values used were $A_1 = 100$, $S_L = .2$, $S_N = .5$.

Figure 5-2 also shows the predictions for trials 3 and 10. Notice that with the two CSs, $V_{sum}$ approaches $A_1$ much more rapidly than in Figure 5-1, and by trial 10 the increments in strength are too small to show in the graph.

The model's prediction of overshadowing can be seen clearly by comparing the course of $V_L$ in Figures 5-1 and 5-2. The only difference between these two conditioning situations is the addition of the noise in the second example. In Figure 5-1, $V_L$ has reached a strength of 89.3 after 10 trials, and with further trials it will approach 100. In Figure 5-2, $V_{sum}$ has nearly reached 100 by trial 10, but because the more salient noise has usurped over 70 units of strength, $V_L$ will never rise above 30. In short, because the total strength of both CSs in the compound can never rise above 100 in this example, the model predicts that the light will be overshadowed—the level of conditioning will never be what it would be in the absence of the noise.

***Blocking.*** The model's explanation of the blocking effect is similar to that of overshadowing. Suppose that in a blocking group, stimulus L receives many pairings with one food pellet in Phase 1, so that by the end of this phase, $V_L$ is approximately 100 (assuming once again that the strength of one food pellet is 100). At the start of Phase 2, the quantity $(A_1 - V_{sum})$ will be close to zero, and so there will be no further changes in conditioned strength for either stimulus: $V_L$ will remain near 100, and $V_T$ will remain at 0.

***Conditioned Inhibition.*** Let us return to the simple case in which a single CS, L, is paired with one food pellet $(A_1 = 100)$. Suppose there have been enough acquisition trials to bring $V_L$ to a value of 90. Now, in the second phase of this experiment, a second CS, T, with a salience the same as L $(S_T = .2)$ is presented in addition to L, but no food pellets are delivered. Figure 5-3 shows that according to the model, T should become a conditioned inhibitor during these extinction trials. The reason is that, despite the presence of T on these extinction trials, the US will be overpredicted because of the conditioned strength of L. The model states that if the US is overpredicted (that is, if $A_j$ is less than $V_{sum}$), then the

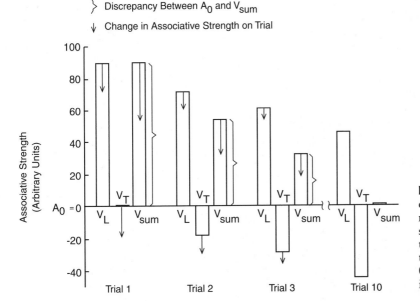

**FIGURE 5-3** Predictions of the Rescorla-Wagner model for a case where T should become a conditioned inhibitor. Parameter values used were $A_0 = 0$, $S_L = .2$, $S_T = .2$, starting value for $V_L = 90$.

strength of all the CSs present on the trial will be decremented. Since $V_T$ is initially 0, any decrements in strength will push $V_T$ into the negative range, making it a conditioned inhibitor. To be more precise, on trial 1, the following equations apply:

$$\Delta V_L = .2 \times (0 - 90) = -18$$

$$\Delta V_T = .2 \times (0 - 90) = -18$$

That is, on this first extinction trial, $V_L$ will lose 18 units of strength (from 90 to 72), and $V_T$ will also lose 18 units (from 0 to −18).

The second trial shown in Figure 5-3 is the first example we have encountered in which both an excitatory CS and an inhibitory CS are present. With $V_L = 72$ and $V_T = -18$, Figure 5-3 shows that $V_{sum} = 54$. The following equations apply to the second extinction trial:

$$\Delta V_L = .2 \times (0 - 54) = -10.8$$

$$\Delta V_N = .5 \times (0 - 54) = -10.8$$

Therefore, on the second extinction trial, $V_L$ will lose 10.8 units of strength (from 72 to 61.2), and $V_T$ will lose 10.8 units (from −18 to −28.8). With additional extinction trials, $V_L$ will become less positive, $V_T$ will become more negative, and $V_{sum}$ will approach an asymptote of zero. But notice that at this asymptote (which Figure 5-3 shows is nearly reached by trial 10), $V_L$ retains an excitatory strength of approximately 50. The inhibitory strength of $V_T$ is approximately −50, and because there is almost no discrepancy between $A_0$ and $V_{sum}$, there will be almost no further changes in the associative strength of either stimulus with additional extinction trials.

*Summary.* The Rescorla-Wagner model might be called a theory about US effectiveness: It states that an unpredicted US is effective in promoting learning, whereas a well-predicted US is ineffective. As the first formal theory that attempted to predict when a US will promote associative learning and when it will not, it is guaranteed a prominent place in the history of psychology. The model has been successfully applied to many conditioning phenomena, but it is not perfect. Some well-established phenomena are difficult for the model to explain. For this reason, other psychologists have proposed alternative theories of classical conditioning that are based on fairly different assumptions about the learning process. We will examine two types of alternative theories in the following sections.

## Theories of CS Effectiveness

The main assumption of this class of theories is that the conditionability of a CS, not the effectiveness of the US, changes from one situation to another. A phenomenon called the **CS preexposure effect** provides one compelling piece of evidence for this assumption.

*The CS Preexposure Effect.* Consider a simple conditioning experiment with two groups of subjects. The control group receives simple pairings of one CS with a US. The only difference in the CS preexposure group is that before the conditioning trials, the CS is presented by itself a number of times. The comparison of interest concerns how quickly conditioned responding develops in these two groups. The common finding, which has been obtained with both animal and human subjects, is that conditioning proceeds more rapidly in the control group than in the CS preexposure group (Lubow & Moore, 1959; Lipp, Siddle, & Vaitl, 1992; Zalstein-Orda & Lubow, 1995). A common sense explanation of this result is that a sort of habituation occurs in the CS preexposure group—because the CS is presented repeatedly but initially predicts nothing, the subject gradually pays less and less attention to this stimulus. We might say that the subject learns to ignore the CS because it is not informative, and for this reason the subject takes longer to associate the CS with the US when conditioning trials begin and the CS suddenly becomes informative.

Although it is a well-established phenomenon, the Rescorla-Wagner model does not predict the CS preexposure effect. Let us examine what the model has to say about the first preexposure trial, on which the CS is presented by itself. Since there have been no prior conditioning trials, the CS elicits no expectation at all, and since no US is presented, the strength of the US is zero. Because the strength of the subject's expectation equals that of the US (both are zero), there should be no learning of any kind on the first preexposure trial, and exactly the same logic applies to all subsequent preexposure trials. In short, the model predicts that no learning will occur when a novel CS is presented by itself. But evidently, subjects do learn something on CS preexposure trials, and what they learn hinders their ability to develop a CS-US association during the later conditioning phase.

One explanation of the CS preexposure effect is that the salience of a CS can change as a result of a subject's experience with that CS. Assuming that the general framework of the Rescorla-Wagner model is correct, the data suggest that the salience of a CS decreases when a CS is repeatedly presented without consequence. We can easily change the salience parameter in the mathematical equation, but what does such a change mean from a psychological perspective? Some learning theorists have proposed that this change consists of a decrease in the organism's attention to the CS. They claim that during the CS preexposure trials, the subject learns that it is pointless to pay attention to that stimulus, so when the stimulus is later paired with a US, it takes longer for an association to develop.

If the CS preexposure effect and other similar phenomena are to be explained by the Rescorla-Wagner model, it seems that the only recourse is to concede that the salience parameter, $S_i$, is not a fixed property of the CS. Rather, this parameter probably reflects both the physical properties of the CS and the subject's previous experience with the CS. Once it is granted that $S_i$ can change, the Rescorla-Wagner model itself becomes, in part, a theory of CS effectiveness (as well as of US effectiveness). However, we will now turn to two other theories that assume that only the effectiveness of the CS, and not that of the US, can change with experience.

*Mackintosh's Theory of Attention.* In cognitive psychology, attention has been a popular concept for many years. The basic notion is that an individual is continually bombarded by numerous stimuli in many sensory modalities, but a person's ability to process this information is fairly limited. As a result, an individual must selectively process some of this information at the expense of ignoring the remainder. A common example that illustrates the phenomenon of selective attention is the so-called **cocktail party phenomenon.** If you are at a party where there are many conversations going on at once, you have the ability to choose which conversation you attend to. Without moving, you could decide to listen to the person in front of you for a while, then listen for a time to a conversation taking place in back of you, and so on. Laboratory experiments have shown that if a subject listens to one of two voices speaking simultaneously, the subject can later recall virtually nothing about what the other voice was saying. At least within the domain of speech, it seems that a person's attentional capacity is very limited, for with only two sources of speech it is difficult or impossible to learn from both simultaneously.

Nonhumans must also have such limits of attentional capacity, and these limits should affect their ability to learn from their experiences. Theories of attention in animals propose that on a conditioning trial where several stimuli are presented simultaneously, the subject will attend to only one or a few of these stimuli, and learning (that is, changes in associations) will only occur for those stimuli to which the animal attends. Without attention, there will be no learning.

Starting with such ideas, Mackintosh (1975) proposed a theory of attention and classical conditioning that is considered to be a major competitor of the Rescorla-Wagner model. Without going into great detail, the major tenets of Mackintosh's theory can be illustrated by showing how it explains Kamin's blocking effect. Mackintosh rejects the most important principle of the Rescorla-Wagner model—that the amount of learning depends on the discrepancy between the strength of the subject's expectation and the strength of the US. Mackintosh instead assumes that $S_i$ changes with experience in the following way. If we have two stimuli, L and T, and L is a better predictor of the US than T, then $S_L$ will increase and $S_T$ will decrease and eventually reach zero. In other words, the subject will attend to the more informative stimulus L and not attend to stimulus T. Now consider what this theory predicts for the second phase of Kamin's blocking experiment, as diagramed in Table 5-1. In the blocking group, stimulus L will be more informative than T by virtue of the conditioning that took place in Phase 1. Therefore $S_L$ will increase and $S_T$ will drop toward zero. If the decline in $S_T$ is rapid, then there will be little learning about T in Phase 2.

A somewhat different theory of CS effectiveness was developed by Pearce and Hall (1980). Details of this theory will not be presented here, but in essence the theory states that CSs become ineffective whenever the US is already well predicted. If the situation is then changed so that the US is again surprising (by making the US more intense, for example), the theory asserts that the CSs will quickly regain their effectiveness, and additional conditioning can then occur. Like Mackintosh's theory, the Pearce-Hall theory predicts that blocking should not occur on the first trial of Phase 2, because a CS cannot lose its effectiveness until it is presented at least once with no surprising consequences.

Experiments designed to distinguish between the Rescorla-Wagner model and the theories of CS effectiveness have produced mixed results, with some of the evidence supporting each theory (Balaz, Kasprow, & Miller, 1982; G. Hall & Pearce, 1983; G. Hall, Kaye, & Pearce, 1985). Perhaps these findings indicate that both classes of theory are partly correct. That is, perhaps the effectiveness of both CSs and USs can change as a result of a subject's experience. If a US is well predicted, it may promote no conditioning, as the Rescorla-Wagner model states. Likewise, if nothing surprising follows a CS, the CS may become ineffective, at least until the situation changes.

## Comparator Theories of Conditioning

Despite their differences, the Rescorla-Wagner model and theories of CS effectiveness have two features in common: (1) Their predictions are based on trial-by-trial calculations, and (2) they assume that the presence of one CS can interfere with the subject's learning about other CSs, as in the blocking procedure. In contrast, another class of theories takes a different position on both points (Balsam & Gibbon, 1988; Gibbon & Balsam, 1981; R. R. Miller & Schachtman, 1985). These theories have been called **comparator theories** because they assume that the animal compares the likelihood that the US will occur in the presence of the CS with the likelihood that the US will occur in the absence of the CS. This idea may sound familiar because it is fairly similar to Rescorla's (1968, 1969) analysis of CS-US correlations, discussed in Chapter 4.

Let us see how comparator theories differ from those already examined. First, comparator theories do not make predictions on a trial-by-trial basis, because they assume that what is important is not the events of individual trials but rather the overall, long-term correlation between a CS and the US. Second, these theories propose that the comparison of CS and context does not affect the learning of a conditioned response but rather its performance. As a simple example, suppose that the probability of a US is .5 in the presence of some CS, but its probability is also .5 in the absence of this CS. The comparator theories predict that this CS will elicit no CR, which is what Rescorla (1968) found, but not because the CS has acquired no excitatory strength. Instead, the theories assume that both the CS and **contextual stimuli**—the sights, sounds, and smells of the experimental chamber—have acquired equal excitatory strengths, because both have been paired with the US 50 percent of the time. The theories also assume that a CS will not elicit conditioned responding unless it has greater excitatory strength than the contextual stimuli. Unlike the Rescorla-Wagner model, however, they assume that an animal in this situation has indeed learned something about the CS—that the US sometimes occurs in its presence—but it will not respond to the CS unless it is a better predictor of the US than the context.

To test comparator theories, one common research strategy is to change the strength of one stimulus and to try to show that the subjects have indeed learned something about another stimulus that was not visible in their previous performance. For example, suppose that after conditioning, an animal exhibits only a weak response to the CS because both the CS and the contextual stimuli have some excitatory strength. According to comparator theories, one way to increase the response to the CS would be to extinguish the excitatory strength of the context by keeping the subject in the context and never presenting the US. Since the response to the CS depends on a comparison of the CS and the context, extinction of the context should increase the response to the CS. Experiments of this type have shown that extinction of the context does increase responding to the CS (Matzel, Brown, & Miller, 1987). In a related experiment by Cole, Barnet, and Miller (1995), one CS was followed by a US every time it was presented, whereas a second CS was followed by a US only 50 percent of the time. At first, the second CS did not elicit much conditioned responding. However, after responding to the first CS was extinguished, conditioned responses to the second CS increased dramatically. The Rescorla-Wagner model does not predict these effects, because it states that the conditioned strength of one CS cannot change if that CS itself is not presented. According to comparator theories, however, subjects may learn an association between a CS and US that cannot initially be seen in their performance, but this learning can be unmasked if the strength of a competing CS is weakened.

Not all studies have supported the predictions of comparator theories (for example, Ayres, Bombace, Shurtleff, & Vigorito, 1985; Rauhut, McPhee, DiPietro, & Ayres, 2000). On the other hand, a growing body of research has provided support for comparator theories by showing that a subject's initial performance does not necessarily demonstrate everything that the subject has learned (Yin, Barnet, & Miller, 1994). Some studies have found evidence for comparator theories by demonstrating a type of spontaneous recovery in which the conditioned response to a CS changes over time (Miller, Jagielo, & Spear, 1993). As the evidence supporting the predictions of comparator theories has accumulated, they have

become credible competitors for such theories as the Rescorla-Wagner model and theories of CS effectiveness. Further research in this area should tell us whether or not the distinction between learning and performance is indeed as critical a variable in classical conditioning as comparator theories contend.

## Summary

In this section we have carefully examined an influential theory of classical conditioning, the Rescorla-Wagner model, and we have taken a briefer look at two alternative types of theories—theories of CS effectiveness and comparator theories. The predictions of these theories are still being tested, and it is not yet possible to say which is best. In dealing with experimental results, each of these theories has its strengths and weaknesses. The weaknesses suggest that a perfect theory of classical conditioning has not yet been formulated.

Nevertheless, substantial progress has been made toward the goal of understanding the process of classical conditioning. Although these three types of theories differ in many ways, they share one common theme: The predictiveness or informativeness of a CS is a critical determinant of whether or not a conditioned response will occur. And the predictiveness or informativeness of a CS cannot be judged in isolation: It must be compared to the predictiveness of other stimuli also present in the animal's environment.

# TYPES OF ASSOCIATIONS

## Associations in First-Order Conditioning

Chapter 4 considered the question of whether an S-S or an S-R association is formed during simple first-order conditioning. Remember that an S-S association would be a link between the CS center and the US center, which are hypothetical areas of the subject's brain activated by these two stimuli. According to the S-S position, a conditioned response occurs because presentation of the CS activates the CS center, which activates the US center, which in turn activates the response center (see

Figure 4-4). According to the S-R position, a direct link between the CS center and the response center is formed during conditioning. Later, activation of the CS center will directly activate the response center through the S-R link, and the US center is not involved. Chapter 4 showed that experiments employing US devaluation (in which the ability of the US to evoke a UR is diminished in one way or another after the CS has been conditioned) tended to support the S-S position. That is, any change that decreases the ability of the US to evoke a response also decreases the ability of the CS to evoke this response. These results favor the S-S position and the more indirect route from CS center to response center in Figure 4-4, because the response-eliciting capacity of the CS seems to be tied to the response-eliciting capacity of the US.

## Associations in Second-Order Conditioning

Compared to the findings on first-order conditioning, studies on the associations formed during second-order conditioning have painted a more complex and confusing picture. Imagine an experiment with rats in which a light is paired with food and the conditioned response to the light is an increase in activity. Food is the US, and light is CS1 (the first-order conditioned stimulus). Next, a tone (the second-order conditioned stimulus, CS2) is repeatedly paired with the light, and second-order conditioning is eventually demonstrated—the tone now also elicits an increase in activity. What sorts of associations make the conditioned response to the tone possible? Based on the discussion in the preceding paragraph, you might guess that the activation of brain centers follows the path: tone → tone center → light center → food center → response center → response. This is a sensible guess, but it is wrong. When Holland and Rescorla (1975) conducted this experiment, they found evidence for a direct S-R association between the tone center and the response center. Their method involved devaluing the US by satiating the rats and then retesting their responses to the tone. Activity responses

in the presence of the tone were not diminished, even though the animals showed little interest in eating the food.

Based on their research, Holland and Rescorla concluded that S-S associations are formed in first-order conditioning, but that S-R associations are formed in second-order conditioning. Other studies have also found evidence for S-R associations in second-order conditioning. In one procedure, after a conditioned response to CS2 is developed, CS1 is extinguished. (This could have been done in the Holland and Rescorla experiment by first extinguishing conditioned responses to the light and then testing the tone.) Some studies have found that conditioned responses to CS2 persisted after extinction of CS1, once again supporting the S-R position (Amiro & Bitterman, 1980; Zamble, Hadad, Mitchell, & Cutmore, 1985).

However, other experiments have found evidence for second-order S-S associations (Rashotte, Griffin, & Sisk, 1977; Rescorla, 1982). Why S-S associations are found in some cases of second-order conditioning and S-R associations are found in others is still not fully understood, but certain procedural differences (such as whether CS2 and CS1 are paired by presenting them simultaneously or in succession) can make a big difference (Holland, 1985; Rescorla, 1982). In any case, one general conclusion we can draw about associations in second-order conditioning is that they do not fall into any single category: Both S-S and S-R associations can and do occur.

## Associations Involving Contextual Stimuli

No experiment on classical conditioning takes place in a vacuum. Besides the stimuli the experimenter uses as CS and US, the experimental chamber inevitably contains a variety of distinctive sights, sounds, and smells that are collectively called *contextual stimuli*. These contextual stimuli are more or less continuously present in the chamber (the experimenter cannot turn them on or off), and it might seem convenient to try to ignore them, but it is becoming increasingly clear that they play an important role in many conditioning situations (see Balsam & Tomie, 1985). Let us briefly consider a few examples of their effects.

When a stimulus is repeatedly presented in one experimental chamber, an association can develop between the contextual stimuli and that stimulus. For instance, if a light is occasionally presented in the chamber, the subject may form a context-light association, and we might say the subject learns to "expect" the light when it is placed in the chamber. If the light is now an expected event, this might help to explain the CS preexposure effect—the finding that if a CS has been repeatedly presented in the experimental context, it becomes harder to condition when it is later paired with a US. The possibility of a context-CS association suggests an explanation of the CS preexposure effect that is somewhat different from Mackintosh's (1975). Mackintosh proposed that the CS preexposure effect occurs because animals stop paying attention to uninformative CSs. According to the present explanation, the problem is not that the CS is uninformative but that it is expected. And just as there is little learning when the US is expected (an idea that is at the heart of the Rescorla-Wagner model), there may be little learning when the CS is expected.

One way to test this theory is to try to extinguish the context-CS association by giving the subject several sessions in the experimental chamber with no CS presentations (a boring phase of the research for both experimenter and subject, no doubt, since nothing happens in the experimental chamber). If the context-US association is weakened, this should reverse the effects of CS preexposure, and the CS should now be easier to condition when paired with a US. Wagner (1978) obtained just such a result in an eyeblink conditioning study with rabbits. Evidence for context-CS associations has been obtained in other ways as well, leaving little doubt that such associations can be formed (Lubow & Gewirtz, 1995; Rescorla, 1984).

Other studies have provided parallel evidence for the existence of context-US associations. For example, if rats receive frequent food presentations in one compartment of a maze, they display increased activity in that compartment (Mustaca, Gabelli, Papini, & Balsam, 1991). This increased activity is a conditioned response that results from an association between the context (the compartment) and food. Other evidence for context-US associations comes from the **US preexposure effect,** which is analogous to the CS preexposure effect discussed above. In the US preexposure effect, conditioning of a CS is slower if the US is repeatedly presented by itself in a particular context before the CS-US pairings begin (Domjan & Best, 1980).

Other research has suggested that, in many ways, associations involving contextual stimuli behave similarly to associations involving CSs and USs. For instance, Rescorla, Durlach, and Grau (1985) demonstrated several standard conditioning phenomena with context-US associations—acquisition, extinction, discrimination, and discrimination reversal (in which the roles of CS$^+$ and CS$^-$ are reversed). Contextual stimuli can also summate with a normal CS, so that the CS elicits stronger conditioned responses when presented in the same context where conditioning originally took place than in a different context (Bouton & Bolles, 1985). They can serve as a point of comparison with a normal CS, as the preceding section on comparator theories showed. In many respects, contextual stimuli are similar to ordinary CSs.

## CS-CS Associations

We have already seen that in a typical conditioning situation, associations may develop between CS and US, between context and CS, and between context and US. If a compound CS (such as a light and tone presented simultaneously) is paired with a US, an association can also form between the two CSs. The existence of sensory preconditioning (Chapter 4) provides one type of evidence for CS-CS associations. An experiment on taste-aversion learning by Rescorla and Cunningham (1978) offered another type of evidence, because it showed that extinction of one element of a compound CS causes a reduction in responding to the other, nonextinguished element. Rats initially drank a solution that was composed of two different tastes, such as salt and quinine, after which they were given an injection of poison to make them ill. This procedure was designed to develop aversions to the salt and quinine tastes. Next, the aversion to one of the two tastes (say, quinine) was extinguished for one group of rats by having them drink a quinine solution in the absence of the poison. A control group received no such extinction sessions with quinine. Finally, when given the opportunity to drink a salt solution, the quinine-extinction group showed less aversion to the salt solution than did the control group.

This result shows that in the initial pairing of the salt-quinine solution with illness, the rats not only developed associations between each taste and illness but also between salt and quinine. Because of this salt-quinine association, a decrease in the aversion to quinine produced a decrease in the aversion to salt. This sort of association between the elements of a compound CS is called a *within-compound association*. Other studies have provided additional evidence for such within-compound associations (Beauchamp, Gluck, Fouty, & Lewis, 1991; Heth, 1985). Rescorla (1986b) has found that stronger within-compound associations develop when the two elements of the compound are perceptually similar (such as two solid colors) than when they are dissimilar (such as a solid color and a striped pattern).

### Occasion Setting

A CS⁺ tends to elicit a conditioned response, and a CS⁻ tends to prevent the occurrence of a conditioned response. For decades it was generally believed that these are the only two ways a CS can affect an animal's behavior. However, experiments by Holland (1983, 1985; R. T. Ross & Holland, 1981) suggest a third possibility. Holland has found that under certain circumstances, a stimulus can control a conditioned response in an indirect way: It can determine whether the subject will respond to another CS. For instance, in one experiment with rats, Ross and Holland (1981) arranged two types of trials. On half of the trials, a light was presented for a few seconds, followed by a tone for a few seconds, followed by food. On

the other trials, the tone was presented by itself, and there was no food. Thus the presence of the light meant that the tone would be followed by food. From previous research, the experimenters knew that when a tone is paired with food, it elicits a distinctive "head-jerk" CR in rats—the animal repeatedly moves its head from side to side (as though it is looking for the source of the sound). In this experiment, Ross and Holland found that the tone elicited this head-jerk response when it was preceded by the light, but not otherwise. In other words, the light seemed to regulate the conditioned response to the tone. Ross and Holland called the light an *occasion setter*, because it signaled those occasions on which the tone would be paired with food (and those occasions on which the tone would elicit a CR).

A few different theories about how an occasion setter does its job have been proposed. Holland has favored the idea that an occasion setter regulates a specific CS-US association. This possibility is illustrated in Figure 5-4, using the stimuli of the Ross and Holland experiment. We can think of the occasion setter (the light) as a sort of switch that must be turned on to complete the connection between tone and food. If this idea is correct, the occasion setter should only influence responding to the tone; it should not affect responding to other CSs (such as a bell that has been paired with food).

As an alternative view, Rescorla (1985) proposed that an occasion setter's role is actually one of **facilitation**—it regulates the degree to which

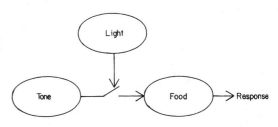

**FIGURE 5-4**   One theory of how a light can act as an occasion setter for a tone. The light might act like a switch that completes the tone-food connection.

which the US center can be activated by any CS, not just the CS that has been paired with the occasion setter in training. If this idea is correct, the occasion setter should increase responding to any CS, not only the one with which it appeared during training. T. L. Davidson and Rescorla (1986) found that an occasion setter can affect the responses to more than one stimulus. They first trained rats in two occasion-setting procedures: A tone served as an occasion setter for a flashing light, and a steady light served as an occasion setter for a clicker. In the test phase, the roles of the two occasion setters were switched, and it was found that the tone now controlled responses to the clicker, and the steady light controlled responses to the flashing light. These results seem to contradict the simple switching idea illustrated in Figure 5-4, because according to this theory, an occasion setter for one stimulus should not affect responses to a different stimulus in any way (just as a switch on one's radio does not control the operation of the television, or vice versa).

The light in the R. T. Ross and Holland (1981) experiment can be called a **positive occasion setter,** because it signaled that food would be available after the tone. If, in another experiment, the tone was followed by food only when it was not preceded by a light, the light would be called a **negative occasion setter,** because it signaled the absence of the US. Holland (1991) showed that a single stimulus can serve as a positive occasion setter for one CS and as a negative occasion setter for another. Speaking loosely, we might say that the occasion setter served as an "on" switch for one CS and as an "off" switch for another CS.

In summary, these studies show that if occasion setters do act as switches, the wiring of these switches must be more intricate than in the simple diagram of Figure 5-4. Indeed, recent studies of occasion setting indicate that they have a number of unusual and interesting properties that are not well understood (Bonardi & Hall, 1994; Maes & Vossen, 1993). Although the nature of occasion setters is still being studied, we can be confident about one conclusion: These stimuli are dis-

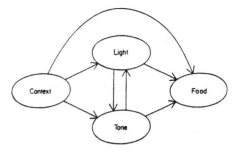

**FIGURE 5-5**   The associations that may form when a compound stimulus composed of a light and a tone are paired with food.

tinctly different from ordinary excitatory or inhibitory CSs.

## Summary

Some of the types of associations we have examined are summarized in Figure 5-5, which depicts the possible consequences of repeatedly pairing a compound CS (a light and a tone) with a food US. In addition to the light-food and tone-food associations, within-compound associations can form between the light and the tone, and each of these three stimuli can become associated with the context. Still other associations can develop in second-order conditioning and occasion-setting situations. In addition, each type of association can be either excitatory or inhibitory. Thus, although classical conditioning might be loosely described as a procedure in which the subject learns to associate a CS and a US, in reality a rich array of associations can develop in any classical conditioning situation.

## BIOLOGICAL CONSTRAINTS ON CLASSICAL CONDITIONING

As discussed in Chapter 1, probably the most fundamental assumption underlying research on animal learning is that it is possible to discover general principles of learning that are not dependent in any important way on an animal's biological makeup. According to this line of reasoning, the same general principles of learning will be discovered regardless of what species of subject, what response, and what stimuli one chooses to study. If this assumption turned out to be incorrect, the extensive research on the arbitrary responses (for instance, eyeblink conditioning, conditioned suppression) of a small number of species (rabbits, rats) in artificial environments would make little sense. Why would psychologists care, for example, about how different CS-US relationships affect a rat's responding in a conditioned suppression procedure if unpredictably different patterns were likely with different mammals, or with different CSs or USs?

During the 1960s, researchers began to report findings that questioned the validity of the general-principle approach to learning. For the most part, these findings took the form of alleged exceptions to one or another well-established general principles of learning. As this type of evidence began to accumulate, some psychologists started to question whether the goal of discovering general principles of learning was realistic (Lockard, 1971; Rozin & Kalat, 1971; Seligman, 1970). Their reasoning was that if we find too many exceptions to a rule, what good is the rule?

This section will examine the evidence against the general-principle approach in the area of classical conditioning, and it will attempt to come to some conclusions about its significance for the psychology of learning. Biological constraints on other types of learning will be discussed in later chapters.

## The Contiguity Principle and Taste-Aversion Learning

As discussed in Chapter 2, the principle of contiguity is the oldest and most persistent principle of association, having been first proposed by Aristotle. We have seen that CS-US contiguity is an important independent variable in classical conditioning: In trace conditioning, the separation of CS and US by only a few seconds can produce large decreases in both the rate and asymptote of conditioning. A popular textbook from the early 1960s summarized the opinion about the importance of contiguity that prevailed at that time: "At the present time it seems unlikely that learning can

take place at all with delays of more than a few seconds" (Kimble, 1961, p. 165).

Given this opinion about the importance of contiguity, it is easy to see why the work of John Garcia and his colleagues on long-delay learning attracted considerable attention. Garcia's research involved a classical conditioning procedure in which poison was the US and some novel taste was the CS. In one study (Garcia, Ervin, & Koelling, 1966), rats were given the opportunity to drink saccharin-flavored water (which they had never tasted before), and they later received an injection of an emetic that produces nausea in a matter of minutes. For different subjects the interval between the termination of drinking and the injection varied from 5 to 22 minutes. Although these durations were perhaps a hundred times longer than those over which classical conditioning was generally thought to be effective, all subjects subsequently exhibited an aversion to water flavored with saccharin. Furthermore, there was no orderly relationship between the CS-US interval and degree of aversion: Subjects with delays of 20 minutes or more showed, on average, just as much suppression of drinking as those with delays of 5 or 10 minutes. (These tests were conducted three days later to make sure that the subjects had completely recovered from their illnesses.)

A second experiment by the same researchers found that aversions to the taste of saccharin could be established with CS-US intervals of over an hour. Later investigators showed that taste-aversion learning was possible with still longer CS-US intervals. For instance, Etscorn and Stephens (1973) found aversions to saccharin when a full 24 hours separated the CS from the poison US.

To make a convincing case that such long-delay learning is possible, it was necessary to rule out some alternative explanations of the results. One possibility was that the actual delays in taste-aversion learning are not really as long as they appear, because some stimulus (such as an aftertaste or the sensation of a full stomach) bridges the delay between ingestion and illness. This possibility has been ruled out through some clever experiments (Garcia, McGowan, & Green, 1972). Another possibility was that the avoidance of the CS was an instance of **sensitization.** That is, perhaps after becoming ill, an animal is hesitant about ingesting *any* substance. This possibility has been disproven in at least two ways. First, aversion to the CS is much greater in experimental groups (in which a specific taste is later followed by poison) than in control groups (which are exposed only to the poison). Second, a taste aversion is specific to the CS; it is not a general avoidance of all foods or all liquids.

It is now generally accepted that taste aversions can be acquired by animals of many different species when the CS-US interval is several hours long, and that this learning is not dependent on any aftertaste or other stimulus that might fill the delay between ingestion and illness. Many writers have argued that such a learning ability is adaptive: If an animal in the wild eats a poisonous food, it may not become ill until many hours later. Creatures that have the ability to associate their illness with what they have previously eaten will be able to avoid that food in the future and thereby have a better chance of survival. Nonetheless, because the effective CS-US intervals are many times longer than in traditional experiments on classical conditioning, some psychologists proposed that taste-aversion learning is a special type of learning, one that does not obey the principle of contiguity. Thus, taste-aversion learning was seen by some as an exception to one of the most basic principles of association. As the next section shows, taste-aversion learning was also involved in a second line of attack on the general-principle approach.

## Biological Preparedness in Taste-Aversion Learning

As already mentioned, a crucial assumption underlying most research on classical conditioning is that the experimenter's choice of stimuli, responses, and species of subject is relatively unimportant. Suppose, for example, an experimenter wishes to test some hypothesis about learning using the salivary conditioning preparation. The subjects will be dogs, and the US will be food powder, but what stimulus should be used as the CS? According to what Seligman and Hager (1972) called the **equipotentiality premise,** it does not matter what stimulus is used; the decision is entirely arbitrary. The following quotation from Pavlov (1928) documents his belief in the equipotentiality premise: "Any natural phenomenon chosen at will may be converted into a conditional stimulus . . . any visual stimulus, any desired sound, any odor, and the stimulation of any part of the skin" (p. 86).

From the outset, we should dismiss a very strict interpretation of the equipotentiality premise. It does not mean that all stimuli and all responses will result in equally rapid learning. Pavlov himself recognized that different CSs will condition at different rates: A bright light will acquire a CR more rapidly than a dim light. Yet although stimuli (or responses) certainly differ in their conditionability, the equipotentiality premise states that a stimulus (or response) that is difficult to condition in one context should also be difficult to condition in other contexts. For example, if a dim light is a poor CS in a salivary conditioning experiment, it should also be a poor CS in an eyeblink conditioning experiment. In short, the equipotentiality premise states that a given stimulus will be an equally good (or equally bad) CS in all contexts.

Although the simplicity of the equipotentiality premise might be appealing, a large amount of evidence has shown that it is incorrect. Garcia and Koelling (1966) conducted an important experiment showing that the same two stimuli can be differentially effective in different contexts. Two groups of rats were each presented with a compound stimulus consisting of both taste and audiovisual components. Each rat received water that had a distinctive flavor, and whenever the rat drank the water, it was presented with flashing lights and a clicking noise. For one group, the procedure consisted of typical taste-aversion learning: After drinking the water, a rat was injected with a poison, and it soon became ill. For the second group, there was no poison; instead, a rat's paws were shocked whenever it drank. Thus both groups of animals received pairings of both taste and audiovisual stimuli with an aversive event, but the aversive event was illness for one group and shock for the other.

Garcia and Koelling wanted to determine how strongly the two types of stimuli (taste and audiovisual) were associated with the two different aversive consequences. To do so, they conducted extinction tests (no shock or poison present) in which the taste and audiovisual stimuli were presented separately. Half of the subjects in each group first received the flavored water without the audiovisual stimulus, and their consumption was measured. Later, they were presented with plain water, but their drinking was now accompanied by the audiovisual stimulus. To control for possible sequence effects, the other half of the subjects received these stimuli in the opposite order.

Figure 5-6 shows the results of this experiment. For each group, the bar graphs show the amount of water consumed in each of the two tests, measured as a percentage of that group's consumption in baseline tests conducted before any poison or shock was presented. The group that received poison showed a greater aversion to the taste stimulus than to the audiovisual stimulus. However, exactly the opposite pattern was observed for the group that received the shock. For these animals, consumption of the flavored water was almost the same as in baseline, but consumption of water accompanied by the audiovisual stimulus decreased to less than 20 percent of its baseline level.

What can we conclude about the stimuli used in this experiment? Which was the better stimulus, taste or the audiovisual stimulus? What was the more effective aversive event, shock or illness? The results shown in Figure 5-6 imply that there is no simple answer to these questions. Taste was a more effective stimulus when the aversive event was poison, but the audiovisual stimulus was more effective when the aversive event was shock. Garcia and his colleagues therefore concluded that before we can predict the strength of a conditioned response, we must know something about the *relationship* between the CS and the US. They suggest that because of a rat's biological makeup, it has an innate tendency to associate illness with the taste of the food it had previously eaten. The rat is much less likely to associate illness with visual or auditory stimuli that are present when a food is eaten. On the other hand, the rat is more likely to associate a painful event like shock with external auditory and visual stimuli than with a taste stimulus.

Seligman (1970) suggested that some CS-US associations might be called **prepared associations** because the animal has an innate propensity to form such associations quickly and easily (for example, a taste-illness association). Other potential associations might be called **contraprepared associations,** because even after many pairings, a subject may have difficulty forming an association between the two stimuli (such as taste and shock). In between are **unprepared associations**—those

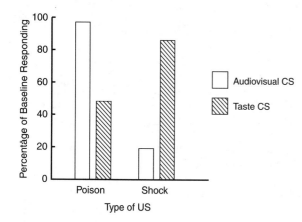

**FIGURE 5-6** Results from the experiment of Garcia and Koelling (1966). The first two bars show the amount of water consumed in the presence of two different CSs by the group for which poison was the US. The second two bars show the consumption by the group with shock as the US.

for which the creature has no special predisposition, but which can nevertheless be formed after a moderate number of pairings. In the Garcia and Koelling experiment, the association between the audiovisual stimulus and shock may be an example of an unprepared association. It is hard to imagine why rats would have an innate predisposition to associate a strange flashing light and clicking sound with shock to the forepaws, but they were able to associate these two stimuli after a number of pairings.

It should be clear that Seligman's concept of preparedness is at odds with the equipotentiality premise. It implies that in order to predict how effective a particular CS will be, it is not enough to know how effective this CS has been in other contexts. We must also know what US will be used and whether this CS-US pair is an example of a prepared, unprepared, or contraprepared association. To complicate matters further, other experiments have shown that the predisposition to associate two stimuli can vary across different species. Although rats may be predisposed to associate taste stimuli with illness, other animals may not be. Wilcoxon, Dragoin, and Kral (1971) compared the behaviors of rats and bobwhite quail when illness followed ingestion of water that had a distinctive (sour) taste, or water with a distinctive (dark blue) color, or water that was both sourtasting and dark blue. As we would expect, rats displayed aversions to the sour taste but not to the blue color. In contrast, quail developed aversions both to the sour water and the blue water, and the blue color was actually the more effective stimulus for these animals.

Wilcoxon and colleagues hypothesized that the differences between rats and quail are related to their respective methods of obtaining food in the natural environment. Rats have excellent senses of taste and smell but relatively poor vision, and they normally forage for food at night. Quail are daytime feeders, and they have excellent vision, which they use in searching for food. It makes sense that those stimuli that are most important for a given species at the time of ingestion are also those that are most readily associated with illness. An implication of this conclusion is that an analysis of a creature's lifestyle in its natural environment may provide clues about which associations are prepared, unprepared, and contraprepared for that creature.

Another implication is that attempting to generalize about preparedness or ease of learning from one species to another can be a dangerous strategy. Note, however, that quail could develop aversions to either the color or taste of water, but that aversions to color developed more easily. Braveman (1977) described a number of studies showing that various mammals, including rats and other rodents, can develop an aversion to the visual appearance of a food or liquid, although several pairings of food and illness may be required. In short, although animals may be predisposed to develop aversions to stimuli of one sensory modality, aversions to stimuli of other modalities can be learned, only with greater difficulty.

## Biological Preparedness in Human Learning

As with animals, some of the best evidence for preparedness in human beings involves taste-aversion learning. People can develop a strong aversion to a food that is followed by illness, even if the illness follows ingestion of the food by several hours. Based on what you know about the past and present eating habits of the human species, which stimulus modality do you suspect is the most likely to be the focus of an illness-induced aversion to certain foods? Logue, Ophir, and Strauss (1981) used questionnaires to query several hundred college students about any food aversions they might have that developed as a result of an illness that occurred after they ate the food. Of the 65 percent who reported at least one aversion, 83 percent claimed that the taste of the food was now aversive to them. Smaller percentages claimed they found other sensory characteristics of the food aversive: The smell of the food was aversive for 51 percent, the texture of the food for 32 percent, and the sight of the food for only 26 percent. These percentages suggest that people are more similar to rats than to quail when it comes to the acquisition of food aversions following illness. In many cases, people develop an aversion to some food even though they know that their illness was caused by something completely unrelated to the food, such as the flu or chemotherapy treatment (Bernstein, Webster, & Bernstein, 1982; Logue, Logue, & Strauss, 1983).

The other major area of research on possible preparedness in human conditioning involves the development of fears, or phobias. Ohman, Dimberg, and Ost (1985) have proposed that human beings have a predisposition to develop fears of things that have been dangerous to our species throughout our evolutionary history, such as snakes and spiders. Quite a few experiments have tested this hypothesis. In one procedure, the conditioned response is a person's skin conductance response (SCR, see Chapter 4), with pictures of snakes and spiders as CSs and a shock as the US. Subjects in one group learn a conditional discrimination in which pictures of snakes are followed by shock and pictures of spiders are not. In a second group, the roles of snakes and spiders are reversed. For the subjects in two control groups, pictures of flowers are followed by shock and pictures of mushrooms are not, or vice versa. The typical result of this type of study is that subjects learn the discrimination and exhibit a strong SCR to the stimulus paired with shock but not to the other stimulus. The rate of discrimination learning is usually just as fast with flowers and mushrooms as it is with snakes and spiders, a result that provides no support for the preparedness hypothesis (McNally, 1987). However, some studies have found greater resistance to extinction in the spider/snake groups compared to the flower/mushroom groups (Ohman and others, 1985; Schell, Dawson, & Marinkovic, 1991). There is also some evidence that fear responses to flowers and mushrooms are quickly extinguished by verbal instructions ("You will receive no more shocks") but fear responses to snakes and spiders are not (Hugdahl & Ohman, 1977). Overall, however, the evidence for human preparedness involving snakes and spiders is fairly weak and inconsistent, and there are other ways to interpret the data that

do not involve biological preparedness (Davey, 1995).

Ohman and colleagues (1985) have also proposed that people are predisposed to associate angry faces with aversive consequences. Their reasoning is that throughout our evolutionary history, when one person stared with an angry expression toward another person, the angry person often followed this expression with some attempt to hurt or intimidate the other person. As a result, human beings have become prepared to produce a fearful or defensive reaction to an angry face. This hypothesis has been tested with discrimination procedures similar to those used for spiders and snakes, except that angry faces are used in one group and happy or neutral faces are used in a control group. Once again, the results have been mixed, with some studies finding support for the preparedness hypothesis (Dimberg & Ohman, 1983) and others finding none (Packer, Clark, Bond, & Siddle, 1991). In summary, compared to the other evidence for preparedness we have examined, the evidence for preparedness in human phobias remains inconclusive. Further research may help to clarify this issue.

## Biological Constraints and the General-Principle Approach

No doubt the findings of Garcia and his colleagues were a surprise to traditional learning theorists—few would have predicted that associative learning could occur with such long delays between stimuli, at least with animal subjects. In retrospect, they have not proven to be damaging to the general-principle approach to learning. It is true that taste-aversion learning can occur with long delays between CS and US, but long-delay learning is not found only in taste-aversion paradigms. In a series of experiments, Lett (1973, 1975, 1979) inserted delays of various lengths between a rat's choice response in a T-maze and the animal's subsequent receipt of food (if the response was correct). During the delay, a rat was returned to its home cage so that no cues in the end of the maze could be used to bridge the delay between choice response and the food. Lett found that rats' choices of the correct arm of the maze increased over trials even when the delay interval was 60 minutes. Other studies have found learning when stimuli are separated by as much as 24 hours (Capaldi, 1966). Studies like these show that, at least in certain circumstances, animals can associate events separated by long delays in situations that do not involve taste aversions.

Besides showing that long-delay learning is not unique to taste aversions, we can also dispute the claim that taste-aversion learning violates the principle of contiguity. In essence, this principle states that individuals will more readily associate two events the more closely the events occur in time. Figure 5-7a shows the results from an experiment in which rats obtained food by pressing a lever and shocks were used to suppress the rats' responding (Baron, Kaufman, & Fazzini, 1969). As the delay between a response and shock increased, there was less and less suppression of responding, as compared to the rats' baseline response rates.

Figure 5-7b shows the results from a study on taste-aversion learning, in which different groups of rats experienced different delays between their initial exposure to a saccharin solu-

tion and a poison injection (Andrews & Braveman, 1975). The graph shows the amount of saccharin consumed in a later test. Observe the similarity in the shapes of the functions in Figures 5-7a and 5-7b. Both sets of results are consistent with the principle of contiguity—the shorter the interval between a response and an aversive event, the stronger is the responding. The only major difference between the two experiments is the scale on the *x*-axis (seconds in Figure 5-7a, hours in Figure 5-7b). Taste aversions were conditioned with considerably longer delays, but this is merely a quantitative difference, not a qualitative one. That is, the results in Figure 5-7b do not require the postulation of a different law to replace the principle of contiguity; they merely require the use of different numbers in describing the relationship between contiguity and learning.

In the 1960s and 1970s, the evidence for biological preparedness in taste-aversion learning (and in other learning situations) was also seen as a problem for the general-principle approach. This research clearly showed that some associations are more easily formed than others. Furthermore, an association (for example, between the visual appearance of a food and illness) that is difficult for one

**FIGURE 5-7**    (a) The effects of delay between a lever press and shock in an experiment on punishment (Baron, Kaufman, & Fazzini, 1969). With increasing delays, the punishment caused less suppression of lever pressing. (b) The effect of delay between saccharin consumption and poison administration in an experiment on taste-aversion learning (Andrews & Braveman, 1975). With increasing delays, the poisoning caused less suppression of saccharin consumption.

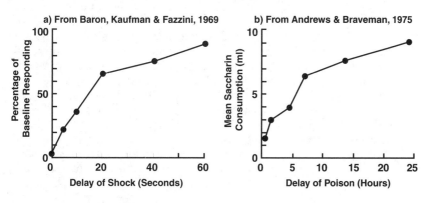

species to learn may be easy for another. Notice, however, that Seligman's continuum of preparedness deals with differences in the speed of learning or the amount of learning, not in the kind of learning that takes place. It is not impossible for rats to develop an association between a visual stimulus and illness; it simply requires more conditioning trials than does a taste-illness association. The same can be said for a taste-shock association. Once again, this alleged evidence against general principles of learning merely amounts to a quantitative difference, not a qualitative one. A description of the learning of prepared, unprepared, and contraprepared associations would require different numbers, but not necessarily different laws.

Seligman and Hager (1972) had proposed that taste-aversion learning is a unique type of learning that does not obey the laws of traditional learning theory. However, in a review of the literature on this topic, Logue (1979) described considerable evidence that there is actually nothing unique about taste-aversion learning. She noted that many of the most familiar phenomena of classical conditioning, including generalization gradients, extinction, conditioned inhibition, blocking, stimulus preexposure effects, and second-order conditioning, have all been observed in taste-aversion learning. Logue concluded that taste-aversion learning violates no traditional principles of learning and requires no new principles of learning. Although some theorists continue to maintain that taste-aversion learning has some unique characteristics (Chambers, 1990), Logue's viewpoint is shared by many researchers on classical conditioning (see Domjan, 1983; Shettleworth, 1983; Revusky, 1977). In fact, taste-aversion learning has joined the conditioned suppression and eyeblink paradigms as a commonly used procedure for investigating the general principles of classical conditioning procedure (for example, Batsell & Batson, 1999; Bevins, Jensen, Hinze, & Besheer, 1999). This fact, perhaps more than any other, should put to rest the notion that taste-aversion learning is inconsistent with the general-principle approach to learning theory.

## THE FORM OF THE CONDITIONED RESPONSE

As we have already seen, predicting the form of a conditioned response has proven to be a difficult task. In some cases, the CR is quite similar to the UR, and in others it is the opposite of the UR. When a CR is the opposite of the UR, it is sometimes called a *compensatory CR*, because it tends to compensate for, or counteract, the UR (just as the b-process in opponent-process theory is thought to counteract the a-process). In this section, we will first investigate how classical conditioning can affect an individual's reaction to a drug. In this area of research, both mimicking and compensatory CRs have been observed. We will then examine some theories that try to explain why CRs assume the variety of forms that they do.

### Drug Tolerance as a Conditioned Response

A heroin user's first injection produces a highly pleasurable response of euphoria, but with later injections of the same dosage, the intensity of this positive emotional response becomes smaller and smaller. The decrease in effectiveness of a drug with repeated use is called **tolerance,** and it is found with many drugs. Several hypotheses about why tolerance occurs have been proposed. Typical pharmacological explanations attribute tolerance to possible physiological changes, such as a change in metabolism that allows the drug to pass through the body more quickly. According to the Solomon and Corbit theory (Chapter 3), drug tolerance is the result of an automatic strengthening of the b-process over trials. Both the pharmacological explanations and the Solomon and Corbit theory therefore attribute drug tolerance to a change in the individual's body that alters the way the body reacts to the drug. However, based on his research on morphine and other drugs, Shepard Siegel (1975, 1999) has proposed a very different explanation of tolerance, one based on classical conditioning. In short, Siegel claims that drug tolerance is, at least in part, due to a compensatory CR that is elicited by contextual stimuli that regularly precede a drug administration. A description of a few of his experiments will illustrate how Siegel came to these conclusions.

One of the URs produced by morphine is **analgesia,** or a decreased sensitivity to pain. In one experiment, Siegel (1975) found that a decrease in analgesia over successive morphine injections (that is, tolerance of the analgesic response) was controlled by contextual stimuli. Siegel's subjects were rats, and he tested their sensitivity to pain by placing them on a metal plate that was heated to an uncomfortably warm temperature of about 54°C. When a rat's paws become painfully hot, the rat makes an easily measurable response—it lifts its forepaws and licks them. By measuring the latency of this paw-lick response, Siegel had a measure of the animal's sensitivity to pain.

Rats in a control group received four test trials (separated by 48 hours) on which they were brought into a special experimental room, given an injection of a saline solution (as a placebo), and later placed on the metal surface. The paw-lick latencies for these control subjects were roughly the same on all four trials, averaging 13 seconds. The procedure for one experimental group was exactly the same, except that these rats received four morphine injections, not saline injections. On the first trial, the average paw-lick latency for this group was 24 seconds—nearly double that of the control group. This result shows that the morphine had its expected analgesic effect. However, the latencies for this group decreased over the next three trials, and on the fourth trial, their latencies were about the same as those of the control group. Thus in four trials, these rats had developed a tolerance to the morphine—it no longer had an analgesic effect.

According to Siegel's hypothesis, this tolerance occurred because the contextual stimuli that accompanied each morphine injection (the sights, sounds, and smells of the experimental room) acquired the capacity to elicit a compensatory CR of **hyperalgesia,** or an increased sensitivity to pain. By trial 4, this compensatory CR of hyperalgesia completely counteracted the UR of analgesia, so the net effect was no change in pain sensitivity. If this hypothesis is correct, it should be possible to eliminate the tolerance simply by changing the contextual stimuli on the final trial. Siegel attempted to do this in a third group by giving these rats their first three morphine injections in their home cages. On trial 4, these rats received their morphine injections in the experimental room for the first time. Since this context was completely novel, it should elicit no compensatory CRs. Indeed, these animals showed a strong analgesic response, and their mean paw-lick latency was 28 seconds! Thus, although this was the fourth morphine injection for these rats, their analgesic response was like that of animals that had never received a morphine injection before. This big difference between the two morphine groups was obtained simply by *changing the room* in which the morphine was injected.

If a rat's tolerance to morphine is indeed a conditioned response, it should be possible to extinguish this response by presenting the CS (the context) without the US (morphine). In another study, Siegel, Sherman, and Mitchell (1980) demonstrated such an extinction effect. Rats first received three daily injections of morphine, during which they developed tolerance to its analgesic effects. They then received nine extinction trials, in which they were transported to the experimental room and were given an injection as usual, except that they received saline instead of morphine. These can be called extinction trials because the CS (the experimental room and injection routine) was presented without the morphine. The extinction trials were followed by one final test with morphine, and the experimenters found that the morphine again produced a modest analgesic response—the rats' tolerance to morphine had been partially extinguished as a result of the saline trials.

Some of the most convincing evidence for the compensatory-CR theory has come from studies in which the CS is presented without the drug US, and a compensatory CR has been observed directly. For instance, Rozin, Reff,

Mack, and Schull (1984) showed that for regular coffee drinkers, the smell and taste of coffee can serve as a CS that elicits a compensatory CR counteracting the effects of caffeine. In addition to its effects on arousal and alertness, caffeine normally causes an increase in salivation. However, for regular coffee drinkers, this increase in salivation is minimal (a tolerance effect). Rozin and colleagues had their subjects drink a cup of coffee that either did or did not contain caffeine (and the subjects were not told which). After they drank coffee with caffeine, subjects showed only a small increase in salivation, as would be expected of habitual coffee drinkers. However, after they drank coffee without caffeine, these subjects showed a substantial *decrease* in salivation. The experimenters concluded that this decrease was a compensatory CR elicited by the stimuli that were usually paired with caffeine (the smell and taste of coffee). In addition, when these subjects drank a cup of hot apple juice containing caffeine, they showed substantial increases in salivation, which shows that they had not developed a general tolerance to the salivation-increasing effects of caffeine—their tolerance was found only when the caffeine was paired with the usual CS, coffee.

In summary, Rozin and coworkers demonstrated that coffee can come to elicit a compensatory CR, a decrease in salivation, after it has been repeatedly paired with caffeine. Similar evidence for compensatory CRs has been obtained with morphine (Mucha, Volkovskis, & Kalant, 1981; Paletta & Wagner, 1986) and with many other pharmacological agents, including adrenalin (Russek & Pina, 1962) and alcohol (Crowell, Hinson, & Siegel, 1981).

If it is generally true that classical conditioning contributes to the phenomenon of drug tolerance, it should be possible to find evidence for this effect in nonlaboratory settings. Siegel and his colleagues (Siegel, Hinson, Krank, & McCully, 1982) presented some evidence from regular heroin users who died, or nearly died, after a heroin injection. Of course, an overdose of heroin can be fatal, but in some cases the dosage that caused a death was one the user had tolerated on the

previous day. Siegel proposes that in some cases of this type, the user may have taken the heroin in an unusual stimulus environment, where the user's previously acquired compensatory CRs to the heroin injection would be decreased. He states that survivors of nearly fatal injections frequently report that the circumstances of the drug administration were different from those under which they normally injected the drug.

In summary, Siegel (1999) proposes that drug tolerance is due, at least in part, to the acquisition of a compensatory CR that tends to counteract the effects of the drug itself. He has demonstrated that morphine tolerance is stimulus-specific, and that it can be acquired and extinguished like any other CR. It is hard to imagine how a theory of drug tolerance focusing on general physiological changes (and not allowing for the contribution of classical conditioning) could account for the phenomena Siegel and others have observed.

Although Siegel's findings provide a strong case that morphine tolerance can come under the control of environmental stimuli, his theory that this tolerance is due to the presence of a compensatory CR has been challenged. Some theorists have proposed that Siegel's results are due to a type of context-specific habituation: Because the context allows the animal to anticipate the upcoming morphine injection, the effects of this injection are diminished (T. B. Baker & Tiffany, 1985). Others have suggested that both the compensatory-CR theory and the context-specific habituation theory may be part of the story of drug tolerance (Paletta & Wagner, 1986).

## Conditioned Opponent Theories

Schull (1979) proposed an interesting theory about compensatory CRs. He called his theory a **conditioned opponent theory** because he accepted most of the assumptions of the Solomon and Corbit theory but made one important change. Schull agreed that a typical emotional experience involves the elicitation of an a-process followed by an opposing b-process. However, he did not accept the idea that the b-process is automatically strengthened with use and weakened with disuse. Instead, he assumed that the b-process may appear to grow because any stimulus that is paired with the emotional experience will become a CS that can later elicit the b-process (but not the a-process, which Schull assumed is not transferable to a CS). To put it another way, whereas Solomon and Corbit proposed that the b-process is increased by a nonassociative strengthening mechanism, Schull proposed that any increase in the size of the b-process is a CR elicited by one or more CSs.

Schull's theory may be easier to understand if we consider a specific example. As discussed in Chapter 3 in the section on the Solomon and Corbit theory, a person's response to an initial heroin injection is a very pleasurable sensation followed by unpleasant withdrawal symptoms. The initial pleasure is the a-process, and the unpleasant aftereffect is the b-process. Now, according to Schull, only the b-process is conditionable. Let us assume that stimuli that accompany the heroin injection—the needle, the room, and so on—serve as CSs that, after a few pairings with heroin, begin to elicit the withdrawal symptoms by themselves. These CSs have several effects. First, they tend to counteract the a-process, so a heroin injection no longer produces much of a pleasurable sensation. Second, they combine with the b-process to produce more severe and longer-lasting withdrawal symptoms. Third, when no heroin is available, the presence of these stimuli can still produce withdrawal symptoms and cravings for the drug. Thus Schull proposed that classically conditioned stimuli may contribute to many of the debilitating characteristics of drug addiction.

Whereas Schull's conditioned opponent theory deals exclusively with the conditioning of b-processes, Wagner and his associates (Donegan & Wagner, 1987; Mazur & Wagner, 1982; Wagner, 1981) have developed a general theory of classical conditioning that is meant to apply to all CRs, whether or not we would want to call them "b-processes." Wagner calls this theory a **sometimes opponent process (SOP)** theory because it predicts that in some cases a CR will be the opposite of the UR, whereas in other cases a CR will mimic the UR. How can we predict what type of CR we will see in a particular conditioning situation? According to SOP, the CR will mimic the UR if the UR is **monophasic,** but it will be the opposite of the UR if the UR is **biphasic.** In essence, the terms monophasic and biphasic concern whether or not a b-process can be observed in the UR. For example, the heart-rate UR to shock is biphasic because it consists of an increase in heart rate when the shock is on, followed by a decrease in heart rate *below baseline* when the shock is terminated. Because the UR exhibits such a "rebound effect," SOP predicts that the CR will be the opposite of the UR, and Black's (1965) research has demonstrated that this is the case. On the other hand, the UR of an eyeblink to a puff of air is monophasic: The eye closes, then opens, but there is no rebound—the eye does not open wider than it was initially. For this reason, SOP predicts that the CR will mimic the UR in eyeblink conditioning, which is of course the case.

If SOP is correct, we should be able to make predictions in two directions. First, by observing the entire UR, we should be able to predict the form of the CR. For instance, a rat's typical response to foot shock is a brief period of hyperactivity followed by a longer period of decreased activity ("freezing"). SOP predicts that the CR will resemble the latter response, freezing, which is the case (Fanselow, 1980). Second, SOP predicts that if a CR appears to be the opposite of the UR, careful observation will reveal that the UR is actually biphasic. For example, whereas decreased activity is typically observed in rats after a morphine injection, stimuli paired with morphine elicit a CR of hyperactivity. By observing rats' activity levels for many hours after a morphine injection, Paletta and Wagner (1986) found that the initial period of decreased activity is indeed followed by a period of hyperactivity, as SOP predicts. Other types of studies have found support for some of the predictions of SOP (Albert, Ricker, Bevins, & Ayres, 1993).

Wagner and Brandon (1989) presented an extension of SOP that offers one additional reason why the form of a CR can be so difficult to predict. They called their revised theory

**AESOP,** which stands for an **affective extension of SOP.** To get a feeling for the basic idea of AESOP, refer back to the diagram of CS and US centers shown in Figure 4-4. This diagram suggests that through classical conditioning, an association may form between a CS center and a US center. According to AESOP, however, a single US can have not one but two centers: one related to the sensory properties of the US and the other related to its emotional properties. These two US centers will activate two different types of unconditioned responses. For example, if the US is a mild shock to the skin near a rabbit's eye, the sensory center may produce a rapid response (an eyeblink), whereas the emotional center may produce a slower but longer-lasting response (such as a mild state of fear). A CS that is paired with the US may develop an association with both the sensory and emotional US centers, but the nature of the two associations will depend on many factors, such as the timing and duration of the CS.

For instance, a 1-second tone may be just the right duration to elicit a strong eyeblink CR, but it may be too brief to elicit much of a fear response (as might be measured by a change in the rabbit's heart rate). Conversely, a 10-second tone may be too long to produce much eyeblink conditioning, but it may elicit a strong fear response. Thus two different CSs may elicit CRs that look quite different, even though they have been paired with the same US.

Since Wagner and Brandon introduced AESOP, a number of studies have found support for its basic premise—that it is essential to take into account both the sensory and emotional features of a US (Brandon, Bombace, Falls, & Wagner, 1991; McNish, Betts, Brandon, & Wagner, 1997). The details of AESOP and the related experiments are complex, and we will not explore them here. For our purposes, the most important point to remember is that, because both the sensory and emotional properties of the US can affect the type of CR elicited by any particular CS, the size and form of the CR may be difficult to predict in advance.

## PHYSIOLOGICAL RESEARCH ON CLASSICAL CONDITIONING

The final topic of this chapter complements each of the previous ones. Regardless of their theoretical perspectives, just about all researchers who study classical conditioning agree that our understanding of this type of learning would be greatly enhanced if we knew what changes take place in the nervous system during the acquisition and subsequent performance of a new conditioned response. This topic has been the focus of intense research efforts in recent years. Much has been learned about the physiological mechanisms of classical conditioning, and the following discussion can provide only a brief survey of some of the major developments in this area.

### Research with Primitive Creatures

Kandel's research on the neural mechanisms of habituation in the mollusk *Aplysia* was discussed in Chapter 3. Kandel and his associates have also studied classical conditioning in *Aplysia* in several different ways. In some early studies, Kandel and Tauc (1964, 1965) produced a conditioning-like effect in a three-neuron configuration of *Aplysia*. Figure 5-8 illustrates their methods. Electrodes were inserted into the cell bodies of neurons 1 and 2, and delivering a weak electrical current through either electrode would cause the corresponding neuron to fire. Before conditioning, it was found that the firing of neuron 1 did not cause neuron 3 to fire, whereas the firing of neuron 2 did cause neuron 3 to fire. However, the firing of neuron 1 did produce a small depolarization in the membrane of neuron 3, which indicated that there was an ineffective synaptic connection between neurons 1 and 3.

Given this initial state of affairs, Kandel and Tauc treated the stimulation of neuron 1 as the CS and the stimulation of neuron 2 as the US, which produced the UR of the firing of neuron 3. After several CS-US pairings (the stimulation of neuron 1, then neuron 2), Kandel and Tauc found that the CS now elicited a

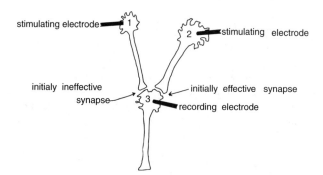

**FIGURE 5-8**　A schematic diagram of the procedure used by Kandel and Tauc (1964) to obtain an effect resembling classical conditioning in only three neurons of *Aplysia*. Before conditioning, stimulation of neuron 2 produced a strong response in neuron 3, but stimulation of neuron 1 did not. After several "conditioning" trials on which neuron 1 and neuron 2 were stimulated in rapid succession, neuron 1 now developed the capacity to produce a response in neuron 3.

response of its own—the stimulation of neuron 1 now caused neuron 3 to fire. This new synaptic association was not permanent: It lasted for about 20 minutes and then disappeared. However, the researchers were able to demonstrate this conditioning-like effect in several sets of neurons. They also showed that the effect depended on the temporal contiguity of CS and US—unpaired stimulations of neuron 1 and neuron 2 did not produce the effect. These results illustrate how simple the neural mechanisms of classical conditioning can be, at least in some cases. Since there are three distinct elements in any classical conditioning situation—the CS, the US, and the response—a minimum of three neurons must be involved. Yet working with this absolute minimum of three neurons, Kandel and Tauc were able to demonstrate something resembling classical conditioning.

In other research, Kandel and his associates have examined classical conditioning in the gill-withdrawal reflex of *Aplysia*. In their conditioning arrangement, the US was a shock to the tail, and the UR was the gill-withdrawal response (see Figure 3-8). The CS was weak stimulation of the siphon, which initially produced only a minor gill-withdrawal response. After several pairings of the CS and US, however, the CS began to elicit a full gill-withdrawal response (Carew, Hawkins, & Kandel, 1983). As in classical conditioning with mammals, the precise temporal arrangement of CS and US was crucial. Optimal learning occurred with short-delay conditioning (with the CS

preceding the US by 0.5 seconds), and there was no evidence of conditioning with a delay of 2 seconds (Hawkins, Carew, & Kandel, 1983). Other studies on the gill-withdrawal reflex have demonstrated more complex conditioning phenomena, such as discrimination learning and second-order conditioning (Hawkins, Greene, & Kandel, 1998).

Kandel and his associates have been able to trace the neural circuitry involved in gill-withdrawal conditioning. They found that the CR in this procedure (the increased response to siphon stimulation) was due to an increase in the amount of transmitter released by the sensory neurons of the siphon. It is interesting to note that precisely the opposite neural change (decreased transmitter release by the sensory neurons) was found to be responsible for habituation of the gill-withdrawal response (see Chapter 3). Further work by Kandel's group showed that the increased transmitter release is caused by an increased flow of calcium into the sensory axon terminal, which is in turn caused by an increased flow of potassium out of the cell. To make matters more complex, however, changes in transmitter release are not the only neural changes that have been observed in *Aplysia*'s nervous system during classical conditioning. Glanzman (1995) has obtained evidence that the dendrites of the postsynaptic neurons in the circuit develop enhanced sensitivity, so they exhibit stronger responses to chemical stimulation. Even in the simple nervous system of *Aplysia*, a number of different physiological mechanisms are involved in a learning episode (Bao, Kandel, & Hawkins, 1998).

Classical conditioning has been studied in other primitive creatures besides *Aplysia*, including two other species of mollusk, *Hermissenda* and *Limax* (Farley, Richards, & Grover, 1990; Hopfield & Gelperin, 1989). Are the neural and chemical mechanisms of classical conditioning similar in these different species? According to Thompson, Donegan, and Lavond (1988), there are both similarities and differences. For example, in both *Aplysia* and *Hermissenda*, classical conditioning involves an increased transmitter release by sensory neurons that are activated by the CS. In both species, the increased transmitter release is triggered by changes in the flow of calcium and potassium ions. On the other hand, the neural circuitry and the specific chemical mechanisms are substantially different in these two species. Thus, the general mechanisms of classical conditioning are similar in these two species of mollusk, but the details are different. These findings provide a clue that we should probably expect even greater diversity in neural circuits when examining more advanced species, whose nervous systems are so much larger and more complex. Nevertheless, Usherwood (1993) has noted that comparisons of the chemical mechanisms of conditioning in mollusks and rabbits have revealed quite a few similarities. These similarities suggest that the research on simple creatures may provide valuable clues about the chemical mechanisms of learning in higher organisms.

## Research with Mammals and Other Vertebrates

Because of the staggering complexity of the nervous systems of higher animals such as mammals, the task of uncovering the physiological mechanisms of classical conditioning is extremely difficult. Nevertheless, substantial progress has now been made, and research on this topic is proceeding in several different directions (Thompson & Krupa, 1994). Our brief review of this topic will focus on five main points.

1. *The neural pathways involved in the CR are often different from those involved in the UR.* This can be shown through procedures that eliminate one of these responses but not the other. For example, in baboons, a certain part of the hypothalamus appears to be intimately involved in the conditioned heart-rate changes elicited by CSs paired with shock. If this part of the hypothalamus is destroyed, heart-rate CRs disappear, whereas unconditioned heart-rate responses are unaffected (O. A. Smith, Astley, DeVito, Stein, & Walsh, 1980).

For another common classical conditioning preparation, rabbit eyeblink conditioning, the neural circuitry has been studied extensively, and the brain locations involved are fairly well understood. The **cerebellum,** a part of the brain that is important for many skilled movements, plays a critical role in eyeblink conditioning (see Canli & Donegan, 1995; Perrett & Mauk, 1995). As in heart-rate conditioning, different neural pathways are involved in eyeblink URs and CRs. The eyeblink UR to an air puff directed at the eye seems to be controlled by two distinct pathways—a fairly direct pathway in the brainstem and a more indirect pathway passing through the cerebellum. Considerable evidence shows that the eyeblink CR is controlled by this second, indirect pathway. If sections of this pathway in the cerebellum are destroyed, eyeblink CRs disappear and cannot be relearned (Knowlton & Thompson, 1992; Lavond, Hembree, & Thompson, 1985). If neurons in this same part of the cerebellum are electrically stimulated, eyeblink responses similar to the CR are produced (Thompson, McCormick, & Lavond, 1986). If this divergence of UR and CR pathways is found in other response systems, it would help to explain why the forms of the UR and CR are often different.

Wagner and Donegan (1989) pointed out that there is an intriguing correspondence between this physiological research and the predictions of Wagner's SOP model. As discussed in the preceding section, SOP suggests that a CR mimics the later portions of the UR but not its initial portions. The findings described above may explain why this is so, at least in the case of eyeblink conditioning: The CR is activated by the neural pathways involved in the later part of the UR but not in the early part. This relationship between SOP and neurophysiological evidence provides an example of how theories of learning and neurophysiological research can be mutually supportive.

2. *Many different brain structures may be involved in the production of a simple CR.* For example, although the cerebellum is important in rabbit eyeblink conditioning, many other brain areas are involved as well. In other species, a number of different brain sites have been implicated in heart-rate conditioning, including parts of the amygdala, hypothalamus, and cingulate cortex (Schneiderman, McCabe, Haselton, Ellenberger, Jarrell, & Gentile, 1987).

3. *Many of the different conditioning phenomena we have studied in this chapter and in Chapter 4 may involve different parts of the brain.* This point has been made in a number of studies with different species of subjects. For example, if the hippocampus is removed from a rabbit, the animal will fail to exhibit the blocking effect (P. R. Solomon, 1977), but removal of the hippocampus does not prevent the development of conditioned inhibition. But with pigeons, hippocampal lesions do not eliminate the blocking effect, whereas they do interfere with the CS preexposure effect (Good & Macphail, 1994). Studies with rats (Phillips & LeDoux, 1992; Wilson, Brooks, & Bouton, 1995) have found that the hippocampal system is essential for certain types of associations involving contextual stimuli, whereas another brain area, the amygdala, seems important for associations involving both contextual stimuli and a typical CS (a tone).

4. *Different conditioned responses involve different brain locations.* For example, the cerebellum seems to be important in eyeblink conditioning, whereas other brain areas seem to be involved in heart-rate conditioning.

5. *Some examples have been found of individual neurons whose activity appears to be related to the acquisition of conditioned responses.* For example, McCormick and Thompson (1984) found that the firing rates of certain cells in the cerebellum are correlated with behavioral measures of the eyeblink CR. That is, when a rabbit is presented with a series of conditioning trials with a CS such as a tone, the activity of these cells increases at about the same rate as eyeblink response. When the eyeblink CR decreases during extinction, so does the activity of these cells. Moreover, the cellular activity within a single presentation of the CS parallels the pattern of the eyeblink, with the neuron's activity preceding the eyeblink response by about 30 milliseconds. Along with other evidence, this finding suggests that these cells play an important role in the development of the CR. Such neurons are not unique to the cerebellum, however, because neurons with similar properties have been found in the hippocampus, a brain structure suspected of playing a role in learning and memory (Berger & Weisz, 1987). The discovery of neurons whose activity is so closely related to overt behavior is an important development. Exactly how neurons in different parts of the brain actually contribute to the conditioning process is not yet known, however.

## Research with Human Subjects

In recent years, there have been growing research efforts to identify the physiological mechanisms of classical conditioning in humans, especially in the eyeblink conditioning preparation (Daum & Schugens, 1996). At least two different research strategies have been used. Some studies have examined human subjects with damage in specific areas of the brain due to accident or illness; these individuals are trained in an eyeblink conditioning paradigm. Another strategy is to condition subjects without brain damage while using modern imaging technologies to measure activity in different parts of the brain (for example, Buchel, Dolan, Armony, & Friston, 1999).

In several respects, the results with human subjects are very similar to those with other mammals. The cerebellum appears to play a crucial role in eyeblink conditioning. For example, one study compared a group of people with damage to the cerebellum to a group of people without such brain damage. The subjects without brain damage quickly learned a conditioned eyeblink response, whereas the subjects with damage to the cerebellum did not learn this response. However, the air puff itself did elicit an eyeblink UR in these subjects, which shows that they had not simply lost motor control of this response (Daum, Schugens, Ackermann, Lutzenberger, Dichgans, & Birbaumer, 1993). The deficit appears to be a problem in forming the necessary associations for the eyeblink CR to a neutral stimulus.

This does not mean, however, that these subjects have suffered a general inability to associate stimuli, because measurements of their heart rates and skin conductance responses show that they have indeed learned the association between CS and the air puff. As in the animal studies, these results indicate that different parts of the brain are involved in the conditioning of different response systems.

When normal human subjects undergo eyeblink conditioning, brain imaging techniques such as positron emission tomography (PET) reveal increased blood flow in one side of the cerebellum (corresponding to the side of the eye involved in conditioning), but there is increased blood flow in many other parts of the brain as well. These results seem to indicate (not too surprisingly) that many brain structures besides the cerebellum are involved in the eyeblink conditioning process, just as they are in animals (Molchan, Sunderland, McIntosh, Herscovitch, & Schreurs, 1994). With other types of human classical conditioning,

**FIGURE 5-9**    A positron emission tomography (PET) image of parts of the human brain that showed increased activity during the extinction of a conditioned fear response, including the medial frontal cortex (MF) and the medial temporal cortex (MT). (From Hugdahl, 1998)

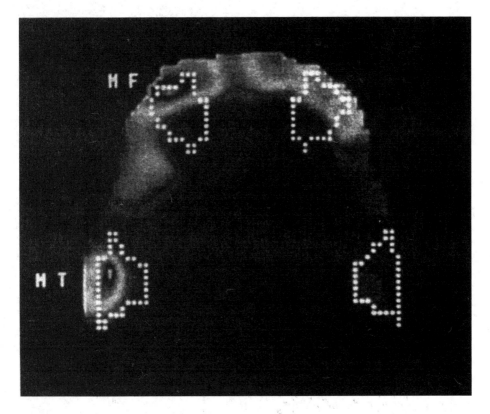

different parts of the brain are activated. Hugdahl (1998) used PET imaging to study the brain activity of adult males during the acquisition and extinction of a conditioned fear response, in which a tone was followed by a shock to the wrist. Figure 5-9 is a PET image that shows some parts of the cerebral cortex where there was increased activity during the extinction phase (when the tone was presented without shock). These brain areas were quite different from those most active during the acquisition phase, leading Hugdahl to suggest that different brain mechanisms may be involved in the acquisition and extinction of conditioned responses.

As we have seen, physiological research on classical conditioning is proceeding on a number of different levels, including research on entire brain structures, on individual neurons, and on chemical mechanisms. Both primitive and more advanced species are being studied. Much is still unknown about the brain mechanisms of classical conditioning, but one point seems certain: Anyone hoping for a simple physiological explanation is going to be disappointed. Classical conditioning, one of the simplest types of learning, appears to involve a very complex system of neural and chemical mechanisms.

## CHAPTER SUMMARY

In Kamin's experiment on the blocking effect, rats first received conditioning trials with a light paired with shock, and then trials with both the light and a tone paired with the shock. In the test phase, presenting the tone alone produced no fear response. To account for this and similar results, the Rescorla-Wagner model states that conditioning will occur only if there is a discrepancy between the strength of the US and the strength of the subject's expectation. This model can account for many conditioning phenomena, such as overshadowing, conditioned inhibition, and the overexpectation effect. However, the model has difficulty explaining certain phenomena, such as the CS preexposure effect. Theories of CS effectiveness, such as Mackintosh's theory of attention, maintain that the conditionability

of a CS decreases if the CS is not informative. Comparator theories propose that subjects may *learn* a CS-US association but not *perform* a conditioned response unless the CS is a better predictor of the US than are the contextual stimuli.

Many different types of associations can occur in classical conditioning procedures, including both S-S and S-R associations, associations with contextual stimuli, and associations between two CSs. Animals appear to be biologically prepared to learn certain conditioned associations more easily than others. In taste-aversion learning, animals and people can learn to associate a taste with illness, even if the illness occurs several hours after eating. Rats can quickly learn an association between a taste and illness or an association between audiovisual stimuli and shock, but they are slow to learn the opposite associations. Although biological constraints cannot be ignored, the same general principles seem to apply to taste-aversion learning and other forms of classical conditioning.

When a CS has been paired with a drug US, the CS will often elicit compensatory CRs—physiological responses that are the opposite of those produced by the drug—and these compensatory CRs can show up as drug tolerance. Conditioned opponent theories have attempted to describe these compensatory CRs and to predict when a CR will mimic the UR and when it will be the opposite of the UR.

Research with simple creatures such as *Aplysia* has discovered some specific neural and chemical changes that occur during conditioning. Research with vertebrates, including humans, has shown that many brain structures may be involved in the development of a simple CR, and that different brain structures seem to be involved for different conditioned responses and different conditioning phenomena.

## REVIEW QUESTIONS

1. Using either nonmathematical rules or the equations, explain how the Rescorla-Wagner model accounts for the blocking effect, overshadowing, and the overexpectation effect.

2. What are some of the different associations that can form in a simple case of classical conditioning? Describe the details of one study that has been used as evidence for one of these types of associations.

3. Why were evidence for long-delay taste-aversion learning and other examples of biological constraints on classical conditioning seen as threats to the general-principle approach to learning? How has this issue been settled?

4. What are some of the main findings and conclusions that can be drawn from physiological research on classical conditioning with simple creatures, mammals, and humans?

## CHAPTER 6

# Basic Principles
# of Operant Conditioning

Unlike classically conditioned responses, many everyday behaviors are not elicited by a specific stimulus. Behaviors such as walking, talking, eating, drinking, working, and playing do not occur automatically and with machinelike regularity in response to any particular stimulus. In the presence of a stimulus such as food, a creature might eat or it might not, depending on a multitude of factors such as the time of day, the time since its last meal, the presence of other members of its species, the other activities available at the moment, and so on. Because it appears that a creature can choose whether or not to engage in behaviors of this type, people sometimes call them "voluntary" behaviors and contrast them with the "involuntary" behaviors that are part of unconditioned and conditioned reflexes. Some learning theorists state that whereas classical conditioning is limited to involuntary behaviors, operant conditioning influences our voluntary behaviors. The term voluntary is difficult to define in a precise, scientific way, and therefore it may be a mistake to use this term to refer to all of our nonreflexive behaviors. However, regardless of what we call nonreflexive behaviors, this chapter should make one thing clear: Just because there is no obvious stimulus preceding a behavior, this does not imply that the behavior is unpredictable. Indeed, the extensive research on operant conditioning might be characterized as an effort to discover general principles that can predict what nonreflexive behaviors a creature will produce and under what conditions.

## THE LAW OF EFFECT

### Thorndike's Experiments

E. L. Thorndike (1898, 1911) was the first researcher to investigate systematically how an animal's nonreflexive behaviors can be modified as a result of its experience. In Thorndike's experiments, a hungry animal (a cat, a dog, or a chicken) was placed in a small chamber that Thorndike called a **puzzle box.** If the animal performed the appropriate response, the door to the puzzle box would be opened, and the animal could exit and eat some food placed just outside the door. For some subjects, the required response was simple—pulling on a rope, pressing a lever, or stepping on a platform. Figure 6-1 shows one of Thorndike's more difficult puzzle boxes, which required a cat to make three separate responses—pulling a string (which lifted one bolt), stepping on the platform (which lifted the other bolt), and reaching through the bars and turning one of the two latches in front of the door. The first

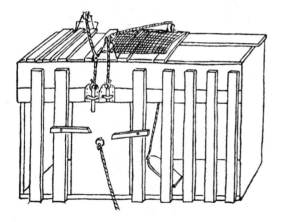

**FIGURE 6-1**   One of Thorndike's puzzle boxes. A cat could escape from this box by pulling a string, stepping on the platform, and turning one of the two latches on the front of the door. (From Thorndike, 1898)

time a subject was placed in a puzzle box (whether simple or complex), it usually took a long time to escape. A typical subject would move about inside the puzzle box, explore the various parts of the chamber in a seemingly haphazard way, and during the course of this activity it would eventually perform the response that opened the door. Based on his careful observations of this behavior, Thorndike concluded that an animal's first production of the appropriate response occurred purely by accident.

To determine how a subject's behavior would change as a result of its experience,

Thorndike would return an individual animal to the same puzzle box many times. His measure of performance was **escape latency**—the amount of time it took the subject to escape on each trial. Figure 6-2 presents a typical result from one of Thorndike's cats, which shows that as trials progressed, the cat's latency to escape gradually declined (from 160 seconds on the first trial to just 7 seconds on the twenty-fourth trial). Thorndike attributed this gradual improvement over trials to the progressive strengthening of an S-R connection: The stimulus was the inside of the puzzle box, and the response was whatever behavior opened the door. To account for the gradual strengthening of this connection, Thorndike (1898) formulated a principle of learning that he called the **Law of Effect:**

> Of several responses made to the same situation, those which are accompanied or closely followed by satisfaction to the animal will, other things being equal, be more firmly connected with the situation, so that, when it recurs, they will be more likely to recur; those which are accompanied or closely followed by discomfort to the animal will, other things being equal, have their connections with that situation weakened, so that, when it recurs, they will be less likely to occur. The greater the satisfaction or discomfort, the greater the strengthening or weakening of the bond. (p. 244)

How are we to know what is satisfying or discomforting for an animal subject? Thorndike was careful to define these terms in a way that did not rely on the observer's intuition:

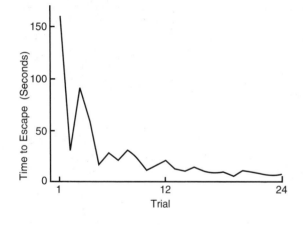

**FIGURE 6-2**   The number of seconds required by one cat to escape from a simple puzzle box on 24 consecutive trials. (From Thorndike, 1898)

By a satisfying state of affairs is meant one which the animal does nothing to avoid, often doing such things as attain and preserve it. By a discomforting or annoying state of affairs is meant one which the animal commonly avoids and abandons. (p. 245)

The application of the Law of Effect to the puzzle-box experiments is straightforward: Certain behaviors, those that opened the door, were closely followed by a satisfying state of affairs, escape and food, so when the animal was returned to the same situation it was more likely to produce those behaviors than it had been at first. In modern psychology, the phrase "satisfying state of affairs" has been replaced by the term **positive reinforcer,** but the Law of Effect (or the principle of **reinforcement**) remains as one of the most important concepts of learning theory.

### Guthrie and Horton: Evidence for a Mechanical Strengthening Process

Two researchers who followed Thorndike, E. R. Guthrie and G. P. Horton (1946), provided more convincing evidence that the learning that took place in the puzzle box involved the strengthening of whatever behavior happened to be followed by escape and food. They placed cats in a puzzle box with a simple solution: A pole in the center of the chamber had only to be tipped in any direction to open the door. A camera outside the chamber photographed the cat at the same instant that the door swung open, thereby providing a permanent record of exactly how the subject had performed the effective response on each trial. The photographs revealed that after a few trials, each cat settled upon a particular method of manipulating the pole that was quite consistent from trial to trial. However, different subjects developed quite a variety of methods for moving the pole—one cat would always push the pole with its left forepaw, another would always rub the pole with its nose, and another would lie down next to the pole and roll over into it. Figure 6-3 shows the results from the first 24 trials for one cat. At first the cat's behavior at the moment of reinforcement varied greatly from trial to trial. By the ninth or tenth

trial, however, the animal began to develop a stereotyped method of operating the pole—it would walk to the left of the pole and brush against it with its backside. This method of moving the pole was produced in a very regular fashion on trials 15 through 24. Figure 6-4 shows the behavior of another cat, beginning on trial 52. This cat had developed the behavior of moving the pole by biting it while standing in a particular position.

The findings of Guthrie and Horton can be summarized by stating that after their subjects mastered the task, there was relatively little variability from trial to trial for a given subject, but considerable variability between subjects. These results provide evidence for a particular version of the Law of Effect that R. Brown and Herrnstein (1975) aptly called the **stop-action principle.** According to this principle, there is a parallel between the action of the camera and the reinforcer in the experiments of Guthrie and Horton. Like the camera, the occurrence of the reinforcer serves to stop the animal's ongoing behavior and strengthen the association between the situation (the puzzle box) and those precise behaviors that were occurring at the moment of reinforcement.

The stop-action principle states that because of this strengthening process, the specific bodily position and the muscle movements occurring at the moment of reinforcement will have a higher probability of occurring on the next trial. Of course, a single reinforcer may not be enough to guarantee the prompt recurrence of a behavior on the next trial, and by chance some other pattern of movement might displace the pole. This is shown by the fact that a cat's behavior varied considerably from trial to trial at first. However, one of these initial behaviors will eventually produce a second reinforcer, thereby further strengthening that S-R association and making it more likely that the behavior will occur again (and be strengthened still further). This sort of positive feedback process should eventually produce one S-R connection that is so much stronger than any other that its particular pattern of response will occur with high probability, trial after trial. This reasoning provides a simple explanation of why different cats developed different stereotyped techniques for moving the pole.

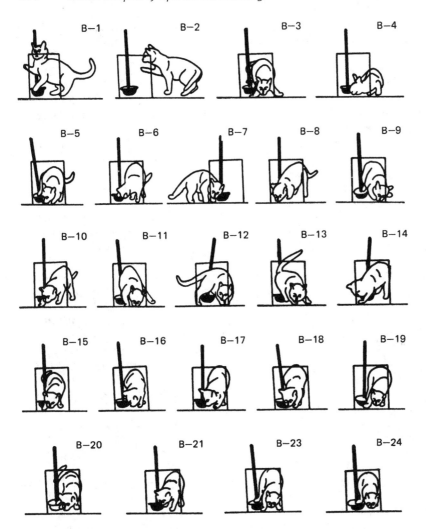

**FIGURE 6-3** The behavior of one cat (Subject B) in the puzzle box of Guthrie and Horton. The 24 pictures show the cat's position at the moment of reinforcement on the cat's first 24 trials in the puzzle box, where any movement of the vertical pole caused the door to open. (From Guthrie & Horton, 1946)

For each cat, whatever random behavior happened to get reinforced a few times would become dominant over other behaviors.

## Superstitious Behaviors

The mechanical nature of the stop-action principle suggests that behaviors may sometimes be strengthened "by accident." We have already seen this sort of fortuitous strengthening at work in the experiments of Guthrie and Horton. Different cats developed different styles of moving the pole, apparently as a consequence of what behaviors happened to precede reinforcement on each cat's first few trials in the puzzle box. The stereotyped way a particular cat responded in the puzzle box is an example of a **superstitious behavior,** because although some behavior that moved the pole was necessary for reinforcement, there was no

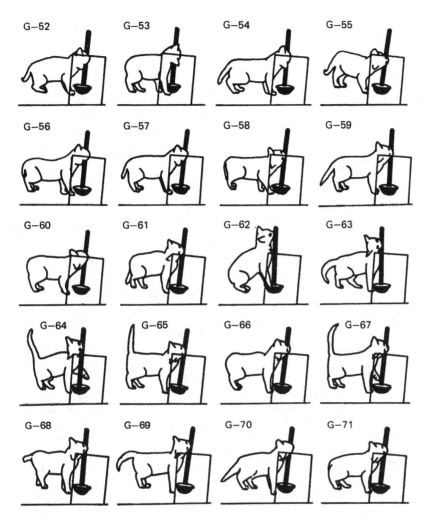

**FIGURE 6-4**　The behavior of another cat (Subject G) at the moment of reinforcement on trials 52 through 71 in the puzzle box. (From Guthrie & Horton, 1946)

requirement that the subject use approximately the same motion each time.

Skinner (1948) conducted a famous experiment, now often called the **superstition experiment,** that made a strong case for the power of accidental reinforcement. The subjects were pigeons, and each was placed in a separate experimental chamber in which grain was presented every 15 seconds regardless of what the pigeon was doing. After a subject had spent some time in the chamber, Skinner ob-

served the animal's behavior. He found that six of his eight subjects had developed clearly defined behaviors that they performed repeatedly between food presentations. One bird made a few counterclockwise turns between reinforcers, another made pecking motions at the floor, and a third repeatedly poked its head into one of the upper corners of the chamber. A fourth bird was observed to toss its head in an upward motion, and two others swayed from side to side. These behaviors occurred repeatedly despite the fact that no behavior was required for reinforcement. Similar results have been found by other researchers who repeated (with some variations) the basic idea of Skinner's experiment (Gleeson, Lattal, & Williams, 1989; Justice & Looney, 1990; Neuringer, 1970).

According to Skinner, these distinctive behaviors developed for the same reasons that the cats of Guthrie and Horton developed distinctive styles of moving the pole: Whatever behavior happened to be occurring when the reinforcer was delivered was strengthened. If the first reinforcer occurred immediately after a pigeon had tossed its head upward, this behavior of head tossing would be more likely to occur in the future. Therefore, there was a good chance that the next reinforcer would also follow a head-tossing motion. The accidental strengthening process is self-perpetuating, because once any one behavior develops a somewhat higher frequency of occurrence than all other behaviors, it has a greater chance of being reinforced, which increases its frequency still further, and so on.

Skinner (1948) proposed that many of the superstitious behaviors people perform are produced by the same mechanism that caused his pigeons to exhibit such peculiar behaviors:

> Rituals for changing one's luck at cards are good examples. A few accidental connections between a ritual and favorable consequences suffice to set up and maintain the behavior in spite of many unreinforced instances. The bowler who has released a ball down the alley but continues to behave as if he were controlling it by twisting and turning his arm and shoulder is another case in point. These behaviors have, of course, no real effect on one's luck or upon a ball half way down an alley, just as in the present case the food would appear as often if the pigeon did nothing—or, more strictly speaking, did something else. (p. 171)

Superstitious behaviors frequently arise when an individual actually has no control over the events taking place, as in card playing or other types of gambling, where winning or losing depends on chance. Lee (1996) had college students play a computer game in which winning or losing points was out of their control (although they did not know this). She found that the students tended to pick the same computer icons after successfully earning points, but to switch icons after a failure, even though the choice of icons had no effect on success or failure. Matute (1994, 1995) has also observed superstitious behaviors in situations where people have no control over events. In one experiment, college students were exposed to unpleasantly loud tones and were told that they could turn off the tones by typing the correct sequence of keys on a keyboard. In reality, the subjects had no control over the tones, which went on and off no matter what keys the subjects typed. Nevertheless, most of the subjects developed superstitious behaviors—they tended to type the same key sequences each time a tone came on. At the end of the experiment, many of the subjects said they believed that their typing responses did turn off the tones. Superstitious behaviors are also common among athletes. In a study of college football, track, and gymnastics teams, Bleak and Frederick (1998) found that an average player performed about 10 different superstitious behaviors, such as wearing a lucky charm or item of clothing, eating the same meal before each competition, or taping a part of the body that was not injured. Some superstitious behaviors occur without the athlete's awareness. When Ciborowski (1997) asked college baseball players to describe the behaviors they performed between pitches while batting (touching parts of the body or clothing, gripping the bat in certain ways, touching the ground or plate with the bat, and so on), the players were able to list most of them, but not all. However, when asked how many times they repeated these behaviors, the players' estimates were too low by a factor of four. Ciborowski found that the average player made 82 such movements in one time at bat.

Richard Herrnstein (1966) refined Skinner's analysis of human superstitions. Herrnstein noted that Skinner's analysis is most applicable to idiosyncratic superstitions, like those of a gambler or an athlete. It seems likely that such personalized superstitions arise out of an individual's own experience with reinforcement. On the other hand, superstitions that are widely held across a society (for example, the belief that it is bad luck to walk under a ladder, or that the number 13 is unlucky) are probably acquired through communication with others, not through individual experience. How these more common superstitions first arose is not known, but Herrnstein suggested that some may be the residue of previous contingencies of reinforcement that are no longer in effect. As an example, he cited the belief that it is bad luck to light three cigarettes on a single match. This superstition arose in the trenches during World War I. At that time, there was some justification for this belief, because every second that a match remained lit increased the chances of being spotted by the enemy. This danger is not present in everyday life, but the superstition is still passed on from generation to generation. Herrnstein speculated that it may be perpetuated by stories of occasional individuals who violate the rule and meet with an unfortunate fate. Thus Herrnstein claimed that some superstitions were originally valid beliefs and are now perpetuated by rumor and/or occasional coincidental events. It is easy to imagine how some superstitions (such as the one about walking under a ladder) may have begun, whereas the origins of others are less clear.

There has been relatively little experimental research on the social transmission of superstitious behaviors. However, in one study, preschool children were taught, either by the words of an adult or by watching another child on videotape, that pressing the nose of a mechanical clown might help them earn marbles (Higgins, Morris, & Johnson, 1989). Actually, this behavior had nothing to do with the delivery of marbles, which the clown presented at varying intervals no matter what a child was doing. Nevertheless, the children continued to perform this "superstitious" response, day after day, as long as a marble was delivered now and then.

Skinner's analysis of his superstition experiment is not the only possible interpretation, and other theories have been proposed. Staddon and Simmelhag (1971) conducted a careful replication of the superstition experiment, recorded the pigeons' behaviors more thoroughly than Skinner did, and came to different conclusions. In their superstition experiment, Staddon and Simmelhag found that certain be-

havior patterns tended to occur frequently in many or all of their subjects during the intervals between food deliveries. They found that these behaviors could be grouped in two major categories, which they called **interim behaviors** and **terminal behaviors.** Interim behaviors were defined as those that were frequent in the early part of the interval, when the next reinforcer was still some time away. Interim behaviors included pecking toward the floor, turning, and moving along the front wall of the chamber. Terminal behaviors were defined as behaviors that seldom occurred early in the interval but increased in frequency as the time of food delivery approached. Two of the most frequent terminal behaviors were orienting toward the food magazine and pecking in the vicinity of the magazine. To recapitulate, interim behaviors are those that occur frequently early in the interval between reinforcers, and terminal behaviors are those that occur frequently toward the end of the interval.

Staddon and Simmelhag proposed that some of the behaviors that Skinner called "superstitious behaviors," such as turning in circles, may actually have been interim behaviors. But interim behaviors are seldom followed by the delivery of food, because they do not often occur at the end of the interval. In other words, Staddon and Simmelhag argued that it is not accidental reinforcement that causes interim behaviors to increase in frequency. Instead, they proposed that interim behaviors are simply behaviors that a subject has an innate predisposition to perform when the likelihood of reinforcement is low. In short, interim behaviors are a reflection of an organism's hereditary endowment, not of the reinforcement process. In addition, certain terminal behaviors, such as pecking, may frequently occur when food is about to be delivered, and their appearance may be unrelated to any accidental reinforcement. Timberlake and Lucas (1985) proposed a similar theory about the possible role of hereditary behavior patterns in Skinner's superstition experiment.

It now seems clear that these alternate accounts of the superstition experiment are at least partly correct. Many studies have shown that the periodic delivery of food or some other reinforcer can give rise to a variety of stereotyped behaviors, which Staddon and Simmelhag called interim and terminal behaviors, and which others have called **adjunctive behaviors**. Thus, not all the behaviors that arise when periodic free reinforcers are delivered are the result of an accidental pairing with reinforcement. Some may simply be innate behaviors that become highly probable when the next reinforcer is some time away and the subject must do something to "pass the time."

On the other hand, it seems equally clear that Skinner's analysis of superstitious behaviors was also partly correct—sometimes behaviors increase in frequency because of the accidental pairing with reinforcement. In the laboratory, experiments with both adults and children have found that some (though not all) subjects developed superstitious behaviors when free reinforcers were periodically delivered (Ono, 1987; G. A. Wagner and Morris, 1987). These superstitious behaviors tended to increase just before a reinforcer was delivered, and they were distinctly different for different subjects (with one child kissing the nose of the mechanical clown that delivered marbles, another child puckering his mouth, and another child swinging his hips). Outside the laboratory, many idiosyncratic superstitions can be easily traced to past reinforcement. The superstitions displayed by many athletes are often the direct result of the success that followed these behaviors in the past, as the athletes themselves will admit.

### Problems with the Stop-Action Principle

Despite the evidence in its favor, it has long been recognized that the stop-action principle has its problems. A number of classic experiments demonstrated that animals learn much more than a single pattern of movements during the course of operant conditioning. In a study by Muenzinger (1928), guinea pigs had to run down an alley and then press a lever in order to obtain a piece of lettuce. Over hundreds of trials, Muenzinger observed the movements a guinea pig used to press the lever, classifying them into three categories—pressing with the left paw, pressing with the

right paw, and gnawing on the lever with the teeth. He reasoned that one of these three categories should eventually dominate the others. To see why, suppose that in the first 50 trials there were 25 left-paw responses, 20 right-paw responses, and 5 teeth responses. These early responses might reflect nothing more than a slight initial preference for the left paw. But since each response is supposedly strengthened by reinforcement, and since the left-paw response received more strengthenings than right-paw responses, the animal's initial preference for the left paw would be amplified. On the second 50 trials, we might expect to see perhaps 30 left-paw responses, 18 right-paw responses, and 2 teeth responses. On later trials, the additional strengthening of left-paw responses should make this behavior more and more frequent.

Muenzinger's results did not follow this pattern, however. Most of his subjects displayed response styles that varied unaccountably over trials, with left-paw responses in the majority at some times, right-paw responses at other times, and teeth responses at still other times. The stop-action principle offers no way to explain this variability in response styles.

One interpretation of Muenzinger's results might run as follows: Reinforcement strengthens not one particular movement pattern but an entire class of interchangeable movements. The three response types Muenzinger observed are all members of the same class because they all have the same effect on the environment—the lever is depressed. Therefore, when one member of the class (for example, a right-paw response) is reinforced, the future probability of all members of the class are strengthened. This analysis provides no explanation of the fluctuations in response types observed by Muenzinger; rather, it treats them as uninteresting, random variations within a class of interchangeable behaviors.

Lashley (1924) conducted a series of studies that provided stronger evidence for this view that reinforcing one specific behavior strengthens an entire class of behaviors with equivalent functions. In one study, rats had to wade through a maze filled with a few inches of water to reach a food reward. After the rats had learned to travel through the maze without errors, the water level was raised so that the rats had to swim instead of wade. If all the rats had learned was a specific set of muscle movements, it would be necessary for them to learn the maze anew, since the muscle movements of swimming are quite different from those used in wading. However, no such relearning was necessary, and the subjects swam through the maze correctly on their first trial with the deeper water. Lashley concluded that what rats learn in a maze is a sequence of turns, each of which brings them closer to the goal. This sequence of turns is not linked to any single pattern of muscle movements.

Studies such as those of Muenzinger and Lashley showed that even the simplest operant responses exhibit a remarkable degree of adaptability and flexibility. If you are not impressed with this flexibility, consider how difficult it would be to build a robot with similar adaptability of movement. If you happen to be skilled in mechanics and electronics, given sufficient time and money you might be able to build a robot that could walk through a maze and learn from its incorrect turns. Yet imagine how much more difficult it would be to build a robot with the adaptability of movement possessed by an average mammal. Such a robot would be able to swim through the maze if it were flooded, to hop on one foot if the other foot were injured, to crawl using its arms and elbows if both legs were paralyzed, and so on. The task of building such a skillful robot would be immense. Similarly, the task of discovering how animals can exhibit such flexibility of movement has proven to be a difficult one for psychologists and physiologists. Chapter 13 will survey some of what is known about how animals and people learn to perform new skilled movements.

## THE PROCEDURE OF SHAPING, OR SUCCESSIVE APPROXIMATIONS

Whereas the experiments of Guthrie and Horton favored the view that a specific set of muscle movements and bodily positions was strengthened at the moment of reinforcement,

Figures 6-3 and 6-4 show that in its strictest sense, this viewpoint is incorrect. Although the stereotyped nature of these cats' behaviors is unmistakable, a certain amount of variability in bodily position from trial to trial is evident as well. This variability in behavior might annoy a meticulous theorist interested in predicting behaviors precisely, but it is actually an indispensable commodity for psychological researchers, animal trainers, and behavior therapists. Variability in behavior provides the means by which a totally new behavior, never performed by an individual before, can gradually be developed. The procedure that makes use of behavioral variability is known as **shaping,** or the technique of **successive approximations.**

### Shaping Lever Pressing in a Rat

Suppose that as part of your laboratory work in a psychology course, you are given a rat in an experimental chamber equipped with a lever the rat can press and a pellet dispenser. You have a remote-control button that, when pressed, delivers one food pellet to the food tray in the chamber. Your task is to train the rat to press the lever at a modest rate. Since you have learned about Thorndike's experiments, you may believe that this task will be very simple: Your strategy is simply to wait until the rat presses the lever by accident and then deliver a food pellet. This reinforcer should strengthen the response of pressing the lever, and your plan is to deliver a food pellet for every lever press, thereby gradually increasing the probability of this response.

Although this plan sounds reasonable, there are at least two ways it might fail. Suppose that after a few minutes in the chamber your rat presses the lever, and you immediately press the button to deliver a food pellet. However, the operation of the pellet dispenser makes a loud click that startles the rat and causes it to freeze for 10 or 15 seconds. About a minute later, the animal finally discovers the food pellet in the tray and eats it. We have seen that the contiguity between response and reinforcer is an important requirement of the Law of Effect—whatever behavior immediately precedes reinforcement will be strengthened. In this case, the behavior that immediately preceded the rat's discovery of the food pellet was not pressing the lever (as you had intended) but rather approaching the food tray. If it did anything, the reinforcer may have strengthened the rat's tendency to approach or explore the food tray.

The problem is that you need a reinforcer that you can be sure the animal will receive immediately after the correct response is made. A common solution to this problem is to develop the sound of the pellet dispenser into a conditioned reinforcer. A **conditioned reinforcer** is a previously neutral stimulus that has acquired the capacity to strengthen responses because that stimulus has been repeatedly paired with food or some other primary reinforcer. (A **primary reinforcer** is a stimulus that naturally strengthens any response it follows. Primary reinforcers include food, water, sexual pleasure, and comfort.) If you repeatedly expose your subject to the sound of the pellet dispenser followed by the delivery of a food pellet, the sound of the dispenser should become a conditioned reinforcer. You can be sure that this has been accomplished when the rat will quickly return to the food tray from any part of the chamber as soon as you operate the dispenser.

At this point, your initial plan might work. If you present the sound of the dispenser immediately after the rat presses the lever, the response of lever pressing should be strengthened. However, there is yet another difficulty you might encounter. Suppose the lever is 5 inches above the floor of the chamber, and it takes an effortful push from your subject to fully depress the lever. Under these circumstances, you might wait for hours and the rat might never depress the lever. And of course, you cannot reinforce a response that never occurs.

It is in this situation that the variability inherent in behavior becomes helpful. A good way to start would be to wait until the rat is below the lever and then to reinforce any detectable upward head movement. After 5 or 10 reinforcers for such a movement, the rat will probably exhibit an upward head movement soon after consuming the previous food pellet.

Once this behavior is well established, the procedure of shaping consists of gradually making your criterion for reinforcement more demanding. For example, the next step might be to wait for an upward head movement of at least half an inch. At first your subject may make a few head movements of less than half an inch (which you do not reinforce), but because of the variability in such behaviors, a movement of the required size will most likely occur. Each reinforcement of such a larger movement will increase the probability of another similar response, and soon the rat will be making these responses regularly. You can then go on to demand upward movements of 1 inch, 1.5 inches, and so on, until the animal is bringing its head close to the lever. The next step might be to require some actual contact with the lever, then contact with one forepaw, then some downward movement of the lever, and so on, until the rat has learned to make a full lever press.

Figure 6-5 provides a graphic illustration of how the procedure of shaping makes use of the variability in the subject's behavior. Suppose that before beginning the shaping process, you simply observed the rat's behavior for 5 minutes, making an estimate every 5 seconds about the height of the rat's head above the floor of the chamber. Figure 6-5 provides an example of what you might find: The $y$-axis shows the height of the rat's head to the nearest half inch, and the $x$-axis shows the number of times this height occurred in the 5-minute sample. The resulting frequency distribution indicates that the rat usually kept its head about 1.5

You can test your skill at shaping the behaviors of two animated creatures at the following Web sites. Which creature is easier to train?

- *http://www.uwm.edu/People/johnchap/oc.htm*
- *http://epsych.msstate.edu/adaptive/Fuzz/fuzzApplet.html*

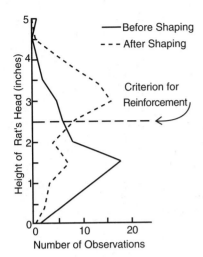

**FIGURE 6-5** Hypothetical distributions showing the height of a rat's head as observed at regular intervals before shaping (solid line) and after selective reinforcement of head heights greater than 2.5 inches (dotted line). Rachlin (1970) presents a similar analysis of the shaping process.

inches from the floor, but sometimes its head was lower and sometimes much higher. Given such a distribution, it might make sense to start the shaping process with a requirement that the rat raise its head to a height of at least 2.5 inches before it is reinforced. Figure 6-5 also illustrates how the frequency distribution would probably shift after the shaping process began.

### Shaping Behaviors in the Classroom

The procedure of successive approximations can be used to produce totally new behaviors in people as well as in laboratory rats. At many colleges and universities, stories abound about how the students in a large lecture course collaborated to shape the behavior of their professor. In one such story, a professor who usually stood rigidly behind the lectern was reinforced by his students for any movement, and by the end of the hour he was pacing back and forth and gesturing wildly with his arms. In another story, a professor in an introductory psychology course lectured from an elevated stage. The students secretly agreed to reinforce the professor for any movement to the left. The reinforcers they used were listening attentively, nodding their heads in apparent understanding of what he was saying, and taking notes. Whenever the professor moved to the right, however, they stopped delivering these reinforcers—they would stop taking notes, yawn, look bored, and look around the room. This systematic delivery of reinforcers for movement to the left was apparently quite successful, for legend has it that about halfway through the lecture the professor fell off the left side of the stage (which was only about 18 inches high).

Stories of this type suggest that shaping can work even when the subject is unaware of what is going on. If the professors in these stories realized what their students were doing, they probably would have resisted this behavioral control (perhaps on the stubborn belief that it is the behavior of students that should be shaped in the classroom, not the professor's).

### Shaping as a Tool in Behavior Modification

Not all examples of shaping are as frivolous as those described in the last section. Shaping is frequently used in behavior therapy for individuals with severe behavior problems. As one example, Isaacs, Thomas, and Goldiamond (1960) used this procedure to reinstate speech in a 40-year-old patient in a mental institution. This patient, who was classified as a catatonic schizophrenic, had not spoken at all since he entered the institution 19 years earlier. At this point, a behavior therapist began to work with the patient, meeting with him about three times a week. More or less by accident, the therapist found that chewing gum could be used as a reinforcer for this patient.

During the first two weeks, the therapist would hold up a stick of gum and wait for the patient's eyes to look toward the gum. As soon as they did, he would give the patient the gum.

By the end of the second week, the patient's eyes looked toward the gum as soon as it was presented. In the third and fourth weeks, the therapist's criterion was any detectable lip movement, and soon lip movements occurred as soon as the gum was presented. The therapist then required any audible vocalization before giving the *gum*, and then attempted to get the patient to say the word gum by holding up the gum and saying, "Say gum, gum." At the end of the sixth week, the patient suddenly said, "Gum, please." He subsequently answered questions about his name and age.

This patient's case was by no means a total success, because after additional reinforcement procedures, he began to talk to other members of the hospital staff but not to other patients or visitors. The difference between these two classes of individuals was that the hospital staff was instructed to respond only to verbal communications of the patient, whereas patients and visitors would reinforce the patient's silent gestures by attempting to understand them and give the patient what he wanted. Of course, these two patterns of behavior provide further support for the effects of reinforcement on the patient's verbal behavior: He would speak in those situations where only speech was reinforced, but he would communicate with gestures in those situations where gestures were reinforced with attention and compliance with his requests.

Some might find it interesting to speculate why this patient had been mute for so many years. In light of his rapid recovery of speech after the first word was spoken, it seems unlikely that the patient was unable to speak. Was it the case, however, that he believed he was unable to speak? Was he mute because he was reinforced for his silence, or because he was punished in some way when he did speak? Unfortunately, we will never know the answers to these questions. What we do know, however, is that 19 years of the standard hospital treatment (along with whatever "common sense" strategies the hospital staff may have used to try to encourage speech) were totally unsuccessful for this patient. In contrast, after only 18 one-hour sessions of behavior therapy, a modest level of speech was restored. Although the technique of successive approximations may sound simple, it is by no means a procedure that is so obvious that it occurs to every professional in the field of mental health. The literature on behavior modification records many such cases where the use of shaping or some other straightforward behavioral technique was never considered by those in charge of a patient, but where the patient made rapid progress once the recommendations of a specialist in behavior modification were followed.

The technique of shaping has become a common component of behavior modification programs. For instance, it has been employed to reduce cocaine use among pregnant women who are cocaine dependent (Elk, Schmitz, Spiga, Rhoades, Andres, & Grabowski, 1995). It has been used as a way to increase school attendance in a mentally retarded teenager (Meyer, Hagopian, & Paclawskyj, 1999), as a replacement for written instructions on how to take a computerized test (Anger, Rohlman, & Sizemore, 1994), and to teach self-care skills to a mentally disabled patient (Katzmann & Mix, 1994). These are just a few of the many cases in which shaping has been used to improve the lives of people with a variety of different problems. Shaping procedures are now also being used to teach computer-controlled robots to learn new skills (Savage, 1998).

## Making Shaping More Precise: Percentile Schedules

As it has been described so far, shaping is more of an art than an exact science. Whether the learner is a person or an animal, it usually takes a skilled and experienced trainer to use shaping effectively. Many split-second decisions must be made about which behaviors to reinforce and which not to reinforce, how quickly the criterion for reinforcement should be increased, how large a step in the criterion should be made, what to do when the learner has a setback, and so on. Naturally, some trainers will be more skilled than others, and no two trainers will use exactly the same techniques. It would certainly be advantageous to make the rules for shaping more precise and explicit, so that two different trainers could use exactly the same techniques and so that the most effective techniques could be quickly learned by an inexperienced trainer.

Galbicka (1994) has suggested that the technique of shaping can be made more precise and more effective through the use of **percentile schedules of reinforcement**. A reinforcement schedule is a rule that states exactly when a reinforcer will or will not be delivered. The most common types of reinforcement schedules will be thoroughly discussed in Chapter 7, but percentile schedules will be examined here because of their connection to the shaping process.

In a percentile schedule, a given response is reinforced if it is better than a certain percentage of the last several responses that the learner has made (Platt, 1973). This abstract definition may be hard to understand, so let us take a specific, if hypothetical, example. Imagine that a boy is doing poorly in school because he is easily distracted from his work and therefore does not complete his assignments on time. A behavior therapist might use a percentile schedule to shape more and more rapid completion of his work. Suppose the student is told to work on a series of math problems, and the therapist records how many problems are correctly completed each minute. In the first six minutes, the boy completes 3, 4, 5, 2, 3, and 2 problems. The therapist then establishes a percentile schedule in which the boy is rewarded each minute if his performance is better than in four of the last six minutes. The reinforcers could be points that can later be exchanged for money, snacks, or some other tangible reinforcers. In this example, the four lowest scores in the last six minutes were 3, 2, 3, and 2 problems, so in the seventh minute, the boy's performance will be reinforced if he completes more than 3 problems.

Every minute, the criterion for reinforcement could change, because it depends on the performance of the last six minutes. Suppose that a bit later in the math class, the boy's scores for the last six minutes are 4, 5, 6, 7, 5, and 4 correct problems. Now, the four lowest scores are 4, 5, 5, and 4, so in the next minute the boy must complete at least 6 problems to receive a reinforcer.

Notice the similarities between this percentile schedule and the more informal shaping procedure. In both cases, the criterion for reinforcement begins at a relatively low level that reflects the learner's current behavior. The criterion is set so that the required behavior is well within the learner's current ability level, but only better performances are reinforced. This selective reinforcement of better performances should cause the learner's performance to improve. The difference from the usual shaping procedure, however, is that the rules for reinforcement are very specific, and nothing is left to the discretion of the trainer. Of course, initial decisions must still be made about how much of the learner's past performance to include (in this example, we arbitrarily used six minutes) and what percentage of the responses to reinforce (here, only responses in the top third of the subject's recent performances were reinforced). Once these decisions are made, however, any reasonably intelligent trainer could apply these rules and presumably obtain the same results.

In fact, Galbicka (1994) has pointed out that even a computer can be programmed to deliver reinforcers according to percentile schedules, as long as the computer is capable of recording and evaluating the learner's responses. The preceding example of training math performance is one that could be easily adapted to a computerized format, and so could many other academic and vocational skills. Some computer software already used in classrooms does adopt the essence of this approach, by keeping track of each student's performance and tailoring the difficulty of the material to each child's rate of improvement. In this way, the slower learners are given additional practice with simpler concepts until they master them, and the faster learners are not held back, but are given more difficult material to keep them challenged.

## Versatility of the Shaping Process

We have already seen that the applicability of classical conditioning is relatively limited as a theory of learned behaviors: Classical conditioning applies only to those behaviors that are reliably elicited by some stimulus (the US). In comparison, the Law of Effect is much more widely applicable, even if we consider only the strict stop-action approach favored by Guthrie and Horton. The stop-action principle applies not only to behaviors that are preceded by a specific stimulus but to any behavior the subject produces. As long as a behavior such as pressing a lever, stepping on a platform, or pulling a chain occurs once in a while, we can patiently wait for the desired behavior to occur, follow it with a reinforcer, and the frequency of that behavior should increase. To put it simply, the stop-action principle can be used to increase the frequency of any behavior that is part of the subject's repertoire. However, once the procedure of shaping is added to the Law of Effect, its applicability is extended still further. The procedure of shaping utilizes the variability inherent in a creature's behavior to develop totally new behaviors, which the subject has never performed before and probably would never perform in the absence of a shaping program. For instance, a rat can be taught to press a lever that is high above its head or one that requires so much effort to operate that the animal must get a running start and throw all of its weight onto the lever. In principle, at least, the applicability of the shaping process is limited only by the capabilities of the subject—if the subject is capable of making the desired behavior, the careful employment of the technique of successive approximations should eventually be successful in producing the appearance of the behavior.

## THE RESEARCH OF B. F. SKINNER

Whereas Thorndike deserves credit for the first systematic investigations of the principle of reinforcement, it was B. F. Skinner who was primarily responsible for the increasing interest in this topic during the middle of the twentieth century. Skinner himself discovered many of the most basic and most important properties of reinforcement. In addition, he trained several generations of students whose ongoing research continues to enrich our knowledge about the ways that reinforcement affects the behavior of people and animals.

Skinner used the terms *operant conditioning* and *instrumental conditioning* to describe the procedure in which a behavior is strengthened through reinforcement. Both of these terms reflect the large degree of control the subject has over the most important stimulus in the environment—the reinforcer. The delivery of the reinforcer is contingent on the subject's behavior—no reinforcer will occur until the subject makes the required response. For example, in Thorndike's puzzle box the reinforcer (escape and food) might occur after 5 seconds or after 500 seconds, depending entirely on when the animal made the appropriate response. The term operant conditioning reflects the fact that the subject obtains reinforcement by operating on the environment in this paradigm. The term instrumental conditioning is suggestive of the fact that the subject's behavior is instrumental in obtaining the reinforcer.

### The Free Operant

In his research on operant conditioning, Skinner modified Thorndike's procedure in a simple but very important way. Research with the puzzle box involved a **discrete trial procedure:** A trial began each time a subject was placed in the puzzle box, and the subject could make one and only one response on each trial. The primary dependent variable was response latency. After each trial, the experimenter had to intervene, physically returning the subject to the puzzle box for the next trial. This procedure was time-consuming and cumbersome, and only a small number of trials could be conducted each day (due to the fatigue of both subject and experimenter). Other operant conditioning procedures that were popular in the early part of the century, such as those involving runways or mazes with a reinforcer at the end, shared these same disadvantages.

Skinner's innovation was to make use of a response that the subject could perform repeatedly without the intervention of the experimenter. When experimenting with rats, researchers of the Skinnerian tradition typically use lever pressing as the operant response. When the subjects are pigeons, the most frequently measured response is the key peck: One or more circular plastic disks, called response keys, are recessed in one wall of the experimental chamber (see Figure 6-6), and the bird's pecks at these keys are recorded. Procedures that make use of lever pressing, key pecking, or similar responses are called **free operant procedures,** so as to distinguish them from the discrete trial procedures of the puzzle box or maze. The distinguishing characteristics of a free operant procedure are that (1) the operant response can occur at any time, and (2) the operant response can occur repeatedly for as long as the subject remains in the experimental chamber. Indeed, responses such as lever pressing and key pecking require so little effort that a subject can make thousands of responses in a single session.

Along with this change in procedures came a change in independent variables: Instead of using latency as a measure of response strength, Skinner used **response rate** (most commonly measured as responses per minute). One major advantage of the free operant procedure, with its large number of responses, is that the experimenter can observe and record the moment-to-moment variations in response rate that occur

**FIGURE 6-6** A pigeon pecking at a lighted key in a typical operant conditioning chamber. Grain is provided as a reinforcer through the square opening beneath the key.

as a subject learns about the experimental situation or as some external stimulus is changed.

## The Three-Term Contingency

In its simplest form, a contingency is a rule that states that some event, B, will occur if and only if another event, A, occurs. Simple classical conditioning provides one example of such a contingency: The US will occur if and only if the CS occurs first. It is sometimes said that in operant conditioning, there is a contingency between response and reinforcer—the reinforcer occurs if and only if the response occurs. Skinner pointed out, however, that there are actually three components in the operant conditioning contingency: (1) the context or situation in which a response occurs (that is, those stimuli that precede the response), (2) the response itself, and (3) the stimuli that follow the response (that is, the reinforcer). To be more specific, Skinner noted that the contingency in operant conditioning usually takes the following form: In the presence of a specific stimulus, often called a **discriminative stimulus,** the reinforcer will occur if and only if the operant response occurs. Because of the three components—discriminative stimulus, response, and reinforcer—Skinner called this relationship a **three-term contingency.**

Suppose a pigeon learns to peck a key for food pellets in a chamber that has a bright yellow light just above the key. When the light is on, each response produces a food pellet, but when the light is off, no food pellets are delivered. If the light is periodically turned on and off during the course of the experiment, the pigeon will learn to discriminate between these two conditions and respond only when the light is on. This type of discrimination learning is important in many real-world situations, because a response that is reinforced in one context may not be reinforced in another. For example, a child must learn that the behavior of telling jokes may be reinforced if it occurs during recess but punished if it occurs during math class. The term **stimulus control,** refers to the broad topic of how stimuli that precede a behavior can control the occurrence of that behavior. Chapter 10 will examine this topic in detail.

### Other Basic Principles: Acquisition, Extinction, Spontaneous Recovery, Generalization, and Conditioned Reinforcement

All of these principles have counterparts in classical conditioning that we have already examined, so a brief discussion of them will suffice here. Thorndike's results (as in Figure 6-2) demonstrate that the acquisition of an operant response, like that of a CR, is usually a gradual process. In operant conditioning, the procedure of extinction involves no longer following the operant response with a reinforcer, and as in classical conditioning, the response will weaken and eventually disappear. If the subject is returned to the experimental chamber at some later time, spontaneous recovery of the operant response will typically be observed. Thus the idealized response patterns shown in Figure 4-6 could represent the acquisition, extinction, and spontaneous recovery of an operant response just as well as a classically conditioned response.

In the preceding section, we saw that discrimination learning can occur in operant conditioning as well as in classical conditioning. The opposite of discrimination, generalization, is also a common phenomenon in operant conditioning. Let us return to the example of the pigeon that learned to discriminate between the presence and absence of a bright yellow light. Suppose the color of the light were now changed to green or orange, and no more reinforcers were delivered. Despite this change in color, the subject would probably continue to peck at the key for a while, until it learned that no more reinforcers were forthcoming. In other words, the pigeon generalized from the yellow light to a light of another color, even though it had never been reinforced for pecking in the presence of this other color. If we tested a number of different colors, we would probably obtain a typical generalization gradient in which responding was most rapid in the presence of yellow and less and less rapid with colors less and less similar to yellow.

In operant conditioning, the phenomenon of conditioned reinforcement (also called **secondary reinforcement**) is in many ways analogous to second-order classical conditioning. As discussed in Chapter 4, if some CS (such as a light) is repeatedly paired with a US, that CS can then take the place of the US in classical conditioning with a second CS (say, a tone). If the tone is now repeatedly paired with a light, the tone will start to elicit CRs, which is the same thing that would happen if the tone were paired with the US itself. We might say that the first-order CS, the light, acts as a surrogate for the US in second-order conditioning.

In operant conditioning, the counterpart to the US is the primary reinforcer. The counterpart to the first-order CS is the initially neutral stimulus that becomes a conditioned reinforcer through repeated pairings with the primary reinforcer. The conditioned reinforcer can then act as a surrogate for the primary reinforcer, increasing the strength of any response that it follows. In an early study on conditioned reinforcement, Skinner (1938) presented rats with repeated pairings of a clicking sound and food. No responses were required of the subjects during this phase of the experiment. In the second phase of the experiment, food was no longer presented; nevertheless, the rats learned to press a lever when this response produced only the clicking sound. Naturally, since the clicking sound was no longer paired with food, it is not surprising that the lever pressing did not persist for long. This is another way in which first-order CSs and conditioned reinforcers are similar: If a conditioned reinforcer is no longer paired with a primary reinforcer, it eventually loses its capacity to act as a reinforcer, just as a first-order CS loses its ability to condition a second-order CS if it is repeatedly presented without the US.

Skinner used the term **generalized reinforcers** to refer to a special class of conditioned reinforcers—those that are associated with a large number of different primary reinforcers. Perhaps the best example of a generalized reinforcer is money. The potency of this reinforcer in maintaining the behaviors of workers in our society is clear—few employees would remain on the job if informed that their employer could no longer pay them any salary. Money is a generalized reinforcer (and a very powerful one) precisely because it can be exchanged for so many different stimuli that are inherently reinforcing for most people—food, clothing, material possessions, entertainment, exciting vacations. Although money is a powerful reinforcer, it should be clear that its power, like that of all conditioned reinforcers, is dependent on its continued association with primary reinforcers. If money could no longer be exchanged for any primary reinforcers, it would be difficult to find individuals willing to work simply to obtain green pieces of paper.

Some everyday human behaviors are maintained by conditioned reinforcers that are several times removed from any primary reinforcer. Consider a college student who is diligently studying for an upcoming midterm exam in elementary calculus. If there is nothing inherently reinforcing about studying calculus for this student, why is the behavior occurring? Skinner would attribute this behavior to the student's past experience with the conditioned reinforcer of a good grade—the student has presumably had numerous experiences throughout her life in which studying for an exam was followed by a good grade on the exam. A good grade on an exam is not a primary reinforcer, however; it simply brings the student one step closer to another conditioned reinforcer—a good final grade in the course. A good course grade makes it more likely that the student will obtain a good job after graduation (another conditioned reinforcer), which will provide a decent salary (another conditioned reinforcer), which can finally be exchanged for a wide range of primary reinforcers. Considering all the steps that separate the behavior of studying from primary reinforcement, it is not surprising that this behavior has a low frequency of occurrence among some students, especially when they have no inherent interest in the subject matter of a course.

## Response Chains

In Chapter 3, we examined the concept of a reaction chain, which is a sequence of innate behaviors that occur in a fixed order. A similar concept involving learned behaviors is the **response chain,** which is defined as a sequence of behaviors that must occur in a specific order, with the primary reinforcer being delivered only after the final response of the sequence. Some of the clearest examples of response chains are displayed by animals trained to perform complex sequences of behavior for circus acts or other public performances. Imagine a hypothetical performance in which a rat climbs a ladder to a platform, pulls a rope that opens a door to a tunnel, runs through the tunnel to another small platform, slides down a chute, runs to a lever, presses the lever, and finally receives a pellet of food. Ignoring for the moment how the rat could be trained to do this, we can ask what maintains the behavior once it has been learned.

The first response, climbing the ladder, brings the rat to nothing more than a platform and a rope. These are certainly not primary reinforcers for a rat. Skinner would claim, however, that these stimuli act as conditioned reinforcers for the response of climbing the ladder because they bring the animal closer to primary reinforcement than it was before. Besides serving as conditioned reinforcers, the platform and rope also act as discriminative stimuli for the next response of the chain, pulling the rope. The conditioned reinforcer for this response is the sight of the door opening, for this event brings the subject still closer to primary reinforcement. Like the platform and rope, the open door also serves a second function—it is a discriminative stimulus for the next response, running through the tunnel.

We could go on to analyze the rest of the response chain in a similar fashion, but the general pattern should be clear by now. Each stimulus in the middle of a response chain is assumed to serve two functions: It is a conditioned reinforcer for the previous response and a discriminative stimulus for the next response of the chain. This analysis is depicted graphically in Figure 6-7, where $S^D$ stands for "discriminative stimulus" and $S^R$ stands for "reinforcing stimulus."

How would an animal trainer go about teaching a rat to perform this sequence? One very effective strategy, sometimes called **backward chaining,** is to start with the last response of the chain and work backward. After

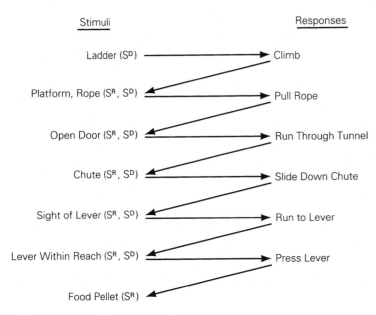

**FIGURE 6-7** The alternating sequence of stimuli and responses in the hypothetical response chain described in the text. Each stimulus within the chain serves as a conditioned reinforcer for the previous response and as a discriminative stimulus for the next response.

teaching the rat where to obtain its food reinforcement and establishing the sound of the food dispenser as a conditioned reinforcer, the trainer could start to shape the last response of the chain, pressing the lever. Once this response was well established, the trainer might place the rat on the bottom of the chute. It is very likely that the rat would move from this position to the lever, since the lever will now act as a conditioned reinforcer (having been previously paired with food). By additional shaping, the animal could be trained to slide down the chute to reach the lever, then to travel through the tunnel to reach the chute, and so on. Some shaping with food as a primary reinforcer might be required for some links of the chain (for instance, pulling the rope). Once the response was established, however, the primary reinforcement could be removed and the behavior would be maintained by the conditioned reinforcement provided by the next stimulus of the chain, a stim-

ulus that signaled that the animal was one step closer to the primary reinforcer.

Backward chaining is one effective way to teach a response chain, but it is not the only way. In **forward chaining,** the teacher starts by reinforcing the first response of the chain, and then gradually adding the second response, the third response, and so on. For example, in learning to use a laundromat, retarded adolescents were first reinforced just for finding an empty washing machine. Next, they were reinforced for finding an empty machine and putting in the soap, then for finding an empty machine, putting in the soap, loading the clothes, and so on (McDonnell & McFarland, 1988). Still another training method is the **total task method;** here the individual is taught all of the steps of a response chain at once, using verbal instructions to prompt the correct response at each step. All these methods for teaching response chains (along with other variations) have been used successfully, and which is most effective seems to depend on exactly what types of behaviors are being taught (Ash & Holding, 1990; Hur & Osborne, 1993).

Response chains are similar in some ways to the innate reaction chains described in Chapter 3. Both consist of an alternating pattern of stimuli and responses (compare Figure 3-5 with Figure 6-7). In both, each successive stimulus acts to terminate the preceding behavior and to "set the occasion" for the next behavior of the chain. A major difference between innate and learned response chains, however, is that only the latter depends on reinforcement for its continued integrity. If a reaction chain is completely innate, its component behaviors are not dependent on any external reinforcer, nor can they be modified by experience—each behavior will continue to be highly probable whenever its eliciting stimuli are present.

In contrast, the behaviors of a learned response chain will eventually disappear if the primary reinforcement is eliminated. It is also interesting to observe what happens if one of the conditioned reinforcers in the middle of the chain is eliminated. The general rule is that all behaviors that occur before the "broken link" of the chain will be extinguished, whereas those that occur after the broken link will continue to occur. For example, suppose that pulling the rope no longer opens the door to the tunnel. The response of rope pulling will eventually stop occurring, as will the behavior of climbing the ladder that leads to the platform and rope. On the other hand, if the rat is placed beyond the broken link (inside the tunnel or at the top of the chute), the remainder of the chain should continue to occur as long as the final response is followed by the primary reinforcer. Because they are the farthest from the primary reinforcer, responses near the beginning of a response chain should be the weakest, or the most easily disrupted. Behavior therapists frequently make use of this principle when attempting to break up a response chain that includes some unwanted behaviors (such as walking to the drugstore, buying a pack of cigarettes, opening the pack, lighting a cigarette, and smoking it). Efforts to interrupt this chain should be most effective if applied to the earliest links of the chain.

## BIOLOGICAL CONSTRAINTS ON OPERANT CONDITIONING

Just as biological factors affect what is learned in classical conditioning, they play an important role in operant conditioning. Two phenomena, instinctive drift and autoshaping, both discovered in the 1960s, raised serious questions about the power of reinforcement to modify and control a creature's behavior. The stories of how these phenomena were discovered and the theoretical debates surrounding them provide us with some valuable lessons about the strengths and limitations of the general principles of learning.

### Instinctive Drift

Learning theorists, especially those who specialize in operant conditioning, have generally believed that reinforcement exerts a simple but powerful influence on behavior: Behaviors that are reinforced will increase in frequency, and those that are not will decrease and eventually disappear. When shaping, generalization, chaining, and other basic principles are added to this idea, it should be possible to teach complex and intricate sequences of behavior to both people and animals. Two psychologists who attempted to apply the principles of operant conditioning outside the laboratory were Keller Breland and Marian Breland. After studying with B. F. Skinner, the Brelands became animal trainers and

Can you tell the difference between everyday examples that do and do not illustrate the principle of positive reinforcement? Quiz yourself at *http://server.bmod.athabascau.ca/html/prtut/reinpair.htm.*

worked with many different species, teaching complex and frequently amusing patterns of behavior. Their animals were trained for zoos, fairs, TV commercials, and other public performances.

The Brelands' business was successful, and over the years they trained several thousand animals. On the surface, at least, it appeared that they had demonstrated that principles from the laboratory were usable in less controlled settings and applicable to creatures ranging from whales to reindeer. Despite the success of their business, however, the Brelands began to notice certain recurrent problems in their use of reinforcement techniques. They referred to these problems as "breakdowns of conditioned operant behavior." In an article entitled "The Misbehavior of Organisms" (Breland and Breland, 1961), they described several of their "failures" in the use of reinforcement. The following is one example:

> Here a pig was conditioned to pick up large wooden coins and deposit them in a large "piggy bank." The coins were placed several feet from the bank and the pig required to carry them to the bank and deposit them, usually four or five coins for one reinforcement. (Of course, we started out with one coin, near the bank.)
>
> Pigs condition very rapidly, they have no trouble taking ratios, they have ravenous appetites (naturally), and in many ways are among the most tractable animals we have worked with. However, this particular problem behavior developed in pig after pig, usually after a period of weeks or months, getting worse every day. At first the pig would eagerly pick up one dollar, carry it to the bank, run back, get another, carry it rapidly and neatly, and so on, until the ratio was complete. Thereafter, over a period of weeks the behavior would become slower and slower. He might run over eagerly for each dollar, but on the way back, instead of carrying the dollar and depositing it simply and cleanly, he would repeatedly drop it, root it, drop it again, root it along the way, pick it up, toss it up in the air, drop it, root it some more, and so on.
>
> We thought this behavior might simply be the dilly-dallying of an animal on a low drive. However, the behavior persisted and gained in strength in spite of a severely increased drive—he finally went through the ratios so slowly that

he did not get enough to eat in the course of a day. Finally it would take the pig about 10 minutes to transport four coins a distance of about 6 feet. This problem behavior developed repeatedly in successive pigs. (p. 683)

This example differs from the instances of contraprepared associations discussed in Chapter 5. Here, the problem was not that pigs had difficulty learning the required response: At first, a pig would carry the coins to the bank without hesitation. It was only later that new, unreinforced behaviors—dropping and rooting the coins—appeared and increased in frequency. The Brelands noted that the intruding behaviors were those that pigs normally perform as part of their food-gathering repertoires. Because these behaviors appeared to be related to the subject's innate responses, they called them examples of **instinctive drift:** With extensive experience, the subject's performance drifted away from the reinforced behaviors and toward instinctive behaviors that occur when the animal is seeking the reinforcer (in this case, food) in a natural environment.

It is interesting to compare the behavior of pigs with that of a raccoon in a similar situation. The task was to pick up coins and place them in a small container. With just one coin, the raccoon learned, with a little difficulty, to pick it up and drop it in the container, after which it received food as a reinforcer. When the raccoon was given two coins simultaneously, however, its behavior deteriorated markedly. Instead of picking up the coins and depositing them quickly (which would provide the most immediate reinforcement), the raccoon would hold onto the coins for several minutes, frequently rubbing them together, and occasionally dipping them into the container and pulling them out again. Although these behaviors were not reinforced, they became more and more prevalent over time, and the swift sequence of depositing the coins that the Brelands desired was never achieved.

You may recognize a similarity between this raccoon's behaviors and those of the pigs. The raccoon's intruding behaviors resemble those that are part of its food-gathering repertoire. A raccoon may repeatedly dip a piece of food in a stream before eating it, and the rubbing motions are similar to those it might use in removing the shell from a crustacean. Notice, however, that in the present context these behaviors were inappropriate in two respects: (1) The coins were not food, the container was not a stream, and there was no shell to be removed by rubbing the coins together, and (2) the intruding behaviors did not produce food reinforcement, and indeed they actually postponed its delivery.

The Brelands reported that they had found numerous other examples of this sort of instinctive drift, and they claimed that these examples constituted "a clear and utter failure of conditioning theory" (1961, p. 683). The problem was perfectly clear: Animals exhibited behaviors that the trainers did not reinforce in place of behaviors the trainers had reinforced.

## Autoshaping

In 1968, P. L. Brown and Jenkins published an article entitled "Auto-shaping of the Pigeon's Key-peck." They presented their findings as simply a method for training pigeons to peck a key that was easier and less time-consuming than manual shaping. Naive pigeons were deprived of food and taught to eat from the grain dispenser. After this, a bird was exposed to the following contingencies: At irregular intervals averaging 60 seconds, the response key was illuminated with white light for 8 seconds, and then the key was darkened and food was presented. Despite the fact that no response was necessary for the delivery of food, all of the pigeons began to peck at the lighted key. The trial on which the first key peck was recorded ranged from trial 6 for the fastest bird to trial 119 for the slowest.

Whereas autoshaping did seem to be an easier way to train the response of key pecking, psychologists soon realized the more important theoretical significance of the Brown and Jenkins result. Key pecking had been used in countless experiments because it was considered to be a "typical" operant response—a response that is controlled by its consequences. Yet here was an experiment in which the key-peck response was not necessary for reinforce-

ment, yet it occurred anyway. Why did the pigeons peck at the key? Several different explanations were proposed.

***Autoshaping as Superstitious Behavior.*** Brown and Jenkins suggested that autoshaping might be an example of a superstitious behavior, as discussed earlier in this chapter. Consider the following scenario: At first, when the key is lit, the pigeon simply *looks toward* the key, and a reinforcer is delivered a few seconds later. This might accidentally strengthen the behavior of looking at the key. On the next trial, the bird might again look up when the key is lit, and when this behavior does not immediately produce the reinforcer, the bird might *approach* the key, and at this moment the reinforcer might occur. On later trials, a bird might *get closer* to the key, *make contact* with the key, and eventually *peck* at the key, and all of these behaviors might be adventitiously reinforced by the food. This scenario depicts a process by which the bird's behavior is gradually shaped into a key peck through the presentation of a reinforcer that is not actually contingent on any response.

Although this hypothesis is ingenious, an experiment by Rachlin (1969) suggested that it is wrong. Using a procedure similar to that of Brown and Jenkins, Rachlin photographed pigeons on each trial at the moment reinforcement was delivered. The photographs revealed no tendency for the birds to get progressively closer to the key and finally peck it. On the trial immediately preceding the trial of the first key peck, a pigeon might be far from the key, looking in another direction, at the moment of reinforcement. There was no hint of a gradual shaping process at work.

More evidence against the superstition interpretation came from a study in which the food reinforcer was eliminated from any trial on which the pigeon pecked at the lighted key (Williams & Williams, 1969). The results of this experiment were quite remarkable: Even though no food ever followed a key peck, pigeons still acquired the key-peck response and persisted in pecking at the lighted key on about one third of the trials. This experiment showed quite convincingly that key pecking in an autoshaping procedure is not an instance of superstitious behavior.

***Autoshaping as Classical Conditioning.*** A number of researchers have proposed that autoshaping is simply an example of classical conditioning intruding into what the experimenter might view as an operant conditioning situation (B. R. Moore, 1973). Several types of evidence support this idea. As most people know, pigeons eat grain by pecking at the kernels with jerky head movements. We might say that pecking is the pigeon's unconditioned response to the stimulus of grain. According to the classical conditioning interpretation, this response of pecking is transferred from the grain to the key because the lighted key is repeatedly paired with food.

Further support for this interpretation comes from studies in which food can be delivered at any time during a session, but the probability of food might be either higher when the key light is on than when it is off, lower when the key light is on, or the same when the key light is on as when it is off. Pigeons will peck at the lighted key in the first condition but not in the other two (Durlach, 1986). These results parallel Rescorla's (1966, 1968) findings from classical conditioning experiments that showed that excitatory conditioning will occur when there is a positive CS-US correlation, but not when there is a zero or negative correlation between CS and US (Chapter 4). Other researchers have found that autoshaping occurs when the lighted key provides information about the upcoming food, but it is reduced or eliminated when the lighted key is redundant with other signals for food (Allaway, 1971; Wasserman, 1973). In short, the data show that autoshaping is successful when the lighted key is predictive of food, but not otherwise. This same general rule applies to the relationship between CS and US in traditional classical conditioning preparations.

Some intriguing evidence that also favors the classical conditioning interpretation of autoshaping comes from experiments in which the researchers either photographed or closely observed the behaviors of their subjects. In an important series of experiments by Jenkins and Moore (1973), illumination of a response key was regularly followed by the presentation of food for some pigeons and by the presentation of water for other pigeons. In both cases the pigeons began to peck at the lighted key. However, by filming the pigeons' responses, Jenkins and Moore were able to demonstrate that the pigeons' movements toward the key differed depending on which reinforcer was used. When the reinforcer was food, a pigeon's response involved an abrupt, forceful pecking motion made with the beak open wide. These movements are similar to those a pigeon makes when eating. When the reinforcer was water, the response was a slower approach to the key with the beak closed or nearly closed. On some trials, swallowing movements and a rhythmic opening and closing of the beak were observed. All of these movements are part of the pigeon's characteristic drinking pattern.

Jenkins and Moore proposed that these behaviors were clear examples of Pavlov's concept of stimulus substitution. The lighted key served as a substitute for either food or water, and responses appropriate for either food or water were directed at the key. In one experiment, they observed these two response styles with a single pigeon in a single session when illumination of the left key signaled water and illumination of the right key signaled food Figure 6-8 shows some representative responses on the left key (top row) and on the right key (bottom row). Notice the different beak and eyelid positions in the two sets of photographs.

Although P. L. Brown and Jenkins (1968) used the term autoshaping to refer to their specific experiment, in which pigeons pecked a lighted key that preceded food, later writers have used the term to refer to any situation in which an organism produces some behavior in response to a signal that precedes and predicts an upcoming reinforcer. Others have called this phenomenon **sign-tracking,** because the animal watches, follows, and makes contact with a signal for an upcoming reinforcer. In this broader sense, autoshaping (or sign-tracking) has been observed in many species, and many of the examples are consistent with the

**FIGURE 6-8** Photographs of a pigeon's key pecks when the reinforcer was water (top row) and when the reinforcer was grain (bottom row). Notice the different beak and eyelid movements with the two different reinforcers. (From Jenkins & Moore, 1973)

stimulus substitution theory of classical conditioning. For example, G. B. Peterson, Ackil, Frommer, and Hearst (1972) videotaped the behavior of rats to a retractable lever that was inserted into the chamber and illuminated 15 seconds before the delivery of each reinforcer. For some rats, the reinforcer was food, and for others it was electrical stimulation of the brain. Both groups of rats made frequent contact with the lever, but the topographies of their responses were distinctly different. Rats with the food reinforcer were observed to gnaw and lick the lever, whereas those with brain stimulation as a reinforcer would touch the lever lightly with paws or whiskers, or they might sniff and "explore" the lever. The gnawing and licking behaviors were, of course, similar to the rats' responses to the food itself. Peterson and coworkers also reported that the behaviors and postures of individual rats in response to the lever when it signaled brain stimulation were frequently similar to their behaviors and postures during the delivery of brain stimulation. Thus the two different reinforcers elicited two different behavior patterns, and

these patterns were mirrored in the rats' responses to the lever that was paired with reinforcement.

***Autoshaping as the Intrusion of Instinctive Behavior Patterns.*** Whereas the studies described in the preceding paragraphs provide support for the stimulus substitution interpretation of autoshaping, other studies do not. Wasserman (1973) observed the responses of 3-day-old chicks to a key light paired with warmth. In an uncomfortably cool chamber, a heat lamp was turned on briefly at irregular intervals, with each activation of the heat lamp being preceded by the illumination of a green key light. All chicks soon began to peck the key when it was green, but their manner of responding was unusual—a chick would typically move very close to the key, push its beak into the key, and rub its beak from side to side in what Wasserman called a "snuggling" behavior. Similar responses were observed in chicks exposed to a negative automaintenance procedure, in which any contact with the key canceled the activation of the heat lamp on that trial. These snuggling responses resembled behaviors a newborn chick normally makes to obtain warmth from a mother hen: The chick pecks at the feathers on the lower part of the hen's body, then rubs its beak and pushes its head into the feathers.

On the surface, this study seems to provide another example of stimulus substitution—a warmth-seeking behavior pattern is displayed to a signal for warmth. The problem, however, is that the chicks in the experiment exhibited a very different set of behaviors in response to the heat lamp itself. When the heat lamp was turned on, there was no pecking or snuggling; instead, a chick would extend its wings (which allowed it to absorb more of the heat) and stand motionless. On other trials, a chick might extend its wings, lower its body, and rub its chest against the floor. Thus, although both snuggling and wing extension are warmth-related behaviors for a young chick, there was essentially no overlap between a chick's responses to the key light and its responses to the heat lamp. For this reason, Wasserman concluded that the stimulus substitution account of autoshaping is inadequate and that the physical properties of the signal also determine the form of autoshaped responses.

Other experiments support Wasserman's conclusions. For example, Timberlake and Grant (1975) observed the behaviors of rats when the signal preceding the delivery of a food pellet was the entry of another rat (restrained on a small moving platform) into the experimental chamber. Since a food pellet elicits biting and chewing responses, the stimulus substitution interpretation of autoshaping predicts that a subject should perform these same biting and chewing responses to the restrained rat, because the rat is a signal for food. Not surprisingly, Timberlake and Grant observed no instances of biting or chewing responses directed toward the restrained rat. However, they did observe a high frequency of other behaviors directed toward the restrained rat, including approach, sniffing, and social contact (pawing, grooming, and climbing over the other rat).

In some of the examples of autoshaping we have reviewed, the signal elicits behaviors that resemble the behaviors produced by the reinforcer, as the stimulus substitution approach would predict. In other cases the behaviors elicited by the signal are different from those elicited by the reinforcer, but they seem to be behaviors involved in obtaining that type of reinforcer in the animal's natural environment. Thus, with rats, which usually feed in groups, the presence of a restrained rat predicting food elicited approach, exploration, and social behaviors—all behaviors that might occur during the course of a food-seeking expedition. With young chicks, a signal preceding the activation of a heat lamp elicited some of these birds' normal warmth-seeking behaviors. Timberlake and Grant (1975) interpreted the results as follows:

> As an alternative to stimulus substitution, we offer the hypothesis that auto-shaped behavior reflects the conditioning of a system of species-typical behaviors commonly related to the reward. The form of the behavior in the presence of the predictive stimulus will depend on which behaviors in the conditioned system are elicited and supported by the predictive stimulus. (p. 692)

Timberlake (1983, 1993) has called this interpretation of autoshaped behaviors a **behavior-systems analysis** to reflect the idea that different reinforcers evoke different systems or collections of behaviors. An animal may have a system of food-related behaviors, a system of water-related behaviors, a system of warmth-seeking behaviors, a system of mating behaviors, and so on. Exactly which behavior from a given system will be elicited by a signal depends in part on the physical properties of that signal. For instance, in Wasserman's study, the characteristics of the response key (such as a distinctive visual stimulus about head high) evidently lent themselves more readily to snuggling than to wing extension, so that the former was observed rather than the latter.

Notice that the predictions of Timberlake's behavior-systems approach are more ambiguous than those of the stimulus substitution approach. It would be difficult (at least for me) to predict in advance whether a green key light would be more likely to elicit wing extension, snuggling, or some other warmth-related behavior. Nevertheless, the behavior-systems approach does make testable predictions because it states that the behaviors provoked by a signal will depend on the type of reinforcer that usually follows the signal. The theory predicts quite clearly that a signal for warmth should elicit behaviors that are part of the animal's warmth-seeking behavior system, not those that are part of its feeding system or its drinking system. Although these predictions are less specific than those of stimulus-substitution theory, they are certainly in closer agreement with the evidence on the form of autoshaped behaviors.

The behavior-systems approach can help to predict what types of behaviors are likely to be seen in many different learning situations. For example, Silva and Timberlake (1997) used this approach to predict that different types of conditioned responses should be seen depending on whether a CS is long or short. They reasoned that with a long-duration CS, behavior systems related to chasing and capturing prey would be evoked, whereas a short-duration CS should evoke behavior systems related to the handling and consumption of food. In support of this prediction, they found that during an 18-second CS, rats tended to approach and touch a moving object, whereas with a 2-second CS, they were more likely to put their noses in the food tray and wait for a food pellet. Timberlake and his colleagues (Silva & Timberlake, 2000; Timberlake & Lucas, 1989) have shown that the behavior-systems approach can be applied to a variety of learning phenomena (including autoshaping, instinctive drift, preparedness, backward conditioning, and others).

*Summary.* Regardless of whether we emphasize the hereditary aspects of autoshaped behaviors or their similarity to classically conditioned CRs, both autoshaped behaviors and instinctive drift seem to pose severe difficulties for operant conditioners. Breland and Breland (1961) summarized the problem nicely: "The examples listed we feel represent clear and utter failure of conditioning theory. . . . The animal simply does not do what it has been conditioned to do" (p. 683).

## Reconciling Reinforcement Theory and Biological Constraints

How do those who believe in the general-principle approach to learning, and especially in the principle of reinforcement, respond to these cases where the general principles do not seem to work? First, let us consider the phenomenon of autoshaping.

As we have seen, early discussions of autoshaped behavior suggested that it posed major problems for the general-principle approach because it seemed to defy the rules of operant conditioning. Later analyses suggested that autoshaping is simply an instance of classical conditioning. Although there may be aspects of autoshaped responses that distinguish them from other types of conditioned responses (Swan & Pearce, 1987; Wasserman, 1973), it is now commonly believed that autoshaping is in fact a good example of classical conditioning. And like taste-aversion learning (see Chapter 5), autoshaping is now widely used as a procedure for studying basic principles of classical conditioning (for example, Locurto, Terrace, & Gibbon, 1981; Nakajima, 2000; Rescorla, 1999). Autoshaping therefore appears to be a type of behavior that is quite consistent with the general-principle approach to learning after all (but with the principles of classical conditioning rather than operant conditioning).

The evidence on instinctive drift in operant conditioning cannot be dealt with so easily. Here, it is not just that reinforced behaviors are slow to be learned. What happens is that totally different, unreinforced behaviors appear and gradually become more persistent. These behaviors are presumably part of the animal's inherited behavioral repertoire. As the Brelands discovered, these behaviors often cannot be eliminated by using standard reinforcement techniques, so it might appear that the principle of reinforcement is simply incorrect—it cannot explain why these behaviors arise and are maintained. Indeed, some researchers have asserted that the concept of reinforcement is inadequate and should be abandoned (Timberlake, 1983, 1984).

How might a psychologist who relies heavily on the concept of reinforcement react to this empirical evidence and the theoretical challenges it poses? The reactions of B. F. Skinner are worth examining. First of all, it is important to realize that Skinner has always maintained that an organism's behavior is determined by both learning experiences and heredity. Well before biological constraints on learning became a popular topic, Skinner had written about the hereditary influences on behavior in several places (Heron and Skinner, 1940; Skinner, 1956b, 1966). Later, Skinner (1977) stated that he was neither surprised nor disturbed by phenomena such as instinctive drift or autoshaping. He asserted that these are simply cases where phylogenetic (hereditary) and ontogenetic (learned) influences on behavior are operating simultaneously: "Phylogeny and ontogeny are friendly rivals and neither one always wins" (p. 1009).

In other words, we should not be surprised that hereditary factors can compete with and sometimes overshadow the reinforcement contingencies as determinants of behavior. For example, if reinforcers are delivered at regular, periodic intervals, a variety of unreinforced behaviors appear between reinforcers. As discussed previously, Staddon and Simmelhag (1971) called these interim and terminal behaviors, and collectively they have been called adjunctive behaviors. Adjunctive behaviors can take a variety of forms. If food is delivered at periodic intervals, and if water is available between the food reinforcers, animals may consume substantial amounts of water (Falk, 1961). Other common adjunctive behaviors include aggression (Cohen & Looney, 1973), wheel running (King, 1974), and retreat from the location of food delivery (Cohen & Campagnoni, 1989). Adjunctive behaviors have also been observed with human subjects. In one study, college students played a game of backgammon in which they had to wait for fixed periods of time (and could not watch) as their opponents made their moves. When these waiting periods were long, several behaviors unrelated to playing the game—bodily movement, eating, and drinking—increased in frequency (Allen & Butler, 1990). Although the causes of adjunctive behaviors are still being debated, the main point is that these be-

haviors appear even though they have nothing to do with earning the reinforcer.

The examples of adjunctive behaviors, autoshaping, and instinctive drift do not mean that the principle of reinforcement is flawed; they simply show that reinforcement is not the sole determinant of a creature's behavior. Critics who use these data to claim that the principle of reinforcement should be abandoned appear to be making a serious logical mistake—they conclude that because a theoretical concept cannot explain everything, it is deficient and should be abandoned. This conclusion does not follow from the premises. It is just as incorrect as the claim of some radical environmentalists (such as Kuo, 1921) that all behaviors are learned, none innate. This chapter (and each of the next several chapters) provides overwhelming evidence that the delivery of reinforcement contingent upon a response is a powerful means of controlling behavior. No amount of evidence on the hereditary influences on behavior can contradict these findings.

There is a growing consensus in the field of learning that the research on biological constraints does not forecast the end of the general-principle approach, but rather that it has provided the field with a valuable lesson (see, for example, Domjan, 1983; Domjan & Galef, 1983; Herrnstein, 1977; Logue, 1988). This research shows that an animal's hereditary endowment plays an important part in many learning situations, and the influence of heredity cannot be ignored. As we learn more about how these biological factors exert their influence, we will be better able to understand and predict a creature's behavior.

## CHAPTER SUMMARY

If a response is followed by a reinforcer, the frequency of that response will increase. Thorndike demonstrated this principle in his experiments with cats in the puzzle box, and he called it the Law of Effect. Using photography, Guthrie and Horton found that whatever motion a cat happened to make at the moment of reinforcement tended to be repeated on later trials. Different cats learned distinctly different styles of making the same response. If a response is strengthened when, by mere coincidence, it is followed by a reinforcer, it is called a superstitious behavior. B. F. Skinner reported seeing superstitious behaviors in a famous experiment with pigeons. Accidental reinforcement may account for the unusual rituals performed by some gamblers and athletes.

The procedure of shaping, or successive approximations, involves reinforcing any small movement that comes closer to the desired response, and then gradually changing the criterion for reinforcement until the desired behavior is reached. Shaping is a common part of many behavior modification procedures.

B. F. Skinner used the term *three-term contingency* to describe the three-part relation between a discriminative stimulus, an operant response, and a reinforcer. Responses can be strengthened by either primary reinforcers or conditioned reinforcers. Contingencies between stimuli and responses can have more than three components, as in a response chain, which consists of an alternating series of stimuli and responses, and only the last response is followed by a primary reinforcer.

While using operant conditioning techniques to train animals, Breland and Breland discovered instinctive drift: the animals would begin to display innate behaviors associated with the reinforcers, even though these behaviors were not reinforced. When Brown and Jenkins repeatedly paired a lighted key with food, pigeons eventually began to peck at the key. They called this phenomenon *autoshaping*. Such examples of biological constraints in operant conditioning do not mean that the principle of reinforcement is incorrect, but they do show that behavior is often controlled by a mixture of learning and hereditary influences.

## REVIEW QUESTIONS

1. What is the stop-action principle? How did Guthrie and Horton demonstrate this principle? Describe an experiment that shows how this principle may account for the development of superstitious behaviors.

2. Give an example to show how the procedure of successive approximations can be used to teach an animal to perform a new response. Give an example of how this procedure can be used in a behavior modification program with a human learner.

3. Explain how response chains include all of the following: discriminative stimuli, operant responses, conditioned reinforcers, and a primary reinforcer. Describe at least two different techniques for teaching a response chain.

4. What are instinctive drift and autoshaping? How do psychologists who study reinforcement respond to critics who say that these examples of biological constraints show that the principle of reinforcement is flawed?

## CHAPTER 7

# Reinforcement Schedules: Experimental Analyses and Applications

Among B. F. Skinner's many achievements, one of the most noteworthy was his categorization and experimental analysis of **reinforcement schedules.** A reinforcement schedule is simply a rule that states under what conditions a reinforcer will be delivered. To this point, we have mainly considered cases in which every occurrence of the operant response is followed by a reinforcer. This schedule is called **continuous reinforcement** (abbreviated CRF), but it is only one of an infinite number of possible rules for delivering a reinforcer. The real world provides countless examples of situations in which a particular response is sometimes, but not always, followed by a reinforcer. A salesman may knock on several doors in vain for every time he succeeds in selling a magazine subscription. A typist may type dozens of pages, comprised of thousands of individual keystrokes, before finally receiving payment for a completed job. A predator may make several unsuccessful attempts to catch a prey before it finally obtains a meal. Recognizing that most behaviors outside the laboratory receive only intermittent reinforcement, Skinner devoted considerable effort to the investigation of how different schedules of reinforcement have different effects on behavior (Ferster & Skinner, 1957).

## PLOTTING MOMENT-TO-MOMENT BEHAVIOR: THE CUMULATIVE RECORDER

Besides developing the free operant procedure, which makes it possible to collect a large amount of data from a single subject each session, Skinner constructed a simple mechanical device, the **cumulative recorder,** which records these responses in a way that allows any observer to see at a glance the moment-to-moment patterns of a subject's behavior. Figure 7-1 shows how the cumulative recorder works. A slowly rotating cylinder pulls a roll of paper beneath a pen at a steady rate, so the *x*-axis of the resultant graph, the **cumulative record,** represents time. If the subject makes no response, a horizontal line is the result. However, each response causes the pen to move up the page by a small increment (in a direction perpendicular to the movement of the paper), so the *y*-axis represents the cumulative number of responses the subject has made since the start of the session.

As Figure 7-1 shows, a cumulative record tells much more than the overall number of responses. Segments of the record that have a fairly even linear appearance correspond to periods in which the subject was responding at a

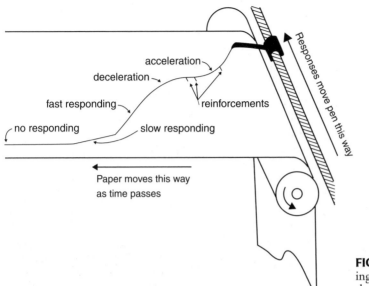

**FIGURE 7-1** A simplified drawing of a cumulative recorder and the type of graph it produces.

steady rate—the greater the slope, the faster the response rate. Figure 7-1 also shows how an acceleration or deceleration in response rate would appear in the cumulative record. Finally, small downward deflections in a cumulative record generally indicate those times at which a reinforcer was delivered. With these points in mind, we can now examine how the schedule of reinforcement determines a subject's pattern of responding.

## THE FOUR SIMPLE REINFORCEMENT SCHEDULES

### Fixed Ratio

The rule for reinforcement in a fixed-ratio (FR) schedule is that a reinforcer is delivered after every *n* responses, where *n* is the size of the ratio. For example, in an FR 20 schedule, every 20 responses will be followed by a reinforcer. If an animal begins with an FR 1 schedule (which is the same as continuous reinforcement) and then the ratio is gradually increased, the subject can be trained to make many responses for each reinforcer. For example, many animals will respond for food reinforce-

ment on FR schedules where 100 or more responses are required for each reinforcer. The behavior of many species (including pigeons, rats, monkeys, and human beings) on FR schedules have been studied, and in most cases the general characteristics of the behavior are similar. After a subject has performed on an FR schedule for some time and has become acquainted with the requirements of the schedule, a distinctive pattern of responding develops. As Figure 7-2 shows, responding on an FR schedule exhibits a "stop-and-go" pattern: After each reinforcer, there is a pause in responding that is sometimes called a **postreinforcement pause.** Eventually, this pause gives way to an abrupt continuation of responding. Once responding begins, the subject typically responds at a constant, rapid rate (note the steep slopes in the cumulative record) until the next reinforcer is delivered.

Outside the laboratory, perhaps the best example of fixed-ratio schedules is the "piecework" method used to pay factory workers in some companies. For instance, a worker operating a semiautomatic machine that makes door hinges might be paid $10 for every 100 hinges made. When I was an undergraduate, I

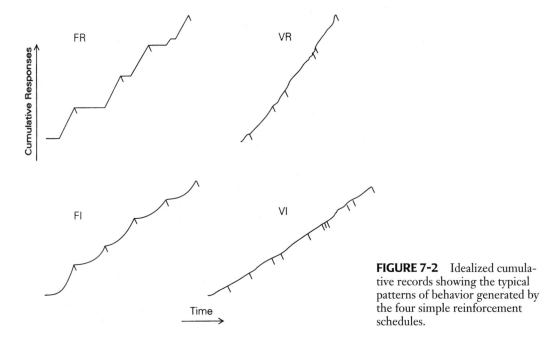

**FIGURE 7-2**   Idealized cumulative records showing the typical patterns of behavior generated by the four simple reinforcement schedules.

worked in a factory for several summers, and I had the opportunity to observe workers who were paid by the piecework system. Their behavior was quite similar to the FR pattern shown in Figure 7-2. Once a worker started up the machine, he almost always worked steadily and rapidly until the counter on the machine indicated that 100 pieces had been made. At this point, the worker would record the number completed on a work card and then take a break—he might chat with friends, have a soda or a cup of coffee, or glance at a newspaper for a few minutes. After this pause, the worker would turn on the machine and produce another 100 hinges. These workers needed very little supervision from their boss. The boss did not have to prod them to work faster or chastise them for taking excessively long breaks. The schedule of reinforcement, which delivered reinforcers in direct proportion to the amount of work done, was sufficient to maintain the performance of these workers.

Several other features of performance on FR schedules deserve mention. First, the average size of the postreinforcement pause increases as the size of the ratio increases. For example, with a pigeon pecking a key, the average pause may be only a second or so with an FR 20 schedule, but it may be several minutes long with an FR 200 schedule. In contrast, the subject's rate of responding after the postreinforcement pause decreases fairly gradually as the size of the ratio increases (Crossman, Bonem, & Phelps, 1987; Powell, 1969). With very large ratios, however, the animal may start to exhibit long pauses at times other than right after reinforcement. The term **ratio strain** is sometimes used to describe the general weakening of responding that is found when large response:reinforcer ratios are used.

### Variable Ratio

The only difference between an FR schedule and a **variable-ratio** (VR) schedule is that on the latter, the number of required responses is not constant from reinforcer to reinforcer. To be specific, the rule for reinforcement on a VR *n* schedule is that *on average*, a subject will receive one reinforcer for every *n* responses, but the exact number of responses required at any moment may vary widely. When an experiment is controlled by a computer, a VR schedule is sometimes implemented by giving the computer a list of possible ratio sizes from which it selects at random after each reinforcer to determine the number of responses required for the next reinforcer. For example, a list for VR 10 might contain the ratios 1, 2, 3, 4, 5, 6, 10, 19, and 40. In the long run, an average of 10 responses will be required for each reinforcer, but on a given trial, the required number may be as few as 1 or as many as 40. In a special type of VR schedule called a **random ratio** (RR) schedule, each response has an equal probability of reinforcement. For instance, in an RR 20 schedule, every response has one chance in 20 of being reinforced regardless of how many responses have occurred since the last reinforcer.

Figure 7-2 shows a typical cumulative record from a VR schedule. The pattern of responding might be described as rapid and fairly steady. The major difference between FR performance and VR performance is the absence of long postreinforcement pauses on VR schedules. Although it is sometimes stated that there are no postreinforcement pauses on VR schedules, this is not strictly correct. With VR schedules of modest length, regular postreinforcement pauses are found (Kintsch, 1965), and they get longer as the size of the ratio gets larger (Blakely & Schlinger, 1988). The important difference, however, is that the pauses on VR schedules are several times smaller than those found on FR schedules with equal response:reinforcer ratios (Mazur, 1983). Intuitively, the reason for the shorter postreinforcement pauses on VR schedules seems clear: After each reinforcer, there is at least a small possibility that another reinforcer will be delivered after only a few additional responses.

Many forms of gambling are examples of VR schedules. Games of chance, such as slot machines, roulette wheels, and lotteries, all exhibit the two important characteristics of VR schedules: (1) A person's chances of winning are directly proportional to the number of times the person plays, and (2) the number of responses required for the next reinforcer is uncertain. It is the combination of these two features that makes gambling an "addiction" for some people—gambling behavior is strong and persistent because the very next lottery ticket or the very next coin in a slot machine could turn a loser into a big winner. Ironically, the characteristics of a VR schedule are strong enough to offset the fact that in most forms of gambling, the odds are against the player, so that the more one plays, the more one can be expected to lose.

Although games of chance are among the purest examples of VR schedules outside the laboratory, many other real-world activities, including most sports activities, have the properties of a VR schedule. Consider the behavior of playing golf. As one who is very fond of this activity, I know that this behavior is maintained by quite a few different reinforcers, such as companionship, exercise, sunshine, fresh air, and picturesque scenery. Most of these reinforcers are delivered on a schedule that is approximately continuous reinforcement—that is, they occur almost every time one goes golfing. Yet these are certainly not the only reinforcers at work, because each of these reinforcers could be obtained just as easily (and without paying greens fees) by taking a hike in the woods with friends. And although I also enjoy a walk in the woods, I can attest (as can, I am sure, millions of other golfers) that the game of golf offers additional reinforcers that a walk in the woods does not. These include the thrill and satisfaction that come from playing well, either through an entire round or on a single shot. Nearly every golfer can boast of a few outstanding shots and of occasional days when every iron shot happened to land on the green and every putt seemed to drop. Regardless of what factors cause such occasional excellent performances, what is important from a behavioral perspective is that they are unpredictable. Each time a golfer walks to the first tee, there is a chance that this round will be his or her best. On each shot when the flagstick is within the golfer's range, there is a chance that the ball will end up in the hole or very close to it. This continual possibility of an outstanding round or at least a spectacular shot is probably an important reason why the average golfer keeps returning to the course again and again.

Some other behaviors reinforced on VR schedules include playing practically any competitive sport; fishing; hunting; playing card games or video games; watching the home team play; going to fraternity parties, and so forth. You should be able to see that the delivery of reinforcers for each of these activities fits the definition of a VR schedule: The occasion of the next reinforcer is unpredictable, but in the long run, the more often the behavior occurs, the more rapidly will reinforcers be received.

### Fixed Interval

In all interval schedules, the presentation of a reinforcer depends both on the subject's behavior and on the passage of time. The rule for reinforcement on a **fixed-interval** (FI) schedule is that the first response after a fixed amount of time has elapsed is reinforced. For example, in an FI 60-second schedule, immediately after one reinforcer has been delivered, a clock starts to time the next 60-second interval. It does not matter whether the subject makes no responses during this interval or 100 responses—none of them will do any good whatsoever. However, at the 60-second mark, a reinforcer is "stored" (that is, the apparatus is now set to deliver a reinforcer), and the next response will produce the reinforcer.

If the subject had either a perfect sense of time or access to a clock, the optimal behavior on an FI schedule would be to wait exactly 60 seconds and then make one response to collect the reinforcer. However, because no subject has a perfect sense of time and because a clock is usually not provided for the subject to watch, subjects on FI schedules typically make many more responses per reinforcer than the one that is required. Figure 7-2 shows the typical pattern of responding found on FI schedules. As on FR schedules, there is a postreinforcement pause, but after this pause, the subject usually starts by responding quite slowly (unlike the abrupt switch to rapid re-

sponding on an FR schedule). As the interval progresses, the subject responds more and more rapidly, and just before reinforcement, the response rate is quite rapid. For obvious reasons, the cumulative record pattern from this class of schedule is sometimes called a **fixed-interval scallop.**

The FI schedule does not have many close parallels outside the laboratory, because few real-world reinforcers occur on such a regular temporal cycle. However, one everyday behavior that approximates the typical FI pattern of accelerating responses is waiting for a bus. Imagine that you are walking to a bus stop and that just as you arrive you see a bus leave. Suppose that you are not wearing a watch, but you know that a bus arrives at this stop every 20 minutes, so in the meantime, you sit down on a bench and start to read a book. In this situation, the operant response is looking down the street for the next bus. The reinforcer for this response is simply the sight of the next bus. (This may seem like a fairly weak reinforcer, but once you see the bus coming, you can walk up to the curb and make sure the driver sees you and stops.) At first, the response of looking for the bus may not occur at all, and you may read steadily for 5 or 10 minutes before your first glance down the street. Your next glance may occur 1 or 2 minutes later, and now you may look down the street every minute or so. After 15 minutes, you may put away the book and stare down the street almost continuously until the bus arrives.

Other situations in which important events occur at regular intervals can produce similar patterns of accelerating behavior. In a clever experiment, Mawhinney, Bostow, Laws, Blumenfeld, and Hopkins (1971) examined one such situation. These researchers measured the study behavior of college students in a psychology course, and they found that the pattern of this behavior varied quite predictably, depending on the schedule of examinations. As mentioned earlier, the conditioned reinforcer of a good grade on an exam is an important reinforcer for studying. So that the students' study behavior could be measured, all the readings for the course were available only in a special room in the library, and the materials could not be taken out of this room. The amount of time each student spent studying in this room was recorded by observers who watched through a one-way mirror.

During the first two weeks of the course, a short quiz (worth 5 points) was scheduled for each class meeting. In the next three weeks there were no quizzes, but a longer exam (worth 60 points) was given at the end of the third week. The second half of the term mimicked the first half, with two weeks of daily quizzes followed by three weeks with a large exam at the end. The weeks with daily quizzes approximated a CRF schedule of reinforcement, for every day of studying might be reinforced with a good grade on the next day's quiz. The exams after three weeks were more like an FI schedule, for there was no immediate reinforcer for studying during the early parts of the three-week period. This arrangement is not exactly like an FI schedule, because on an FI schedule, no response except the last has any effect, whereas studying early in the three-week period presumably had some beneficial effect in terms of the grade on the exam. Despite this difference, Figure 7-3 shows that the patterns of the students' study behavior during the two three-week periods were similar to typical FI performance—there was little studying during the early parts of the three-week period, but the amount of studying steadily increased as the exam approached. In contrast, study behavior was more stable from day to day when the students had daily quizzes. This experiment demonstrates that an instructor's selection of a schedule of quizzes or exams can have a large effect on the study behavior of the students in the course.

Although an accelerating response pattern is a common result when FI schedules are in effect, this scalloping pattern is not always found. For example, some research with both human and animal subjects has found cases in which FI performance looks more like the stop-and-go pattern that is characteristic of FR schedules (Baron & Leinenweber, 1994). In other cases, human subjects exhibit long pauses and very low response rates. The reasons for these different response patterns on FI schedules are still not well understood, but one important factor may be what types of alternative behaviors are available during the intervals between reinforcers. Barnes and Keenan (1993) found the classic scalloped patterns when subjects could read or watch TV during these intervals, but when these activities were not available, subjects made just a few responses toward the end of the interval.

### Variable Interval

**Variable-interval** (VI) schedules are like FI schedules except that the amount of time that must pass before a reinforcer is stored varies unpredictably from reinforcer to reinforcer. For example, in a VI 60-second schedule, the time between the delivery of one reinforcer and the storage of another might be 6 seconds for one reinforcer, then 300 seconds for the next, 40 seconds for the next, and so on. As on FI schedules, the first response to occur after a reinforcer is stored collects that reinforcer, and the clock does not start again until the reinforcer is collected.

As Figure 7-2 shows, VI schedules typically produce a steady, moderate response rate. At an intuitive level, this manner of responding seems sensible in light of the characteristics of the schedule. Since a reinforcer might be stored at any moment, a long pause after reinforcement would not be advantageous. By maintaining a steady response rate, the subject will collect each reinforcer soon after it is stored, thus keeping the VI clock moving most of the time. On the other hand, a very high response rate, such as that observed on a VR schedule, would produce only a minor increase in the rate of reinforcement.

An example of an everyday behavior that is maintained by a VI schedule of reinforcement is checking for mail. The reinforcer in this situation is simply the receipt of mail. Most people receive mail on some days but not on others, and the days when one will find something reinforcing (such as letters, as opposed to junk mail or bills) in the mailbox are usually impossible to predict. The delivery of mail approximates a VI schedule because (1) it is unpredictable, (2) if a reinforcer is stored (the mail has been delivered), only one response is required to collect it,

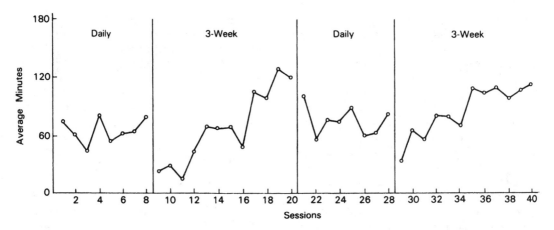

**FIGURE 7-3**    Results obtained by Mawhinney and colleagues (1971) in their experiment on the study habits of college students. The *y*-axis shows the average number of minutes of study per day when the instructor gave daily quizzes and when a larger exam was given at the end of a three-week period.

and (3) if the reinforcer has not yet been stored, no amount of responding will bring it forth. The resultant behavior is moderate and steady: Most people check the mail every day, but only once a day (or at most only a few times a day if there is some uncertainty about whether the mail carrier has come yet).

### Extinction and the Four Simple Schedules

Suppose that an experimenter takes five pigeons and trains them on five different schedules—one on a CRF and one each on an FR, VR, FI, and VI schedule. Each subject receives 10 sessions, and each session, regardless of the reinforcement schedule, lasts until 50 reinforcers have been delivered. For each subject, the eleventh session starts with the same schedule as before, but after five reinforcers have been delivered, each animal is switched to an extinction schedule. Which subject (ignoring the possibility of individual differences among the pigeons) will make the most responses during extinction before quitting? How many responses will the different subjects make?

Of course, the answers to these questions would depend in part on the numerical value of each schedule (for instance, whether the FR

schedule was FR 5 or FR 100), but some general rules about the **resistance to extinction** of the different simple schedules can be stated. One general finding is that extinction is more rapid after CRF than after a schedule of intermittent reinforcement. This finding is called the **partial reinforcement effect,** an effect that seemed paradoxical to early researchers because it violates Thomas Brown's principle of frequency. Why should a response that is only intermittently followed by a reinforcer be stronger (more resistant to extinction) than a response that has been followed by a reinforcer every time it has occurred? This dilemma has been named **Humphrey's paradox,** after the psychologist who first demonstrated the partial reinforcement extinction effect.

One explanation of the partial reinforcement effect is called the **discrimination hypothesis** (Mowrer & Jones, 1945). It states that in order for a subject's behavior to change once extinction begins, the subject must be able to discriminate the change in reinforcement contingencies. With CRF, where every response has been reinforced, the change to extinction is easy to discriminate, and so it does not take long for responding to disappear. For example, a vending machine usually dispenses reinforcers (candy, soda) on a schedule of continuous reinforcement: Each time the correct change is inserted, a reinforcer is delivered. If the schedule is switched to extinction (the machine breaks down), a person will not continue to put coins in the machine for long.

Compare this situation to a slot machine, which dispenses reinforcers on a VR schedule. If a slot machine broke down in such a way that it appeared to be functioning normally but could never produce a jackpot, a gambler might continue to pour many coins into the machine before giving up. It would take a long time for the gambler to discriminate the change from a VR schedule to extinction.

Although the discrimination hypothesis may be easy to understand, the experimental evidence suggests that a slightly different hypothesis, the **generalization decrement hypothesis** (Capaldi, 1966) is better. Generalization decrement is simply a term for the decreased responding one observes in a generalization test when the test stimuli become less and less similar to the training stimulus. For instance, if a pigeon is reinforced for pecking at a yellow key, we should observe a generalization decrement (less rapid responding) if the key is blue in a generalization test. According to the generalization decrement hypothesis, responding during extinction will be weak if the stimuli present during extinction are different from those that prevailed during reinforcement, but strong if these stimuli are similar to those encountered during reinforcement.

According to Capaldi, there is a large generalization decrement when the schedule switches from CRF to extinction, because the subject has never experienced a situation in which its responses were not reinforced. In other words, the animal quickly stops responding because it has never been taught to keep responding when its initial responses are not reinforced. However, suppose an animal has been reinforced on a VR 50 schedule, and now the schedule has been switched to extinction. Here, there will be much less generalization decrement because on many occasions in the past the animal has made a long run of unreinforced responses, and eventually a reinforcer

was delivered. For this animal, the stimuli present during extinction (long stretches of unreinforced responses) are quite similar to the stimuli present during the VR schedule. For this reason, the animal will probably continue to respond for a longer period of time.

## Other Reinforcement Schedules

Although the four simple reinforcement schedules have been the most thoroughly investigated, they are only four of an infinite number of possible rules for delivering reinforcement. Many other rules for reinforcement have been named and studied, and we can examine a few of the more common ones.

Under a schedule of **differential reinforcement of low rates** (DRL), a response is reinforced if and only if a certain amount of time has elapsed since the previous response. For example, under DRL 10 seconds, every response that occurs after a pause of at least 10 seconds is reinforced. If a response occurs after 9.5 seconds, this not only fails to produce reinforcement but it resets the 10-second clock to zero, so that now 10 more seconds must elapse before a response can be reinforced. As you might imagine, DRL schedules produce very low rates of responding, but they are not as low as would be optimal. Since subjects cannot estimate the passage of time perfectly, the optimal strategy would be to pause for an average of 12 or 15 seconds and then respond. In this way, if the subject erred from this average on the short side, the pause might still be longer than 10 seconds and produce a reinforcer. The usual finding, however, is that the average pause is somewhat less than the required duration, and as a result, considerably more than half of the subject's responses go unreinforced (Richards, Sabol, & Seiden, 1993). Some subjects seem to use a regular sequence of behaviors to help pace their operant responses. For example, a pigeon on a DRL 5-second schedule might peck at the key, then peck at each of the four corners of the chamber, then peck at the key again.

The opposite of the DRL contingency is the **differential reinforcement of high rates**

(DRH), whereby a certain number of responses must occur within a fixed amount of time. For example, a reinforcer might occur each time the subject makes 10 responses in 3 seconds or less. Since rapid responding is selectively reinforced by this schedule, DRH can be used to produce higher rates of responding than those obtained with any other reinforcement schedule.

Other common reinforcement schedules are those that combine two or more simple schedules in some way. In a **concurrent schedule,** the subject is presented with two or more response alternatives (for instance, several different levers), each associated with its own reinforcement schedule. With more than one reinforcement schedule available simultaneously, psychologists can determine which schedule the subject prefers and how much time is devoted to each alternative. In **chained schedules,** the subject must complete the requirement for two or more simple schedules in a fixed sequence, and each schedule is signaled by a different stimulus. For instance, in a chain FI 1-minute FR 10, a pigeon might be presented with a yellow key until the FI requirement is met, then a blue key until 10 more responses are made, and then the reinforcer would be presented. The subject's behavior during each link of the chain is usually characteristic of the schedule currently in effect (an accelerating response pattern during the FI component, and a stop-and-go pattern during the FR component). As in the response chains discussed earlier, the strength of responding weakens as a schedule is further and further removed from the primary reinforcer. Thus an FI schedule will produce less responding if instead of leading to reinforcement it simply leads to an FR schedule.

## FACTORS AFFECTING PERFORMANCE ON REINFORCEMENT SCHEDULES

The preceding sections have shown that different reinforcement schedules produce very different rates and patterns of behavior. It is now time to recognize, however, that many other factors besides the schedule itself can af-

fect performance on a reinforcement schedule. We will begin with a brief review of a few of the most important factors.

It is certainly true that the effectiveness of a reinforcement schedule depends on the nature of the reinforcer that is delivered, and three important features of any reinforcer are its quality, its rate of presentation, and its delay. Neef, Shade, and Miller (1994) investigated the effects of these features on the performance of emotionally disturbed teenagers. The teens were referred to these researchers because they needed practice in math skills and, more generally, in completing school assignments promptly. Computers were programmed to present math problems to each teenager, and the computer reinforced completed problems according to a VI schedule. The **quality** of the reinforcers was varied by using either money (which all subjects preferred) or points exchangeable for privileges or items in the school store (which were less preferred). **Rate of reinforcement** was varied by using VI schedules of different lengths. **Delay of reinforcement** was manipulated by delivering reinforcers either immediately after the math session was over or not until the next day. (The teenagers always could choose between two problems that offered reinforcers of different reinforcer quality, rate, or delay, but we can ignore the details of this choice procedure.)

Different subjects had somewhat different preferences, but in general, they spent more time working on the math problems (1) when the quality of the reinforcer was higher, (2) when the rate of reinforcement was faster, and (3) when the delay was shorter. Neef and colleagues also investigated the factor of **response effort** by varying the difficulty of the math problems, and they found that the students preferred to work on the problems that required less effort.

Another important factor is the **amount of reinforcement.** In the laboratory, animals will usually make more responses on a given reinforcement schedule if the reinforcer is a large amount of food than if it is a small amount of food. In the business world, a salesperson may invest substantial time and effort trying to finalize the sale of a large and expensive item, but will not invest so much effort for a smaller and cheaper item. Finally, the individual's **level of motivation** is an important determinant of how much operant behavior will be seen. A rat that has just eaten a large amount of food will not exhibit much lever pressing; a student who does not care about his grades will not do much studying, no matter what the exam schedule may be.

Many of these points may seem obvious, but other factors that can affect performance on reinforcement schedules are not so obvious. Next, we will examine some factors that can easily be overlooked.

## Behavioral Momentum

When a heavy object starts moving, it acquires momentum, and it becomes difficult to stop. Nevin (1992, 1998) has argued that there is an analogy between the momentum of a moving object and the **behavioral momentum** of an ongoing operant behavior. Nevin has found that a behavior's resistance to change (which is a measure of behavioral momentum) depends on the association between the discriminative stimulus and the reinforcer (that is, on how frequently the behavior has been reinforced in the presence of a certain discriminative stimulus).

An experiment with pigeons (Nevin, 1974) illustrates the concept of behavioral momentum. The pigeons earned food by pecking on a response key that was sometimes green and sometimes red. VI schedules delivered 60 food presentations per hour when the key was green, but only 20 food presentations per hour when the key was red. As expected, the pigeons pecked more rapidly when the key was green. Then, Nevin interrupted the green and red keys with periods during which free food was delivered. In one condition, when the free food deliveries were very rapid, the pigeons' rates of key pecking decreased by about 60 percent when the key was green, but by over 80 percent when the key was red. According to Nevin, pecking on the green key had greater momentum because it was associated with a higher rate of reinforcement, so this behavior

was less disrupted by the free food deliveries than was pecking on the red key.

Nevin and Grace (2000) have proposed that the concept of behavioral momentum has a number of implications for attempts to change behavior outside the laboratory. Behavior therapists frequently want to make sure that a newly-trained behavior (such as working steadily on one's job during work hours) will persist in the presence of potential disruptors (distractions by friends, reinforcers for competing behaviors, and so on). The newly-trained behavior will have more momentum, and be more likely to persist despite such potential disruptors, if the worker has developed a strong association between the work environment and reinforcement for appropriate work-related behavior.

As another example, the concept of behavioral momentum may help to explain why some behaviors, such as taking illegal drugs, are prone to relapse when a patient leaves a treatment center and returns home. The undesired behavior, taking drugs, is strongly associated with a specific discriminative stimulus (the patient's neighborhood and friends). Although the patient may have little problem refraining from drugs in the treatment facility, the association between the patient's neighborhood and drugs has not been broken. Because drug-taking behavior has strong momentum when the individual is in his old neighborhood, it may persist in that environment despite the treatment the patient has received elsewhere. Nevin and Grace (2000) propose that more effective behavior therapies will depend on a better understanding of how behaviors develop momentum and how the momentum of unwanted behaviors can be disrupted.

## Contingency-Shaped versus Rule-Governed Behaviors

Every reinforcement schedule specifies its own unique three-way connection among discriminative stimulus, operant response, and reinforcer, which B. F. Skinner called a three-term contingency. For example, the contingency for a pigeon responding on an FI schedule can be stated roughly as follows: If one minute has passed since the last reinforcer, a single response will be followed immediately by the reinforcer. In this example, the discriminative stimulus is the passage of time, the operant response is pecking the response key, and the reinforcer is food. And as we have seen, each reinforcement schedule tends to produce its own characteristic pattern of behavior (Figure 7-2). For those who first studied reinforcement schedules, it seemed logical to conclude that these distinctive behavior patterns were the result of the different contingencies specified by each schedule. For instance, the contingencies in effect under an FI schedule cause an accelerating pattern of responding; the contingencies in effect under an FR schedule cause a stop-and-go pattern of responding. B. F. Skinner called these behavior patterns **contingency shaped,** because in his studies he watched as an animal's behavior was gradually shaped into its final form as it gained more and more experience with a particular reinforcement schedule (Ferster & Skinner, 1957).

The problem with this analysis of reinforcement schedules is that some experiments, especially those with human subjects, have found behavior patterns that were quite different from the typical patterns shown in Figure 7-2. But if these behavior patterns are shaped by the reinforcement contingencies, why should the same reinforcement schedule produce different behavior patterns from different subjects? Do people and animals react to the same reinforcement schedule in different ways? Are other factors besides the reinforcement contingencies involved?

When adult human subjects work on simple reinforcement schedules in a laboratory setting, their behaviors are often varied and unpredictable. For example, under FI schedules, some humans show the accelerating pattern found with animals, but others respond very quickly throughout the interval, and others make only a few responses near the end of the interval (Leander, Lippman, & Meyer, 1968; Lowe, Harzem, & Bagshaw, 1978). Similar discrepancies between human and animal behaviors have been found with other reinforcement schedules as well (Lowe, 1979).

One hypothesis states that the discrepancies between animal and human performance on reinforcement schedules occur because people are capable of both contingency-shaped behavior and **rule-governed** behavior. The distinction between contingency-shaped and rule-governed behavior was first made by Skinner (1969). He proposed that because people have language, they can be given verbal instructions or rules to follow, and these rules may or may not have anything to do with the prevailing reinforcement contingencies. For example, a mother may tell a child, "Stay out of drafts or you will catch a cold," and the child may follow this rule for a long time, regardless of whether it is truly effective in preventing colds. With respect to laboratory experiments on reinforcement schedules, this theory states that human subjects may behave differently from animals because they are following rules about how to respond (such as "Press the response button as rapidly as possible," or "Wait for about a minute, and then respond"). Subjects may form these rules on their own, or they may get them from the instructions the experimenter provides before the experiment begins. Once a human subject receives or creates such a rule, the actual reinforcement contingencies may have little or no effect on his or her behavior. For instance, if the experimenter tells the subject, "Press the key rapidly to earn the most money," the subject may indeed respond rapidly on an FI schedule even though rapid responding is not necessary on this schedule.

Several types of evidence support the idea that human performance on reinforcement schedules is often rule governed, at least in part. Many studies have shown that the instructions given to subjects can have a large effect on their response patterns (for instance, Bentall & Lowe, 1987; Catania, Matthews, & Shimoff, 1982). If subjects are given no specific rule to follow, they may form one on their own. Human subjects have sometimes been asked, either during an experiment or at the end, to explain why they responded the way they did. Some studies of this type have found a close correspondence between a subject's verbal descriptions and his or her actual response patterns (Wearden, 1988). Other research has shown that infants or young children behave much more like animals than like older children or adults under simple schedules of reinforcement (Lowe, Beasty, & Bentall, 1983). This may be because the youngest children do not have language at all, and because the language skills of the slightly older youngsters are too meager for them to develop and follow a verbal rule for responding (Pouthas, Droit, Jacquet, & Wearden, 1990).

Not all the evidence supports the hypothesis that the differences between human and nonhuman schedule performance are due to the use of rules by human subjects. Sometimes when subjects are asked to explain what rule they were following, they can give no rule, or the rule they give does not describe their actual behavior pattern (Matthews, Catania, & Shimoff, 1985). It therefore seems likely that other variables also contribute to the differences between human and nonhuman performance on reinforcement schedules. For instance, animal subjects are usually food-deprived and then given a chance to earn a primary reinforcer, food. With human subjects, the reinforcers in many experiments have been conditioned reinforcers—points that may later be exchanged for small amounts of money. In addition, animal and human subjects usually come to the laboratory with very different reinforcement histories, as discussed below.

### Reinforcement History

In many laboratory experiments with animals, the subjects have never before been exposed to a reinforcement schedule of any sort. In contrast, adult humans have a long and complex history of exposure to various reinforcement schedules outside the laboratory. Is it possible that the differences between human and nonhuman behavior patterns that are sometimes found with the same reinforcement schedules are a product of these different reinforcement histories? If so, it should be possible to change the response patterns of either human or nonhuman subjects by giving them prior experience with different reinforcement schedules.

This responding has been used in several experiments with both people and animals. Weiner (1964) had human subjects press a response key to earn points in 10 one-hour sessions. Some subjects worked on an FR 40 schedule (on which more rapid responding led to more reinforcers). Other subjects worked on a DRL 20-second schedule (on which only pauses longer than 20 seconds were reinforced). Then all subjects were switched to an FI 10-second schedule. The subjects with FR experience responded rapidly on the FI schedule, but those with DRL experience responded very slowly. These large differences persisted even after 20 sessions with the FI schedule.

Similar effects of prior reinforcement history have been found with animals (Freeman & Lattal, 1992; LeFrancois & Metzger, 1993). In a study by Wanchisen, Tatham, and Mooney (1989), one group of rats received many sessions with only one reinforcement schedule, FI 30 seconds, and all of these rats developed the accelerating pattern that is typical for FI schedules. A second group of rats first received 30 sessions with a VR 20 schedule, and then 30 sessions with the FI 30-second schedule. Some of these rats responded rapidly on the FI schedule, and some responded very slowly, but none showed an accelerating response pattern. Wanchisen and her colleagues concluded that prior experience with one reinforcement schedule can alter how subjects, both animal and human, perform on another schedule, and these effects may persist even after long exposure to the new schedule.

### Summary

A large number of variables can affect the type of behavior that is seen with any reinforcement schedule. Factors such as the size and quality of the reinforcer, the effort involved in the operant response, the individual's level of motivation, and the availability of alternative behaviors can all affect the rate and temporal pattern of an operant response. With human subjects, it may be important to know what instructions they were given and what rules about responding they may have formed on their own. With both animal and human subjects, it may be important to know what reinforcement schedules they have encountered previously, and for how long. Since Skinner's pioneering research, reinforcement schedules have been intensely studied, and there is no doubt that they can exert powerful control over an individual's behavior. It is important to recognize, however, that operant behavior is affected by a multitude of variables, and this makes the task of analyzing the behavior more complex and more challenging.

## THE EXPERIMENTAL ANALYSIS OF REINFORCEMENT SCHEDULES

Throughout the preceding discussions of reinforcement schedules, the explanations of why particular schedules produce specific response patterns have been casual and intuitive. For example, we noted that it would not "make sense" to have a long postreinforcement pause on a VR schedule, or to respond at a very rapid rate on a VI schedule. This level of discussion can make the basic facts about reinforcement schedules easier to learn and remember. However, such imprecise statements are no substitute for a scientific analysis of exactly which independent variables (which characteristics of the reinforcement schedule) control which dependent variables (which aspects of the subject's behavior). This section presents a few examples that show how a scientific analysis can either improve upon intuitive explanations of behavior or distinguish among different explanations, all of which seem intuitively reasonable.

### The Cause of the FR Postreinforcement Pause

Why do animal subjects pause after reinforcement on FR schedules? Several possible explanations seem intuitively reasonable. Perhaps the postreinforcement pause is the result of fatigue: The subject has made many responses, has collected a reinforcer, and now it rests to alleviate its fatigue. A second possibility is satiation: The consumption of the food reinforcer causes a slight decrease in the animal's level of hunger, which results in a brief interruption in responding. A third explanation of the postreinforcement pause emphasizes the fact that on an FR schedule, the subject is farthest from the delivery of the next reinforcer immediately after the occurrence of the previous reinforcer. According to this position, a subject's behavior on an FR schedule is similar to a response chain. We have already seen that the initial responses in the chain, those farthest removed from the primary reinforcer, are the weakest. For convenience, let us call these three explanations of the FR postreinforcement pause the **fatigue hypothesis,** the **satiation hypothesis,** and the **remaining-responses hypothesis.**

Each of these hypotheses sounds plausible, but how can we determine which is correct? Several types of evidence help to distinguish among them. First, there is the finding that postreinforcement pauses become larger as the size of the FR increases. This finding is consistent with both the fatigue and remaining-responses hypotheses, but it contradicts the satiation hypothesis. Because the subject can collect reinforcers at a faster rate on a small FR schedule, its level of hunger should be lower, so according to the satiation hypothesis, pauses should be longer on shorter FR schedules, not on larger FR schedules.

Data that help to distinguish between the fatigue and remaining-responses hypotheses are provided by studies that combine two or more different FR schedules into what is called a multiple schedule. In a **multiple schedule,** the subject is presented with two or more different schedules, one at a time, and each schedule is signaled by a different discriminative stimulus. For example, Figure 7-4 illustrates a portion of a session involving a multiple FR 10 FR 100 schedule. When the response key is blue, the schedule is FR 100; when it is red, the schedule is FR 10. The key color remains the same until a reinforcer is earned, at which point there is a .50 probability that the key color (and schedule) will switch.

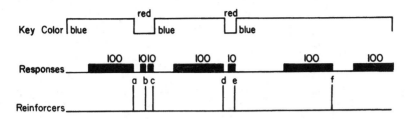

**FIGURE 7-4**    A hypothetical but typical pattern of response from a multiple schedule where the blue key color signaled that the schedule was FR 100 and the red key color signaled that the schedule was FR 10. The text explains how results like these can be used to distinguish between different theories of the postreinforcement pause.

The behavior shown in Figure 7-4, though hypothetical, is representative of the results from several studies that used multiple FR schedules (Crossman, 1968; Mintz, Mourer, & Gofseyeff, 1967). Examine the postreinforcement pauses that occurred at points a, b, c, d, e, and f. Half of these pauses occurred after a ratio of 100 (a, d, f) and half after a ratio of 10 (b, c, e). Notice that there is a long pause at f, as might be expected from the fatigue hypothesis, but contrary to this hypothesis, there are only short pauses after FR 100 at points a and d. The pause after FR 10 is short at point b, but long at points c and e. It turns out that we are unable to predict the size of the postreinforcement pause by knowing how many responses the subject has produced in the *preceding* ratio. This fact forces us to reject the fatigue hypothesis.

On the other hand, it is possible to predict the size of the pause by knowing the size of the *upcoming* ratio. Notice that the pause is short whenever the key color is red (points a, b, and d), which is the discriminative stimulus for FR 10. The pause is long when the key color is blue (points c, e, and f), the discriminative stimulus for FR 100. This pattern is exactly what would be predicted by the remaining-responses hypothesis: The size of the postreinforcement pause is determined by the upcoming FR requirement.

This type of analysis has demonstrated quite clearly that the size of the postreinforcement pause depends heavily on the upcoming ratio requirement, and that the factors of satiation and fatigue play at most a minor role.

## Comparisons of VR and VI Response Rates

We will now turn from a question with a fairly clear answer to one the answer to which is still being debated. Experiments with both human and animal subjects have shown that if a VR schedule and a VI schedule deliver the same number of reinforcers per hour, subjects usually respond faster on the VR schedule (Matthews, Shimoff, Catania, & Sagvolden, 1977). For example, W. M. Baum (1993) presented both VR and VI schedules to the same pigeons, varying the rates of reinforcement from about 20 to several thousand reinforcers per hour. Figure 7-5 shows the results from a typical pigeon. As can be seen, the pigeon consistently responded faster on the VR schedules, although the differences between VR and VI tended to disappear with the very high rates of reinforcement (when reinforcers were occurring every few seconds). The question we will try to answer is: Why is responding faster on VR schedules than on VI schedules when the rates of reinforcement are the same?

One theory about this difference in response rates can be classified as a **molecular** theory, which means that it focuses on small-scale events—the moment-by-moment relationships between responses and reinforcers.

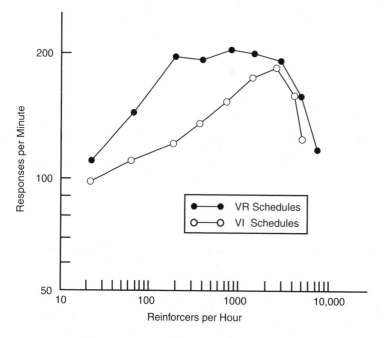

**FIGURE 7-5** Response rates of a typical pigeon in Baum's (1993) experiment, showing faster responding on VR schedules than on VI schedules that delivered about the same number of reinforcers per hour.

The other theory is a **molar** theory, or one that deals with large-scale measures of behavior and reinforcement. Of course, the terms small-scale and large-scale are relative, but to be more specific, molecular theories usually discuss events that have time spans of less than one minute, whereas molar theories discuss relationships measured over at least several minutes and often over the entire length of an experimental session. The issue of VI and VR response-rate differences is one of several areas where there are opposing molar and molecular explanations, and we will encounter others in later chapters.

For the present issue, the most popular molecular theory is the **IRT reinforcement theory,** where IRT stands for **interresponse time**—the time between two consecutive responses. In essence, this theory states that response rates are slower on VI schedules than on VR schedules because long IRTs (long pauses between responses) are more frequently reinforced on VI schedules. This theory was

first proposed by Skinner (1938), and among its more recent proponents are Anger (1956), Shimp (1969), and Platt (1979).

Imagine that a subject has just been switched from CRF to a VI schedule. Some of this subject's IRTs will be short (for instance, less than 1 second will elapse between two responses) and others will be larger (for example, a pause of 5 or 10 seconds will separate two responses). On the VI schedule, which of these two responses is more likely to be reinforced— a response after a pause of 0.5 seconds or a response after a pause of 5 seconds? The answer is the latter, because the more time that elapses between two responses, the greater is the probability that the VI clock will time out and store a reinforcer. For example, if the schedule is VI 60 seconds, the probability of reinforcement is roughly 10 times higher for an IRT of 5 seconds than for an IRT of 0.5 seconds. The direct relationship between IRT size and the probability of reinforcement on VI schedules is not theory but fact. IRT reinforcement theory states that as a consequence of this relationship, longer IRTs will be selectively strengthened on VI schedules.

Next, let us examine the relationship between IRT size and the probability of reinforcement on a VR schedule. Stated simply, there is no such relationship, because time is irrelevant on a VR schedule—the delivery of reinforcement depends entirely on the number of responses emitted, not on the passage of time. Therefore, unlike VI schedules, there is no selective strengthening of long pauses on VR schedules, and this in itself could explain the VI-VR difference. However, Skinner (1938) went a bit further by noting that when a subject is first switched from CRF to a VR schedule, its responses are not distributed uniformly over time. Instead, responses tend to occur in clusters, or "bursts," perhaps simply because the subject makes several responses while in the vicinity of the key or lever, then explores some other part of the chamber, then returns and makes a few more responses, and so on.

Skinner suggested that this tendency to respond in bursts could lead to a selective strengthening of short IRTs on a VR schedule. For simplicity, let us suppose that each burst consists of exactly five responses, each separated by 0.5 seconds, and each pause between bursts is at least 5 seconds long. In each burst of responses, there is only one chance for a long IRT to be reinforced (the first response after the pause), but there are four chances for a 0.5-second IRT to be reinforced (the next four responses). Skinner therefore concluded that short IRTs were selectively strengthened on a VR schedule simply because they were reinforced more frequently.

To provide empirical support for their viewpoint, proponents of IRT reinforcement theory have arranged schedules that reinforce different IRTs with different probabilities. For example, Shimp (1968) set up a schedule in which only IRTs between 1.5 and 2.5 seconds or between 3.5 and 4.5 seconds were reinforced. As the theory of selective IRT reinforcement would predict, IRTs of these two sizes increased in frequency. In another experiment, Shimp (1973) mimicked the pattern of

IRT reinforcement that occurs in a typical VI schedule: He did not use a VI clock, but simply reinforced long IRTs with a high probability and short IRTs with a low probability. The result of this "synthetic VI" schedule was a pattern of responding indistinguishable from that of a normal VI schedule—moderate, steady responding with a mixture of long and short IRTs.

Critics have raised a number of objections against IRT reinforcement theory, some of which are too lengthy and technical to repeat here. However, one objection is that even in situations where only long IRTs are reinforced, such as in DRL schedules, subjects typically continue to produce a large number of short IRTs. That is, the tendency to respond in bursts is not completely eliminated even when this manner of responding is never reinforced. At the very least, this finding implies that other factors besides the probability of reinforcement influence the sizes of IRTs a subject produces.

A molar theory of the VI-VR difference might be called the **response-reinforcer correlation theory.** Instead of focusing on the last IRT to occur before reinforcement, this theory emphasizes a relationship between responses and reinforcement of a much more global nature (W. M. Baum, 1973; Green, Kagel, & Battalio, 1987). Figure 7-6 depicts the properties of VI and VR schedules that underlie the response-reinforcer correlation theory, and it shows the relationship between a subject's average response rate and overall reinforcement rate for a typical VR schedule and a typical VI schedule. On VR 60, as on all ratio schedules, there is a linear relationship between response rate and reinforcement rate. For instance, a response rate of 60 responses per minute will produce 60 reinforcers per hour, and a response rate of 90 responses per minute produces 90 reinforcers per hour. The relationship on the VI 60-second schedule (as on all VI schedules) is very different. No matter how rapidly the subject responds, it cannot obtain more than the scheduled 60 reinforcers per hour. The reason that reinforcement rate drops with very low response rates is that the VI clock will sometimes be stopped (having

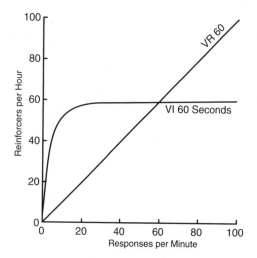

**FIGURE 7-6**   The relationship between a subject's rate of response and the rate of reinforcement on a VR 60 schedule and a VI 60-second schedule.

stored a reinforcer), and it will not start again until the subject makes a response and collects a reinforcer. But as long as the subject responds at a modest rate, it will obtain close to 60 reinforcers per hour.

It should be emphasized that the relationships depicted in Figure 7-6 apply only in the long run. Because of the variable nature of VI and VR schedules, in the short run the actual rate of reinforcement will often be much higher or much lower. According to the response-reinforcer correlation theory, however, the organism is able to ignore these short-term fluctuations and learn about the long-term relationships between response rate and reinforcement rate. To see how this could cause the response rate difference between VI and VR, suppose that after extensive experience on VR 60, a pigeon's response rate stabilizes at about 60 responses per minute (where the two functions cross in Figure 7-6), producing about 60 reinforcers per hour. Now suppose the schedule is switched to VI 60 seconds, under which this same response rate would also produce 60 reinforcers per hour. However, the subject's response rate is not completely steady, and by occasionally responding

at rates above and below 60 responses per hour, the subject learns that variations in response rate have little effect on reinforcement rate on the VI schedule. The subject's behavior may gradually drop to, say, 20 responses per hour without a substantial decrease in the rate of reinforcement. Speaking loosely, we could say that on VI 60 seconds, the subject has learned that the extra 40 responses per hour are "not worth it," for they would produce only a negligible increase in reinforcement rate.

Critics of the response-reinforcer correlation theory have argued that it makes excessive intellectual demands on the subject: animals may not be capable of making accurate long-term estimates of response rate and reinforcement rate. However, rather than speculate about what animals can or cannot do, a better strategy is to conduct an appropriate experiment. One way to decide between the molar and molecular theories is to use a schedule in which the molar contingencies favor rapid responding and the molecular contingencies favor slow responding (or vice versa). This is not possible with normal VR or VI schedules, but experiments by Vaughan (1987) with pigeons and by Cole (1999) with rats used some complex schedules that had these properties. For instance, one schedule used by Vaughan had the molar features of a VR schedule (with more reinforcers for faster response rates) but the molecular features of a VI schedule (with reinforcement more likely after a long IRT). As predicted by IRT reinforcement theory, pigeons responded slowly on this schedule (and thereby lost reinforcers in the long run). Cole's experiment with rats obtained similar results. Conversely, Vaughan found that pi-

Selected articles from the *Journal of the Experimental Analysis of Behavior* are available at *http://www.envmed.rochester.edu/wwwvgl/ jeab_articles/jeab_articles.htm*.

Online articles are available in the *Experimental Analysis of Human Behavior Bulletin* at *http://www.eahb.org/BulletinHomepage.htm.*

geons responded rapidly on a schedule in which the molecular contingencies favored rapid responding (short IRTs) but the molar contingencies favored slow responding (so once again the pigeons lost reinforcers in the long run). These results clearly favor the molecular approach, for they indicate that the animals were sensitive to the short-term consequences of their behavior, but not to the long-term consequences.

## APPLICATIONS OF OPERANT CONDITIONING

Within the field of behavior modification, operant conditioning principles have been applied to so many different behaviors that they are too numerous to list, let alone describe in any detail, in a few pages. Operant conditioning principles have been used to help people who wish to improve themselves by losing weight, smoking or drinking less, or exercising more. They have been applied to a wide range of children's problems, including classroom disruption, poor academic performance, fighting, tantrums, extreme passivity, and hyperactivity. They have been used in attempts to improve the daily functioning of adults and children who have more serious behavioral problems and must be institutionalized. These principles have also been applied to problems that affect society as a whole, such as litter and pollution, the waste of energy and resources, workplace accidents, delinquency, shoplifting, and other crimes. In light of the number and diversity of these applications, it should be clear that this section can do no more than describe a few representative examples. For those who wish to know more, there are many books devoted primarily or exclusively to the system-

atic use of operant conditioning principles in real-world settings (Ammerman & Hersen, 1995; Hersen, Eisler, & Miller, 1994; Martin & Pear, 1999; Miltenberger, 1997).

## Teaching Language to Autistic Children

**Autism** is a severe disorder that affects about 2 to 4 of every 10,000 children (Wing, 1972), usually appearing when a child is a few years old. One major symptom of autism is extreme social withdrawal. The child shows little of the normal interest in watching and interacting with other people. Autistic children do not acquire normal language use: They either remain silent or exhibit **echolalia,** which is the immediate repetition of any words they hear. Autistic children frequently spend hours engaging in simple repetitive behaviors such as rocking back and forth or spinning a metal pan on the floor. Despite considerable research, the causes of autism remain a mystery, but one certainty is that typical psychiatric and institutional care produce little if any improvement in these children (Kanner, Rodriguez, & Ashenden, 1972). Individuals diagnosed as autistic frequently spend all of their childhood and adult lives in a state institution.

During the 1960s, Ivar Lovaas developed an extensive program based on operant conditioning principles designed to train autistic children to speak, to interact with other people, and in general to behave more normally (Lovaas 1967, 1977). Lovaas's program makes use of many of the operant conditioning principles we have already discussed, plus some new ones. At first, a therapist uses a spoonful of ice cream or some other tasty food as a primary reinforcer, and starts by reinforcing the child simply for sitting quietly and looking at the experimenter. Next, using the procedure of shaping, the therapist rewards the child for making any audible sounds, and then for making sounds that more and more closely mimic the word spoken by the therapist. For instance, if the child's name is Billy, the therapist may say the word "Billy" as a discriminative stimulus, after which any verbal response that approximates this word will be reinforced. To avoid the necessity of relying entirely on the primary reinforcer of food (which would lose its effectiveness rapidly because of satiation), the therapist begins to develop other stimuli into conditioned reinforcers. Before presenting the food, the therapist might say "Good!" or give the child a hug—two stimuli that can eventually be used as reinforcers by themselves.

Early in this type of training, the therapist might use her hand to aid the child in his mouth and lip movements. This type of physical guidance is one example of a **prompt.** A prompt is any stimulus that makes a desired response more likely. In this example, the therapist's prompt of moving the child's lips and cheeks into the proper shape makes the production of the appropriate response more likely. Whenever a prompt is used, it is usually withdrawn gradually, in a procedure known as **fading.** Thus the therapist may do less and less of the work of moving the child's lips and cheeks into the proper position, then perhaps just touch the child's cheek lightly, then not at all. This type of training demands large amounts of time and patience on the part of the therapist, especially in the beginning, when progress is slowest. It may take several days of training, conducted for several hours each day, before the child masters his first word. It may be a few more days before a second word is mastered, and a few more before the therapist can say either of the two words and reliably receive the appropriate imitative response (assuming that the child is not echolalic to begin with). However, the pace of a child's progress quickens as additional words are introduced, and after a few weeks the child may master several new words each day.

At this stage of training, the child is only imitating words he hears, and the next step is to teach him the meanings of these words. The training begins with concrete nouns such as *nose, shoe,* and *leg.* The child is taught to identify the correct object in response to the word as a stimulus (for example, by rewarding an appropriate response to the instruction, "Point to your nose"), and to produce the appropriate word when presented with the object (Therapist: "What is this?" Billy: "Shoe."). As in the imitative phase, the child's progress accelerates as the labeling phase proceeds, and soon the child is learning the meanings of several new words each day. Later in training, similar painstaking techniques are used to teach the child the meanings of verbs and adjectives, of prepositions such as *in* and *on,* and of abstract concepts such as *first, last, more, less, same,* and *different.* This program can produce dramatic improvements in the behavior of children who typically show negligible improvement from any other type of therapy. Over the course of several months, Lovaas's typical result is that a child who was initially aloof and completely silent becomes friendly and affectionate and learns to use language to answer questions, to make requests, or to tell stories. Autistic children can also be taught other communication skills, such as how to ask questions when they need information about an unfamiliar object or situation (Taylor & Harris, 1995).

How successful is this behavioral treatment in the long run? Lovaas (1987) compared children who had received extensive behavioral treatment for autism (40 hours a week for 2 or more years) with children who had received minimal treatment (10 hours a week or less). The children were assigned to these "treatment" and "control" groups at random. At age 6 or 7, all children were given some standard IQ tests, and their performance in school was evaluated. The differences between groups were dramatic: Nearly half of the children from the treatment group had normal IQs and academic performance, as compared to only 2 percent of the children from the control group. A follow-up 6 years later, when the children were about 13 years old, found that the children in the treatment group continued to maintain their advantage over those in the control group. Some of the children in the treatment group performed about as well as average children of the same age on tests of intelligence and adaptive behavior (McEachin, Smith, & Lovaas, 1993). These results are very encouraging, for they suggest that if extensive behavioral treatment is given to young autistic children, it can essentially eliminate the autistic symptoms in some of them (though not all). Lovaas proposed that the chances for success are best if the behavioral treatment begins at the earliest possible age.

## The Token Economy

In a **token economy,** the principle of conditioned reinforcement is used in an attempt to improve the behaviors of entire groups of individuals. Token economies have been employed in classrooms, mental institutions, prisons, and homes for juvenile delinquents (see Kazdin, 1977, for a comprehensive review). What all token economies have in common is that each individual can earn tokens by performing any of a number of different desired behaviors, and can later exchange these tokens for a variety of "backup" or primary reinforcers. The tokens may be physical objects such as poker chips or gold stars on a bulletin board, or they may simply be points added in a record book.

An early report by Schaefer and Martin (1966) provides a good example of a token system. In a large state hospital, Schaefer and Martin studied the behavior of 40 adult female patients diagnosed as chronic schizophrenics. They noted that one of the major characteristics of hospitalized schizophrenics is that they appear "apathetic" and seem to lack "interest and motivation": For instance, a patient may stare at a wall all day, or may continually pace around the ward. Schaefer and Martin sought to determine whether the contingent delivery of tokens for more varied and normal behaviors would improve the behavior of these patients. The patients were randomly divided into two groups. Patients in the control group received a supply of tokens regardless of their behavior. Patients in the experimental group were reinforced with tokens for specific behaviors from three broad categories: personal hygiene, social interaction, and adequate work performance. Some examples of reinforced behaviors in the first category were thoroughness of showering, brushing teeth, combing hair, use of cosmetics, and maintenance of an attractive appearance. Among the reinforced social behaviors were everyday greetings (such as "Good morning"), speaking in group-therapy sessions, and playing cards with other patients. Work assignments that were reinforced with

tokens varied from individual to individual, but some examples were emptying wastepaper baskets, wiping tables, and vacuuming. Notice that all of the reinforced behaviors would generally be considered normal and desirable not only within the hospital but also in the outside world. The tokens were used to purchase both necessities and luxuries, including food, cigarettes, access to TV, recreational activities, and so on. The token program remained in effect for 3 months, and nurses on the ward periodically made observations of the patients in both the experimental and control groups.

The single most important finding of this study was that over the 3-month period, the variety and frequency of "adaptive" behaviors increased in the experimental group, whereas there was no visible change in the control group. The results of this and many other studies on token economies in mental institutions leave no doubt that such procedures can produce impressive improvements in the personal, social, and work-related behaviors of patients. An important question, however, is whether patients who are exposed to a token economy ultimately fare better when they are released from the hospital—that is, whether their more adaptive behaviors will generalize to the outside world, where there are no tokens for good hygiene or for performing household chores.

Although the evidence is not as overwhelming as we might hope, a number of findings suggest that there may be long-term benefits from carefully designed token economies. For example, Paul and Lentz (1977) compared the effectiveness of token economies to other types of treatment, including the traditional care that is provided for psychiatric patients. They found that patients who were exposed to the token economy needed less medication, spent less time in the hospital, and remained out of the hospital longer once released. Schaefer and Martin found that only 14 percent of the patients in the experimental group who were eventually discharged later returned to the hospital, as compared to the hospital's average return rate of 28 percent. Not all accounts of token economies have reported such long-term benefits. However, it seems that those token economies from which the patient is removed gradually rather than abruptly, and those that stress independence and self-reliance, are the most likely to produce lasting improvements (Kazdin, 1983).

Since about 1980, the use of token economies in mental hospitals and other institutions has declined. Today, only a small percentage of psychiatric patients receive this type of treatment, despite the evidence that token economies lead to improvements in behavior (LePage, 1999). Glynn (1990) discussed several factors responsible for the dwindling use of token economies. First, token economies require a long time to produce lasting behavioral change, whereas the average duration of hospitalization has decreased greatly over the years. Second, token economies are difficult to implement, and to succeed they require the cooperation and hard work of a well-trained staff. There has been an increasing emphasis on pharmacological treatment for psychiatric patients, and as a result, behavior therapists—those most likely to use token economies—have had less involvement with these patients than in the past. There have also been some court rulings that restrict what can legally be done within a token-economy system. For these reasons and others, it seems unlikely that token economies will be used extensively in mental institutions in the near future.

Although their use with psychiatric patients has declined, token economies are commonly used in classrooms. Tokens may be delivered for good academic performance or for good behavior (Swain & McLaughlin, 1998). In one example, the classroom behavior of special education students was improved by giving them tokens for such behaviors as paying attention, using appropriate language, cooperating with others, and following instructions (Cavalier, Ferretti, & Hodges, 1997). Teachers can set up a system in which tokens are exchanged for snacks, small prizes, or access to special activities.

For over two decades, a token system of behavior management has been used in a student housing cooperative at the University of Kansas. This residence hall for 30 students has achieved lower rents and high student satisfac-tion by giving the students responsibility for many of the tasks needed to keep the house functioning. The students are in charge of advertising vacancies, collecting rents, purchasing food and preparing meals, cleaning, making routine repairs, and many other tasks. To make certain that these chores get done, detailed job descriptions have been created for every work assignment, supervisors check to see that the tasks are completed correctly and record the performance of each worker, and the students earn rent reductions by doing their assigned tasks. At the same time, monetary fines are imposed if a student fails to perform a large percentage of his assigned tasks.

To determine whether this behavior-management system was indeed responsible for the smooth functioning of the residence, the token system was suspended for a period of 4 weeks, and students received their maximum rent reductions whether or not they completed their tasks (Johnson, Welsh, Miller, & Altus, 1991). Figure 7-7 shows the results of this experiment. For 5 weeks in which the behavior management system was in effect, the students completed about 85 percent of their assigned tasks. During the 4 weeks in which the system was suspended, the number of completed tasks steadily declined to under 60 percent. (The only worker whose performance did not deteriorate was the food shopper, who was evidently under strong social pressure to maintain an adequate supply of food in the house.) Performance quickly improved when the system was reinstated, and a follow-up 5 years later showed a continued high level of task completion. One especially encouraging feature of this project is that the students took an active role in designing the behavior management system, and the system continued to function successfully with only minimal supervision by a behavior analyst.

## Reinforcing Employee Performance

In recent years, many businesses, both large and small, have begun to use the principles of operant conditioning to increase productivity and to decrease employee absen-

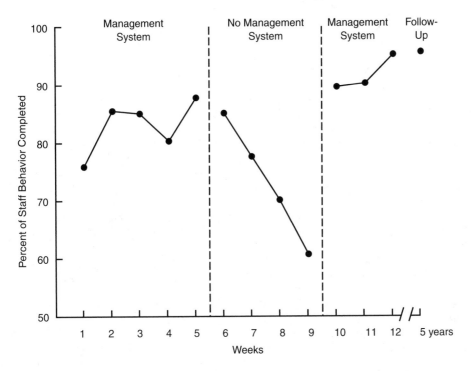

**FIGURE 7-7**   The percentage of tasks in a student housing cooperative that were completed when a behavior-management system was in effect, when the system was suspended, and when it was reinstated. (From Johnson, Welsh, Miller, & Altus, 1991)

teeism and workplace accidents. A study by Wallin and Johnson (1976) illustrates the potential benefits of this approach. In a small electronics company where worker tardiness and absenteeism had become a problem, workers were allowed to participate in a monthly lottery if their attendance record had been perfect for the past month. The names of all workers who had perfect attendance records were placed in a basket, and a random drawing determined the winner of a $10 prize. Since the lottery was an example of an RR schedule, we might predict that it should produce steady behavior, assuming that the size of the reinforcer was sufficient. Apparently it was, for in the first 11 months of the lottery system, employee absenteeism was 30 percent lower than in the previous 11 months. This simple program, which cost only $110, saved the company over $3,100 in sick-leave expenditures during the initial 11-month period.

But monetary reinforcers are not always necessary. Werner (1992) found that simply recognizing employees with good attendance by awarding them certificates and displaying these certificates publicly could produce a substantial decrease in absenteeism.

Reinforcement procedures have also been used to decrease workplace accidents. For instance, Fox, Hopkins, and Anger (1987) described how workers in two open-pit mines were given trading stamps (exchangeable for various types of merchandise) in return for accident-free performance. The workers could earn stamps in a variety of ways: by completing a year without a lost-time accident, by following safety standards, and so on. They lost stamps if someone in their group had an accident or damaged equipment. Following the adoption of the trading-stamp program, lost-time accidents decreased by more than two thirds in both mines and continued at this lower level over a period of several years. The program was also very cost effective for the mining companies: The monetary savings from reduced accident rates were at least 15 times greater than the cost of the trading-stamp program. Quite a few other studies have found that such reinforcement programs can both reduce workplace accidents and save companies substantial amounts of money (McAfee & Winn, 1989; Sulzer-Azaroff, Loafman, Merante, & Hlavacek, 1990).

## Behavioral Marital Therapy

Since about the mid-1970s, some behavior therapists have used behavioral principles to aid couples who seek help because they are having marital problems. Jacobson and Dallas (1981) recognized that in unhappy married couples, each spouse tends to resort to threats, punishment, and retaliation in an attempt to get what he or she wants from the other. For this reason, the initial phases of therapy are designed to promote more positive interactions between partners. To encourage a reciprocal exchange of reinforcers between spouses, a contingency contract is often used. A **contingency contract** is a written agreement that lists the duties (behaviors) required of each party and the privileges (reinforcers) that will result if the duties are performed (Stuart, 1971). In most cases, both spouses play active roles in creating the contract and indicate their agreement with the terms of the contract by signing it.

A contingency contract can help to encourage the exchange of reinforcers and to let each partner know what behaviors the other desires. For instance, the husband may agree to do the dishes in the evening if and only if the wife took the children to school that morning. Conversely, the wife agrees to take the children to school the next morning if and only if the husband did the dishes the night before. Jacobson and Dallas (1981) claim that the use of a written contract has several advantages: "it constitutes a public commitment to change; it decreases the likelihood of forgetting; and it prevents each spouse from retrospectively distorting the terms of the agreement" (p. 390). This part of behavioral marital therapy is called **behavior exchange** because each

spouse makes an effort to perform specific behaviors that will please the other.

Behavior exchange is just one part of behavioral marital therapy. Another important component is training in **communication and problem-solving skills.** N. S. Jacobson (1977) explains that unhappy couples often have difficulty communicating, and they find it difficult to solve even the simplest of problems that may arise. As part of their therapy, a couple first reads a book about problem solving in marriage, and then they try to solve a very minor problem as the therapist watches. For instance, the wife may complain that she does not like always having to remind the husband to take out the garbage. The couple then try to find a solution to this small problem that satisfies both spouses, and whenever one spouse responds in an inappropriate way, the therapist interrupts, points out the flaw, and suggests a better alternative. After a little trial and error, the couple usually finds a solution to this minor problem. Over time, they gradually work up to bigger problems, and as "homework assignments" they are instructed to hold nightly problem-solving sessions and take notes on their results.

Behavior therapy seems to offer a promising approach to the treatment of marital discord: One review of 17 separate studies concluded that a couple's chances of successfully resolving their marital difficulties more than doubled if the couple received behavioral marriage therapy (Halweg & Markman, 1988). Jacobson and Addis (1993) found that both components of behavioral marital therapy—behavior exchange and training in problem solving and communication—are essential to the long-term success of the treatment. Although these techniques do not work for everyone, they can help many unhappy couples improve the quality of their marriages.

As with most types of behavior modification, behavioral marital therapy is not a fixed and unchanging system; it continues to evolve as therapists experiment with new techniques and measure their effectiveness. Because behavioral marital therapy usually will not work if the partners are hostile, uncooperative, and inflexible, a variation known as **integrative**

Selected articles from the *Journal of Applied Behavior Analysis* are available online at *http://www.envmed.rochester.edu/wwwvgl/jaba_articles/jaba_articles.htm.*

**couple therapy** adds an initial phase called *acceptance* to the techniques already described (Christensen & Jacobson, 2000). During the acceptance phase of treatment, the therapist helps the partners learn to tolerate each other's flaws and imperfections (within limits), and to view differences in attitudes, feelings, and preferences as a healthy part of a marriage, not as something that must be eradicated. In other words, the partners are asked to accept the premise that no spouse is perfect, and some differences must be accepted for any marriage to work. Preliminary findings suggest that integrative couple therapy has a higher success rate than behavioral marital therapy that does not include the acceptance phase (Jacobson, Christensen, Prince, Cordova, & Eldridge, 2000).

### Summary

The successful application of the principles of reinforcement to a wide array of behavioral problems provides one of the strongest pieces of evidence that the research of the operant conditioning laboratory is relevant to real-world behavior. However, one common criticism of behavior modification is that these principles are nothing new—that people have always used reward and punishment to try to control the behavior of others. Kazdin (1980) argues that this criticism is unfair for several reasons. First of all, many people are apparently quite unaware of how their own actions affect the behavior of others, and as a result, they inadvertently reinforce the very behaviors they would like to eliminate. The parent who eventually gives in to a child's demands after the child whines or has a tantrum is reinforcing whining and tantrums on a VI schedule.

The psychiatric nurse who listens sympathetically when a patient complains of imaginary illnesses or tells unbelievable stories is reinforcing this unusual verbal behavior with attention. These and countless other examples show that many people have little understanding of the basic principles of reinforcement.

Kazdin also notes that whereas the rules for reinforcement are applied systematically and consistently in a behavior-modification program, they seldom are when the average person uses reinforcers. A parent may begin with a rule that a child can earn an allowance by drying the dishes each night. However, the parent may sometimes excuse the child and give the allowance anyway if the child complains of being tired (and complaining is thereby reinforced). On another day, when the parent is in a bad mood, the same complaint of being tired might result in the child being spanked.

One final argument against the statement that the principles of operant conditioning are "common sense" ideas is that knowing something about the principles of reinforcement is not the same as knowing everything. Behavior modifiers certainly do not know everything about how reinforcement works, but they do know much more than the average person. Consider how many of the principles of operant conditioning you understood (at least at a common sense level) before you started this chapter compared to those you know now. You may have had some idea of how primary and conditioned reinforcers can alter behavior, but unless you have had experience training animals, you were probably unfamiliar with the principles of shaping, backward chaining, prompting, fading, and discrimination learning. You would probably find it difficult to predict the different behavior patterns produced by the four simple reinforcement schedules, either during acquisition or subsequent extinction. (If you do not believe this, try describing the four simple schedules to a friend with no training in psychology to see whether he or she can predict the different behaviors these schedules generate.) The subtleties and complexities of operant behavior are not obvious, and it has taken careful experiments to uncover them.

With further research in this area, psychologists should continue to develop a more complete understanding of how "voluntary" behaviors are affected by their consequences.

## CHAPTER SUMMARY

A fixed-ratio (FR) schedule delivers a reinforcer after a fixed number of responses, and it typically produces a postreinforcement pause followed by rapid responding. A variable-ratio (VR) schedule delivers a reinforcer after a variable number of responses, and it typically leads to rapid, steady responding. On a fixed-interval (FI) schedule, the requirement for reinforcement is one response after a fixed amount of time. Subjects often exhibit a postreinforcement pause and then an accelerating response pattern. Variable-interval (VI) schedules are similar except that the time requirement is variable, and they typically produce moderate, steady responding.

Performance on a reinforcement schedule can be affected by the quality and amount of reinforcement, response effort, and the individual's level of motivation and past experience. People may also respond according to rules they have been taught or have learned on their own. When reinforcement is discontinued, extinction is usually rapid after continuous reinforcement, slower after FI or FR, and slowest after VI or VR.

Experimental analysis has shown that the postreinforcement pause on FR schedules occurs primarily because each reinforcer is a signal that many responses must be completed before the next reinforcer. Regarding the question of why VR schedules produce faster responding than VI schedules, IRT reinforcement theory states that long pauses are often reinforced on VI schedules, whereas bursts of rapid responses are more likely to be reinforced on VR schedules. A different theory states that subjects learn that more rapid responding yields more reinforcers on VR schedules, but not on VI schedules.

Reinforcement schedules are frequently used in behavior therapy. Autistic children have been taught to speak by using positive reinforcement, shaping, prompting, and fading. Token economies and other reinforcement techniques have been used in some psychiatric hospitals, schools, and businesses. In behavior therapy for couples, contingency contracts help partners increase the exchange of positive reinforcers.

## REVIEW QUESTIONS

1. For each of the four basic reinforcement schedules, describe the rule for reinforcement, the typical response pattern, and the rate of extinction, and give a real-world example that approximates this schedule.

2. What are some factors, other than the schedule itself, that can affect performance on a reinforcement schedule? List at least four factors, and give a concrete example to illustrate each.

3. What is the difference between molecular and molar theories of behavior? Describe both a molecular theory and a molar theory of why responding is usually faster on VR schedules than on VI schedules.

4. Give a few examples of how the principles of operant conditioning have been used in behavior therapy. In describing the methods, identify as many different terms and principles of operant conditioning as you can.

## CHAPTER 8

# Avoidance and Punishment

Chapters 6 and 7 were entirely devoted to the topic of positive reinforcement, a procedure in which a response is followed by a particular stimulus (a reinforcer) and the response is strengthened as a result. Skinner has noted, however, that positive reinforcement is only one of four possible relationships between a behavior and its consequences. Figure 8-1 presents these four possibilities in the form of a two-by-two matrix. First, after a behavior occurs, a stimulus can be presented, or a stimulus can be removed or omitted. In each of these cases, the result could be either an increase or a decrease in the behavior, depending on the nature of the stimulus that is either presented or removed. We have already thoroughly examined the procedure in cell 1 of the matrix (positive reinforcement). This chapter will focus on the other three cells.

We can begin with some definitions. With **negative reinforcement** (cell 3), a behavior increases in frequency if some stimulus is removed after the behavior occurs. One example of negative reinforcement is when an individual takes a Tylenol, and this is followed by the termination of a headache. In this case, the individual **escapes** from the pain of the headache by performing some behavior. As a result, this behavior should be strengthened in the future: The next time the person has a headache, he is likely to take a Tylenol again. The term *negative reinforcement* also encompasses instances of **avoidance,** in which a response prevents an unpleasant stimulus from occurring in the first place. For example, the behavior of paying one's income tax avoids the unpleasant consequences of failing to do so. It has been conclusively shown that both positive and negative reinforcement act to strengthen or increase the likelihood of the behavior involved. The term *positive* indicates that a stimulus is presented if a behavior occurs; the term *negative* indicates that a stimulus is subtracted (removed or avoided entirely) if a behavior occurs.

Procedurally, cells 2 and 4 are similar to cells 1 and 3, respectively, except that the opposite type of stimulus is used. Cell 2 represents the procedure of **punishment,** in which a behavior is followed by an unpleasant stimulus. To emphasize the fact that a stimulus is presented, we might call this procedure *positive punishment,* but this term is seldom used. Cell 4 represents **negative punishment,** in which a pleasant stimulus is removed or omitted if a behavior occurs. The term **omission** is often used instead of negative punishment. An example of negative punishment is when a parent refuses to give a child his or her usual weekly allowance after the child has performed some undesirable behavior (such as staying out too late).

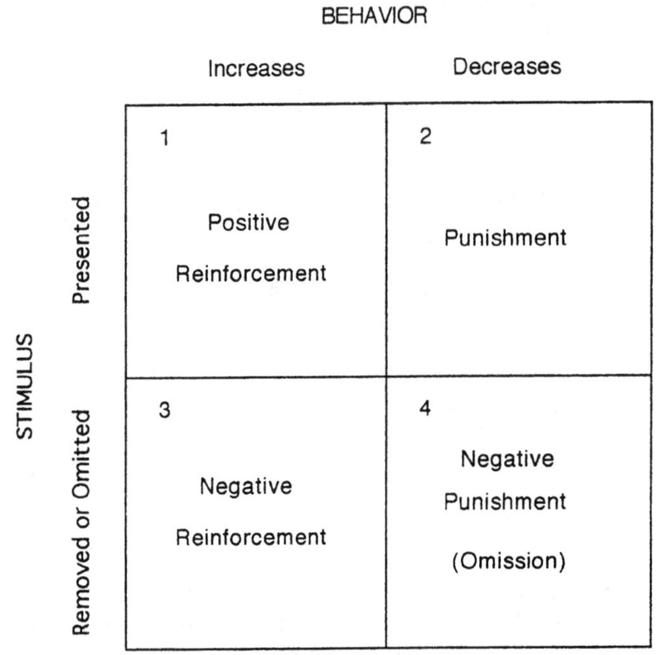

BEHAVIOR

**FIGURE 8-1** A two-by-two matrix depicting two types of reinforcement and two types of punishment.

The first part of this chapter surveys a number of experiments on negative reinforcement, and it discusses some of the theoretical issues about avoidance that psychologists have debated over the years. Next, we will look at the two types of punishment procedures. Although punishment is, in theory, the opposite of reinforcement, some psychologists have concluded that in practice, punishment is not an effective form of behavioral control. We will consider the evidence and attempt to draw our own conclusions. Finally, we will examine some of the ways that punishment has been used in behavior modification.

## AVOIDANCE

### A Representative Experiment

R. L. Solomon and Wynne (1953) conducted an experiment that illustrates many of the properties of negative reinforcement. Their subjects were dogs, and their apparatus a **shuttle box**—a chamber with two rectangular compartments separated by a barrier several inches high. A subject could move from one compartment to the other simply by jumping over the barrier. Each compartment had a metal floor that could be electrified to deliver an unpleasant stimulus, a shock. The only other noteworthy features of the chamber were two overhead lights that separately illuminated the two compartments. In each experimental session, a dog received 10 trials on which it could either escape or avoid a shock by jumping over the barrier to the other compartment. Every few minutes, the light above the dog was turned off (but the light in the other compartment remained on). If the dog remained in the dark compartment, after 10 seconds the floor was electrified and the animal received a shock until it hopped over the barrier to the other compartment. Thus the dog could *escape* from the shock by jumping over the barrier. However, the dog could also *avoid* the shock completely by jumping over the barrier before the 10 seconds of darkness had elapsed. On the next trial the contingencies were the same, except that the response required to escape or avoid the shock was jumping back into the first compartment.

On each trial, Solomon and Wynne measured the latency of the hurdling response from the moment the light above the dog went out. The latencies for a subject's first few trials were usually longer than 10 seconds, so they could be classified as **escape responses**—the hurdling response occurred only after the shock had begun. However, by perhaps the fifth trial, a dog's response latency decreased to less than 10 seconds, so now it was making an **avoidance response**—by hurdling soon after the light went out, the animal did not receive the shock.

After a few dozen trials, a typical dog's response latencies declined to an average of about 2 or 3 seconds, and they might be consistently less than 10 seconds for the last several sessions of the experiment. In fact, Solomon and Wynne found that many dogs never again experienced a shock after their first avoidance response—all subsequent latencies were less than 10 seconds. Results such as these had led earlier theorists (Mowrer, 1947; Schoenfeld, 1950) to ponder a question that is sometimes called the **avoidance paradox:** How can the nonoccurrence of an event (shock) serve as a reinforcer for the avoidance response? Notice that escape responses pose no problem for a reinforcement analysis, because here the response produces a change in a hedonically important stimulus—the presence of shock changes to the absence of shock when the escape response is made. On the other hand, consider a trial on which one of Solomon and Wynne's dogs made a response 5 seconds after the light was turned off. Such an avoidance trial involved no change in the shock conditions—there was no shock before the response, and no shock after the response. The early avoidance theorists felt it did not make sense to say that a shock that is not experienced can act as a reinforcer for some behavior. It was this puzzle about what motivated avoidance responses that led to the development of an influential theory of avoidance known as **two-factor theory,** or **two-process theory.**

## Two-Factor Theory

The two factors, or processes, of this theory are classical conditioning and operant conditioning, and according to the theory, both are necessary for avoidance responses to occur (Mowrer, 1947). The proposed role of each of these factors can be illustrated by referring to the experiment of Solomon and Wynne. One unconditioned response to shock is fear, and this response plays a critical role in the theory. Through classical conditioning, this fear response is transferred from the US (shock) to some CS (a stimulus that precedes the shock). In the Solomon and Wynne experiment, the CS was clearly the 10 seconds of darkness that preceded each shock. After a few trials, a dog would presumably respond to the darkness with fear. This conditioning of a fear response to an initially neutral stimulus is the first process of the theory.

Mowrer reasoned that besides being a response, fear has various stimulus properties—a subject can sense changes in heart rate, breathing, and other visceral responses. Everyone will probably agree that the sensations that accompany a fear reaction are unpleasant. According to Mowrer, a so-called avoidance response is reinforced by the reduction in fear that accompanies the removal of the fear-eliciting CS. In the Solomon and Wynne experiment, a dog could escape from a dark compartment to an illuminated compartment by jumping over the barrier. Thus the operant conditioning component of two-factor theory is the reinforcement of an avoidance response by the reduction in fear that occurs when the CS (darkness in this example) is terminated.

It should be emphasized that in two-factor theory, what we have been calling "avoidance responses" are redefined as escape responses. The reinforcer for an avoidance response is supposedly not the avoidance of the shock but rather the escape from a fear-eliciting CS. This theoretical maneuver is two-factor theory's solution to the avoidance paradox. If the theory is correct, we no longer have to wonder how the nonoccurrence of an event such as shock can reinforce a behavior. The removal of a fear-evoking CS is an observable change in the stimulus environment that certainly might act as a negative reinforcer. In short, according to two-factor theory, the termination of the signal for shock in avoidance behavior has the same status as the termination of the shock in escape behavior—both are actual changes in stimulation that can serve as reinforcers.

### Evidence Supporting Two-Factor Theory

Because the role of the fear-eliciting CS is so crucial to two-factor theory, it is not surprising that many experiments have investigated how CSs can influence avoidance behavior. This research has provided support for two-factor theory in several ways. One class of experiments (Rescorla & LoLordo, 1965; Weisman & Litner, 1969) has involved creating a fear-eliciting CS in one context and observing its effects when it is presented during a different situation, where an animal is already making avoidance responses. For example, Rescorla and LoLordo (1965) first trained dogs in a shuttle box where jumping into the other compartment postponed a shock. Then the dogs received conditioning trials in which a tone was paired with shock. Finally, the dogs were returned to the avoidance task, and occasionally the tone was presented (but no longer followed by shock). Whenever the tone came on, the dogs dramatically increased their rates of jumping over the barrier. This result shows that a stimulus that is specifically trained as a CS for fear can amplify ongoing avoidance behavior.

Other experiments supporting two-factor theory have shown that the signal for shock in a typical avoidance situation does indeed develop aversive properties, and that animals can learn a new response that produces the removal of that signal. In an early experiment, N. E. Miller (1948) attempted to develop a white compartment into an aversive stimulus by shocking rats while they were in that chamber. From this point on, no further shocks were presented, but Miller found that a rat would learn a new response, turning a wheel, when this response opened a door and allowed the rat to escape from the white chamber. In the next phase, wheel turning was no longer an effective response; instead, a subject could escape from the white chamber by pressing a lever. Eventually, Miller's subjects learned this second novel response.

Miller reported that the rats learned these new responses by "trial and error": Whatever response produced the opportunity to escape from the white chamber eventually increased in frequency. You should see the parallel between Miller's results and the experiments of Thorndike, where food was used as the reinforcer. Here, the only consequence of a response was the chance to escape from the white chamber, and since the appropriate response increased, this was by definition an example of negative reinforcement. Miller concluded that fear is an "acquirable drive," and that fear reduction can serve as a reinforcer.

The studies just described provide support for two-factor theory by showing that a CS for shock can accelerate ongoing avoidance behavior, and its removal can reinforce totally new responses. However, not all the evidence on two-factor theory has been favorable, and the next section discusses some of the major problems with the theory.

### Problems with Two-Factor Theory

*Avoidance Without Observable Signs of Fear.* One problem with two-factor theory concerns the relationship between fear and avoidance responses. It has long been recognized that this relationship is not as neat as the theory predicts. If the theory is correct, we should be able to observe an increase in fear when the signal for shock is presented, and then a decrease in fear once the avoidance response is made. To conduct such a study, an experimenter must select some objective measure that is thought to be a measure of fear. An animal's heart rate is a commonly used measure. In a study that supported two-factor theory, Soltysik (1960) found heart-rate increases in dogs before the avoidance response and decreases after the response. Unfortunately, the results of other studies are not as encouraging for two-factor theory. Black (1959) observed that dogs' heart rates continued to increase after the avoidance responses were made. In a study with human subjects, Bersh, Notterman, and Schoenfeld (1956) found no heart-rate increases when the signal for shock was presented to well-practiced subjects.

Beginning with some of the earliest studies on avoidance learning, evidence began to accumulate that observable signs of fear disappear as subjects become more experienced. For example, R. L. Solomon and Wynne (1953) noted that early in their experiment, a dog would exhibit various signs of fear (whining, urination, shaking) when the light was turned off. However, once the animal became proficient in making the avoidance response, such overt signs of emotion disappeared. But according to two-factor theory, fear should be greatest when avoidance responses are the strongest, since fear is supposedly what motivates the avoidance response. Other studies have corroborated the observations of Solomon and Wynne (for example, Starr & Mineka, 1977).

***Extinction of Avoidance Behavior.*** As described earlier, many of the dogs in the Solomon and Wynne experiment quickly became proficient at the avoidance task, so that after a few trials, they never again received a shock. From the perspective of two-factor theory, each trial on which the shock is avoided is a classical-conditioning extinction trial: The CS (darkness) is presented, but the US (shock) is not. According to the principles of classical conditioning, the CR (fear) should gradually weaken on such extinction trials until it is no longer elicited by the CS. But if the darkness no longer elicits fear, the avoidance response should not occur either. Thus two-factor theory predicts that avoidance responding should gradually deteriorate after a series of trials without shock. However, once avoidance responses fail to occur, the subject will again receive darkness-shock pairings, and the CR of fear should be reconditioned. Then, as soon as avoidance responses again start to occur, the fear of the darkness should once again start to extinguish. In short, two-factor theory seems to predict that avoidance responses should repeatedly appear and then disappear in a cyclical pattern.

Unfortunately for two-factor theory, such cycles in avoidance responding have almost never been observed. Indeed, one of the most noteworthy features of avoidance behavior is its extreme resistance to extinction. The classic work of Solomon and Wynne provided a good example of this resistance to extinction. They report that after producing an initial avoidance response, many of their dogs responded for several hundred trials without receiving a shock (Solomon, Kamin, & Wynne, 1953; R. L. Solomon & Wynne, 1954). In addition, they found that response latencies continued to decrease during these trials even though no shock was received. This suggests that the strength of the avoidance response was increasing, not decreasing, during these shock-free trials.

Such findings were troublesome for two-factor theory, and many psychologists viewed the slow extinction of avoidance behavior as a major problem for the theory. It is therefore not surprising that other theories of avoidance behavior were developed. Two major alternatives to two-factor theory are discussed next.

## One-Factor Theory

To put it simply, **one-factor theory** states that the classical conditioning component of two-factor theory is not necessary. There is no need to assume that fear reduction is the reinforcer for an avoidance response, because, contrary to the assumptions of two-factor theory, avoidance of a shock can in itself serve as a reinforcer. The experiments of Sidman (1953) and Herrnstein and Hineline (1966) are among the best known studies relevant to one-factor theory.

***The Sidman Avoidance Task.*** Murray Sidman (1953) developed an avoidance procedure that is now called either by his name or by the term **free-operant avoidance.** In this procedure, there is no signal preceding shock, but if the subject makes no responses, the shocks occur at perfectly regular intervals. For instance, in one condition of Sidman's experiment, a rat would receive a shock every 5 seconds throughout the session if it made no avoidance response (see Figure 8-2a). However, if the rat made an avoidance response (pressing a lever), the next shock did not occur until 30 seconds after the response.

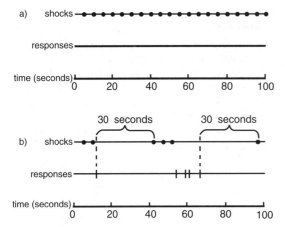

**FIGURE 8-2** The procedure in one condition of Sidman's (1953) avoidance task. (a) If the subject makes no responses, a shock is delivered every 5 seconds. (b) Each response postpones the next shock for 30 seconds.

Each response postponed the next shock for 30 seconds (Figure 8-2b). By responding regularly (say, once every 20 to 25 seconds), a rat could avoid all the shocks. In practice, Sidman's rats did not avoid all the shocks, but they did respond frequently enough to avoid many of them.

On the surface, these results seem consistent with one-factor theory and problematic for two-factor theory because there is no signal before a shock. If there is no stimulus to elicit fear, why should an avoidance response occur? Actually, it is easy to construct an answer that is consistent with two-factor theory, as Sidman himself realized. The logic proceeds as follows: Although Sidman provided no external stimulus, the passage of time could serve as a stimulus because the shocks occurred at regular intervals. That is, once a subject was familiar with the procedure, fear might increase as more and more time elapsed without a response. The animal could associate fear with the stimulus "a long time since the last response," and it could remove this stimulus (and the associated fear) by making a response.

To make a stronger case for one-factor theory, we need an experiment in which neither an external stimulus nor an unobservable stimulus such as the passage of time might function as a CS for fear. The next experiment meets these requirements.

***The Herrnstein and Hineline (1966) Experiment.*** The procedure of this experiment was complex, but in essence, by pressing a lever, a rat could switch from a schedule that delivered shocks at a rapid rate to one that delivered shocks at a slower rate. For example, in one condition the probability of a shock after each 2-second interval was .3 if the rat had not recently pressed the lever, but only .1 if the rat had recently pressed the lever. Clearly, to reduce the number of shocks, the animal should remain on the .1 schedule as much as possible. A single response switched the animal to the .1 schedule, which remained in effect until, by chance, a shock finally occurred. Then the animal was switched back to the .3 schedule, where it remained until another lever press occurred.

A hypothetical 100-second segment of a session is shown in Figure 8-3. The imaginary subject began the session on the .3 schedule and received four shocks in the first 20 seconds before a response switched the animal to the .1 schedule. The animal's second response had no effect, since it was still on the .1 schedule. The .1 schedule remained in effect for 22 seconds, after which a shock occurred and the .3 schedule was reinstated. Notice that during these 22 seconds on the .1 schedule, the animal avoided four shocks that would have occurred on the .3 schedule. A third response at about 55 seconds switched the animal to the

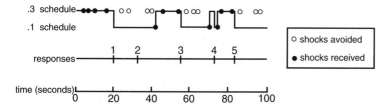

**FIGURE 8-3** A hypothetical 100-second segment of a session in the Herrnstein and Hineline (1966) experiment. Each response temporarily switched a rat from a schedule where the probability of shock was .3 every 2 seconds to a schedule where the probability was .1. A subject could avoid many shocks (open circles) by responding, but a response did not guarantee any specific amount of shock-free time.

.1 schedule for another 14 seconds, during which three more shocks were avoided. But responding is not always reinforced by a shock-free period. The animal's fourth response was, by chance, followed almost immediately by a shock delivered by the .1 schedule. This example shows that responses in this procedure only produced a lower rate of shocks on the average; they did not guarantee any fixed shock-free time.

Herrnstein and Hineline (1966) found that 17 of their 18 rats eventually acquired the avoidance response. They concluded (1) that animals can learn an avoidance response when neither an external CS nor the passage of time is a reliable signal for shock, and (2) to master this task, animals must be sensitive to the average shock rates in the presence and absence of responding. According to Herrnstein (1969), if animals are sensitive to these two rates of shock, then postulating that an unobservable fear controls the behavior is a needless complication: Why not simply assume that a reduction in shock rate is the reinforcer for the avoidance response? The one-factor theorist's solution to the avoidance paradox is thus to deny that it is a paradox.

***Slow Extinction as a Failure of Discrimination.*** One-factor theory, which relies solely on the principles of operant conditioning, has a simple explanation for the slow extinction of avoidance responses. Recall (from Chapter 7) that one popular explanation of why extinction is slower after variable schedules of reinforcement than after fixed schedules is that it is more difficult for the subject to discriminate a change in the contingencies. This same explanation can be extended to the extinction of avoidance responses. We have seen that once an avoidance response is acquired, the subject may avoid every scheduled shock by making the appropriate response. Now suppose that at some point the experimenter turns off the shock generator. From the subject's perspective, the subsequent trials will appear no different from the previous trials: The stimulus comes on, the subject responds, the stimulus goes off, no shock occurs. Since the subject can discriminate no change in the conditions, there is no change in behavior either, according to this reasoning.

## Cognitive Theory

Seligman and Johnston (1973) developed a **cognitive theory of avoidance** that they suggested was superior to both two-factor and one-factor theories. Seligman and Johnston proposed that a subject's behavior will change in an avoidance task whenever there is a discrepancy between expectancy and observation (so on a very general level, the theory bears some resemblance to the Rescorla-Wagner model, described in Chapter 5). To be more specific, Seligman and Johnston proposed that there are two important expectations in an avoidance situation: (1) an expectation about the consequences of a response, and (2) an expectation about the consequences of not responding. On the first trial of a signaled avoidance experiment, a subject can have no expectation that a particular response will avoid a shock nor that shock will occur if it does not respond. Consequently, the subject makes no avoidance response on the first trial. However, over the course of the acquisition phase, the subject gradually develops the expectations that (1) no shock will occur if a response is made, and (2) shock will occur if a response is not made. Assuming that the animal prefers situation 1 over situation 2 (a very reasonable assumption), the animal will make a response.

Once these two expectations have been formed, Seligman and Johnston assumed that the animal's behavior will not change until one or both of the expectations are violated. This assumption can account for the slow extinction of avoidance behavior. As long as the animal responds on each extinction trial, it can observe only that a response is followed by no shock. This observation is consistent with the animal's expectation, so there is no change in its behavior. Presumably, extinction will only begin to occur if the subject eventually fails to make a response on some trial (perhaps by mistake or because the subject is distracted by a random noise, by an itch, and so on). It is only on such trials that the subject can observe an outcome (no response followed by no shock) that is inconsistent with the animal's expectations.

***The Procedure of Response Blocking (Flooding).*** The slow extinction of avoidance responses is not inevitable: An experimenter can hasten the course of extinction by using a procedure called **response blocking,** or **flooding.** As its name suggests, response blocking involves presenting the signal that precedes shock but preventing the subject from making the avoidance response. For example, Page and Hall (1953) conducted an avoidance experiment in which rats learned to avoid a shock by running from one compartment to another. After the response was learned, one group of rats received normal extinction trials. A second group had the extinction trials preceded by five trials in which a subject was retained in the first compartment for 15 seconds, with the door to the second compartment closed. Thus these subjects were prevented from making the avoidance response, but unlike in the acquisition phase, they received no shocks in the first compartment. Page and Hall found that extinction proceeded much more rapidly in the response-blocking group. The other term for this procedure, flooding, connotes the fact that subjects are "flooded" with exposure to the stimulus that used to precede shock. (In the Page and Hall experiment, this stimulus was simply the inside of the first compartment.) Considerable evidence now suggests that response blocking is an effective way to speed the extinction of avoidance responses (M. Baum, 1966, 1976).

Cognitive theory provides a convenient explanation of why response blocking works. The subject is forced to observe a set of events—no response followed by no shock—that is discrepant from the animal's expectation that no response will be followed by shock. A new expectation, that no shock will follow no response, is gradually formed, and as a result, avoidance responses gradually disappear.

Can the other theories of avoidance behavior account for the effects of response blocking? An obvious explanation based on two-factor theory is that the forced exposure to the CS produces extinction of the conditioned response of fear. An explanation based on one-factor theory might proceed as follows: Normal avoidance extinction is slow because there is no discriminative stimulus that signals the change from acquisition to extinction conditions. The procedure used to prevent the avoidance response represents a drastic stimulus change: There is now a closed door that prevents the animal from entering the other compartment. This change in stimuli gives the subject a cue that things are now different from the preceding acquisition phase. It is therefore not surprising that subsequent extinction proceeds more quickly.

***When Avoidance Responses Become Ineffective.*** According to cognitive theory, a second way to hasten the extinction of avoidance responses would be to present the shock whether or not a response occurs. This contingency would violate a subject's expectation that a response leads to no shock, and therefore avoidance responding should decline. Several studies have shown that following avoidance responses with shock does lead to rapid extinction of those responses (Davenport & Olson, 1968; Seligman & Campbell, 1965). Of course, this result is not surprising, and you should be able to see that both two-factor theory and one-factor theory can easily account for this finding. The presentation of a shock following an avoidance response is a dramatic change in conditions that should quickly produce changes in the subject's behavior.

## Biological Constraints in Avoidance Learning

As if the theoretical analysis of avoidance were not already confusing enough, the picture is further complicated by evidence that biological constraints can also play an important role in avoidance learning, just as they can in classical conditioning and with the use of positive reinforcement. Robert Bolles (1970) proposed that animals exhibit a type of preparedness in avoidance learning. In this case, the preparedness does not involve a stimulus-stimulus association, but rather a propensity to perform certain behaviors in a potentially dangerous situation. Bolles was highly critical of traditional theories of avoidance learning, especially two-factor theory. He suggested that a two-factor account of avoidance learning in the wild might go as follows: A small animal in the forest is attacked by a predator and is hurt but manages to escape. Later, when the animal is again in this part of the forest, it encounters a CS—a sight, sound, or smell that preceded the previous attack. This CS produces the response of fear, and the animal runs away to escape from the CS, and it is reinforced by a feeling of relief. According to the two-factor account, then, avoidance behavior occurs because animals learn about signals for danger (CSs) and then avoid those signals. Bolles (1970) claimed, however, that this account is

> utter nonsense. . . . Thus, no real-life predator is going to present cues just before it attacks. No owl hoots or whistles 5 seconds before pouncing on a mouse. And no owl terminates its hoots or whistles just as the mouse gets away so as to reinforce the avoidance response. Nor will the owl give the mouse enough trials for the necessary learning to occur. What keeps our little friends alive in the forest has nothing to do with avoidance learning as we ordinarily conceive of it or investigate it in the laboratory. . . . What keeps animals alive in the wild is that they have very effective innate defensive reactions which occur when they encounter any kind of new or sudden stimulus. (pp. 32–33)

Bolles called these innate behavior patterns **species-specific defense reactions** (SSDRs). As the name implies, SSDRs may be different for different animals, but Bolles suggested that they usually fall into one of three categories—freezing, fleeing, and fighting (adopting an aggressive posture and/or behaviors). Bolles proposed that in laboratory studies of avoidance, an avoidance response will be quickly learned if it is identical with or at least similar to one of the subject's SSDRs. If the required avoidance response is not similar to an SSDR, the response will be learned slowly or not at all. To support this hypothesis, Bolles noted that rats can learn to avoid a shock by jumping or running out of a compartment in one or only a few trials. The rapid acquisition presumably reflects the fact that for rats, fleeing is a highly probable response to danger. In comparison, it may take a rat 100 trials to learn to avoid shock in a shuttle box. The greater difficulty may arise because this situation requires the rat to reenter a chamber where it was just shocked, and returning to a dangerous location is not something a rat is likely to do. It is even more difficult to train a rat to avoid shock by pressing a lever, presumably because this response is decidedly unlike any of the creature's typical responses to danger.

It is important to understand that the difficulty in learning new responses such as lever pressing depends on the nature of the reinforcer. When the reinforcer is avoidance of shock, lever pressing is a difficult response for rats to acquire, and some rats never learn it. Yet when the reinforcer is food or water, lever pressing is a relatively easy response for rats to learn. With other species, researchers have found similar variations in the difficulty of acquiring a response that depend on what reinforcer is used. We have seen that key pecking is an operant response that is frequently used with pigeons, partly because it is fairly easy to shape a pigeon to peck a key when food is the reinforcer. In comparison, it is very difficult to train a pigeon to peck a key to avoid a shock. The problem is apparently that a pigeon's most usual response to an intense aversive stimulus is to fly away, a response that has almost nothing in common with standing in place and pecking. Because of examples like this, Fanselow (1997) has argued that the basic principle of negative reinforcement (which states that any response that helps to avoid an aversive event will be strengthened) is not especially useful when SSDRs take over: Even a simple response such as pressing a lever or pecking a key may be difficult for the animal to learn.

A few studies have shown that it is possible to train animals to make an arbitrary operant response in an avoidance situation by somehow making the desired response more compatible with the SSDRs of that species. For example, in response to mild shock, a pigeon may exhibit SSDRs from the "fighting" category, including flapping its wings. Beginning with this response of wing flapping, Rachlin (1969) trained pigeons to operate a "key" that protruded into the chamber in order to avoid the shock. With rats, Modaresi (1990) found that lever pressing was much easier to train as an avoidance response if the lever was higher on the wall, and especially if lever presses not only avoided the shocks but produced a "safe area" (a platform) on which the rats could stand. Through a careful series of experiments, Modaresi showed that these two features coincided with the rats' natural tendencies to stretch upward and to seek a safe area when facing a potentially painful stimulus. Both of these studies are consistent with Bolles's claim that the ease of learning an avoidance response

depends on the similarity between that response and one of the subject's SSDRs.

## Conclusions About the Theories of Avoidance

First, let us consider once again the difference between one-factor theory and cognitive theory. Seligman and Johnston claim that one-factor theory makes no specific predictions about such matters as extinction and response blocking. However, we have seen that the predictions of cognitive theory are just as ambiguous as those of one-factor theory. In the final analysis, the differences between these two theories are to a large extent semantic: Wherever cognitive theory speaks of a violation of expectations or a change in expectations, one-factor theory can point to changes in discriminative stimuli. Those who like to speculate about an animal's expectations will probably favor cognitive theory; strict behaviorists, who avoid such speculation about internal events, will prefer the terminology of one-factor theory.

Over the years, two-factor theory has been a popular theory of avoidance behavior, but it suffers from several weaknesses. Avoidance learning can occur when there is no external signal for shock (Herrnstein & Hineline, 1966). Although fear plays a crucial role in this theory, the bulk of the evidence suggests that fear disappears yet avoidance responses continue as subjects become experienced at the avoidance task. Finally, two-factor theory has difficulty explaining the slowness of extinction in avoidance tasks.

Both one-factor theory and cognitive theory avoid the major problems of two-factor theory by assuming that fear is not an indispensable part of avoidance behavior. However, we have reviewed a number of studies showing that fear does play a role in some avoidance situations (N. E. Miller, 1948; Rescorla & LoLordo, 1965). More recently, Levis (1989; J. E. Smith & Levis, 1991) has argued that fear is involved in all avoidance situations, and that if the animals show no measurable signs of fear, this is because researchers do not have the ability to measure very small levels of fear.

These small levels of fear could still be enough to motivate subjects to continue performing the avoidance response. Levis concluded that the rejection of two-factor theory has been premature.

Other learning theorists have also argued that two-factor theory has its advantages. Stasiewicz and Maisto (1993) proposed that the theory can be applied to many cases of drug abuse by assuming that taking the drugs allows abusers to avoid negative emotional states. Zhuikov, Couvillon, and Bitterman (1994) developed a mathematical version of two-factor theory, and they concluded that the theory makes accurate predictions about many details of avoidance responding that cannot be made if one of the factors is eliminated.

In summary, after several decades of research and debate, the question of which theory of avoidance is best has not been settled to everyone's satisfaction. This may be a sign that each theory is partially correct. Perhaps fear does play an important role in some avoidance situations, but it is not a necessary role—avoidance responding may sometimes occur in the absence of fear, as the one-factor and cognitive theories propose.

## Flooding as Behavior Therapy

Regardless of which theory best accounts for the effects of response blocking or flooding, this procedure has been adopted by some behavior therapists as a treatment for phobias. The major difference between flooding and systematic desensitization (Chapter 4) is that the hierarchy of fearful events or stimuli is eliminated. Instead of beginning with a stimulus that elicits only a small amount of fear, a therapist using a flooding procedure starts immediately with a highly feared stimulus and forces the patient to remain in the presence of this stimulus until the patient's external signs of fear subside. For example, an individual with a snake phobia might be required to remain in a small room where the therapist is handling a live snake. Of course, it is the therapist's duty to describe the details of the flooding procedure to the patient in advance, to point out that the fear the patient will experience may be quite unpleasant, and to obtain the patient's consent before proceeding. In spite of these safeguards for protecting the rights of the patient, the use of flooding in behavior therapy has been challenged on both practical and moral grounds. Morganstern (1973) reviewed a number of studies that compared the effectiveness of flooding and systematic desensitization, and he concluded that these procedures are about equally effective. Since systematic desensitization (which never allows the patient to experience a high level of fear) is clearly a more pleasant form of therapy, Morganstern argued that there is little justification for using flooding in therapy.

Whereas Morganstern's position seems reasonable, flooding can sometimes succeed in eliminating a phobia when systematic desensitization has failed. Yule, Sacks, and Hersov (1974) report the case history of an 11-year-old boy who had a fear of loud noises—balloons bursting, cap guns, motorcycles, pneumatic drills, and so on. Several weeks of systematic desensitization had produced little improvement. As a last resort, the therapists described a flooding procedure, and the boy agreed to try it. In the first session, the boy entered a small room filled with some 50 balloons. The mere sight of the balloons made the boy very nervous, and he began to cry when the therapist started to break them, one at a time. The therapist continued, however, and eventually he persuaded the boy to break the balloons, first with his feet (while covering his ears with his hands) and later with his hands. The first session ended after several dozen balloons had been broken. At the beginning of the second session, the boy still appeared anxious, but the therapist reported that after breaking several hundred more balloons the boy almost seemed to enjoy it. After the second session, the boy no longer seemed to fear loud noises, so the therapy was discontinued. A follow-up inquiry 25 months later found that the boy had experienced no recurrences of the phobia.

Although flooding was successful in this case, Yule and colleagues suggest that it should be used with caution. They suggest that long-duration sessions are essential—the therapist

You can test your understanding of the concept of negative reinforcement at *http://www.mcli.dist.maricopa.edu/proj/nru/nru_web.html.*

should first observe the onset of fear, and then continue with the procedure until a definite reduction in fear is seen. If the session is terminated too soon, the patient's phobia might actually increase. Indeed, there are a few reports of cases where patients' fears worsened after short-duration therapy sessions of this type (Staub, 1968). Despite these drawbacks, flooding can be an effective form of treatment for phobias when used carefully (J. E. James, 1986; Morris & Kratochwill, 1983).

## LEARNED HELPLESSNESS

Aversive stimuli can do more than produce fear and avoidance responses. Considerable research with both animals and people has shown that repeated exposure to aversive events that are unpredictable and out of the individual's control can have long-term debilitating effects. Seligman and his colleagues (Maier & Seligman, 1976; Overmier & Seligman, 1967) have proposed that in such circumstances, both animals and people may develop the expectation that their behavior has little effect on their environment, and this expectation may generalize to a wide range of situations. Seligman calls this general expectation **learned helplessness.**

Consider the following experiment. A dog is first placed in a harness where it receives several dozen inescapable shocks. On the next day, the dog is placed in a shuttle box, where it receives escape/avoidance trials very similar to those administered by R. L. Solomon and Wynne (1953): Ten seconds of darkness is followed by shock unless the dog jumps into the other compartment. But whereas the dogs in Solomon and Wynne's study learned the task within a few trials, about two thirds of the animals in Seligman's procedure never learned either to

escape or avoid the shock. (In Seligman's procedure, the shock ended after 60 seconds if a dog did not respond.) For a few trials, a dog might run around a bit, but eventually the subject would simply lie down and whine when the shock came on, making no attempt to escape. Seligman's conclusion was that in the initial training with inescapable shock, the dog developed an expectation that its behavior has no effect on the aversive consequences it experiences, and this expectation of helplessness carried over to the shuttle box. This type of learned helplessness after inescapable shock has been found with many different species, even with creatures as primitive as cockroaches (Brown, Hughes, & Jones, 1988).

Parallel experiments have been conducted with human subjects. For instance, in one study (Hiroto & Seligman, 1975), college students were first presented with a series of loud noises that they could not avoid. They were then asked to solve a series of anagrams. These students had much greater difficulty solving the problems than students who were not exposed to the unavoidable noises. A typical control subject solved all the anagrams, and got faster and faster as the trials proceeded. A typical subject in the noise group would fail on most of the problems, apparently giving up on a problem before the allotted time had expired. Eventually, after many trials, a subject in the noise condition might begin to make some slow progress on the anagrams.

Seligman's explanation is the same for both of these examples: Early experience with uncontrollable aversive events produces a sense of helplessness that carries over into other situations, leading to learning and performance deficits. To be more specific, Maier and Seligman (1976) claimed that there are three components of learned helplessness: motivational, cognitive, and emotional. By a motivational impairment, they meant that subjects lose the motivation to try to control events in their environment, or if they do try at first, they give up easily. The cognitive impairment is a lowered ability to learn from one's experience. Some studies have shown that even when "helpless" subjects are given the same number of successes as control subjects, they learn more slowly. For example, one study found that exposure to inescapable shocks later impaired rats' abilities to learn which of two arms in a maze would allow them to escape from a shock (Jackson, Alexander, & Maier, 1980). After a few successful anagram solutions, students in the helpless group did not improve as rapidly on subsequent problems as did control subjects.

Finally, Maier and Seligman (1976) summarized a number of emotional problems that have been shown to follow exposure to inescapable aversive events: Rats developed ulcers, cats ate less, humans experienced temporary increase in blood pressure, and monkeys became ill. Seligman proposed that this complex pattern of motivational, cognitive, and emotional problems is the result of exposure to inescapable aversive events.

Seligman (1975) suggested that this laboratory phenomenon is similar to the severe and prolonged periods of depression some people experience. As one example, he described the case of a middle-aged woman whose children had gone off to college and whose husband was often away on business trips. These unpleasant events were out of the woman's control—nothing she did could bring her family back. Apparently as a result of these experiences, the woman developed a case of profound depression. She often stayed in bed most of the day, for just getting dressed seemed like a great chore. As with Seligman's dogs, the simplest of tasks became difficult for this woman. Since Seligman's initial work, hundreds of studies have been published on learned helplessness in humans, and this research has branched in many directions. Psychologists have applied the concept of learned helplessness to the problems of patients suffering from long-term illnesses (Chaney, Mullins, Uretsky, Pace, Werden, & Hartman, 1999), the ability of the elderly to cope with their problems (K. Solomon, 1990), the work efficiency and satisfaction of industrial employees (Sahoo & Tripathy, 1990), and many other situations where people might feel that they have little control over important events in their lives.

The theory of learned helplessness has even been applied to the performance of professional football teams. What happens after a team loses a game by a lopsided score? Using common sense, we might expect that in the next game, the team will rebound and perform better than expected, perhaps because the players work harder in preparation, or because the coaching staff makes adjustments. The theory of learned helplessness makes the opposite prediction, however. A bad loss one week should lead to feelings of helplessness, and the team's performance in the next game should also be below average. Reisel and Kopelman (1995) tested these opposing predictions using 3 years' worth of data from all teams in the National Football League, and the results supported the theory of learned helplessness. They found that (1) if a team was badly beaten in one game, the team tended to perform worse than expected in the next game, and (2) this was especially true if the team faced a difficult opponent in the next game. (According to the theory, learned helplessness should indeed be most pronounced when the upcoming task appears insurmountable.)

Seligman and his colleagues have suggested that there may be differences between helplessness in humans and in animals (Abramson, Seligman, & Teasdale, 1978). They proposed that helplessness in humans can vary along three dimensions: (1) The sense of helplessness may be specific to one situation or fairly global, (2) the person may attribute his or her helplessness to internal or external factors, and (3) the person may view this helplessness as stable (long-term) or unstable (short-term). The severity of the problem and strategy for treatment will depend heavily on which one of these characteristics applies in a given case. For instance, if a student attributes his failure in math to specific, external factors ("That was a very difficult course"), this will be less debilitating than if the failure is attributed to internal, global factors ("I'm just incapable of college-level work"). Seligman and his colleagues admit that they do not know whether these three dimensions are applicable to helplessness in animals.

Despite these possible differences between animal and human helplessness, many research projects have used Seligman's procedures to establish learned helplessness in animals, and then to examine possible connections between brain chemistry and depression. Animals that are given certain pharmacological agents show less learned helplessness than control animals (Besson, Privat, Eschalier, & Fialip, 1999; Siuciak, Lewis, Wiegand, & Lindsay, 1997). This research may provide a better understanding of depression in humans, and it may lead to better treatments for this disorder.

Seligman's work has also suggested possible remedies for helplessness that do not involve drugs. One form of treatment has already been alluded to: If helpless dogs are guided across the barrier for enough trials, they will eventually start making the response on their own. In more general terms, Seligman suggests that the best treatment is to place the subject in a situation where it cannot fail, so that gradually an expectation that one's behavior has some control over the consequences that follow will develop. More interesting are studies showing that learned helplessness can be prevented in the first place by what Seligman calls "immunization." That is, the subject is first exposed to a situation where some response (such as turning a wheel) provides escape from shock. Thus the animal's first exposure to shock occurs in a context where the animal can control the shock. Then, in a second situation, inescapable shocks are presented. Finally, the animals are tested in a third situation where a new response (say, switching compartments in a shuttle box) provides escape from shock. It has repeatedly been shown that this initial experience with escapable shock blocks the onset of learned helplessness (Maier & Seligman, 1976; J. L. Williams & Lierle, 1986).

As one possible implication of this finding, Seligman (1975) suggests that feelings of helplessness in a classroom environment may be prevented by making sure that a child's earliest classroom experiences are ones where the child succeeds (ones where the child demonstrates a mastery over the task at hand). McKean (1994) has made similar suggestions for helping college students who exhibit signs of helplessness in academic settings. Such students tend to view course work as uncontrollable, aversive, and inescapable. They assume that they are going to do poorly, and give up easily whenever they experience difficulty with course assignments or other setbacks. To assist such students, McKean suggests that professors should make their courses as predictable and controllable as possible (for example, by clearly listing all course requirements on the syllabus, by explaining the skills students will need to succeed in the course, and by suggesting how to develop these skills). Initial course assignments should be ones that students are likely to complete successfully, so they gain confidence that they have the ability to master the requirements of the course.

## PUNISHMENT

Figure 8-1 suggests that punishment has the opposite effect on behavior as positive reinforcement: Reinforcement produces an increase in behavior, and punishment produces a decrease in behavior. Whether punishment is indeed the opposite of reinforcement is an empirical question, however, and such illustrious psychologists as Thorndike and Skinner have concluded that it is not. Based on their own research, each concluded that the effects of punishment are not exactly opposite to those of reinforcement. However, their experiments are not very convincing.

For example, Skinner (1938) placed two groups of rats on VI schedules of lever pressing for three sessions, and then each animal had two sessions of extinction. For one group, nothing unusual happened during extinction, and this group produced the upper cumulative record in Figure 8-4: Responding gradually decreased over the two sessions. For the second group, however, each lever press during the first 10 minutes of extinction was punished—whenever a rat pressed the lever, the lever "slapped" upward against the rat's paws. This mild punishment was enough to reduce the number of responses during these 10 minutes to a level well below that of the first group. However, when the punishment was removed, response rates increased, and by the end of the second session, the punished animals had made just about as many responses as the unpunished animals. From these results, Skinner concluded that the effects of punishment are not permanent, and that punishment

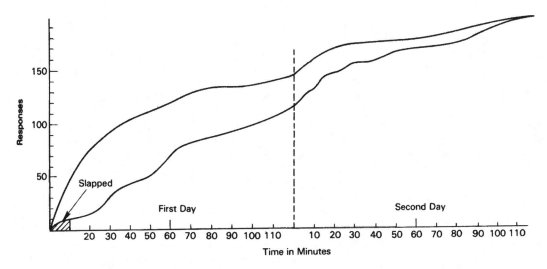

**FIGURE 8-4** Cumulative records during 2 days of extinction from the two groups of rats in Skinner's (1938) experiment on punishment. The upper record is from the group that received normal extinction. The lower record is from the group whose responses were punished during the first 10 minutes of extinction.

produces only a "temporary suppression" of responding.

The problem with Skinner's conclusion is that although the effects of punishment were certainly temporary, so was the punishment itself. We know that the effects of positive reinforcement are also "temporary" in the sense that operant responses will extinguish after the reinforcer is removed. Since Skinner's early experiment, many studies have addressed the question of whether punishment is the opposite of reinforcement in its effects on behavior. The following section describes a few of these studies.

### Is Punishment the Opposite of Reinforcement?

We can attempt to answer this question by examining the two words used by Skinner—"temporary" and "suppression." If, unlike in Skinner's experiment, the punishment contingency is permanent, is the decrease in behavior still temporary? Sometimes it is, for a number of studies have shown that subjects may habituate to a relatively mild punisher (Azrin, 1960; Rachlin, 1966). In Azrin's (1960) experiment,

once pigeons were responding steadily on a VI schedule, punishment was introduced—each response produced a mild shock. Response rates decreased immediately, but over the course of several sessions, they returned to their preshock levels. Despite such results, there is no doubt that suitably intense punishment can produce a long-term decrease or disappearance of the punished behavior. When Azrin used more intense shocks, there was little or no recovery in responding over the course of the experiment.

Although Skinner did not define the term "suppression," later writers (Estes, 1944) took it to mean a decrease in behavior that does not depend on a contingency between the behavior and the aversive event. It does not take a punishment contingency to cause a decrease in behavior. For example, in the frequently used conditioned-suppression procedure, a CS for shock is presented as an animal is responding for food reinforcement. After a few pairings of the CS and shock, responding for food slows or stops completely during the CS, even though these responses are not punished, and no behavior on the part of the subject can prevent the shock. In short, an aversive event can cause a general decrease in a subject's ongoing behavior. Does a contingency between a specific behavior and an aversive event do more than this? Does it cause a greater decrease in this behavior than the same event delivered on a noncontingent basis? An experiment by Schuster and Rachlin (1968) investigated this question. Pigeons could sometimes peck at the left key in a Skinner box, and at other times they could peck at the right key. Both keys offered identical VI schedules of food reinforcement, but then different schedules of shock were introduced on the two keys. When the left key was lit (signaling that the VI schedule was available on this key), some of the pigeon's key pecks were followed by shock. On the other hand, when the right key was lit, shocks were presented regardless of whether the pigeon pecked at the key. Under these conditions, responding on the left key decreased markedly, but there was little change in response rate on the right key.

Studies like this have firmly established the fact that a punishment contingency does more than simply cause a general decrease in activity. When a particular behavior is punished, that behavior will exhibit a large decrease in frequency while other, unpunished behaviors show no substantial change in frequency. To summarize, contrary to the predictions of Thorndike and Skinner, empirical results suggest that the effects of punishment are directly opposite to those of reinforcement: Reinforcement produces an increase in whatever specific behavior is followed by the hedonically positive stimulus, and punishment produces a decrease in the specific behavior that is followed by the aversive stimulus. In both cases, we can expect these changes in behavior to persist as long as the reinforcement or punishment contingency remains in effect.

## Factors Influencing the Effectiveness of Punishment

We now know a good deal more about punishment besides the fact that its effects can be permanent and that the response-punisher contingency is important. Operant conditioners have examined a number of variables that

determine what effects a punishment contingency will have. Azrin and Holz (1966) reviewed some of these variables, and to their credit all of their major points appear as true now as when their findings were published. Several of these points are described next.

***Manner of Introduction.*** If one's goal is to obtain a large, permanent decrease in some behavior, then Azrin and Holz recommend that the punisher be immediately introduced at its full intensity. We have already seen that subjects can habituate to a mild punisher, and several studies have shown that this habituation seems to generalize to higher intensities of punishment. The end result is that a given intensity of punishment may produce a complete cessation of behavior if introduced suddenly, but it may have little or no effect on behavior if it is gradually approached through a series of successive approximations. Azrin, Holz, and Hake (1963) reported that a shock of 80 volts following each response was sufficient to produce a complete suppression of pigeons' key-peck responses if the 80-volt intensity was used from the outset. However, if the punishment began at lower intensities and then slowly increased, the pigeons would continue to respond even when the intensity was raised to as much as 130 volts. Since a behavior modifier's goal when using punishment is to eliminate an undesirable behavior, not to shape a tolerance of the aversive stimulus, the punisher should be at its maximum intensity the first time it is presented.

***Immediacy of Punishment.*** Just as the most effective reinforcer is one that is delivered immediately after the operant response, a punisher that immediately follows a response is most effective in decreasing the frequency of the response. Baron, Kaufman, and Fazzini (1969) studied the behavior of rats who were responding on a Sidman avoidance task. Some of the rats' avoidance responses were punished with shock, but in different conditions the delay between a response and the punishment was varied between 0 and 60 seconds. There was an orderly relationship between punishment delay and response rate: The more immediate the punishment, the greater the decrease in responding. The importance of delivering punishment immediately may explain why many common forms of punishment are ineffective. For example, the mother who tries to decrease a child's misbehavior with the warning, "Just wait until your father gets home" is describing a very long delay between a behavior and its punishment. It would not be surprising if this contingency had little effect on the child's behavior. The same principle applies in the classroom, where a scolding from the teacher is most effective if the teacher scolds a child immediately after the child has misbehaved, not after some time has passed (Abramowitz & O'Leary, 1990).

***Schedule of Punishment.*** Like positive reinforcers, punishers need not be delivered after every occurrence of a behavior. Azrin and Holz conclude, however, that the most effective way to eliminate a behavior is to punish every response rather than to use some intermittent schedule of punishment. In one experiment, rats pressed levers to earn food, but some lever presses were punished with a brief shock. The shocks were delivered on FR schedules ranging from FR 1 (every response followed by shock) to FR 1000 (every thousandth response followed by shock). As you might expect, the smaller FR punishment schedules produced the greater decreases in responding (Azrin, Holz, & Hake, 1963). The same general rule applies to human behavior: Using an intermittent schedule of punishment may sometimes be enough to eliminate an unwanted behavior, but the most powerful way to reduce behavior is to punish every occurrence (Cipani, Brendlinger, McDowell, & Usher, 1991).

The schedule of punishment can affect the patterning of responses over time as well as the overall response rate. When Azrin (1956) superimposed an FI 60-second schedule of punishment on a VI 3-minute schedule of food reinforcement, he found that pigeons' response rates declined toward zero as the end of each 60-second interval approached. In other words, the effect of the FI schedule of punishment (a decelerating pattern of responding)

was the opposite of that typically found with FI schedules of reinforcement (an accelerating pattern of responding). In a similar fashion, Hendry and Van-Toller (1964) punished rats' lever presses on an FR 20 schedule and found that response rates decreased as the twentieth response was approached. Response rates increased suddenly after each shock was delivered. This pattern is also the opposite of that produced by FR reinforcement schedules, in which there is a pause after each reinforcer is delivered. In other research, Galbicka and his colleagues showed that certain lengths of interresponse times (IRTs) could be decreased through punishment: When long IRTs were punished, monkeys produced fewer long IRTs and more short IRTs (Galbicka & Branch, 1981; Galbicka & Platt, 1984). This result parallels the studies showing that certain durations of IRTs can be increased through selective reinforcement (Chapter 7).

These and other studies on schedules of punishment bolster the argument that punishment is the opposite of reinforcement in its effects on behavior: Where a particular reinforcement schedule produces an accelerating response pattern, the same schedule of punishment produces a decelerating pattern; where reinforcement produces a pause-then-respond pattern, punishment produces a respond-then-pause pattern; where reinforcement increases IRTs of certain sizes, punishment decreases them.

***Motivation to Respond.*** Azrin and Holz note that the effectiveness of a punishment procedure is inversely related to the intensity of the subject's motivation to respond. Azrin, Holz, and Hake (1963) demonstrated this point quite clearly by observing the effects of punishment on pigeons' food-reinforced responses when the birds were maintained at different levels of food deprivation. Punishment had little effect on response rates when the pigeons were very hungry, but when these animals were only slightly food-deprived, the same intensity of punishment produced a complete cessation of responding. This finding is not surprising, but it does emphasize a strategy for increasing the effectiveness of a punishment procedure without increasing the amount of punishment:

Attempt to discover what reinforcer is maintaining the behavior, and decrease the value of that reinforcer. Thus, if a mother believes that her young child engages in destructive behaviors as a way of getting the mother's attention, she can (1) punish the undesired behaviors and simultaneously (2) give the child more attention before the youngster resorts to the undesirable behaviors. A related strategy, as discussed next, is to deliver the same reinforcer for a different, more desirable response.

***Availability of Alternative Behaviors.*** Azrin and Holz reported a result that we might easily predict using common sense. A pigeon could peck at a single response key for food reinforcement on an FR 25 schedule. When each response was punished by a mild shock, the subject's response rate decreased, but only by about 10 percent. However, in another condition, a second key also provided food on an FR 25 schedule, but only responses on the first key were punished. It should come as no surprise that the pigeon ceased responding on the first key and responded exclusively on the second. The more general point, however, is that punishment is much more effective when the subject is provided with an alternative way to obtain the reinforcer that has been maintaining some unwanted response. For this reason, when behavior modifiers decide it is necessary to use punishment to eliminate some unwanted behavior (such as fighting among children), they almost always pair this punishment with reinforcement for an alternative behavior that is incompatible with the unwanted behavior (for instance, cooperative play).

***Punishment as a Discriminative Stimulus.*** This observation is less obvious than those of the last few paragraphs. Besides having aversive properties, a punisher can also sometimes function as a discriminative stimulus—a signal predicting the availability of other stimuli, either pleasant or unpleasant. Imagine an experiment in which a pigeon's responses go unpunished during some portions of the session but are followed by shock during other parts of the session. Each time the shock begins, the pigeon's response rate increases! This behavior seems paradoxical until we learn that the pigeon can obtain food only during those periods when its responses are punished; an extinction schedule is in effect during the periods when responses are not shocked (Holz and Azrin, 1961). In other words, the shocks following responses served as discriminative stimuli for the availability of food reinforcement, for they were the only stimuli that differentiated between the periods of reinforcement and extinction. Azrin and Holz suggest that similar explanations may account for some instances of **masochism**—self-injurious behaviors that appear equally paradoxical at first glance. Because self-injurious behaviors often bring to the individual the reinforcers of sympathy and attention, the aversive aspects of this type of behavior (pain) may serve as discriminative stimuli that reinforcement is imminent.

## Disadvantages of Using Punishment

Although Azrin and Holz conclude that punishment can be a method of behavior change that is at least as effective as reinforcement, they warn that it can produce a number of undesirable side effects. First, they note that punishment can elicit several emotional effects, such as fear and anger, that are generally disruptive of learning and performance. In one study, college students performing a memory task worked more slowly and made more mistakes when each mistake was punished by a shock than when each mistake was simply signaled by a tone (Balaban, Rhodes, & Neuringer, 1990). Therefore, if the teacher's goal is to reduce mistakes and increase correct responses, the strategy of punishing mistakes can backfire. Second, punishment can sometimes lead to a general suppression of all behaviors, not only the behavior being punished. Imagine that a child in a classroom raised his hand, asked a question, and the teacher replied, "Well, that's a very stupid question." The teacher's remark might be intended to try to reduce the number of stupid questions that children ask, but the likely result would be a decrease in all questions, good or bad, both from that child and from everyone else in the class.

A third disadvantage is that in real-world situations, the use of punishment demands the continual monitoring of the individual's behavior, whereas the use of reinforcement does not necessarily demand such monitoring. This is because it is in the individual's interest to point out instances of a behavior that is followed by a reinforcer. If a child receives a reinforcer for cleaning up her room, she will probably make sure her parents see the room after it is cleaned. On the other hand, if the child is punished for a messy room, she is unlikely to call her parents to see the messy room so that the punishment contingency can be enforced.

Along the same lines, a practical problem with the use of punishment is that individuals may try to circumvent the rules or escape from the situation entirely. Azrin and Holz described the behavior of a clever rat that was scheduled to receive shocks for some of its lever presses while working for food reinforcement. The rat learned to avoid the shocks by lying on its back while pressing the lever, thereby using its fur as insulation from the shocks delivered via the metal floor of the chamber. We might expect people to be even more ingenious in their tricks to circumvent a punishment contingency. If punishment is a teacher's primary method of behavioral control, a child may try to hide evidence of misbehavior. In addition, the child may attempt to escape from the situation by feigning sickness or by playing hooky.

Another problem with using punishment is that it can lead to aggression against either the punisher or whomever happens to be around. The constant risk of bodily harm faced by prison guards (and by prisoners) attests to this fact. Aggression as a response to aversive stimulation is not unique to humans. Ulrich and Azrin (1962) reported a study in which two rats were placed in an experimental chamber. The animals behaved peaceably until they began to receive shocks, at which point they began to fight. Similar results have been obtained with pigeons, mice, hamsters, cats, and monkeys.

A final problem with using punishment (one not mentioned by Azrin and Holz) is that

in institutional settings, the people who must actually implement a behavior modification program may be reluctant to use punishment. Various studies have examined the attitudes of personnel who work with institutionalized patients, such as developmentally handicapped individuals. The staff in such institutions preferred other techniques for changing behavior, such as instruction, modeling, and reinforcement, over punishment (Davis & Russell, 1990). Perhaps these individuals have learned, through their daily work experiences, about some of the disadvantages of punishment described in the preceding paragraphs.

Given the numerous disadvantages of punishment, Azrin and Holz suggest that it should be used reluctantly and with great care. A final argument against using punishment is an ethical one. If an individual's behavior can be changed in the desired way with either reinforcement or punishment, why should the more unpleasant procedure of punishment be used? Unfortunately, there are cases in which reinforcement is ineffective, and in these cases punishment is sometimes used as a last resort. As will be discussed at the end of this chapter, some people believe that aversive techniques should never be used as a means of controlling another person's behavior. Perhaps they are right, but Azrin and Holz point out that punishment will always be a part of our environment. It might be possible to legislate punishment out of existence in institutions such as prisons, schools, and psychiatric hospitals. It would be much more difficult, however, to eliminate punishment in everyday interpersonal interactions (between parent and child, between spouses, and so forth). Finally, the physical environment is full of potential punishers that are impossible to eliminate. Just think of the possible punishing consequences that might follow the wrong behavior while one is driving a car, walking through a forest, swimming, skiing, cooking, or performing almost any behavior. Since punishment cannot be eliminated from our environment, it is important for behavioral psychologists to continue to study this phenomenon so as to increase our understanding of how it influences behavior.

## Negative Punishment

Cell 4 in Figure 8-1 represents the procedure of negative punishment, or omission, in which some stimulus is removed if a response occurs, resulting in a decrease in responding. In one study on omission, pigeons pecked a key for food on a VI schedule, but occasionally the color of the response key would turn blue, which signaled that further pecking would result in a 10-minute time-out (during which reinforcement was not available). However, the subject could avoid the time-out by not pecking when the key was blue. As the pigeons became familiar with this contingency, response rates dropped to zero when the key was blue, even though the VI schedule was still in effect during this stimulus (Ferster, 1958).

As with positive punishment, omission procedures are most effective if the omission occurs immediately after the undesired behavior, every time the behavior occurs. In one case, therapists used time-outs to discourage a mentally retarded adult from putting his hands in his mouth (which caused them to become red and swollen). Time-outs reduced hand mouthing to near-zero levels if they occurred on a schedule of continuous punishment, but they had much less effect if they were delivered on fixed-interval schedules (Lerman, Iwata, Shore, & DeLeon, 1997). Thus with both positive and negative punishment, immediacy and consistency are important. Because it is a means of reducing behavior without using an aversive stimulus, negative punishment has become a popular tool in behavior modification, as discussed at the end of this chapter.

## BEHAVIOR DECELERATORS IN BEHAVIOR THERAPY

The term **behavior decelerators** is sometimes used to refer to all techniques that can lead to a slowing, reduction, or elimination of unwanted behaviors. Punishment and omission are two of the most obvious methods for reducing undesired behaviors, but they are by no means the only ones. Behavior therapists have cataloged a variety of other useful behavior deceleration techniques, and we will examine some of the most common ones. The examples that follow also provide further support for Azrin and Holz's rules about punishment.

## Positive Punishment

Wherever possible, behavior therapists avoid using punishment because the comfort and happiness of the patient is one of their major concerns. However, if a behavior is dangerous or otherwise undesirable, and if other techniques are impractical or unsuccessful, the use of punishment may be deemed preferable to doing nothing at all. This section describes some representative situations in which behaviors have been reduced or eliminated with punishment. As will be seen, the aversive stimuli employed are often quite mild.

*Punishment of "Voluntary" Behaviors.* One nonphysical form of punishment that is frequently used by parents and teachers is scolding and reprimanding a child for bad behavior. This tactic can certainly influence a child's behavior, but not always in the way the adult wants. The problem is that a reprimand is a form of attention, and we have already seen that attention can be a powerful reinforcer. Furthermore, a child who is scolded or reprimanded frequently also receives attention from siblings or classmates, and this attention from peers may serve as further reinforcement for the undesired behavior. O'Leary, Kaufman, Kass, and Drabman (1970) found that the manner in which a reprimand is given is a major factor determining its effectiveness. Most teachers use loud or public reprimands that are heard not only by the child involved but by all others in the classroom. However, when second-grade teachers were instructed to used "soft" or private reprimands wherever possible (that is, to walk up to the child and speak quietly, so that no other children could hear), they observed a 50 percent decrease in disruptive behavior.

Stronger forms of punishment are sometimes necessary when a child's behavior is a more serious problem than a mere classroom disturbance. For example, some retarded, autistic, or schizophrenic children engage in

**self-injurious behaviors** such as repeatedly slapping themselves in the face, biting deep into their skin, or banging their heads against any solid object. The causes of these behaviors are not clear, but because of the risk of severe injury, these children are sometimes kept in physical restraints around the clock except when a therapist is in the immediate vicinity. A report by Prochaska, Smith, Marzilli, Colby, and Donovan (1974) describes the treatment of one 9-year-old profoundly retarded girl named Sharon, who would hit her nose and chin with her fist at a rate of about 200 blows per hour if she was not restrained. Behavior therapists first tried to decrease her head banging with negative punishment and with positive reinforcement for other behaviors, but with Sharon, these procedures were ineffective. They then began to use a shock to Sharon's leg as a punisher for head banging, and her rate of head banging decreased dramatically. Unfortunately, Azrin and Holz's observation about the need for continual monitoring was supported in this case, because there was little generalization of this learning to Sharon's home or school environments. Evidently, Sharon had learned that head banging was punished only in the clinic, with the electrodes on her leg and with the therapist watching her.

To reduce Sharon's head banging in her normal environments, the therapists made use of a remote-control unit to deliver the shocks, and her behavior was continuously monitored at school and at home. Under these new conditions, Sharon's head banging dropped to zero within a week. The disappearance of head banging generalized to times when the shock generator was removed, and eventually the punishment procedures were terminated with no return of the behavior. The elimination of head banging was accompanied by improvements in other behaviors—Sharon's crying spells (previously frequent) ceased, so she could now go with her parents to public places such as shopping malls and restaurants.

The use of shock as a punisher with children is a controversial matter, but to be fair, the aversive features of this procedure must be weighed against the negative consequences of failing to implement the punishment procedure. In Sharon's case, the pain of several dozen half-second shocks seems small when compared to the alternative—a life of self-injury, physical restraint, and the inability to play with peers or go out in public.

One promising development in the treatment of self-injurious behaviors is the finding that sometimes punishers much milder than electric shock can be effective. For example, Fehr and Beckwith (1989) found that head-hitting by a 10-year-old handicapped boy could be reduced by spraying a water mist in the child's face. This treatment was especially effective when used in combination with reinforcement for other, better behavior. Water mist has also been successfully used to reduce aggression and other unwanted behaviors (Matson & Duncan, 1997).

***Punishment of "Involuntary" Behaviors.*** You may be surprised to learn that so-called involuntary or reflexive behaviors, which seem to occur automatically in response to some stimulus, can be reduced through punishment. Heller and Strang (1973) described the use of a mild punisher to reduce the frequency of bruxism in a 24-year-old male. **Bruxism** is the gnashing and grinding of one's teeth while asleep, a problem found in about 5 percent of all college students. This behavior sometimes results in serious tooth damage. To measure the rate of bruxism automatically, Heller and Strang used a voice-operated relay that was activated by the sound of the teeth grinding. The client wore an earplug while he slept, and each instance of bruxism recorded by the voice-operated relay was followed immediately by a 3-second burst of noise in the client's ear. As soon as this punishment contingency was introduced, the rate of bruxism decreased from a baseline rate of about 100 occurrences per hour to about 30 per hour. The therapists reported that the remaining instances of bruxism were often too soft to trigger the equipment and therefore went unpunished. It is interesting to note that although the client was asleep when the bruxism occurred, the character of this behavior changed in a way that partially circumvented the punishment contingency (it became quieter). Presumably, the rate of bruxism would have decreased further if more sensitive recording equipment had been employed.

Aversive stimuli have also been used to eliminate other types of involuntary behavior, such as chronic coughing or sneezing that are not due to any obvious medical problem (Creer, Chai, & Hoffman, 1977; Kushner, 1968). Punishment techniques have been used to treat involuntary muscle spasms (Sachs & Mayhall, 1971), frequent vomiting (Cunningham & Linscheid, 1976), gagging (Glasscock, Friman, O'Brien, & Christopherson, 1986), and hallucinations (Bucher & Fabricatore, 1970). Of course, we should not expect a punishment contingency to eliminate a symptom caused by some physical disorder (for example, coughing due to a respiratory illness). However, if physicians have determined that no medical problem is responsible for a persistent behavioral symptom, punishment may be an effective (albeit unpleasant) treatment.

## Negative Punishment: Response Cost and Time-out

It is easy to incorporate a negative punishment contingency in any token system: Whereas tokens can be earned by performing desirable behaviors, some tokens are lost if the individual performs an undesirable behavior. The loss of tokens, money, or other conditioned reinforcers following the occurrence of undesirable behaviors is called **response cost**. Token economies that include a response-cost arrangement have been used with children, prison inmates, and patients in mental institutions. E. L. Phillips (1968) described how response cost was used as part of a token system for "predelinquent" boys. These boys, in their early teens or younger, had each been guilty of minor violations of the law, and authorities believed that their behaviors would get worse unless some action were taken. They were therefore sent to Achievement Place, a home in the community supervised by two "house parents." While at Achievement Place, each boy was on a token system under which he could earn points through such behaviors as doing homework, getting good grades, keeping his room clean, and doing household chores. The points could be used to purchase snacks or an allowance, or for privileges such as watching TV, staying up late, or going into town. Behaviors that lost points were arguing or fighting, disobeying the house parents, displaying poor manners, or being late. For example, a boy lost a certain number of points for every minute he was late in returning from school or late in going to bed. By recording the boys' behaviors before and after the response-cost contingency went into effect, Phillips showed conclusively that this contingency improved their behaviors. As might be expected, the loss of points affected only those behaviors that were included under the rule. For instance, when fines were established for being late from school, the boys became prompt in returning home from school, but not in returning from errands.

Probably the most common form of negative punishment is the **time-out**, in which one or more desirable stimuli are temporarily removed if the individual performs some unwanted behavior. In one case study, time-out was combined with reinforcement for alternative behaviors to eliminate the hoarding behavior of a patient in a psychiatric hospital (Lane, Wesolowski, & Burke, 1989). This case study illustrates what researchers call an **ABAB design**. Each "A" phase is a baseline phase in which the patient's behavior is recorded, but no treatment is given. Each "B" phase is a treatment phase. Stan was brain-injured, and he frequently hoarded such items as cigarette butts, pieces of dust and paper, food, and small stones by hiding them in his pockets, socks, or underwear. In the initial 5-day baseline phase, the researchers observed an average of about 10 hoarding episodes per day (see Figure 8-5). This was followed by a treatment phase (days 6 through 15) in which Stan was rewarded for two alternative behaviors—collecting baseball cards and picking up trash and throwing it away properly. During this phase, any episodes of hoarding were punished with a time-out period, in which Stan was taken to a quiet area for 10 seconds. As Figure 8-5 shows, the number of hoarding episodes decreased

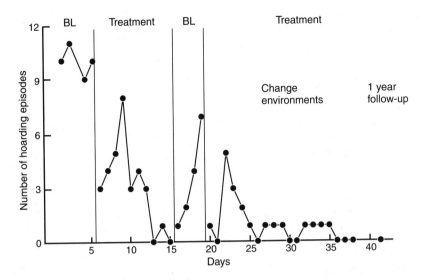

**FIGURE 8-5** The number of hoarding episodes per day of a brain-injured man during two baseline (BL) phases and two treatment phases in which hoarding was punished with time-outs and alternative behaviors were reinforced. The second treatment phase took place in a changed environment, a different lunch area. (From Lane, Wesolowski, & Burke, 1989)

during this treatment phase. In the second baseline phase, the treatment was discontinued, and during these 4 days, Stan's hoarding behavior increased. Finally, in the second treatment phase, the time-outs and reinforcement for alternative behaviors resumed, and Stan's hoarding gradually declined and eventually stopped completely. In a follow-up 1 year later, no hoarding was observed. This ABAB design demonstrated the effectiveness of the treatment procedures, because Stan's hoarding occurred frequently in the two baseline phases and decreased dramatically in the two treatment phases.

Time-out is often used with children, as when a parent tells a child to go to his or her room for misbehaving. Time-outs in which a child is sent to an isolated room can reduce aggressive or disruptive behaviors in classroom situations. Time-outs can also be effective if they simply remove a child from some ongoing activity. For example, because fourth-grade children in one elementary school were constantly unruly and disruptive during gym class, their teachers set up a time-out contingency.

Any child who behaved in a disruptive way was immediately told to stop playing and to go sit on the side of the room, where he or she had to remain until all the sand had flowed through a large hourglass (which took about 3 minutes). Children who repeatedly misbehaved also lost free play time and other desirable activities (a response-cost contingency). This omission procedure was very effective, and disruptive behavior during gym class soon dropped by 95 percent (White & Bailey, 1990).

In a few cases, time-out procedures used in schools have been challenged in court, with parents claiming that the schools do not have the right to exclude their children from academic activities, even if the children are being disruptive. Yell (1994) reviewed these cases and reported that in every instance, the courts ruled that time-out can be used in classrooms, provided that it is used appropriately. Nevertheless, Yell recommends that educators be aware of state and local policies about the use of time-out, and he suggests a number of guidelines that should be followed when using this procedure. Although these procedures may be criticized by some, both time-out and response cost have become increasingly popular with teachers and behavior therapists because they are effective ways to reduce unwanted behaviors without presenting any aversive stimulus.

## Other Techniques for Behavior Deceleration

*Overcorrection.* In some cases, if an individual performs an undesired behavior, the parent, therapist, or teacher requires several repetitions of an alternate, more desirable behavior. This technique is called **overcorrection,** and it often involves two elements: restitution (making up for the wrongdoing) and positive practice (practicing a better behavior). The corrective behavior is usually designed to require more time and effort than the original bad behavior. For example, Adams and Kelley (1992) taught parents how to use an overcorrection procedure to reduce aggression against siblings. After an instance of physical or verbal aggression against a sibling, restitution might consist of an apology, and the positive practice might involve sharing a toy, touching the sibling gently, and saying something nice. This positive practice was repeated several times. If the child did not practice these behaviors appropriately, the practice trials started over from the beginning. This procedure produced a significant reduction in aggression between siblings, but not complete elimination.

Overcorrection has frequently been used with mentally handicapped individuals to reduce aggression and other undesirable behaviors. For example, Sisson, Hersen, and Van Hasselt (1993) used overcorrection as part of a treatment package to teach profoundly retarded adolescents to package items and sort them by zip code. Maladaptive behaviors included stereotyped motions such as hand flapping, rocking back and forth, and twirling and flipping the items. After each occurrence of such a behavior, the therapist guided the patient through three repetitions of the correct sequence of behaviors. Overcorrection can also

be effective in treating involuntary behaviors, such as bruxism (T. S. Watson, 1993).

Overcorrection meets the technical definition of a punishment procedure, because a sequence of events (the correction procedure) is contingent on the occurrence of an undesired behavior, and the behavior decreases as a result. A difference from other punishment techniques, however, is that during the corrective exercises, the learner is given repeated practice preforming a more desirable behavior. This may be the most beneficial component of the overcorrection procedure, because, as discussed below, providing the learner with a more desirable alternative behavior is an important ingredient in many behavior reduction treatments.

*Extinction.* If an undesired behavior occurs because it is followed by some positive reinforcer, and if it is possible to remove that reinforcer, the behavior should eventually disappear through simple extinction. One of the most common reinforcers to maintain unwanted behaviors is attention. In the home, the classroom, or the psychiatric hospital, disruptive or maladaptive behavior may occur because of the attention it attracts from parents, peers, teachers, or hospital staff. These behaviors will sometimes disappear if they are ignored by those who previously provided their attention. For example, Ayllon and Haughton (1964) reported the cases of two psychiatric patients who continually complained of various bodily ailments (although medical exams found nothing wrong). When hospital staff was instructed to stop reinforcing these complaints with attention and sympathy and to ignore them instead, the number of complaints decreased greatly.

In another case, a woman had a skin rash that did not go away because she continually scratched herself in the infected areas. The therapist suspected that this scratching behavior was maintained by the attention the woman received concerning her rash from her family and fiancé (who applied skin cream to the rash for her). The therapist asked her family and fiancé to avoid all discussion of the rash and not to help her treat it. The scratching behavior soon extinguished, and the rash disappeared (Walton, 1960).

Other maladaptive behaviors may be maintained by negative reinforcement—the behaviors allow the individual to avoid or escape certain events or activities. For example, therapists at one institution found that a few children with developmental disabilities would engage in self-injurious behavior (head banging, hand biting, and so on) whenever they were instructed to work on educational tasks, and by doing so they escaped from their lessons. The therapists therefore began an extinction procedure in which the child's tutor would ignore the self-injurious behavior, tell the child to continue with the lesson, and manually guide the child through the task if necessary. In this way, the reinforcer (escape from the lesson) was eliminated and episodes of self-injurious behavior decreased dramatically (Pace, Iwata, Cowdery, Andree, & McIntyre, 1993).

In reviewing the use of extinction as a behavior decelerator, Ducharme and Van Houten (1994) noted that this technique is not free of problems. Extinction is sometimes slow, especially if the unwanted behavior has been intermittently reinforced in the past. In addition, the unwanted behaviors sometimes increase rather than decrease at the beginning of the extinction process. (Parents who decide to ignore tantrums in an effort to extinguish them may initially witness one of the worst tantrums they have ever seen.) As with any extinguished behavior, episodes of spontaneous recovery may occur. Nevertheless, Ducharme and Van Houten concluded that, when used properly, extinction can be a very useful method of eliminating unwanted behaviors. One of the most effective ways to use extinction is to combine it with the reinforcement of other, more desirable behaviors.

***Response Blocking.*** For behaviors that are too dangerous or destructive to wait for extinction to occur, an alternative is response blocking, which is physically restraining the individual to prevent the inappropriate behavior. Most parents of young children probably use response blocking quite often to prevent their youngsters from doing something that would

be harmful to themselves or to others. Behavior therapists have used response blocking to reduce or eliminate such behaviors as self-injury, aggression, and destruction of property by children or adults with mental retardation (Fisher, Lindauer, Alterson, & Thompson, 1998; Smith, Russo, & Le, 1999).

Response blocking can have both short-term and long-term benefits. First, by preventing the unwanted behavior, immediate damage or injury can be avoided. Second, as the individual learns that the behavior will be blocked, attempts to initiate this behavior usually decline. For example, to prevent a mentally retarded girl from poking her fingers in her eyes, Lalli, Livezey and Kates (1996) had the girl wear safety goggles. Unlike cases of response blocking in which the therapist manually restrains the patient, this use of goggles had the advantage of blocking the unwanted behaviors even when the girl was alone. After she stopped trying to poke at her eyes, the goggles were gradually replaced with her normal eyeglasses, and her eye-poking did not reappear.

***Reinforcement of Alternative Behavior.*** A classic study by Ayllon and Haughton (1964) offers a good illustration of how extinction of inappropriate behaviors can be combined with reinforcement of more appropriate behaviors. These researchers worked with patients in a psychiatric hospital who engaged in psychotic or delusional speech. They found that this inappropriate speech was often reinforced by the psychiatric nurses through their attention, sympathy, and conversation. Ayllon and Haughton therefore conducted a two-part study. In the first part, the nurses were explicitly instructed to reinforce psychotic speech with attention and tangible items (gum, candy, and so on). As shown in Figure 8-6, psychotic speech increased steadily during this part of the study. In the second phase, the nurses were told to ignore psychotic speech, but to reinforce normal speech (such as conversations about the weather, ward activities, or other everyday topics). Figure 8-6 shows the large increases in normal speech and decreases in psychotic speech that resulted. This study demonstrated both the power of attention as a reinforcer and how attention can be

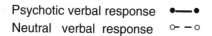

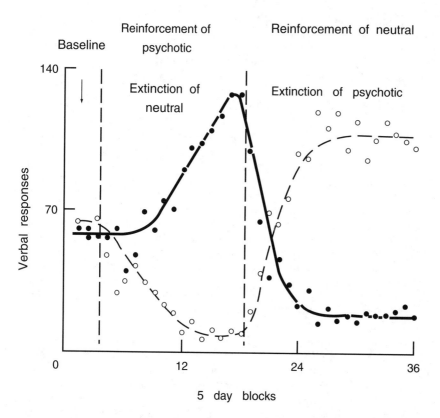

**FIGURE 8-6**    The number of instances of psychotic speech and of normal speech in psychiatric patients when nurses were instructed to reinforce psychotic speech and when they ignored psychotic speech and reinforced normal speech. (From Ayllon & Haughton, 1964)

withheld from inappropriate behaviors and de-livered for more desirable alternative behaviors.

In recent studies, reinforcement of alterna-tive behaviors has been effectively used in combination with **noncontingent reinforce-ment**—the delivery of free reinforcers at ran-dom times. Marcus and Vollmer (1996) used this method to reduce the aggressive and dis-ruptive behaviors in three young children with severe behavior problems. Every few minutes, a child would be given a toy or other reinforcer, regardless of what the child was doing. The toy could also be obtained imme-diately if the child asked for it politely—this

was the alternative behavior the therapists wanted to reinforce. This treatment produced a significant reduction in the aggressive and disruptive behaviors and increases in polite requests for toys.

This chapter has already mentioned sev-eral other cases in which reinforcement of al-ternative behaviors has been successfully combined with other behavior-deceleration techniques. In modern behavior therapy, re-inforcement of alternative behaviors is a very common part of treatment packages for be-havior reduction. The logic is that most be-havior-reduction techniques teach a person

Information about graduate programs in applied behavior analysis can be found at *http://www.wmich.edu/aba/GTD/Training Directoryhome.htm.*

*what not to do*, but they do not teach the patient *what to do*. Reinforcement of alternative behaviors remedies this deficiency, and it provides more acceptable behaviors to fill the "behavioral vacuum" that is created when one behavior is reduced.

***Stimulus Satiation.*** If it is not feasible to remove the reinforcer that is maintaining an undesired behavior, it is sometimes possible to present so much of the reinforcer that it loses its effectiveness due to satiation. Ayllon (1963) described a female psychiatric patient who hoarded towels in her room. Despite the nurses' efforts to remove them, she usually had more than 20 towels in the room. A program of stimulus satiation was begun in which the nurses brought her many towels each day. At first, the woman seemed to enjoy touching, folding, and stacking them, but soon she started to complain that she had enough, and that the towels were in her way. Once the number of towels in her room reached about 600, she started removing them on her own. The nurses then stopped bringing her towels, and afterward, no further instances of hoarding were observed.

One unusual example of stimulus satiation involved no physical objects at all. A psychiatric patient who complained of hearing voices was given ample time to listen to these voices. For 85 half-hour sessions, the patient was instructed to sit in a quiet place and record when the voices were heard, what they said, and how demanding the tone of voice was. By the end of these sessions, the rate of these hallucinations was close to zero (Glaister, 1985). This version of stimulus satiation has also been used to treat obsessional thoughts.

## The Aversives Controversy

The question of whether punishment can be an effective way of controlling behavior has been settled. This chapter has presented numerous studies, from both inside and outside the laboratory, that have demonstrated that punishment can change behavior and, in many cases, change it permanently. However, showing that punishment can be used successfully is not the same as showing that it should be used as a technique of behavioral control. In recent years, the controversy over whether behavior therapists should be allowed to use aversive stimuli to control the behavior of their patients has intensified. Much of the controversy has focused on the treatment of mentally retarded or developmentally disabled persons, with whom aversive stimuli are sometimes used in an effort to eliminate self-destructive or other dangerous behaviors. On one side of the debate are those who claim that punishment is sometimes the only effective way to control and improve the functioning of people with severe behavior problems (such as the retarded girl, Sharon, described previously). On the other side are those who argue, on legal and ethical grounds, that the use of aversive stimuli is never acceptable and that alternative treatments should always be used.

One line of argument against the use of aversives is based on legal principles. In the United States, an important principle is the "right to refuse treatment." This principle states that even if a treatment is known to be effective, and even if the treatment is clearly in the best interests of the individual, that individual has the right to refuse the treatment. For example, a person could refuse to have an infected tooth extracted even if failure to remove the tooth could cause a life-threatening spread of the infection. It is easy to imagine a person refusing a behavioral treatment that involved aversive stimuli, even if the treatment would be beneficial in the long run. However, in the case of mentally retarded individuals, the issue is more complicated, because such individuals are usually classified as "incompetent" to make their own decisions, and treatment decisions must be made by their legal guardians. Furthermore, for complex legal reasons, the "legal guardian" in cases involving the use of aversive treatments is often not the individual's parents or caretakers but the courts. Court decisions regarding the use of aversives have been inconsistent, with some judgments allowing the treatments to proceed and others prohibiting them. Often, the decision depends on whether the judge is convinced that the use of aversives is "a professionally accepted form of treatment," and this proves to be a difficult matter to decide (Sherman, 1991).

Those who work with the developmentally disabled are divided on this issue (see Jacob-Timm, 1996). Some practitioners are against the use of aversives under any circumstances for ethical reasons. For example, Freagon (1990) asserted: "The use of severe punishment or aversives needs to be defined as abuse, just as it is defined as abuse when applied with people without disabilities" (p. 154). Conversely, others argue that it would be unethical to restrict the use of the most effective treatments available, even if they involve aversives, and that such restrictions could have unfortunate consequences for the patients involved (Axelrod, 1990).

Opinions also differ about the effectiveness of aversive treatments and how they compare to nonaversive procedures. Some workers maintain that various nonaversive techniques are available, including reinforcement of alternative behaviors, stimulus control, satiation, prompting, fading, teaching of communication skills, and so on. They propose that these non-aversive techniques can be just as effective as aversive procedures, and therefore there is no excuse for using aversive procedures (La Vigna & Donnellan, 1986; Lohrman-O'Rourke & Zirkel, 1998). Others disagree; they maintain that the existing data have not yet shown that nonaversive techniques can be equally effective for severe behavior problems (Yates, 1991).

It should be emphasized that no one advocates the unrestricted and indiscriminate use of aversive stimuli as a means of behavior control. Opinions of those who work with the developmentally disabled "range from those who support exclusive use of nonaversive procedures to others who support the use of aversive proce-

dures only as a last resort" (Alberto & Andrews, 1991, p. 220). It seems likely that as time passes, a combination of ethical debate, court decisions, and more data about the effectiveness of alternative techniques will help to settle this issue. Whether aversive techniques will continue to be used in therapeutic settings cannot now be predicted.

## CHAPTER SUMMARY

In negative reinforcement, an aversive stimulus is removed or eliminated if a response occurs. Two variations of negative reinforcement are escape and avoidance. The two-factor theory of avoidance states that avoidance involves (1) learning to fear a previously neutral stimulus, and (2) responding to escape from this stimulus. A number of studies have supported the two-factor theory, but some findings pose problems for the theory: Well-practiced subjects continue to make avoidance responses while showing no measurable signs of fear, and extinction of avoidance responses is very slow.

The one-factor theory of avoidance states that removing a fear-provoking CS is not necessary for avoidance responding and that avoidance of the aversive event is in itself the reinforcer. Studies supporting one-factor theory have shown that animals can learn avoidance responses when there is no CS to signal an upcoming shock. The cognitive theory of avoidance states that subjects learn to expect that (1) if they respond, no aversive event will occur, and (2) if they do not respond, an aversive event will occur. To teach a subject that the second expectation is no longer correct, response blocking (or flooding) can be used.

Seligman showed that if animals are presented with aversive stimuli that they cannot avoid, they may develop learned helplessness. He suggested that unavoidable aversive events can lead to helplessness and depression in people, and this theory has been applied to many aspects of human behavior.

In punishment, an aversive stimulus is presented if a response occurs, and the response is weakened. Many factors influence the effectiveness of punishment, including its intensity, immediacy, schedule of presentation, and the availability of alternative behaviors. There are a number of disadvantages to using punishment: It requires continual monitoring of the subject, and it can lead to undesirable side effects, such as aggression, a decrease in other behaviors, or attempts to escape from the situation.

Behavior therapists usually do not use punishment unless there is no feasible alternative, but it can be an effective way of reducing a variety of unwanted behaviors, such as aggression, classroom misbehavior, and some involuntary behaviors, such as bruxism and chronic coughing. Other methods for reducing unwanted behaviors include response cost, time-out, overcorrection, extinction, response blocking, reinforcement of alternative behavior, and stimulus satiation.

## REVIEW QUESTIONS

1. What factors comprise the two-factor theory of avoidance? What types of evidence support two-factor theory? What are the main pieces of evidence that pose problems for the theory?

2. What is one-factor theory, and how does this theory account for (a) the acquisition of avoidance responses, and (b) the slowness of extinction of avoidance responses? How does the cognitive theory of avoidance account for these effects?

3. Name several factors that determine the effectiveness of a punishment procedure. Give a concrete example to illustrate each factor. What are some potential disadvantages of using punishment?

4. Describe some examples of how punishment has been successfully used in behavior therapy, and discuss some details that probably helped ensure the success of the procedures. What are some behavior-reduction techniques used by behavior therapists that do not involve aversive stimuli?

## CHAPTER 9

# Theories and Research on Operant Conditioning

The theoretical issues examined in this chapter are very broad, and they deal with matters of importance to the entire field of learning. The topics concern such basic issues as what ingredients, if any, are essential for learning to take place, and under what conditions will a supposed reinforcer strengthen the behavior it follows. Most of the issues we will examine have been pondered by learning theorists for many years. Some have now been fairly well resolved, but others are the subject of continuing research.

The issues of this chapter can be divided into three general categories. First, we will consider whether both the performance of a response and the reinforcement of that response are necessary for learning to take place. Hypotheses about the importance of the reinforcer have varied enormously. Some writers have suggested that reinforcement is essential for any learning to occur, others that reinforcement is involved in operant conditioning but not in classical conditioning, and still others that reinforcement is not essential for either type of learning. We will weigh the relative merits of each of these positions. Second, we will trace the history of attempts to develop a method for predicting which stimuli will be effective reinforcers for a given subject and which will not. A successful method for predicting the effectiveness of a reinforcer would

have obvious practical utility, and we will see that it would be equally important from a scientific standpoint. Finally, we will survey recent efforts to analyze the effects of reinforcers using concepts from economics.

## THE ROLE OF THE RESPONSE

Operant conditioning might be described as "learning by doing": An animal performs some response and experiences the consequences, and the future likelihood of that response is changed. For Thorndike, the performance of the response was a necessary part of the learning process. After all, if a response does not occur, how can it be strengthened by reinforcement? Convinced that a pairing of response and reinforcer is essential for learning, Thorndike proposed the following experiment:

> Put the rat, in a little wire car, in the entrance chamber of a maze, run it through the correct path of a simple maze and into the food compartment. Release it there and let it eat the morsel provided. Repeat 10 to 100 times according to the difficulty of the maze under ordinary conditions.... Then put it in the entrance chamber free to go wherever it is inclined and observe what it does. Compare the behavior of such rats with that of rats run in the customary manner. (1946, p. 278)

Thorndike predicted that a rat that was pulled passively through a maze would perform like a naive subject in the later test, since the animal had no opportunity to perform a response. On this and several other issues, Thorndike's position was challenged by Edward C. Tolman (1932, 1951, 1959), who might be characterized as an early cognitive psychologist (although he worked decades before the emergence of the field of cognitive psychology). According to Tolman, operant conditioning involves not the simple strengthening of a response but the formation of an expectation. In a maze, for example, a rat develops an expectation that a reinforcer will be available in the goal box. In addition, Tolman proposed that the rat acquires a **cognitive map** of the maze—a general understanding of the spatial layout of the maze. Tolman proposed that both of these types of learning could be acquired by passive observation as well as by active responding, so that animals should be able to learn something in the type of experiment Thorndike described.

One study fashioned according to Thorndike's specifications was conducted by McNamara, Long, and Wike (1956), who used two groups of rats in an elevated T-maze. Subjects in the control group ran through the maze in the usual fashion, and a correct turn at the choice point brought the animal to some food. If the subject went to the wrong arm of the maze, it was confined there for one minute. Control subjects received 16 trials in the maze, and by the end of training, they made the correct turn on 95 percent of the trials. Subjects in the experimental group received 16 trials in which they were transported through the maze in a wire basket. Each experimental subject was paired with a control subject; that is, it was transported to the correct or incorrect arm of the maze in exactly the same sequence of turns that its counterpart in the control group happened to choose (therefore receiving the same number of reinforcers as its counterpart). This training was followed by a series of extinction trials in which all subjects ran through the maze, but no food was available. During extinction, control subjects chose the previously correct turn on 64 percent of the trials, and ex-

perimental subjects on 66 percent of the trials. Thus the experimental animals performed equally well despite the fact that they had never been reinforced for running through the maze.

Similar findings of learning without the opportunity to practice the operant response have been obtained in other studies (Dodwell & Bessant, 1960; Keith & McVety, 1988). Dodwell and Bessant found that rats benefited substantially from riding in a cart through a water maze with eight choice points. This shows that animals can learn not only a single response, but also a complex chain of responses, without practice. These studies make it clear that, contrary to Thorndike's prediction, active responding is not essential for the acquisition of an operant response.

## THE ROLE OF THE REINFORCER

### Is Reinforcement Necessary for Operant Conditioning?

From a literal point of view, the answer to this question is obviously yes, since by definition operant conditioning consists of presenting a reinforcer after the occurrence of a specific response. But we have seen that, loosely speaking, operant conditioning can be called a procedure for the learning of new "voluntary" or nonreflexive behaviors. A better way to phrase this question might be: "Is reinforcement necessary for the learning of all new voluntary behaviors?" Prominent early behaviorists such as Hull (1943), Mowrer (1947), and Thorndike believed that it was, but on this issue as well, Tolman took the opposite position. A famous experiment by Tolman and Honzik (1930), called the **latent learning experiment,** provided evidence on this issue.

In the Tolman and Honzik experiment, rats received 17 trials in a maze with 14 choice points, one trial per day. The rats were divided into three groups. Group 1 was never fed in the maze; when they reached the goal box they were simply removed from the maze. Rats in Group 2 received a food reinforcer in the goal box on every trial. In Group 3, the conditions were switched on day 11: For the first 10 trials

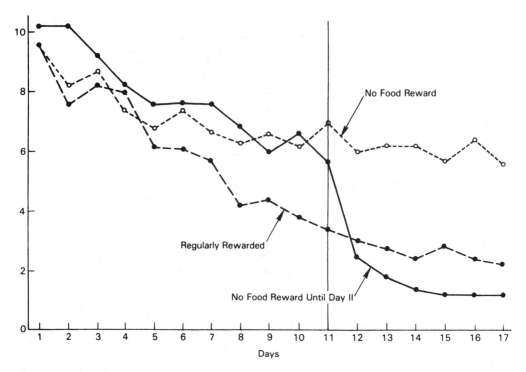

**FIGURE 9-1**    Mean number of errors on each trial for the three groups in the Tolman and Honzik (1930) experiment on latent learning.

there was no food in the goal box, but on trials 11 through 17 food was available.

On each trial, Tolman and Honzik recorded the number of errors (wrong turns) a rat made; Figure 9-1 shows the averages from each group. Rats in Group 2 (consistently reinforced) displayed a typical learning curve, with the number of errors decreasing to about three per trial by the end of the experiment. Rats in Group 1 (never reinforced) showed much poorer performance. Their error rate dropped slightly but leveled off at about seven errors per trial. The results from Group 3 are the most interesting. On the first 11 trials, their results resembled those of Group 1. This makes sense since both groups received no food on trials 1 to 10, and on trial 11, subjects in Group 3 had no way of knowing that food was available until they reached the goal box. On trial 12, however (that is, after only one reinforced trial), the performance of Group 3 improved dramatically, and their average number of errors was actually slightly lower than that of Group 2 for the remainder of the experiment. In other words, as soon as rats in Group 3 learned that food was available in the goal box, their performance became equal to that of rats that had been consistently reinforced since the beginning of the experiment.

Since Group 2 required some 12 trials to drop to an error rate of three per trial, it would be implausible to propose that Group 3 learned an equivalent amount on a single trial (trial 11). Instead, Tolman and Honzik asserted that although the subjects in Group 3 received no food on trials 1 to 10, they nevertheless learned just as much about the maze as subjects in Group 2. However, because they initially received no food in the maze, Group 3 subjects were not motivated to display what they had learned. Only after food was available did subjects in Group 3 translate their learning

To experience what it is like to learn a simple maze, click on "Maze Experiment" at *http://www.olemiss.edu/psychexps/Exps/experiments.html.*

into performance. Tolman and Honzik concluded that reinforcement is not necessary for the *learning* of a new response, but it is necessary for the *performance* of that response. Several dozen experiments on latent learning were conducted between the 1920s and 1950s, most of which found evidence that learning can occur when the experimenter provides no obvious reinforcer such as food (MacCorquodale & Meehl, 1954). All learning theorists are now acutely aware of the distinction between learning and performance, largely because of Tolman's influential work.

## Expectations about the Reinforcer

Although latent learning can occur without a reinforcer, the strengthening power of a reinforcer is shown most clearly when a reinforcer is presented after the required response is made. In such situations, exactly what is the function of the reinforcer? Some theorists, such as Thorndike (1946) and Hull (1943), suggested that the reinforcer is merely a sort of catalyst—it strengthens an S-R association between the discriminative stimulus and the operant response, but the reinforcer itself is not included in that association. Opposing this view is the idea that a reinforcer not only stimulates associative learning but also becomes a part of the associative network (Mackintosh & Dickinson, 1979; Tolman, 1932). If so, the associative learning in operant conditioning would involve three distinct elements—the discriminative stimulus, the operant response, and the reinforcer. According to this view, we might say that the animal "develops an expectation" that a particular reinforcer will follow a particular response.

An early experiment by Tinklepaugh (1928) tested these competing ideas. A monkey was first trained on a discrimination task in which a slice of banana was placed beneath one of two containers. After waiting a few seconds, the monkey could choose one of the containers, earning the slice of banana if it chose correctly. The monkey almost always succeeded on this easy task. Then, on a test trial, the experimenter secretly replaced the slice of banana with a piece of lettuce (a less potent reinforcer for the monkey). If the monkey had learned nothing more than an S-R association (between the correct container and the reaching response), then the switch to lettuce should go unnoticed. If, however, the monkey had developed an expectation about the usual reinforcer, the lettuce should come as a surprise. Tinklepaugh found that the switch in reinforcers did indeed affect the animal's behavior: The monkey appeared surprised and frustrated, and it refused to accept the lettuce. The monkey had evidently developed a strong expectation about what type of reinforcer was forthcoming.

Colwill and Rescorla (1985) obtained similar findings with rats under more controlled conditions. Two different responses produced two different reinforcers: Pressing a lever earned food pellets and pulling a chain earned a few drops of sugar water. The rats learned to make both responses. Later, each rat was given either free food pellets or free sugar water (with the lever and chain unavailable), and then each animal was made ill with a poison. This procedure was designed to devalue one of the two reinforcers by associating that food with illness. In the test phase, each rat was again presented with the lever and the chain, but this time no food was available. The question of interest was whether a subject would respond more on one manipulandum than on the other in the extinction test. Colwill and Rescorla found that rats poisoned after eating food pellets made few lever presses but many chain pulls, and the opposite was true for those rats poisoned after drinking sugar water. They concluded that the rats associated lever pressing with food pellets and chain pulling with sugar water, and the animals avoided whichever response was associated with the food paired with illness.

This research shows quite clearly that reinforcers are more than catalysts that strengthen S-R associations. During operant conditioning, animals develop associations between specific responses and specific reinforcers. The response-reinforcer association is an important part of the learning, because if the reinforcer is devalued, the response will be weakened. In other words, animals will not produce responses that were reinforced in the past if they no longer value the reinforcer that was used to strengthen those responses.

Other studies by these researchers have provided a more complete picture of the different associations formed during operant conditioning (Colwill, 1996; Rescorla, 1998). In a series of experiments, Colwill and Rescorla (1986, 1988) found that pairwise associations are formed among all three components of Skinner's three-term contingency (the discriminative stimulus, the operant response, and the reinforcer). For instance, they found that rats learned to associate two different discriminative stimuli with two different reinforcers (a light with food pellets and a noise with sugar water, or vice versa). Similarly, animals can learn to associate a particular response with a particular discriminative stimulus. These findings parallel those that demonstrate the existence of associations among the three main components of classical conditioning situations—the CS, the US, and the response (see Chapter 5).

In addition, Colwill and Rescorla (1990) have found evidence that a discriminative stimulus can become associated, not just with the operant response or reinforcer individually, but with a particular response-reinforcer pair. The designs of these experiments are complex, but here is a relatively simple example. A rat might be taught that in the presence of a light (one discriminative stimulus), pulling a chain produces food pellets, and pressing a lever produces sugar water. In the presence of a noise (a second discriminative stimulus), the outcomes are reversed: Chain pulls produce sugar water, and lever presses produce food pellets. Next, sugar water might be devalued by pairing it

with a poison. Can you keep track of the associations in this experiment? Evidently the rats could, because in a subsequent extinction test, a rat given this treatment would tend to make chain pulls when the light was presented and to make lever presses when the tone was presented. In other words, for each discriminative stimulus, the rat tended to make the response that had been previously associated with food pellets and to avoid the response associated with the now devalued sucrose reinforcer.

These experiments demonstrate conclusively that in operant conditioning, animals learn something more complex than merely "In the presence of stimulus A, make response B." They evidently learn the three-term contingency "In the presence of stimulus A, response B is followed by reinforcer C." Furthermore, if more than one stimulus, response, and reinforcer are used, animals can keep track of several three-term contingencies at once. If the value of one reinforcer changes, they can adjust their behavior appropriately. Thus in operant conditioning, just as in classical conditioning, subjects appear to develop a richer and more diverse array of associations than was once supposed.

## Is Reinforcement at Work in Classical Conditioning?

The diversity of associations is only one feature shared by classical and operant conditioning. A number of phenomena, including extinction, spontaneous recovery, generalization, discrimination, and others, are found with both conditioning procedures. Because of these similarities, a persistent issue debated by learning theorists is whether these two procedures correspond to two different learning processes or whether a single learning process is at work in both procedures. In theoretical debates that began before theories of avoidance learning were developed (Chapter 8), two-factor theorists were those who believed that the two conditioning procedures depend on two different learning processes. On the other hand, one-factor theorists believed that a common learning mechanism is at work in both classical and operant conditioning.

Among those who favored the two-factor position were S. Miller and Konorski (1928), Skinner (1935), Mowrer (1947), and Kimble (1961). For example, Konorski and Miller (1937) proposed that although operant responses are clearly controlled by their consequences, classically conditioned responses are not. They asserted that the appearance of a CR depends only on temporal contiguity between CS and US, whereas the appearance of an operant response depends on the reinforcement of that response.

One prominent one-factor theorist was Clark Hull (1943), who maintained that reinforcement is a necessary part of both operant and classical conditioning. Hull proposed that although the experimenter does not explicitly program a reinforcer in classical conditioning, there are nevertheless hidden reinforcers that strengthen and maintain the CR, and without such reinforcers no CR would appear. In effect, Hull was claiming that classical conditioning is actually a disguised form of operant conditioning, and that the one factor common to both procedures is reinforcement. Similar positions have been taken by others (Kendler & Underwood, 1948; N. E. Miller, 1951a; K. Smith, 1954).

It does not take much imagination to speculate about the "built-in" reinforcers that might operate in some common classical conditioning paradigms. In Pavlov's experiments on salivary conditioning, the US was dry food, so it seems plausible that, by salivating, a dog could increase the palatability of the food (Hebb, 1956). Such increased palatability would be a reinforcer that was contingent on the response: The food would be more palatable on trials with a salivary response and less palatable on trials without salivation. Could it be that this CR of salivation is actually an operant response? In eyeblink conditioning, it seems very likely that a CR might alter the aversiveness of the US, particularly when the US is an air puff to the eye that can be avoided by closing the eyelid (Schlosberg, 1937). Is eyeblink conditioning actually an example of avoidance learning? Other CRs might be the by-products of operant responses. For instance, when a CS is repeatedly paired with shock, human subjects exhibit a change in the electrical conductance of the skin, called the skin conductance response. K. Smith (1954) suggested that the skin conductance response is actually a byproduct of muscular tensing that occurs in anticipation of the shock. The reinforcer for these muscular responses might be a decrease in the painfulness of the shock.

If CRs are controlled by their consequences, as one-factor theorists maintain, then it should be possible to increase or reduce the frequency of CRs by adding an explicit reinforcer to a classical conditioning situation. Gormezano and Coleman (1973) describe several experiments of this type. In one, they used rabbits in an eyeblink conditioning procedure, with a shock near the eye as the US. Rabbits in what we will call the classical group received a 5-mA shock as the US on every trial, whether they made a response or not. (In other words, this group received normal classical conditioning, in which the US was not dependent on the subject's behavior.) However, in what we will call the omission group, a subject could eliminate the US entirely by making a conditioned eyeblink response to the CS, a tone. That is, in this group the US intensity was 5 mA if there was no CR, but 0 mA if a CR did occur.

A one-factor analysis of this experiment might proceed as follows. In the classical group, eyeblink CRs will appear because these responses somehow produce a reduction in the aversiveness of the shock. In the omission group, acquisition should be more rapid and the asymptote of learning should be higher, because for these subjects, the reinforcer for a CR is the complete avoidance of a shock. The results of Gormezano and Coleman did not support these predictions, however. Acquisition was slower in the omission group, and at asymptote, CRs occurred on about 80 percent of the trials, compared to nearly 100 percent in the classical group. The poorer performance of the omission group is understandable in terms of the principles of classical conditioning (since some trials had no US and were therefore "extinction trials"), but it is exactly the opposite of what a reinforcement analysis would predict.

Results like this weaken the one-factor position, for they indicate that CRs are not easily influenced by experimenter-controlled reinforcers or punishers. Such results do not completely settle the issue, because as Kimble (1961) has noted, one can always propose that some reinforcer is at work in classical conditioning. Nevertheless, these results make it awkward to maintain that reinforcement controls all classically conditioned responses, and nowadays this viewpoint has few supporters.

## Can Reinforcement Control Visceral Responses?

This question, like that of the previous section, initially arose out of attempts to find a clear behavioral distinction between classical conditioning and operant conditioning. Two-factor theorists, such as Konorski and Miller (1937) and Mowrer (1947), suggested that reinforcement can control the behavior of the skeletal muscles (those involved in movement of the limbs) but not visceral responses (the behavior of the glands, organs, and the smooth muscles of the stomach and intestines). On the other hand, one-factor theorists claimed that reinforcement controls all learned behaviors, including visceral responses.

For many years it was impossible to perform a meaningful experiment on this question because scientists had no way to separate skeletal and visceral responses. Suppose a misguided one-factor theorist offered to deliver a reinforcer, a $20 bill, if you increased your heart rate by at least 10 beats per minute. You could easily accomplish this by running up a flight of stairs or by doing a few push-ups. This demonstration of the control of heart rate through reinforcement would not convince any two-factor theorist, who would simply point out that what the reinforcer increased was the activity of the skeletal muscles, and the increase in heart rate was an automatic, unlearned response to the body's increase in activity. That is, the increase in heart rate was not a direct result of the reinforcement; rather, it was a by-product of skeletal activity. To perform a convincing study, it would be necessary to eliminate any possible influence of the body's skeletal muscles.

During the 1960s, Neal Miller and his colleagues devised a procedure that met this requirement. Their subjects were rats that were temporarily paralyzed by an injection of a drug called **curare.** Curare blocks movement of the skeletal muscles, including those necessary for breathing, so an artificial respirator was needed to keep the subjects alive. The normal activity of the glands and organs is not affected by curare, so it might be possible to observe the direct control of visceral responses by reinforcement. But what could serve as an effective reinforcer for a paralyzed rat? To solve this problem, Miller made use of a finding by Olds and Milner (1954) that a mild, pulsating electrical current delivered via an electrode to certain structures in the brain acts as a powerful reinforcer. Although it is not known why **electrical stimulation of the brain** (ESB) is a reinforcer, it can be used to strengthen responses in many species of subjects. Rats will press a lever at high rates for many hours, ceasing only at the point of exhaustion, if ESB is made contingent on this response.

Figure 9-2 shows the experimental procedure used by Miller and his colleagues in many of their experiments. A curarized rat is artificially respirated, has an electrode implanted in its brain for the delivery of ESB, and is connected to recording equipment to monitor heart rate (or other visceral responses). In an early set of experiments, N. E. Miller and DiCara (1967) attempted to increase or decrease the heart rates of different rats, using ESB as reinforcement. After measuring a rat's baseline heart rate (which averaged about 400 beats per minute), the experimenters began a shaping procedure. If the goal was an increase in heart rate, reinforcement would be provided for some small (for instance, 2 percent) increase. The criterion for reinforcement was then gradually raised. With other rats, Miller and DiCara used a similar procedure to try to shape heart-rate decreases. They obtained substantial heart-rate changes in both directions: By the end of a session, the average heart rate was over 500 beats per minute for subjects reinforced for a rapid heart rate, and about 330 beats per minute for subjects reinforced for a slow heart rate.

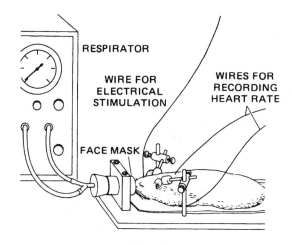

**FIGURE 9-2** The experimental arrangement used by Miller and DiCara in their experiments on the operant control of heart rate. (From DiCara, 1970)

Miller's research group also found that reinforcement could control many visceral responses besides heart rate (see DiCara, 1970, for a review). They found that curarized rats could either dilate or constrict the blood vessels of the skin, increase or decrease the activity of the intestines, and increase or decrease the rate of urine production by the kidneys. The specificity of these responses made it difficult to argue that they were caused by some general property of the drug, of the artificial respiration procedure, and so forth. It would be very difficult to explain how some property of curare could cause an increase in heart rate in one subject (with no change in intestinal activity), a decrease in heart rate in another subject (with no change in intestinal activity), an increase in intestinal activity in yet another subject (with no change in heart rate), and so on. It seems much more reasonable to accept the position that these visceral responses were being influenced by the ESB reinforcement. Furthermore, Miller's group used shock avoidance as a reinforcer in some of their studies to show that the results were not limited to ESB as a reinforcer.

Unfortunately, later studies by both Miller and others found it difficult to replicate the early results showing control of heart rate by ESB reinforcement. Sometimes such control was demonstrated, but often it was not, and there was no obvious pattern in the successes and failures (N. E. Miller & Dworkin, 1974).

Thus the operant control of heart rate, which appeared to be robust and easily obtainable in the early studies, later proved to be a perplexingly evanescent phenomenon. Since the mid-1970s, there has been little further research on this issue. If we must try to draw some conclusions from the data that are available, it seems that reinforcement can exert direct control over some visceral responses when the activity of the skeletal muscles has been eliminated, but this control is not as easy to obtain as the early studies seemed to suggest.

Despite these unresolved theoretical issues, interest in the practical and therapeutic applications of visceral learning has grown at an enormous rate. If individuals can learn to control such visceral responses as heart rate, blood pressure, and intestinal activity (through operant conditioning or any other means), the potential health benefits are numerous. Interest in these matters has given rise to a new term, biofeedback, and a new area of intense research activity.

## Biofeedback

Chapter 3 discussed the importance of feedback in behaviors ranging from simple reflexes to reaction chains. Sensory feedback is essential for the smooth execution of most movements. Imagine how difficult it would be to write a letter or walk around a house in complete darkness, or to eat a meal without biting your tongue or gums after a dentist has anesthetized a large portion of your mouth. Recognizing the importance of feedback in the control of movement, many psychologists have speculated that one reason we have so little control over many of our bodily functions is that feedback from our organs and glands is weak or nonexistent. The term **biofeedback** encompasses any procedure designed to supply the individual with amplified feedback about some bodily process. The reasoning is that with this improved feedback may come the possibility of better control.

The general design of many biofeedback experiments can be illustrated by examining one study on the control of muscle tension in the forehead. Excessive tension in the forehead muscles is the cause of muscle contraction headaches, which some people experience at a high frequency. Budzynski, Stoyva, Adler, and Mullaney (1973) attempted to train a group of individuals who suffered from chronic muscle-contraction headaches to relax these muscles. These people experienced some headache pain almost every day before the start of treatment. During therapy sessions, each patient received **EMG (electromyogram) biofeedback**—electrodes attached to the patient's forehead monitored muscle tension, and the level of tension was translated into a continuous train of clicks the patient could hear. The patient was instructed to slow down the rate of clicking, thereby decreasing the tension in these muscles. Patients learned to accomplish this task almost immediately, and their average muscle tension levels were about 50 percent lower in the first biofeedback session than in the preceding baseline sessions.

Although this finding is interesting in its own right, the important therapeutic questions are the following:

1. Could patients continue to relax forehead muscles in the absence of the biofeedback?
2. Did their headaches become less frequent?
3. Did the treatment produce long-term benefits?
4. How does EMG biofeedback compare to other treatment procedures for tension headaches?

Regarding the first question, Budzynski and colleagues showed that after biofeedback training, patients could produce low forehead tension without the biofeedback equipment, and this ability was retained in a 3-month follow-up. Patients were instructed to practice this muscle relaxation at home, twice a day for about 20 minutes. In answer to questions 2 and 3, this combination of biofeedback training and home practice led to a marked reduction in headache activity in about 75 percent of the patients, and these improvements were maintained in a 3-month follow-up. On the average, patients reported a decrease of about 80 percent in the frequency and severity of their headaches, and many were able to decrease or eliminate medication they had been taking.

The answer to the fourth question is not as clear. Some studies have found that other procedures, such as deep-muscle relaxation, were just as effective as EMG biofeedback for tension headaches. If so, it would be fair to ask whether the biofeedback training (which involves expensive equipment and therapist time) is necessary at all. However, biofeedback techniques are still being refined, and one study found that feedback from neck and shoulder muscles was a particularly effective treatment: All subjects trained with this technique showed reductions in headaches, whereas less than half of the subjects given deep-muscle relaxation showed improvement (Arena, Bruno, Hannah, & Meador, 1995). This result suggests that EMG biofeedback may be more effective than simple relaxation techniques in the treatment of tension headaches.

For a different class of medical problems, the superiority of EMG biofeedback over other therapeutic techniques has been more firmly established. H. E. Johnson and Garton (1973) used biofeedback to treat 10 patients from hemiplegia (paralysis on one side of the body), who could walk only with the aid of a leg brace. All of them had suffered from this problem for at least a year, and they had failed to improve with traditional muscular-rehabilitation training. With electrodes connected to the paralyzed muscles of the leg, a patient received auditory feedback on the level of muscle tension (which was initially very low, of course). Any increase in muscle tension would produce a louder sound, and a patient's task was to increase the loudness of the signal. All patients rapidly learned how to do this. They received daily biofeedback sessions, first in the hospital and later at home with a portable EMG feedback device. All patients showed some improvement in muscle functioning, and five improved to the point where they could walk without the leg brace. This study and others have demonstrated quite convincingly that EMG biofeedback can be a useful supplement to traditional rehabilitation therapy for certain muscular disorders, producing improvements that would not be obtained without the biofeedback.

Feedback from an EMG device is only one of many types of biofeedback; some other examples include feedback on heart rate, cardiac irregularities, blood pressure, skin temperature, electrical activity of the brain, stomach acidity, and intestinal activity. Biofeedback has been tried as a treatment for many different problems, with varying degrees of success (Good, 1998; Schwartz, 1995). In one study, a combination of skin temperature biofeedback and training in other skills (including progressive relaxation techniques) produced substantial improvement in patients suffering from irritable bowel syndrome—a disorder with symptoms that include frequent intestinal pain, gas, and diarrhea (Schwartz, Taylor, Scharff, & Blanchard, 1990). In another interesting study, biofeedback was used with children diagnosed with either hyperactivity, attention-deficit disorder, or a learning disability (Linden, Habib, & Radojevic, 1996). Children with these diagnoses were given 40 sessions of **EEG (electroencephalogram) biofeedback** (which measures the electrical activity of the brain). The purpose of the biofeedback training was to increase a particular brain wave pattern called **beta waves,** which are thought to be associated with an attentive and alert mental state. A child received feedback whenever beta waves were present in the EEG recording. After their training sessions were completed, these children obtained higher scores on an IQ test and exhibited greater attentive-

ness. The potential importance of this finding is obvious, but the experimenters caution that this was just a preliminary study, and more research on this technique is needed. EEG biofeedback is also being tested as a treatment for a variety of other medical problems, such as epilepsy and chronic pain (Carmagnani & Carmagnani, 1999).

Not all attempts to treat medical problems with biofeedback have been successful. For instance, some attempts to use biofeedback as a treatment for high blood pressure have not obtained good results, whereas others have found substantial decreases in blood pressure levels in most patients (Nakao, Nomura, Shimosawa, Fujita, & Kuboki, 2000). Weaver and Mc-Grady (1995) suggested that it may be possible to use various measures to identify which patients will respond to biofeedback for high blood pressure and which will not. If so, then biofeedback treatment could be targeted at those individuals who are most likely to benefit from the treatment.

Research on biofeedback has grown substantially over the years, and biofeedback techniques have been applied to an increasingly diverse array of medical disorders. Of course, it would be foolish to assume that biofeedback will be beneficial for any type of medical problem. Evaluations of the effectiveness of biofeedback must be made on a problem-by-problem basis. For some medical problems, biofeedback may be totally ineffective. For other problems, it may be only as effective as other, less expensive treatments. For still others, it may produce health improvements that are superior to those of any other known treatment.

A good source of information on biofeedback is the Web site of the Association for Applied Psychophysiology and Biofeedback: *http://www.aapb.org*.

# HOW CAN WE PREDICT WHAT WILL BE A REINFORCER?

The past several chapters should leave no doubt that the principle of reinforcement is one of the most central concepts in the behavioral approach to learning. This concept has also been the subject of considerable debate and controversy between behavioral psychologists on one hand and critics of the behavioral approach on the other. Critics have frequently argued that the definition of reinforcement is circular, and therefore that the concept is not scientifically valid (Chomsky, 1959, 1972b; Postman, 1947). This is a serious criticism, so let us examine what they mean by the term *circular*.

A brief definition of a reinforcer is "a stimulus that increases the future probability of a behavior which it follows." Suppose a behavioral psychologist presents a stimulus, a small quantity of beer, to a rat each time the rat presses a lever, and the probability of lever pressing increases. By the foregoing definition, the psychologist would conclude that beer is a reinforcer for the rat. This conclusion, however, provides no explanation; it is nothing more than a restatement of the facts. If asked, "Why did the rat's lever pressing increase?" our behaviorist would answer, "Because it was reinforced by the presentation of beer." If asked, "How do you know beer is a reinforcer?" the reply would be, "Because it caused an increase in lever pressing." The circularity in this sort of reasoning should be clear: A stimulus is called a reinforcer because it increases some behavior, and it is said to increase the behavior because it is a reinforcer. As stated, this simple definition of a reinforcer makes no specific predictions whatsoever. If there were no increase in lever pressing in the beer experiment, this would pose no problem for the behavioral psychologist, who would simply conclude, "Beer is not a reinforcer for the rat."

If there were nothing more to the concept of a reinforcer than this, then critics would be correct in saying that the term is circular and not predictive. Because of the seriousness of this criticism, behavioral psychologists have made several attempts to escape from this circularity by developing independent criteria for determining which stimuli will be reinforcers and which will not. The problem boils down to finding some rule that will tell us in advance whether a stimulus will act as a reinforcer. If we can find such a rule, one which makes new, testable predictions, then the circularity of the term reinforcer will be broken. Several attempts to develop this sort of rule are described next.

## Need Reduction

In his earlier writings, Clark Hull (1943) proposed that all primary reinforcers are stimuli that reduce some biological need, and that all stimuli that reduce a biological need will act as reinforcers. The simplicity of this rule is appealing, and it is certainly true that many primary reinforcers serve important biological functions. We know that food, water, warmth, and avoidance of pain are all primary reinforcers, and each also plays an important role in the continued survival of an organism. Unfortunately, it does not take much thought to come up with exceptions to this rule. For example, sexual stimulation is a powerful reinforcer, but despite what you may hear some people claim, no one will die if deprived of sex indefinitely. (To be sure, sexual behavior is essential to the survival of a species, so any species for which sex was not a reinforcer would probably become extinct very quickly. However, the principle of need reduction is meant to apply to the survival needs of an individual creature, not of an entire species.) Another example of a reinforcer that serves no biological function is saccharin (or any other artificial sweetener). Saccharin has no nutritional value, but because of its sweet taste it is a reinforcer for both humans and nonhumans. People purchase saccharin and add it to their coffee or tea, and rats choose to drink water flavored with saccharin over plain water.

Besides reinforcers that satisfy no biological needs, there are also examples of biological necessities for which there is no corresponding reinforcer. One such example is vitamin $B_1$ (thiamine). Although intake of thiamine is essential for maintaining good health, animals such as rats apparently cannot detect the presence or absence of thiamine in their food by smell or taste. As a result, rats suffering from a thiamine deficiency will not immediately select a food that contains thiamine. If they have the opportunity to sample various diets over a period of days, however, they will eventually settle on the diet that improves their health (Rodgers & Rozin, 1966). This result shows that it is better health, not the presence of thiamine in the rat's food, that is actually the reinforcer for selecting certain foods.

It makes sense that most biological necessities will function as reinforcers, because a creature could not survive if it were not strongly motivated to obtain these reinforcers. As a predictor of reinforcing capacity, however, the need-reduction hypothesis is inadequate because there are numerous exceptions to this principle—reinforcers that satisfy no biological needs, and biological needs that are not translated into reinforcers.

## Drive Reduction

Recognizing the problem with the need-reduction hypothesis, Hull and his student Neal Miller (1948, 1951b) became two of the most vigorous advocates of the **drive-reduction theory** of reinforcement. This theory states that strong stimulation of any sort is aversive to an organism, and any reduction in this stimulation acts as a reinforcer for the immediately preceding behavior. The term drive reduction was chosen because many of the strong stimuli an animal experiences are frequently called drives (the hunger drive, the sex drive, and so on). Of course, the theory asserts that other strong stimuli, which are not normally called drives (such as loud noise, intense heat, and fear), will also provide reinforcement when their intensity is reduced. A reduction in stimulation of any sort should serve as a reinforcer.

There are at least two major problems with the drive-reduction theory. First, it is not always easy to measure the intensity of stimulation (or a reduction in stimulation) objectively. Suppose we place an animal in a chamber where the temperature is 100°F, and an operant response lowers the temperature to 75°F

for a few minutes. The animal would probably produce the operant response at a steady rate, thereby keeping the temperature at 75°F most of the time. This behavior is consistent with the drive-reduction hypothesis, because the reinforcer consists of a reduction in a certain stimulus, namely heat. Now suppose the temperature of the chamber is 25°F, and the operant response again produces a 25°F reduction in temperature, to 0°F. Most animals would not make the operant response in this case, evidently preferring an air temperature of 25°F to one of 0°F. In this case, the reduction in stimulation does not act as a reinforcer.

An advocate of drive-reduction theory would undoubtedly argue that this example portrays a naive interpretation of what is meant by a reduction of stimulation, since living organisms are not thermometers. As discussed in Chapter 2, fairly good evidence shows that animals have some sensory receptors that are stimulated by heat and other receptors that are stimulated by cold. A drive-reduction theorist might propose that a reduction in either type of stimulation (extreme heat or extreme cold) acts as a reinforcer, and experimental results verify this idea. If we accept this logic, however, we are once again in the position where we cannot predict in advance whether a given reduction in temperature will serve as a reinforcer—we must know something about the subject's sensory receptors and how they operate.

The second problem with drive-reduction theory is more serious. There are numerous examples of reinforcers that either produce no decrease in stimulation or actually produce an increase in stimulation. Sheffield, Wulff, and Backer (1951) found that male rats would repeatedly run down an alley when the reinforcer was a female rat in heat. This reinforcer produced no decrease in the male's sex drive because the rats were always separated before ejaculation occurred, yet the male rat's high speed of running continued trial after trial. Similarly, we know that sexual foreplay is reinforcing for human beings even when it does not culminate in intercourse. People will engage in a variety of behaviors for the opportunity to engage in sexual activities that do not include orgasm and the resultant reduction in sex drive. The popularity of pornographic magazines and films provides further evidence on this point.

Reinforcers that consist of an actual increase in stimulation are common for creatures of a wide range of species and ages. Human infants, kittens, and other young animals spend long periods of time playing with toys and other objects that produce ever-changing visual, auditory, and tactile stimulation. Butler (1953) found that monkeys would learn a complex response when the reinforcer was simply the opening of a window that let them see outside the experimental chamber. Myers and Miller (1954) observed that rats would press a lever when the reinforcer was the chance to explore a novel environment. Adult humans are reinforced by a great variety of stimuli and activities that increase their sensory stimulation—music, engaging in sports and exercise, mountain climbing, skydiving, horror films, and the like. There seems to be no way to reconcile these facts with the drive-reduction hypothesis.

### Trans-situationality

The failures of both need-reduction and drive-reduction theories suggest that there is no simple way to classify reinforcers and non-reinforcers on the basis of their biological or stimulus properties. The problem is compounded by the existence of individual differences within a given species—horror films may be reinforcers for some people but not for others. Because of these difficulties, theorists such as Paul Meehl (1950) turned to a more modest theoretical position, but one that still offered the possibility of making new predictions and thereby avoiding the circularity of the term reinforcer. Meehl invoked the concept of **trans-situationality,** which simply means that a stimulus that is determined to be a reinforcer in one situation will also be a reinforcer in other situations. Suppose that at the outset, we do not know whether water sweetened with saccharin will be a reinforcer for a mouse. By performing a simple experiment, we might find that the mouse will learn to run in an activity wheel if every several revolutions of the wheel are reinforced with a few seconds of access to the saccharin solution. After we have determined that saccharin is a reinforcer in this one experiment, the principle of trans-situationality implies that we should be able to make new predictions. For instance, we should be able to use saccharin as a reinforcer for lever pressing, climbing a ladder, learning the correct sequence of turns in a maze, and so on.

In reality, the principle of trans-situationality works quite well in many cases. Reinforcers such as food, water, and escape from pain can be used to strengthen a multitude of different behaviors. Nevertheless, cases exist in which a reinforcer in one situation will not act as a reinforcer in another situation. The first person to document clear exceptions to the principle of trans-situationality was David Premack, whose influential experiments and writings changed the way many psychologists think about reinforcement.

### Premack's Principle

The procedure of reinforcement is frequently said to include a contingency between a behavior (the operant response) and a stimulus (the reinforcer). An implication of this description is that the two elements of a reinforcement contingency are members of two distinct classes of events—reinforceable behaviors on one hand and reinforcing stimuli on the other. One of Premack's major contributions was to demonstrate that there is no clear boundary between these two classes of events, and in fact it may be counterproductive to talk about two separate classes at all. Premack followed the lead of earlier writers such as Sheffield (Sheffield, 1948; Sheffield, Wulff, & Backer, 1951) in pointing out that nearly all reinforcers involve both a stimulus (such as food) and a behavior (such as eating), and it may be the latter that actually strengthens the operant response. Is it water or the act of drinking that is a reinforcer for a thirsty animal? Is a toy a reinforcer for a child or is it the behavior of playing with the toy? Is a window with a view a reinforcer for a monkey or is it the behavior of looking? Premack proposed that it is more accurate to characterize the reinforcement procedure as a contingency between one behavior and another than as a contingency between a behavior and a stimulus. For example, he would state that in many operant conditioning experiments with rats, the contingency is between the behavior of lever pressing and the behavior of eating—eating can occur if and only if a lever press occurs.

At least for the moment, let us accept Premack's view and see how it relates to the principle of trans-situationality. If the principle is correct, then there must be some subset of all behaviors that we might call *reinforcing behaviors* (for instance, eating, drinking, playing) and another subset of behaviors that are *reinforceable behaviors* (for example, lever pressing, running in a wheel, pecking a key). According to the principle of trans-situationality, any behavior selected from the first subset should serve as a reinforcer for any behavior in the second subset. However, Premack's experiments have shown a number of ways in which trans-situationality can be violated.

To replace the principle of trans-situationality, Premack proposed an alternative theory (1959, 1965), now called **Premack's principle,** which provides a straightforward method for determining whether one behavior will act as a reinforcer for another. The key is to measure the durations of the behaviors in a baseline situation, where all behaviors can occur at any time without restriction. Premack's principle states that *more probable behaviors will reinforce less probable behaviors.* The phrase "more probable behavior" means the behavior that the subject performed for a larger fraction of the time in the baseline session. Premack suggested that instead of postulating two categories of behaviors—reinforceable behaviors and reinforcing behaviors—we should rank behaviors on a scale of probability that ranges from behaviors of high probability to those of zero probability. Behaviors higher on the probability scale will reinforce behaviors lower on the probability scale.

A study Premack (1963) conducted with Cebus monkeys highlights the advantages of Premack's principle and the weaknesses of the trans-situationality principle. These monkeys are inquisitive animals that will explore and manipulate any objects placed in their environment. Premack therefore used the manipulation of different mechanical objects as the tested behaviors. His findings can be illustrated by examining the results from one monkey, Chicko. Figure 9-3 shows that in baseline conditions, operating a lever had the highest probability, operating a plunger had the lowest, and opening a small door had an intermediate probability.

In subsequent contingency sessions, different pairs of items were presented. One item served as the "operant response" and the other as the potential "reinforcer"—the reinforcer was locked and could not be operated until an operant response occurred. In six different phases, every possible combination of operant response and reinforcer was tested, and Figure 9-3 shows the results. The lever served as a reinforcer for both door opening and plunger pulling. Door opening reinforced plunger pulling but it did not reinforce lever pressing. Plunger pulling did not reinforce either of the other behaviors. You should see that each of these six results is in agreement with the principle that more probable behaviors will reinforce less probable behaviors.

In addition, notice that door opening, the behavior of intermediate probability, violated the principle of trans-situationality. When it was contingent on plunger pulling, door opening was a reinforcer. When it led to the availability of lever pressing, it played the role of a reinforceable response. Which was door opening, then—a reinforcer or a reinforceable response? Premack's answer is that it can be either, depending on the behavior's relative position on the scale of probabilities. A behavior will act as a reinforcer for behaviors that are lower on the probability scale, and it will be a reinforceable response for behaviors higher on the probability scale. For this reason, Premack's principle is sometimes called a principle of **reinforcement relativity:** There are no absolute categories of reinforcers and reinforceable responses, and which role a behavior plays depends on its relative location on the probability scale.

L = Lever Pressing
D = Door Opening
P = Plunger Pulling

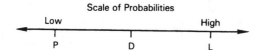

Scale of Probabilities

| Contingency Conditions | Result | Conclusion |
| --- | --- | --- |
| 1. D → L | D Increases | L Reinforces D |
| 2. P → L | P Increases | L Reinforces P |
| 3. L → D | L Does Not Increase | D Does Not Reinforce L |
| 4. P → D | P Increases | D Reinforces P |
| 5. L → P | L Does Not Increase | P Does Not Reinforce L |
| 6. D → P | D Does Not Increase | P Does Not Reinforce D |

**FIGURE 9-3** The procedure used in Premack's (1963) experiment, and the results from one monkey, Chicko. The notation D → L means that Chicko was required to open the door before being allowed to operate the lever.

***Premack's Principle and Punishment.*** Premack (1971a) proposed a principle of punishment that is complementary to his reinforcement principle: *Less probable behaviors will punish more probable behaviors.* Since a subject may not perform a low-probability behavior if given a choice, it is necessary to require that the low-probability behavior be performed to demonstrate that this principle is correct. One way to accomplish this is to use a **reciprocal contingency,** which ensures that two behaviors occur in a fixed proportion. An experiment conducted by the author (Mazur, 1975) illustrates the characteristics of a reciprocal contingency. In one condition, a rat was required to engage in 15 seconds of wheel running for every 5 seconds of drinking. This reciprocal contingency therefore required approximately three times as much running as drinking. Notice, however, that the total durations of these activities were completely controlled by the subject—the rat could spend most of its time either running or drinking, or it could choose not to perform these behaviors at all.

The results from one typical rat will show how this experiment simultaneously verified Premack's reinforcement and punishment rules.

In baseline sessions, this rat spent about 17 percent of the session drinking and about 10 percent of the session running, as shown in Figure 9-4. In the reciprocal contingency described in the preceding paragraph, the percentage of time spent running increased to 16 percent, while drinking time decreased to just over 5 percent of the session time. In other words, the higher probability behavior, drinking, reinforced running, and at the same time, the running requirement punished drinking. Naturally, the exact percentages varied from subject to subject, but for all five rats, drinking was the behavior with the higher probability in baseline. In the reciprocal contingency, drinking time decreased and running time increased for all subjects, as Premack's principles of reinforcement and punishment predict. Other studies have provided similar support for Premack's rules (Terhune and Premack, 1970).

***The Use of Premack's Principle in Behavior Modification.*** Although we have focused on the theoretical implications of Premack's principle, this theory has had a large impact on the applied field of behavior modification, in several ways. First, it has stressed that behav-

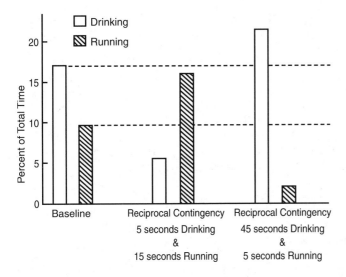

**FIGURE 9-4** The performance of one rat in Mazur's (1975) experiment. In the first reciprocal contingency, running time increased and drinking time decreased compared to their baseline levels. In the second reciprocal contingency, running time decreased and drinking time increased compared to their baseline levels.

iors themselves can serve as reinforcers, thereby encouraging behavior therapists to use such reinforcers in their work. Therapists now frequently instruct clients to use "Premackian reinforcers," such as reading, playing cards, phoning a friend, or watching television, as reinforcers for desired behaviors such as exercising, studying, or avoiding smoking. Premackian reinforcers have also been widely adopted in institutional settings. Imagine the difficulties the staff of a mental institution would face in setting up a token economy if they relied only on tangible reinforcers such as food, beverages, cigarettes, money, and the like. The costs of reinforcing patients with such items would be prohibitive, and problems of satiation would be commonplace. However, by making certain activities contingent upon good behavior, therapists gain access to a wide variety of inexpensive reinforcers.

Another advantage of Premack's principle is that it provides therapists with clues about what events will be reinforcers for individuals who may not be affected by typical reinforcers. For example, Mitchell and Stoffelmayr (1973) used Premack's principle to improve the behavior of a group of extremely inactive schizophrenics. These patients spent most of their time sitting motionless, and occasionally they would pace up and down the ward, but they did little else. The therapists tried to get the patients to en-

gage in some productive work (not to obtain a source of free labor, of course, but for therapeutic reasons). These patients refused items such as candies, cigarettes, fruit, and biscuits, so they could not be used as reinforcers. However, since sitting was a highly probable behavior for these patients, the therapists decided to make sitting contingent on a small amount of labor. A patient was required to work for a few minutes on a simple task and was then allowed to sit down for a while. Using this passive behavior as a reinforcer, Mitchell and Stoffelmayr succeeded in getting these patients to engage in some useful activity for the first time. This example illustrates how a therapist can discover effective reinforcers simply by observing what a patient normally does.

In a very different setting, Homme, deBaca, Devine, Steinhorst, and Rickert (1963) used Premack's principle to control the behavior of a class of nursery-school children. Among the most probable behaviors of these children were running around the room, screaming, pushing chairs about, and so on. The teacher's instructions and commands initially had little impact on the children's behaviors. A program was then established in which these high-probability behaviors were made contingent on low-probability behaviors, such as sitting quietly and listening to the teacher. After a few minutes of such a low-probability behavior, the teacher would ring a bell and give the instructions "Run and scream," at which point the children could perform these high-probability behaviors for a few minutes. Then the bell would ring again, and the teacher would give instructions for another behavior, which might be either one of high or low probability. (One of their favorite high-probability behaviors was pushing the teacher around in a desk chair with casters.) After a few days, the children's obedience of the teacher's instructions was nearly perfect.

These examples illustrate just a few of the many ways that Premack's principle has been used in applied settings. Although we shall soon see that this principle has its limitations, it has proven to be a successful rule of thumb for deciding which events will be reinforcers and which will not.

## Response Deprivation Theory

Research has shown that Premack's principle will reliably predict reinforcement and punishment effects (1) if a schedule requires more of the low-probability behavior than of the high-probability behavior, or (2) if a schedule requires equal amounts of the two behaviors. However, if a schedule requires much more of the high-probability behavior than the low-probability behavior, Premack's principle may be violated. My experiment with rats in a reciprocal contingency between running and drinking (Mazur, 1975) illustrates how this can happen.

Recall that one rat spent about 17 percent of the time drinking and 10 percent running in baseline sessions (Figure 9-4). This animal's ratio of drinking time to running time was therefore about 1.7 to 1. In one of the reciprocal contingencies, 45 seconds of drinking were required for every 5 seconds of running. Notice that this reciprocal contingency demanded a 9:1 ratio of drinking to running, which is higher than the ratio exhibited in the unrestricted, baseline conditions. Figure 9-4 shows that in this reciprocal contingency, running time decreased to about 2 percent of the session time, while drinking time actually increased to 21 percent. Thus, contrary to

Premack's principle, in this case a low-probability behavior actually reinforced a high-probability behavior. Eisenberger, Karpman, and Trattner (1967) were the first to show that this can happen if a schedule requires large amounts of the high-probability behavior and small amounts of the low-probability behavior.

To accommodate results of this type, Timberlake and Allison (1974; Allison, 1993) proposed the **response deprivation theory** of reinforcement, a theory that is actually a refinement of Premack's principle. To see how the theory works, let us consider once again the results from the rat shown in Figure 9-4. According to response deprivation theory, the baseline ratio of the two behaviors is a crucial number. For this subject, the baseline ratio of drinking time to running time was 1.7:1. Timberlake and Allison would assume that the rat preferred this ratio of drinking to running above all others, since in baseline the animal was free to choose any ratio. Response deprivation theory therefore predicts that any schedule that lowers this ratio is depriving the animal of its preferred level of drinking. It is this restriction on the opportunities for drinking that makes drinking a reinforcer.

For example, in the condition where 5 seconds of drinking alternated with 15 seconds of running, the drinking:running ratio was 1:3, a large decrease from the baseline ratio. Notice that if the animal simply maintained its baseline amount of running (10 percent), its drinking time would be only 3.3 percent, compared to a baseline level of 17 percent. Timberlake and Allison propose, in effect, that the animal strikes a compromise between drinking and running—it increases its running time (to 16 percent in this case) so as to bring its drinking time somewhat closer to its baseline level (to just over 5 percent in this case). Upon observing this increase in running time compared to baseline, we say that drinking has reinforced running.

Response deprivation theory accounts for the reinforcement of drinking by running using similar logic: Whenever the required drinking:running ratio is *larger* than in baseline, this amounts to a deprivation of running, so running can serve as a reinforcer. In the condition requiring a 9:1 ratio of drinking to running, Subject 1 had relatively little opportunity for running, so by increasing its drinking time above baseline levels, the animal earned a bit more running time.

In summary, response deprivation theory states that unless a schedule happens to require exactly the same ratio of two behaviors that a subject chooses in baseline conditions, one of the behaviors becomes a relatively precious commodity because of its restricted availability. Regardless of whether it is the high- or low-probability behavior, the more restricted behavior will act as a reinforcer for the less restricted behavior.

Although it may be a bit more difficult to understand than Premack's principle, response deprivation theory is the most reliable predictor of reinforcer effectiveness of all the theories we have examined. The theory allows us to predict whether an activity will serve as a reinforcer by observing the probability of that behavior (and of the behavior to be reinforced) in a baseline situation. This theory has been tested both in laboratory experiments with animals and in applied settings with people, and it has proven to be an accurate way to predict when a contingency will produce an increase in a desired behavior and when it will not (Timberlake & Farmer-Dougan, 1991). For example, Konarski (1987) set up different contingencies between two behaviors in a population of mentally retarded adults, and this allowed him to make a direct comparison of the predictions of Premack's principle and response deprivation theory. The predictions of Premack's principle succeeded in some cases and failed in others, but the predictions of response deprivation theory proved to be correct almost 100 percent of the time. Because response deprivation theory allows us to make predictions in advance that are usually correct, the circularity of the term *reinforcer* is avoided.

## The Functional Analysis of Behaviors and Reinforcers

Response deprivation theory offers a good way to predict when an activity will serve as an effective reinforcer. However, a different problem that often challenges behavior therapists is to determine what reinforcer is maintaining some undesired behavior. Those who work with children or adults who have autism or mental retardation often see bizarre or inappropriate behaviors that seem to occur for no obvious reason. Examples include the destruction of toys or other objects, aggression against peers or caregivers, screaming, self-injurious behaviors, chewing on inedible objects, and many others. One useful first step toward eliminating these behaviors is to conduct a **functional analysis,** which is a method that allows the therapist to determine what reinforcer is maintaining the unwanted behavior.

These maladaptive behaviors may occur for many possible reasons. An aggressive act may allow a child to seize a desired toy (a positive reinforcer). Destroying objects may lead to attention from the caregiver (another positive reinforcer). Screaming or disruptive behavior may produce an interruption in an unwanted lesson or activity (a negative reinforcer). In addition, some behaviors (such as chewing on inedible objects, repetitive motions, or self-injurious behaviors) may produce what is called **automatic reinforcement;** that is, sensory stimulation from the behavior may serve as its own reinforcer (Fisher, Adelinis, Thompson, Worsdell, & Zarcone, 1998).

How can the cause of a particular maladaptive behavior be determined? Using the method of functional analysis, the patient's environment is systematically changed in ways that allow the therapist either to support or to rule out possible explanations of the inappropriate behavior. For example, Watson, Ray, Turner, and Logan (1999) used functional analysis to evaluate the self-injurious behavior (SIB) of a mentally disabled 10-year-old boy. In his classroom, the boy would frequently bang his head on the table, slap his face, and scratch at his face with his fingernails. On different days, the boy's teacher reacted to episodes of SIB in different ways. On some days, the teacher immediately said "Don't do that" after each instance of SIB, to see if the behavior was being reinforced by the teacher's attention. On other days, the boy was given a toy or other item after each instance of SIB, to see if tangible reinforcers might be strengthening this behavior. To assess the possibility that the SIB might be producing automatic reinforcement, the boy was sometimes placed in a room by himself, where he could receive no attention or tangible reinforcers if he engaged in SIB. Finally, on some days, whatever task the boy was working on was terminated after an instance of SIB, to determine whether the behavior might be reinforced by escape from unpleasant tasks.

Figure 9-5 shows the results of these tests. Compared to the normal classroom situation (labeled "baseline"), the rate of SIB was much lower in the situations testing the effects of attention, tangible reinforcers, and automatic reinforcement, but it was higher when it allowed the boy to terminate the ongoing task. The researchers therefore concluded that the SIB was actually escape behavior. As a treatment, they instructed the boy's teacher to allow him to end a nonpreferred task and switch to a more preferred task if he completed it without any instance of SIB. After this approach was adopted, the boy's SIB virtually disappeared.

Functional analysis must be done on a case-by-case basis, because the same behaviors may occur for different reasons for different people. In one survey of over 100 individuals who engaged in SIB, functional analysis found that for about a third of them, the behavior was being maintained by attention from the caregiver. For these individuals, the SIB was greatly reduced by having the caregiver ignore instances of SIB, but give the patients attention when they were engaged in other behaviors (Fischer, Iwata, & Worsdell, 1997). In another example of functional analysis, researchers found that finger sucking by two children was being maintained, not by attention or by escape from unpleasant tasks, but by automatic reinforcement (the sensory stimulation of the fingers). When bandages or rubber gloves were put on the children's fingers, their finger sucking decreased (Ellingson and others, 2000).

The power of functional analysis is that the therapist need not simply watch helplessly and wonder why a maladaptive behavior is occurring. By the appropriate manipulation of the environment, possible sources of reinforcement can be evaluated, and based on this information, an appropriate treatment plan can be tailored to the needs of each individual.

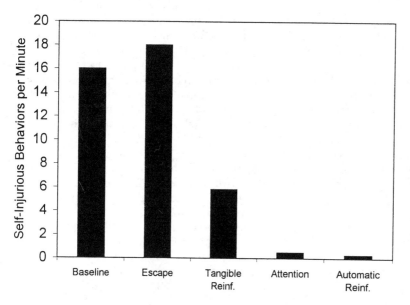

**FIGURE 9-5**   The rates of self-injurious behavior exhibited by a mentally-disabled boy in five different experimental conditions. (From Watson, Ray, Turner, & Logan, 1999)

# BEHAVIORAL ECONOMICS

This chapter has described quite a few different theories about reinforcement. In an effort to achieve a better understanding of this concept, some psychologists have turned to theories from the field of economics. Microeconomics, which is concerned with the behavior of individual consumers, and the study of operant conditioning, which is concerned with the behavior of individual organisms, have several common features (Lea, 1978). Both disciplines examine how the individual works to obtain relatively scarce and precious commodities (consumer goods in economics, reinforcers in operant conditioning). In both cases, the resources of the individual (money in economics, time or behavior in operant conditioning) are limited. Both disciplines attempt to predict how individuals will allocate their limited resources so as to obtain scarce commodities.

Because of these common interests, some psychologists and economists have begun to share theoretical ideas and research techniques. The field of **behavioral economics** is a product of these cooperative efforts (Bickel, Green, & Vuchinich, 1995; Green & Kagel, 1996). This section describes a few of the ways in which economic concepts have been applied to human and animal behavior, both inside and outside the laboratory.

## Optimization: Theory and Research

*Optimization as a Basic Assumption in Microeconomics.* A basic question for microeconomists is how individual consumers will distribute their incomes among all the possible ways it can be spent, saved, or invested. Suppose a woman brings home $500 a week after taxes. How much of this will she spend on food, on rent, on household items, on clothing, on entertainment, on charitable contributions, and so on? Optimization theory provides a succinct and reasonable answer: The consumer will distribute her income in whatever way maximizes her "subjective value" (or loosely speaking, in whatever way gives her the most satisfaction). Although this principle is

easy to state, putting it into practice can be extremely difficult. How can we know whether buying a new pair of shoes or giving that same amount of money to a worthy charity will give the woman greater satisfaction? For that matter, how does the woman know? Despite these difficulties, optimization theory maintains that people can and do make such judgments and then distribute their income accordingly.

A simple example may help to illustrate the assumptions of optimization theory. Suppose that you are an avid reader of both autobiographies and science fiction, and that as a birthday present you receive a gift certificate good for any 10 paperbacks at a local bookstore. How many autobiographies will you buy, and how many books of science fiction? Naturally, optimization theory cannot give us a definite answer, but it does provide some guidelines. A common assumption is that as a consumer obtains more and more items of a given type, the value of each additional item of that same type decreases. For example, the value of one new science fiction novel may be relatively high, but a second science fiction novel will be a bit less valued, and the tenth new science fiction novel may have fairly little value. This assumption is based on the concept of satiation—you may grow weary of vicariously traveling to yet another unexplored planet in the twenty-third century.

Similarly, your first new autobiography should be the most valued, the second a bit less valued, and so on. These assumptions are illustrated graphically in the two left panels of Figure 9-6. The *y*-axis shows the (hypothetical) cumulative value of different numbers of science fiction novels (left panel) and autobiographies (center panel). The steps depict the additional value provided by one more paperback of each type. The consistently higher curve for science fiction novels means that for this illustration, we will assume that you enjoy science fiction novels somewhat more than autobiographies. From these two graphs, the total value of any possible combination of science fiction novels and autobiographies can be calculated. The results are plotted in the right panel of Figure 9-6. Even before looking at this graph, you should realize that the optimal

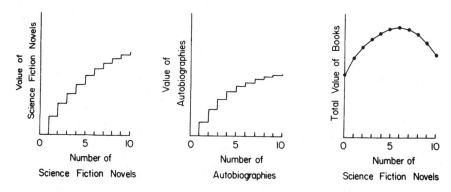

**FIGURE 9-6** An illustration of the predictions of optimization theory for a case where a person must choose any combination of science fiction novels and autobiographies, for a total of 10 books. The left panel shows that the subjective value of a set of science fiction novels increases with each additional novel, but the increment in value is progressively smaller. The center panel shows a similar pattern for autobiographies. The right panel shows that a person with precisely these preferences for the two types of books would maximize subjective value by choosing six science fiction novels and four autobiographies.

package will consist of some mixture of the two types of books, since the first autobiography has more value than the tenth science fiction novel, and the first science fiction novel has more value than the tenth autobiography. For the specific functions drawn in the two left panels, it turns out that the combination of six science fiction novels and four autobiographies leads to the highest total value. Optimization theory therefore predicts that this combination would be chosen by a person who had this particular set of preferences for the two types of books.

The decisions of anyone who earns an income are obviously much more complex than in this simple example, but optimization theory suggests that the decision-making process is essentially the same—the consumer searches for the maximum subjective value. Although a good deal of economic theory is based on this principle, uncertainty about the exact shape of any individual's value functions makes the principle of optimization difficult to test. The next section shows that the principle has also been applied to animal behavior, where researchers have been able to gather concrete evidence to support it.

***Optimization and Behavioral Ecology.***
Behavioral ecologists study the behaviors of animals in their natural habitats or in semi-naturalistic settings, and they attempt to determine how the behavior patterns of different species are shaped by environmental factors and the pressures of survival. It is easy to see why the concept of optimization is appealing to behavioral ecologists, with their interest in the relationship between evolution and behavior: Animals whose behaviors are more nearly optimal should increase their chances of surviving and of breeding offspring that will have similar behavior tendencies. Behavior ecologists have documented many cases where an animal's behaviors are close to optimal, involving such varied pursuits as foraging for food, searching for a mate, and choosing group size (Krebs & Davies, 1978). Two quite different examples are described below.

When searching for its prey, any predator must make decisions. If a large prey is encountered, it should of course be captured. On the other hand, if a small prey is encountered, the predator's decision is trickier. If a long time is required to chase, capture, and eat the small prey, it may not be worthwhile to go after it, because during this time the predator will miss the opportunity to capture any larger prey that might come along. Theorists have developed complex equations specifying the optimal choice for a predator in any particular situation (Charnov, 1976; Schoener, 1971), but perhaps you can get a feel for their predictions without resorting to any mathematics. A general rule is that if the density of large prey is low (so that encounters with large prey are rare), the predator should go after any prey, large or small. If the density of large prey is high, however, the predator should ignore all small prey, because in chasing them it would lose valuable time during which a large prey might come along.

Werner and Hall (1974) tested these predictions by placing 10 bluegill sunfish in a large aquarium with three sizes of prey (smaller fish). When prey density was low (20 of each type), the sunfish ate all three types of prey as often as they were encountered. When prey density was high (350 of each type), the sunfish ate only the largest prey. When prey density was intermediate (200 of each type), the sunfish ate only the two largest prey types. By measuring the time the sunfish required to capture and eat prey of each type, Werner and Hall were able to show that the behaviors of the sunfish were exactly what optimization theory predicted for all three situations.

In an ingenious (if not enviable) piece of field research, Parker (1978) applied optimization theory to the mating behavior of the dung fly. This insect is so named because the female deposits its fertilized eggs in cow dung, where the larvae then develop. Dung flies generally mate in the vicinity of a fresh pat of cow dung, because females prefer fresh deposits over older ones. The males tend to locate themselves near a fresh pat and wait for a female to arrive. Parker calculated the optimal time a male should wait near one pat before moving to a fresher pat, based on the behavior he observed in the females and on the level of competition among males for the prime locations. The amounts of time the males actually stood pat before moving on were close to the optimal durations. Other aspects of the dung flies' behaviors, such as the amount of time spent

copulating as opposed to searching for another mate, were also approximately optimal.

These examples show how scientists have applied optimization theory to the behaviors of animals in naturalistic settings. Operant conditioning experiments have also provided some support for the theory (Silberberg, Bauman, & Hursh, 1993). In the psychological laboratory, optimization theory can be put to a more rigorous test, and its predictions can be compared to those of alternative theories. Some of this research will be described in Chapter 14.

## Elasticity and Inelasticity of Demand

In operant research, many studies have been done on how behavior changes as the requirements of a reinforcement schedule become more severe, as when a ratio requirement is increased from FR 10 to FR 100. This question is very similar to the economic question of how the **demand** for a commodity changes as its price increases. Economists say the demand for a commodity is **elastic** if the amount purchased decreases markedly when its price increases. Demand is typically elastic when close substitutes for the product are readily available. For example, the demand for a specific brand of cola would probably drop dramatically if its price increased by 50 percent, because people would switch to other brands, which taste about the same. Conversely, demand for a product is called **inelastic** if changes in price have relatively little effect on the amount purchased. This is generally the case for products with no close substitutes. In modern society, the demand for gasoline is fairly inelastic because many people have no alternative to driving their cars to work, school, shopping centers, and so on.

Lea and Roper (1977) conducted an experiment with rats that demonstrated a similar relation between the availability of substitutes and elasticity of demand. By pressing one lever, rats could earn food pellets on FR schedules, which ranged from FR 1 to FR 16 in different conditions. The availability of a substitute food was also varied across conditions. When no substitute was available, demand for the food pellets was fairly inelastic: On FR 16, the rats earned almost as many pellets as on FR 1, even though the price was 16 times higher. When a fairly close substitute (sucrose pellets) could be obtained by pressing a second lever, demand for the food pellets was more elastic, with a greater decrease in the number of food pellets earned with the higher ratios. Finally, demand was very elastic when a perfect substitute (identical food pellets) could be earned by pressing the second lever. Lea and Roper therefore obtained, in this simple experiment with rats, the same relation between substitution and elasticity that economists find when people purchase goods in the marketplace. Other laboratory experiments with animals have found a similar connection between substitute availability and elasticity (Green & Freed, 1993; Hursh & Bauman, 1987).

## Behavioral Economics and Drug Abuse

Animal experiments can often provide valuable information about matters that are of great importance to human behavior. One such area involves the effects of addictive drugs on an individual's behavior. Many laboratory experiments have examined how animals respond when given the opportunity to work to obtain drugs such as alcohol, heroin, or cocaine. One general finding is that these drugs can serve as powerful reinforcers for animals ranging from rats to monkeys. In addition, it is possible to use economic concepts to analyze the effects of a drug more precisely. For example, some of studies have used animal subjects to measure the elasticity of different drugs. Animals may be allowed to work for drugs on FR schedules of different sizes, to determine how the "price" of the drug affects consumption. A common finding is that demand for addictive drugs is fairly inelastic: As the amount of work required for each dose of the drug increases, the animals will make more responses, so that their total level of drug consumption does not decrease much at all. However, if the price gets high enough (a very large

FR must be completed for a small dose of the drug), consumption of the drug will finally decrease.

Experiments have also found that other factors besides price can affect an animal's demand for a drug, such as the availability of substitutes and competition from other reinforcers. For instance, in one study, baboons had to choose between food and intravenous injections of heroin. When both were plentiful (a choice was available every 2 minutes), the baboons chose the two alternatives about equally often, and as a result they consumed a good deal of heroin. But when the two reinforcers were less plentiful (a choice was available only every 12 minutes), the baboons chose food most of the time, and their consumption of heroin decreased dramatically (Elsmore, Fletcher, Conrad, & Sodetz, 1980). Studies of this type show that even addictive drugs conform to standard economic principles of supply and demand, and that drug consumption will decrease if the cost gets high enough. Furthermore, it does not always take a manipulation as extreme as decreasing the availability of food to reduce drug consumption. Carroll (1993) showed that rhesus monkeys' demand for the drug PCP could be substantially reduced simply by giving them access to saccharin as an alternative reinforcer, and similar results have been obtained with other addictive drugs.

Research using the behavioral economic approach to drug addiction has also been conducted with human subjects, involving such drugs as nicotine, caffeine, alcohol, and heroin. As with the animal studies, this research has shown that economic principles can be applied to drugs just as well as to other commodities. For instance, as the price of a drug increases, or as substitute reinforcers become more available, drug consumption declines (Bickel, DeGrandpre, & Higgins, 1995). Sometimes these economic analyses produce surprising results: For example, DeGrandpre, Bickel, Hughes, and Higgins (1992) reviewed 17 studies that manipulated the nicotine content of cigarettes, and they plotted economic demand functions to show the effects of changing nicotine levels. Their analysis showed that if smokers are given reduced-nicotine cigarettes in place of their usual cigarettes, they smoke more cigarettes per day, and thereby expose themselves to more cigarette smoke (and greater health risks). Conversely, if smokers are given cigarettes with higher nicotine levels, they smoke fewer cigarettes per day. The researchers concluded that unless the use of reduced-nicotine cigarettes eventually helps a smoker quit smoking altogether, this practice can actually be a health risk rather than a benefit.

Laboratory studies and economic principles can also be used to analyze drug interactions and substitutability. For instance, consider the strategy of treating heroin addicts by giving them methadone as a substitute. In economic terms, methadone is an imperfect substitute for heroin because it delivers some but not all of the reinforcing properties of heroin. More specifically, methadone prevents the withdrawal symptoms associated with heroin abstinence, but it does not provide the euphoria or "high" that heroin does. In addition, for a drug user, the clinical setting in which methadone is administered may not be as reinforcing as the social environment in which heroin is typically used (Hursh, 1991). For these reasons, it would be a mistake to expect the availability of methadone treatment to eliminate heroin use, even if the treatment were freely and easily available to all those who currently use heroin.

Vuchinich (1999) has argued that to reduce drug abuse in our society, a multifaceted approach is best. First, the cost of using drugs should be increased through stricter drug enforcement policies that reduce the supply. Second, the community must make sure that reinforcers are available for other, non-drug activities. For young people who may be tempted to experiment with drugs, sports and recreational programs that require participants to avoid drugs may be effective. For recovering addicts, the alternative reinforcers can be provided by supportive family and friends, and a job that demands a drug-free employee. Third, Vuchinich emphasizes that the reinforcers for non-drug activities should be ones that can be delivered promptly, because delayed reinforcers are notoriously ineffective.

Besides drug abuse, behavioral economic principles have been applied to other behavior problems, including alcoholism, smoking, overeating, and compulsive gambling (Bickel & Vuchinich, 2000). One important theme of the behavioral economic approach is that although it can sometimes be difficult to change such behaviors, it is not impossible. Behavioral economists argue that these problem behaviors should not be viewed as incurable diseases, but rather as economic behaviors that follow the same principles as do other behaviors. Whether one uses the terminology of economics (supply, demand, elasticity) or of learning theory (reinforcement, punishment, stimulus control), these behaviors can be changed by appropriate modifications in the individual's environment.

## CHAPTER SUMMARY

Thorndike predicted that a subject must actively respond for learning to occur, but experiments in which animals were passively transported through mazes showed that they learned without active responding. In the latent learning experiment of Tolman and Honzik, rats showed immediate improvement in their performance once food was presented at the end of a maze. Tolman and Honzik concluded that the rats had learned the maze without reinforcement, but that reinforcement was necessary before they would perform the correct responses.

Studies have shown that animals develop expectations about what reinforcer will be delivered, and may appear surprised if the reinforcer is changed. Other research has shown that animals develop specific associations among all three components of the three-term contingency—the discriminative stimulus, the operant response, and the reinforcer.

Studies with animals found that reinforcement can control visceral responses such as heart rate and stomach activity, but some of these findings have been difficult to replicate. Nevertheless, research with human patients has found many useful medical applications of biofeedback, in which a person is given continuous feedback about some bodily process and attempts to control it. Biofeedback has been successfully used for tension headaches, some types of muscular paralysis, stomach and intestinal disorders, and a variety of other ailments.

How can we predict what will be a reinforcer? Hull's need-reduction and drive-reduction theories have obvious shortcomings. The principle of trans-situationality states that a reinforcer in one situation will be a reinforcer in other situations. Premack's principle states that more probable behaviors will reinforce less probable behaviors. But the best general rule for predicting what will be a reinforcer seems to be response deprivation theory, which states that whenever a contingency is arranged between two behaviors, the more restricted behavior should act as a reinforcer for the less restricted behavior.

The field of behavioral economics combines the techniques of operant research and the principles of economics. Optimization theory, which states that individuals will distribute their money, time, or responses in a way that optimizes subjective value, has been applied to many cases of animal behavior in natural settings. Other research has tested economic principles about supply and demand, elasticity, and substitutability among reinforcers, using animal subjects in controlled environments.

## REVIEW QUESTIONS

1. How were the three different groups of rats treated in Tolman and Honzik's classic experiment on latent learning? How did each of the three groups perform, and what did Tolman and Honzik conclude?

2. Describe two experiments, using different procedures, that showed that animals develop expectations about the reinforcer in operant conditioning.

3. Describe an experiment designed to test whether reinforcement can control visceral responses in rats. Describe one biofeedback procedure used to treat a medical problem. What type of feedback is given, how do subjects respond, and how effective is the treatment in the long run?

4. What are need-reduction theory, drive-reduction theory, and the principle of trans-situationality? What are their weaknesses? How do Premack's principle and response deprivation theory predict what will serve as a reinforcer?

## CHAPTER 10

# Stimulus Control and Concept Formation

The relationship between stimuli and the behaviors that follow them is the topic of this chapter, a topic frequently called **stimulus control.** As we have seen throughout this book, predicting what response will occur in the presence of a given stimulus is a challenging task, even when the same stimulus is presented again and again in a controlled laboratory environment. But in the real world, all creatures are repeatedly confronted with stimuli and events they have never experienced before, and their survival may depend on an adaptive response. The topic of stimulus control also encompasses research on how creatures respond to such novel stimuli. In previous chapters we used the term *generalization* to describe a subject's tendency to respond to novel stimuli in much the same way that it has previously responded to similar, familiar stimuli. It is now time to examine the process of generalization more closely.

In its overall organization, this chapter progresses from simple to increasingly complex relations among stimuli. We will begin with analyses of generalization among stimuli that differ only in their location on a single physical continuum, such as size or wavelength of light. Next, we will examine a more abstract sort of generalization in which the stimuli presented in two tasks are completely different and it is only the structures of the tasks that are similar. For instance, if a subject first masters a task in which one color signals reinforcement and another color signals extinction, will this facilitate the learning of a subsequent discrimination task involving not colors but lines of different orientations? Finally, we will consider the topic of concept formation, which involves the classification of different objects into a single category (for instance, "trees"), even though their visual appearances may sometimes have little in common.

## GENERALIZATION GRADIENTS

### Measuring Generalization Gradients

Suppose that we have trained a pigeon to peck at a yellow key by reinforcing pecks with food on a VI 1-minute schedule, and the bird now pecks at the key at a fairly steady rate. Now we wish to determine how much generalization there will be to other key colors, such as blue, green, orange, and red. How can we collect this information? This answer is not as simple as it may seem. Suppose we switch to a red key light, intending to measure the pigeon's response rate over a 5-minute period. The animal may start to respond, but do we deliver food for pecks at the red key or not? If we do, then we will be measuring the effects of the reinforcement as well as generalization. If we deliver no reinforcers, then any pecking at the red key will surely start to extinguish.

To overcome these problems as much as possible, researchers have relied on two major techniques for obtaining generalization gradients. In both, the test stimuli are always presented under extinction conditions. In the first technique, test trials, or **probe trials,** with the unreinforced stimuli are occasionally inserted among reinforced trials with the training stimulus. For instance, each trial might consist of 10 seconds of exposure to one of the key colors, with successive trials being separated by a 5-second intertrial interval in which the key is dark. Ninety percent of the trials might involve the yellow key light and the VI 1-minute schedule, and the other 10 percent of the trials would include different key colors and an extinction schedule. The advantage of embedding probe trials among reinforced trials with the training stimulus is that the procedure can continue indefinitely without the threat of extinction until sufficient data are collected. The main disadvantage of this procedure is that the subject may begin to form a discrimination between the yellow key and all other key colors, so that there will be

progressively less generalization as the training proceeds.

The other main technique for obtaining generalization gradients is exemplified by an experiment conducted by Guttman and Kalish (1956). The training stimulus was a yellow key light of a wavelength of 580 nanometers. (One nanometer, abbreviated nm, equals one billionth of a meter.) After the pigeons had learned to respond steadily to the yellow key light, a series of extinction trials began that included the yellow light and 10 other colors of both shorter wavelengths (the blue end of the spectrum) and longer wavelengths (the red end of the spectrum). The trick was to obtain enough trials with each wavelength before responding extinguished. Guttman and Kalish accomplished this by limiting the duration of each trial to 30 seconds. The first block of 11 trials included one trial with each color, presented in a random order. This procedure continued for 12 blocks, so that each color was presented 12 times. Response rates declined across the 12 blocks, but because each stimulus was presented throughout the extinction period, the effects of extinction were approximately balanced across colors. As Figure 10-1 shows, Guttman and Kalish obtained a fairly symmetrical generalization gradient, with the most responding to the yellow training stimulus and less responding to colors of shorter or longer wavelengths.

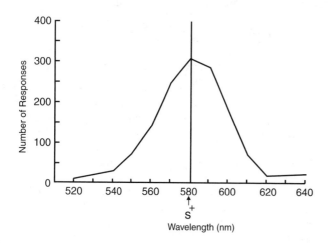

**FIGURE 10-1** A generalization gradient for wavelength of light from the Guttman and Kalish (1956) experiment with pigeons. After training in which pecks at a 580-nm key light were reinforced, this and 10 other wavelengths were tested under extinction conditions.

## What Causes Generalization Gradients?

Having examined two techniques for obtaining generalization gradients, we can now ask why such gradients occur in the first place. Why should reinforcement of a behavior in the presence of one stimulus cause this behavior to occur to similar stimuli that have never been used in training? Pavlov's (1927) answer was that generalization is an automatic by-product of the conditioning process. His explanation was based on his physiological theory about the "spread of excitation" across neurons in the cerebral cortex, a theory now known to be incorrect. Nevertheless, Pavlov's more general view that generalization is an inherent property of the nervous system cannot be so easily dismissed, and some modern theories also try to explain the shapes of generalization gradients using reasonable assumptions about the wiring of the nervous system (Gluck, 1991). Chapter 2 described the work of Hubel and Wiesel, some of which involved recording the electrical responsiveness of single neurons in a cat's visual cortex. Hubel and Wiesel found that different cells were responsive to different features in the visual environment. For instance, one cell might fire most rapidly when a line at a 45-degree angle was presented. The cell would fire more slowly if the orientation of the line was 35 degrees or 55 degrees, and still more slowly if it was 25 degrees or 65 degrees. Notice that if Hubel and Wiesel plotted the cell's responsiveness as a function of line orientation, they would obtain a function quite similar to the typical generalization gradient.

Now let us imagine that the appropriate conditioning experience, such as reinforcing the cat for a lever press in the presence of a 45-degree line, were somehow to strengthen a chain of associations between this cell (and perhaps many others like it) and the motor neurons involved in a lever press (through physiological mechanisms that are at best only dimly understood). Because of the properties of the "45-degree angle detector" in the cat's visual cortex, we might expect some generalization of lever pressing to lines of similar ori-

entations. Of course, we should not take this simplistic physiological hypothesis very seriously because it is a far cry from the responsiveness of a single cortical cell to an animal's overt behavior. There is no reason why a behavioral generalization gradient should bear any resemblance to the response characteristics of any single neuron.

A hypothesis quite different from Pavlov's was proposed by Lashley and Wade (1946). They theorized that some explicit discrimination training along the dimension in question (such as wavelength of light or frequency of tone) is necessary before the typical peaked generalization gradient is obtained. For instance, if the dimension of interest is color, they would claim that subjects must receive experience in which reinforcement occurs in the presence of one or more colors but not in their absence. Without such discrimination training, Lashley and Wade proposed that the generalization gradient would be flat—the subject would respond just as strongly to all the novel test stimuli as to the training stimulus. Thus, whereas Pavlov proposed that generalization gradients are innate, Lashley and Wade proposed that they are dependent upon learning experiences.

*How Experience Affects the Shape of Generalization Gradients.* An experiment that provides some support for the position of Lashley and Wade was conducted by Jenkins and Harrison (1960). Two groups of pigeons responded on a VI schedule in the presence of a 1000-Hz tone. Three pigeons received **nondifferential training**, in which every trial was the same—the key light was lit, the 1000-Hz tone was on, and the VI schedule was in effect. Five other pigeons received **presence-absence training**, which included two types of trials: (1) trials with the 1000-Hz tone that were exactly like those of the other group, and (2) trials without the tone, during which the key light was lit as usual, but no reinforcers were delivered.

After training, both groups received a series of extinction trials similar to those of Guttman and Kalish, where the different trials included different tone frequencies, and some trials included no tone at all. The results are presented in Figure 10-2. As Lashley and Wade predicted, the nondifferential training produced generalization gradients that were basically flat: Response rates were roughly the same at all tone frequencies. On the other hand, the presence-absence training produced typical generalization gradients with sharp peaks at 1000 Hz.

To explain their results, Jenkins and Harrison suggested that it is useful to consider what

discriminative stimuli might be expected to control responding in each condition. As we saw in Chapters 4 and 5, a general rule of classical conditioning is that the stimulus that is the best predictor of the US is likely to become the most effective CS. Extrapolating to an operant conditioning situation, we might expect that the discriminative stimulus that is the best predictor of reinforcement will exert the strongest control over responding. For the pigeons that received nondifferential training, many stimuli were equally good predictors of

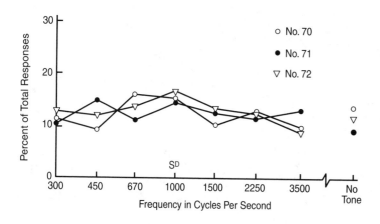

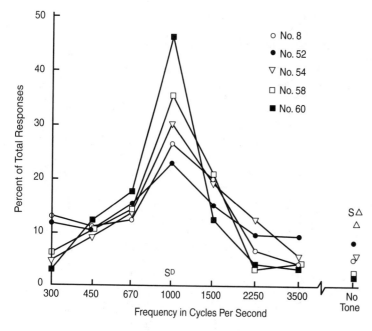

**FIGURE 10-2** Generalization gradients for tone frequency in the Jenkins and Harrison (1960) experiment after nondifferential training (top panel) and presence-absence training (bottom panel) with a 1000-Hz tone.

the reinforcer—the tone, the illuminated key light, and the many other sights, sounds, and smells of the experimental chamber. If all of these stimuli shared in the control of key pecking, then changing or removing one of them (the tone) should have little effect. In addition, if one of these stimuli (such as the key light) happened to be particularly salient, it might overshadow the other stimuli, just as one CS may overshadow another in classical conditioning. Perhaps the illuminated key light did indeed overshadow the tone in the nondifferential group, for the tone exerted no control over responding—the pigeons pecked just as rapidly when the frequency of the tone was changed, or when there was no tone at all.

On the other hand, for the pigeons that received presence-absence training, the tone was the only stimulus reliably correlated with reinforcement. Because it was the best signal for the availability of reinforcement, the tone came to exert control over the subject's responding, as witnessed by the sharp declines in response rate that occurred when one feature of the tone (its frequency) was altered.

Another experiment by Jenkins and Harrison (1962) provided further information about the effects of experience on generalization gradients. Two pigeons received discrimination training in which the 1000-Hz tone was an $S^+$ (a discriminative stimulus for reinforcement) and a 950-Hz tone was an $S^-$ (a discriminative stimulus for the absence of reinforcement). In other words, nonreinforced trials with the 950-Hz tone replaced the no-tone trials of the presence-absence group in the previous experiment. The term **intradimensional training** has been used to label discrimination training in which $S^+$ and $S^-$ come from the same stimulus continuum (tone frequency in this case). In a subsequent extinction test, these two pigeons produced much narrower generalization gradients than those from the presence-absence training. There was little responding to the 950-Hz tone or to those of lower frequency, a sharp increase in responding to tones in the vicinity of 1000 Hz, and little responding to tones above 1100 Hz. These gradients were at least five times narrower than those from the differential group in the bottom of Figure 10-2.

These results provided further evidence on the effects of experience on generalization gradients, and once again Jenkins and Harrison (1962) interpreted the results in terms of the different stimuli that might compete for control of the pigeon's responding. After presence-absence training, the 1000-Hz tone was the only stimulus reliably correlated with reinforcement, but Jenkins and Harrison pointed out that this tone had many separate features—its frequency, its loudness, its location, and so on. To the extent that responding was controlled by features of the tone other than its frequency, we should expect responding to persist at other frequencies, as it did after presence-absence training. When the $S^-$ was a tone of slightly different frequency, however, the only reliable predictor of reinforcement was the frequency of the 1000-Hz tone, so the other features of this tone, such as loudness and location, should lose their control over responding. The sharper gradients from the pigeons that received intradimensional training are consistent with this analysis.

In summary, the Jenkins and Harrison results support Lashley and Wade's hypothesis that generalization gradients are dependent on experience. With nondifferential training, tone frequency exerted no control over responding. After presence-absence training, tone frequency exerted modest control, and typical peaked generalization gradients were obtained. With intradimensional training, very sharply peaked gradients were obtained. Unfortunately for the Lashley and Wade theory, however, other studies have shown that peaked generalization gradients can sometimes be obtained with nondifferential training. We have already encountered one study of this type: In the Guttman and Kalish (1956) experiment, peaked gradients along the dimension of wavelength were obtained after nondifferential training with a 580-nm key light. These results seem to support Pavlov's theory that no special training is necessary for generalization gradients to appear.

It is not difficult to think of ways to reconcile the results of Guttman and Kalish (and others like them) with the Lashley and Wade theory. As Lashley and Wade themselves suggested, although subjects might receive only nondifferential training within an experiment, they may have learned from their everyday experiences prior to the experiment that different stimuli along the dimension in question can signal different consequences. Thus the pigeons in the Guttman and Kalish experiment might have learned from their everyday experiences that color is frequently an informative characteristic of a stimulus, and as a result they were predisposed to "pay attention to" the color of the key in the experimental chamber.

### *How Sensory Deprivation Affects the Shape of Generalization Gradients.*

Once the possibility of pre-experiment learning is entertained, the Lashley and Wade theory becomes quite difficult to test: It becomes necessary to prevent the possibility of discrimination learning along the dimension in question from the moment a subject is born. Peterson (1962) conducted such an ambitious experiment by raising four ducklings in an environment that was illuminated with a monochromatic yellow light of 589 nm. Because this special light emitted only a single wavelength, all objects appeared yellow regardless of their actual color in white light. (To envision what this visual experience is like, imagine watching a black-and-white movie while wearing yellow-tinted glasses: Everything on the screen would appear as a mixture of yellow and black.) After training the ducklings to peck at a yellow key for water reinforcement, Peterson conducted a generalization test with key lights of different colors. These ducklings produced flat generalization gradients, indicating that color exerted no control over their behavior. Two ducklings reared in white light produced more normal, peaked generalization gradients. However, several attempts to replicate Peterson's experiment have been unsuccessful (Malott, 1968; Tracy, 1970). For instance, Rudolph, Honig, and Gerry (1969) raised chickens and quail under monochromatic light and found more sharply peaked generalization gradients than in a control group reared under ordinary white light. There seems to be no way to reconcile these results with the Lashley and Wade theory.

To summarize, research on the relationship between experience and generalization gradi-

ents has yielded a variety of findings. The experiments employing sensory restriction showed that, at least with birds, stimulus control by wavelength of light can occur even when a subject has had no previous exposure to more than one color. These studies contradict the extreme form of the Lashley and Wade theory, which states that no stimulus control will occur without some discrimination training involving the relevant stimulus dimension. At the other extreme is Pavlov's theory that peaked generalization gradients are derived from an inherent characteristic of the nervous system, and this theory is also incorrect. Jenkins and Harrison found no stimulus control along the dimension of tone frequency without some form of prior discrimination training (presence-absence training, intradimensional training) with tone frequency. The results suggest a compromise position: In some cases, discrimination learning may be necessary before stimulus control is obtained, and in other cases, no experience may be necessary. The evidence that, for birds, such experience is necessary for tones but not for colors is consistent with the idea that vision is a dominant sensory modality for these creatures. Perhaps we might say that birds are "prepared" to associate the color of a stimulus with the consequences that follow, but are "unprepared" to associate the pitch of a tone with subsequent events.

Whether or not experience is necessary before a particular creature exhibits stimulus control along a particular stimulus dimension, one certainty is that explicit discrimination training can change the shape of a generalization gradient. We have already seen how intradimensional training can sharpen stimulus control. The next section explores some theories and evidence about exactly what a subject learns when it receives intradimensional discrimination training.

## IS STIMULUS CONTROL ABSOLUTE OR RELATIONAL?

Consider a simple experiment on discrimination learning in which a chicken is presented with two discriminative stimuli, a light gray card and a dark gray card. If the chicken approaches the light gray card it is reinforced, but if it approaches the dark gray card it is not. This procedure is called **simultaneous discrimination** training because the two stimuli are presented together and the subject must choose between them. With sufficient training, the chicken will learn to choose the light gray card. But exactly what has the animal learned? According to the **absolute theory** of stimulus control, the animal has simply learned about the two stimuli separately: It has learned that choosing the light gray color produces food and choosing the dark gray color produces no food.

On the other hand, according to the **relational theory** of stimulus control, the animal has learned something about the *relationship* between the two stimuli—it has learned that the lighter gray is associated with food. The absolute position assumes that the animal responds to each stimulus without reference to the other; the relational position assumes that the animal responds to the relationship between the two. C. Lloyd Morgan (1894), an early writer on animal behavior, favored the absolute position because he believed that nonhumans are simply not capable of understanding relationships such as lighter, darker, larger, or redder. These relationships are abstract concepts that are not part of any single stimulus, and he felt that animals do not have the capacity to form such abstractions. A major advocate of the relational position was the German psychologist Wolfgang Kohler (1939). Let us look at the evidence on both sides of this debate and attempt to come to some resolution.

### Transposition and Peak Shift

In support of the relational position, Kohler (1939) presented evidence for a phenomenon he called **transposition**. After training several chickens on the simultaneous discrimination task just described, Kohler gave the chickens several trials on which the two stimuli were (1) the light gray card that had previously served as the $S^+$, and (2) a card with a still lighter gray (which we can call the "very light gray stimulus"). Which stimulus would a chicken choose?

If the absolute position is correct, the chicken should choose the gray that had been the $S^+$, since the animal had been reinforced for choosing this stimulus, but it had never been reinforced for choosing the very light gray card (since it had never seen this stimulus before). On the other hand, if the animal had learned to respond to the relation between the two training stimuli (choosing the lighter gray), it should choose the novel, very light gray stimulus. Across several extinction trials, all of Kohler's subjects showed a preference for the novel stimulus over the previously reinforced stimulus. The term transposition is meant to convey the idea that the subject has transferred the relational rule ("Choose the lighter gray") to a new pair of stimuli (one of which happens to be the previous $S^+$).

Kohler also found evidence for transposition with chimpanzees, and other studies have found such evidence with rats (Lawrence and DeRivera, 1954) and with children (Alberts & Ehrenfreund, 1951). Besides the brightness of different grays, transposition has also been found when the different discriminative stimuli varied along the dimension of size (Gulliksen, 1932). These results constitute one of the main pieces of evidence for the relational theory.

In research on generalization gradients, a phenomenon that is in some ways similar to transposition was first reported by Hanson (1959), who referred to it as **peak shift**. Notice that whereas transposition is found in simultaneous discrimination tasks, generalization gradients are usually obtained by presenting the various stimuli one at a time, in what is called a **successive discrimination** procedure. In Hanson's experiment, pigeons in the control group received several sessions of training in which pecking at a 550-nm key light occasionally produced food on a VI schedule. These pigeons had no training with any other key color until the generalization test. In an experimental group, pigeons received intradimensional training with the 550-nm key light as $S^+$ and a 555-nm key light as $S^-$. After this training, Hanson measured the birds' responses to a range of different key colors during extinction so as to obtain generalization gradients.

Results from both groups are shown in Figure 10-3. The control group produced a typical generalization gradient with a peak at 550 nm, as expected. In contrast, the group that received intradimensional training produced a peak around 530 to 540 nm rather than at the previously reinforced wavelength. In fact, there was very little responding to the 550-nm key light in the generalization test. The term peak shift thus refers to a shift in the generalization gradient in a direction away from the S+.

Peak shift has also been observed with many other stimuli besides colors, such as stimulus duration (Spetch & Cheng, 1998) and the number of objects in an array (Honig & Stewart, 1993). It has been found with many species, including humans (McLaren, Bennett, Guttman-Nahir, Kim, & Mackintosh, 1995).

Let us try to decide how the results shown in Figure 10-3 relate to the absolute and relational views of stimulus control. The absolute position would seem to predict a peak at 550 nm for both groups, since this was the stimulus that had previously signaled the availability of reinforcement. On the other hand, the peak shift might provide some support for the relational position, for the following reason. Lights of both 550 nm and 555 nm are greenish-yellow, but the shorter wavelength is a bit greener. Thus according to the relational position, the pigeons that received intradimensional training might have learned that the greener of the two stimuli was a signal for reinforcement. This would explain why they responded more to the 530- and 540-nm stimuli, which are greener still. Unfortunately, the relational position cannot explain why responding was markedly lower to wavelengths between 500 and 520 nm, which are the purest greens. In summary, at this point in our discussion, Hanson's results do not seem to be completely consistent with either the absolute or the relational positions.

## Spence's Theory of Excitatory and Inhibitory Gradients

A clever version of the absolute theory developed by Kenneth Spence (1937) can account quite nicely for both transposition and peak shift. The essence of the absolute position is that the subject learns only about the two stimuli individually and learns nothing about the relation between the two. Beginning with this assumption, Spence proposed that in intradimensional training, an excitatory gener-

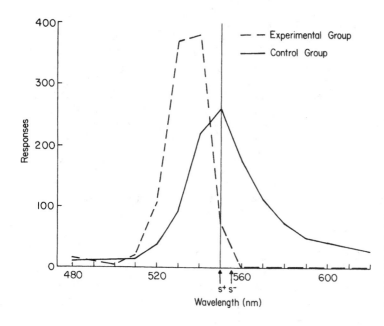

**FIGURE 10-3** Generalization gradients for wavelength of light in the experiment of Hanson (1959). The control group was trained only with a 550-nm key light as S+, whereas the experimental group was trained with a 550-nm key light as S+ and a 555-nm key light as S−.

alization gradient develops around the S⁺, and an inhibitory gradient develops around the S⁻. Let us see how this process might apply to Hanson's experiment. Figure 10-4a depicts an excitatory generalization gradient around 550 nm and an inhibitory gradient centered around 555 nm. The term *associative strength* refers to the ability of each stimulus to elicit a response. Spence proposed that the net associative strength of any stimulus can be determined by subtracting its inhibitory strength from its excitatory strength. For each wavelength, the result of this subtraction is shown in Figure 10-4b.

Notice that the S⁺, at 550 nm, has the highest excitatory strength, but it also has a good

**FIGURE 10-4**   An analysis of peak shift based on Spence's (1937) theory. (a) Intradimensional training is assumed to produce an excitatory gradient around S⁺ (550 nm) and an inhibitory gradient around S⁻ (555 nm). (b) The net associative strength of each wavelength equals the difference between its excitatory strength and inhibitory strength. Because of the inhibitory gradient around S⁻, the peak of this gradient is shifted from S⁺ in a direction away from S⁻.

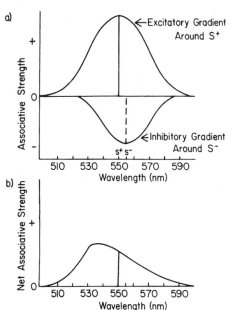

deal of inhibitory strength because of its proximity to the S⁻. On the other hand, a stimulus in the vicinity of 530 to 540 nm has considerable excitatory strength but relatively little inhibitory strength (because it is farther away from the S⁻). The result is that stimuli around 530 to 540 nm actually have a higher net associative strength than the S⁺ of 550 nm. If we assume (as Spence did) that the strength of responding in the presence of any stimulus depends on its associative strength, then Figure 10-4b predicts the type of peak shift that Hanson actually obtained.

Recall that the relational theory cannot explain why responding was so low with stimuli of 500 to 520 nm. Spence's theory has no problem explaining these results, however. As Figure 10-4 shows, we need only assume that these wavelengths are so far from both S⁺ and S⁻ they acquired little excitatory or inhibitory strength. In short, Spence's theory can explain both the peak shift and the decreased responding with stimuli farther away from S⁺. It does a very good job of accounting for the results from successive discrimination experiments.

## The Intermediate-Size Problem

Whereas Spence's theory does a good job of accounting for the results from experiments on transposition and peak shift, it fails to predict the results on what is called the **intermediate-size problem**. Gonzalez, Gentry, and Bitterman (1954) conducted an experiment on the intermediate-size problem with chimpanzees. Their stimuli were nine squares of different sizes. Their smallest square (which they called Square 1) had an area of 9 square inches, and their largest square (Square 9) had an area of about 27 square inches. During training, the chimpanzees were always presented with Squares 1, 5, and 9, and they were reinforced if they chose the intermediate square, Square 5. (Of course, the left-to-right locations of the squares varied randomly from trial to trial so that a subject could not use position as a discriminative stimulus.)

On test trials, the chimpanzees were presented with different sets of three squares, and they were reinforced no matter which square they chose. As an example, suppose the three squares on one trial were Squares 4, 7, and 9. The predictions of the relational position are straightforward: If the chimps had learned to choose the square of intermediate size, they should choose Square 7. Figure 10-5 helps to explain the predictions of Spence's theory. The initial training should have produced an excitatory gradient around Square 5 and inhibitory gradients around Squares 1 and 9. Because Square 5 is flanked on each side by an inhibitory gradient, there is no peak shift in this case; instead, the inhibitory gradients simply sharpen the gradient of net associative strength around Square 5. Thus a subject

**FIGURE 10-5**   An application of Spence's (1937) theory to the intermediate-size problem. (a) In initial training, an excitatory gradient develops around S⁺ (Square 5) and inhibitory gradients develop around the two S⁻s (Squares 1 and 9). (b) Because of the two symmetrical inhibitory gradients, there is no peak shift in the gradient of net associative strength. There is only a sharpening in the generalization gradient.

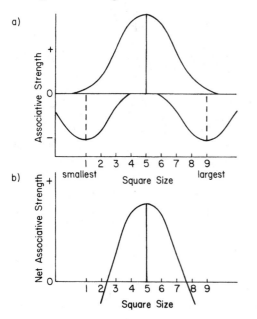

should choose whichever stimulus is closer to Square 5 (Square 4 in the above example).

The actual results of Gonzalez, Gentry, and Bitterman (1954) favored the relational theory over Spence's theory. To summarize the results briefly, the chimps usually chose the square of intermediate size on test trials regardless of which three squares were presented. In short, they behaved as though they were responding to the relationships among the stimuli, not their absolute sizes.

### Evaluating the Two Theories

Both the relational theory and Spence's absolute theory of stimulus control have strengths and weaknesses. Studies on the peak shift favor Spence's theory, because the relational theory cannot explain why responding decreases with stimuli that are far removed from S⁺ in a direction away from S⁻. Further support for Spence's theory comes from studies that show that an inhibitory generalization gradient does indeed develop around the S⁻ (see Rilling, 1977, for a review of the abundant evidence for inhibitory stimulus control). For example, Honig, Boneau, Burstein, and Pennypacker (1963) obtained a good example of an inhibitory generalization gradient with pigeons. In the training for one group of pigeons, the S⁺ was a plain white key, and the S⁻ was a white key with a black vertical line down the middle. For a second group, the stimuli serving as S⁺ and S⁻ were reversed. In a subsequent extinction test, the responses of both groups were measured to black lines that had different orientations ranging from vertical to horizontal. Figure 10-6 shows the results for each group. The group for which the vertical line was S⁺ produced a typical peaked gradient centered around this stimulus. The group for which the vertical line was S⁻ produced a gradient of the opposite shape: Responses were fewest to the vertical line, and they became more numerous to lines whose orientations were farther and farther from vertical (even though the pigeons had never been reinforced for pecking at white keys with lines on them). Honig and colleagues concluded

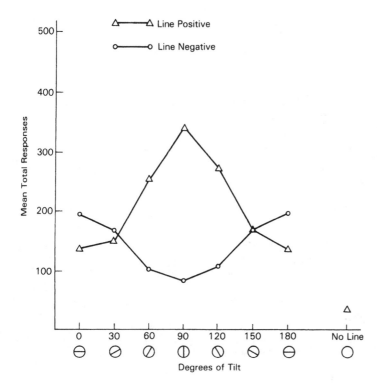

**FIGURE 10-6** Generalization gradients along the dimension of line orientation from the experiment of Honig and coworkers (1963). The triangles show the results from the group with a vertical line on the response key as S⁺ and a blank key as S⁻. The circles show the results from the group with a blank key as S⁺ and a vertical line as S⁻.

that the more similar a test stimulus was to the S⁻, the greater was its capacity to inhibit responding.

One strong piece of evidence for the relational theory comes from the intermediate-size problem, which poses great difficulties for Spence's theory. Other results favoring a relational position come from more recent studies by Thomas and his colleagues, who have obtained peak shifts in successive discriminations with college students as subjects. They found that the peak of a generalization gradient tended to shift toward the middle of the range of the test stimuli, and that this peak shift could be controlled by what test stimuli the experimenter chose to use. For example, if S⁻ was a dim light and S⁺ was a bright light, a peak shift toward brighter lights was observed when the range of test stimuli included some very bright lights (Thomas, Mood, Morrison, & Wiertelak, 1991). Thomas (1993) accounted for these results with an **adaptation-level the-ory,** which states that subjects tend to adapt to the range of stimuli that are presented, and this adaptation is reflected in where the peak of the generalization gradient appears.

In summary, both Spence's theory and the relational theory are supported by some experimental results but not others. The relational theory appears to have the advantage in simultaneous discriminations (where two or more stimuli are presented together, and it is therefore easy to compare them). Spence's absolute theory seems to be most applicable in successive discriminations (where the stimuli are presented one at a time, and it is therefore more difficult to compare them). In this situation, it is not surprising that subjects might rely on the absolute features of the stimuli, because the relationships between stimuli are less salient under these circumstances. Perhaps it is most accurate to conclude that animals can use both the absolute and relational properties of stimuli when learning discriminations, and which they use most heavily depends on which are easiest to use in any given circumstance.

## BEHAVIORAL CONTRAST

The existence of peak shift shows that it is often impossible to predict how a subject will respond in the presence of one stimulus simply by knowing the reinforcement schedule associated with that stimulus. It is often essential to know what other stimuli have been presented and what reinforcement contingencies were associated with them. Thus, in Figure 10-3, a 550-nm key light produced substantial responding in one group but only minimal responding in a second group (for which a 555-nm key light served as an S⁻). The phenomenon of **behavioral contrast** (Reynolds, 1961) offers another example of how the reinforcement contingencies operating in the presence of one stimulus can affect responding in the presence of a different stimulus.

An experiment by Gutman (1977) provides a convenient example of behavioral contrast. Like many experiments on behavioral contrast, Gutman's study used a special type of successive discrimination procedure, otherwise known as a **multiple schedule.** As discussed in Chapter 7, in a multiple schedule, two or more reinforcement schedules are presented one at a time, in an alternating pattern, and each schedule is associated with a different discriminative stimulus. The different reinforcement schedules that comprise a multiple schedule are called the **components** of the multiple schedule. In Phase 1 of Gutman's experiment, rats were exposed to a two-component multiple schedule in which the component schedules were identical: One VI 30-second schedule was signaled by a noise, and a separate VI 30-second schedule was signaled by a light. The light and noise were alternately presented every 3 minutes throughout a session. Not surprisingly, response rates to the noise and light were about the same in this first condition, as shown in Figure 10-7. In Phase 2, the only change was that the schedule operating during the noise was switched from VI 30 seconds to extinction. Figure 10-7 shows that, as expected, respond-

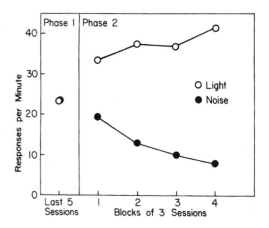

**FIGURE 10-7**    Results from Gutman's (1977) experiment on behavioral contrasts in rats. When both the light and the noise signaled VI 30-second schedules (Phase 1), response rates were about the same for both stimuli. When the noise signaled a period extinction (Phase 2), response rates declined toward zero when the noise was present but increased substantially above those of Phase 1 when the light was present.

ing became slower and slower during the noise. What was more surprising, however, was that response rates increased dramatically in the presence of the light, even though the reinforcement schedule for the light was exactly the same as in the first condition. This phenomenon, in which responding to one stimulus changes as a result of a change in the reinforcement conditions for another stimulus, is called behavioral contrast.

To be more specific, Gutman's study provided an example of **positive contrast,** because it involved an increase in responding during the unchanged light component. The opposite effect has also been observed. For example, suppose the noise schedule was switched and three times as many reinforcers were delivered in the presence of the noise. The likely result would be an increase in response rate during the noise and a decrease in response rate during the light. This decrease in response rate during the unchanged light component would be called **negative contrast.**

There are plenty of theories about why behavioral contrast occurs. We will consider three distinctly different theories. One possibility is that positive contrast is due to the slower responding that occurs in the component that is changed to extinction. Perhaps this slower responding allows the animal to respond faster in the changed component. The slower responding in the extinction component might allow the subject to recover from fatigue, so the "well-rested" animal can respond faster in the unchanged component. In addition, during the extinction component, the animal may be able to spend more time performing various activities that would normally compete for its time in the unchanged component (for instance, grooming, exploring the chamber). That is, the animal may pack more of these extraneous behaviors into the extinction component, so it has more time to perform the operant response in the unchanged component (Ettinger & Staddon, 1982). Although some evidence supports this theory (Dougan, McSweeney, & Farmer-Dougan, 1986), response-rate changes in adjacent components do not seem to be the primary cause of behavioral contrast. This has been shown, for example, by switching the adjacent component from a VI schedule to one that delivers free reinforcers at the same rate. Naturally, response rates decline dramatically under the free-reinforcer schedule, but behavioral contrast is not observed in the unchanged component (Halliday & Boakes, 1971).

A second theory of behavioral contrast is **additivity theory** (Gamzu & Schwartz, 1973). In essence, this theory states that positive contrast occurs when autoshaped or classically conditioned responses are added to the subject's normal operant responses on the VI schedule. In their famous experiment on autoshaping, Brown and Jenkins (1968) found that pigeons would peck at a lighted key that signaled an upcoming reinforcer (Chapter 6). According to additivity theory, during the second phase of Gutman's experiment, the light had the same status as the illuminated key in the Brown and Jenkins experiment. That is, the light signaled that reinforcers were available, and the absence of the light (when the noise was on instead) signaled that no reinforcers were available. Because the light was positively correlated with the availability of food, we might expect it to elicit "autoshaped" lever presses, and when added to the rat's operant responses this would produce an increased response rate.

A third theory of behavioral contrast focuses on the decrease in reinforcement in the changed component (Herrnstein, 1970). According to this account, an animal's rate of response in one component of a multiple schedule depends not only on the reinforcement available during that component, but also on the rate of reinforcement in the adjacent components. To speak loosely, it is as though the subject judges the value of one component by comparing it to its neighbors. In the first phase of Gutman's experiment, the schedule during the light component was "nothing special," since the same schedule was available during the noise component. The light therefore produced only a moderate rate of response. On the other hand, during the second phase of the experiment, the light component was quite attractive compared to the extinction schedule of the noise component, so the light produced a high response rate.

In a review of the substantial body of research on behavioral contrast, Williams (1983) concluded that there may be more than one cause of contrast. It is not possible to review all the evidence here, but there is support both for the additivity theory and for the view that the rate of reinforcement in adjacent components is important. As research results have continued to accumulate, it has become increasingly clear that no single theory can account for all of the data on behavioral contrast (see, for example, McSweeney & Melville, 1991; Williams, 1991). Behavioral contrast is a complex phenomenon, and it is probably the product of a few different factors.

Although its causes are not completely understood, behavioral contrast demonstrates once again that it can be dangerous to study reinforcement schedules as though they were isolated entities. A subject's behavior on one schedule may be greatly influenced by events occurring before and after the schedule is in effect.

## "ERRORLESS" DISCRIMINATION LEARNING

Given what you have learned thus far about operant conditioning and discrimination learning, consider the following problem. Suppose that as a laboratory exercise for a course on learning, your assignment is to teach a pigeon a strong discrimination between red and green key colors. The red key will signal a VI 1-minute schedule, and you would like moderate, steady responding to this key color. The green key will signal extinction, so you would like no responding during the green key. You might begin by training the bird to eat from the food hopper when it was presented, and then you might use a shaping procedure to train the bird to peck the red key. At first, you would reinforce every response, and then gradually shift to longer and longer VI schedules (such as VI 15 seconds, then VI 30 seconds, and finally VI 1 minute). After several sessions with a VI 1-minute schedule on the red key, the pigeon would probably respond steadily throughout the session, and you could then introduce the green key color and its extinction schedule. From now on, sessions might alternate between 3-minute red components and 3-minute green components. At first, we would expect the pigeon to respond when the key was green because of generalization, but eventually responses to this color should decrease to a low level.

This might sound like a sensible plan for developing a good red/green discrimination, but Terrace (1966) listed several reasons why it is not ideal. One major problem is that this method of discrimination training takes a long time, and along the way the subject makes many "errors" (unreinforced responses on the green key). Because the training must continue for several sessions before a good discrimination is achieved, there are likely to be many setbacks owing to the spontaneous recovery of responding to the green key at the start of each session. Perhaps because of the numerous errors, it appears that this type of discrimination

training is aversive for the subject. For one thing, the pigeon may exhibit aggressive behavior, such as wing flapping. If another pigeon is present in an adjacent compartment, the subject may engage in an aggressive display and eventually attack the other animal. Such attacks typically occur soon after the transition from $S^+$ to $S^-$. Further evidence that the procedure is aversive comes from the finding that if the pigeon can turn off the $S^-$ by pecking at another key, it will do so. A final problem with this procedure is that even after months of training, the animal's performance is usually not perfect—there are occasional bursts of responding to the $S^-$.

The criticisms of this method of discrimination training would be of little use if there were no better method of discrimination training, but Terrace (1963) showed that there is one. He named this alternative **errorless discrimination learning** because the subject typically makes few or no responses to the $S^-$. The errorless discrimination procedure differs from the traditional procedure in two major ways. First, rather than waiting for strong, steady responding to the $S^-$, the experimenter introduces the $S^-$ early in the training procedure. Terrace first presented the $S^-$ within 30 seconds of the pigeon's first peck at the red key. Second, a fading procedure is used to make it unlikely that the subject will respond to the $S^-$. Notice that in the procedure described above, the green key would remain on for 3 minutes the first time it was presented. This would give the subject ample time to respond to this key color. In Terrace's procedure, however, the $S^-$ was presented for only 5 seconds at a time at first, which gave the pigeon little chance to respond in its presence. In addition, Terrace made use of the fact that the pigeon was unlikely to peck at a dark response key: At first, the $S^-$ was not an illuminated green key but a dark key. Using a fading procedure, Terrace gradually progressed from a dark key to a dimly lit green key, and over trials the intensity of the green light was increased. In summary, in Terrace's procedure the $S^-$ was introduced early in training, it was presented very briefly at first, and it was initially a stimulus that was unlikely to elicit responding.

Terrace's errorless discrimination procedure is effective in decreasing the number of responses to the S$^-$ and improving the subject's long-term discrimination performance. In one experiment, subjects trained with a conventional discrimination procedure made an average of more than 3,000 responses to the S$^-$ during 28 sessions. Subjects trained with the errorless procedure averaged only about 25 responses in the same number of sessions. In addition to enormous differences in responding to the S$^-$, Terrace (1972) proposed that his errorless procedure produces several other performance differences compared to traditional procedures. He claimed that with the errorless procedure, the S$^-$ does not become aversive, and so aggressive behaviors and responses to escape from the S$^-$ do not occur. He also claimed that the S$^-$ does not develop inhibitory properties, so after errorless discrimination training, there is no peak shift in the generalization gradient. Finally, he claimed that positive behavioral contrast to the S$^+$ does not occur if the S$^-$ never elicits responses. In short, Terrace proposed that none of the "by-products" of traditional discrimination learning occur with his errorless discrimination procedure.

Rilling (1977) has disputed each of Terrace's claims about the "by-products" of discrimination learning. Rilling and his colleagues have conducted a series of experiments showing that after errorless discrimination learning, subjects may exhibit aggressive responses during the S$^-$, responses to escape from the S$^-$, peak shift in their generalization gradients, and positive behavioral contrast. Based on these results, Rilling concluded that Terrace's claim that the errorless procedure produces a qualitatively different type of discrimination learning is unfounded. Nevertheless, Rilling conceded that Terrace's procedure does produce some quantitative differences in performance: With this procedure, there is generally *less* aggressive behavior, *less* behavioral contrast, and perhaps *less* inhibition to the S$^-$. Rilling's evidence suggests that these differences are due mainly to the early introduction of the S$^-$, and that the fading procedure Terrace used is less important.

Although Terrace's assertion about the by-products of errorless discrimination learning may have been exaggerated, it is certainly true that his procedure generates excellent stimulus control in a minimum amount of time. For this reason, variations of Terrace's techniques have been used in educational settings. B. F. Skinner maintained that classroom curricula should be designed so that the student almost never makes a mistake. His reasoning is that if we do not want children to avoid learning experiences, and if making an incorrect response (and thereby failing to receive reinforcement) is aversive, then we should try to eliminate these aversive episodes as much as possible.

In one example of an educational application of errorless discrimination learning, Duffy and Wishart (1987) used a fading procedure to teach children with Down syndrome to identify basic shapes such as ovals and rectangles. Some of the children were taught using a conventional trial-and-error method, using cards with three shapes, such as the right-hand card in Figure 10-8. A child would be asked to "point to the rectangle" and would be praised if he or she made a correct response. If the child made an error (which happened frequently in the conventional procedure), the teacher would say, "No, that is not right. Try again the next time." The errorless learning procedure was exactly the same, except that at first the cards had only the correct shape and two blank spaces, as on the left-hand card in Figure 10-8. Not surprisingly, the children had little problem pointing to the correct shape. Then, very small incorrect shapes were added, as on the center card in Figure 10-8, and over trials the sizes of the incorrect shapes were gradually increased until they were the same size as the correct shape. Duffy and Wishart found that with the errorless procedure, the children made very few mistakes during training, and their performance remained slightly better at the end of training. They also reported that the children's attitudes toward the learning situation seemed to be better with the errorless procedure, perhaps because they did not suffer many failures.

Because of these advantages, errorless learning procedures, along with other tech-

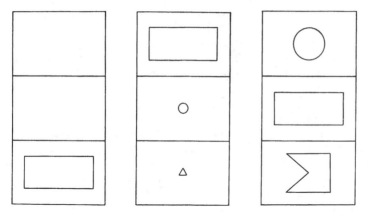

**FIGURE 10-8**   Examples of the types of cards used by Duffy and Wishart to teach children with Down syndrome the names of shapes. Errorless learning started with only the correct shape (left), then small incorrect shapes were added (center), and the incorrect shapes gradually became larger until they were the same size as the correct shape (right).

niques that gradually increase the difficulty of the discriminations, have frequently been incorporated in teaching procedures for mentally handicapped children (Conners, 1992; Zygmont, Lazar, Dube, & McIlvane, 1992). It has also been used to reteach adults information they have lost as a result of Alzheimer's Disease or other brain disorders (Jackson, 1999; Winter & Hunkin, 1999). However, there may be some drawbacks to using errorless discrimination procedures with these children. For example, after errorless training, the children may have difficulty learning discrimination reversals, in which the roles of S⁺ and S⁻ are reversed (McIlvane, Kledaras, Iennaco, McDonald, & Stoddard, 1995). They may also have difficulty generalizing and maintaining their discrimination skills in new situations (Jones & Eayrs, 1992). Educators must therefore carefully consider the advantages and disadvantages when deciding whether to use errorless discrimination training or alternative techniques.

## TRANSFER OF LEARNING AFTER DISCRIMINATION TRAINING

In the examples of generalization and discrimination discussed thus far in this chapter, the S⁺, S⁻, and all test stimuli varied along some simple physical dimension such as color, tone frequency, or size. We will now turn to situations where the physical characteristics of the training stimuli and test stimuli may be totally different, and where the similarity between the training phase and the testing phase is more abstract. Therefore, if a subject exhibits "savings" from one task to the next, this will be evidence for a more sophisticated capacity to generalize from previous learning experiences.

Harry Harlow (1949) was the first to demonstrate that animals can learn much more in a discrimination task than which stimulus dimension they should attend to. Harlow's subjects were primates that were typically tested on many different discrimination problems. For instance, in a famous experiment, Harlow presented two monkeys with over 300 different discrimination problems. Two different stimulus objects were presented on a trial. The choice of one stimulus led to food, and the choice of the other did not. The same objects were used as S⁺ and S⁻ for six trials, which constituted one discrimination problem. Then another two objects served as S⁺ and S⁻ for the second discrimination problem (another six trials), then another two objects for the third problem, and so on. On the first few discrimination problems, the monkeys' performance improved gradually over trials, reaching a level of about 75 percent correct by the sixth and final trial. This shows that six trials were not enough to produce high levels of performance on the early discrimination problems. However, on later problems, the monkeys acquired each new discrimination more and more quickly. After about 250 discrimination problems, they were able to master each new discrimination by trial 2 (that is, after only one trial of learning).

Harlow called this improvement in the rate of learning across several different discrimination problems by several different names, including a **learning set, learning to learn,** and **transfer from problem to problem.** It is important to see that although the S⁺ and S⁻ were different from one problem to the next, each of the several hundred discrimination problems had a number of features in common: One and only one choice was correct on each trial, the same object was correct for all six trials of each problem, the positions of the objects were irrelevant, and so on. Evidently, the monkeys were able to learn that each problem had these similar properties, because by the end of the experiment, their performance was nearly optimal: They needed only one trial to determine which stimulus object was the S⁺, and starting with trial 2, they chose this object nearly 100 percent of the time. This performance suggests that the monkeys had learned a "strategy" that they could apply to each new problem: If your choice is reinforced on trial 1, choose this same object on the next five trials; if not, choose the other object on the remaining trials.

Some evidence suggests that different species vary considerably in their ability to develop learning sets. Warren (1965) compared the results of learning-set experiments with several different species (conducted by a number of different researchers), and his findings are shown in Figure 10-9. After a few hundred discrimination problems, rhesus monkeys chose the correct stimulus on trial 2 almost 90 percent of the time. Other animals, such as cats, develop learning sets more slowly, and rats and squirrels showed only modest transfer from problem to problem, even after more than a thousand discrimination tasks. Warren noted that there is a clear tendency for animals higher on the phylogenetic scale to develop stronger learning sets. It seems that one noteworthy characteristic of higher species is the ability to acquire more abstract information from a learning situation. That is, besides learning which specific stimuli are S⁺ and S⁻ in each discrimination problem, the higher species may be better at recognizing the similarities between problems and at developing a behavioral strategy that improves performance on subsequent problems.

Such cross-species comparisons must be viewed with caution, however, because the success or failure of one species may depend on exactly how the experiment was conducted. Although Figure 10-9 suggests that rats show little transfer even after extended training, more recent studies with rats found substantial transfer after only a few dozen problems when olfactory cues or spatial locations were used instead of visual stimuli (Fagan, Eichenbaum,

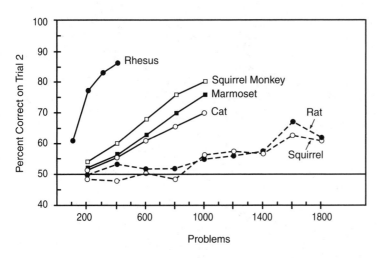

**FIGURE 10-9** Warren's (1965) comparison of the performances of several different species in experiments on learning sets. If subjects learn that the structure of each new discrimination problem is similar to that of previous problems, they should begin to perform above chance level on the second trial of a new problem. The speed and amount of improvement varied considerably across species.

& Cohen, 1985; Zeldin & Olton, 1986). These results show that with stimuli of the right modality, rats can develop substantial learning sets after all.

Harlow's (1949) procedure of repeated discrimination problems provides just one example of a learning set. Another situation in which a learning set can develop is the **discrimination reversal** procedure. In this procedure, a subject first acquires one discrimination, and then the roles of S⁺ and S⁻ are periodically switched. For example, Harlow studied the behavior of eight monkeys in an experiment where S⁺ and S⁻ were switched every 7, 9, or 11 trials. Early in the experiment, the monkeys performed incorrectly for several trials after each reversal (which is not surprising since they had previously been reinforced for choosing the now-incorrect stimulus). However, after many reversals, they needed only one trial to correct their behavior—after one unreinforced choice, they would switch to the other stimulus. In short, they had learned how to perform this task with a minimum number of errors.

Researchers have investigated a number of other discrimination tasks in which animals appear to learn something more abstract than simply which stimulus is S⁺ and which is S⁻. For example, in an **alternation task,** the stimuli serving as S⁺ and S⁻ switch roles each trial, so the subject must learn to choose the stimulus that was incorrect on the previous trial (Hunter, 1920). In a **double alternation task,** S⁺ and S⁻ are switched every two trials. For example, Schlosberg and Katz (1943) studied rats in discrimination tasks where the left lever was S⁺ for two trials, then the right lever was S⁺ for two trials, and so on. The rats learned to perform quite well on this task, exhibiting a rudimentary ability to count trials. More recent studies on animals' abilities to learn such abstract relations will be discussed in Chapter 11.

## CONCEPT FORMATION

Many of the discrimination tasks we have considered in this chapter might seem quite artificial for three reasons: (1) The stimuli involved were simple, idealized images that an animal would be unlikely to encounter in the natural environment (such as a perfect square, uniformly red, on a plain white background); (2) only a small number of stimuli were used (the simplest of discrimination tasks involves only two stimuli, S⁺ and S⁻); (3) from an objective point of view, the distinction between positive and negative instances was well-defined and unambiguous. For instance, the S⁺ might be a red square and the S⁻ a green square, and the subject would not be presented with any objects other than squares nor with any squares that were a mixture of red and green.

In more recent work on the topic of **concept formation** or **categorization,** all three of these restrictions have been removed. This research is designed to mimic more closely the types of discrimination an animal must learn in the natural environment. For example, when an animal learns to discriminate between predators and nonpredators or between edible plants and poisonous plants, there may be countless examples from each category, they will generally not be simple, idealized forms, and the distinction between positive and negative instances of a category may not always be easy to make. Research on concept formation is designed to investigate how individuals learn to make such complex discriminations.

This distinction between discrimination learning and concept formation is not always clear-cut, but the single most important difference is the number of stimuli used in training. Instead of using just one S⁺ and one S⁻ during discrimination training, experiments on concept formation make use of many stimuli, which are divided into two categories—a set of **positive instances** (which are followed by reinforcement) and a set of **negative instances** (which are not followed by reinforcement). To

You can try an interesting experiment on concept formation at *http://coglab.psych.purdue .edu/coglab/Labs/Prototypes.html.*

perform well on such a task, a subject must learn what characteristics distinguish the members of the two categories. The following sections examine research on concept formation involving both human and nonhuman subjects.

## The Structure of Natural Categories

Eleanor Rosch (1973, 1975, 1977) has conducted a series of experiments on how people respond to different members of "natural" categories—categories of objects found in the real world, such as birds, vegetables, or vehicles. Two of her most important conclusions are that the boundaries of these categories are not distinct, and that people tend to judge some members of a category as "good" or "typical" examples of the category and others as "bad" or "atypical" examples. Rosch used the terms **central** and **peripheral instances** to refer to typical and atypical examples, respectively. In one experiment, Rosch (1973) simply asked subjects to estimate the typicality of different examples of various categories. A 7-point rating scale was used, with 1 signifying a very typical instance and 7 a very atypical example.

Rosch reported that subjects found this an easy task, and different instances received very different rankings. For example, in the category of birds, *robin* received a mean ranking of 1.1, *chicken* a mean ranking of 3.8, and *bat* a mean ranking of 5.8. Thus robins were judged to be typical birds, chickens much less typical, and bats were treated as very marginal examples of birds. The example of bats illustrates how the boundaries of a natural category may be indistinct. Whereas taxonomically speaking, bats are not birds, many people probably do not know this, and they may consider bats as (atypical) members of the bird category. Conversely, whereas an olive is a fruit, many people do not classify it as such, and in Rosch's study it received a mean rating of 6.2.

Rosch described three important characteristics of natural categories. First, people tend to agree about which examples are central and which are peripheral. A second characteristic, related to the first, is that when people are asked to list the members of various categories, they list central instances more frequently. For instance, when Battig and Montague (1969) asked people to make lists of birds, *robin* was listed by 377 subjects, *chicken* by 40 subjects, and *bat* by only 3 subjects. A third characteristic is that in reaction-time tests, subjects take longer to decide that peripheral examples are members of the category.

It is interesting to speculate about how children learn to identify members and nonmembers of various natural categories. Language presumably plays an important role: A parent may point to a robin and say "That is a bird." Later, the parent may tell the child that it is a robin, and that robins are one type of bird. Yet whereas language is certainly important for human concept formation, it cannot explain why natural categories have the structure they do (with central instances, peripheral instances, and ambiguous boundaries). Consider the fact that a child may be repeatedly taught "A robin is a bird" and "A chicken is a bird," yet the child will still judge the latter to be an atypical bird, and will be a bit slower to agree that a chicken is a bird. How can we explain this behavior? Some theories of human concept formation (Franks & Bransford, 1971) propose that people judge whether a given instance is a member of a category by comparing its features to those of an idealized category member. For instance, through our numerous experiences with birds, we may decide that the "ideal" bird has the following characteristics, among others: It has wings, feathers, a beak, and two legs, it sings, it flies, it perches in trees. A robin has all of these features, so it is judged to be a typical bird; a chicken does not, so it is judged to be less typical.

Regardless of how people manage to classify natural objects, the task is a complex one. Consider the natural concept of *tree*. For many people, the ideal tree might be something like a full-grown maple tree, with a sturdy brown trunk and a full canopy of large green leaves. Yet people can correctly identify objects as trees even when they have none of the characteristics of this ideal tree (for example, a small sapling with no leaves, half-buried in snow). The human ability to categorize natural objects is remarkable, and scientists have not yet been able to build a machine that even approximates this ability. Recognizing the impressive concept-formation abilities that people possess, some psychologists wondered whether other animals (who do not use language and therefore cannot label objects as "bird" or "vegetable") have the ability to learn natural concepts.

## Animal Studies on Natural Concept Formation

Quite a few experiments have examined natural concept learning by animals. Herrnstein and his colleagues have conducted several such experiments with pigeons as subjects (Herrnstein & Loveland, 1964; Herrnstein, Loveland, & Cable, 1976). In Herrnstein's procedure, a pigeon would perform in an ordinary experimental chamber containing a translucent screen onto which slides could be projected from behind. In one experiment, Herrnstein (1979) chose to study the natural concept of *tree*: If a slide contained one tree, several trees, or any portion of a tree (such as a branch, a part of the trunk), it was a positive instance, and pecking at the response key was reinforced on a VI schedule. If the slide contained no tree or portion of a tree, it was a negative instance, and extinction conditions were in effect. To avoid indiscriminate pecking in the presence of both positive and negative slides, there was a further restriction that a negative slide would remain on the screen until 2 seconds elapsed without a peck.

In each session, a pigeon saw 80 different slides, half positive instances and half negative. In most sessions, the same 80 slides were presented, but in several generalization tests, some completely new slides were used. The first thing Herrnstein found was that the pigeons quickly learned to discriminate between positive and negative instances. After only a few sessions, the pigeons were responding significantly faster to the positive slides than to negative slides.

Let us consider how the pigeons might have mastered this task. One possibility is that the pigeons did not learn anything about the general category of tree, but simply learned about the 80 stimuli individually. However, the re-

sults of generalization tests showed that the pigeons' accurate discrimination was not limited to the 80 slides used in training. When presented with slides they had never seen before, the pigeons responded about as rapidly to the positive slides and about as slowly to the negative slides as they did to old positive and negative slides, respectively. In other words, they were able to classify new slides as trees or nontrees about as well as the old slides.

Similar concept formation experiments with pigeons have used a variety of categories besides trees. Among the concepts pigeons have successfully learned are *people* (Herrnstein & Loveland, 1964), *water*, a *particular woman* (Herrnstein, Loveland, & Cable, 1976), *fish* (Herrnstein & de Villiers, 1980), and *artificial objects* (Lubow, 1974). They have also been trained to distinguish among the different letters of the alphabet (Blough, 1982) and between triangles and squares (Towe, 1954). Although pigeons have been used in much of this research, the ability to form natural concepts has also been observed in other species, including the parrot (Pepperberg, 1981), the mynah (Turney, 1982), and the monkey (Schrier & Brady, 1987; Yoshikubo, 1985).

What makes natural concept learning so difficult for psychologists to analyze is the lack of a simple way to characterize the distinction between positive and negative instances. It would be easy to relate natural concept learning to traditional discrimination experiments if some simple feature or set of features was present in all positive slides but not in any negative slides. For instance, if all slides of trees included the color green, or some leaves, or a brown trunk, we might conclude that pigeons mastered the problem by attending to the relevant features. In Herrnstein's experiments, however, there were no features common to all positive slides. Some slides of trees included green leaves, but some slides of nontrees also included large green patches (such as a large grassy area). Some negative slides actually included green, leafy objects, such as a stalk of celery. In positive slides taken during the fall, the leaves were red and orange, and in some taken during the winter, there were no leaves. In some positive slides a large tree filled the center of the picture, and still others showed only distant treetops across a large body of water. Because of this great variability, Herrnstein concluded that there were no "common elements" in either the positive or negative slides.

How, then, did the pigeons manage to discriminate between pictures with trees and pictures without them (or between the presence and absence of water, or people, or artificial objects)? When people sort pictures of objects into categories, they treat these two-dimensional stimuli as representations of three-dimensional objects, and sort them accordingly. Herrnstein, Loveland, and Cable (1976) proposed that their pigeons did much the same thing: They responded to these complex visual patterns as though they represented objects in a three-dimensional world. By doing so, they were able to classify the visual patterns into the positive or negative categories, depending on whether or not a particular real-world object (such as a tree, a person) was represented in each picture.

Not everyone accepts this conclusion. Some psychologists doubt that the animals in these studies actually treated the two-dimensional slides as representations of three-dimensional objects (Cerella, 1982). As an alternative hypothesis, some have suggested that the animals were simply responding to a complex set of features, both positive and negative, and that they were able to generalize to new slides because they shared some of these features (colors, shapes, patterns) with the training slides (see D'Amato & Van Sant, 1988). Another possibility is that the animals memorized individual positive and negative pictures, and then responded to new pictures based on their similarity to the memorized pictures (Kendrick, Wright, & Cook, 1990). Both of these alternative hypotheses provide a plausible explanation of how animals could perform well on a concept-formation task without actually seeing the relation between the pictures and three-dimensional objects.

The issue of whether animals recognize the correspondence between two-dimensional slides or pictures and three-dimensional objects is difficult to answer, but some research suggests that they can (for example, Herzog & Hopf, 1986). In an ingenious study by Delius (1992), pigeons were presented with actual three-dimensional objects that were either spherical (marbles, peas, ball bearings, and so on) or nonspherical (dice, buttons, nuts, flowers, and so on), and each choice of a spherical object was reinforced with food. The pigeons quickly learned to choose the spherical objects. They were then tested with photographs or black-and-white drawings of spherical and nonspherical objects, and they chose the pictures of spherical objects with a high level of accuracy. In a related study, Honig and Stewart (1988) found that pigeons responded to photographs taken at two distinctive locations in ways that suggested they had formed concepts of the actual physical locations represented in the photographs. These studies suggest that, at least under certain conditions, animals can learn the correspondence between pictures and three-dimensional objects.

Two other studies provide further insights into how pigeons categorize two-dimensional stimuli. Kirkpatrick-Steger, Wasserman, and Biederman (1996) taught pigeons to discriminate between line drawings of four objects—a watering can, an iron, a desk lamp, and a sailboat. They then tested the birds with line drawings in which the pieces of these objects were scrambled in various ways, to see if the pigeons could still discriminate the objects. The pigeons' correct and incorrect responses showed some interesting patterns. For example, one bird performed well with scrambled drawings of the watering can as long as the handle was above the base, but poorly if the handle was below the base. With drawings of the sailboat, this bird performed well when the two sails were properly aligned, side by side, but poorly if they were misaligned. Other birds showed similar sensitivity to the spatial arrangement of the objects' parts. These results indicate that the pigeons were not just responding to individual features in isolation—the relationships among the features were also important in their ability to recognize the objects.

In a clever experiment by Watanabe, Sakamoto, and Wakita (1995), pigeons were taught to discriminate between the paintings of two artists, the impressionist Monet and the abstract painter Picasso. After they learned this discrimination with one set of paintings for each artist, they were able to correctly categorize new paintings by Monet and Picasso that they had not seen before. Furthermore, without further training, they were also able to distinguish between the works of other impressionist painters (Renoir and Cezanne) and other abstract painters (Matisse and Braque). The experimenters also tested the birds with some familiar paintings, but presented upside down or reversed left to right. With the abstract paintings of Picasso, this had little effect on the birds' accuracy. However, with Monet's paintings, which depict more realistic three-dimensional objects to the human eye, the birds made more errors with the upside-down or reversed images. This finding provides more evidence that pigeons can respond to the two-dimensional images as representations of three-dimensional objects.

If animals do have the ability to respond to two-dimensional images as if they were three-dimensional objects, then there is a parallel between this ability and the adaptability of movement discussed in Chapter 6 in the section on "Problems with the Stop-Action Principle." There we saw that when a particular sequence of movements is reinforced, the future likelihood of different movements that have the same effect on the environment is increased. To put it another way, as far as responses are concerned, animals tend to use interchangeably all responses that have the same effect in their three-dimensional environment. As far as stimuli are concerned, animals may have the ability to group together all visual images that represent the same type of object in their three-dimensional environment. In both cases, how these impressive feats might be accomplished is not well understood. In both cases, it has proven difficult to develop machines with similar abilities.

## Developing Stimulus Equivalence

We have seen that both people and animals have a fairly easy time learning natural categories, such as trees, water, or even artists' styles. But what would happen if subjects were asked to learn a "category" of arbitrarily chosen objects—stimuli that have nothing in common except that the experimenter chose to put them all in a single group? Can subjects learn to treat an arbitrary group of objects as a category, and exactly what will they learn about the relationships among individual stimuli? The answer seems to depend on both who the subjects are and how they are taught.

If the subjects are human, a phenomenon known as **stimulus equivalence** can develop. Stimulus equivalence refers to a situation in which subjects learn to respond to all stimuli in a category as if they are interchangeable, even though they have been taught only a few relations between stimuli, not all possible relations. This is a fairly abstract statement, so let us take a concrete example. Suppose a young child is trained with six different geometrical shapes as stimuli. The shapes are not related in any way, but we will call them A, B, C, D, E, and F. On every trial, one shape is presented as a stimulus, and the child must choose between two other shapes by touching one or the other. On some trials, shape A is the stimulus, and the correct response is B (with either D, E, or F as the incorrect alternative). On other trials, B is the stimulus, and the correct response is C (again with either D, E, or F as the incorrect alternative). The child is also taught to pick E if D is the stimulus, and to pick F if E is the stimulus. This training has therefore involved only four relations: If A pick B, if B pick C, if D pick E, and if E pick F. After this training, the child is tested with new choices that he or she has not seen before. If C is the stimulus and the possible choices are B and D, the child will choose B. If A is the stimulus and the possible choices are C and F, the child will choose C. Do you see the pattern that is emerging?

Using a training procedure similar to this one and then testing with new combinations of stimuli and responses, Sidman and Tailby (1982) found that the children in their experiment had formed two equivalence sets, with A, B, and C in one set and D, E, and F in the other, and they treated all members of one set as interchangeable. (Actually, Sidman and Tailby used more than six stimuli and two equivalence sets, but this simplified description gives the general idea of their experiment.) The important point is that these equivalence sets emerged even though the children were only trained with a few of the possible stimulus-response combinations.

This exercise with arbitrary shapes may sound like a strange intellectual game for children, and you may wonder why some psychologists are interested in the development of stimulus equivalence. One reason is the belief of some researchers that the ability to learn equivalence sets is similar to the ability to learn language. After all, written and spoken words are arbitrary stimuli that refer to objects or events in the world. For example, a child in elementary school must learn that the spoken word "six," the written word "six," the number "6," and the Roman numeral "VI" all refer to the same quantity. These different symbols constitute an equivalence set: They can be used interchangeably by a person who understands spoken and written English.

All language involves learning an arbitrary connection between some object or event in the world and a sound—the spoken word for that object or event. Some psychologists have therefore suggested that the ability to learn equivalence sets is closely related to the ability to learn language, and animals that do not use language should not exhibit stimulus equivalence. This issue has been the focus of much debate, and the evidence is mixed. Some studies with nonhumans have found no evidence for the development of stimulus equivalence, even after extended training (Sidman, Rauzin, Lazar, Cunningham, Tailby, & Carrigan, 1982). One experiment found some fragmentary signs of stimulus equivalence in a chimpanzee that had received training with an artificial language (Yamamoto & Asano, 1995), but another study with language-trained chimps found none (Dugdale & Lowe, 2000). In contrast, one study with rats did find some characteristics of stimulus equivalence (Nakagawa, 1999).

Vaughan (1988) tried to show that pigeons could form equivalence sets if they were given suitable training. He presented 80 slides of trees to the pigeons, and he randomly assigned 40 slides to the positive category (in which

pecking led to food) and another 40 to the negative category (in which pecking did not lead to food). Within a few sessions, the pigeons learned to peck at the positive slides and not to peck at the negative slides. This showed that the pigeons could learn the correct response for 80 individual slides, but it does not tell us whether they had learned to associate the 40 slides of each category. Vaughan then repeatedly reversed the positive and negative roles of all 80 slides every few days (with all positive slides becoming negative and vice versa). After a while, the pigeons demonstrated that they had learned to partition the 80 slides into two categories, which we might call equivalence sets. On any given day, if the first several slides of one category were positive, the birds would peck when other slides from that category were presented. Conversely, if the first several slides of one category were negative, the birds would not respond to other slides from that category. Vaughan concluded that the birds had learned two equivalence sets of 40 slides each.

Vaughan's results remain controversial, in part because his procedure was very different from those of previous studies on equivalence sets. Some have argued that his procedure does not constitute an adequate test of stimulus equivalence (S. C. Hayes, 1989). In fact, there is considerable disagreement among the experts regarding how equivalence sets should be defined and tested (O'Mara, 1991). Reviewing all the data from animals, Zentall (1998) concluded that although their performance may not meet the strictest definitions of stimulus equivalence, animals nevertheless show an impressive ability to group unrelated stimuli into categories and to treat the members of a category as if they were interchangeable.

## STIMULUS CONTROL IN BEHAVIOR MODIFICATION

Almost every instance of behavior modification involves stimulus control in one way or another. For instance, treatments of phobias are designed to eliminate a response (a fear reaction) that is under the control of a certain class of stimuli (the phobic objects or situations). What is special about the following examples, however, is that one of the main features of the behavioral treatment is the development of appropriate stimulus control.

### Stimulus Equivalence Training

Procedures that were first used to teach stimulus equivalence in laboratory experiments, as described in the preceding section, are now being used in a variety of therapeutic settings. In some cases, stimulus equivalence training can assist children who are having difficulty learning to read. For example, one group of children was given practice in matching written words to spoken words and in writing printed words by copying them. After this practice, they were able to read the written words (which they could not do before), even though the practice did not involve reading the written words out loud. Evidently, this training helped the children learn equivalences between (1) hearing a spoken word, (2) seeing the written word, and (3) reading the word out loud. Besides learning to read the words they had practiced, the children were also able to read other words that used the same syllables in different combinations (Melchiori, de Sousa, & de Rose, 2000). Stimulus equivalence training has also been used to teach developmentally disabled individuals to distinguish between vowels and consonants (Lane & Critchfield, 1998), and even to learn the sequence of behaviors to follow when shopping for food in a supermarket (Taylor & O'Reilly, 2000). If stimulus equivalence training continues to produce encouraging results such as these, it will surely be used in more behavior therapy settings in the future.

### Study Behavior

There are many different reasons why some students do poorly in school, but one frequent problem among poor students is that no matter where they are, studying is a low-probability behavior. Such a student may intend to study regularly but may actually succeed in doing productive work only rarely. The problem is simply that there are no stimuli that reliably occasion study behavior. A student may go to her room after dinner, planning to study, but may turn on the TV or stereo instead. She may go to the library with her reading assignments but may find herself socializing with friends or taking a nap instead of reading.

Recognizing that poor study habits are frequently the result of ineffective stimulus control, L. Fox (1962) devised the following program for a group of college students who were having difficulty. Each student gave the therapist a detailed weekly schedule, and the therapist found one hour that the student was free each day. The student was instructed to spend at least a part of this hour studying his most difficult course every day. Furthermore, this studying was to be done in the same place every day (usually in a small room of a library or a classroom building). The student was told to take only materials related to the course into that room, and not to use that room on other occasions. A student was not necessarily expected to spend the entire hour in that room: If the student began to daydream or became bored or restless, he was to read one more page and then leave immediately. The importance of leaving the room promptly if he was not studying was emphasized to the student. The purpose of this procedure was to establish a particular time and place as a strong stimulus for studying a particular subject by repeatedly pairing this time and place with nothing but study behavior. Fox's reasoning was that other stimuli did not lead to study behavior because they were associated with competing activities (watching TV, talking with friends), so it was best to select a new setting where it would be difficult for competing activities to occur.

Not surprisingly, at first students found it difficult to study for long in this new setting, and they would leave the room well before the hour was over. Gradually, however, their study periods grew longer, and eventually they could spend the entire hour in productive study. At this point, the therapist chose the student's second most difficult course, and the stimulus control procedure was repeated. That is, the student was told to study this subject at a specific time of day in a different special location. Before long, each student was studying each of his courses for one hour a day at a specific time and place. If the student needed to spend more time on any course, he could do this whenever he wished, but not in the special room.

All of Fox's students exhibited considerable improvement in their grades. The smallest gain in semester grades was one full grade above those of the previous semester. It is impossible to tell how much of this improvement was due to better stimulus control, because the students were also given training in other techniques, including the SQ3R method (survey, question, read, recite, and review) of reading new material. Other evidence suggests that teaching students only stimulus control techniques may not be particularly effective, but combining these with other behavioral methods such as self-reinforcement can lead to improved academic performance (Richards, 1981).

## Insomnia

Most people have experienced occasional insomnia, but persistent, severe insomnia can be a serious problem. A person who lies in bed awake most of the night is unlikely to function well the next day. Although some cases of chronic insomnia are due to medical problems, many are the result of inappropriate stimulus control. That is, the stimulus of one's bed does not reliably produce the behavior of sleeping. The role of stimulus control becomes apparent if we compare the behavior of insomniacs with those of people without sleeping problems. A normal person exhibits one sort of stimulus control—she is able to sleep well in her own bed, but may have some difficulty falling asleep in a different place, such as on a couch or in a hotel room. An insomniac may exhibit exactly the opposite pattern—he may have difficulty falling asleep in his own bed, but may fall asleep on a couch, in front of the television, or in a different bed. This pattern shows that insomnia is often not a general inability to fall asleep, but a failure to fall asleep in the presence of a particular stimulus, one's own bed.

The reason a person's own bed may fail to serve as a stimulus for sleeping is fairly clear: The bed may become associated with many activities that are incompatible with sleeping, including reading, watching television, eating, and thinking about the day's events or one's problems. To make one's bed a more effective stimulus for sleeping, some behavior therapists recommend that the client never do anything but sleep there. Bootzin (1972) described the case of a man who would lie in bed for several hours each night worrying about everyday problems before falling asleep with the TV on. The man was instructed to go to bed each night when he felt sleepy, but not to watch TV or do anything else in bed. If he could not get to sleep after a few minutes, he was to get out of bed and go into another room. He could then do whatever he liked, and he was not to go back to bed until he felt sleepy. Each time he went to bed, the same instructions were to be followed: Get up and leave the room if you do not fall asleep within a few minutes. At first, the client had to get up many times each night before falling asleep, but after a few weeks he would usually fall asleep within a few minutes the first time he got in bed.

This treatment has been used with many insomniac patients with good results (Morin, Culbert, & Schwartz, 1994). The procedure is effective for at least two reasons. First, since the clients are instructed to remain out of bed when they cannot sleep, their need for sleep increases early in the program, when they spend a good portion of the night out of bed. Thus, when they go to bed, their chances of falling asleep are greater. Second, since the bed is used only for sleeping, its associations with other behaviors gradually decrease and at the same time its association with sleep increases. Of course, stimulus control is only one of many techniques of behavior control, and some treatments for insomnia also include other procedures, such as progressive relaxation and learning to avoid worrisome thoughts (Davies, 1991; Hryshko-Mullen, Broeckl, Haddock, & Peterson, 2000).

The usefulness of these procedures for training stimulus control may hinge on the reduction of incompatible behaviors. The student in a quiet room of the library will have little to do but study. In addition, those few behaviors other than studying that can occur (such as daydreaming) are prevented because

A self-help manual that explains how to use stimulus-control techniques to modify your own behavior can be found at *http://mental help.net/psyhelp/chap11/chap11b.htm#b.*

the student is instructed to leave the room immediately if he or she stops studying. Similarly, the therapy for insomnia involves preventing the client from engaging in any behavior other than sleeping in one's bed. In a sense, then, these stimulus-control techniques are the opposite of the procedure of reinforcing incompatible behaviors so as to eliminate an undesirable behavior. In the former, incompatible behaviors are prevented, and in the latter, they are reinforced.

## CHAPTER SUMMARY

Pavlov proposed that generalization is an automatic by-product of the conditioning process, whereas Lashley and Wade proposed that experience is necessary for typical gradients to occur. Each theory seems to be correct in some cases and wrong in others. Some experiments found that discrimination training was necessary before typical generalization gradients appeared. However, experiments on sensory deprivation supported Pavlov's position by finding generalization gradients for color with birds that were raised in an environment with only one color.

The debate over absolute versus relational stimulus control also has a mixed resolution. Spence's theory of absolute stimulus control can account for peak shift by assuming that an excitatory gradient develops around the $S^+$ and an inhibitory gradient develops around the $S^-$. However, this theory cannot explain results from the intermediate-size problem, which favor the position that animals can respond to relationships between stimuli.

Terrace developed an "errorless" discrimination training procedure, in which the $S^-$ is introduced very early in training, but under conditions in which the subject is not likely to respond to this stimulus. Errorless discrimination training has been successfully used in behavior-modification programs with mentally handicapped children and other populations.

Concept formation occurs when individuals learn to treat one class of stimuli as positive and another class as negative. Studies with pigeons and other animals show that they can learn such categories as tree, water, and people. Human subjects can also learn equivalence sets, in which random stimuli are arbitrarily assigned to different categories. Some psychologists have proposed that only humans can learn such arbitrary categories, but others claim to have evidence that animals can also learn them.

Stimulus control techniques are used in behavior modification when a desired response seldom occurs in the presence of the appropriate stimulus. For poor students, a special location can be trained as a strong discriminate stimulus for study behavior. If a person's insomnia is due to poor stimulus control, the person's bed can be trained as a strong discriminative stimulus for sleeping.

## REVIEW QUESTIONS

1. What was Pavlov's theory about the cause of generalization gradients? What is another theory about them? What do experiments on discrimination training and on sensory deprivation tell us about this issue?

2. Describe the difference between the absolute and relational theories of stimulus control. What do studies on transposition, peak shift, and the intermediate-size problem indicate about these theories?

3. Describe some findings about natural categories in humans and some findings about natural category learning by pigeons. What do these studies demonstrate about concept formation by animals?

4. Give one example of how stimulus control techniques have been used in behavior-modification programs. Describe some specific procedures that the client must practice in order for the treatment to work.

## CHAPTER 11

# Comparative Cognition

Considering the current popularity of cognitive psychology, the title of this chapter should come as little surprise. In recent years there has been increasing interest in applying concepts from cognitive psychology (which in the past has employed human subjects almost exclusively) to animals. Through this interest a new field has emerged, and it has been called **animal cognition** (W. A. Roberts, 1998; Vauclair, 1996) or **comparative cognition** (Kesner & Olton, 1990; Roitblat, 1987). The word *comparative* is especially revealing, because a major purpose of research in this field is to compare the cognitive processes of different species, including humans. By making such comparisons, researchers hope to find commonalities in the ways different species receive, process, store, and use information about their world (Rilling & Neiworth, 1986). Thus, although the cognitive and behavioral approaches to animal learning differ in some significant ways, they share one very fundamental goal: to discover general principles that are applicable to many different species. Of course, when psychologists compare species as different as humans, chimps, rodents, and birds, differences in learning abilities are likely to emerge as well, and these differences can be just as informative as the similarities. The comparative approach can give us a better perspective on those abilities that we have in common with other species, and it can also help us understand what makes the human species unique.

Although we have already encountered the cognitive approach in several different places in this book, this chapter is entirely devoted to the topic of comparative cognition. We will survey some of the major topic areas of traditional cognitive psychology, including memory, problem solving, reasoning, and language. We will try to determine how animals' abilities in each of these domains compare to those of people.

## MEMORY

A prevalent view about human memory is that it is important to distinguish between **long-term memory,** which can retain information for months or years, and **short-term memory,** which can only hold information for a matter of seconds. The facts in your long-term memory include such items as your birthday, the names of your friends, the fact that 4 + 5 = 9, the meaning of the word *rectangle*, and thousands of other pieces of information. On the other hand, an example of an item in short-term memory is a phone number you have just looked up for the first time. If someone distracts your attention for a few seconds after you have looked up the number, you will probably forget the number and have to look it up again. Researchers who study animal memory have also found it important to distinguish between long-term and short-term memory, so it will be convenient for us to examine these two types of memory separately in the following sections. We will also examine animal research on rehearsal, a process that is important for both types of memory.

## Short-Term Memory, or Working Memory

Besides being short-lived, short-term memory is also said to have a very limited capacity compared to the large capacity of long-term memory. Although your short-term memory is large enough to hold a seven-digit phone number long enough to dial it, you would probably have great difficulty remembering two new phone numbers at once. (If you do not believe this, look up two phone numbers at random and try to recall them 10 seconds later.) According to cognitive psychologists, because of the brevity and limited capacity of short-term memory, information must be transferred to long-term memory if it is to have any permanence.

In both human and animal research, the term **working memory** is now frequently used instead of short-term memory (Bower, 1975). This change in terminology reflects the view that the information in working memory is used to guide whatever tasks the individual is currently performing. For example, suppose you are working on a series of simple addition problems, without the aid of a calculator. At

You can measure your short-term memory span for words, letters, and other types of information at *http://coglab.psych.purdue.edu/ coglab/Labs/MemorySpan.html.*

any given moment, your working memory would contain several different pieces of information: that you are adding the hundreds column, that the total so far is 26, that the next number to be added is 8, and so on. Notice that the information must continually be updated: Your answers would be incorrect if you remembered the previous total rather than the present one, or if you failed to add the hundreds column because you confused it with the hundreds column of the previous problem. In many tasks like this, people need to remember important details about their current task and to ignore similar details from already-completed tasks. In a similar way, a butterfly searching for nectar may need to remember which patches of flowers it has already visited today, and it must not confuse today's visits with yesterday's.

Modern research suggests that similar brain mechanisms may be involved in working memory in humans and other primates. Studies with rhesus monkeys have found that individual neurons in two areas of the cerebral cortex (specifically, the prefrontal cortex and the parietal cortex) were active when the monkeys had to remember the location of an object, whereas neurons in different areas were active when the monkeys had to remember the visual characteristics of the object (Funahashi, Bruce, & Goldman-Rakic, 1989; Wilson, O'Scalaidhe, & Goldman-Rakic, 1993). Studies with humans using brain imaging techniques (PET and MRI) have found similar differences in which parts of the cerebral cortex were most active for tasks that required memory for the type of object versus those that required memory for spatial location (Smith, 2000). These studies not only show a correspondence between working memory and brain activity; they also show that different parts of the cortex may be involved depending on what types of information must be remembered.

Other research with animals has examined different properties of working memory, such as its duration, its capacity, and factors that affect accuracy of performance. The following sections describe two techniques that are frequently used to study working memory in animals.

*Delayed Matching to Sample.* As an introduction to this procedure, Figure 11-1a diagrams the simpler task of **matching to sample** as it has been used in experiments with pigeons. A suitable experimental chamber is one with three response keys mounted in one wall. Before each trial, the center key is lit with one of two colors (for instance, red or green). This color is called the **sample stimulus.** Typically, the subject must peck at this key to light the two side keys: The left key will then become green and the right key red, or vice versa. These two colors are called the **comparison stimuli.** The pigeon's task is to peck at the side key that has the same color as the center key. A correct response produces a food reinforcer; an incorrect response produces no food. Matching to sample is an easy task for pigeons and other animals, and at asymptote they make the correct choice on nearly 100 percent of the trials (Blough, 1959).

Figure 11-1b diagrams the slightly more complex procedure of **delayed matching to sample (DMTS).** In this case, the sample is

**FIGURE 11-1** (a) The procedure of simple matching to sample. The right key matches the center key, so a peck at the right key is the correct response. (b) Delayed matching to sample. A peck at the right key is again the correct response, but now the pigeon must remember the sample color through the delay interval.

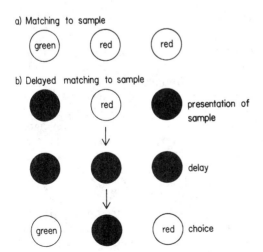

a) Matching to sample

b) Delayed matching to sample

presentation of sample

delay

choice

presented for a certain period of time, then there is a delay during which the keys are dark, and finally the two side keys are lit. Once again, the correct response is a peck at the comparison stimulus that matches the sample, but because the sample is no longer present, the pigeon must remember its color through the delay if it is to perform better than chance. Since one of the two keys is correct, chance performance is 50 percent. If the animal is correct more than 50 percent of the time, this means it has remembered something about the sample through the delay interval.

By using delays of different durations in the DMTS procedure, we can measure how long information about the sample is retained in working memory. The answer is different for different species. For example, the filled circles in Figure 11-2a show the accuracy of pigeons in an experiment by Grant (1975), in which the delay was varied from 0 seconds to 10 seconds. The average percentage of correct choices decreased steadily with longer delays, and with the 10-second delay, the pigeons made the correct choice about 66 percent of the time. The results from a similar study with three capuchin monkeys (D'Amato, 1973) are shown in Figure 11-2b. These monkeys were able to perform well with much longer delays, maintaining about a 66 percent success rate with delays of 60 seconds.

It is important to realize that functions like those in Figure 11-2 do not depict a fixed or immutable time course of working memory for these species, because many factors can significantly alter the rate at which performance deteriorates as a function of delay. For example, the performance of pigeons on DMTS improves if the sample is presented for a longer duration (W. A. Roberts & Grant, 1978). This improvement may occur because the subject has more time to study the sample and thereby strengthen its representation in working memory.

Performance on this task can also be affected by the presence of other stimuli that interfere with the memory of the sample. In human memory tasks, two types of interference have long been recognized—retroactive interference and proactive interference.

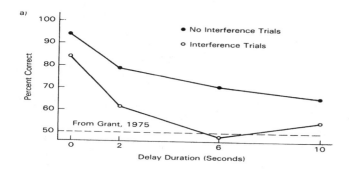

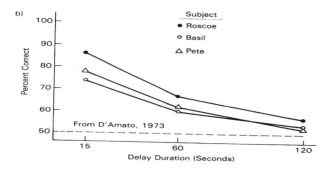

**FIGURE 11-2** (a) Performance of pigeons in a delayed matching-to-sample task, where the delay between sample and choice stimuli was varied. (b) Performance of three capuchin monkeys in a delayed matching-to-sample task. Note that the scale on the *x*-axis is different in the two panels.

**Retroactive interference** occurs when the presentation of some new material interferes with the memory of something that was learned earlier. (That is, the interfering material works backward in time—retroactively—to disrupt previously learned material.) For example, suppose that in a list-learning task like the one used by Ebbinghaus (Chapter 2), a subject memorizes List A, then List B, and then is tested on List A. The memorization of List B will impair the subject's memory of List A and lead to poorer performance than if the subject simply rested instead of learning List B. **Proactive interference** occurs when previously learned material impairs the learning of new material. (In this case, the interfering material works forward in time—proactively—to disrupt subsequent learning.) For example, it might be easy to memorize one list, List D, in isolation, but this list may be much harder to learn if it is preceded by the memorization of Lists A, B, and C.

Both types of interference have been found with animals in DMTS. Retroactive interference can be demonstrated by presenting vari-

ous sorts of stimuli during the delay interval. Not surprisingly, when the sample and comparison stimuli are different colors, matching performance is impaired if colored lights are presented during the delay interval (Jarvik, Goldfarb, & Carley, 1969; Kendrick & Rilling, 1984). In fact, any sort of surprising or unexpected stimulus presented during the delay interval is likely to impair performance on the matching task.

To demonstrate the existence of proactive interference in DMTS, one must show that stimuli presented *before* the sample can impair performance. Grant's (1975) experiment with pigeons, discussed above, provides one such demonstration. This study included a condition in which each test trial was immediately preceded by one or more interference trials, on which the opposite color was correct. The open circles in Figure 11-2a show the results from this condition. As can be seen, performance was considerably worse when these interference trials were added; evidently, the memory of the preceding trials interfered with the pigeons' performance on later trials.

So far we have examined some factors that affect performance on DMTS, but we have not discussed exactly what strategy the animal uses when performing on this task. For a human observer, it is tempting to conclude that the animal follows a simple rule: "Choose the comparison stimulus that matches the sample." Notice that this is a general rule, which could be applied to any sample and comparison stimuli the animal might encounter. However, it is also possible that the animal has learned two more specific rules: "After a red sample, choose red" and "After a green sample, choose green." If the animal has learned the general rule, it should be able to transfer this learning to a new set of stimuli (for example, blue and yellow keys instead of red and green). If it has only learned the two specific rules, such transfer to new stimuli should not occur. When tested for transfer to new stimuli, pigeons generally show some degree of savings—they learn the new task more quickly—but not the immediate and complete success with new stimuli that we would expect if they had developed a general rule for responding to "sameness" (Wilkie, 1983; Zentall & Hogan, 1978). Even monkeys have difficulty in transfer tests if the new stimuli are very different from the original stimuli (D'Amato, Salmon, & Colombo, 1985). For example, after DMTS training with different shapes as stimuli, some monkeys showed immediate transfer when the new stimuli were other shapes, but not when they were a steady green light and a flashing green light (Iverson, Sidman, & Carrigan, 1986). If these monkeys had developed a rule about responding to sameness, it was general enough to apply to new shapes but not to other types of stimuli.

A slightly different procedure, in which it is not possible to follow a general rule about sameness, is called either **conditional discrimination** or **symbolic DMTS**. The latter name, though widely used, is not really appropriate, because the sample and comparison stimuli are completely different in this task, so no "matching" is involved. For example, the sample stimuli might be red and green, and the comparison stimuli might be a horizontal black line and a vertical black line, each on a white background. The correct response rules might be: "If red, choose horizontal" and "If green, choose vertical." In analyzing performance on this task, psychologists have tried to determine whether animals use retrospective or prospective coding to retain information in working memory. **Retrospective coding** involves "looking backward" and remembering what has already happened (for example, "The sample was red"). **Prospective coding** involves "looking forward" and remembering what response should be made next (for example, "Peck the key with the horizontal line").

An experiment by Roitblat (1980) found evidence that pigeons use a prospective strategy on a conditional discrimination task. In this experiment, there were three possible sample stimuli (red, orange, and blue) and three comparison stimuli (black lines that were horizontal, vertical, and almost vertical). The correct response rules were: If red, choose horizontal; if orange, choose almost vertical; and if blue, choose vertical. A pigeon using a retrospective strategy (looking back and remembering the sample color through the delay interval) would be expected to make more errors with the red and orange samples, since these colors are more similar to each other than either is to blue. On the other hand, a pigeon using a prospective strategy (looking ahead and remembering which line orientation to choose) would tend to make more errors when the correct comparison stimulus was either vertical or almost vertical, since these are more similar to each other than either is to horizontal. Roitblat found greater confusion with the similar line orientations than with the similar colors, which suggested that his pigeons were using a prospective strategy. To put it simply, the animals appeared to be remembering which response to make, not which color they had seen.

A number of other studies have found further evidence for prospective coding (for example, Honig & Dodd, 1983; Urcuioli & Zentall, 1992). However, it would be a mistake to conclude that pigeons always use prospective coding in conditional discrimination procedures. Some studies have found evidence for retrospective coding when the sample stimuli were easy to discriminate and the comparison stimuli were not (Urcuioli & Zentall, 1986; Zentall, Urcuioli, Jagielo, & Jackson-Smith, 1989). The researchers concluded that pigeons are capable of both prospective and retrospective coding, and that they may rely more heavily on one or the other, depending on which is more useful in a particular task.

*The Radial-Arm Maze.* The DMTS task is quite different from anything an animal is likely to encounter in its natural environment. A somewhat more realistic task that involves working memory is provided by the radial-arm maze: It simulates a situation in which an animal explores a territory in search of food. Figure 11-3 shows the floor plan of an eight-arm maze for rats used by Olton and his associates. The entire maze is a platform that rests a few feet above the floor, and the maze has no walls, so the rat can see any objects that may be in the room (windows, doors, desks, and so on). At the end of each arm is a cup in which a bit of food can be stored. In a typical experiment, some food is deposited at the end of each arm. The rat is placed in the center area to start a trial and is given time to explore the maze and collect whatever food it can find. Once the rat collects the food in one arm, it will find no

more food in that arm if it returns later during the same trial. The most efficient strategy for obtaining food is therefore to visit each arm once and only once.

The role of working memory in this situation should be obvious: To collect food efficiently, the rat must remember either which arms it has already visited on the current trial (if it is using retrospective coding) or which arms it has not yet visited (if it is using prospective coding). This information must be continually updated, and visits on the current trial must not be confused with visits on a previous trial. Perhaps the most remarkable feature of an average rat's performance on this task is its accuracy. Let us call the first visit to any arm a correct response and any repeat visit an error. If a trial is ended after the rat visits eight arms (including any repeat visits), it will usually make seven or eight correct responses (Olton, 1978). This performance means that the rat is very skillful at avoiding the arms that it has already visited on the current trial. With a larger, 17-arm maze, rats still average about 15 correct responses out of 17 visits (Olton, Collison, & Werz, 1977), and similar performance has been obtained from gerbils (Wilkie & Slobin, 1983).

The first question we must ask about this exceptional performance is whether the animals rely on some external cues or special strategies to make the task easier. For instance, if a rat simply started at one arm and then went around the maze in a clockwise pattern, it could visit all the arms and make no errors, but this strategy would place few demands on working memory. However, there is good evidence that rats do not follow this type of strategy. Instead, they seem to select successive arms in a haphazard manner (Olton, 1978). Other studies have shown that rats do not use the smell of food to guide them, and that they do not use scent markings to avoid repeat visits. What they do use to orient their travels within the maze are visual landmarks in the room surrounding the maze. The landmarks help the animals identify individual arms and keep track of which ones they have already visited (Brown, 1992; Mazmanian & Roberts, 1983).

**FIGURE 11-3**   The floor plan of an eight-arm maze for rats.

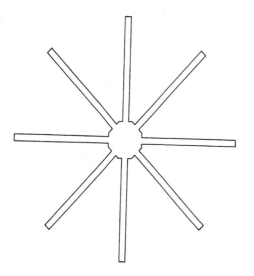

Experiments with the radial-arm maze have provided considerable information about the capacity and duration of animals' working memory for spatial locations. It is commonly said that human working memory can retain only about seven unrelated items at once (for example, seven words, or seven random digits). With this number as a point of comparison, the nearly flawless performance of rats in a 17-arm maze is especially impressive. Equally impressive are the time intervals over which rats can remember which arms they have visited. Beatty and Shavalia (1980) allowed rats to visit four arms of an eight-arm maze, after which they were removed from the maze. If they were returned to the maze as much as 4 hours later, the rats were almost perfect in their selection of the four arms they had not previously visited. This experiment, and others like it, show why working memory is probably a more appropriate term than short-term memory. In research with people, short-term memory has generally referred to information that is lost in a matter of seconds (Peterson & Peterson, 1959), but an animal's memory for its travels in the radial-arm maze can last 100 times longer.

Do rats use retrospective or prospective coding in the radial-arm maze? One way to answer this question is to look at the occasional errors a subject makes in the maze. If the animal is using retrospective coding (remembering which arms it has already visited), it is more likely to forget (and therefore revisit) an arm that was visited early in the trial than one that was recently visited. On the other hand, if the animal is using prospective coding (remembering which arms are still to be visited), the order of previous visits should have nothing to do with the errors it makes.

Several studies have shown that early visits are most likely to be forgotten, as would be expected with retrospective coding (Olton, 1978; Olton & Samuelson, 1976). However, Cook, Brown, and Riley (1985) found evidence for both types of coding, using a 12-arm maze for rats. Each 12-visit trial was interrupted for 15 minutes after either 2, 4, 6, 8, or 10 visits. An interruption after 6 visits produced more errors than interruptions either earlier or later in

a trial. In addition, the pattern of errors suggested that the rats used primarily retrospective coding during the first 6 visits or so, and then switched to primarily prospective coding. Notice how this switch in coding strategies can serve to lessen the demands on working memory. For example, after 2 visits, a rat could either use retrospective coding to remember these 2 arms, or it could use prospective coding to list the 10 yet-to-be-visited arms. Obviously, the retrospective strategy is easier. But later in the trial, when faced with the choice of remembering, say, 9 visited arms or 3 to-be-visited arms, the prospective strategy of remembering the to-be-visited arms is easier. Zentall, Steirn, and Jackson-Smith (1990) obtained similar results from pigeons performing a task that was analogous to a radial-arm maze: They too appeared to use retrospective coding at the beginning of a trial and prospective coding at the end.

*Summary.* Research with DMTS and the radial-arm maze has substantially increased our understanding of animal working memory, which turns out to have many of the same properties as human working memory. Depending on the species and the task at hand, information in working memory may last only a few seconds or as long as several hours. Because the amount of information that can be stored in working memory is quite small, this information is very susceptible to disruption by either proactive or retroactive interference. Many studies have investigated exactly what type of information is stored in working memory, and these studies have provided evidence for both retrospective coding (remembering what has just happened) and prospective coding (remembering what remains to be done). Which type of coding dominates in a particular situation often seems to depend on which is easier to use in that situation.

### Rehearsal

The concept of **rehearsal** is easy to understand when thinking about human learning. We can rehearse a speech by reading it aloud or by reading it silently. It seems natural to think of rehearsal as overt or silent speech in which we repeatedly recite whatever we wish to remember. Theories of human memory state that rehearsal has two main functions: It keeps information active in short-term memory, and it promotes the transfer of this information into long-term memory.

Because we tend to equate rehearsal with speech, it may surprise you to learn that psychologists have found strong evidence for rehearsal in animals. Since animals do not use language, what does it mean to say that they can engage in rehearsal? With animals, rehearsal is more difficult to define, but it refers to an active processing of stimuli or events after they have occurred. Rehearsal cannot be observed directly; its existence can only be inferred from an animal's behavior on tasks that make use of short- or long-term memory. To demonstrate the existence of rehearsal in animals, researchers have tried to show (1) that animals can choose whether to engage in rehearsal, just as they can choose whether to perform any operant behavior, and (2) that rehearsal can be disrupted by distracting the animal.

Rehearsal seems to serve the same two functions for animals as it does for people. For this reason, Grant (1984) has suggested that we should distinguish between **maintenance rehearsal,** which serves to retain information in short-term memory, and **associative rehearsal,** which promotes long-term associative learning (as when an animal learns to associate a CS and US in classical conditioning). The evidence for rehearsal in animals can be divided into these two categories.

### Evidence for Maintenance Rehearsal.

We have already examined evidence that information is retained in working memory for a short period of time and then is lost. Some researchers have attempted to show that animals have at least partial control over how long information is retained in working memory. Their purpose is to demonstrate that working memory involves more than a passive memory trace that decays over time; rather, by using rehearsal, an animal can actively maintain information in working memory (Grant, 1981;

Maki, 1981). This process of rehearsal can be thought of as a sort of covert behavior that an animal can learn to use or not use as the situation demands.

One line of evidence that animals use rehearsal to keep information in working memory is the observation that animals can remember "expected" stimuli (stimuli they have repeatedly encountered before) better than "suprising" stimuli (events that they have not experienced before). The premises underlying these experiments are that (1) rehearsal helps refresh the animal's short-term memory for recent events, and (2) surprising events receive more rehearsal than expected events (Maki, 1981; Terry & Wagner, 1975).

Perhaps the best evidence for maintenance rehearsal comes from a technique called **directed forgetting,** which can be demonstrated with the conditional discrimination procedure. The purpose of this technique is to teach the animal that on some trials it is important to remember the sample stimulus, and on other trials it is safe to forget the sample. To accomplish this, either a "remember cue" or a "forget cue" is presented during the delay that follows the sample stimulus. The remember cue tells the animal that it is important to remember the sample because a test is coming up (that is, the comparison stimuli will soon follow). The forget cue tells the animal that it is safe to forget the sample because there will be no test on this trial. Thus the animal is "directed" either to remember or to forget the sample. If an animal can choose whether or not to engage in rehearsal, it should eventually learn to follow the directions and rehearse the sample when it sees the remember cue but not when it sees the forget cue. For the experimenter, the trick is to find a way to show that the animal is indeed rehearsing in one case but not the other.

An experiment with pigeons by Maki and Hegvik (1980) illustrates how this can be done. Figure 11-4 diagrams the procedure. The two sample stimuli in this experiment were not key colors but rather the presence or absence of food. Each trial started with the presentation of the sample, then there was a delay of a few seconds, and finally the comparison stimuli

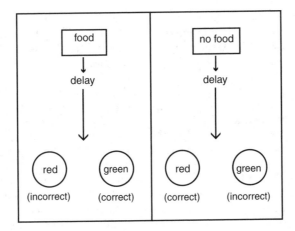

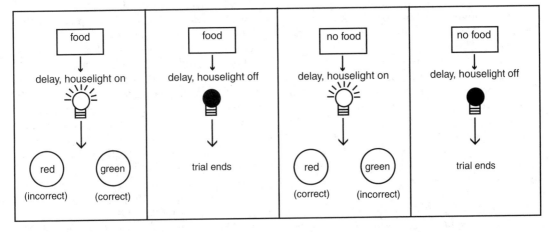

**FIGURE 11-4** The procedures used in the Maki and Hegvik (1980) experiment on directed forgetting. The top row shows the two types of trials used in the initial training. The bottom row shows the four types of trials used in the second phase, which taught the pigeons to "forget" on trials with the houselight off.

(red and green keys) were presented. The response rules for reinforcement were: After a food sample, peck green; and after a no-food sample, peck red. Once the pigeons had mastered this task, remember and forget cues were introduced during the delays. For half the birds, the remember cue was houselight-on, and the forget cue was houselight-off. For the other birds, these two cues were reversed. As Figure 11-4 shows, the red and green comparison stimuli were presented after the remember cue, and a correct choice was reinforced. After

the forget cue, no comparison stimuli were presented, and the trial simply terminated with no possibility of reinforcement. After several sessions of training with this procedure, occasional "probe trials" were included, during which the comparison stimuli did follow the forget cue, and a correct choice was reinforced. Maki and Hegvik reasoned that if the animals had learned not to bother rehearsing on trials with the forget cue, they should perform poorly on these occasional surprise quizzes. This is just what they found: On probe trials that followed the forget cues, the pigeons averaged about 70 percent correct choices, compared to about 90 percent on trials with the remember cue.

Evidence for directed forgetting has been obtained in a number of experiments with pigeons and several other species (Grant, 1982; Roberts, Mazmanian, & Kraemer, 1984). Nevertheless, the poor performance that follows a forget cue could be caused by factors that have nothing to do with rehearsal (Zentall, Roper, & Sherburne, 1995). For example, the poor performance could occur because the forget cue is distracting, or because the animals do not expect to receive reinforcement and therefore are not motivated to respond accurately.

To eliminate some of these alternative explanations, Roper and her colleagues have developed procedures for pigeons that more closely resemble the methods used to study directed forgetting with human subjects (Roper, Kaiser, & Zentall, 1995; Roper & Zentall, 1993). There is certainly an advantage in copying the procedures used with human subjects, because one important goal of this research is to compare animal and human memory processes under conditions that are as similar as possible. With these procedures, the researchers found convincing evidence for directed forgetting in pigeons, but only if the pigeons were required to do a different memory task on trials with the forget cue. These results are similar to those obtained with human subjects, and they suggest that directed forgetting occurs because the subjects are rehearsing other information on trials with the forget cue.

***Evidence for Associative Rehearsal.*** Research on human memory has shown that rehearsal increases the strength of long-term memory. If a person is first presented with a list of items to remember and is then given a distraction-free period (in which the subject presumably recites or rehearses the material in some way), this person's ability to recall the list items at a later time will be improved. In a clever series of experiments, Wagner, Rudy, and Whitlow (1973) demonstrated that rehearsal also contributes to the strength of long-term learning in classical conditioning

with rabbits. They demonstrated that the acquisition of a CR proceeds more slowly if some **posttrial episode (PTE)** that "distracts" the animal occurs shortly after each conditioning trial. They also showed that surprising PTEs are more distracting (have a greater decremental effect on learning) than expected PTEs.

In one experiment, Wagner, Rudy, and Whitlow first developed two surprising and two expected PTEs. The expected PTEs were sequences of stimuli that the rabbits had seen many times, whereas the surprising PTEs were rearrangements of these stimuli that the animals had not seen before. In the test phase, all rabbits received a series of classical conditioning trials on which a new CS was paired with a US (a mild shock in the vicinity of the eye, which produced an eyeblink). For all subjects, a PTE occurred 10 seconds after each conditioning trial. However, for half of the subjects, the PTE was an expected sequence of stimuli, and for the other half, it was a surprising sequence of stimuli. Wagner and colleagues found that eyeblink conditioning to the CS developed much more slowly in the subjects that received surprising PTEs.

Wagner, Rudy, and Whitlow used the following reasoning to interpret their findings: (1) In order for a long-term CS-US association to develop, an animal needs a distraction-free period after each conditioning trial, during which rehearsal takes place; (2) this rehearsal process utilizes the animal's working memory, which has a limited capacity; (3) attending to an event such as a PTE also utilizes the animal's working memory, and so the processing of a PTE competes with the rehearsal of the previous conditioning trial; and (4) surprising events attract more attention than do expected events, so they have a greater disruptive effect on the animal's rehearsal of the previous conditioning trial. Thus the subject's greater attention to a surprising PTE presumably decreased the amount of rehearsal that was devoted to the events of the previous conditioning trial, and so acquisition was slower.

If rehearsal is necessary for conditioning, and if a surprising PTE interferes with this rehearsal to some extent, then the sooner the

PTE occurs after the conditioning trial, the greater should be the disruption of conditioning. To test this prediction, Wagner, Rudy, and Whitlow varied the time between the trial and the surprising PTE from 3 to 300 seconds for different groups of subjects. Figure 11-5 shows the median percentages of CRs to the new CS over the first 10 conditioning trials. As can be seen, the PTEs had their greatest disruptive effects when they closely followed each conditioning trial, and thereby kept rehearsal to a minimum.

### Long-Term Memory, or Reference Memory

Nearly all of the experiments described in this book relate to long-term memory. Whether behavior is modified through habituation, classical or operant conditioning, or observational learning, a cognitive psychologist would attribute a long-term change in behavior to a change in the individual's long-term memory. Long-term memory has also been called **reference memory,** because an individual must refer to the information in long-term memory when performing almost any task (Honig, 1984; Roitblat, 1987). Consider once again the task of performing a series of addition problems. Whereas you use working memory to keep track of which steps you have completed, you must refer to long-term memory to know what the sum of any two digits is, how to carry digits from one column to the next, and so on.

Besides their different durations, probably the biggest distinction between short- and long-term memory is their different storage capacities. In contrast to the very limited size of short-term memory, the storage capacity of long-term memory is very large. It is probably safe to say that no one has yet found a way to measure and quantify this capacity for either animals or people (as can be easily done for a computer, which might have the capacity to store, for instance, 40 megabytes of information). Although we do not know how much information can be stored in an animal's long-term memory, some studies have demonstrated impressive feats of learning and remembering. For example, Vaughan and Greene (1983, 1984) trained pigeons to classify slides of everyday scenes as either "positive" (because responses to these slides were reinforced with food) or "negative" (because responses to these slides were never reinforced). They decided whether each slide would be positive or negative simply by flipping a coin. Therefore, the first time a pigeon saw a slide, it had no way of knowing whether

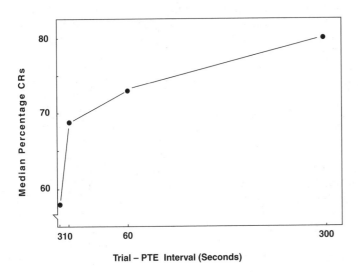

**FIGURE 11-5**   The four data points show the percentage of conditioned eyeblink responses in four different groups of rabbits in the Wagner, Rudy, and Whitlow (1973) experiment. For each group, the *x*-axis shows the amount of time that elapsed between each conditioning trial and a surprising posttrial episode (PTE).

it was positive or negative, and on subsequent presentations the bird could respond correctly only if it remembered that specific slide.

In one study, Vaughan and Greene started with 80 slides, randomly divided into 40 positive and 40 negative instances. After about 10 sessions (with each slide appearing twice a session), the birds were discriminating between positive and negative instances with better than 90 percent accuracy. Then the birds were presented with a new set of 80 slides, which they learned even faster. The procedure was successfully repeated with two more sets of 80 slides, which were learned in just a few sessions each. Finally, the birds were tested with all 320 slides, and their accuracy was still above 90 percent. Since there was no way to succeed on this task without remembering the individual slides, the experiment showed that pigeons can remember at least several hundred visual stimuli. Even when tested after a 2-year delay, the pigeons responded with over 70 percent accuracy, which was significantly better than the chance level of 50 percent. Equally impressive memory for pictorial materials has been found with human subjects (Shepard, 1967).

Studies with other species of birds have demonstrated similar feats of memory, often involving memory for **caches**—sites where the birds have stored food (Sherry, 1984; Shettleworth & Krebs, 1982, 1986). For example, a bird known as Clark's nutcracker gathers over 20,000 pine seeds each fall and stores them in the ground in several thousand different locations. To survive the winter, the bird must recover a good portion of these seeds. Field observations and laboratory experiments have shown that nutcrackers do not use random searching or olfactory cues in recovering their caches. Although they may use certain characteristics of cache sites to aid their searches (such as the appearance of the soil above a cache), the birds' memories of specific visual landmarks are much more important (Kamil & Balda, 1985; Vander Wall, 1982).

Other studies with animals have investigated the time course of forgetting from long-term memory, just as Hermann Ebbinghaus tested his recall of nonsense syllables after different intervals to construct a forgetting curve

(see Chapter 2 and Figure 2-2). The general shape of forgetting curves for animals is similar to that of Ebbinghaus: Forgetting is rapid at first, with a substantial loss during the first 24 hours, but subsequent forgetting proceeds at a much slower rate (Gleitman, 1971; Thomas & Lopez, 1962).

What causes the forgetting of information in long-term memory? For humans, a prevalent view is that interference from similar stimuli or events is a major cause of forgetting (Keppel, 1968), and this view has substantial empirical support. It is therefore of interest to note that both proactive and retroactive interference have been observed in studies of animal long-term memory (Honig, 1974; Thomas, 1981). As an example of proactive interference, suppose that a pigeon receives several days of training on a discrimination task in which S⁺ is a pure green and S⁻ is a slightly bluer green. Then the roles of S⁺ and S⁻ are reversed for one session, and the bird learns to respond to the blue-green stimulus. If the bird is then tested on the following day, the early training with green as the S⁺ is likely to interfere with the bird's memory of the more recent training, and it may respond more to green and less to blue-green. This is an instance of proactive interference because the memory of prior training impairs the memory of subsequent training.

If an individual forgets something that was learned long ago, is this because the memory has been lost forever, or is the problem one of retrieval failure (the memory is still there but it is difficult to find)? In research on human memory, there is evidence that many instances of forgetting are really cases of retrieval failure. Although you may not be able to recall some information on your first attempt (for instance, the Democratic nominee for president in 1980), you may succeed if you are given a hint (for instance, peanuts).

There is similar evidence from animal studies that forgetting is often a problem of retrieval failure, and that "forgotten" memories can be recovered if the animal is given an appropriate clue or reminder (Gordon, 1983; Spear, 1971). For example, Gordon, Smith, and Katz (1979) trained rats on an avoidance task in which a subject had to go from a white room to a black room to avoid a shock. Three days after training, rats in one group were given a reminder of their previous avoidance learning: They were simply confined in the white compartment for 15 seconds, with no shock. Rats in a control group were not returned to the test chamber. Twenty-four hours later, both groups were tested in extinction to see how quickly they would move into the black chamber. The rats that had received the reminder treatment entered the black room significantly faster, presumably because the reminder served to revive their memories of their earlier avoidance training. Similar effects of reminder treatments have been obtained in classical conditioning situations (Gordon, McGinnis, & Weaver, 1985). The general conclusion from this line of research is that any stimulus that is present during a learning experience (such as the room or chamber in which the learning takes place) can later serve as a reminder and make it more likely that the experience will be remembered.

When people are asked to remember a list of items and then recall them in any order they wish (a **free-recall** procedure), they tend to remember the items near the beginning and near the end of the list better than those in the middle. The good recall of words at the beginning of the list is called the **primacy effect,** and the good recall of words at the end of the list is called the **recency effect.** Similar primacy and recency effects have been obtained from pigeons and monkeys when they were presented with lists of stimuli to remember (Castro & Larsen, 1992; Wright, Santiago, Sands, Kendrick, & Cook, 1985). Although the procedures were necessarily somewhat different from those used in typical list-learning experiments with people, these results nevertheless provide further examples of the similarities between human and nonhuman memory (Wright, 1994).

Although our survey of animal memory is now finished, both short- and long-term memory are important for many of the other cognitive tasks we will now consider. Whether an animal is solving a problem, learning an abstract concept, or counting stimuli, it must rely

on long-term memory for background information about the current task, and on short-term memory for information about what has already happened and what is likely to happen next.

## TIME, NUMBER, AND SERIAL PATTERNS

Can animals sense the passage of time and estimate the duration of an event? Can they count objects, and if so, how many and how accurately? Can they detect orderly sequences of events in their environment? These questions are interesting because they all deal with abstract properties of stimuli. A 30-second television commercial may have nothing in common with a 30-second traffic light, yet a person can easily understand the abstract feature (duration) that makes these two events similar. In the same way, even young children can recognize what four blocks, four cookies, and four crayons have in common, even though the physical properties of these objects are very different. Determining whether animals can also recognize and respond to such abstract dimensions as time and number is not an easy task, but substantial progress has been made in recent years.

### Experiments on an "Internal Clock"

On a fixed-interval schedule, responding typically gets faster and faster as the time for reinforcement approaches (see Chapter 7). Research by Dews (1962) has shown that, for pigeons, the passage of time serves as a discriminative stimulus that controls this response pattern. More recent studies have provided additional information about animals' timing abilities. Try to imagine what would happen in the following experiment. A rat is first trained on an FI 40-second schedule. A light is turned on to signal the start of each 40-second interval, and after the reinforcer, the light is turned off during an intertrial interval, and then the next trial begins. Training on this schedule continues until the animal's response rate in each interval consistently shows the accelerating pattern that is typical of FI performance.

Now the procedure is changed so that on occasional trials no reinforcer is delivered—the light remains on for about 80 seconds, and then the trial ends in darkness. With further training, the animal will learn that a reinforcer is available after 40 seconds on some trials, but not on others. For the first 40 seconds, however, both types of trials look exactly alike, and there is no way to tell whether a reinforcer will be available or not. How do you think the animal will respond on nonreinforced trials? Will it respond faster and faster throughout the 80-second period? Will it cease responding after 40 seconds have elapsed without reinforcement?

Figure 11-6 presents the results from an experiment like the one just described (S. Roberts, 1981). The open circles show that on trials without reinforcement, response rates started low, increased for a while, reached a maximum at about 40 seconds, and then declined. The location of the peak indicates that the rats were able to estimate the passage of time fairly accurately, since they responded the fastest at just about the time a response might be reinforced. It was no coincidence that the peak occurred at about 40 seconds. On other trials, a tone was presented instead of the light, and the tone usually meant that a reinforcer was available on an FI 20-second schedule. The filled circles in Figure 11-6 show the results from nonreinforced test trials with the tone, which also lasted for about 80 seconds.

Again, response rates first increased and then decreased, but on these trials the peak response rate occurred at about 20 seconds. These results show that the rats had learned that the tone signaled a 20-second interval and the light signaled a 40-second interval, and in both cases they could estimate these intervals fairly well. This procedure for studying animal timing abilities is called the **peak procedure** because the peak of the response-rate function tells us how accurately the animals could time the intervals.

How accurately can animals distinguish between two events that have different durations? A conditional discrimination procedure can be used to answer this question. Suppose a rat is reinforced for pressing the left lever after a 5-second tone and for pressing the right lever after an 8-second tone. Even a well-trained rat will make some errors on this task, but if the animal makes the correct response most of the time (for instance, on 75 percent of the trials), we can conclude that the rat can discriminate between the two different durations. Experiments using this type of procedure with both rats and pigeons have shown that they can discriminate between two stimuli if their durations differ by roughly 25 percent (Church, Getty, & Lerner, 1976; Stubbs, 1968). This finding illustrates a principle of perception called **Weber's law,** which says that the amount a stimulus must be changed before the change is detectable is proportional

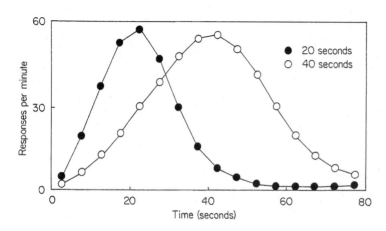

**FIGURE 11-6** Pigeons's response rates in S. Roberts's (1981) experiment using the peak procedure. The filled circles show the results from trials with a tone that usually signaled an FI 20-second schedule. The open circles show the results from trials with a light that usually signaled an FI 40-second schedule. (From S. Roberts, 1981)

to the size of the stimulus. Thus an animal may be able to discriminate between a 4-second tone and a 5-second tone (which differ by 25 percent), but not between a 10-second tone and an 11-second tone (which differ by only 10 percent), even though there is a 1-second difference in both cases. On temporal discrimination tasks, the timing abilities of pigeons are remarkably similar to those of humans: For both species, Weber's law describes the results fairly well for durations greater than about 1 second. Temporal discrimination is much worse with brief stimuli, and both pigeons and people need much more than a 25-percent difference to tell which of two durations is longer (Fetterman & Killeen, 1992).

This research shows that animals are fairly good at judging durations, but it does not tell us exactly how they measure the passage of time. Some psychologists have proposed that every animal has an "internal clock" that it can use to time the duration of events in its environment (Church, 1978; S. Roberts, 1983). This internal clock is said to include a **pacemaker** that, much like a metronome, pulses at a steady rate and allows the animal to measure durations. Church (1984) and S. Roberts (1983) have proposed that in some respects an animal's internal clock is analogous to a stopwatch. Like a stopwatch, the internal clock can be used to time different types of stimuli. S. Roberts (1982) trained rats to press one lever after a 1-second tone and another after a 4-second tone. When the stimuli were then changed to 1- and 4-second *lights*, the rats continued to choose correctly without additional training. Like a stopwatch, the internal clock can be stopped and then restarted. S. Roberts (1981) demonstrated this point with his peak procedure. Recall that on most trials, a light signaled an FI 40-second schedule, but on a few trials, the light stayed on for 80 seconds or more and no reinforcer was available. In one experiment, Roberts included occasional nonreinforced trials in which the light was turned on for 10 or 15 seconds, then turned off for 5 or 10 seconds, then turned back on for the remainder of the 80-second trial. The rats' response patterns indicated that they stopped timing the 40-second interval during the blackout and then picked up where they left off when the light was turned back on.

The theory of Church, Roberts, and their associates states that animals can measure durations because they can, in effect, sense the pulsing of their internal pacemakers. A different theory of animal timing, called the **behavioral theory of timing**, was proposed by Killeen and Fetterman (1988; Killeen, 1991). The details of this theory are complicated, but in essence the theory states that animals use their own behaviors to measure durations. For example, if a reinforcement schedule requires that the animal wait for 5 seconds and then make a response (a DRL 5-second schedule; see Chapter 7), the animal might walk to all four corners of the experimental chamber and then make the operant response. In this way, the animal could time the 5-second interval with reasonable accuracy. The behavioral theory of timing also includes an internal clock that supposedly "sets the tempo" of the animal's overt behaviors. However, this internal clock is paced, not by an internal pacemaker, but by the rate at which the animal is currently receiving reinforcers. In short, this theory states that the rate of reinforcement controls the rate of the internal clock, which in turn controls the rate of the animal's behaviors, and the animal uses these behaviors to measure the passage of time. A series of experiments by Fetterman and Killeen (1991) showed that pigeons' accuracy on timing tasks was determined by the rate of reinforcement, just as their theory predicted.

The debate between those who favor the theory of an internal pacemaker and those who favor the behavioral theory of timing has not been resolved. Nevertheless, the experiments we have reviewed show that animals have fairly versatile timing abilities. They can discriminate between stimuli of slightly different durations, and they can transfer this skill from a visual stimulus to an auditory stimulus. They can time the total duration of a stimulus that is temporarily interrupted. They can time the total duration of a compound stimulus that begins as a light and then changes to a tone (S. Roberts, 1981). An animal's ability to time events is certainly far less accurate than an ordinary wristwatch, but then so is a person's.

## Counting

Many of the techniques used to study animals' counting abilities are similar to those used to study timing, and the results are similar as well. A conditional discrimination procedure can be used to determine whether an animal can discriminate between two different quantities (for example, five light pulses versus eight light pulses). As with the discrimination of durations, animals can generally discriminate between two quantities if they differ by about 25 percent or more, but Weber's law is only approximately supported, because this percentage decreases slightly with large numbers. That is, it may be easier for an animal to discriminate between 40 and 50 than between 4 and 5 (Hobson & Newman, 1981).

Procedures that require animals to count their own responses have shown that they can do so in an approximate way, just as the peak procedure showed that animals can roughly time the absolute durations of stimuli. In one procedure, Mechner (1958) used a variation of a fixed-ratio schedule in which a rat had to switch from one lever to another after completing the ratio requirement. For example, if 16 responses were required, on half of the trials, the sixteenth consecutive response on lever A was reinforced. On the other half of the trials, the rat had to make 16 or more consecutive responses on lever A and then one response on lever B to collect the reinforcer. If the rat switched too early (say, after 14 responses), there was no reinforcer, and the rat had to start from the beginning and make another 16 responses on key A before a reinforcer was available. In four different conditions, either 4, 8, 12, or 16 consecutive responses were required. For these four conditions, Figure 11-7 shows one rat's probability of switching to lever B after different run lengths (where a run is a string of consecutive responses on lever A). We can see that as the ratio requirement increased, the average run length also increased in a systematic way. When 4 responses were required, the most common run length was 5;

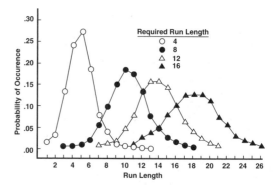

**FIGURE 11-7** One rat's probability of switching from lever A to lever B after different run lengths in Mechner's (1958) experiment. The required run length is the number of consecutive responses required on lever A before a switch to lever B would be reinforced. (From Mechner, 1958)

when 16 responses were required, the most common run length was 18. Producing run lengths that were, on the average, slightly longer than required was a sensible strategy because the penalty for switching too early was severe.

Because of the many similarities between animals' timing and counting abilities, Church and Meck (1984) proposed that these two skills may be different manifestations of the same cognitive mechanism. That is, they suggested that an animal's internal clock may operate in a "continuous" mode to measure the duration of a single stimulus, or it may operate in a "discrete" mode to count the number of stimuli. Studies with pigeons showed that they could either count a series of flashing lights or time their durations, whichever the task required (W. A. Roberts, Coughlin, & Roberts, 2000). Besides the parallels already mentioned, Meck and Church (1983) noted that timing and counting are similarly affected by the drug methamphetamine. Judging by their responses in a choice situation, rats' estimates of both duration and number were about 10 percent longer after an injection of methamphetamine. And as with timing, rats show cross-modal transfer in a counting task. After rats learned to discriminate between two and four sounds, they needed no additional training to respond correctly when the stimuli were switched to two or four light pulses (Church & Meck, 1984).

This cross-modal transfer of a counting skill has important theoretical implications. It shows that the rats had formed, at least in a rudimentary way, an abstract concept of number—one that was not tied to the physical characteristics of the stimuli being counted. To put it simply, the rats were able to respond to the abstract feature that four sounds and four lights had in common—the attribute of "fourness." Nevertheless, in some ways this ability to respond to the number of stimuli is quite primitive compared to the counting abilities of people, even young children. For one thing, the counting abilities we have examined so far are not exact: The rats in Mechner's research did not switch to lever B after they had made exactly the right number of responses on lever A. On some trials they switched too early, and on others they made more responses on lever A than necessary. In contrast, a person could learn to switch after exactly the right number of responses each time by simply counting responses.

Can animals learn to count objects in an exact rather than approximate way? A few studies suggest that they can, at least with small numbers. Davis and Albert (1986) found that rats were able to learn a discrimination in which three bursts of noise served as the S+ and either two or four bursts served as S−. Davis and Bradford (1991) taught three different groups of rats to eat exactly three, four, or five food pellets per trial by reinforcing this behavior and punishing any attempt to eat more than the correct number of pellets. In another study on counting, Capaldi and Miller (1988) found evidence that the rats learned abstract concepts of number that could transfer from one type of stimulus to another. Some writers have proposed that counting is a skill that animals can learn only with difficulty, but Capaldi and Miller concluded just the opposite, stating that "rats assign abstract number tags to reinforcers readily, easily, and under most, if not all, circumstances" (1988, p. 16).

Other evidence for an exact counting ability was presented by Pepperberg (1987), who trained a parrot, Alex, to respond to any number of objects from two through six by actually saying the appropriate number. In training, a number of objects (such as keys, small pieces of paper or wood, corks) would be placed on a tray, and Alex was reinforced if he said the correct number. For instance, the experimenter might present three corks and ask, "What's this?" The correct response would be "Three corks." Different objects were used on different trials so that Alex would not simply learn to say "three" whenever he saw corks. After a few months of training, Alex was responding correctly on about 80 percent of the trials. To show that Alex's counting ability was not limited to the training stimuli, new objects were presented on test trials. In some cases, Alex did not even know the names of the objects (such as wooden beads or small bottles), but he was able to give the correct number of objects on about 75 percent of the test trials with new stimuli. With somewhat less accuracy, Alex could count subsets of heterogeneous objects (for instance, with three keys and two corks, he would be asked either "How many keys?" or "How many corks?"). By arranging the objects on the tray in many different ways, Pepperberg was able to show that Alex was not responding to other cues, such as the length of a row of objects or the overall shape of the group (such as a diamond shape that might be formed by four objects). All in all, Pepperberg has made a convincing case that Alex can count up to six objects, whether familiar or novel, with a high degree of accuracy.

Matsuzawa (1985) has reported a similar counting skill in a chimpanzee (although naturally the chimp did not speak, but rather pressed response keys with the numbers 1 through 6 on them). Brannon and Terrace (2000) taught macaques to point to arrays of abstract shapes in order of increasing number: To receive a reward, the monkey had to first point to the array with one shape, then to the arrays with two, three, and four shapes. After learning this task, they were able to transfer this ability to arrays with between five and nine shapes, even though they had received no training with these larger numbers. These studies, along with Pepperberg's research with

Alex, provide the best evidence available for accurate counting by animals.

## Serial Pattern Learning

Suppose you are taking a calculus course with an eccentric professor who assigns a certain number of homework problems at the end of each class. He assigns 14 problems in the first class, 7 in the second class, 3 in the third, 1 in the fourth, and 0 in the fifth. In the next 10 classes, the numbers of problems assigned are 14, 7, 3, 1, 0, 14, 7, 3, 1, and 0. After 10 or 15 classes, you may detect the repeating pattern of five numbers and thereby be able to predict how many problems will be assigned in each future class.

Hulse and Campbell (1975) wanted to know whether rats can detect such repeating serial patterns. They trained rats to run down a long runway that had food at the end. (The food could not be seen until a rat reached the end of the runway.) For one group of rats, the number of pellets available on each trial in the runway followed the repeating pattern described in the previous paragraph (14 pellets on the first trial, 7 on the second, and so on). With enough training, these rats showed that they had learned something about the cyclical pattern: They ran fast on trials with 14, 7, or 3 pellets, more slowly on trials with 1 pellet, and very slowly on trials with no pellets. The same was true for a second group of rats that was trained with the reverse pattern (0, 1, 3, 7, and 14 pellets). For a third group, the number of pellets on each trial was chosen randomly (that is, there was no pattern to be learned), and these rats ran at about the same rate on every trial.

It is clear that the rats in the first two groups had learned something about the serial pattern, but exactly what had they learned? One possibility (Capaldi, Verry, & Davison, 1980) is that they simply learned associations between adjacent items (that is, that 14 pellets were followed by 7 pellets, 7 pellets by 3 pellets, and so on). Another possibility is that they learned a more abstract rule, such as "The number of pellets steadily decreases over trials until there are none." To support this possibil-

ity, Hulse and Dorsky (1979) showed that rats were able to learn a steadily increasing or decreasing sequence in fewer trials than a sequence that decreased, increased, and decreased again—14, 1, 3, 7, and 0 pellets. Their explanation is that the learning was slower with this pattern because a more complex rule is needed to describe it.

A third possibility is that besides learning a rule about a decreasing or increasing pattern, the rats learned something about the overall structure of the sequence—that it is five trials long, that three pellets occur in the exact middle of the sequence, and so on. Roitblat, Pologe, and Scopatz (1983) provided evidence for this idea by first training rats with the steadily decreasing sequence (14, 7, 3, 1, 0) and then occasionally presenting test trials on which one trial somewhere in the middle of the sequence delivered no pellets (for example, 14, 0, 3, 1, 0). The experimenters reasoned that if the rats had learned only associations between adjacent items or a simple rule about decreasing pellets, then a trial with no pellets in the middle of the sequence should disrupt the rats' performance for the rest of the sequence. What they found, however, was that the no-pellet trials had no detectable effect—running rates on the remaining trials of the sequence were the same as on normal trials. They concluded that in addition to any learning of trial-to-trial associations or a rule about decreasing numbers of pellets, the rats had some understanding of the overall structure of the sequence, so that an occasional odd trial did not disrupt their performance during the rest of the sequence.

## Chunking

A common idea in human cognitive psychology is that memorizing is easier if a long list of information is divided into portions of more manageable size called **chunks** (Miller, 1956). For example, the telephone number 711-2468 consists of seven digits, which is about all that human short-term memory can hold at once. However, the burden on memory is lightened if "711" reminds you of the name of a chain of convenience stores, and if you remember "2468" as the first four even numbers. In this way, the problem of remembering seven pieces of information is reduced to remembering two chunks of information. Many studies of human memory have shown that organizing a list into chunks can help people remember more information more accurately.

Can animals also recognize chunks of information, and can they use the strategy of chunking to help them learn and remember a long list? Various experiments have shown that they can. In a series of experiments, Terrace studied how chunking can help pigeons learn and remember (Terrace, 1991; Terrace & Chen, 1991). The pigeons' task was basically a list-learning exercise: Five stimuli were presented in random locations on a translucent screen, and a pigeon had to peck the five stimuli in the correct order to obtain a food pellet (see Figure 11-8a). Some of the stimuli were different colors, and others were white shapes on a black background (a horizontal line and a diamond). In his first experiment, Terrace (1991) wanted to see whether pigeons could learn the list of five stimuli faster if it were divided into two chunks, with only colors in one chunk and only shapes in the other. Terrace used five groups of pigeons, and each group learned a different list of colors and/or shapes. As Figure 11-8b shows, the list for Group II was nicely divided into two chunks—the first three stimuli were colors, and the last two were shapes. The list for Group IV was divided into one large chunk of four colors, followed by the diamond shape. The lists for the other three groups were not organized into chunks: For Group I, the list had only colors, and for Groups III and V, colors and shapes were intermixed.

As Terrace expected, the two groups that had lists divided into chunks (Groups II and IV) required significantly less practice to learn the correct pecking sequence. In addition to the faster acquisition, Groups II and IV also demonstrated faster performance at the end of their training: They could complete the correct five-peck sequence more quickly. As further evidence that the pigeons in these two groups had divided their lists into two chunks,

**FIGURE 11-8** (a) In Terrace's (1991) experiment, five visual stimuli were arranged randomly in any of eight locations on a rectangular screen, and a pigeon received food only if it pecked the stimuli in exactly the correct sequence. (b) For the five groups of pigeons, the correct sequence is shown. (The letters inside the circles indicate stimuli of different colors: R = red, G = green, B = blue, Y = yellow, V = violet.)

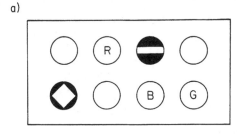

Terrace found that the longest hesitation between pecks occurred at the switch between colors and shapes. For instance, in Group II, the pigeons would peck the three colored stimuli quickly, then hesitate briefly, then peck the two shapes in rapid succession.

In later experiments, Terrace and Chen (1991) found that once pigeons learned a chunk in one list, they could use this chunk in another list. For example, pigeons in an experimental group that first learned a list with chunks, RED-GREEN-YELLOW-line-diamond, were then quick to learn a second list with the same color chunk, RED-GREEN-YELLOW-dots-diagonal lines. (That is, they learned the new list more quickly than a control group that first had to learn a list without chunks, RED-GREEN-YELLOW-BLUE-ORANGE.) Even more interesting was the finding that after learning the three-color chunk, pigeons in the experimental group could use this chunk to help them learn a new list with all colors: RED-GREEN-YELLOW-BROWN-VIOLET. Once again, they learned this new list much faster than pigeons in the control group, even though the first list for both groups began with RED-GREEN-YELLOW. Terrace and Chen concluded that having learned to respond to RED-GREEN-YELLOW as a single chunk, the pigeons in the experimental group could use this chunk in a list which, from an objective standpoint, had no chunks at all.

These experiments show that if a list is already organized into chunks, pigeons can make use of that organization to help them learn the list. Similar results have been obtained with rats (Capaldi, Miller, Alptekin, & Barry, 1990; Stempowski, Carman, & Fountain, 1999). But even if a set of stimuli is not organized into chunks, animals may develop their own chunks if they are free to select items in any order they choose (Macuda & Roberts, 1995). For example, Dallal and Meck (1990) found evidence for chunking by rats in a 12-arm radial maze. Four arms (in different parts of the maze) had sunflower seeds at the end, four had food pellets, and four had rice puffs. For one group of rats, the locations of the different types of food were changed every trial, so there was no consistent pattern for the rats to learn. For a second group, the locations of the different types of food were the same trial after trial. Dallal and Meck found that, with practice, the rats in this second group tended to select the arms in chunks based on the different food types. For example, a rat might first go to the four arms with sunflower seeds, then the four with food pellets, and finally the four with rice puffs. A typical rat's performance was usually not so perfectly organized, but rats in the second group showed a strong tendency to group the arms by food type. As a result, their overall performance in the maze was better than that of the group with random food locations—they made fewer repeat visits to arms where they had already consumed the food. Their improved performance was especially evident when all rats were given four consecutive trials in the same maze on one day. By the second and third trials, the group with random food locations started to make many errors (repeat visits to now-empty arms), presumably because of proactive interference from the previous trial(s). The group with consistent food locations made substantially fewer errors. Dallal and Meck concluded that by chunking the arms of the maze on the basis of food type, these rats were able to decrease the burdens on their working memories and thereby perform more accurately.

All of these studies involved chunking in laboratory situations, but some animals may use chunking as a learning strategy in their natural environments. H. Williams and Staples (1992) studied how young male zebra finches learned songs up to 15 syllables long from older male finches. They found that the older finches tended to divide their songs into chunks of about three syllables, the younger finches would copy these chunks, and eventually they could put the chunks together into a complete song.

Human beings are much better at learning lists than the animals in these experiments. For instance, a child can memorize a list of five items without much effort, but the pigeons in Terrace's experiment required over 100 sessions to do so. Still, the research on chunking by animals adds to our list of similarities between human and animal memory: (1) If a list is already organized into chunks, both animals and people can learn the list faster. (2) If an already-learned chunk reappears in a new list, the new list will be learned even faster. (3) If a set of items is not already organized, both animals and people may group similar items together, and this will help to improve memory and avoid mistakes.

## LANGUAGE AND REASONING

Finding a creative solution to a difficult problem, communicating through language, and engaging in logical reasoning are among the most sophisticated learned behaviors that people can perform. Cognitive psychologists have studied these classes of behavior extensively, almost always with human subjects. Over the years, however, a few psychologists have attempted to determine whether animals are capable of these complex behaviors. Regardless of how this question is ultimately answered, the research with animals should give us a better perspective on the most advanced of human cognitive skills.

### Teaching Language to Animals

Most people would probably credit animals with at least some rudimentary problem-solving abilities, since the challenge of surviving in the wild frequently poses obstacles that demand creative solutions. On the other hand, many have claimed that the ability to use language is one skill that only human beings possess (for example, Chomsky, 1972a). For this reason, attempts to teach language to chimpanzees and other animals have received tremendous attention. This section describes some of the most important studies and discusses some of the controversies that have arisen about animals' linguistic abilities.

***Some Representative Studies.***    In the earliest attempts to teach language to chimpanzees, researchers tried to get the animals to speak (Hayes, 1951; Kellogg & Kellogg, 1933). For the most part, these studies were unsuccessful,

although the chimps eventually learned to say a few words. The main problem was that a chimpanzee's vocal apparatus does not permit it to make many human speech sounds. To avoid this problem, Allen and Beatrice Gardner (1969, 1975) decided to try to teach their chimpanzee, Washoe, to use American Sign Language (ASL). Washoe was about 1 year old when the Gardners obtained her, and she lived in an enclosed yard and a small trailer. She was trained by a number of different people, all of whom were moderately proficient in ASL. The trainers tried to teach Washoe signs, but they also played games with her and got her to participate in a variety of activities. During Washoe's waking hours, a trainer was always with her. By relying on a mixture of modeling, manual guidance, and a good deal of patience, the trainers were able to teach Washoe to produce signs for quite a few different words, including nouns (such as *flower, toothbrush, hat*), verbs (*go, listen, tickle*), adjectives (*sweet, funny, more*), pronouns (*you, me*) and prepositions (*in, out*). To make sure that the trainers were not seeing more in Washoe's signs than was really there, the Gardners conducted tests in which one person showed Washoe a picture of some object while another person, who could not see the picture, watched and interpreted Washoe's response. On these tests, Washoe was often correct on better than 70 percent of the trials. After 4 years with the Gardners, Washoe had learned about 130 signs. This was quite an impressive vocabulary (though still small compared to that of the average 4-year-old child, who knows several thousand words).

After being taught a sign in a few contexts, Washoe sometimes used it in a new context without further training. For instance, she was taught the sign for *more* in combination with a few different signs (including *more tickle* and *more swinging*), and she later began to use the sign to ask for more food and for more of other activities. The Gardners reported that Washoe occasionally used creative combinations of words, as when she signed *water bird* upon seeing a swan (for which she had learned no sign). We cannot assume, however, that Washoe was using this novel phrase to describe the swan, because she was looking at a scene in which both water and a bird were present.

Although Washoe's vocabulary of signs was substantial, and although she frequently used signs in various combinations, the order in which she used the signs in a "sentence" was quite inconsistent. For example, she might sign the phrase *food eat* on some occasions and *eat food* on others, with no apparent reason for the different word orders. In contrast, both children and adults tend to use consistent word orders whether they are using spoken or sign language. In short, Washoe had a good vocabulary but poor (perhaps nonexistent) grammar.

Using a very different training situation, David Premack (1971b, 1983) obtained much more encouraging evidence that chimpanzees can learn at least some rules about grammar and word order. Instead of using ASL, Premack constructed a language consisting of different plastic shapes that represented different words. Sentences were created by placing the shapes (which had metal backings) on a magnetic board in a specific order. Premack's pupil, a 6-year-old chimpanzee named Sarah, learned to respond appropriately to many different configurations of these symbols. Unlike Washoe, who learned ASL in an informal outdoor setting from trainers who were also playmates and companions, Sarah lived in a cage and received more rigorous and systematic training. Sarah's trainers started by teaching her to associate symbols with different objects or events, and they progressed slowly to short sentences and then to longer and more complex ones.

The order of symbols was a critical part of the language Sarah learned, and she demonstrated an impressive ability to respond on the basis of symbol order. For instance, after Sarah learned the symbols for several different colors, her trainer introduced a symbol for *on*. Symbols for *green on red* were put on the board, and then the trainer gave Sarah a green card and got her to place it on top of a red card. Sarah was then taught to produce the opposite response to the symbol sequence *red on green*. Eventually, she learned to respond appropriately to either sequence when given the red and green cards at once. This performance

in itself shows that her responses were controlled by the order of the symbols, not just by the symbols themselves. Having succeeded at this task, Sarah was then able to respond correctly to new symbol strings such as *blue on yellow* with no further training. Sarah had learned not only that the order of symbols was important but that this same order could be applied to other symbols. In a simple way, this example illustrates an understanding of a grammatical rule—an abstract rule about sentence structure that applies to entire classes of words.

In another case where word order was important, Sarah learned to respond to a complex sentence of symbols, *Sarah insert banana pail apple dish*, by putting a banana in a pail and an apple in a dish. To respond correctly, Sarah had to pay attention to word order; otherwise, she would not know what to insert into what. It is instructive to examine some of the training steps that were used to achieve this level of complexity. Once Sarah had learned the relevant symbols, her trainers started with the simpler sentence *Sarah insert banana pail*, and the appropriate response was reinforced. On different trials, symbols for *apple* and *dish* were also used, in different combinations (*banana in dish, apple in pail,* and so on). Later, Sarah was presented with two sentences side by side— *Sarah insert banana pail* and *Sarah insert apple dish*—and she learned to respond to each in turn. Then the two sentences were combined into one long one, *Sarah insert banana pail Sarah insert apple dish*, and in successive steps the symbols we would consider redundant (the second occurrences of *Sarah* and *insert*) were removed.

This example illustrates the type of procedure Premack used to train Sarah to respond appropriately to long and difficult sentences. You may have noticed that this technique is really an advanced version of the familiar operant procedure of successive approximations— each change is just a small step harder than something the subject has already mastered. Premack (1971b) explained that his procedure involved "one-to-one substitution"—each new type of sentence would differ in only one way from sentence forms Sarah had already learned. Using this technique, Premack and his associates trained Sarah to respond appropriately to a wide range of grammatical forms and concepts, including plurals, yes-no questions, and quantifiers (*all, some, none,* and *several*). One disappointing feature of Sarah's performance, however, was that she seldom initiated a conversation. Her use of the symbol language was almost exclusively confined to answering questions posed by the experimenters. Furthermore, if one of her trainers placed a question on the board and then left the room, Sarah would usually either give an incorrect response or none at all. She was hardly bursting with enthusiasm about the power of her newly acquired communication skills, eager to use them wherever she could. This behavior contrasts quite starkly with that of young children, who spontaneously practice and use the words they have learned, whether anyone is listening or not.

In addition to the work of the Gardners and Premack, there have been many other attempts to teach language to chimpanzees and other primates, including a gorilla and an orangutan (for example, Miles, 1983; Patterson, 1978; Rumbaugh, 1977; Savage-Rumbaugh, 1984). ASL has been used in some cases, and pictorial symbols in others. Some research with chimpanzees has also used spoken English words. The animals could not learn to speak, of course, but they did demonstrate an understanding of the words spoken by humans (Brakke & Savage-Rumbaugh, 1995). In many of these studies, the animals were able to learn well over a hundred signs. Patterson and Linden (1981) reported that a gorilla named Koko had mastered over 400 signs. There have also been some studies with nonprimates. Herman, Richards, and Wolz (1984) trained two bottlenosed dolphins to respond to about two dozen manual gestures by engaging in the appropriate activities. For example, a trainer might make the gestures for *frisbee fetch basket,* and the dolphin would then find the frisbee and put it in the basket. The dolphins could also answer questions about whether a particular object was or was not present in the tank (Herman & Forestell, 1985). Similar work has been done with sea lions (Schusterman & Krieger, 1984). And the parrot Alex, whose counting abilities have already been

A Web site devoted to Pepperberg's research on Alex the parrot can be found at: *http://www.cages.org/research/pepperberg/index.html.*

described, learned to say about 50 English words and use them appropriately to make requests ("Gimme tickle") and answer questions (Trainer: "What's this?"; Alex: "Clothespin"). Alex could also answer questions about the physical properties of objects, describing either an object's shape or color depending on what question his trainer asked (Pepperberg, 1983, 1999).

***Criticisms.*** Despite these accomplishments, some have argued that the ways these animals learned to use signs are not really comparable to human language. One researcher who has articulated this view quite forcefully is Herbert Terrace (1979, 1985). Over a 4-year period, Terrace and his associates taught ASL to a chimpanzee who was called Nim Chimpsky (a name with a curious resemblance to that of Noam Chomsky, the linguist who claimed that only people can learn language). Nim's training sessions were frequently videotaped so that his signs and the context in which they occurred could later be carefully analyzed. In many respects, Nim's performance was impressive. He learned about 125 signs for nouns, verbs, adjectives, pronouns, and prepositions. He frequently used these signs in combinations of two or more, and Terrace's analysis revealed that Nim had learned to use some primitive grammatical rules. The evidence for grammatical rules was the consistency of sign order in Nim's two-sign "sentences." For example, of all the two-sign sentences that included the sign for *more,* this sign occurred first in 85 percent of the cases (*more drink, more tickle,* and so on). Similarly, when Nim used the sign for *me* in combination with a transitive verb (*hug, give*), *me* occurred in the second position 83 percent of the time. This consistency of sign order also occurred at a more general level involving whole classes of words of similar grammatical categories. For instance, when Nim made a two-sign sentence including an action and an agent, the sign for the action usually came first, whereas in sentences involving an action and a place, the sign for the action usually came second. This consistency of sign order suggested that Nim was following certain grammatical rules (though not necessarily those used in the English language) in his two-sign sentences.

Unfortunately, in Nim's sequences of three or more signs, inconsistency was the rule. For example, in three-sign sequences involving *eat, me, Nim,* and *more,* these signs occurred in almost every possible order. Out of a large sample of Nim's behavior, *me more eat* and *more eat Nim* both occurred 19 times, *eat me Nim* 48 times, *Nim me eat* 27 times, *eat Nim eat* 46 times, and *me Nim eat* 21 times. As Terrace pointed out, Nim's sequences of signs were different from the short sentences spoken by a typical 2- or 3-year-old child in several ways. First, there was no consistency of word order. Second, there were pointless repetitions of signs, and redundant signs (*me* and *Nim* used in a single sequence). Third, the average length of Nim's sign sequences (corresponding to what psycholinguists call the **mean length of utterance**) leveled off at about 1.5 signs per sequence and never increased again. In contrast, a child's mean length of utterance steadily increases with age. Fourth, when a child's sentences increase in length, the amount of information conveyed by each sentence also increases, but this was not the case with Nim. When Nim did produce a longer sequence of signs, it tended to include only repetitions of a few signs, in no particular order. An extreme example is the longest string the experimenters recorded, involving 16 signs: *give orange me give eat orange me eat orange give me eat orange give me you.* No ordinary child, whether speaking or using ASL, would ever produce such a redundant and chaotic string of words.

Terrace (1979) also reported that Nim's performance differed from a typical child's in

other ways. The proportion of a child's utterances that are full or partial repetitions of what an adult just said decreases with age. Nim's repetitions, however, increased from an already high 38 percent when he was 26 months old to 54 percent at 44 months. In addition, only a small percentage of Nim's utterances were spontaneous; most were immediately preceded by a sign from his trainer. In fact, Nim frequently interrupted his trainer by starting to gesture while the trainer was in the middle of a sequence of signs. This suggests that Nim did not understand the turn-taking character of most human conversation.

Based on his analyses of Nim's behavior, as well as those of Washoe, Sarah, and other chimps, Terrace (1979) concluded that the "language" these animals had learned lacked many of the essential characteristics of human language. He asserted that the chimps had learned only the most primitive grammatical rules, and that for the most part they would string together signs in a random order. They relied heavily on imitation and on prompting by their trainers, and showed little spontaneous use of language. The complexity of their utterances did not increase with additional training. Not surprisingly, some have agreed with the general tone of Terrace's evaluation of the chimp language projects (R. Brown, 1985), whereas others have strongly disagreed (Premack, 1986; Rumbaugh, Savage-Rumbaugh, & Sevcik, 1994).

***Some Tentative Conclusions.*** Terrace was almost surely correct in saying that, so far, the linguistic capacities that animals have demonstrated are quite limited compared to those of humans. On the positive side, however, two points can be made. First, this research has shown that animals have at least some measure of linguistic ability. Animals of several species have demonstrated the ability to use words, signs, or symbols to represent objects, actions, and descriptions. Second, the limitations of the initial research could prove to be more the fault of the training and testing procedures used than of the animals themselves. Even if it is correct to say that no ape has yet generated a "true sentence" (Terrace, Petitto, Sanders, &

Bever, 1979), it would be foolhardy to claim that no ape can ever be taught to do so.

Evidence is starting to accumulate that Terrace's assessment of animal language abilities may have been too pessimistic. Although Nim and some of the other chimpanzees may have relied heavily on imitation, Miles (1983) has reported that an orangutan named Chantek, who had learned a few dozen signs, almost never engaged in direct imitation. Although Nim and other chimps seldom initiated a conversation, over one third of Chantek's utterances were classified as "spontaneous"—not immediately preceded by a trainer's utterance. In addition, the mean length of Chantek's utterances, unlike those of Nim, steadily increased over a period of about 16 months. In another example of the spontaneous use of symbols, two pygmy chimpanzees (not the same species as ordinary chimpanzees) learned to use several dozen pictorial symbols on a keyboard without any explicit training by humans. These animals learned by watching others use these symbols, and they could use the symbols to refer to objects and events not present (Savage-Rumbaugh, McDonald, Sevcik, Hopkins, & Rubert, 1986). There is also growing evidence that a number of different species (pygmy chimpanzees, dolphins, and parrots) can learn at least some basic principles of grammar, such as the use of prepositions and demonstratives (Herman & Uyeyama, 1999; Kako, 1999).

Terrace (1979) has claimed that language-trained animals used their language only to obtain reinforcers, not to communicate information. However, a number of subsequent findings suggest that these animals do sometimes use their signs to communicate with other animals or with people. Fouts, Fouts, and Schoenfield (1984) reported that five chimpanzees who had been taught ASL signs would use these signs to communicate with one another, even when no human beings were present to prompt or reinforce these behaviors. Greenfield and Savage-Rumbaugh (1993) found that two different species of chimpanzees used the symbols they were taught by humans to express a variety of different functions, such as agreement, requests, and promises. These chimpanzees often displayed the sort of turn-taking in the use of symbols that is typical of human conversations. Two other studies found that chimpanzees can use their signs to describe behaviors they have just performed, or are about to perform (Premack, 1986; Savage-Rumbaugh, 1984). It therefore seems that some features of language that may have been absent from the early chimpanzee studies—spontaneity, use of signs purely for the sake of communication, and reference to objects and events not present—have in fact been found in subsequent studies. Given this trend, it seems likely that future research will find additional similarities in the ways people and animals can learn to use language.

## Reasoning by Animals

This topic follows naturally from the preceding discussion, because many of the tests of animals' reasoning abilities have been conducted with animals who have first been given some training in language. Premack (1983, 1988) has found that language-trained chimpanzees can succeed on some reasoning tasks that non–language-trained chimpanzees cannot. On other tasks, however, language-trained and non–language-trained animals perform identically. Premack attempted to explain these differences by proposing that language training, with its use of abstract symbols, gives chimpanzees a vocabulary for describing relations among objects rather than simply responding to the physical properties of objects. In Premack's terms, non–language-trained chimpanzees use only an **imaginal code** (one related to the visual properties of objects), whereas language-trained chimpanzees learn to use an **abstract code.** On tasks that can be solved with an imaginal code, chimps with and without language training can perform equally well. If the task requires an understanding of abstract relations, however, only language-trained animals will succeed. Premack's theory is controversial, but it is certainly worth examining in more detail. We will look at some reasoning tasks for which language training makes a difference, and some for which it does not.

### Reasoning about the Locations of Objects.
Premack (1983) described an experiment in which chimpanzees faced the following situation. A chimp was shown two containers at opposite ends of a room, and the chimp watched as a trainer placed an apple in one container and a banana in the other. The chimp was then briefly taken out of the room, and when she returned she saw the trainer standing in the middle of the room, eating either an apple or a banana. The trainer then left, and the chimp was allowed to go to either of the two containers. Would the chimp infer that the fruit the trainer was eating was from one of the containers, and would she therefore go to the other container?

Premack's chimps (all of whom were at least 6 years old) made the correct choice on this type of problem, both those that had received language training and those that had not. Premack argued that all chimps were able to solve this problem because, even without language training, they have the ability to reason about physical similarity and object locations: They could infer that the fruit the trainer was eating was the same as the fruit that had been placed in one of the containers. Although this problem may not require an understanding of abstract relations, it is not trivially easy. As a point of comparison, Premack found that 5-year-old children also succeed on this task, whereas some children who are 4 years old or younger do not—they are just as likely to go to either container.

### Object Permanence.
Related to the preceding topic is the concept of **object permanence,** an understanding that objects continue to exist even when they are not visible. The developmental psychologist Jean Piaget proposed that during the first 2 years of life, human infants proceed through six different stages, in which their understanding of object permanence becomes more and more complete. In the sixth stage, a child will search for a hidden toy until it is found because the child understands that the toy has not ceased to exist just because it is not seen.

Piaget developed a series of tests to determine which of the six stages an infant has reached, and these tests can be adapted quite easily for use with animals. Research with a number of different species, including cats and dogs, has shown that they follow more or less the same sequence of stages as human infants, eventually reaching stage six (Dore & Dumas, 1987). This level of competence is not limited to mammals, because Pepperberg and Funk (1990) found that birds of four different species (a parrot, a macaw, a cockatiel, and a parakeet) could also solve stage-six problems. For example, a cockatiel might watch a trainer hide a small toy in her hand and then move her hand under three different pieces of newspaper (so the bird could not see where the toy was hidden). The bird might then search under the last piece of newspaper, or it might search systematically under each piece of newspaper in succession. Pepperberg and Funk found that these birds showed about the same level of competence as Alex, the language-trained parrot. They concluded that language training is not necessary for animals to correctly solve problems involving object permanence.

### Analogies.
An analogy is a statement of the form "A is to B as C is to D." To test someone's ability to understand analogies, we can give the person two or more choices for D and ask which is correct. For example, consider the analogy, "Lock is to key as can is to _____." Is *paint brush* or *can opener* a more appropriate answer? On this type of problem, the ability to make judgments about physical similarity is usually not enough. In physical terms, a can opener is not especially similar to a key, a lock, or a can. To solve this analogy, one must understand (1) the relation between lock and key, (2) the relation between can opener and can, and (3) the similarity of the two relations (that is, that the second item of each pair is used to open the first). In other words, to understand an analogy, one must be able to understand a relation (similarity) between two relations.

Gillan, Premack, and Woodruff (1981) tested Sarah, the language-trained chimpanzee, with analogies that involved either perceptual relations or functional relations between objects. The analogy in the previous paragraph involves functional relations because it requires an understanding of the functions the different objects serve, and it was one of the analogies given to Sarah (see Figure 11-9). An example of a perceptual analogy is the following: Large yellow triangle is to small yellow triangle as large red crescent is to (small red crescent or small yellow crescent)? This analogy also requires an understanding of the relations between objects, but in this case the relations pertain only to the perceptual properties of the objects (their relative sizes).

Sarah was fairly successful at solving both types of analogies. In contrast, non–language-trained chimpanzees were never significantly better than chance (50 percent correct), even though they were tested on very simple perceptual analogies. This finding is consistent with Premack's hypothesis that without language, an animal cannot understand abstract relations between objects.

**FIGURE 11-9**  Pictures presented to the chimpanzee Sarah, which represent the analogy, "Lock is to key as can is to what?" Two possible answers, can opener and paint brush, were presented below the line, and Sarah chose the correct answer.

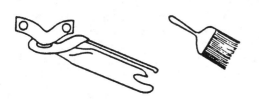

*Transitive Inference.*  If Alex is shorter than Bill, and if Bill is shorter than Carl, then it follows that Alex is shorter than Carl. This conclusion is justified because inequalities of size are **transitive.** That is, they conform to the following general rule: if A < B and B < C, then A < C. If we draw the correct conclusion about the heights of Alex and Carl without ever having seen them side by side, we are displaying the capacity for **transitive inference.**

Gillan (1981) tested whether three non–language-trained chimpanzees were capable of transitive inference by first training them with containers of different colors, which had food in some situations but not others. For instance, one chimp was taught that blue was better than black, black was better than red, and so on. In the test for transitive inference, a chimp had to choose between two containers that had never been paired before. For instance, when given a choice between blue and red, would the chimp choose blue? Gillan found that the chimps were capable of making such inferences. Premack claimed that this result is neither evidence for or against his theory, because this type of problem can be solved by using either abstract reasoning or visual imagery (for instance, by imagining the different colored containers in a row, and choosing the container closest to the "better" end of the row). Premack's view is that whereas only language-trained chimps are capable of abstract reasoning, those without language training can solve this problem using the simpler visual strategy.

Actually, it appears that neither language training nor a primate brain is required to solve this type of problem. Studies using tests similar to Gillan's have demonstrated this same type of transitive inference in both rats (Davis, 1992; W. A. Roberts & Phelps, 1994) and pigeons (von Fersen, Wynne, Delius, & Staddon, 1991). There are different theories about how animals are able to master this task, but there is general agreement that they can (Zentall & Sherburne, 1994; Wynne, 1995).

*Conclusions.*  Chimpanzees with language training seem to be capable of solving at least some reasoning tasks that chimpanzees without language training cannot. It is not yet clear exactly why this is so. Premack has argued that language training teaches chimpanzees to use an abstract code instead of (or in addition to) an imaginal code. Others have concluded, however, that language training simply makes the chimps better test-takers, since this training involves extensive experience with answering questions, following instructions, and so on (Thompson, Oden, & Boysen, 1997). One study with rhesus monkeys demonstrated the big difference that test-taking experience can make. Both young and elderly monkeys were given a variety of discrimination and concept-formation tests. Some of the elderly monkeys were experienced test-takers, and some were not. The experimenters found that the inexperienced elderly monkeys performed more poorly than juvenile monkeys, whereas the experienced elderly monkeys outperformed the juveniles on many tasks (Novak, Suomi, Bowman, & Mohr, 1991).

Premack has also proposed that only primates are capable of using an abstract code, and that therefore only primates are capable of abstract reasoning. This claim has met even more strenuous opposition. Many lines of evidence suggest that nonprimates can learn a variety of tasks that involve abstract reasoning. These include the learning of natural concepts by several species of birds (Chapter 10), accurate counting of objects by a parrot, and language learning by dolphins and sea lions. It seems likely that more examples of abstract reasoning will be found in other species in future research.

Perhaps the moral is that it is always risky to claim, "Here is a problem in abstract reasoning that only humans (or only primates) can solve." The danger is that some clever researcher will find a way to teach a bird or ro-

dent to solve exactly that problem. Although no one would seriously question the vast differences between human and nonhuman intellectual abilities, some of the apparent limitations of animals' reasoning abilities might be attributed to deficiencies in current training or testing procedures, not to the animals.

## CHAPTER SUMMARY

Two procedures used to study short-term memory in animals are delayed matching to sample (DMTS) and the radial-arm maze. In DMTS, performance accuracy declines quickly as the delay between sample and comparison stimuli increases. Studies using radial-arm mazes have shown that rats can generally avoid repeat visits to arms of a maze where they have already collected the food, even when a maze has as many as 17 arms. Other studies have found evidence for both maintenance rehearsal and associative rehearsal in animals. Experiments on long-term memory have shown that pigeons can remember several hundred slides with a high degree of accuracy. Other studies have demonstrated that long-term memory can be improved if an animal is given an appropriate stimulus as a reminder of a previous learning experience.

A variety of experiments on timing has demonstrated that the duration of a stimulus can control an animal's behavior with reasonable accuracy, and so can the number of stimuli. Animals can also detect repeating serial patterns of stimuli, and they can learn lists of stimuli through chunking.

When researchers have tried to teach language to animals, the responses resemble human language abilities in some respects but not in others. Some chimpanzees have learned to use over 100 signs or symbols for words, but they seldom use any consistent word order or grammar. David Premack obtained better grammar from a chimpanzee by reinforcing only the correct word order (using different plastic shapes to represent words). Other studies have shown that several species (the gorilla, the dolphin, and the parrot) can learn the meanings of gestures, symbols, or spoken words.

A list of resources on animal cognition is maintained by Dr. Robert Cook at *http://www.pigeon.psy.tufts.edu/psych26/alinks.htm*.

Premack proposed that chimpanzees that receive language training can use a type of abstract reasoning that nontrained chimpanzees cannot, and some studies have supported his theory. However, other studies have found signs of abstract reasoning ability in animals without language training. For instance, pigeons can solve problems of transitive inference, and cats, dogs, and birds can perform tasks involving object permanence.

## REVIEW QUESTIONS

1. Describe how delayed matching to sample and the radial-arm maze can be used to study animal short-term memory, and discuss some of the main findings that have been obtained with these procedures.

2. What are maintenance rehearsal and associative rehearsal? Describe one experiment that appears to demonstrate each type of rehearsal in animals.

3. Describe some experiments on animal timing, counting, and chunking abilities, and discuss their results.

4. Describe the strengths and the limitations of the language abilities of chimpanzees trained to use American Sign Language. How did Premack's procedures differ from the sign-language studies, and what did he find? What did Premack conclude about chimpanzees that are given language training?

## CHAPTER 12

# Learning
# by Observation

Let there be no mistake about it: A large proportion of human learning occurs, not through classical conditioning or as a result of reinforcement or punishment, but through observation. Two psychologists whose writings and experiments repeatedly emphasized this fact are Albert Bandura and Richard H. Walters. In their classic book, *Social Learning and Personality Development* (1963), Bandura and Walters argued that traditional learning theory was grossly incomplete because it neglected the role of observational learning. As we have seen, traditional learning theory emphasizes the importance of individual experience: An individual performs some behavior and experiences the consequences that follow. The point of Bandura and Walters is that a good deal of learning occurs through vicarious rather than personal experience: We observe the behavior of others, observe the consequences, and later we may imitate their behavior. In short, Bandura and Walters claim that the traditional approach to learning, which stresses personal experience and practice, is insufficient—it can account for some types of learning but not all.

As the title of their book implies, Bandura and Walters were interested in how people develop different personalities (for instance, why some people are extroverted and others intro-verted, some peaceful and others aggressive, some industrious and others lazy). They suggested that while some personality differences have a hereditary basis, most are due to an individual's learning experiences. They rejected the Freudian or psychodynamic approach to personality, which emphasizes the interactions of unconscious psychic forces in determining an adult's personality. Like Freud, Bandura and Walters believed that early childhood experiences can have a profound influence on adult personality, but they proposed that these experiences exerted their influence through the principles of **social learning theory.** By social learning theory, Bandura and Walters meant a combination of (1) the traditional principles of classical and operant conditioning, plus (2) the principles of **observational learning,** or **imitation.** Thus, they felt that they were not rejecting the principles of traditional learning theory but rather were adding one more important principle of learning to the list.

Later in this chapter we will examine some of a large body of evidence collected by Bandura and Walters and others that shows that observational learning is indeed an important contributor to personality differences among individuals. To begin, however, we will survey a number of different theories about why imitation occurs in the first place.

## THEORIES OF IMITATION

### Imitation as an Instinct

Some early psychologists suggested that people and other animals have an innate propensity to imitate behaviors they see others perform (McDougall, 1908; Morgan, 1896). William James (1890) stated: "This sort of imitativeness is possessed by man in common with other gregarious animals, and is an instinct in the fullest sense of the term . . ." (p. 408). This belief that imitation was an innate tendency stemmed in part from evidence that young infants may imitate the movements of an adult. For instance, McDougall (1908) reported that his 4-month-old son would stick out his tongue when an adult in front of the child did the same. Of course, it is possible that the infant might have learned this response because it was reinforced (with the smiles and laughter of adults). More recent research provides much stronger evidence for an innate tendency to imitate.

In some carefully controlled experiments, Meltzoff and Moore (1977, 1983) sought to determine whether 12- to 21-day-old infants would imitate any of four gestures made by an adult tester—lip protrusion, mouth opening, tongue protrusion, and sequential finger movement. The tester made one of these gestures at a time, then waited to see whether the infant would copy it. The infant's behavior was videotaped and subsequently scored by people who did not know which of the four gestures the infant had observed on a given trial. Meltzoff and Moore found a reliable tendency for the infants to imitate the specific behavior that they had just seen. Because of the young ages of these infants, it seems very unlikely that such imitative behaviors had been reinforced by their parents. In fact, all of the parents claimed that they had never seen imitative behavior in their infants, and most felt that it was not possible at such a young age.

The results of Meltzoff and Moore have been replicated several times, and it is now fairly clear that newborn infants have a tendency to repeat certain gestures made by adults, especially tongue protrusion (Field, Woodson, Greenberg, & Cohen, 1982). There is disagreement over how to interpret this behavior, however, and some researchers have suggested that it does not necessarily show that infants have a general ability to imitate gestures (Anisfeld, 1991). One hypothesis is that imitation of lip protrusion (and possibly a few other facial expressions) is an inborn fixed-action pattern (as described in Chapter 3), which is triggered when the infant sees someone else make the same gesture. However, Meltzoff and Moore (1989) believe that their findings may be evidence of a general ability to imitate gestures and movements. If so, this ability is a remarkable one, because it suggests that humans are born with the capacity to associate a visual input (the sight of an adult making a certain gesture) with a set of muscle movements that allows the infant to mimic that visual input. Notice that the infant cannot see its own face when it opens its mouth or sticks out its tongue. Indeed, most of the infants studied by Meltzoff and Moore probably had never seen their own faces in a mirror. More research is needed to determine whether newborn infants have the ability to imitate a wide range of different gestures and facial expressions or just a few special ones, such as lip protrusion.

As the quotation from William James showed, he believed that other animals were also capable of learning by imitation. In the last 100 years, hundreds of experiments on imitation by animals have been conducted, with such diverse subjects as primates, cats, dogs, rodents, birds, and fish (see M. Robert, 1990; Whiten & Ham, 1992). The learning tasks in these studies span quite a large range of complexity, and it will be helpful to consider three categories of observational learning proposed by Thorpe (1963).

The simplest of Thorpe's categories is **social facilitation,** in which the behavior of one individual prompts a similar behavior from another individual, but the behavior is one that is *already in the repertoire* of the imitator. For instance, Turner (1964) exposed newly hatched chicks to a mechanical "hen" that pecked at a piece of grain that was orange for some chicks and green for others. Turner found that the chicks pecked at grain of the same color about twice as frequently as grain of the other color. (The kernels were glued to the floor, so that the chicks' pecking responses would not be reinforced by the ingestion of food.) This example of imitation is labeled social facilitation because the chicks already knew how to peck. Similarly, Wyrwicka (1978) trained mother cats to eat some unusual foods (bananas and mashed potatoes), and their kittens also began to eat these foods.

Thorpe's second category of observational learning is **local enhancement,** in which the behavior of a model directs the attention of the learner to a particular object or place in the environment. As a result, a response that might otherwise have been learned through trial and error is acquired more rapidly. For instance, Warden, Fjeld, and Koch (1940) trained some monkeys to earn food reinforcers by making responses such as pulling a chain. An untrained monkey was then placed in an identical test chamber adjacent to the chamber with a trained monkey. In many cases, the untrained monkey would observe the other monkey make the required response and immediately imitate it. The untrained monkeys would probably have eventually learned the correct responses by trial and error, but their learning was accelerated by watching another, more experienced monkey. Local enhancement has also been observed in birds (S. B. Johnson, Hamm, & Leahey, 1986). It is not necessary for the model to be the same species as the learner. Bullock and Neuringer (1977) found that pigeons could learn to produce a two-response chain (pecking two keys in a specific order) by observing a human hand demonstrate the appropriate sequence.

Thorpe's third category of imitation, which he called **true imitation,** is not clearly distinguishable from local enhancement, but it refers to the imitation of a behavior pattern that is very unusual or improbable for the species, so that it would seldom be learned through trial and error. Kawai (1965) described several examples of true imitation observed in a troop of monkeys living on an island off the coast of Japan. For example, when grains of wheat were spread along the beach, the monkeys would pick them out of the sand one by one and eat them. However, one monkey learned to separate the wheat from the sand more efficiently by picking up a handful of the mixture and throwing it in the water. The sand would sink and the wheat would float, so it could be collected easily. Soon many of the other monkeys of the troop were imitating this behavior. Kawai reported that several other novel behaviors spread quickly through the troop as a result of observational learning, including washing the sand off sweet potatoes and bathing in the ocean (which the monkeys had never done until one pioneer took up this activity). Examples of true imitation have also been seen in gorillas and orangutans. Orangutans in captivity have imitated many complex behaviors of their human caretakers, such as "sweeping and weeding paths, mixing ingredients for pancakes, tying up hammocks and riding in them, and washing dishes or laundry" (Byrne & Russon, 1998, p. 678).

Anecdotal evidence reported by Fisher and Hinde (1949) seems to provide a convincing example of true imitation by birds. In 1921, residents of a village in southern England first reported that some birds had begun to obtain milk by piercing the covers of milk bottles left out on doorsteps. Over several years, this behavior spread through parts of England, Ireland, Wales, and Scotland, and it was observed in several different species of birds. Since it makes little sense to propose that all of these birds suddenly learned this behavior on their own, the behavior must have been acquired

Short videos showing observational learning by a chimpanzee can be viewed at *http:// epsych.wsstate.edu/adaptive/LearningBy Observation/index.html.*

and transmitted through observational learning. More recently, researchers have reported examples of true imitation in rats and other species (for example, Heyes, Jaldow, & Dawson, 1994).

In summary, the ability to learn through observation is by no means unique to human beings, and the tendency to imitate the behavior of others can be observed at a very young age in many species. There seems to be some truth to the claims of early psychologists that the tendency to imitate is instinctive. The problem with this account, however, is that it tells us nothing about when imitation will occur and when it will not. More recent theories of imitation have tried to answer this question.

## Imitation as an Operant Response

In a well-known book, N. E. Miller and Dollard (1941) claimed that observational learning is not an additional type of learning (besides classical and operant conditioning) but rather that it is simply a special case of operant conditioning. We have already seen that discriminative stimuli play a crucial role in operant conditioning both inside and outside the laboratory. For instance, a laboratory animal may learn to make one response in the presence of a red light, another response in the presence of a green light, and yet another response in the presence of a yellow light. (A person driving a car has also learned different responses to these three stimuli.) According to Miller and Dollard, observational learning involves situations where the discriminative stimulus is the behavior of another person, and the appropriate response just happens to be a similar behavior on the part of the observer.

One of Miller and Dollard's many experiments will illustrate their approach. First-grade children participated in this experiment in pairs, with one child being the "leader" and the other the "learner." On each of several trials, the two children would enter a room in which there were two chairs with a large box on top of each. The leader was instructed in advance to go to one of the two boxes, where there might be a piece of candy. The learner

could see where the leader went, but not whether the leader obtained any candy. Next, it was the learner's turn to go to one of the two boxes, where he or she might or might not find a piece of candy. Half of the learners were in an *imitation group*—they were reinforced for making the same choice as the leader. The other learners were in the *nonimitation group*—they obtained reinforcement if their choice was opposite that of the leader.

The result of this simple experiment was not surprising: After a few trials, children in the imitation group always copied the response of the leader, and those in the nonimitation group always made the opposite response. Miller and Dollard concluded that, like any other operant response, imitation will occur if an individual is reinforced for imitating. Conversely, nonimitation will occur if nonimitation is reinforced. In both cases, the behavior of some other person is the discriminative stimulus that indicates what response is appropriate. Similar follow-the-leader behavior has been observed in rats and other animals (see Hake, Donaldson, & Hyten, 1983). According to Miller and Dollard, then, imitative learning fits nicely into the Skinnerian three-term contingency of discriminative stimulus, response, and reinforcement. There is no need to claim that observational learning is a separate class of learning that is different from operant conditioning.

## Imitation as a Generalized Operant Response

As Bandura (1969) has pointed out, Miller and Dollard's analysis of imitation applies only to those instances in which a learner (1) observes the behavior of a model, (2) immediately copies the response, and (3) receives reinforcement. Many everyday examples of imitation do not follow this pattern. For instance, suppose a little girl watches her mother make herself a bowl of cereal: The mother takes a bowl out of the cabinet, pours in the cereal, and then adds milk and sugar. The next day, when the mother is not in the kitchen, the girl may decide to make herself a bowl of cereal, and she may do so successfully. Here we have an example of imitation, of learning by observation, but notice that if the girl had never performed this sequence of behaviors before, she obviously could not have been reinforced for these behaviors. This example therefore illustrates a case of learning without prior practice of the response and without prior reinforcement.

Just as the principle of reinforcement cannot explain why a rat makes its first lever press (before receiving any reinforcers for that behavior), it cannot, *by itself*, explain the first occurrence of any response learned by observation. However, the principle of reinforcement can account for some instances of novel behavior if we now include the concept of generalization. That is, some novel responses may be nothing more than variations of similar responses that have been reinforced in the past. Chapter 6 showed that reinforcing one response can serve to strengthen an entire class of similar responses. In Lashley's (1924) experiment, after rats had been reinforced for wading correctly through a water maze, they were able to swim through the same maze with deeper water without further training. We might say that the correct swimming responses were the result of generalization from previously learned wading responses. In a similar fashion, we could propose that the young girl had been previously reinforced for imitating the behavior of her parents, and so her imitation of the behaviors involved in making a bowl of cereal is nothing more than an example of generalization. This explanation seems plausible considering that most parents frequently reinforce their children for imitation. Imitating a parent's behavior of speaking a word or phrase, of solving a puzzle, of holding a spoon correctly, and the like, may be reinforced with smiles, hugs, and praise. It would not be surprising if this history of reinforcement led to the imitation of other behaviors.

Generalized imitation has been demonstrated in a number of experiments. For example, Baer, Peterson, and Sherman (1967) reinforced several profoundly retarded children for imitating a variety of behaviors performed by the teacher (standing up, nodding yes, opening a door). After establishing imitative responses

(which required several sessions), the teacher occasionally performed various new behaviors, and the children would also imitate these behaviors although they were never reinforced for doing so. A study with normal infants about 1 year old found that they could learn to imitate the sounds made by their parents, and that this imitation increased if the parents reinforced it with praise (Poulson, Kymissis, Reeve, Andreatos, & Reeve, 1991). This type of generalized vocal imitation may play an important part in a child's language learning. Other studies have also demonstrated generalized imitative behavior (Kymissis & Poulson, 1994; Weisberg, Stout, Hendler, 1986).

## Bandura's Theory of Imitation

Bandura has maintained that the theory of generalized imitation, like the other theories of imitation, is inadequate. His reasons can be nicely illustrated by considering a famous experiment on the imitation of aggressive behaviors by 4-year-olds (Bandura, 1965). The children participated in the experiment individually. Each child first watched a short film (projected onto a TV screen) in which an adult performed four distinctive aggressive behaviors against a large Bobo doll. For each aggressive behavior, the adult spoke distinctive words. For example, in one segment, the adult sat on the doll and punched it in the face, while saying, "Pow, right in the nose, boom, boom."

Some of the children then saw the adult model being reinforced by another adult: He was given soda, candies, and other snacks and was called a "strong champion." Other children saw the model being punished for his aggressive behavior: The model was scolded for "picking on that clown," was spanked, and was warned not to act that way again. For children in a third group, the film contained no consequences for the model's aggressive behavior.

Immediately after viewing the film, a child was brought into a room that contained a Bobo doll and many other toys. The child was encouraged to play with the toys and was left alone in the room, but was observed through a one-way mirror. Many instances of aggressive behaviors against the Bobo doll were recorded, and most of these resembled those of the adult model in the film (see Figure 12-1). In many cases, the children's words were also similar to those used by the model. Boys exhibited significantly more aggression than girls.

So far, these results do not contradict the theory of generalized imitation, but Bandura claimed that two additional findings cannot be explained by this theory. First, the consequences to the model made a difference—children who saw the model being punished exhibited less imitation than children in the other two groups. According to Bandura, the theory of generalized imitation states that children (or adults) imitate others *because imitation has been reinforced in the past,* but it says nothing about how reinforcement or punishment *of the model* should affect the learner. Second, in the final phase of Bandura's study, the experimenter offered to reward the child if he or she would imitate the behavior of the model in the film. With this incentive, children in all three groups produced large and equal amounts of aggressive behavior. Bandura concluded that reinforcement is not necessary for the *learning* of new behaviors through observation, but that the expectation of reinforcement is essential for the *performance* of these new behaviors. Bandura claimed that the theory of generalized imitation makes no provisions for distinguishing between the learning and the performance of imitative behaviors.

Before trying to decide whether Bandura's criticisms of the generalized imitation theory are justified, let us examine the theory he proposes as an alternative. Bandura's (1969, 1986) theory can definitely be called a cognitive theory, for it proposes several processes that can never be observed in an individual's behavior. It states that there are four factors that determine whether imitative behavior will occur:

1. *Attentional Processes.* The learner must pay attention to the appropriate features of the

**FIGURE 12-1**  The top row shows frames from a film in which an adult model exhibits a number of different aggressive behaviors toward a Bobo doll. The two bottom rows show children imitating the model after having watched the film. (From Bandura, Ross, & Ross, 1963)

model's behavior if imitation is to occur. A young girl may watch her mother make a bowl of cereal, but if she did not pay attention to where the sugar came from and how much to put in, she may be quite unsuccessful in her attempt at imitation.

2. *Retentional Processes.* It is obvious that an individual must retain some of the information that is gained through observation if imitation is to occur at a later time. Bandura states that rehearsal can be important here. Thus the little girl may say to herself, "First the cereal, then the milk, then the sugar." Notice that this information is stated in a fairly abstract way, and Bandura assumes that some abstraction of this type is indeed all that is remembered. Thus the child may not remember exactly where in the refrigerator the milk was, or exactly where on the table her mother placed the bowl, but such specific information is not usually necessary for successful imitation.

3. *Motor Reproductive Processes.* It is obvious that the learner must have the appropriate motor skills in order to imitate a model. In other words, the learner must be able to translate general knowledge ("Put a bowl on the table"; "Pour in some cereal") into a coordinated pattern of muscle movements. In the examples of children making cereal or hitting a Bobo doll, this translation of knowledge into action poses no problem, because the children already possessed the required motor skills (handling objects, pouring, kicking, punching, and so on). In other cases of observational learning, however, the motor reproductive processes must not be taken for granted. For example, a model may demonstrate slowly and in a step-by-step manner the sequence of movements involved in juggling three balls, and the learner may retain this information in an abstract form (that is, he or she may be able to recite the necessary sequences), but may still be unable to produce the appropriate movements without extensive practice. Similarly, imitating such behaviors as doing a cartwheel, landing an airplane, or smoothly plastering a wall may be impossible because the observer lacks the necessary motor skills. Chapter 13 will have more to say about how these skills are learned.

4. *Incentive and Motivational Processes.* According to Bandura, the first three processes are all that are necessary for an individual to acquire the capability to perform some new behavior, but this capability will not be reflected in the learner's behavior without the appropriate incentive. Bandura states that the individual must have an expectation that the performance of this new behavior will produce some type of reinforcement. Bandura's (1965) study on aggressive behavior provided a clear example of the role of incentive. Children who saw the adult model being punished for his aggressive play with the Bobo doll presumably developed the expectation that such behavior would lead to unpleasant consequences, so they exhibited less imitation than the other groups of children. When the experimenter changed the expectations of the children by offering reinforcement if the children imitated the model, these children exhibited just as much imitation as the other two groups. These results are similar to those of the Tolman and Honzik (1930) latent learning experiment (Chapter 9), in which rats displayed their ability to run through a maze without errors only after food became available in the goal box.

## Which Theory of Imitation Is Best?

As we have seen, the theory that imitation is an instinctive tendency says nothing about when imitation will or will not occur. The theory of imitation as simple operant conditioning cannot explain why a learner imitates a behavior for which he has never been reinforced. However, the two other theories—imitation as a generalized operant response and Bandura's theory—are much harder to refute.

Bandura has claimed that two problems with the theory of generalized imitation are (1) that it does not explain why observers will imitate a reinforced model more readily than a punished model, and (2) that it does not distinguish between the learning and performance of an imitative behavior. In my opinion, both of these criticisms are weak. It is true that in its simplest form the theory of generalized imitation states only that new imitative responses occur because similar imitative responses have been reinforced in the past. But this theory certainly needs more details before it can make any specific predictions. Based on what we know about generalization, it seems reasonable to make the following, more specific prediction: Imitation will most likely occur when the current situation is similar to situations in which the observer has been reinforced for imitation in the past. Conversely, imitation will least likely occur when the current situation is similar to situations in which the observer has been punished in the past.

Let us try to apply these two principles to the results of Bandura's (1965) experiment. Why did children frequently fail to imitate the adult model who was punished? A plausible answer from the theory of generalized imitation is that children have been punished for imitation in similar situations in the past. For instance, a boy might watch his older sister take some ice cream out of the refrigerator without permission, and get punished for doing so. Later, the boy might try the same behavior, and get the same result. After a number of such learning experiences, the boy might learn to avoid imitating someone who has been punished. Similarly, the boy might learn that he is frequently reinforced for imitation when the model is also reinforced. For example, his sister cleans up her room and is rewarded by her parents; the boy cleans up his room and is similarly rewarded.

In short, the theory of generalized imitation can easily explain why children imitate models that are reinforced but not models that are punished. In reviewing the different theories of imitation, Kymissis and Poulson (1990) concluded that, unlike earlier theories, the theory of generalized imitation can account for all types of imitative behavior, using only well-established principles of operant conditioning. Bandura would disagree, of course, arguing that his theory offers the most satisfactory account of imitation. What makes Bandura's theory different (and what gives his theory its cognitive tone) is its speculation about the abstract rules an individual sup-

posedly forms as a result of a learning experience. Thus Bandura might suggest that the children in his 1965 experiment had previously learned the general rules "If you imitate someone who is rewarded, you are also likely to be rewarded" and "If you imitate someone who is punished, you are also likely to be punished." Having already developed these expectations, the children in the different groups behaved appropriately. On the other hand, a behaviorist might say that the children had learned a complex set of contingencies concerning imitation and were simply generalizing to a new situation. The behaviorist might go so far as to say that the children were acting as if they were following the general rules just quoted, but that since we cannot actually see how information is retained in their memories, there is no point in speculating about this.

The fact that children in all groups exhibited large amounts of imitation when offered rewards poses no real problem for a behavioral analysis either. At least since the Tolman and Honzik (1930) experiment, behaviorists have recognized the distinction between learning and performance, and some have concluded that reinforcement is not essential for learning but it is essential for the performance of learned behaviors. Although the children were not actually reinforced until after they had displayed their imitative responses, this is another instance in which generalization from past experiences may have been at work. The children may have learned that when a responsible adult promises you a reward for certain behaviors, the adult frequently keeps his or her promise. Bandura would say the children had an "expectation of reinforcement"; behaviorists would say that the children were generalizing from similar experiences in the past.

In summary, Bandura's claim that the theory of generalized imitation cannot explain his results is not correct. Both theories can account for the results, but they do so in slightly different ways. As in other debates between the cognitive and behavioral approaches, the debate over explanations of imitative behavior is partly about terminology and partly about how much we should speculate about processes that we cannot observe directly.

## FACTORS THAT AFFECT THE LIKELIHOOD OF IMITATION

Young children usually have more contact with their parents than with anyone else, but they are also exposed to a wide range of other potential models, including siblings, classmates, teachers, grandparents, television personalities, cartoon characters, and sports stars. It is obvious that children do not imitate everyone to an equal degree. What characteristics of these potential models make a difference?

Mischel (1971) has summarized some of the most extensively studied factors. One theory is that a model's "rewardingness" plays an important role in imitation. Perhaps children tend to imitate their parents because they receive so many reinforcers from their parents. Bandura and Huston (1961) tested this idea in an experimental setting. Nursery-school children had individual meetings with a woman who acted in either a "nurturant" manner (for some children) or a "nonnurturant" manner (for other children). In the nurturant condition, the woman was affectionate and attentive to the child, but in the nonnurturant condition she was aloof. Several days later, each child was asked to participate in a game with the same woman, and during the game the woman made a number of distinctive gestures and verbalizations. Bandura and Huston found that children in the nurturant condition imitated the woman's behaviors significantly more often.

It has also been suggested that children tend to imitate their parents because they are powerful figures in their lives. Mischel and Grusec (1966) put this idea to a test. Some nursery-school children met a woman who was introduced as their "new teacher," and this woman emphasized the fact that they would be seeing a lot of her in the future. In another condition, different children were introduced to the same woman as a "visiting teacher from out of town" whom they would not see again.

In both cases, the woman played a game with the children, and later the children were observed at play when the woman was absent. Those children who were told that the woman was their new teacher (and would therefore have considerable control over them) imitated the woman's behaviors and mannerisms considerably more.

The concept of control or power is closely related to the concept of dominance within a social group. Abramovitch and Grusec (1978) found a high correlation between the teacher's ranking of a child's dominance and the number of times that child was imitated by other children in a free-play situation. The tendency to imitate dominant children has been found in children as young as 1 year of age (Russon & Waite, 1991).

In an interesting comparative study, Russon and Galdikas (1995) found that these same factors affect patterns of observational learning among wild orangutans. Orangutans were most likely to imitate parents and older siblings, to whom they had strong attachments. They were less likely to imitate friends and least likely to imitate strangers. They also frequently imitated dominant members of their group.

Besides rewardingness and dominance, another important variable is the model's similarity to the learner. For instance, it has been shown that a child is more likely to imitate a model who is the same sex, the same age, or who seems to have similar interests (Burnstein, Stotland, & Zander, 1961; E. S. Davidson & Smith, 1982). Yet another variable is the model's sincerity—in one study, children imitated a model who appeared sincere more than one who appeared insincere (Klass, 1979).

This brief review of characteristics of the model that influence imitation is by no means exhaustive, but it is easy to see how these variables can be explained by both Bandura's theory and by the generalized imitation theory. For instance, if a child has dealt with a dominant parent or peer, the child may have learned that this dominant individual will reinforce imitation (or punish nonimitation). It is also plausible to assume that in the past the child may have been reinforced for imitating children of the same sex or the same age, but punished for imitating some behaviors of individuals of the opposite sex or of very different ages. Finally, a child may have learned that it is unwise to imitate people who appear insincere. According to the generalized imitation theory, each of these variables reflects the effects of a child's past experiences; according to Bandura's theory, they reflect the child's expectations of future reinforcement.

## INTERACTIONS BETWEEN OBSERVATIONAL LEARNING AND OPERANT CONDITIONING

In much of their book, Bandura and Walters (1963) surveyed research findings that showed how the behavior of parents affects a child's personality development. They presented research on such characteristics as dependency, aggressiveness, sexual preferences and behaviors, delinquency, and industriousness. They suggested that there are two main ways a parent can shape a child's personality—by the control of rewards and punishments and by serving as a model whom the child can imitate. Bandura and Walters contended that in order to predict how upbringing will affect a child's personality, it is necessary to take both of these factors into account. They maintained that in some cases direct reinforcement and observational learning can work in concert, and in other cases they may work in opposite directions. We will briefly consider one case of each type.

### Achievement Motivation

Bandura and Walters claimed that direct reinforcement and observational learning work together in shaping what we might call self-discipline and a high achievement motivation. These terms encompass such characteristics as an individual's willingness to work and make sacrifices so as to obtain long-term goals, to set high standards for oneself and attempt to achieve them, and to be independent and self-reliant. Bandura and Kupers (1964) conducted an experiment that illustrates how an adult model can influence a child's self-discipline in

a situation that allowed the child to reinforce herself for good (or perhaps not so good) behavior. First, a child watched an adult play a bowling game in which the scores could range between 5 and 30. For children in one group, the adult would reward himself by taking a candy from a bowl for every score of 20 or better. For a second group, the adult was more lenient, rewarding himself for any score above 10. As in most studies of this type, the adult left the room before the child began to play the game, and the child was secretly observed. The children tended to use the same criteria for rewarding themselves as those they had observed the adult use. Children in a third group, who observed no model, tended to reward themselves no matter what score they obtained.

This study showed that children can learn to apply either strict or lenient standards of self-discipline by observing a model, and Bandura and Walters speculate that numerous learning experiences of a similar type must occur as children observe their parents' behaviors over a period of many years. Of course, besides serving as models, parents may directly reinforce either strict or lenient standards of achievement and self-discipline in their children. A study by Rosen and D'Andrade (1959) is instructive. These researchers measured the achievement orientation of 9- to 11-year-old boys by administering a type of questionnaire, and then they observed the boys perform on several tasks in the presence of their parents.

For example, in one task, a boy was blindfolded and asked to build a tower by stacking as many blocks as he could. As partial validation of the questionnaire results, Rosen and D'Andrade found that boys with a higher achievement-motivation score built higher towers. There were several significant correlations between a boy's level of achievement motivation and his parents' behaviors. The first related to the parents' level of aspiration for their son. They were told that an average boy of their son's age could build a tower of eight blocks, and were then asked to guess how many blocks their son would use. Parents of the boys with higher achievement motivation made higher estimates. Second, there were differences in the way the parents of high-achievement boys acted during the tasks. They appeared to be more concerned with their son's performance and gave more encouragement as the boy worked on the tasks. When the boy did well, they responded with more approval and affection, and they showed more irritation and disapproval if the boy did poorly. In short, the parents of boys with high achievement motivation made more use of reinforcers and punishers to encourage high standards of performance in their sons. More recent research is consistent with the findings of Rosen and D'Andrade. For instance, one study on 9- to 13-year-old children found that those who grew up in homes where there was a strong emphasis on learning and intellectual activities were more highly motivated to achieve academic success (Gottfried, Fleming, & Gottfried, 1998).

The combined influences of reinforcement and modeling on achievement motivation may operate not only within families but across entire societies. McClelland (1961) noted that folk tales and stories in children's readers from some societies emphasize the achievement of excellence, whereas those from other societies do not. In an ingenious and extensive piece of research, McClelland had readers score the stories of different countries (which were disguised so that the country could not be identified) for achievement-related themes. These stories had all been published during the 1920s. He also developed measures of economic growth in these countries that were based on increases in per capita income and per capita electrical use between the years of 1925 and 1950. McClelland found a significant correlation between the average level of achievement motivation depicted in a country's children's stories and its rate of economic growth over the next 25 years.

Of course, there is nothing in McClelland's research that implies that either achievement motivation or economic growth is desirable. The rapid economic growth of industrialized nations over the past century or so has brought with it the problems of toxic waste, acid rain, nuclear weapons, and other concerns. What the results do suggest, however, is that the val-ues a society emphasizes via its stories, legends, and heroes can have a substantial influence on the level of achievement motivation (and probably other characteristics) in its next generation.

## Aggression

Bandura and Walters (1963) presented evidence that parents' behaviors can influence the aggressiveness of their children in conflicting and seemingly paradoxical ways. The apparent paradox is that parents who use the most severe punishment for aggressive behaviors tend to produce more aggressive children. This result has been obtained in many different studies (Sears, Maccoby, & Levin, 1957; Vienero & Lagerspetz, 1984). Glueck and Glueck (1950) found that the use of severe punishment was correlated with juvenile delinquency in young boys. On the surface, this seemed to suggest that punishment is ineffective as a deterrent for aggressive behaviors, a finding that conflicts with the ample evidence showing that punishment is an effective procedure for eliminating unwanted behaviors (see Chapter 8).

Bandura and Walters (1959) pointed out that this apparent paradox is resolved when we realize that parents who use physical punishment with their children are providing their children with models of aggressive behavior. They showed that children whose parents punished aggressive behaviors usually avoided aggressive behaviors when their parents were present, but they were aggressive in their interactions outside the home. When parents use threats and physical force to discipline their children, the children use these same techniques in dealing with peers (Hoffman, 1960). In addition, the children of parents who make use of force so severe it must be termed **child abuse** are more likely to resort to physical punishment and child abuse when they become parents (Eron, 1987; Lefkowitz, Huesmann, & Eron, 1978). All of these results are consistent with the view that when they discipline their children, parents are serving as models as well as controlling agents.

These findings do not mean, however, that parents should feel helpless when they see aggressive behaviors in their children. Chapter 8 described several procedures for reducing unwanted behaviors that do not make use of physical punishment or other aversive stimuli, including differential reinforcement for incompatible behaviors, response cost, and timeout. Research has shown that such techniques can successfully reduce aggressive behaviors and that parents of unusually aggressive children can be trained to use those techniques (Patterson, Chamberlain, & Reid, 1982; Patterson & Reid, 1973). The advantage of these techniques is that besides reducing unwanted behaviors, they provide the child with a model whose reaction is firm yet moderate and nonviolent when displeased with someone else's behavior.

## THE INFLUENCE OF TELEVISION

As we have seen, much of the work of Bandura and his associates examined how aggressive behavior could be encouraged through the actions of a model. This research set the stage for the continuing debate over whether violence on television makes the people who watch it more violent. This has proven to be a difficult question to answer, but there is now substantial evidence that TV viewing can affect the attitudes and behavior of both children and adults. For instance, Gerbner and his colleagues (Gerbner, Gross, Eleey, Jackson-Beck, Jeffries-Fox, & Signorielli, 1977) found that heavy viewers (those who average over 6 hours of TV viewing a day) have different perceptions of the world than do less frequent viewers. Based on their responses to questionnaires, it seems that heavy viewers see the world as a meaner place, inhabited by more violent and selfish people. They are also more likely to own a gun and to say that it is all right to hit people when you are angry at them.

This research, along with much of the research on the connection between television viewing and aggressive behavior, is based on correlational evidence. For instance, studies with children and adolescents have found a positive correlation between the amount of television they watch and their level of aggressiveness in everyday life. The problem with correlational evidence, however, is that correlation does not imply causation. That is, a correlation between two variables does not necessarily mean that the first variable is the cause of the second. Thus a correlation between TV violence and aggressive behavior in children might or might not mean that watching TV violence causes aggressive behavior. Another possibility is that aggressive tendencies are the cause and watching TV violence is the effect: Perhaps those children who have more aggressive personalities to begin with (for reasons we need not consider now) choose to watch more TV violence than less aggressive children, because the aggressive children find it more enjoyable. Still another possibility is that both variables, watching TV violence and aggressiveness, might be influenced by some third variable, such as a stressful living situation.

To avoid the weaknesses of correlational evidence, those who study the effects of TV violence have used a number of strategies. One strategy is to conduct a **longitudinal study,** in which the relevant variables are measured at different points in time. For example, in a well-known study, Eron, Huesmann, Lefkowitz, and Walder (1972) examined the TV-viewing habits and aggressive tendencies of more than 200 third-grade boys, and then they reexamined these same boys 10 years later. They found a moderate correlation between preference for violent TV in the third grade and aggressiveness 10 years later. Conversely, they found no correlation between aggressiveness in third grade and preference for violent TV 10 years later. This pattern of results suggests that watching violent TV can lead to later aggressiveness, not the reverse. Some similar studies have corroborated these findings (Huesmann, Lagerspetz, & Eron, 1984), but others have not (Milavsky, Stipp, Kessler, & Rubens, 1982).

Another strategy in this area of research has been to conduct **controlled experiments** in which subjects are randomly assigned to experimental and control groups. The experiment of Bandura, Ross, and Ross (1963) that we already reviewed is an example of this type of research. Studies of this type have generally found increases in aggressiveness after children watch violent TV programs (Wood, Wong, & Chachere, 1991). The problem with these laboratory experiments, however, is that both the TV viewing and the measurement of aggressiveness take place in very brief time periods and restricted environments, and it is not clear how much applicability they have to real life. To deal with this problem, some researchers have conducted **field experiments,** in which the TV viewing and the measurement of aggressive behaviors occur in more realistic settings. For example, children have been exposed to either violent or nonviolent TV programs over a period of several weeks, and their aggressiveness has been assessed in normal activities, such as free-play time at school. In general, the results of field experiments show a modest effect of TV violence on aggressive behavior (Friedrich-Cofer & Huston, 1986).

After analyzing the results of many previous studies, Hogben (1998) concluded that some types of television violence are more strongly correlated with viewer aggression than others. Stronger correlations with viewer aggression are found for television programs in which the violence seems justified (as when the character is fighting for a good cause), and weaker correlations are found when a program emphasizes the unpleasant consequences of violence (the suffering of the victim or punishment of the aggressor). It appears that it is not simply the presence of violence in a television program but how the violence is portrayed that is important. If so, there should be ways to lessen the negative effects of TV violence. Among the ideas being explored are changing the content of TV programs so that perpetrators of violence are stigmatized rather than glorified, and teaching children to watch television with a more critical attitude (Hoberman, 1990).

A related issue that concerns many parents is how children may be affected by playing video games that include violent actions. Many popular video games portray graphic acts of violence, such as engaging in hand-to-hand combat or shooting and killing realistic human figures. Of course, children know that what takes place in a video game is not real; still, aggression in game playing may lead to a tendency to be more aggressive in real life. Compared to the extensive research on television violence, so far there have not been many studies on the effects of video games. However, the available data suggest that there is indeed a correlation between playing violent video games and aggressive behavior in children (Dill & Dill, 1998). In fact, it may turn out that playing violent video games has a greater effect on aggressive behavior in children than does watching violence on television, because video games involve active participation on the part of the players.

Watching television and playing video games can, of course, affect children in many other ways as well. Children who sit and watch TV for many hours each day are using up time that might be spent more productively. One extensive correlational study found an inverse relationship between the amount of television that children watched and their reading comprehension scores on standardized tests, with much lower test scores for children who watched more than 4 hours of television a day (Neuman, 1988). However, the effects of television can sometimes be beneficial. Educational programs such as *Sesame Street* can give young children valuable information about letters and words, numbers, and social skills. A longitudinal study (designed so that cause and effect could be sorted out, as discussed above) found that children who were regular viewers of *Sesame Street* between the ages of 3 and 5 had higher vocabulary skills 2 years later than those who did not watch this program as often (Rice, Huston, Truglio, & Wright, 1990).

It should come as no surprise that television can have many different effects on the viewer.

The National Television Violence Study: Executive Summary can be read at *http://www.ccsp/ucsb.edu/ntvs.htm.*

A good overview of the effects of television violence has been prepared by Dr. John P. Murray and is available at *http://www.ksu.edu/humec/impact.htm.*

As with most examples of modern technology, it is not the device itself but how it is used that determines whether the effects will be desirable or undesirable.

## WHAT CAN BE LEARNED THROUGH OBSERVATION?

It is the contention of social learning theorists like Bandura and Walters that an individual's characteristic ways of responding to different situations, which some call the individual's "personality," are developed to a large extent during childhood through the interacting influences of operant conditioning and observational learning. Since Bandura and Walters' influential book was published, hundreds of studies have attempted to demonstrate the effects of observational learning on a person's personality traits, problem-solving skills, aesthetic preferences, and so on. Let us examine a few areas in which the effects of observation and imitation have been investigated.

### Phobias

Rachman (1977) has summarized several pieces of evidence that suggest that phobias can be acquired vicariously; most of the studies demonstrate that members of the same family frequently have similar fears. Several studies have found high correlations between the fears of a mother and her children, or among the children of one family (May, 1950). Interviews with children who have dental phobias suggest that these fears are often learned from their parents (Milgrom, Mancl, King, & Weinstein, 1995). During World War II, Grinker and Spiegel (1945) reported a number of case studies of fighter pilots who developed phobias after observing a crewmate's fear reaction during or after a mission. When individuals who suffer from phobias are asked about the origins of their phobias, a substantial number say that they acquired the phobia by watching someone else who was fearful of the same object or situation (Merckelbach, Arntz, & de Jong, 1991). As can be seen, evidence for the vicarious acquisition of phobias is based on correlational evidence, case studies, and retrospective reports, and this is not the strongest type of evidence. However, several experiments with animals have obtained more convincing evidence. For example, Mineka, Davidson, Cook, and Kerr (1984) reported that monkeys rapidly developed a long-lasting fear of snakes by observing another monkey's fearful reactions to a snake. Thus, in this case, the evidence for observational learning may actually be stronger for animals than for people.

### Drug Use and Addictions

Many types of evidence suggest that Bandura's social learning theory can help to account for the acquisition of various addictive behaviors, including smoking, alcoholism, and drug abuse. Notice that simple principles of reinforcement and punishment can explain why an addiction is maintained once it has been established. As described in Chapter 3 during the discussion of the Solomon and Corbit theory, cessation of smoking or drug use after an addiction has been established frequently causes aversive withdrawal symptoms that can be escaped (all too conveniently) by further intake of the addictive substance. On the other hand, observational learning and social reinforcement can help to explain why such addictions are developed in the first place.

For example, consider the fact that smoking one's first cigarette is usually an aversive event, involving harsh and burning sensations. Why then does a person ever smoke again? One answer is based on observational learning: Even when very young, many children are exposed to parents, older siblings, TV personalities, and others who smoke. The consequences of this behavior may appear to be positive: Some people say they started smoking because smokers seemed to be more mature, sophisticated, or attractive. Perhaps these advantages outweigh a little burning in the throat for the beginning smoker. In addition, among teenagers, peers often deliver strong social reinforcers for smoking: They may encourage nonsmokers to begin and ridicule those who do not. These joint factors of observational learning and social reinforcement are frequently cited as major contributors to the onset of smoking, and it has repeatedly been found that the tendency to smoke is correlated with the smoking habits of one's parents, spouse, and peers (Ennet, Bauman, & Koch, 1994; Hunter, Vizelberg, & Berenson, 1991).

The principles of social learning theory also appear to be important in the development of alcoholism and drug abuse. For instance, it has been found that about 20 percent of all heroin addicts have one or more family members who are also addicted (Hekimian & Gershon, 1968). Similarly, attitudes about drinking among a person's family and peers have been shown to be predictors of alcohol use in young adults (Holman, Jensen, & Capell, 1993). Of course, either learning or hereditary factors could cause similar patterns of drug and alcohol use within a family. However, several types of evidence show that similar drug use among family members is not entirely due to heredity. Andrews, Hops, and Duncan (1997) found that adolescents who have good relationships with their parents are more likely to imitate their use of cigarettes, marijuana, and alcohol than those who have poor relationships. Furthermore, similar drug and alcohol use among peers cannot be due to hereditary factors if the members of a peer group are not related. In fact, researchers have found that drug and alcohol use among adolescents is more highly correlated with the habits of their peers than with the habits of their parents (Windle, 2000), which suggests that observational learning and social reinforcement play an important role.

## Cognitive Development

Many developmental psychologists, such as Jean Piaget (1926, 1929), have suggested that as children grow, they pass through a number of stages of cognitive ability, and that the passage from one stage to the next depends heavily on growth, maturation, and personal experience. In contrast, social learning theorists such as Rosenthal and Zimmerman (1972, 1978) claim that observational learning plays a major role in the development and refinement of cognitive skills. As a representative test of

cognitive development, let us consider the well-known **conservative task.** In one version of this task, a child is shown three clear cylindrical beakers, as illustrated in Figure 12-2. Beakers A and B are identical, and they contain the same amount of water. The test begins by asking the child which has more water, and the child usually says that A and B have the same amount. Then, as the child watches, the contents of B are poured into beaker C, a taller and thinner beaker. The child is then asked whether A or C has more water. Children are said to have mastered the concept of conservation of volume if they say that A and C have the same amount of water. However, children who are younger than about age 7 usually say there is more water in C. They are apparently misled by the higher water level in C. These children are called **nonconservers** because they have not yet learned that liquids retain a constant volume regardless of the shape of the container they are in.

Rosenthal and Zimmerman have tried to demonstrate that a child's mastery of the conservation task depends on more than simply maturation and personal experience. They maintain that observational learning is a major

**FIGURE 12-2** The steps of a test for conservation of volume. After seeing the contents of B poured into C, the child is asked which container, A or C, has more water.

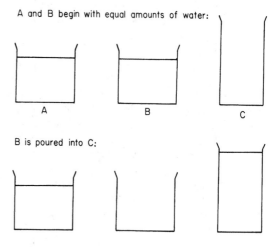

A and B begin with equal amounts of water:

A          B          C

B is poured into C:

determinant of a child's ability to perform well on the conservation task and others like it. To demonstrate the potential of observational learning, they had children who were nonconservers observe a model (an adult female) perform correctly on the conservation task. In one group, the model gave an explanation for her answer that A and C had the same amount of water (for instance, "Because they were the same in the first place"), and in another group she gave no explanation. In a subsequent test, children in both groups showed improved performance on conservation tasks, and those who heard the model explain her choices improved the most. In one of the Rosenthal and Zimmerman studies, the children were only 4 to 5 years old, well below the age at which children typically master the conservation task.

Rosenthal and Zimmerman found that the children's improved performances generalized to other types of conservation tasks (for example, a conservation-of-number task, which involves an understanding that the number of objects in a row does not change if the row is made longer by spacing the objects farther apart). There is also considerable evidence that many other cognitive skills besides conservation can be improved through observational learning. Numerous studies have shown that children can learn grammatical rules, abstract concepts, and problem-solving skills by observing a model (Rivera & Smith, 1987; Zimmerman & Blom, 1983).

### Moral Standards and Behavior

Bandura has proposed that a child's judgments about what behaviors are good and what ones are bad are largely learned by observation. Thus, a child whose parents are impeccably honest in all financial matters may learn to behave the same way. A child who sees and hears his parents cheat on their taxes, steal from their employers, and ignore their bills wherever possible may decide that these are acceptable or even desirable activities. A number of experiments have shown that the behavior of a model can influence the behavior of observers in situations where morally laudable or deplorable behaviors are involved. For in-

stance, it has been found that children are more altruistic after observing an altruistic model (Israely & Guttman, 1983), and that both children and adults are more likely to break rules or laws after observing a model do so (Lefkowitz, Blake, & Mouton, 1955; Waiters, Leat, & Mezei, 1963).

Research by D. P. Phillips (1982) provides a striking example of how observing a model can increase a person's likelihood of performing an action that many consider to be both gravely immoral and irrational. Using statistics from the year 1977, Phillips found a significant increase in the number of suicides, motor vehicle deaths, and serious motor vehicle injuries in the several days that followed the suicide of a character in a nationally broadcast soap opera. For each instance of a soap opera suicide, Phillips used the preceding week as a baseline period, and he was careful to correct his data for seasonal fluctuations, to exclude data from holiday periods, and so on. Phillips's explanation of his results is that soap operas are widely watched, that many viewers identify themselves with the characters, and that the suicide of a character leads some (admittedly few) viewers to attempt to imitate this behavior. He interprets the increased motor vehicle accidents as disguised suicides or attempted suicides. The largest increases in suicides and motor vehicle accidents occurred among females living in urban environments, who were also the heaviest viewers of soap operas. Similar increases in suicides and suicide attempts have been found in the days that follow TV movies or news stories about suicide. Other research has found similar effects of suicides in the media (Martin, 1998), but some psychologists dispute these findings (Joiner, 1999), and the topic is still being debated. Still, this research raises some serious policy issues for the producers of TV dramas and news programs.

## MODELING IN BEHAVIOR THERAPY

Largely because of Bandura's influential work, modeling has assumed its place as one of the major tools available to the behavior therapist. Bandura and Walters suggested that a model can influence an observer's behavior in three main ways, and each of these is utilized by behavior therapists. First, a model's behavior can facilitate responses the observer already knows how to perform. This category is similar to Thorpe's (1963) concept of social facilitation, mentioned earlier. Second, an observer may learn how to produce totally new behaviors (as in Thorpe's local enhancement and true imitation). Finally, undesired responses, such as fear reactions to harmless objects or situations (phobias), can be reduced or eliminated through observational learning. The following sections give some samples of the large and growing literature on the different therapeutic applications of modeling.

### Facilitation of Low-Probability Behaviors

O'Connor (1969) used filmed models in an attempt to increase the sociability of nursery-school children who were characterized as being socially withdrawn. In a classroom setting, the children would keep to themselves and only rarely interact with other children or adults. Children in the experimental group saw a 23-minute film depicting a child of similar age engaging in a series of social interactions. The film began with relatively calm activities, such as two children sharing a book or toy while seated at a table. It progressed through more involved and energetic social interactions, eventually ending with a scene in which six children were shown throwing toys around the room with obvious enjoyment. This method of progressing from simple to more demanding behaviors is called **graduated modeling,** and it is a frequent component in many modeling programs. Naturally, every scene depicted a situation in which the model experienced favorable consequences during the social interaction. Children in a control group saw a film of equal length about dolphins at Marineland that contained no human characters. Immediately after viewing one of the films, the children returned to their classrooms, where observers recorded their behaviors. There was a fivefold increase in the number of social interactions for children in the

experimental group, and no increase in the control group.

Modeling is also used in **assertiveness training** for people who are overly submissive in certain situations and want to develop the ability to stand up for their rights. For example, some wives (or husbands) may do whatever their spouses decide is best regardless of what they think about a decision. Some young adults may be bullied by their parents into occupations or lifestyles they do not really like. Some people have difficulty refusing unreasonable requests made by friends, employers, coworkers, relatives, or strangers. The goal of assertiveness training is to help people deal with these situations more effectively. It frequently consists of a combination of modeling, role playing, and behavioral rehearsal, in which the therapist describes a hypothetical situation, models an appropriate response, asks the client to imitate this response, and evaluates the client's performance. A few sessions of such assertiveness training can have long-term benefits (Goldsmith & McFall, 1975; Wolpe & Lazarus, 1966). In one study, Kirkland and Caughlin-Carver (1982) found that mentally retarded adults who received 14 sessions of training showed significant improvement in their ability to refuse unreasonable requests politely, and these improvements were maintained in observations made 12 weeks after the end of training. Assertiveness training also seems to be an effective method for training juveniles and adults in correctional institutions, who need to learn how to be assertive without being aggressive (Beidleman, 1981).

### Acquisition of New Behaviors

Perhaps the best therapeutic example of the training of totally new behaviors through modeling comes from the work of Lovaas (1967) and others who have taught autistic children to speak, as described in Chapter 7. This therapy makes use of a large number of behavioral techniques, such as shaping, prompting, fading, and discrimination training, but the teacher's modeling of speech is indispensable at every stage of therapy. The teacher repeatedly models the desired words and the child is reinforced for successful imitation. To obtain an appreciation for the importance of modeling in this training, imagine how much more difficult it would be to train an autistic child to say "My name is Billy" if the teacher were required to remain completely quiet and rely only on reinforcers and the process of successive approximations. Even when training a simple response such as a lever press, shaping can be a time-consuming process; shaping language skills would be a virtual impossibility without the opportunity to model the appropriate speech patterns. Of course, many new behaviors besides speech can be taught through modeling, and Lovaas, Freitag, Nelson, and Whalen (1967) described how they used modeling (along with manual prompting) to teach autistic children such nonverbal behaviors as playing games, washing, brushing their hair, making their beds, and preparing snacks.

## Elimination of Fears and Unwanted Behaviors

As a treatment for phobias, modeling sometimes offers several advantages over systematic desensitization (see Chapter 4): It can be used with very young patients, who may not be able to follow the therapist's instructions during deep-muscle relaxation training. It can be a more rapid procedure and require less of the therapist's time, especially when films or videotapes are used. Because of the realistic nature of some modeling procedures (as described below), there may be better generalization to real-world situations.

Bandura and his colleagues conducted some of the earliest experiments assessing the therapeutic potential of modeling. Bandura, Grusec, and Menlove (1967) attempted to reduce excessive fears of dogs in young children. Subjects were divided into four groups. The first group received eight 3-minute sessions of graduated modeling in which they observed a child of their own age engage in more and more demanding interactions with a friendly dog. The child approached the dog, petted it, fed it biscuits, walked around with the dog on a leash, and finally climbed into the dog's pen

and played with it. In this group, the modeling sequences took place in a party context (with party hats, balloons, cookies, and prizes) to reduce anxiety. A second group of children observed the same modeling sequences without the party context. A third group experienced the party context with the dog present but with no model (to control for exposure to the dog). A fourth group experienced the party context but without the dog and the model. All children then received two posttreatment behavioral tests in which they were asked to imitate the model, one immediately and a second a month later. Figure 12-3 shows the results. Both groups with the model were superior to the two groups without a model, and there was no significant difference between the party context and the neutral context. For the two groups that watched the model, these improvements remained essentially unchanged a month later. Similar results were obtained when children watched a film of different children interacting with dogs (Bandura & Menlove, 1968).

Modeling has also been used to eliminate phobias in adults. In a variation called **participant modeling,** the patient imitates the behavior of the model in each step of the treatment, and the patient's involvement with the object of the phobia becomes more demanding each time. For example, Bandura, Blanchard, and Ritter (1969) used this procedure with snake phobics. During the treatment, the therapist fearlessly handled a large king snake. The patient was first asked to touch the therapist's arm as he held the snake, then to touch his hand, then to touch the snake itself, and so on, until the patient took over the handling of the snake and held the snake in his or her lap. Bandura and colleagues reasoned that participant modeling should be especially effective because of the realistic experience it gives the patient. In fact, they found that participant modeling produced about twice the improvement of both a model presented on film and a systematic desensitization treatment. Participant modeling has been successful when used to treat other types of phobias, such as fears of spiders, birds, needles, or dentists, and in some instances a single treatment session is all that is

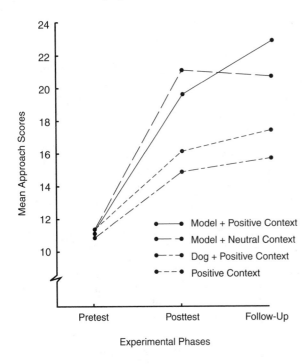

**FIGURE 12-3** Results from the four groups in the Bandura, Grusec, and Menlove (1967) study on the use of modeling in the treatment of children's fear of dogs.

needed to produce long-lasting benefits (Ollendick & King, 1998; Ost, 1989). As we might expect, the effectiveness of participant modeling depends on how similar the treatment conditions are to those in the individual's normal environment. One study found that after treatment, patients' fears of spiders were greater when they were exposed to spiders in a situation that was very different from the one in which they received treatment (Mineka, Mystkowski, Hladek, & Rodriguez, 1999).

Modeling can also be used to eliminate responses other than fear reactions. Middleton and Cartledge (1995) used modeling in combination with other behavioral techniques, such as reinforcement of incompatible behaviors, to reduce aggressive behaviors in 6- to 9-year-old boys. Another example comes from the work of Meichenbaum and Goodman (1971), who have attempted to improve the academic performance of first-grade children who might be described as "impulsive" or "hyperactive." These children often do poorly in school, partly because they tend to behave erratically

or carelessly when working on a challenging task. The goal of Meichenbaum and Goodman was to reduce or eliminate such reckless and error-prone behaviors. They noted that hyperactive children exhibit less self-instruction than do average children of their age. For instance, when painting a picture, a typical first-grader might be heard to utter self-instructions such as "Don't spill the paint" or "I want to make a nice, straight line." Meichenbaum and Goodman observed that in hyperactive children, either such self-instructions are absent or, if present, they are nevertheless followed by the wrong behavior. Their treatment therefore consisted of having a child watch an adult model who gave himself overt self-instructions while performing various tasks. The following self-instructions were used by a model during a simple task of copying a line drawing:

Okay, what is it I have to do? You want me to copy the picture with the different lines. I have to go slowly and carefully. Okay, draw the line down, down, good; then to the right, that's it; now down some more and to the left. Good, I'm doing fine so far. Remember, go slowly. Now back up again. No, I was supposed to go down. That's okay. Just erase the line carefully. . . . Good. Even if I make an error I can go on slowly and carefully. I have to go down now. Finished. I did it! (Meichenbaum & Goodman, 1971, p. 117)

Later, the adult would give the child similar instructions as the child worked on the task, and eventually the child was trained to give himself such instructions as he worked. The modeling of self-instruction was also given for more complex tasks. After this training, these children showed significant improvements on a number of standardized tests, and this improvement was maintained in a 1-month follow-up. As with most cases in which a behavior therapist wishes to eliminate one behavior pattern (careless performance in this case), the modeling techniques used by Meichenbaum and Goodman involved teaching an alternative behavior pattern (following one's self-instructions to work carefully) that was incompatible with the unwanted behavior. Other studies have provided further evidence that modeling and self-instruction can be effective treatments for hyperactive and aggressive children (Miranda & Presentacion, 2000).

### Videotape Self-Modeling

In recent years, a variation of modeling called **videotape self-modeling** has become an increasingly popular technique used by behavior therapists. The goal of this technique is to increase the performance of desired behaviors by having clients watch themselves correctly perform these behaviors on videotape. For example, Dowrick and Raeburn (1995) used this technique with children who had severe physical disabilities, such as cerebral palsy or muscular dystrophy. First, each child was asked to perform some practical skill that needed improvement, such as maintaining a good posture, walking, balancing, writing, or dressing. This behavior was videotaped, and the therapist gave the child instructions on

how to perform, encouragement, and, when necessary, assistance in completing the task. Next, each child's videotape was edited to remove all examples of errors and inappropriate behaviors, as well as all segments in which the therapist gave the child assistance. What remained, therefore, was a tape in which the child was seen performing the behavior correctly, with no help from anyone else. This is an important feature of videotape self-modeling, because the goal is to teach only correct, unassisted behaviors. After the editing, the children watched themselves on the videotapes, which were shown to them six times over a 2-week period. The researchers found substantial improvement in most of the children on the self-modeled tasks. They also found that watching the videotapes, not just performing the behaviors in front of a camera, was a crucial part of the treatment. (Each child was actually videotaped performing two different skills, but only one of the videotapes was shown to the child. Improvement on the self-modeled skill was much greater than on the one that was not shown.)

Videotape self-modeling has been used successfully for a variety of skills with both children and adults (Dowrick, 1999). The procedure has been used to decrease stuttering (Bray & Kehle, 1998), to reduce the fidgeting, distractibility, and inappropriate talking by boys with attention-deficit hyperactivity disorder (Woltersdorf, 1992), and to improve the walking skills and mobility of elderly patients (Neef, Bill-Harvery, Shade, Iezzi, & De-Lorenzo, 1995).

Why is self-modeling an effective technique? Bandura (1994) suggested that self-modeling has two desirable characteristics. First, by repeatedly showing only correct instances of the behavior, it gives the learner information about how to perform the desired skills. Second, seeing one's own behavior gives the learner a sense of **self-efficacy,** which is Bandura's term for confidence that one can successfully perform the task at hand. This is related to the fourth factor in Bandura's theory of imitation, incentive and motivational processes. People are most likely to imitate a model when they are confident that they can perform the behavior successfully and effectively. Seeing oneself succeed on the videotape is, according to Bandura, an ideal way to instill this sense of self-efficacy.

## CONCLUSIONS: THE SOPHISTICATED SKILL OF LEARNING BY OBSERVATION

The increasing popularity of modeling as a technique of behavior modification is a reflection of the power of this method of inducing change in behavior. Learning by observation is the most sophisticated type of learning we have considered in this book. Its relative advantages can be appreciated by reviewing the major categories of learning we have examined. We began with habituation, a form of learning so primitive it is found in one-celled organisms. It consists of nothing more than a decrease in the probability of a reflexive response after repeated presentations of the eliciting stimulus. Classical conditioning is considerably more complex, for it typically consists of the transfer of an old response to a new (conditioned) stimulus. Still, no new responses can be taught using classical conditioning, because the form of the response is determined by the learner, not the teacher. With operant conditioning, we finally have a mode of learning in which the teacher can select the response: Any arbitrary response the learner makes can be reinforced, and its probability should increase. And when the techniques of successive approximations and response chaining are added to the principle of reinforcement, the teacher can gradually build up complex behavior patterns that the learner would probably never produce on his or her own. In Chapter 6, it was stated that, in principle, any behavior a learner is capable of performing can be taught using the technique of successive approximations.

What is possible in principle is not always feasible in practice, however. Teaching a child how to speak, a college student how to write a computer program, or a figure skater how to do a triple jump would be next to impossible if the teacher's intervention were limited to the delivery of reinforcers for successive approximations to the desired goal. However, if the learner is capable of learning through observation, as people and many animals are, the task of teaching such complex behaviors becomes many times easier. The beauty of observational learning is that learners can develop some understanding of the desired behavior well before they actually produce this behavior themselves. To modify a cliché, it is probably not an exaggeration to say that one model is worth a thousand successive approximations.

Closely related to observational learning, though still more advanced, is the human ability to learn new behavior patterns through the spoken or written word. Since most types of formal education rely heavily on these modes of learning, enormous amounts of research have been directed toward the goal of making them more effective. Treatment of this vast topic is well beyond the scope of this book, but the relationship between these types of learning and observational learning should be clear. We have seen that the behavior of even young children can be altered if they (1) watch a live model, (2) watch a filmed model, or (3) listen to a verbal account of the model's behavior. When they are a bit older, children can learn by reading about the behavior of a model and the consequences that followed. In each case, the children are presumably learning about the contingencies of reinforcement—the stimulus-response-reinforcer relationships—that are found in their world. The advantage of education via observation or the spoken or written word is that the individual can learn about these relationships without having to experience them firsthand.

## CHAPTER SUMMARY

One theory of imitation states that it is an instinctive tendency, and there is evidence that animals and even newborn infants can learn by imitation. A second theory states that people imitate when they are reinforced for imitation. A third theory states that imitation is a generalized operant response: People imitate in situations that are similar to those where imitation has been reinforced in the past. Bandura's theory states that four factors determine whether imitative behavior will occur: attentional processes, retentional processes, motor abilities, and incentive and motivational processes.

Characteristics of the model, the learner, and the situation all affect when imitation will or will not occur. Children are more likely to imitate a model who is reinforced than one who is punished. Children are also more likely to imitate models who are affectionate, powerful, or similar to themselves.

Observational learning and operant conditioning can either work together or work in opposite directions. They may work in opposite directions when parents try to use physical punishment for aggressive behavior: Their children may become more aggressive because the parents serve as models of aggression when they use harsh physical punishment. Observational learning can also affect the development of phobias, alcohol and drug use, thinking skills, and moral standards.

Many different variations on modeling techniques have been used successfully in behavior therapy, including graduated modeling, participant modeling, and videotaped self-modeling. Through modeling, shy children can learn better social skills, adults can learn to be more assertive, autistic children can be taught to speak, and phobias can be eliminated.

## REVIEW QUESTIONS

1. Explain the theory that imitation is a simple operant response, and the theory that imitation is a generalized operant response. Which theory is better, and why?

2. What are the four factors necessary for imitation, according to Bandura's theory? What are Bandura's main criticisms of the generalized operant theory of imitation? Are these criticisms valid? Why or why not?

3. What are some characteristics of the model, the learner, and the situation that determine whether or not imitation will occur?

4. Give one specific example to show how modeling has been used in behavior therapy to effect the following: (a) facilitating low-probability behaviors, (b) acquiring new behaviors, and (c) eliminating unwanted behaviors.

# CHAPTER **13**

# Learning Motor Skills

Motor skills are an essential ingredient for all types of learned behaviors. Classical eyeblink conditioning will fail if a neurological deficit prevents a rabbit from blinking its eye. Reinforcement for correct turns in a water maze will be ineffective if the subject cannot swim. Imitation is impossible if the learner does not have the ability to mimic the actions of a model. These points are obvious, but people often take for granted their abilities to perform complex sequences of movement. The bicyclist seldom marvels at her ability to remain upright on two thin wheels. The typist seldom wonders how he can coordinate 10 fingers to produce five or more keystrokes a second, usually in the correct order. Likewise, in previous chapters we have generally taken for granted a subject's response-production abilities. This chapter will examine these abilities in some detail.

Scientists have employed a variety of strategies to study motor-skill learning, and we can group these strategies into three categories that parallel the three major approaches to the study of learning in general—the behavioral, physiological, and cognitive approaches. Much of the early research on motor-skill learning (beginning with the work of E. L. Thorndike and continuing through the first half of the twentieth century) had a behavioral character. Researchers were interested in discovering the relationships between various independent variables (such as the amount of practice, the distribution of practice) and dependent variables (speed of learning, quality of final performance). They had relatively little interest in speculating about what internal, unobserved processes were involved in the learning and performance of a new skill. There were also, however, physiologists who were interested in the neural mechanisms of movement. They tried to discover what brain, spinal cord, and bodily structures were involved in movement. Lastly, with the rise of cognitive psychology in the second half of the century, many theorists have adopted the information-processing approach in analyzing motor skills. There has been much discussion of processes that are not directly observable, such as attention, short-term memory, sensory processing, and response sequencing mechanisms. All three approaches to motor-skill learning have produced many interesting findings, and this chapter will sample some from each category.

## THE VARIETY OF MOTOR SKILLS

The skilled movements that people are capable of learning are indeed diverse. Consider the following examples of motor skills: balancing—on a bicycle, on a log, or on an icy sidewalk; shooting a foul shot in basketball; putting a golf ball; pressing a stopwatch as a runner crosses the finish line; slamming on the brakes of an automobile during an emergency; typing; playing the piano or some other musical instrument. Before reading further, pause for a moment and think about these different skills. What features do some of these movements have in common? Along what dimensions do they differ?

One obvious characteristic of a movement is its duration. Some motor skills are called discrete because they are completed shortly after they have begun (pressing a stopwatch, slamming on the brakes). Others are called continuous because they extend for an indefinitely long period of time (balancing). The terms discrete and continuous represent two ends of a continuum, and many behaviors fall between these two extremes. Another dimension that is closely related to a movement's duration deals with whether or not the individual receives feedback from the environment while the movement is in progress. Chapter 3 described the basic concepts of feedback theory, and it may be helpful to review that section now. Recall that behaviors such as the wood louse's humidity-seeking behavior are called closed-loop feedback systems because the organism continuously receives feedback from the environment about whether its movements are bringing it closer to or farther from its goal.

Similarly, most (but not all) movements other than discrete movements can be called **closed-loop movements** because the individual continually receives and can react to feedback about whether the movement is proceeding correctly. Balancing on a log is a good example: If you feel yourself tipping to the right, you can immediately compensate by shifting your weight to the left. In contrast, many discrete movements (such as slamming on the brakes) occur so rapidly that a person has no time to react to any possible error. In the terminology of feedback theory, these are called **open-loop movements,** and they are characterized by the fact that once the movement begins, it is too late to make any corrections.

One further difference among motor skills is that some require exactly the same movement every time, whereas others demand that the movement be modified to suit the situation. Compare the skills of shooting a foul shot and putting a golf ball. The movements required in a foul shot are always the same, for the player always stands 15 feet from the basket, which is 10 feet above the floor. If one motion is successful on one foul shot, an exact replica of this movement will be successful on any future foul shot. On the other hand, the movements required to sink a putt can vary considerably from one putt to the next. The ball may be a different distance from the hole, at a different angle, and the slope of the green may be different. The golfer must take all of these factors into account and then produce a stroke that has the appropriate force and direction. Motor-skill researchers have studied both types of tasks—those that require accuracy on a single, repetitive movement, and those that demand the flexibility to adapt the movement to fit the occasion.

The motor skills mentioned above all have practical utility in one real-world activity or another, but such everyday movements are not usually the ones studied in the laboratory. Instead, researchers frequently choose to study more artificial tasks, such as turning a knob 90 degrees in 150 milliseconds, or tracking a dot on a rotating turntable with a pointer. The reasons motor-skill researchers study these unusual tasks are similar to the reasons operant conditioners study simple responses in a barren Skinner box. First, these tasks are selected to be representative of a wide range of everyday movements—the knob-turning task involves a discrete, open-loop movement, and the tracking task involves a continuous, closed-loop movement. Second, these tasks are selected to be as simple as possible, so that unnecessary complexities will not make the results difficult to interpret. Third, since it is unlikely that subjects will have encountered these tasks outside the laboratory, the researcher can witness the acquisition of a new motor skill. If a researcher chose to study a more familiar task, such as steering a car, it could be difficult to sort out the contribution of innate ability, previous driving experience, and practice during the experiment itself.

## VARIABLES AFFECTING MOTOR LEARNING AND PERFORMANCE

We will begin our survey of motor-skill research with what can be characterized as the behavioral approach. We will examine some factors that determine how quickly a motor skill is learned and how adroitly it is performed.

### Reinforcement and Knowledge of Results

*The Law of Effect and Motor Learning.* E. L. Thorndike, who is best known for his experiments with the puzzle box (Chapter 6), also conducted some of the earliest research on human motor learning (Thorndike, 1927). In one experiment, subjects were blindfolded, and their goal was to draw a line exactly 3 inches long. Thorndike wanted to see how the accuracy of two groups of subjects changed over trials. One group received reinforcement for each line whose length was within 1/8 inch of 3 inches, plus or minus: Immediately after a subject drew such a line, the experimenter said, "Right." If the line did not meet this criterion, the experimenter said, "Wrong." Subjects in the second group experienced no consequences for accurate or inaccurate lines. They received as many trials as the first group, but they had no way of knowing which lines were close to 3 inches and which were not.

Thorndike viewed this experiment as a test of two principles: the Law of Effect (with which we are already familiar) and the "Law of Practice." Although it is often said that "practice makes perfect," Thorndike found that practice without verbal reinforcement was completely ineffective: Subjects in the second group showed no improvement over trials. On the other hand, subjects in the reinforcement group showed a substantial increase in accuracy over trials. Thorndike's conclusion was that the Law of Effect is just as important in human motor learning as it was for his animals in the puzzle box. In both cases, reinforcement

"stamps in" or strengthens the correct response, so this response is more likely to be repeated in the future.

***What Can Be Better Than Reinforcement?*** Trowbridge and Cason (1932) challenged Thorndike's conclusion that reinforcement is the crucial variable in the acquisition of a motor skill. They argued that, although saying "Right" after a response might serve as a reinforcer in some circumstances, in Thorndike's experiment it was important because it gave the subject information or **feedback** about the accuracy of each response. In the literature on motor-skill learning, this type of feedback is usually called **knowledge of results** (abbreviated KR). In short, Trowbridge and Cason proposed that the information provided by the words "Right" and "Wrong" was what produced the subjects' improved accuracy, not the reinforcing and punishing aspects of the words.

In Thorndike's experiment, the informational and reinforcing properties of the experimenter's words could not be separated, but Trowbridge and Cason devised an ingenious way to distinguish between these two variables. In their experiment, the task was the same as in Thorndike's, to draw a 3-inch line while blindfolded. Two of their groups were the same as Thorndike's: The group that received practice only was called the *No KR Group*, and the group that was told "Right" or "Wrong" was called the *Qualitative KR Group* (because subjects received no quantitative feedback on the size of their errors). In addition, Trowbridge and Cason included a *Quantitative KR Group*, in which subjects were told the direction and magnitude of each error, to the nearest eighth of an inch. For instance, if a line was 7/8 inch longer than 3 inches, the experimenter would say "Plus seven." If a line was 5/8 inch shorter than 3 inches, the experimenter would say "Minus five." Trowbridge and Cason reasoned that the Quantitative KR Group received more information than the Qualitative KR Group, but not more reinforcement. Finally, a fourth group, the *Irrelevant KR Group*, received useless "feedback" after each trial—a meaningless nonsense syllable.

Each group received 100 trials, and the results are shown in Figure 13-1. Neither the No KR nor the Irrelevant KR groups showed any improvement over trials. In the Qualitative KR Group, there was clear improvement: The size of the average error decreased from about 1 inch at the start of the experiment to about one-half inch at the end. Figure 13-1 shows, however, that the performance of the Quantitative KR Group was vastly superior to that of the Qualitative KR Group. From this pattern of results, we can conclude that information, not reinforcement, was the crucial factor, and that the more precise, quantitative KR produced much better performance than the less precise, qualitative KR.

***Different Ways to Deliver Knowledge of Results.*** From the preceding experiment, you might conclude that delivering precise KR on every trial is the best way to teach a motor skill. However, if quantitative KR is given after every trial, the learner may actually become too reliant on this constant feedback, and may be less skillful if he or she later has to perform without feedback. Winstein and Schmidt (1990) gave some subjects quantitative KR

after each trial of a motor-learning experiment, whereas other subjects received quantitative KR on only 67 percent of the trials. During the learning phase, the performance of the group with constant feedback was slightly better. However, in a test 2 days later, *with no feedback given on any trial,* the group that had previously received 67 percent feedback actually performed better. Similar results have been obtained in other studies (Lee, White, & Carnahan, 1990; Wulf & Schmidt, 1989).

To explain these results, Salmoni, Schmidt, and Walter (1984) developed the **guidance hypothesis** of KR. According to the guidance hypothesis, KR provides information that helps the subject learn the new motor skill. KR that is given on every trial provides more guidance than KR given on only a portion of the trials, so performance during the acquisition phase is more accurate with 100 percent KR. However, the subject becomes very dependent on this constant KR and cannot perform well in a later test without KR.

In contrast, subjects who do not receive KR on every trial must rely more on their own ability to detect errors in their movements (since they have no other feedback on some trials), so they perform better on a test with KR completely absent. If this hypothesis is

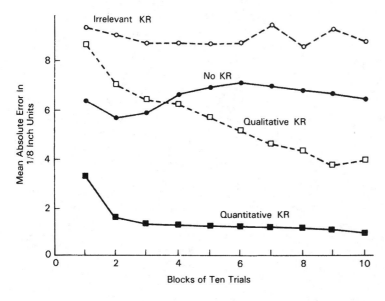

**FIGURE 13-1** Results from the four groups of the Trowbridge and Cason (1932) experiment.

correct, it has implications for those who teach motor skills to athletes, musicians, dancers, and so on. The coach should probably give feedback to the athlete or performer on some practice trials, but not on every trial, so that the performer can learn to detect and correct errors in performance without the coach's help. In this way, the performer can continue to perform well when the coach is not there to give feedback. We will return to the importance of learning to judge one's own performance when we examine theories of motor-skill learning later in this chapter.

***Delaying Knowledge of Results.***   Since receiving KR seems to be such an important part of learning a new motor skill, we might expect that acquisition will be impaired if there is a delay between the performance of a response and the delivery of KR. For some types of motor skills, this is indeed the case. In tasks where the individual usually receives continuous immediate feedback, even small delays in this feedback can produce marked deterioration in performance. A number of studies have examined how a subject's speech is affected when auditory feedback from the subject's voice is delayed by a fraction of a second. (The subject listens to his or her own voice through headphones that delay the transmission of the speech.) The typical result is that subjects begin to stutter and to speak more slowly and in a halting manner (Lee, 1950). In addition, subjects show little improvement with practice (Goldiamond, Atkinson, & Bilger, 1962). K. U. Smith (1962) examined subjects' performances on various tracking tasks with delayed feedback. For instance, a subject might have to trace a curving figure with a pencil while watching his or her performance on a TV screen that delays the visual feedback of the subject's movements. Not surprisingly, Smith found that performance worsened as delays in feedback got longer.

In contrast to the above results, there is little or no impairment of learning when a delay is imposed between a response and feedback that normally comes after the response (which we have been calling KR). Many studies on delayed KR have employed **slow positioning tasks,** in which the subject must move a sliding knob or pointer a certain distance, with no time limit. The knob or pointer is usually out of the subject's sight, so the subject must rely on tactile or kinesthetic cues rather than visual ones. In general, if KR is delayed after each trial (by a few seconds, a few minutes, or even longer), this seems to have little effect on the subject's accuracy (Bilodeau, 1966; Mulder & Hulstijn, 1985a).

We have already seen that delays of only a few seconds can greatly hinder learning in both classical and operant conditioning. The failure to find similar detrimental effects of delayed KR was therefore quite puzzling. This mystery remained unsolved for several decades, but now there appears to be an answer. In one experiment, subjects performed a timing task, in which they tried to move a slide from one position to another in exactly one second (Swinnen, Schmidt, Nicholson, & Shapiro, 1990). After each trial, the subjects received quantitative KR—the actual movement time was displayed, in thousandths of a second. For one group, the time was displayed immediately after a trial, but for another group the time was displayed after an 8-second delay. Both groups showed similar improvements in accuracy over 90 acquisition trials. Two days later, both groups were tested again, but this time they received no KR about their movement times. In this delayed test of their performance, the group that had previously received the delayed KR was actually more accurate than the immediate-KR group.

To explain why performance can be better after delayed KR than after immediate KR, Swinnen and his associates relied on the guidance hypothesis of KR that was discussed in the preceding section. Immediate KR may help to guide subjects during acquisition, but they may become overly dependent on this immediate feedback and never learn to rely on their own senses to estimate the accuracy of their movements. But the subjects with delayed KR had an 8-second period after each trial in which they could try to estimate the accuracy of their movements, and therefore could improve their skills at detecting their own errors. To strengthen his case that error detection is the critical factor, Swinnen (1990) has shown that if subjects are required to make verbal estimates of their errors during the 8-second delay during acquisition, they perform even better in a later test without KR. In contrast, if they are distracted during the 8-second delays (so they do not have time to estimate the accuracy of their movements), their performance on a later test is impaired.

Perhaps so many of the older studies found little effect of delaying KR because the disadvantages of not getting prompt feedback were offset by the opportunity that subjects had to practice estimating their errors during the delay. In fact, some studies have found that delaying KR can indeed slow down the *acquisition* of a motor skill, but, as in the study just described, later *performance* without KR is greatly improved in the delayed-KR conditions (Schmidt, Young, Swinnen, & Shapiro, 1989). The problem with immediate KR seems to be the same as the problem with getting KR on every trial: An overreliance on immediate KR (or on KR given after every trial) may lead to improved performance during the acquisition of a new motor skill, but it seems to hurt performance in a later test when the subject must perform without external feedback.

## Knowledge of Performance

It is often possible to give a subject many types of feedback besides information on how close the movement came to some goal. Consider, for example, the many useful pieces of information a coach might be able to give a pole-vaulter after each vault in practice. The coach might discuss various details related to the athlete's take-off, approach, pole placement, ascent, limb positions, and the like, and each piece of information might help to improve the athlete's future performances. The delivery of such information about the sequence of components of a complex movement is called **knowledge of performance (KP).** Hatze (1976) provided one illustration of the usefulness of this type of detailed feedback in a laboratory setting. The subject's task was to stand in front of a target, and then to raise his right foot and kick the target as

rapidly as possible. For the first 120 trials, the subject received quantitative KR—he was told his time after each trial. As Figure 13-2 shows, the subject's movement time decreased over these trials and leveled off at about 800 milliseconds. After trial 120, the subject was shown a videotape of his performance, and his motions were compared to a stick figure performing the response in the best possible way. After receiving this feedback, the subject began a new phase of improvement, and as Figure 13-2 shows, his movement times decreased to about 500 milliseconds. These results suggest that a comparison between the individual's movements and those of an ideal performer is a particularly effective form of feedback.

KP is now commonly used in the training of Olympic athletes. For instance, a discus thrower might be videotaped as he practices, and later his performance can be reviewed and compared to the motions of a computer-generated figure that demonstrates the movements that would maximize the distance the discus is thrown. In addition, there has been an increasing interest in providing athletes with various types of special feedback to determine which are the most effective (den Brinker, Stabler, Whiting, & Van Wieringen, 1986; Zubiar, Ona, & Delgado, 1999). In some cases, techniques similar to biofeedback (in which the learner is given amplified or quantitative feedback about his movements; see Chapter 9) can assist the acquisition of a novel motor skill (Mulder & Hulstijn, 1985b).

To investigate what types of feedback are most useful to someone learning a new motor skill, Kernodle and Carlton (1992) had four groups of subjects learn to throw a ball with their nondominant hands (that is, with the left hand for subjects who were naturally right-handed throwers, and vice versa). The goal was to throw the ball in a straight line as far as possible. One group received normal KR: They were told the exact distance of each throw. A second group received KP: After each throw, they watched a videotape replay of their throwing motion on that trial. A third group received the same type of KP, but in addition they were told to focus their attention on a

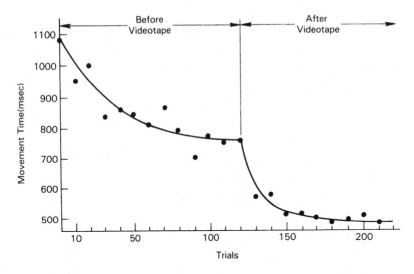

**FIGURE 13-2** Results from the experiment of Hatze (1976) before and after the subject viewed a videotape comparing his leg movements with the best possible movements.

particular part of the throwing motion while watching the replay. During the training, they were told to focus on 10 different components of a good throw, such as "Focus on the hips during the throwing phase." A fourth group also received KP, but while watching the replay, they were instructed on what to do to improve their motion on the next trial, such as "Stride forward with the right foot toward the target area." All four groups were given 12 training sessions over a 4-week period. The researchers found that the fourth group, which received KP plus instructions on how to improve, showed the greatest improvement, both in the length of their throws and in judge's ratings of their throwing form.

Sometimes a single critical piece of information can prove very valuable in learning a new skill. For example, Schmidt and Young (1991) had subjects practice operating a device that simulated swinging a bat at a moving ball. One group received KR—information about the distance the ball was hit. The other group received both KR and KP, with the KP consisting of information about the length of the backswing. Subjects were initially told that the optimal backswing was 165 degrees, and after

each swing they were told the angle of the backswing. Figure 13-3 shows that subjects who received this extra information performed substantially better, both on the two learning days and on the third day, when no KR or KP was given to either group.

More research of this type should help to determine what types of feedback are most useful to the learner. The answers will almost surely vary depending on exactly what type of skill is being learned. In fact, for some skills, providing simple KR may be more helpful than more detailed KP (Tzetzis, Kioumourtzoglou, & Mavromatis, 1997). However, a general conclusion we can draw from this research is that although quantitative KR can be

Information about graduate training and careers in exercise and sport psychology can be found at *http://www.apa.org/about/division/div47.html.*

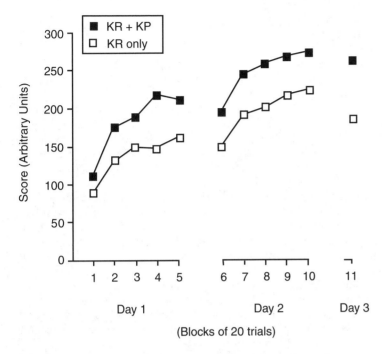

**FIGURE 13-3** Scores on a simulated batting task are shown for a group that received only KR (feedback about the distance the ball was hit) and a group that received KR plus KP (feedback about how the angle of each backswing compared to the optimal angle). (From Schmidt & Young, 1991)

quite helpful in learning a motor skill, more elaborate types of feedback can produce even greater improvements in performance.

### Distribution of Practice

One of the most heavily researched areas in motor learning from the turn of the century through the 1950s was how the temporal distribution of practice affects learning. One reason for the interest in this topic was strictly pragmatic: Researchers wanted to find the most efficient method of learning a new skill. For example, suppose a supervisor has 4 hours in which to teach a new employee to operate a semiautomatic machine. Will the employee's performance be best if he or she practices steadily for the 4 hours, or if the employee alternates between 30-minute practice periods

and 30-minute rest periods, or with some other distribution of practice and rest? As a general rule, the laboratory studies found that performance is better if rest periods are interspersed among fairly brief practice periods than if practice occurs in one continuous block. In short, **distributed practice** is better than **massed practice.** It is interesting to note that Ebbinghaus (1885) obtained a similar result in his research on the memorization of lists of nonsense syllables, a very different type of task.

To explain the effects of distributed practice, Hull (1943) developed the concept of **reactive inhibition,** which is in fact very similar to the average person's concept of fatigue. Hull proposed that as a person continues to practice at some task without a break, reactive inhibition steadily builds up and artificially depresses performance. He suggested that re-active inhibition dissipates spontaneously during any rest period (again, notice the similarity to fatigue), so that overall performance will be better if frequent rest periods are allowed. Indeed, in learning motor skills there is often an improvement in performance immediately after a rest period.

Experiments on the distribution of practice would have important implications for people learning new motor skills were it not for one major qualification: The disadvantages of massed practice appear to be in large part transitory. Subjects who receive massed practice do substantially worse during that practice, but after a sufficient rest period, their performance is usually about as good as that of subjects who initially received distributed practice (Adams & Reynolds, 1954; Rider & Abdulahad, 1991). In summary, the distribution of practice and rest periods has a large temporary effect, but it seems to have little or no effect on long-term performance.

## Observational Learning of Motor Skills

As with many other types of learned behaviors, some motor skills can be acquired through observation. Not surprisingly, simply observing someone else perform a motor skill is not as effective as practicing it yourself. Nevertheless, observational learning can be beneficial, especially when combined with direct practice. In one experiment, people could make the cursor on a computer screen move either left or right by pressing two different keys, and their goal was to keep the cursor on a moving dot on the screen. A group of subjects who practiced this task themselves performed better on the test day than subjects who watched another person learning the task. However, those who only observed the task performed much better than control subjects who neither practiced nor observed the task until the test day. Furthermore, subjects who first observed the task and then practiced it themselves performed better than all the other groups on a transfer test in which the movement of the dot was different during the test

phase (Shea, Wright, Wulf, & Whitacre, 2000). In short, both individual practice and observation contributed to the subjects' acquisition of this new skill.

Another experiment examined the effects of having learners practice a new skill in pairs. The task was to balance on an unstable platform and try to keep it as level as possible on each 30-second trial. The paired subjects took turns practicing the skill, observing their partners, and discussing each other's performance. These subjects performed better on the test day than those who practiced individually. Evidently, the turn-taking routine of the subjects who practiced in pairs was important, because these subjects also performed better than those who practiced in pairs where one learner received all of his trials first, and then the second learner took all of his trials (Shea, Wulf, & Whitacre, 1999). The benefits of practicing with others are apparently well known among athletes, who frequently train together and share pointers and strategies.

## Transfer from Previous Training

In motor-skill research, the topic of **transfer of training** is similar to the topic of generalization in animal-learning research. In both cases, the question is how experience with one set of stimuli will affect performance with a new set of stimuli. Early theorists (Osgood, 1949) believed that it should be possible to observe **positive transfer** (in which practice in one task aids the acquisition of a similar task) in some situations, and **negative transfer** (in which practice on one task interferes with the acquisition of a similar task) in other situations. From an intuitive standpoint, both possibilities seem reasonable. For instance, it seems likely that learning to drive a car with a three-speed manual transmission should make it easier to learn to drive a car with a four-speed transmission. The topic of negative transfer reminds me of the discussions I had with friends when I was young about how playing baseball early in the day would be detrimental to a golf game later in the day. Our theory was that the flat swing of a baseball bat would interfere with one's ability to produce the relatively upright golf swing shortly afterward.

Quite a few studies have found evidence for positive transfer (see Schmidt, 1988, pp. 407–411). As we might expect, the amount of positive transfer from one task to another depends on the similarity of the two tasks. An experiment demonstrating this point was conducted by Baker, Wylie, and Gagne (1950). The subject's task was to turn a crank at a speed that kept a pointer in contact with a target. For each subject, the number of crank revolutions that were needed to move the pointer a certain distance varied from the training phase to the test phase. Not surprisingly, there was more positive transfer when there was a fairly small change in speed in the test phase than when there was a large change in speed. More recent studies have shown that there can be positive transfer across different muscle groups and different movement patterns. Latash (1999) had college students practice mirror writing, in which they had to write a sentence while looking in a mirror and so that the words read correctly as seen in the mirror. After practicing this task for several days with their normal writing hands, the students showed large transfer effects when they had to switch to their other hands. Palmer and Meyer (2000) found positive transfer when experienced pianists learned a new piece of music, but then were asked to play a variation of the melody that required them to use different hand and finger movements. These researchers concluded that motor learning is not simply a matter of learning specific muscle movements, because experienced learners can transfer their skills to new situations that require them to produce the same general patterns of movements using different muscle groups.

Somewhat surprisingly, it has proven to be quite difficult to find experimental evidence for negative transfer in motor-skill tasks. When it is found, negative transfer is often very fleeting, sometimes lasting only a trial or two (Blais, Kerr, & Hughes, 1993). One demonstration of this phenomenon was provided by Lewis, McAllister, and Adams (1951). The subject's task in this experiment was to use a joystick to move several green lights on a display toward different targets. In the initial phase of the experiment, moving a joystick in one direction caused a green light to move in the same direction (for instance, moving the joystick to the upper left made the light move toward the upper left). With practice, subjects became faster at moving the lights toward their targets. In the second (interference) phase, subjects in several experimental groups received a number of trials in which the action of the joystick was reversed (moving the joystick to the upper left made the light move to the lower right). Here, too, subjects' performances improved with practice. Subjects in a control group received no trials with the controls reversed. The test of negative transfer came in the third phase of the experiment, in which the original operation of the joystick was restored. Subjects in the experimental groups performed more poorly than they had at the end of the first phase, and they required several trials to regain their previous performance levels. There was no such drop in the performance of control subjects, which shows that the decrements were not simply due to the passage of time without practice.

Although it is difficult to make any definitive statements about when positive and negative transfer effects will be observed, the following principles may be useful guidelines: Positive transfer is most likely to be found when two tasks involve similar or identical movements in response to a similar stimulus situation. In the experiment of Baker and associates, for example, the stimulus was identical in both tasks (a moving target), and the required motions were similar (turning the same crank in the same direction, only at different speeds). On the other hand, negative transfer is most likely to be observed when two tasks demand antagonistic or incompatible responses to a similar stimulus situation. Thus the strong negative transfer found by Lewis and colleagues probably occurred because a particular stimulus (such as a green light below its target) required one response in the original task and the opposite response in the interfering task.

The difficulty in applying these rules, however, is that it is often not obvious whether two movements (such as swinging a baseball bat and swinging a golf club) should be considered similar or antagonistic. In many cases, two skills may include a mixture of both similar and antagonistic responses. For instance, in one study, subjects in an experimental group practiced the skills of short tennis and lawn tennis for a few hours each, and a control group practiced lawn tennis only. Then both groups were tested in lawn tennis skills. The researchers found that the experimental subjects were better at certain lawn tennis skills and the control subjects were better at others, thus providing evidence for both positive and negative transfer in the same experiment (Coldwells & Hare, 1994).

### Ironic Errors in Movement

People sometimes tend to make the very movement they are trying to avoid. If someone hands you a full cup of coffee and says, "Be careful not to spill it on my new rug," it may be harder to avoid spilling a drop than if you are carrying the cup outdoors across the lawn. According to Wegner (1997), this is not just because you are more nervous when carrying the cup over a new rug. Wegner has proposed a theory of **ironic errors,** which states that people have a tendency to make a false movement that they are trying hard to avoid, especially if their attention is distracted by some competing task. Wegner, Ansfield, and Pilloff (1998) tested this theory in an experiment where subjects tried to putt a golf ball toward a target. One group of subjects was simply told to try to get the ball as close as possible to the target. A second group was told to be particularly careful not to hit the ball past the target. Under conditions of a "mental load" (in which they had to remember a six-digit number while making the putt), those who were specifically instructed not to hit the ball past the target were more likely to do so. In another experiment, these researchers asked people to hold a weight on a string above a target for 30 seconds. A group that was specifically instructed to avoid left or right movements (as opposed to forward or backward movements) tended to make more left or right movements than a

group that was simply instructed to hold the weight as steady as possible. This was especially true when subjects performed the task under a mental-load condition.

Ironic errors can be frustrating and embarrassing, and they can make us look awkward and clumsy. They can also affect the performance of athletes who are trying to perform at the peak of their abilities. To avoid ironic errors, Janelle (1999) recommends that coaches could use a variety of strategies, such as making sure that athletes are thoroughly familiar with all the possible situations that can arise during a game, so the need to make novel decisions (which would constitute a mental load) is minimized. Further research may show whether these strategies can help to reduce the errors that an athlete is trying hardest to avoid.

## THEORIES OF MOTOR-SKILL LEARNING

Thus far we have considered some factors that determine how quickly and how well a new skill will be learned, but we have entertained few hypotheses about what takes place inside the individual during such learning episodes. We will now turn to some theories that deal with this question.

### Adams's Two-Stage Theory

Jack Adams (1971) proposed an influential theory of motor learning that has generated both numerous experiments and substantial theoretical debate. To make the discussion of Adams's theory more understandable, it will be helpful to relate some of Adams's terms to the terminology of control systems theory introduced in Chapter 3. One important concept of Adams's theory is the **perceptual trace,** which corresponds to the reference input of control systems theory. According to Adams, when a person begins to learn a new motor skill, the perceptual trace or reference input is weak or nonexistent. Consider any simple task in which KR is delivered after the movement is completed, such as Thorndike's line-drawing task. The blindfolded subject knows that the task is to draw a 3-inch line, but does not yet know what it "feels like" to draw a line of this length. Adams proposed that an important part of the learning of such a skill is the development of an appropriate perceptual trace. In the line-drawing task, the perceptual trace is presumably a memory of the sensations produced by the sensory neurons of the hand and arm when a line of the appropriate length was drawn.

A second important concept in Adams's theory is the **motor trace** (which Adams actually called the **memory trace**). The motor trace relates to the workings of the action system of control systems theory. The basic idea is that in addition to learning what it feels like to produce the correct movement, a person must also learn to coordinate his or her muscles so that the movement is indeed produced. For instance, in the line-drawing task, the subject must learn to move the pencil so as to reduce the discrepancy between actual input and reference input without overshooting the reference input. It will do the subject little good to say, "I know what it feels like to draw a 3-inch line, but I accidentally moved the pencil about an inch too far." If this statement were true, though, it would suggest that the subject had developed a good perceptual trace but needed to improve the movements of his or her action system, the hand and arm.

Other motor skills provide much clearer illustrations of how an individual may have an accurate perceptual trace but a poorly functioning action system. A beginning pianist may listen to a recording of a difficult piece again and again, until she has a firm idea of what an excellent rendition sounds like. (That is, she develops the ability to discriminate between a very good rendition and an excellent rendition, much as the judges in a competition attempt to do.) Having reached this point, however, it may take long hours of painstaking practice before she can even approximate a good rendition on her own. As another example, having hit thousands of golf balls over the years, I believe I can distinguish between the sensations that accompany a good golf swing and those that accompany a bad swing. A good swing involves a certain rhythm of the wrists, arms, hips, and knees that causes the clubhead to "snap" at the ball, and I can tell the shot is a good one before looking up to see where the ball has gone. My problem is that although I can recognize a good swing when I feel one, my action system does not produce one every time. In fact, I sometimes go through an entire round without ever experiencing the sensations of a good swing.

According to Adams's theory, there are two stages in the learning of a typical motor skill. The first stage is called the **verbal-motor stage,** because in this stage improvement depends on the delivery of feedback, usually in a verbal form. That is, the instructor must supply the learner with KR, because the learner does not have an accurate perceptual trace, and therefore cannot discriminate a good trial from a bad one. The verbal-motor stage is the time when improvement depends on constant feedback from the piano teacher, the pitching coach, or the gymnastics instructor. Without this feedback, the learner cannot tell whether the movement was good, or what was wrong with it.

J. A. Adams (1976) described the end of the verbal-motor stage in this way:

> The Verbal-Motor Stage has a somewhat indefinite end point, and it will vary from subject to subject, but it comes to an end when knowledge of results has been signifying trivial error for some time and that the response is being successfully made. At this point the subject can switch wholly to the perceptual trace as a reference for responding because it now defines the correct response. The subject can now behave without knowledge of results. . . . (p. 205)

Adams calls this second stage the **motor stage.** At this point, the individual can rely on an internal perceptual trace to judge the accuracy of a movement in the absence of external KR. Adams goes on to say that in addition to maintaining his current performance level in the absence of KR, the learner can actually improve his performance by refining the precision of the motor trace (that is, by becoming more skillful in producing the desired movement).

Adams's theory predicts that during the first stage of motor learning, if subjects receive KR only intermittently, the perceptual trace will be strengthened on trials when KR is delivered, but it will tend to decay on trials without KR. Sparrow and Summers (1992) found just such a pattern with a slow positioning task in which some subjects received KR after every fifth trial and others after every tenth trial. The subjects' accuracy was highest immediately after a trial with KR, then it gradually deteriorated during the trials without KR, it improved again after the next trial with KR, and so on.

This experiment shows that KR is essential when a new motor skill is first being learned. However, there is also solid evidence that KR can become unnecessary later in training. The best evidence comes from studies in which KR is withdrawn at some point in the middle of the experiment. For example, Newell (1974) had subjects practice a discrete movement—moving a slide 9.5 inches in 150 millisec-

onds—for 77 trials. One group of subjects received quantitative KR on all trials, whereas in five other groups, quantitative KR was withdrawn after either 2, 7, 17, 32, or 52 trials. Figure 13-4 shows that in the group with uninterrupted KR, errors steadily decreased to a low level. At the other extreme, two trials with KR were clearly not enough to establish a perceptual trace. This group showed some improvement at first, but then performance deteriorated after many trials without KR. This pattern suggests that the subjects began to establish a perceptual trace, but it was later "forgotten." The results from the groups with 7, 17, or 32 trials with KR suggest that these groups derived some permanent benefits from this initial KR. There was some deterioration in performance when the KR was removed, but these groups continued to perform better than the 2-trial group. The results from the

**FIGURE 13-4**    Results from the six groups of the Newell (1974) experiment. Each group received a different number of trials with KR.

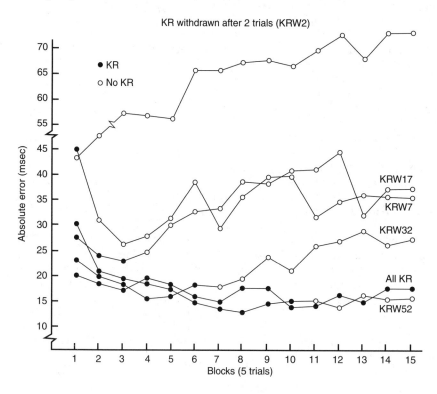

group with 52 trials with KR are probably the most interesting. This group showed no decreases in accuracy when KR was removed, and its performance equaled that of the group with uninterrupted KR throughout the experiment. Adams's interpretation is that subjects in this group had progressed to the motor stage, where an internal perceptual trace replaced external KR as a means of evaluating their performances on each trial.

Adams's theory is also supported by more recent studies (discussed in previous sections) showing that delivering KR on only a fraction of the acquisition trials, or delaying KR for a few seconds, can lead to better performance on later tests when subjects must perform without KR. These results can be interpreted using Adams's theory as follows: Subjects who received less frequent or delayed KR presumably had more of an opportunity to develop accurate perceptual traces (that is, to use sensory cues to judge their performances), since external KR was frequently unavailable. On the other hand, subjects who received KR on every trial may have had it too easy: They may have failed to develop a keen ability to judge their own performances because the experimenter always provided them with immediate, external KR. These results seem to support Adams's theory that the development of an accurate perceptual trace is an important part of learning a motor skill.

Once a person has reached the motor stage, feedback from the piano teacher, the pitching coach, or the gymnastics instructor becomes less important. Of course, the instructor can continue to provide helpful feedback to correct minor flaws in one's technique or to make further refinements in one's style. At the same time, however, the learner can also improve through practice on his or her own by relying on internal feedback in place of the coach's feedback. Perhaps the most important contribution of Adams's theory is that it distinguishes between the two types of learning that take place during the acquisition of most motor skills—learning to recognize what it feels like to make an accurate response and learning to produce such a response consistently. The strongest support for this theory

comes from studies that separate these two types of learning (Newell, 1974, 1976).

## Schmidt's Schema Theory

Adams's two-stage theory represented an important advance in the analysis of motor-skill learning. Yet all theories have their limitations, and a major limitation of Adams's theory is that it seems to be limited to the acquisition of single, repetitive movements (that is, to movements of the foul-shot type, where the stimulus conditions and the required movement are exactly the same, trial after trial). The theory says nothing about how people can acquire skills that involve the production of different responses on different trials so as to deal with different stimulus conditions. Consider the tennis player's response to an approaching ball, a bird's response to the diversionary tactics of a flying insect it is chasing, a hiker's response to the irregular terrain of a rocky hillside, or a driver's response to an unfamiliar winding road. In all of these cases and many others, the individual is confronted with new and different stimulus conditions and must generate a response to suit these conditions. It seems clear that more is involved in the acquisition of such skills than the development of a single perceptual trace and a single motor trace. In an effort to go beyond Adams's theory and deal with these more flexible motor skills, Richard Schmidt (1975) developed his schema theory of motor-skill learning.

Schmidt's theory retains the most novel part of Adams's theory—the idea that two types of learning take place during the acquisition of most motor skills (learning to recognize the correct response and learning to produce it). However, to deal with more flexible motor skills, such as those discussed above, Schmidt proposed that people can acquire general rules (which he called **schemas**) as they practice. Schmidt borrowed the term schema from Bartlett (1932), an early writer on the topic of memory. Bartlett proposed that our memories consist to a large extent of abstractions and generalizations rather than specifics and details. Similarly, Schmidt proposed that people do not retain information about specific past movements and their consequences but rather that they develop what I will call **perceptual schemas** and **motor schemas.** (These are not the terms Schmidt used, but I will use them to be as consistent as possible with the terminology used in describing Adams's theory.)

To make these concepts more concrete, let us consider how a golfer learns to putt a ball the appropriate distance (ignoring the problem of moving the ball in the appropriate direction). The golfer must learn to stroke the ball with different amounts of effort, depending on how far the ball is from the hole. In practice, the golfer may use different amounts of effort on different trials and observe the result (the distance the ball travels). This situation is illustrated in Figure 13-5a. Each point represents a single practice trial: The x-axis represents the golfer's estimate of the effort used in the stroke, and the y-axis represents the golfer's estimate of the distance the ball traveled.

According to Schmidt, these individual data points are soon forgotten, but what the golfer develops and retains is a general rule or motor schema about the relationship between effort and the distance the ball moves (as signified by the solid line in Figure 13-5a). Furthermore, Schmidt states that motor schemas may consist of more than a single function, because other situational variables can affect the outcome of a particular movement. In the example of putting, one such variable is the slope of the green. Figure 13-5b shows a simplified illustration of the more complex motor schema a golfer might develop by practicing level, uphill, and downhill putts. A skillful golfer's motor schema would be much more complex than this, of course, because the slope of a green can vary continuously, and other factors such as the length of the grass and any moisture on the green must be taken into account. The advantage of such a schema is that it allows the individual to respond to new situations with a reasonable chance of success. Thus, although a golfer may never have practiced a 22-foot putt on a moderately slow green with a downhill slope of 4 degrees, the motor schema allows the golfer to generalize from similar past experiences, so as to produce a reasonably suitable response.

Schmidt's theory states that besides developing such a motor schema, learners also develop perceptual schemas that allow them to

**FIGURE 13-5**    (a) A hypothetical illustration of how, according to Schmidt's schema theory, a person might learn a general rule or schema about the relationship between the effort of a putting stroke and the distance the golf ball moves. Each data point represents the learner's estimates of effort and distance on one practice trial, and the line represents the general rule the learner supposedly retains from these trials. (b) This figure makes the point that a successful golfer's schema for putting would have to include different rules for downhill, flat, and uphill putts. In reality, the golfer's schema would have to be considerably more complex to account for continuous variations in the slope of the putting surface.

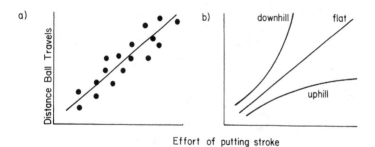

Effort of putting stroke

use sensory feedback to predict whether the appropriate movement was produced. The perceptual schema is simply a generalized version of the perceptual trace in Adams's theory that is applicable to more than one situation. Such a perceptual schema presumably allows a golfer to predict before seeing the result whether the stroke was too strong, too weak, or about right, regardless of whether the distance to the hole was 5 feet, 10 feet, or 40 feet. Indeed, in professional golf tournaments, one frequently sees a golfer stroke a putt and then immediately start walking toward the hole in disgust, knowing before the ball has traveled very far that the putt was not a good one.

The development of a perceptual schema may not seem particularly important in putting because the golfer can always see the result as the ball approaches the hole anyway. In other situations, however, the ability to compare the immediate sensory feedback from a movement with some perceptual schema can be valuable. For example, basketball players frequently remark that the shooter is the first person to know whether a shot will go into the basket. All the players can watch the flight of the ball and try to estimate whether it will hit or miss, but only the shooter has the additional sensory feedback provided by the shooting motion itself. The shooter can take advantage of this information by moving in position to grab the rebound if he or she determines that the shot will bounce off the rim.

The ability to deal with open-ended classes of movements, such as putting golf balls and shooting baskets from different parts of the court, makes Schmidt's theory more versatile than Adams's. But what scientific evidence is there that people do in fact learn such motor schemas? To test the theory, several different research strategies have been used. Some studies have tested whether people soon forget the specific examples that they practice but nevertheless retain a general schema (as illustrated in Figure 13-5). For example, Chamberlin and Magill (1992) taught subjects a timing task that involved pressing a sequence of three buttons that were a total of either 15 cm, 45 cm, or 135 cm apart. For all three distances, the subjects' goal was to complete the task in exactly

1.2 seconds, and they received extensive practice with each distance. The subjects were then tested one day later, and again one week later, on both these well-practiced distances and with new distances that they had never tried before (for instance, 30 cm and 90 cm). Chamberlin and Magill found that their subjects were just as accurate with the new distances as with the well-practiced distances. This finding is quite consistent with the prediction of schema theory that people can learn a general rule for movement and not just individual movement patterns.

Schmidt's theory also makes some predictions that are different from those of Adams's theory. One difference concerns the possibility of "learning from one's mistakes." The question is whether a person can benefit from practice trials on which the individual makes a response that is far off target and then receives KR indicating the size of the error. As a concrete example, think of a slow positioning task where the subject moves a slide 18 inches instead of the goal of 10 inches. According to schema theory, this trial can be a beneficial learning experience despite the magnitude of the error, because it still contributes to the development of the subject's perceptual and motor schemas. On the other hand, Adams's theory suggests that such errant movements will be detrimental to learning because the sensory feedback from these trials will interfere with the subject's perceptual trace, which is nothing more than the memory of the sensations produced by a correct movement. Speaking loosely, we might say that, according to Adams, errant movements are detrimental because they make the subject forget what it feels like to produce the correct movement. Shapiro and Schmidt (1982) reviewed the evidence on variability in practice and concluded that subjects benefit about as much from practicing a variety of different responses as from practicing the single correct response in a positioning task. These results are consistent with schema theory but not with Adams's theory.

Several experiments have provided support for schema theory's prediction that variable practice is beneficial. For example, Kerr and Booth (1978) had children toss bean bags at a target without visual feedback, and they were given quantitative KR by the experimenter. One group of children received **specific training,** in which they always aimed for a target that was 3 feet away. A second group received **variable training,** in which the target was sometimes 2 feet away and sometimes 4 feet away. Both groups later received test trials with the 3-foot target distance, and the group that had received variable training performed more accurately, even though subjects had never practiced with the 3-foot distance. Kerr and Booth suggested that the variable training helped the children develop stronger schemas than did the specific training.

Lee, Magill, and Weeks (1985) discovered that the way variable training is scheduled can have a large impact on its effectiveness. When the different variations of a behavior were practiced in separate blocks (for instance, a block of 2-foot throws, then a block of 4-foot throws), the benefits of this variable training were minimal. On the other hand, when the different variations were randomly intermixed (2-foot throws intermixed with 4-foot throws), this variable training proved to be superior to specific training. This pattern suggests that if you want to reap the greatest benefits from variable practice (such as practicing different shots on a basketball court), you should randomly intermix the different behaviors you practice (changing your position on the court after each shot).

To summarize, a major strength of Schmidt's schema theory is that it provides a framework for understanding how people develop flexible motor skills that allow them to make successful responses when confronted with situations they have never experienced before. The theory states that this ability develops as a person acquires general rules or schemas that describe the relations between different stimulus conditions, possible movements, and their expected consequences.

## LEARNING MOVEMENT SEQUENCES

In this section we will consider motor skills involving sequences of movements that must be performed in a specific order. Some skills of this type are walking, swimming, typing, or playing a musical instrument. In the first two of these examples, the appropriate sequences of movement are cyclical or repetitive, whereas in the second two they are usually not. In all of these examples, however, successful performance depends on producing the sequence of movements in the correct order and with the correct timing. For instance, in performing the breast stroke, a swimmer must coordinate the movements of the arms and legs to move through the water efficiently. A pianist will not get much credit for playing all of the notes in a score if they are not played in the correct sequence, and with the correct tempo.

One of the most obvious characteristics of such skilled movements is that people become more proficient in performing them with practice. The learning curve in such tasks is similar in form to learning curves in classical and operant conditioning. For instance, in learning to type, a beginner's average number of words per minute increases rapidly at first and then more gradually as it approaches some asymptotic level of performance (Thurstone, 1919). The challenge for motor-skill researchers is to explain why people become more skillful in performing such sequences of movement with practice.

### The Response Chain Approach

One major approach to the topic of movement sequences is based on the concept of a response chain, which was discussed in Chapter 6. The relationship should be clear, since a response chain was defined as a sequence of behaviors that must occur in a specific order, with a primary reinforcer following the completion of the last behavior of the chain. According to the standard analysis, what keeps the behaviors of the chain in their correct sequence is the fact that each response produces a distinctive stimulus that acts as a discriminative stimulus ($S^D$) for the next response of the chain. For instance, the beginning of a maze may serve as a discriminative stimulus for running, and running may bring an animal to a choice point, which is a discriminative stimulus to turn left. If the animal is then reinforced with a bit of food, the entire sequence of behaviors is strengthened.

It is easy to see how this analysis could be applied to some skilled-movement sequences, such as walking. The sight or feeling of having one's right leg in front might serve as a discriminative stimulus to shift one's weight to this leg and bring the left leg forward. The opposite might be true when one's left leg is in front. Of course, the movements of walking could be broken down further into a complex sequence of muscle contractions. Nevertheless, the principles of a response chain analysis would remain the same: The visual, tactile, or kinesthetic feedback from one muscle contraction might serve as a discriminative stimulus for the next muscle contraction in the sequence. Why, according to this analysis, does a person's ability to perform a sequence of movements improve with practice? The answer is that the appropriate stimulus-response associations are strengthened by reinforcement. For instance, to achieve the maximum propulsion in the breast stroke, a swimmer must begin to move his or her hands forward at a particular point during each stroke. If we assume that swimming speed is the reinforcer, then through the process of successive approximations, the swimmer should eventually learn exactly what cues signal that the forward movement of the hands should begin.

The response chain analysis of movement sequences is compatible with theories such as those of Adams and Schmidt, which emphasize the role of feedback in the control of movement. Chapter 3 showed how a response chain can be viewed as a series of feedback loops, with the completion of one loop leading to the start of the next. Yet although the response chain approach provides a satisfactory analysis for many response sequences (as in Figure 6-7), several types of evidence now suggest that it cannot account for all examples of behavior sequences.

## Motor Programs

The strongest line of attack against the response chain approach to movement sequencing is based on evidence for the existence of **motor programs**. Those who favor the concept of motor programs suggest that the response chain approach is incorrect because some movement sequences do not depend on continual sensory feedback for their proper execution. After presenting evidence for the existence of movement sequences that do not rely on sensory feedback, Keele (1973) introduced the concept of a motor program as follows:

> If neither visual nor kinesthetic feedback is needed for the execution of patterns of movement, then the movement patterns must be represented centrally in the brain, or perhaps in some cases in the spinal cord. Such representation is called a motor program. As a motor program is executed, neural impulses are sent to the appropriate muscles in proper sequence, timing, and force, as predetermined by the program, and the neural impulses are largely uninfluenced by the resultant feedback. (p. 124)

To clarify the distinction between a response chain and a motor program, let us consider a concrete example of a movement sequence—the typing of the word *the*. A response chain analysis might proceed as follows: Upon seeing the word *the* in the text to be typed, a typist responds by striking the *t* key with the left forefinger. This movement produces sensory feedback (kinesthetic feedback from the finger and perhaps auditory feedback from the typewriter) that serves as a discriminative stimulus to make the next response—striking the *h* key with the right forefinger. Sensory feedback from this response serves as a stimulus for the final response of striking the *e* key with the left middle finger.

Advocates of the motor program approach might agree that this analysis is correct for a beginning typist, but that after typing *the* many, many times, a skilled typist may develop a motor program for producing this response sequence. The idea is that when the skilled typist sees the word *the*, this motor program is activated and sends a series of commands to the muscles of the left forefinger, the right forefinger, and the left middle finger. These commands are timed so that the three movements are performed in the correct sequence, but this timing does not depend on sensory feedback from each successive movement in the sequence. One obvious advantage of the motor program is an increase in speed: The typist can begin to produce the second keystroke before receiving sensory feedback from the first keystroke.

***Evidence for Motor Programs.*** One of the first advocates of the concept of a motor program was Karl Lashley (1951), who described several types of evidence that a response chain analysis cannot explain all movement sequences. For one thing, Lashley argued that human reaction times are too slow to support the idea that sensory feedback from one response can serve as the stimulus for the next response in a rapid sequence. The minimum reaction time for a person to respond to kinesthetic stimulation is over 100 milliseconds (Glencross, 1977), and reaction times are no faster for other sensory modalities. Yet Lashley pointed out that musicians can produce as many as 16 finger movements per second. His point is that this rate could never be achieved if the musician had to wait for sensory feedback from one movement before beginning the next. Similar arguments have been made for the skill of typing (Shaffer, 1978). However, recent studies have suggested that human reaction times can sometimes be faster than previously believed possible, so this argument for motor programs is not quite as convincing as it once seemed (Bruce, 1994; Gao & Zelaznik, 1991).

A second argument made by Lashley was that skilled movements and sequences of movements are still possible for individuals who have lost sensory feedback. He reported the case of a man who had lost all sensation in the area of the knee as a result of a gunshot wound. Despite the loss of sensation, the man could move and position his leg as accurately as an uninjured person (Lashley, 1917). Other evidence that complex movements can continue in the absence of sensory feedback comes from animal studies in which sensory nerve fibers are severed before they enter the spinal cord. For example, Taub and Berman (1968) surgically removed all sensory feedback from both forelimbs of several monkeys. After this surgery, the monkeys were still able to use these limbs to walk and climb (even when blindfolded, which removed the possible influence of visual feedback). The monkeys could coordinate the movements of their senseless forelimbs with their normal hindlimbs. This research provides strong evidence that sensory feedback is not always necessary for skilled movements. However, it should be noted that the movements of the forelimbs were less fluid and clumsier than normal (Bossom, 1974), which suggests that kinesthetic feedback does contribute to the smoothness of movement.

Further evidence for movement sequencing without sensory feedback has involved lower animals. Wilson (1961) found that locusts can continue to produce coordinated, rhythmical wing beating when all sensory nerves in their wings are severed. He concluded that the timing of the wing-beating motions is controlled by a motor program. In research on various songbirds, Nottebohm (1970) determined that young birds will not develop the normal song of their species unless they (1) have the opportunity to hear other members of their species sing, and (2) can hear themselves sing as they first learn the song. However, if the birds are deafened after they have learned the song, they can continue to sing the song with only minor deterioration of their performance. One interpretation is that auditory feedback is necessary while a motor program for the song is being developed, but once it is developed, auditory feedback is no longer necessary.

Lashley's third argument for motor programs concerns the types of errors frequently found in rapid-movement sequences. He noted that many typing mistakes are errors of anticipation or transposition. For instance, I sometimes type *hte* when I intend to type *the*. It is difficult to explain this sort of error with a response chain analysis. If the stimulus for striking the *h* key was the sensory feedback from the movement of striking the *t* key, the second movement should never precede the first. Instead, Lashley would argue that the separate movements were sequenced by a motor program, but that the synchronization of the movements became distorted somewhere along the line from command to execution. In short, Lashley suggested that any errors that indicate the individual was planning ahead support the notion of a motor program but are inconsistent with the response chain approach.

To summarize, Lashley presented three types of evidence for the existence of motor programs: (1) Some movement sequences appear to occur too rapidly to make use of sensory feedback to guide the movement; (2) some movements and sequences of movements can occur when sensory feedback has been removed; and (3) errors of anticipation or transposition in movement sequences suggest that the individual is planning ahead and is not waiting for feedback from one movement as a stimulus to start the next.

A fourth type of evidence, not known to Lashley, is that the amount of time needed to begin a sequence of movements depends on the number of separate movements that are part of the sequence. For instance, a person needs more time to begin a sequence that involves four discrete motions than one that involves only two motions (Ulrich, Giray, & Schaffer, 1990). The explanation usually offered for this effect is that the person is constructing a motor program for all of the motions at the beginning, and it takes more time to preprogram four movements than two movements. If the subject were only planning the first movement before beginning, why would it take longer to plan this single movement in one case than in the other? Starting times are slower for longer movement sequences even when such sequences have been practiced extensively (Fischman & Lim, 1991).

An experiment on handwriting found evidence of this last type (Portier, van Galen, & Meulenbroek, 1990). Subjects were taught to "write" six different patterns, each composed of three letter-like characters (see Figure 13-6). Subjects wrote with a pen that was connected to sophisticated recording equipment that could detect the exact location of the pen at each instant. Not surprisingly, with practice, subjects got faster at writing the patterns. However, writing speed increased substantially for the second and third characters of each pattern, whereas writing speed for the initial character did not increase very much. Why should it take subjects so long to write the first character, which had a relatively simple shape? The experimenters concluded that this was because subjects were not simply learning to write the three individual characters; they were developing motor programs for each pattern as a whole. The first character presumably took longer to write because subjects were simultaneously planning the rest of the pattern. The experimenters also found that the speed of writing the first character was slower if the third character was a mirror image of the first (as in panels E and F of Figure 13-6) than if the third character was the same as the first (panels C and D) or a completely different shape (panels A and B). The effect of the third character on the speed of writing the first character is convincing evidence that subjects

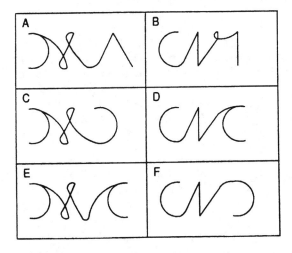

**FIGURE 13-6** Six patterns, each composed of three letter-like characters, that subjects in an experiment on handwriting practiced extensively. (From Portier, van Galen, & Meulenbroek, 1990)

were planning ahead, and planning ahead is precisely what the theory of motor programs predicts we should see with well-practiced movements.

*A Modern View of Motor Programs.* Although the existence of motor programs is now accepted by most theorists, more recent conceptions of motor programs are a bit different from Lashley's. Early theorists described motor programs as sequences of movements produced without reference to any sensory feedback, but more recently there has been a recognition that feedback can play a role in motor programs in several different ways (Schmidt, 1988; Summers, 1981).

First, sensory feedback is needed to give the individual information about the starting conditions—for example, about where the typist's fingers are before the typing of the next word begins. Second, we have seen that feedback after a movement is important for learning, and this is equally true for movement sequences. A typist can use either visual feedback (from the typed page) or tactile feedback (from the fingers) to determine whether the appropriate letters were typed in the correct order. If you know how to touch-type, then you undoubtedly have a first-hand understanding of how it is possible to recognize from tactile stimuli alone that you have made an error. Third, sensory feedback during the execution of a motor program may let the individual know that the current movement will fail to meet its goal and that a correction will be needed. For example, Summers (1981) suggests that walking is usually controlled by a motor program, but when a person's foot unexpectedly strikes an object, sensory feedback tells the person he or she is about to fall. "To avoid falling the person must consciously attend to his movements and make a rapid correction to the motor program" (Summers, 1981, p. 49).

Recent findings also suggest that besides feedback, additional planning can modify a motor program during its execution. That is, if a sequence involves several separate movements, the individual may plan part of the sequence in advance (as the concept of a "motor program" would demand), but later parts of the sequence may continue to be planned or modified even as the early parts of the sequence are being performed (Garcia-Colera & Semjen, 1988).

Because of the duration of human reaction times, it would typically take a person about 200 milliseconds to respond to a stimulus (such as the foot meeting an impediment while walking) and make the necessary correction in one's movement. However, there is evidence that feedback at the level of the spinal cord may allow an individual to make rapid adjustments in a motor program (in the order of 50 milliseconds) while the program is being executed. Marsden, Merton, and Morton (1972) had subjects move their thumbs back and forth rhythmically while the experimenters recorded both the position of the thumb and EMG activity from the single muscle controlling this movement. At unpredictable points during this motion, the apparatus suddenly applied increased resistance to the thumb movement. The researchers observed an increase in EMG activity about 50 milliseconds after the resistance was increased. In other words, the muscle began to compensate for the change in resistance very rapidly. This compensatory action was presumably controlled at the spinal level by the feedback loops such as those involved in the spinal reflex arc (Chapter 3). This muscular action has been characterized as a reflexive adjustment that does not depend on attention or voluntary movement.

There is also evidence that subjects can learn chunking strategies (see Chapter 11) and use them during the execution of a long sequence of movements. Verwey and Dronkert (1996) had subjects learn a sequence of nine key presses using nine different fingers. During the training phase, one group was required to practice the sequence in two chunks (four presses, a pause, then five presses), and a second group was required to use three chunks (three presses, a pause, three presses, a pause, then three more presses). Next, in the test phase, subjects were told to respond as quickly and accurately as possible. Even though they were no longer required to do so, the subjects continued to pause in the same places in the sequence as they did in training. These results suggested that the two groups had learned to chunk the sequence in two different ways.

As in many other areas of learning, physiological research is beginning to provide insights about the neural basis of motor programs. Research with the marine snail *Aplysia* has identified groups of neurons that appear to control motor programs that coordinate feeding movements. Different groups of neurons control motor programs for different parts of the body, but there is also coordination among the different groups of neurons (Perrins & Weiss, 1996). With humans, Jennings (1995) used a reaction-time task to compare the performance of normal adults and those suffering from Parkinson's disease, which causes impairments in motor coordination. The task involved pressing three keys in the correct sequence as quickly as possible, after receiving a signal that indicated which sequence to produce. Subjects with Parkinson's disease actually made the first response of the sequence faster than normal subjects, but they were slower to make the second and third responses. This observation, plus other details about their performances, led Jennings to conclude that patients with this disease tend to start the first movement in the sequence before the entire motor program has been planned, and as a result they have difficulty completing a smooth, coordinated sequence of movements. By using what is known about the neurophysiology of Parkinson's disease, Jennings was able to make some preliminary hypotheses about how different parts of the brain may contribute to the execution of motor programs. Another change in modern conceptions of motor programs is related to Schmidt's schema theory. Even in seemingly repetitive sequences of movements, such as typing the word *the*, different movements will be required on different occasions. The spacing between keys and the force and amount of movement required to operate them can vary considerably from one keyboard to the next. Nevertheless, an experienced typist will have little difficulty transferring his or her skills from one keyboard to another. The individual can also adapt reasonably well to a keyboard that is 6 inches below the waist or

12 inches above the waist, although the relationships among forearms, wrists, and fingers will be considerably different. For a motor program to be useful in such variable conditions, it cannot simply specify one fixed pattern of muscle movements. Instead, theorists have suggested that motor programs provide a general framework (or schema) about the proper timing and sequencing of movements, but the details of the movement sequence can (and must) be adapted to suit the current situation. A motor program that can be adapted to a variety of different situations is called a **generalized motor program,** and recent studies have investigated the best ways to learn such adaptable skills (Lai & Shea, 1998; Whitacre & Shea, 2000). For instance, as when teaching simpler motor skills, providing KR on only a portion of the trials may be better than providing KR continuously (Schmidt & Wulf, 1997).

The concept of a generalized motor program is reminiscent of the finding in operant conditioning that animals can easily make substitutions among responses that have the same effect on the environment although they may involve very different muscle movements. Within the realm of motor skills, a good example of this adaptability is the observation that people's handwriting styles retain their individuality whether they are writing 1/4-inch letters on a piece of paper or 5-inch letters on a blackboard. The schema theory takes an initial step toward an understanding of how this adaptability is possible. It suggests that individuals can generalize from their past experience with different stimulus conditions, different movements, and the results of those movements so as to select a new movement to meet the requirements of a new situation. Thus, in handwriting, an individual has presumably already learned what muscle movements are needed to draw a 1/4-inch oval, a 5-inch oval, or one of any other size (within limits). According to Schmidt, once these relationships are learned, the production of letters of any height requires only the selection of the appropriate parameters within an existing motor program.

The different lines of evidence against the response chain approach that we have consid-

A good source of information about the field of human movement science is the Web site of the International Society of Biomechanics at *http://isb.ri.ccf.org.*

ered by no means imply that the response chain approach is completely wrong. Rather, they simply suggest that in some cases individuals learn more than is specified by a strict response chain analysis. The evidence for motor programs suggests that some well-practiced behavior sequences may no longer depend on continual sensory feedback.

## CHAPTER SUMMARY

Thorndike believed that reinforcement was an important variable in motor skill learning, but later research showed that knowledge of results (KR) is really the critical variable. Giving subjects more detailed information about specific parts of their performance (knowledge of performance) can produce even better learning than simple KR. People learn motor skills more quickly with distributed practice than with massed practice, but this advantage disappears in later tests of their performance. Studies in which subjects are trained on one motor task and then tested on a somewhat different task have found evidence for both positive and negative transfer.

Adams's two-stage theory states that motor-skill learning first involves a verbal motor stage, in which feedback from a teacher or coach is essential, and later a motor stage, in which the learner can continue to improve without external feedback. Studies in which KR is either delivered on a percentage basis or

withdrawn at different points during training have provided support for Adams's theory. Schmidt's schema theory states that by practicing different variations of the same response, people develop general rules (schemas) that allow them to perform responses they have never practiced. Schema theory has been supported by various types of evidence, such as the finding that variable training often leads to better performance than practicing exactly the same movement over and over.

According to the response chain theory, in a sequence of movements, sensory feedback from one movement serves as a stimulus for the next response in the chain. Lashley presented several types of evidence against this theory, such as errors of anticipation that suggest a person is planning ahead. The theory of motor programs maintains that well-practiced sequences of movements can become a single unit that can be executed without sensory feedback from each individual response.

## REVIEW QUESTIONS

1. Describe a study showing that knowledge of results is an important variable in motor-skill learning. What happens when KR is delayed, and when it is given on only a percentage of the trials?

2. What is knowledge of performance (KP)? Describe a few different types of KP that have been found to be useful in helping people learn new motor skills.

3. What are the two stages of Adams's theory of motor-skill learning? What is Schmidt's schema theory, and how does it differ from Adams's? Describe some research that supports each theory.

4. What is the response chain theory of movement sequences? What is a motor program? Describe several different types of evidence that Lashley used to argue against the response chain theory and for the existence of motor programs.

## CHAPTER 14

# Choice

It is not much of an exaggeration to say that all behavior involves choice. Even in the most barren of experimental chambers, an animal can choose among performing the operant response, exploring, sitting, standing, grooming, sleeping, and so on. For creatures outside the laboratory, the choices are much more numerous. At any moment, an organism can choose to either continue with its current behavior or switch to another. The consequences of some choices (such as to pick up a piece of food with the left or right paw) may be fleeting and insignificant, whereas other choices (for instance, to flee or fight an opponent) can have important and irreversible consequences. In either case, however, it should be clear that an understanding of how creatures make choices is essential to an understanding of behavior itself.

Since about the 1960s, a large number of experiments on operant conditioning have dealt with choice behavior, as a quick perusal of titles in such periodicals as *Journal of the Experimental Analysis of Behavior* or *Animal Learning and Behavior* will demonstrate. Although it will not be possible to do justice to this large and growing body of knowledge, this chapter will attempt to present a representative sample of some of the important experiments, theories, and points of controversy in this area.

One of the most remarkable characteristics of the behavior of animals in choice situations is its orderliness and predictability. Much of my own research deals with choice behavior, and when I give students or visitors a tour of the laboratory, they frequently ask, "Can these pigeons and rats really understand the complex choices you present to them and respond in anything but a haphazard way?" The answer is that they certainly can (and research on choice behavior would not have flourished if animals did not behave in an orderly way). Perhaps the reason people ask this question so often is that the behavior of animals in the wild can appear to be haphazard and unpredictable to a casual observer. If you watch the behavior of a pigeon on a city sidewalk, it may be difficult to discern any order in its movements. It may walk forward, turn left, turn right, stop, turn around, and so on, in no obvious pattern. It may peck at various objects on the ground, it may approach or move away from another pigeon, it may fly away with no apparent provocation. Although the pigeon's selection of behaviors may seem to be random, this may be largely due to the complexity and randomness of its natural environment, because if this same pigeon were brought into the operant laboratory, its behavior in a simplified choice situation would almost certainly show some striking regularities.

One fairly simple mathematical expression that captures some of the regularities of behavior in many choice situations is the matching law, developed by Richard Herrnstein. The next several sections describe the matching law, illustrate how it has been applied to several types of experimental results, and discuss some theories about why matching behavior is such a prevalent result in experiments on choice.

## THE MATCHING LAW

### Herrnstein's (1961) Experiment

Herrnstein used a pigeon chamber with two response keys located a few inches apart on one wall, a red key on the left and a white key on the right. Beneath and midway between the two keys was an opening in the wall where grain could be presented as a reinforcer. The experiment consisted of a series of conditions in which each key was associated with its own VI schedule of reinforcement. For example, in one condition, pecks at the left key were reinforced on a VI 135-second schedule, and pecks at the right key were reinforced on a VI 270-second schedule. (Technically, this schedule is called a concurrent VI 135-second VI 270-second schedule. In general, any situation in which two or more reinforcement schedules are presented simultaneously can be called a **concurrent schedule.**) The schedules on the two keys were completely independent—that is, each key had its own VI timer. As in a typical VI schedule, once a reinforcer was stored, the VI timer for that key would be stopped until that reinforcer was collected. In this condition, the birds received approximately 27 reinforcers per hour from the left key and 13 reinforcers per hour (half as many) from the right key.

Herrnstein's main question was: After the birds have learned all that they can about this choice situation, how will they distribute their responses? He therefore gave them many days of training with the same two VI schedules, and then measured their responses. As in most VI schedules, the birds made many responses for each reinforcer they received. What is of interest, however, is that in this condition, where about two thirds of the reinforcers came from the left key, the birds made approximately two thirds of their responses on the left key. That is, the proportion of responses on the left key equaled, or *matched*, the proportion of reinforcers delivered by the left key.

In another condition of this experiment, two birds received only about 15 percent of their reinforcers from the left key, and, on average, the birds made about 15 percent of their responses on this key. Once again, the percentage of left-key responses approximately matched the percentage of left-key reinforcers. Based on results like these, Herrnstein proposed the following general principle, now known as the **matching law:**

$$\frac{B_1}{B_1 + B_2} = \frac{R_1}{R_1 + R_2} \qquad (14\text{-}1)$$

$B_1$ is the number of responses of type 1 (for instance, left-key responses), and $B_2$ is the number of responses of type 2 (for example, right-key responses). Similarly, $R_1$ is the number of reinforcers obtained by making response 1, and $R_2$ is the number of reinforcers obtained by making response 2. Equation 14-1 states that in a two-choice situation, the proportion of responses directed toward one alternative should equal the proportion of reinforcers delivered by that alternative.

Figure 14-1 plots the results from all of the conditions of Herrnstein's experiment. The *x*-axis represents the percentage of left-key reinforcers and the *y*-axis the percentage of left-key responses. According to the matching law, the data points should fall along the diagonal line, since this is where these two percentages are equal. As can be seen, the data points do not lie exactly on the line, but all the points are close to the line. Furthermore, the deviations from the predictions of the matching law appear to be random rather than systematic. We can conclude, therefore, that the matching law provided a good description of the subjects' behavior, except for the sort of random variations found in any psychological experiment.

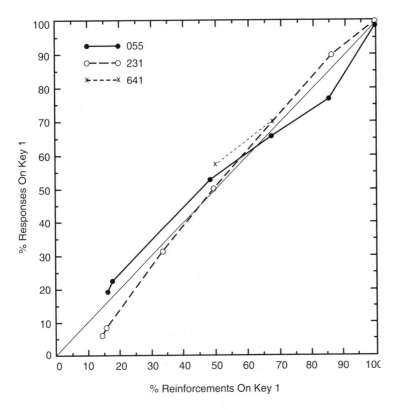

**FIGURE 14-1**   Results from three pigeons in Herrnstein's (1961) experiment on concurrent VI VI schedules. Each data point shows the results from a different condition. The diagonal line shows the predictions of the matching law (Equation 14-1), which predicts that response percentages will match reinforcement percentages.

## Other Experiments on Matching

One reason that many researchers have come to view the matching law as an important principle of choice behavior is that it has been applied with reasonable success in a wide range of experiments with both animals and humans (see Davison & McCarthy, 1988). One experiment examined the social interactions of college students (Conger & Killeen, 1974). Groups of four students sat around a table and had a 30-minute discussion about drug abuse. The discussants knew that the proceedings were being videotaped and would later be analyzed by the experimenters. However, three members of the group were not

real subjects but confederates working for the experimenter. The task of the confederate sitting across from the subject was simply to keep the discussion going. The tasks of the confederates to the left and right of the subject were to deliver verbal reinforcers to the subject on two different VI schedules. For instance, whenever the confederate on the left received a signal (a light only he could see), he would reinforce the next statement of the subject by saying something like "That's a good point." The same was true for the confederate on the right. Conger and Killeen later had observers view the videotapes and measure the amount of time the subject spent talking to the confederate on the left, and the amount of time talking to the confederate on the right. This procedure was repeated with five different subjects.

In the first 15 minutes of the discussion, the confederate on the left delivered about 82 percent of the reinforcers. By the end of the 15 minutes, subjects were spending about 78 percent of the time talking to the confederate on the left (approximately matching the reinforcement percentage). In the second 15 minutes, the confederate on the left now delivered fewer reinforcers than the confederate on the right (about 38 percent of the total). By the end of this half of the experiment, the subjects were spending an average of about 29 percent of the time talking to the confederate on the left. This approximate matching is impressive considering the brief duration of the experiment and the many possible confounding variables (for example, one confederate might have appeared inherently more friendly or more likable than the other, excluding any consideration of the verbal reinforcers they delivered).

The idea that people tend to talk more with those who agree with them is not new (Homans, 1961). Nevertheless, Conger and Killeen's study provides a nice demonstration of how the matching law can be rigorously tested in a controlled yet realistic setting. The matching law has also been applied to a variety of real-world situations. For instance, it has been used to analyze conflicts between career and family (Redmon & Lockwood, 1986) and to explain the success of profit-sharing programs, in which workers are rewarded for increased productivity with a share of their company's profits (Mawhinney & Gowen, 1990).

## Deviations from Matching

Not all experiments have produced results that are consistent with Equation 14-1. W. M. Baum (1974, 1979) listed three ways that the results of experiments have deviated from strict matching, each of which is depicted graphically in Figure 14-2. The most common of these deviations is **undermatching**, in which response proportions are consistently less extreme (that is, closer to .5) than reinforcement proportions. In the idealized example of undermatching shown in Figure 14-2, when the proportion of left reinforcers is .8, the proportion of left responses is only .6. When the proportion of left reinforcers is .3, the proportion of left responses is .45. In other words, undermatching describes the case where a subject's preferences are closer to indifference than they should be according to the matching law.

To understand one common explanation of undermatching, it is necessary to consider one additional feature of Herrnstein's (1961) ex-

**FIGURE 14-2** In each panel, the broken diagonal line shows where data points would fall if a subject's behavior conformed perfectly to the matching law (Equation 14-1). The solid curves illustrate three types of deviation from perfect matching.

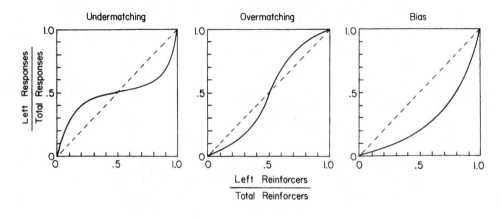

periment that was not previously mentioned. Herrnstein included a 1.5-second **changeover delay,** which was, in effect, a penalty for switching between keys. Suppose a reinforcer was stored on the right key while a pigeon was pecking on the left key. If the bird then switched to the right key, it would not receive the reinforcer for its first peck. Because of the changeover delay, no reinforcer could be collected for 1.5 seconds after a switch, but the first peck after 1.5 seconds had elapsed would produce the reinforcer.

Herrnstein included the changeover delay because he found that without it the birds tended to develop the habit of alternately pecking the left key, then the right key, then the left key, and so on, regardless of the sizes of the two VI schedules. Herrnstein suggested that this alternating pattern might be an example of a superstitious behavior. For instance, if a bird pecked left, then right, then received a reinforcer, the left-right sequence might be adventitiously reinforced even though only the right response was necessary for that particular reinforcer. Once the changeover delay was added, however, a subject had to make at least two consecutive responses on a key before collecting a reinforcer, thereby making the adventitious reinforcement of switching behavior less likely.

Another hypothesis about undermatching is that animals may occasionally attribute a reinforcer to the wrong response (Davison & Jenkins, 1985). For instance, in the short time between making a response and collecting the reinforcer, a pigeon may forget which key it pecked. Other explanations of undermatching have also been proposed (Baum, 1979; Myers & Myers, 1977), and there is no general agreement about why it occurs.

The opposite of undermatching is **overmatching,** in which a subject's response proportions are more extreme than the reinforcement proportions. For example, in the illustration of overmatching in Figure 14-2, a reinforcer proportion of .8 produces a response proportion of .9, and a reinforcer proportion of .3 produces a response proportion of .15. Overmatching is not as common as matching or undermatching, but it has been

observed in situations where there is a substantial penalty for switching between schedules. For example, W. M. Baum (1982) found overmatching when pigeons had to walk around a barrier and over a hurdle to switch from one key to the other. As the effort involved in switching keys was increased, the pigeons switched between keys less and less, and spent most of their time responding on the better VI schedule, which resulted in overmatching.

In the third type of deviation from matching, **bias,** a subject consistently spends more time on one alternative than predicted by the matching equation. Figure 14-2 illustrates the sort of results that might be obtained if a subject has a bias for the right key. When 80 percent of the reinforcers come from the left key, the subject makes only 50 percent of its responses on the left key. When 30 percent of the reinforcers come from the left key, the subject makes only 10 percent of its responses on the left key. Regardless of the reinforcer percentage, the subject makes more responses on the right key than predicted by the matching law. Many factors can produce a bias, such as a preference for a particular side of the chamber, for a particular response key (if one key requires a bit less effort than the other), or for a particular color (if the two response keys have different colors).

## Varying the Quality and Amount of Reinforcement

All of the experiments described thus far in this chapter have dealt with two alternatives that deliver exactly the same reinforcer (such as food or verbal approval), but at different rates. In such experiments, the presence of bias might be considered a nuisance that must be corrected for with appropriate counterbalancing. On the other hand, if bias is treated as an indication of preference for one alternative, the matching law can be used to measure a subject's preferences for different types of reinforcers. An interesting study by Harold Miller (1976) showed how this can be done. Like Herrnstein (1961), Miller used different pairs of VI schedules, but the two schedules offered the pigeons two different types of grain as reinforcers. In some conditions, the choice was between hemp and buckwheat; in others it was between wheat and buckwheat; in still others it was between hemp and wheat.

In choices between wheat and buckwheat, for example, Miller found a strong preference (bias) for the wheat, but he suggested that the matching equation could take this bias into account if it were modified in the following way:

$$\frac{B_1}{B_1 + B_2} = \frac{Q_1 R_1}{Q_1 R_1 + Q_2 R_2} \quad (14\text{-}2)$$

where $Q_1$ and $Q_2$ stand for the qualities of the reinforcers available on the two keys. This equation states that a subject's distribution of behavior is determined by both the rate of reinforcement and the quality of reinforcement delivered by the different schedules. Miller arbitrarily assigned a value of 10 to $Q_b$, the quality of buckwheat, and he found that Equation 14-2 provided a good description of the results if $Q_w$, the quality of wheat, was given a value of about 14. He interpreted this number as meaning that each wheat reinforcer was worth about 1.4 times as much as each buckwheat reinforcer. Miller made similar calculations for conditions where the alternatives were hemp and buckwheat, and he estimated that $Q_h$, the quality of hemp, was about 9.1, or slightly less than that of buckwheat. Miller suggested that his estimates of $Q_b$, $Q_w$, and $Q_h$ were measures of the strengths of these different grains as reinforcers, but how do we know they were not simply meaningless numbers? Miller's answer to this question was the same as the one discussed in Chapter 9 as a way of avoiding a tautological definition of reinforcement: The numbers become meaningful and useful if they lead to new predictions that would not be possible without them. The new predictions Miller made were for the third set of choices, those between hemp and wheat. For example, in one condition, both grains were delivered at a rate of 30 reinforcers per hour. With $Q_w$ = 14 and $Q_h$ = 9.1, Equation 14-2 predicts that subjects should allocate about 61 percent of their responses to the key delivering wheat. For this condition and four others with different VI schedules, the predictions of Equation

14-2 were very close to the subjects' actual behaviors. The matching law has been used in other studies to measure preferences among reinforcers of different qualities, with subjects as different as humans (Neef, Mace, Shea, & Shade, 1992) and cows (Foster, Temple, Robertson, Nair, & Poling, 1996).

Besides the rate of reinforcement and the quality of reinforcement, another variable that can affect preference is the amount or size of each reinforcer. If one key delivers two food pellets as a reinforcer and the other key delivers only one, this should certainly affect a subject's choices. Several researchers (Baum & Rachlin, 1969; Killeen, 1972) have suggested that when amount of reinforcement is the independent variable, it can be used in place of rate of reinforcement in the matching equation:

$$\frac{B_1}{B_1 + B_2} = \frac{A_1}{A_1 + A_2} \quad (14\text{-}3)$$

where $A_1$ and $A_2$ are the amounts of reinforcement delivered by the two alternatives. Catania (1963) found results that were quite consistent with Equation 14-3 in a study where pigeons' access to grain was varied between 3 and 6 seconds per reinforcer. Other studies, however, have found large deviations from the predictions of Equation 14-3: Substantial undermatching and overmatching have both been observed (Davison & Hogsden, 1984; Schneider, 1973). As with other deviations from matching, a number of explanations have been offered, but there is no consensus about why they occur (de Villiers, 1977; R. M. Dunn, 1982; Logue & Chavarro, 1987).

## An Application to Single Schedules

It may appear that the matching law, which makes predictions for choice situations, has nothing to say about cases where there is only one reinforcement schedule. However, Herrnstein (1970, 1974) developed a way to use the matching law to make predictions about behavior on single VI schedules. To see how Herrnstein's analysis works, let us start with a few arbitrary assumptions. Suppose that a particular pigeon pecks a key at a rate of 2 pecks per second whenever it is responding on a VI schedule. That is, if the bird pecked the key without pausing, it would make 120 pecks per minute. Second, let us assume that although the only way the pigeon can obtain food reinforcers is by pecking the key, there are "built-in" reinforcers (we might call them "Premackian reinforcers") for performing other behaviors such as grooming, exploring, resting, and so on. Herrnstein suggested that whereas the experimenter can control the number of food reinforcers, the built-in reinforcers for nonpecking behaviors are out of the experimenter's control, and they occur at a fairly constant rate.

Although these background reinforcers are not food, in order to perform the necessary calculations, we need to measure them in the same units as the food reinforcers. For this example, let us imagine that all behaviors other than pecking provide the pigeon with built-in reinforcers having a value equivalent to 30 food reinforcers per hour. Similarly, although the pigeon's various behaviors, such as grooming and exploring, are quite different from key pecking, we need to measure them on a common scale. A useful strategy is to measure all behaviors in units of time, thereby translating Equation 14-1 to the following:

$$\frac{T_1}{T_1 + T_2} = \frac{R_1}{R_1 + R_2} \tag{14-4}$$

Let $T_1$ represent the time spent key pecking and $T_2$ the total time spent in all other behaviors, so that $T_1 + T_2$ equals the total session time. $R_1$ is the rate at which food reinforcers are delivered by the VI schedule, and $R_2$ is the equivalent reinforcing value of all the built-in reinforcers (which equals 30 in our example).

We are now ready to make predictions for different VI schedules. If the pigeon is exposed to a VI schedule that delivers 30 reinforcers per hour, Equation 14-4 predicts that the bird will spend half of its time pecking and half of its time engaging in other behaviors (because $R_1$ and $R_2$ both equal 30). Since we have assumed that the pigeon pecks at a rate of 2 responses per second, the bird should average

about 60 responses per minute during the session. If the bird is now presented with a VI schedule that delivers 90 reinforcers per hour, Equation 14-4 states that it should spend 75 percent of its time pecking, which would result in an average response rate of 90 responses per minute. Similar predictions can be made for any size of VI schedule the experimenter might arrange. The solid curve in Figure 14-3 shows the predictions for our hypothetical example for all reinforcement rates between 0 and 500 food reinforcers per hour. It shows that as the rate of reinforcement increases, Equation 14-4 predicts that response rates will climb toward the animal's full-time rate of 120 pecks per hour. Of course, these predictions are based on specific assumptions about the pigeon's pecking rate and the values of all nonpecking behaviors. Suppose we took this same pigeon and put it in a more interesting chamber where $R_2$ was equal to 60 (perhaps because this second chamber had a window through which the subject could watch another pigeon). With the increased value of nonpecking behaviors, Equation 14-4 now predicts that the bird will spend less time pecking on all VI schedules, as shown by the broken line in Figure 14-3.

Herrnstein (1970) applied this analysis to the results of an experiment by Catania and Reynolds (1968) in which six pigeons responded on several different VI schedules (presented one at a time, for several sessions each). Figure 14-4 shows the results of the Catania and Reynolds study (data points), and the curves are the predictions of Equation 14-4. The close correspondence between predictions and data points in Figure 14-4 is impressive. De Villiers and Herrnstein (1976) performed similar analyses of the results from several dozen experiments involving single schedules of reinforcement. These experiments were conducted by many different researchers, and they featured a variety of species, operant responses, and reinforcers. In nearly all cases, the correspondence between the predictions of the matching law and the results was about as good as it was for the Catania and Reynolds (1968) experiment. Herrnstein's analysis of single-schedule behavior has

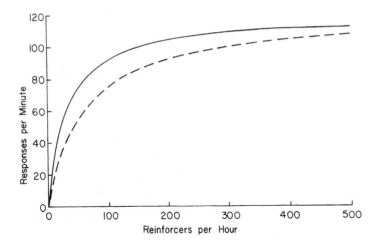

**FIGURE 14-3** The two curves depict some representative predictions from Herrnstein's (1970) equation for single reinforcement schedules (Equation 14-4). This equation predicts how response rates should change as reinforcement rates are varied. The solid curve represents a case where there are relatively few reinforcers for behavior other than pecking ($R_2$ = 30 in Equation 14-4). The broken curve represents a case where there are more reinforcers for behaviors other than pecking ($R_2$ = 60), so the subject's rate of pecking should be slower.

also been applied to human behavior in natural settings (Beardsley & McDowell, 1992; McDowell, 1988). For example, Martens and Houk (1989) showed that Equation 14-4 nicely predicted the relation between a mentally disabled girl's behavior and the amount of reinforcement delivered by her teacher.

Herrnstein's theory can be stated quite simply: An operant response must compete with all other possible behaviors for the individual's time. As the reinforcement for the operant response increases, the individual will devote more and more time to this behavior. Thus, Herrnstein suggests that responding on a single VI schedule can be explained using exactly the same principles that apply to choice in a concurrent VI VI situation.

Not everyone accepts Herrnstein's interpretation (Catania, 1973; Killeen, 1982). For example, some studies have found that the asymptotes in response rate, such as those shown in Figure 14-4, can increase substantially if the amount or quality of the reinforcer is increased, which contradicts Herrnstein's assumption that the asymptotes represent the highest response rates an animal can achieve (Dallery, McDowell, & Lancaster, 2000). Although this theoretical debate has not yet been resolved, the matching law does have some clear implications for real-world behavior. One important implication is that it is impossible to predict how a reinforcer will affect a behavior without taking into account the context—the other reinforcers that are simultaneously available for other behaviors. This principle is illustrated in Figure 14-3, which shows two different predictions for each VI schedule, depending on the amount of reinforcement available for nonpecking behaviors. As a real-world parallel, try to predict how a young child's behavior would be altered by giving him a new reinforcer—a yo-yo, for example. To make any sensible prediction, we need to know something about the context. If the yo-yo is given on an average rainy day in August, the child may play with the yo-yo for hours, because he may be bored with all his other toys and indoor activities. On the other hand, if the yo-yo is given on Christmas and the context includes a host of new toys—trucks, video games, puzzles—the amount of time spent playing with the yo-yo will probably be small. The rich supply of other reinforcers will attract most of the child's time.

Other examples where the total reinforcement context plays a major role are easy to imagine. Many people claim that they tend to eat more when they are bored. This presumably happens not because the reinforcing value of food actually increases when one is bored, but rather because there are few reinforcers available to compete with eating. As another example of a situation where the reinforcement context is meager, imagine that you are

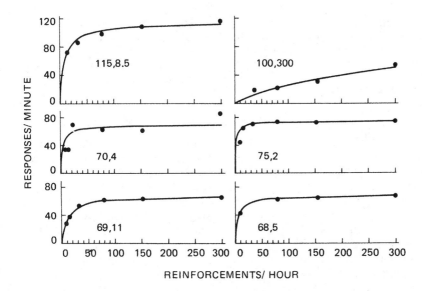

**FIGURE 14-4** Each panel shows the results from one of six pigeons in the Catania and Reynolds (1968) experiment. Each point shows the reinforcement rate and response rate on one VI schedule. For each subject, the curve shows the predictions of Equation 14-4, using the best-fitting estimates of the bird's full-time pecking rate and of $R_2$. The numbers in each panel are the best-fitting estimates of these two quantities. The pattern of results for each subject is well described by Equation 14-4. (From Herrnstein, 1970)

sitting in a reception area waiting for an appointment with someone who is running behind schedule (such as your mechanic or your optometrist). There is little to do but wait, and if you are like me, you may find yourself reading magazines you would not ordinarily spend your time on, such as 2-year-old issues of *Newsweek*, *Good Housekeeping*, or *Optometry Today*. What little reinforcement value these outdated magazines offer takes on added significance in the absence of any alternative sources of reinforcement.

## THEORIES OF CHOICE BEHAVIOR

In many areas of science, it is important to distinguish between *descriptions* of a phenomenon and *explanations* about the mechanisms that underlie the phenomenon. For example, the statement that water increases in volume when it freezes is simply a description—it does not explain why this expansion occurs. Such descriptive statements can be extremely useful in their own right, for they can help us to predict and control future events (for instance, avoiding the bursting of outdoor water pipes by draining them before they freeze). On the other hand, a statement that attributes this expansion to the crystalline structure that hydrogen and oxygen molecules form when in a solid state can be called an explanation: It is a theory about the molecular events that underlie this phenomenon.

In principle, the matching equation can be viewed as either simply a description of choice behavior or as a theory about the mechanisms of choice behavior. We have seen that as a description of behavior in certain choice situations, the matching equation is fairly accurate. We will now consider the possibility that the matching law is an explanatory theory, and we will compare it to a few other theories that have been presented as possible explanatory theories of choice.

## Matching as an Explanatory Theory

In his earlier writings, Herrnstein (1970, 1974) suggested that the matching equation is also a general explanatory theory of choice behavior. The idea is quite simple: It is possible that animals exhibit matching behavior because they are built to do so. That is, in any choice situation, an animal might measure the value of the reinforcement it receives from each alternative (where "value" encompasses such factors as the rate, size, and quality of the reinforcers), and the animal then might distribute its behavior in proportion to the values of the various alternatives. According to such a theory, matching is not just a description of behavior in concurrent VI VI schedules. It is a general principle that explains how animals make choices in all situations, in the laboratory and in the wild.

Having put forward this theory of choice behavior, let us now examine one reason why Herrnstein later decided that it is incorrect. The problem concerns cases where an animal must choose between two ratio schedules (such as VR 20 and VR 100). The matching equation predicts that the animal will make all of its responses on one of the two alternatives, but it does not specify which. Whether the animal makes 100 percent of its responses on the VR 20 schedule or 100 percent of its responses on the VR 100 schedule, it will receive 100 percent of its reinforcers from that schedule, and so the matching equation will be satisfied. However, Herrnstein and Loveland (1974) found that pigeons always choose the smaller VR schedule in such situations, never the larger. Shah, Bradshaw, and Szabadi (1989) obtained similar results with human subjects working for money on pairs of VR schedules. This is not surprising, because a VR 100 schedule will require, on average, five times as many responses per reinforcer as a VR 20 schedule. However, these findings show that we need a theory that predicts that with two VR schedules, individuals will always show ex-

clusive preference for the smaller VR, never the larger VR. To deal with this matter, Herrnstein and Vaughan (1980; Vaughan, 1981, 1985) developed a refinement of the matching law that they called melioration.

## Melioration Theory

To meliorate is to "make better," and in essence the principle of **melioration** states that animals will invest increasing amounts of time and/or effort into whichever alternative is better. This principle sounds simple enough, but let us see how it can be put into practice.

It is easy to show that Equation 14-1 is equivalent to the following equation:

$$\frac{R_1}{B_1} = \frac{R_2}{B_2} \tag{14-5}$$

This equation emphasizes the fact that at the point of matching, the ratio of reinforcers received to responses produced is equal for both alternatives. We might say that the "cost" of each reinforcer is the same for both alternatives. The principle of melioration states that if these ratios are not equal, the animal will shift its behavior toward whichever alternative currently has the higher reinforcer:response ratio. Suppose that a subject begins by making approximately equal numbers of responses on each key in a concurrent VI 30-second VI 120-second schedule. Let us say that the VI 30-second schedule delivers 118 reinforcers for 1,000 responses in the first hour-long session, and the VI 120-second schedule delivers 30 reinforcers for 1,000 responses. Since the reinforcer:response ratio is larger on the VI 30-second schedule, the principle of melioration predicts that the subject will start to make more of its responses on the VI 30-second key. You should be able to demonstrate for yourself that the animal's behavior will continue to shift toward the VI 30-second key until about 80 percent of the responses are made on this key. At that point, Equation 14-5 is satisfied, so there should be no further shifts in behavior (except for inevitable random variations). In short, the principle of melioration predicts that matching behavior will occur in concurrent VI VI schedules.

Now let us consider concurrent VR VR schedules, which posed problems for the matching law. If the two schedules are VR 30 and VR 120, for example, then their respective reinforcer:response ratios are 1:30 and 1:120. These ratios will not change, no matter how the subject distributes its behavior, so the principle of melioration predicts that the subject's behavior will continue to shift toward the VR 30 key until there is no more behavior to shift (that is, until it is responding exclusively at that key). The predictions are the same for any pair of VR schedules: The subject should eventually respond exclusively on the schedule with the more favorable reinforcer:response ratio. In summary, the principle of melioration correctly predicts matching behavior in a choice between two VI schedules, and it predicts exclusive preference for the better of two VR schedules.

Herrnstein (1990) has proposed that (1) people use the principle of melioration in many everyday decisions, and (2) as a result, their decisions are often not optimal. He offers the example of a tennis player who has two options whenever his opponent moves toward the net during a match—a lob or a passing shot. Both shots are more effective when they are surprising: If the player uses a passing shot frequently, the opponent will expect it and prepare for it, and the same is true for the lob. Given these options, how would you choose between lobs and passing shots? Herrnstein reported that when asked this question, most people say they would use some of each shot, depending on which seemed to be more effective. If lobs were more effective, they would start using more lobs; if passing shots then became more effective, they would increase the number of passing shots. This strategy of increasing whichever shot is working better is an example of melioration. A tennis player using this principle might end up, for example, using 70 percent lobs and 30 percent passing shots. However, Herrnstein showed that using the principle of melioration will not necessarily lead to the best performance. It might be the case that the combined effectiveness of lobs

and passing shots is greatest if they are used in some other proportion, such as 40 percent lobs and 60 percent passing shots. To put it simply, a tennis player who wants to maximize performance should not ask "Which shot is currently more effective?" but rather "What mixture of the two shots is most effective?" According to Herrnstein, people seldom ask themselves the latter question.

For most of us, the decisions we make during a tennis match or in other sports are not the most significant decisions of our lives. However, Herrnstein and Prelec (1991) argued that people also use the principle of melioration in more important decisions, such as in personal relationships, shopping, gambling, and business decisions. And just as in the tennis example, using the principle of melioration may result in decisions that are far from optimal. It should therefore be clear why melioration theory (and the closely related principle of matching) are viewed as competitors for optimization theory, which states that people tend to make decisions that maximize their satisfaction.

## Optimization Theory as an Explanation of Matching

As discussed in Chapter 9, some psychologists have proposed that optimization theory is a general explanatory theory of choice for both humans and nonhumans. It is easy to see that optimization theory predicts exclusive preference for the better of two VR schedules—this behavior maximizes reinforcement and minimizes effort. Some psychologists have proposed that optimization theory can also explain why matching occurs on concurrent VI VI schedules (Rachlin, Green, Kagel, & Battalio, 1976; Silberberg, Thomas, & Berendzen, 1991). Before examining their reasoning, it is important to understand the implications of their position. Supporters of optimization theory propose that although the matching law may provide a satisfactory description of behavior in these situations, optimization theory actually provides an explanation of matching behavior. They assert that optimization is the basic mechanism of choice behavior, and the only reason matching occurs in some situations is that it is the optimal thing to do. For those who favor optimization-theory, matching behavior is just one more example of the optimization process at work.

To examine this logic, imagine a pigeon on a concurrent VI 30-second (left-key) VI 120-second (right-key) schedule. Rachlin and coworkers (1976) conducted a series of computer simulations to determine how different ways of distributing responses between the two keys would affect the total rate of reinforcement. The results of these simulations are presented in Figure 14-5. To convince yourself that these simulations are at least approximately correct, first consider what would happen if a pigeon made all of its responses on the left key. The left key would provide about 120 reinforcers per hour, and no reinforcers would be collected from the right key, so the total from the two keys would be about 120 reinforcers per hour (the point at the extreme right in Figure 14-5). If the bird responded only on the right key, it would collect reinforcers only from the VI 120-second schedule, so its total reinforcement rate would be about 30 per hour (the point at the extreme left in Figure 14-5). However, by making some responses on each key, the bird could collect many of the reinforcers from both schedules. The computer simulations of Rachlin and colleagues pro-

jected that the maximum total reinforcement rate would be obtained by allocating 80 percent of one's responses to the left key, which is also the point of matching behavior. The reason for the lower rates of reinforcement with other response proportions is that while responding on one key, the VI clock for the other key might be stopped (with a reinforcer available), and any stoppage of either clock will lower the total reinforcement rate. For instance, if a bird spent 90 percent of its time on the VI 120-second key, the clock for the VI 30-second key would frequently be stopped, so substantially fewer than 120 reinforcers would be obtained from the latter.

Speaking more generally, Rachlin and his colleagues have proposed that in any typical concurrent VI VI schedule, matching behavior will maximize the rate of reinforcement. Of course, it should take a pigeon some time (perhaps many daily sessions) to determine what manner of responding is optimal. According to optimization theory, an animal in this sort of situation will try different ways of distributing its behaviors (for instance, 50 percent left, 80 percent left, 90 percent left, and so on) and eventually stabilize around the distribution that maximizes the overall rate of reinforcement. With concurrent VI VI schedules, it just so happens that the maximum rate of reinforcement can be obtained by matching.

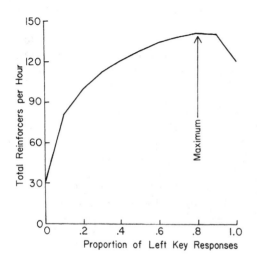

**FIGURE 14-5** Predictions of the computer simulations of Rachlin, Green, Kagel, and Battalio (1976) for a concurrent VI 30-second (left-key) VI 120-second (right-key) schedule. If these predictions are correct, a subject on this schedule would maximize the rate of reinforcement by making 80 percent of its responses on the left key.

*A Test of Optimization Versus Matching.*
The standard concurrent VI VI situation is not a good one in which to contrast the predictions of the matching law and optimization theory, because the two make very similar predictions—both predict matching behavior, or something close to it. To determine which of these principles is a more fundamental rule of choice, it would be best to arrange a choice situation in which the matching law makes one set of predictions and optimization theory makes a very different set of predictions. We could then observe the subjects' behaviors and determine which set of predictions proved more accurate. A number of experiments of this type have been conducted (Herrnstein & Vaughan, 1980; Heyman & Herrnstein, 1986), but an experiment of my own (Mazur, 1981) is probably the easiest to describe.

This experiment was not very different in design from Herrnstein's (1961) experiment. Pigeons could peck at either of two keys, and occasionally a response produced a *dark-key period*, in which the red and green key lights were turned off, and food might or might not be presented. The major differences from Herrnstein's experiment were (1) food was not presented in some dark-key periods, and (2) the dark-key periods on both keys were controlled by a single VI timer, not by two separate VI timers as in Herrnstein's experiment. Figure 14-6 outlines the procedure of my experiment. Each time the VI 45-second timer reached the end of an interval, it would stop and assign a dark-key period to one of the two keys on a random basis. The VI timer would not run again until the subject pecked the appropriate key and collected the dark-key period. (The procedure also included a changeover delay of 3 seconds.) The only thing that was changed from condition to condition was the probability that dark-key periods would include a food reinforcer.

In the first condition, all dark-key periods included food. The subjects received about 32 reinforcers per hour on each key, and they made about 50 percent of their responses on each key. This result is not surprising, and it is consistent with both optimization theory and the matching law. The second condition was more revealing. In this condition, only 10 percent of the dark-key periods that followed a red-key response included food; the other 90 percent provided no reinforcer. All dark-key periods that followed a green-key response continued to include food. The matching law predicts that a bird should begin to make many more responses on the green key, since this key will now provide about 10 times as many reinforcers. But if a bird shows a preference for the green key, this will lower the total rate of reinforcement. The reason is that if the bird spends long periods of time pecking at the green key, the VI timer will frequently be stopped because a dark-key period has been assigned to the red key. The optimal strategy in this condition (and in all conditions of the experiment) would therefore be to switch back and forth between the two keys frequently, making about 50 percent of one's responses on each key. This strategy would ensure that the VI timer would be running most of the time.

If subjects did not change their behavior between Conditions 1 and 2, they would have received about 32 green-key reinforcers and 3.2 red-key reinforcers per hour (since the only change was that now only 10 percent of the red dark-key periods would include food). However, the birds' behaviors did shift, and at the end of the condition they made an average of 86 percent of their responses on the green key (which delivered about 92 percent of the reinforcers). Because of this shift, the birds received only about 23 reinforcers per hour from the green key and 2 reinforcers from the red key. Thus, by showing a strong preference for the green key (as predicted by the matching law), the birds lost about 29 percent of their reinforcers. In some other conditions of the experiment, the birds lost 75 percent or more of their potential reinforcers.

The procedure of this experiment was quite complex, but the results can be stated simply: Although optimization theory predicted that the birds would always make about 50 percent of their responses to each key, the birds consistently showed a preference for whichever key delivered more reinforcers, as predicted by the matching law. The birds' choices produced substantial decreases in the total rate of

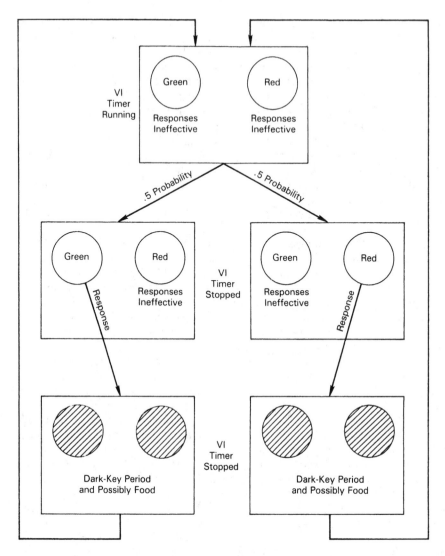

**FIGURE 14-6**    A schematic diagram of the procedure in Mazur's (1981) experiment.

reinforcement, exactly the opposite of what optimization theory predicted should happen.

***Other Tests of Optimization Theory.*** Psychologists have used a variety of other experimental procedures to compare the predictions of the matching law and optimization theory. For example, in choice situations involving both a VI schedule and a VR schedule, optimization theory predicts that animals will make most of their responses on the VR schedule, because most of the responses on any VI schedule are wasted, whereas every response on a VR schedule brings the animal closer to reinforcement. A number of experiments with animal subjects failed to support this prediction, but they were consistent with the predictions of the matching law (DeCarlo, 1985; Vyse & Belke, 1992). Similar results were obtained in a study with college students working for money: The students spent more time on the VI schedule than predicted by optimization theory, and their choices were closer to the predictions of the matching law (Savastano & Fantino, 1994).

Several other experiments, some with animals and some with humans, have failed to support the predictions of optimization theory (for example, Ettinger, Reid, & Staddon, 1987; Jacobs & Hackenberg, 2000). On the other hand, some experiments have found results that favored optimization theory (Jacobs & Hackenberg, 1996; Sakagami, Hursh, Christensen, & Silberberg, 1989), and behavioral ecologists have provided ample evidence that the choices made by animals in many real-world situations are close to those predicted by optimization theory. It is not yet clear how these conflicting findings can be reconciled, and because the evidence is ambiguous, some psychologists continue to favor optimization theory, whereas others favor matching (or melioration) theory.

Because they deal with a subject's overall distribution of responses over long periods of time (such as over an entire experimental session), matching theory, melioration theory, and optimization theory can be classified as molar theories (see Chapter 7). Some researchers now believe that more complete explanations of choice behavior will be found in molecular theories, which attempt to predict moment-to-moment behavior, and which assume that short-term consequences have a large influence on choice. For example, after failing to find empirical support for optimization theory, Ettinger and others (1987) concluded that "animals may not be sensitive to the molar rates of responding and reinforcement. . . . Our animals were sensitive to the schedules at a molecular level, and it is to this molecular level that we should direct our attention" (p. 366). One molecular theory of choice is presented in the next section.

## Momentary Maximization Theory

In its most general sense, **momentary maximization theory** states that at each moment, an organism will select whichever alternative has the highest value *at that moment*. The value of an alternative will usually depend on many factors: the size and quality of the reinforcer, the subject's state of deprivation, and so on. Although both momentary maximization theory and optimization theory state that animals attempt to maximize the value of their choices, the two theories frequently make different predictions because the best choice in the short run is not always the best choice in the long run. As a simple example, consider a dieter who must choose between Jell-O or a strawberry sundae for dessert. The strawberry sundae may appear more attractive at the moment, but the Jell-O might be the more beneficial alternative for the dieter in the long run. Choices that involve a conflict between short-term and long-term benefits will be examined in detail later in the chapter; this issue is raised now only to show that the strategies of momentary maximization and overall optimization may lead to very different decisions.

To understand what sorts of predictions the momentary maximization hypothesis makes for a concurrent VI VI situation, it will be helpful for you to take part in the following hypothetical gambling game. Imagine that you are allowed to play this game for nine trials. You are seated in front of a panel with two small doors, and on each trial you are allowed to open one of the two doors. There may be a dollar behind the door (which you win) or there may be no money. The following rules determine whether a dollar is deposited behind a door or not: There is a modified roulette wheel for each door, which is spun before each trial begins. The probability of winning is .1 on the roulette wheel behind door 1, and .2 on the wheel for door 2. Therefore, on trial 1 of the game, there may be a dollar behind both doors, behind one door, or behind neither door, depending on the outcome of the wheel for each door. Which door do you choose on trial 1?

Two additional rules apply for the next eight trials:

1. Once a dollar is deposited behind a door, it will remain there until you collect it. Thus, if a dollar is deposited behind door 1 on trial 4, it will

remain there until you choose door 1; say, on trial 7.

2. There will never be more than one dollar behind a door at one time. For instance, if a dollar is deposited behind door 1 on trial 4 and you do not collect it until trial 7, the spinning of the wheel is irrelevant on trials 5, 6, and 7, since no more dollars will be deposited behind door 1. However, the spinning of the wheel for door 2 will continue to be important on these trials, since it might pay off on any trial. In other words, door 2 is not affected by what is happening at door 1, and vice versa.

Before reading further, write down what door you would choose on each of the nine trials.

For a situation like this, momentary maximization theory predicts that a subject will choose whatever alternative has the higher probability of reinforcement on each trial. On trial 1, the probability of reinforcement for door 1 (which will be denoted as $p_1$) is .1, and the probability of reinforcement for door 2 ($p_2$) is .2, so momentary maximization theory predicts a choice of door 2. On the second trial, the situation is somewhat different. Assuming door 2 was chosen on trial 1, $p_2$ is still .2, regardless of whether a dollar was collected on trial 1 or not. But $p_1$ will be higher on trial 2 because there are two ways a dollar might be deposited—the roulette wheel for door 1 might have paid off on trial 1 (and waits to be collected) or it might have paid off on trial 2. It can be shown (using some elementary rules of probability theory that will not be explained here) that $p_1$ will be .19 on trial 2. This is still slightly less than $p_2$, so momentary maximization theory predicts that door 2 will again be chosen.

It can be shown that after two choices of door 2, $p_1$ will equal .271 and $p_2$ will equal .2 (because there are now three trials on which a dollar might be deposited at door 1). A momentary maximizer would therefore choose door 1 on trial 3. On trial 4, however, there are two ways to win at door 2 (from a payoff on either trial 3 or 4), so $p_2$ is again greater than $p_1$, and door 2 should be chosen. It turns out that the pattern followed by a momentary maximizer on the nine trials would be 2, 2, 1, 2, 2, 1, 2, 2, 1, and this cyclical pattern would be repeated on any additional trials. You can check

to see whether your choices followed the momentary maximizing strategy.

This hypothetical gambling game is quite similar to a concurrent VI VI schedule. The two roulette wheels are similar to two independent VI timers, and like VI clocks, the roulette wheels will only store one reinforcer at a time. You can therefore probably anticipate what momentary maximizing theory predicts about a subject's behavior on a concurrent VI VI schedule: It predicts that there should be an orderly and cyclical pattern to an animal's moment-by-moment choices. Of course, advocates of momentary maximizing theory (Shimp, 1966, 1969; Silberberg, Hamilton, Ziriax, & Casey, 1978) recognize that animals have limited memorial and decision-making capacities, and they do not expect perfect momentary maximizing behavior to occur. (After all, even people have difficulty determining the probabilities in situations like the gambling game described above.) What they do predict, however, is that animals will show at least some tendency to choose the alternative that has the higher probability of reinforcement. For example, after an animal has made several consecutive responses on the better of two VI schedules, it should show a tendency to switch to the other VI (since a reinforcer may have been stored on this VI during the interim). According to momentary maximizing theory, matching behavior is simply an incidental by-product of an animal's orderly moment-by-moment choices. In contrast, molar theories of choice do not predict that an animal's moment-to-moment behavior will exhibit any orderly patterns, because these theories assume that an animal's behavior is controlled by variables (for instance, total reinforcement rate) that do not change from moment to moment.

When animals exhibit matching behavior, are there orderly moment-by-moment patterns in their behavior, or are there not? It may seem that it should be easy to obtain an answer to this question, but the results of several experiments have been anything but clear-cut. Some studies have found such patterns (Shimp, 1966; Silberberg and others, 1978), but others have not (Heyman, 1979; Nevin,

1969, 1979). For example, Nevin (1979) analyzed his data in several different ways in search of orderly sequences of responses, but found none. At the molar level, however, the data were quite orderly: The pigeons' overall choice proportions were well described by the matching law. Nevin concluded that the momentary maximizing theory does not provide the correct explanation of why animals match, because matching behavior sometimes occurs even when animals' choices appear to be random from moment to moment.

In a subsequent article, Hinson and Staddon (1983) used a different method of analysis and came to a different conclusion. Instead of looking at sequences of responses, as was done in all previous studies, Hinson and Staddon continually recorded the time since a pigeon sampled (pecked at) each of two VI keys. They reasoned that time is the critical independent variable, since on VI schedules it is the passage of time and not the number of responses that actually determines the availability of a reinforcer. They showed that their pigeons could follow a momentary maximizing strategy if they used a fairly simple rule: If schedule 1 delivers, for example, *three times* as many reinforcers as schedule 2, you should check schedule 2 if the time since you last checked it is more than *three times longer* than the time since you last checked schedule 1. Hinson and Staddon showed that their pigeons' behaviors were by no means perfect from the standpoint of momentary maximization theory, but a majority of their responses did follow this rule.

Momentary maximizing theory has been applied to other behaviors besides matching. For example, Silberberg, Warren-Boulton, and Asano (1988) proposed that the theory can explain why interresponse times (IRTs) and response rates on VI schedules are moderate, rather than very long or very short. An IRT can be thought of as a delay, during which the animal must wait before making a response and possibly collecting a reinforcer. With long IRTs, the delay is long but the probability of reinforcement is high. With short IRTs, the delay is short but the probability of reinforcement is low. Silberberg and coworkers suggested that animals maximize the "momentary value" of each response by producing IRTs of intermediate duration, which involve only a moderate delay yet have a reasonable probability of reinforcement.

## Other Theories of Choice

As a result of the intense interest in choice behavior among those who study operant conditioning, quite a few different theories have been proposed besides those that we have already examined. Some of these theories involve fairly complex mathematics, and we will not go into their details here. However, we can take a brief look at some of the major trends in this area of research.

Not all molecular theories of choice assume that animals follow the principle of momentary maximization. Although animals' choices may be influenced by how quickly the reinforcer is delivered, they may or may not always choose the alternative with the shorter delay or the higher momentary probability. As one example of an alternative molecular theory, Vaughan (1985; Vaughan & Miller, 1984) suggested that different choice responses are strengthened to different degrees by their short-term consequences. A choice response that is followed by a delayed reinforcer will be strengthened less than one followed by an immediate reinforcer, and as a result the first response will be chosen more often in the future. Yet unlike momentary maximizing theory, Vaughan's theory does not predict exclusive preference for the response with greater strength—as long as each has some strength, each will be chosen some of the time.

Other theories of choice might be called *hybrid* theories, because they assume that both molar and molecular variables affect choice. For example, a popular theory known as **delay-reduction theory** (Fantino, 1969; Fantino, Preston, & Dunn, 1993) includes the basic idea of the matching law, but in addition it assumes that animals' choices are directed toward whichever alternative produces a greater reduction in the delay to the next reinforcer. In other words, this theory includes both a molar component (matching of response proportions to reinforcement proportions) and a molecular component (control by the shorter delay to reinforcement). Other theories of this type include Killeen's (1982) incentive theory and Grace's (1994) contextual choice model. Another recent trend in the research on choice has been an increasing interest in the dynamics of choice—how choice behavior adapts to a change in the reinforcement alternatives (Couvillon & Bitterman, 1991; Devenport & Devenport, 1994; Dragoi & Staddon, 1999). Considerable work is now being conducted to try to evaluate the strengths and weaknesses of different mathematical theories of choice (Mazur, 2000).

Regardless of which theory of choice proves to be most accurate, no one can dispute the more general assertion of molecular theories that short-term factors have a large effect on choice behavior. This should come as no surprise, because previous chapters have shown that response-reinforcer contiguity is very important in operant conditioning. The next section shows that when a small but immediate reinforcer is pitted against a large but delayed reinforcer, the small, immediate reinforcer is frequently chosen.

## SELF-CONTROL CHOICES

Every day, people make many choices that involve a conflict between their short-term and long-term interests. Consider the situation of a college student who has a class that meets early Monday morning in a course where it is important to attend each lecture. On Sunday evening, the student sets her alarm clock so that she can awaken early enough to get to class on time. The student has chosen going to class (and the improved chances for a good grade this will bring) over an hour of extra sleep. This may sound like the prudent choice, but unfortunately the student has plenty of time to change her mind. When the alarm clock rings on Monday morning, the warmth and comfort of the bed seem more appealing than going to class, and the student turns off the alarm and goes back to sleep. Later in the day, she will probably regret her choice and vow not to miss class again.

This example is a typical **self-control choice** situation, or one involving a choice between a small, proximal reinforcer and a larger but more distant reinforcer. The small reinforcer is the extra hour of sleep, and the larger, delayed reinforcer is the better grade that will probably result from going to class. One noteworthy characteristic of self-control situations is that an individual's preferences may exhibit systematic changes over time. On Sunday evening, the young woman in our example evidently preferred going to class (and its long-term benefits) over an extra hour of sleep, since she set the alarm for the appropriate time. The next morning, her preference had changed, and she chose the extra hour of sleep. Later that day, she regrets this choice, and decides to make a different decision in the future.

In case you are not convinced that self-control situations are commonplace, consider the following everyday decisions. You should be able to identify the small, more immediate reinforcer and larger, delayed reinforcer in each case:

1. To smoke a cigarette or not to smoke.
2. To keep the thermostat at 65°F during the winter months, or set it at a higher temperature and face a larger fuel bill at the end of the month.
3. When on a diet, to choose between low-fat yogurt or ice cream for dessert.
4. To shout at your roommate in anger or control your temper and avoid saying something you do not really mean.
5. To save money for some big item you want (such as a car) or spend it on parties each weekend.

For each example, you should also be able to see how one's preference might change over time. It is easy to say you will begin a diet—tomorrow. On Monday or Tuesday, it is easy to decide you will have a frugal weekend and begin saving for that car. It is much harder, however, to keep these commitments when the time comes to make your final choice. Herrnstein and Mazur (1987) have argued that this tendency to switch preferences over time in self-control choices is one of the strongest pieces of evidence against optimization theory. If people followed the strategy that optimized their satisfaction in the long run, they would consistently choose one alternative or the other.

People seem to differ in their willingness to wait for larger but delayed rewards. In one study, Green, Fry, and Myerson (1994) asked people of different ages a series of questions about hypothetical amounts of money, such as, "Would you rather receive $500 today or $1,000 in one year?" They found that adults in their sixties were more likely to choose the larger, delayed reward than 20-year-old college students, and 12-year-old children were still less likely to choose the delayed reward. Other studies have found that smokers are more likely than non-smokers or ex-smokers to choose the smaller, more immediate amount of money when asked questions like the one above (Bickel, Odum, & Madden, 1999; Mitchell, 1999). Although these are correlational studies, they suggest the possibility that the tendency to make an **impulsive choice** (selecting the smaller, more immediate reward) may transfer across different types of choice situations.

Why do people's preferences change over time in such self-control situations? Is there anything people can do to improve their self-control, to make it less likely that they will make an impulsive decision (in favor of the small, proximal reinforcer)? In attempting to answer questions like these, Howard Rachlin (1970, 1974) and George Ainslie (1975) independently developed similar ideas about self-control. The **Ainslie-Rachlin theory,** as it is sometimes called, suggests that changes of preference in self-control situations are understandable if we consider how delay changes a reinforcer's effectiveness.

### The Ainslie-Rachlin Theory

The example of the student who must choose between sleep and an important class can be used to illustrate the features of this theory. Its first assumption is that the value of a reinforcer decreases as the delay between making a choice and receiving the reinforcer increases. The upper panel of Figure 14-7 shows that the value of a good grade is high at the end of the term, but on the Sunday and Monday in question, its value is much lower because it is so far in the future. In the lower panel, the value of an hour of extra sleep at different points in time is also shown, and the same rule applies to this reinforcer: With

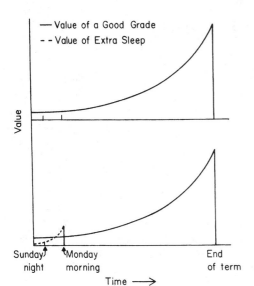

**FIGURE 14-7** An application of the Ainslie-Rachlin model to the hypothetical example described in the text. The top panel shows how the subjective value of a good grade increases as the time of its delivery gets closer. The bottom panel shows that the value of a bit of extra sleep also increases as the time of its delivery gets closer. Because of these changes in value, a person may prefer the good grade at some times (such as Sunday evening) and the extra sleep at other times (say, Monday morning).

greater delays between choice and the delivery of the reinforcer, its value decreases. The second and (very reasonable) assumption of the theory is that a subject will choose whichever reinforcer has the higher value at the moment a choice is made. Notice that the way the curves are drawn in Figure 14-7, the value of the good grade is higher on Sunday evening, which explains why the student sets the alarm with the intention of going to class. On Monday morning, however, the value of an hour of extra sleep has increased substantially because of its proximity. Because it is now greater than that of the good grade, the student chooses the more immediate reinforcer.

If you find the curves in Figure 14-7 difficult to understand, it may help to draw an analogy between time and distance. Figure 14-8 shows a sketch of a long street with two buildings on the left. The buildings are analogous to the two reinforcers in a self-control situation. Building number 2 is clearly larger, but for a person standing at point A, building number 1 would subtend a greater visual angle. We might say that from the perspective of point A, building 1 appears larger (although people obviously have the ability to take their distances into consideration, and so would not be fooled by this illusion). On the other hand, if the person walked to point B, both buildings would appear smaller, but now the visual angle subtended by building 2 would be the larger of the two. Thus, by stepping back from both buildings, a person can get a better perspective on their relative sizes. Similarly, by examining two reinforcers (say, an extra hour of sleep and a better grade) from a distance (for example, the night before a class), a person "gets a better perspective" on the values of the two reinforcers, and is more likely to choose the larger one.

As you can probably see, the student's problem is that she is free to change her mind on Monday morning, when the proximity of the extra hour of sleep gives her a distorted perspective on its value. If she had some way of making her decision of Sunday evening a binding one, she would have a better chance of obtaining the larger, delayed reinforcer. One

technique that exploits this possibility is called **precommitment**—the individual makes a decision in advance, which is difficult or impossible to change at a later time. For example, on Sunday evening the student might ask a friend from the same class to come and get her on the way to class Monday morning, and not to take "no" for an answer. This would not make it impossible for the student to change her mind, but would make it more difficult and more embarrassing to stay in bed. In short, the student could make a precommitment to go to class by having a friend pick her up. The technique of precommitment is a useful way to avoid making an impulsive choice, and the next section shows that it can work for animals as well as people.

### Animal Studies on Self-Control

A good deal of the research supporting the Ainslie-Rachlin theory has involved animal subjects, and this research shows how it is often possible to design simple laboratory analogs of complex real-world situations. Probably the major difference between the self-control situations described above and the

**FIGURE 14-8**    For a person standing at point A, building 1 subtends a larger visual angle than building 2. The opposite is true for a person standing at point B. This situation is somewhat analogous to a self-control situation if we replace physical distance with time and think of the large distant building as a large, delayed reinforcer and the small, closer building as a small, more immediate reinforcer.

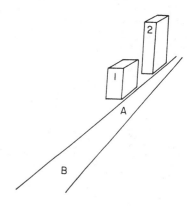

following animal research is the time scale involved. With pigeons, rats, and other animals, a delay of a few seconds can often make the difference between self-control and impulsiveness.

A study by Green, Fischer, Perlow, and Sherman (1981) demonstrated the sort of preference reversals we would expect if the Ainslie-Rachlin theory is correct. Pigeons received many trials each day, and on each trial a bird made its choice by pecking just once at one of two keys. A peck at the red key delivered 2 seconds of grain, and a peck at the green key delivered 6 seconds of grain. There was, however, a short delay between a peck and the delivery of the reinforcer. For example, in one condition there was a 2-second delay for the 2-second reinforcer and a 6-second delay for the 6-second reinforcer. In this condition, the birds showed impulsive behavior on nearly every trial, choosing the 2-second reinforcer. This choice did not speed up subsequent trials, because trials occurred every 40 seconds regardless of which choice was made. It should be clear that this behavior was inconsistent with optimization theory, since the optimal solution would have been to choose the 6-second reinforcer on every trial. By consistently choosing the smaller but more immediate re-inforcer, the birds lost about two thirds of their potential access to grain.

In another condition, the experimenters simply added 18 seconds to the delay for *each* reinforcer, so the delays were now 20 seconds and 24 seconds. When they had to choose so far in advance, the birds' behaviors were more nearly optimal—they chose the 6-second reinforcer on over 80 percent of the trials. This shift in preference when both reinforcers are farther away is exactly what the Ainslie-Rachlin model predicts.

Ainslie (1974) conducted an ingenious experiment showing that at least some pigeons can learn to make use of the strategy of precommitment to avoid impulsive choices. Ainslie's procedure is diagrammed in Figure 14-9. Each pigeon received 50 trials a day, and each trial lasted for exactly 19 seconds, no matter what the pigeon did. The top of Figure 14-9 shows the sequence of events that would occur if the bird did not peck the response key at all. The key would first be lit green for a few seconds, then it would be dark for a few seconds, then it would be lit red for 3 seconds, and then the bird would receive 4 seconds of access to grain. Thus by doing nothing, the bird was certain to receive 4 seconds of food. The middle section of Figure 14-9 shows,

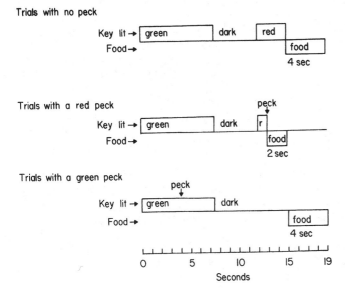

**FIGURE 14-9** A diagram of Ainslie's (1974) procedure. The three sections show, from top to bottom, the events on trials with no pecks, with a peck at the red key, and with a peck at the green key.

however, that if the bird pecked at the key at any time when it was red, it would immediately receive 2 seconds of grain. Ainslie found that each pigeon would almost always peck the key when it was red, thereby exhibiting impulsive behavior—an immediate 2 seconds of food was evidently preferred over 4 seconds of food delivered after a delay of only 3 seconds. When the key turned red, the birds pecked it more than 95 percent of the time.

As the bottom of Figure 14-9 shows, the purpose of the initial period when the key was green was to give a subject the chance to make a precommitment for the larger reinforcer. Notice that when the key was green, both reinforcers were several seconds away, so the 2-second reinforcer should not be so tempting. By making one peck at the green key, a bird made an irreversible choice of the 4-second reinforcer—the key never turned red, so there was no opportunity to peck the red key and get an immediate 2 seconds of food. Three of Ainslie's 10 pigeons learned to use the precommitment option, pecking the green key on more than half of the trials. The other subjects did not peck the green key at any substantial rate.

Part of the reason Ainslie's precommitment procedure was difficult for some birds to master was that making a precommitment required an active response (a peck at the green key), whereas failing to make a precommitment required nothing more than the passage of time. We might suspect that if pigeons had to make an active choice for or against precommitment before the trial would continue, they might use the precommitment strategy more often. An experiment by Rachlin and Green (1972) showed this to be the case. On each trial, a bird had either to peck one key and make a precommitment for a large reinforcer, or peck a second key and later receive a choice between the large reinforcer and a smaller but more immediate reinforcer. In this procedure, four of five pigeons chose the precommitment key on a majority of trials, and the fifth subject also chose this key on occasional trials. In summary, the precommitment procedure seems to work because the individ-

ual can make an irreversible choice when neither reinforcer is immediately available—when the individual has "a better perspective" on the relative sizes of the reinforcers (as illustrated in Figures 14-7 and 14-8). When the alternatives in a self-control situation are punishers rather than reinforcers, they have the reverse effect on choice. In one study, rats tended to choose a large delayed shock over a smaller but more immediate one. However, when they could make a precommitment a few seconds before the trial began to the smaller but more immediate shock, they frequently did so (Deluty, Whitehouse, Mellitz, & Hineline, 1983). This study provides one more example of how reinforcers and punishers have symmetrical but opposite effects on behavior.

Other research with animals has examined factors that may make a subject more or less likely to choose a more preferred but delayed reinforcer. Grosch and Neuringer (1981) used a procedure similar to Ainslie's, except that there was no possibility of precommitment: A pigeon could either wait 15 seconds and then eat a preferred grain, or it could peck a key and receive a less preferred type of grain immediately. (Thus another difference was that the two reinforcers differed in their quality rather than their amount.) The pigeons must have had a substantial preference for the delayed reinforcer, because Grosch and Neuringer found that they would wait for this reinforcer on about 80 percent of the trials. The experimenters then made one small change in the procedure: The two types of food were now placed where they were visible to the pigeons (behind a transparent barrier) throughout the waiting period. With the reinforcers in plain sight, the pigeons became much more impulsive, and they waited for the preferred reinforcer on only 10 or 15 percent of the trials. The sight of the food evidently provided too much of a temptation to resist. In another study, Grosch and Neuringer found that stimuli associated with the food reinforcers had a similar effect. In this case, no food was visible during the waiting interval, but the food hoppers were lit with the same colored lights that normally accompanied the presentation of food. Like the presence of food itself, the colored lights made the pigeons more likely to choose the immediate, less desirable grain.

Grosch and Neuringer also found that their pigeons were more likely to wait for the delayed reinforcer if they had the opportunity to engage in some specific activity during the delay. We have seen that with the food in sight, the pigeons would wait for the preferred grain on only about 15 percent of the trials. Grosch and Neuringer then taught the birds to peck at a key in the rear of the chamber, which at first delivered food on an FR 20 schedule. Not surprisingly, the birds found it easier to wait for preferred grain when they could spend the delay working on the FR 20 schedule. More surprising was the fact that when the rear key no longer delivered any reinforcers, the birds continued to peck at it during the delays for the rest of the experiment with no signs of extinction.

These studies illustrate a few of the factors that have been found to affect the self-control choices of animal subjects. The next section shows that these same factors affect children's choices.

## Factors Affecting Self-Control in Children

The experiments of Grosch and Neuringer were patterned after a series of experiments conducted by Walter Mischel and his colleagues with children (Mischel, 1966, 1974). In one experiment (Mischel & Ebbesen, 1970), preschool children (tested one at a time) were given a choice between waiting 15 minutes for a preferred reinforcer (such as pretzels) or receiving a less preferred reinforcer (such as cookies) immediately. During the 15-minute wait, a child could terminate the trial at any time and get the less preferred snack. Like the pigeons of Grosch and Neuringer, the children found it considerably more difficult to wait when the reinforcers were visible (in an open cake tin in front of the child).

In another study with one different reinforcer, Mischel, Ebbesen, and Zeiss (1972) told some children that they could "think

about the marshmallow and the pretzel for as long as you want." Other children were given no such instructions. The children who were encouraged to think about the reinforcers chose to terminate the trial and obtain the less preferred reinforcer more frequently. Mischel and coworkers also found that children were more likely to wait for the preferred reinforcer when given an activity to engage in during the delay (some children were given a slinky to play with).

Studies by Mischel and others have determined that there are substantial individual differences among children in their self-control abilities: Some children will wait for quite a while for a delayed reinforcer, and others will not. These individual differences can be found in children as young as 2 (Silverman & Ragusa, 1990). It seems that some 2- or 3-year-olds have already learned the strategy of diverting their attention away from the desired objects as a way of avoiding an impulsive choice (Cournoyer & Trudel, 1991). Mischel's research has uncovered a number of other variables that are related to a child's choice in self-control situations. He found that the tendency to wait for a large delayed reinforcer is correlated with age, IQ, the presence of the child's father in the home, and other factors (Mischel, 1961, 1981, 1983). Another study found that the quality of a toddler's interactions with his or her mother is related to self-control ability four years later. Children who had "responsive, cognitively stimulating parent-toddler interactions" at age 2 tended to be less impulsive at age 6 (Olson, Bates, & Bayles, 1990).

Mischel (1966) has also showed that a child's behavior in a self-control situation can be influenced by observational learning. Fourth and fifth graders were asked to participate in a "study of consumer behavior." Each child first observed an adult make choices between such items as a set of plastic chess pieces versus wooden pieces, with the latter not available for two weeks. The child then made similar choices, but with items appropriate for children. The youngster was told to take his or her decisions seriously because he or she would actually receive one of the choices.

Some children observed an adult who consistently chose the immediate reinforcer, making such statements as, "Chess figures are chess figures. I can get much use out of the plastic ones right away." Other children observed an adult who chose the delayed reinforcers, noting their better quality and remarking, "I usually find that life is more gratifying when one is willing to wait for good things." Mischel found that children's choices were greatly affected by the adult model's behavior. Furthermore, the model's influence was long-lasting, for most children continued to follow the example of the model they observed when tested 4 weeks later in a different context. Like so many other behaviors, self-control choices are heavily influenced by observational learning.

Modeling is, of course, only one way to teach children to tolerate a delay. Schweitzer and Sulzer-Azaroff (1988) taught a group of impulsive preschoolers to wait for a larger, delayed reinforcer by beginning with very short delays and progressively increasing the delays as the training proceeded. Similar procedures have been used with developmentally disabled adults (Dixon, Hayes, Binder, Manthey, Sigman, and Zdanowski, 1998). Other techniques for training self-control have also been used (Eisenberger & Adornetto, 1986). But regardless of how it is learned, acquiring the ability to wait for delayed reinforcers at an early age may have long-lasting effects. Mischel, Shoda, and Rodriguez (1989) found that self-control ability at age 4 was correlated with a variety of personality characteristics during adolescence, including the ability to concentrate on a task, to pursue goals, to resist temptation, and to tolerate frustration. We should view these findings with caution because they are based on correlational evidence, but it is easy to imagine how learning to tolerate delays might help a child develop these other desirable traits.

## Techniques for Improving Self-Control

Behavior therapists can offer quite a few suggestions to clients who wish to avoid impulsive behaviors in such varied realms as dieting, maintaining an exercise program, studying regularly, saving money, and avoiding excessive drinking or smoking. Let us look at some of these strategies and see how they relate to the Ainslie-Rachlin model and to the research described above.

We have already seen how a student can make a precommitment to attend an early morning class by arranging to have a classmate meet her and insist that she go. The strategy of precommitment can be used in many other self-control situations. People who wish to lose weight are advised to shop for food when they are not hungry, and to purchase only foods that are low in calories and require some preparation before they can be eaten (Stuart, 1967). The role of precommitment in this case should be obvious. A dieter cannot impulsively eat some high-calorie snack if there are none in the house. If a food item requires, say, an hour of cooking, this delay between the time of choice and the time of eating may decrease the value of the food enough so that sticking to the diet seems preferable. People who habitually spend money impulsively are advised to make a list before they go shopping, to take only enough money to buy what they need, to destroy their credit cards, and to avoid going to a shopping mall without some definite purpose in mind (Paulsen, Rimm, Woodburn, & Rimm, 1977). All of these strategies make it more difficult for the person to buy something on the spur of the moment because it seems appealing at the time.

As Figure 14-7 suggests, impulsive behaviors occur when the value of a delayed reinforcer is too small to compete with the currently high value of an immediate reinforcer. It follows that any strategy which either increases the value of the delayed alternative or decreases the value of the immediate alternative should make the choice of the delayed reinforcer more likely. One useful strategy is therefore to make an additional, more immediate reinforcer contingent upon the choice of the large, delayed reinforcer. For instance, a dieter may make an agreement with himself that he will watch his favorite early evening television program only on those days when he forgoes dessert. A college student who wishes to improve her study habits may allow herself to go out with friends for a snack only after she has studied in the library for two solid hours. Psychologists have labeled this type of strategy **self-reinforcement** because it is the individual who delivers his or her own reinforcers for the appropriate behaviors. Although self-reinforcement can work, a frequent problem is that it is easy to "cheat"—to give yourself the reinforcer even when you have failed to perform the appropriate behavior. For this reason, it is advisable to enlist the help of a friend or family member. The dieter's wife might make sure he only watches his TV program if he did not have dessert. The college student may go to the library with a conscientious roommate who makes sure she has spent 2 hours studying (rather than reading magazines or talking with friends) before they go out for a snack.

The complementary strategy is to make the value of the impulsive option lower by attaching some form of punishment to it. Ross (1974) reports a case in which this technique was used to cure a woman of a nail-biting problem. The woman was unhappy with the way her nails looked after she chewed on them, but as with many nail biters, she found the behavior inherently reinforcing in the short-run (for reasons that are unclear). As part of her treatment, the woman gave the therapist a deposit of $50, and the woman was told that the money would be donated to an organization she intensely disliked (The American Communist Party) if her nails did not grow a certain length each week.

Another strategy for improving self-control relates to the finding of Mischel and his colleagues that observing or even thinking about reinforcers can increase their attractiveness. Although Mischel found that thinking about both reinforcers increased impulsiveness, it has frequently been suggested that selectively thinking about the large, delayed reinforcer can forestall an impulsive action (Ainslie, 1975; Watson & Tharp, 1985). For instance, a person on a diet may be advised to visualize the attractive, healthy body he or she is striving for before sitting down to eat. A similar tactic is to tape on the refrigerator door a picture of an at-

Instructions on how to conduct a self-improvement project based on behavioral principles are available at *http://mentalhelp.net/psyhelp/chap11*.

tractive person in a swimsuit to remind you of your long-term goal each time you have the urge for a snack. A person trying to save money to buy a large item (such as a camera) might tape a picture of the item to the inside of his wallet, to be seen whenever he reaches for some money. The idea behind all of these tactics is that a picture or visual image somehow bridges the gap between the present and the long-term goal, thereby increasing the subjective value of that goal.

We have surveyed some of the major strategies recommended by behavior therapists for improving self-control. Readers interested in more details and additional strategies can refer to behavioral self-management books such as the one by Watson and Tharp (1985). All of these strategies show that there is more to self-control than simple determination and willpower. People who blame their impulsive behaviors on a lack of willpower may actually be lacking only the knowledge of how to apply the appropriate strategies.

## OTHER CHOICE SITUATIONS

Without the Ainslie-Rachlin model, people's behavior in self-control situations might appear paradoxical: Why should an individual's preference vacillate between a small, proximal reinforcer and a larger, more distant reinforcer? Which is the individual's true preference? With the help of the Ainslie-Rachlin model, however, self-control choices become less mysterious. An individual's vacillations in preference are seen as straightforward consequences of the changing delays to the two alternatives. To conclude this chapter on choice behavior, we will examine a few other situations where people's or animals' decisions seem paradoxical. In some cases, their decisions appear to be inconsistent; in others, they are self-defeating. We will examine how psychologists have tried to analyze these situations.

## Preference for Variability

It is often said that "variety is the spice of life," and this maxim is true for animals as well as people. Some studies with pigeons have shown that they prefer situations in which they have more choices (more response alternatives), even when the total amount of reinforcement is no greater than when there were fewer choices (Catania, 1975). In some cases, however, animals appear to take preference for variable outcomes to an extreme and choose a variable alternative even when it is disadvantageous. As an example, consider a situation in which a pigeon must peck either a red key or a green key. The consequences of pecking the red key are always the same: There is a 10-second delay, and then food is delivered. The consequences of pecking the green key are variable: On half of the trials, there is a 1-second delay before food is delivered, and on the other half there is a 19-second delay before food is delivered. Notice that the average of 1 second and 19 seconds is 10 seconds, so in the long run, both keys deliver one food reinforcer for every 10 seconds of delay. Nevertheless, using situations similar to this, I have found that pigeons showed strong preferences, choosing a variable delay of either 1 or 19 seconds over a fixed delay of 10 seconds (Mazur, 1984). The details of my procedure are not important, but through a series of tests, I was able to estimate that the fixed delay had to be reduced to about 3 or 4 seconds before it was equally preferred to the variable option. In other words, a variable delay that averaged 10 seconds was about equally preferred to a fixed delay of only 3 or 4 seconds.

Similar results have been obtained with ratio and interval schedules: Animals prefer VI schedules over equally long FI schedules, and they prefer VR schedules over equally long FR schedules (Fantino, 1967; Herrnstein, 1964).

For example, in one study I found that pigeons preferred a VR 60 schedule over an FR 30 schedule (Mazur, 1986). Therefore, the animals preferred the variable schedule even when it required twice as much work per reinforcer.

How can we explain this strong preference animals show for variable alternatives at the expense of substantial time or effort? The principles of delayed reinforcement described in the previous section on self-control choices can be applied here as well. Figure 14-10a shows the familiar relationship between delay and value: As the delay between a choice response and delivery of the food increases, the value of the food decreases. If the food will be delayed 19 seconds, its value at the moment of choice is small. The food's value is a little greater if it will be delivered in 10 seconds; its value is much greater if it will be delivered in only 1 second. The bar graph in Figure 14-10b is taken directly from this delay curve, and the heights of the bars show the values of food reinforcers with the different delays. But what is the value of food that might be delayed either 1 or 19 seconds? In my analysis, I assumed that it is the *average value* of the two possible delays (that is, the average of the heights of the 1-second bar and the 19-second bar, as shown in the last bar in Figure 14-10b). As can be seen, this average value is substantially greater than the value of a 10-second delay, which may explain why the variable delay is preferred over the fixed delay of 10 seconds. According to this theory, the reason animals prefer variable delays over fixed delays is that only variable delays offer the possibility of a fairly immediate reinforcer, and fairly immediate reinforcers have very high value, as Figure 14-10a shows. The same logic can be applied to preference for other variable schedules, such as VR schedules.

With people, preference for variability can be seen in the powerful effects that VR schedules have on their behavior. Chapter 7 suggested that one reason many sports and games are such strong reinforcers is that these activities deliver reinforcers on VR schedules. That chapter also described how some employers use VR schedules to increase desirable behaviors in their employees, such as regular atten-

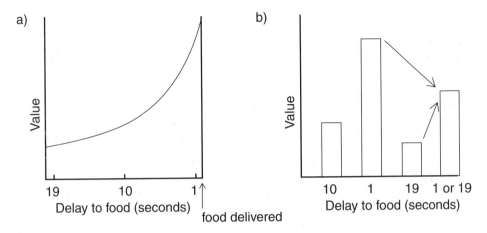

**FIGURE 14-10**   (a) A theoretical curve showing how the value of a reinforcer decreases as its delay increases (compare to Figure 14-7). (b) The hypothetical values of food delivered after 10, 1, and 19 seconds are shown. The last bar shows the value of food that is sometimes delivered after 1 second and sometimes after 19 seconds.

dance and adherence to safety rules. But perhaps the best evidence for the power of variable reinforcers comes from gambling situations, as discussed in the next section.

### Risk Taking

In many everyday decisions, the outcomes are not certain. If you invest in a company, you cannot be certain whether its stock will increase or decrease in value. If you leave home without your umbrella, you cannot be certain whether it will rain. If you go to a party, you cannot be certain whether you will enjoy yourself. An interesting fact about choices involving uncertain consequences is that sometimes people seem to prefer a risky alternative, and sometimes they prefer a safe alternative instead. The same has been found for animals. Researchers have tried to understand why individuals are sometimes **risk-prone** (preferring a risky alternative) and sometimes **risk-averse** (preferring a safer alternative).

In one experiment on this topic, Caraco, Martindale, and Whittam (1980) presented juncos (small birds) choices of the following type. Every trial, a junco could go to one of

two feeding sites. If it went to one feeding site, it would receive one millet seed every time. If it went to the other feeding site, the bird had a 50 percent chance of finding two seeds, and a 50 percent chance of finding none. Caraco and colleagues found that if the trials followed one another rapidly (so there were plenty of opportunities to obtain food), the birds preferred the single, guaranteed millet seed. However, if the trials were separated by longer delays (so there were fewer opportunities to obtain food), the birds preferred the 50 percent chance of getting two seeds. Caraco concluded that these strategies maximize a junco's chances of survival in the wild. When food is plentiful, there is no need to take a risk, because choosing small but certain food sources will guarantee that the bird has enough to eat. When food is scarce and the safe food sources do not provide enough food, the bird will choose riskier options with larger possible payoffs because the bird has "nothing to lose"—getting lucky with the risky option is the bird's only chance of survival.

Some research with other species has obtained results that supported Caraco's theory (Ito, Takatsuru, & Saeki, 2000), but other studies have not (Case, Nichols, & Fantino,

1995). Risk taking may be one choice situation where different species tend to use different strategies. As far as humans are concerned, March and Shapira (1992) suggested that both individuals (for example, politicians) and groups (for example, companies) are likely to take large risks when their survival (in a political campaign, in the marketplace) is at stake. However, March and Shapira also proposed that besides being concerned merely with survival, individuals and groups also have aspiration levels (goals they wish to achieve), and their level of risk taking may depend on how close they are to their goals. For instance, a company may take large risks if its profits for the year are far below its goal, but if its profits are close to the goal, it may behave more conservatively. If the company's profits have exceeded the goal by a comfortable margin, it may then start to take greater risks once again. March and Shapira also proposed that other factors affect the level of risk taking by an individual or group, such as past habits, previous successes or failures, and self-confidence.

Considering all of these factors, it is no wonder that it can be difficult to predict how a person will behave in a risky situation. When it comes to games of chance, however, the choices of many people are all too predictable. Many people enjoy gambling—in casinos, in office pools, in state lotteries. Betting a few dollars a week may be harmless, but for some people, gambling becomes excessive, and they create financial ruin for themselves and their families because of their gambling losses. Excessive betting on lotteries or in casinos makes little financial sense, because the average gambler has to lose money (since state lotteries and casinos always make a profit). Why do people gamble, sometimes heavily, despite the fact that the odds are against them in the long run? Rachlin (1990) suggested that a preference for gambling is similar to the preference for variability discussed in the previous section. Consider the "instant lottery" games found in some states, in which you have a chance of winning money immediately (usually a fairly small amount) each time you buy a ticket. If you buy a ticket every day, you may sometimes go for weeks before you get a winner. But there is a small chance that you will win the very first time you play. Rachlin therefore proposed that buying a lottery ticket is an attractive option for some people for the same reason that food presented after a variable delay is an attractive option for an animal: In both cases, there is a chance that a reinforcer will be delivered almost immediately. Experiments with both animals and people have provided support for the idea that risky alternatives (those that deliver a reinforcer on some trials but not others) are quite similar to reinforcers that are delivered after variable delays (Mazur, 1991; Rachlin, Raineri, & Cross, 1991).

To summarize, we have now examined several choice situations in which the immediacy of a reinforcer is a crucial factor. In self-control choices, people and animals often choose a small immediate reinforcer over a delayed reinforcer that would be better for them in the long run. In the experiments on preference for variability, the possibility of obtaining a quick reinforcer leads animals to choose variable schedules over fixed schedules that would actually require less time or effort in the long run. Finally, the possibility of winning a prize the very next time you place a bet makes gambling attractive, even though you are likely to lose money in the long run. The next section describes some additional situations in which people may choose short-term gains at the expense of larger long-term losses.

## The Tragedy of the Commons

When a person makes an impulsive choice in a self-control situation, the person is acting against his or her long-term interests. The following situations are similar, except here, by acting in their short-term interests, people make choices that are detrimental to society as a whole.

In an article entitled "The Tragedy of the Commons," Garrett Hardin (1968) described a situation that has far too many parallels in modern society. In many villages of colonial America, the commons was a grasslands owned by the village, where residents could allow their cows to graze freely. The commons was thus a public resource that benefited everyone as long as the number of grazing animals did not grow too large. This might not happen for decades or for centuries, but according to Hardin, it was inevitable that eventually there would be more animals than the commons could support. Then, because of overgrazing, the grass becomes scarce, erosion occurs, and the commons is destroyed, to the detriment of everyone.

Why did Hardin believe this unhappy scenario was inevitable? His reasoning was that it is to each herder's benefit to have as many cows as possible, for this will maximize one's income. Now suppose an individual must decide whether to add one more cow to the herd. What are the benefits and costs to consider? The benefits are the profits to be earned from this cow, which go entirely to the owner of the cow. The cost is the extra strain imposed upon the commons, but one additional cow will not make much of a difference, and besides, this cost is shared by everyone who uses the commons. Hardin therefore concluded that the herder will experience a net gain by adding the additional cow to the herd, and by adding a second cow, and so on.

> But this is the conclusion reached by each and every rational herdsman sharing a commons. Therein is the tragedy. Each man is locked into a system that compels him to increase his herd without limit—in a world that is limited. Ruin is the destination toward which all men rush, each pursuing his own best interest in a society that believes in the freedom of the commons. Freedom in a commons brings ruin to all. (Hardin, 1968, p. 1244)

The tragedy of the commons is a play that has been acted out many times in our civilization. The buffalo herds on the American plains were hunted nearly to the point of extinction. Excessive fishing has ruined many of the world's richest fishing areas. Whalers are killing off whales at a rate that could lead to their extinction, which, besides being deplorable in its own right, will of course put the whalers out of business. With every acre of forest land that is turned into a highway or a shopping mall, there is less wilderness for everyone to enjoy.

Most problems of pollution have a similar structure. A company that must pollute the air in order to manufacture its product cheaply keeps the profits of its enterprise to itself; the air pollution is shared by everyone. Before we condemn big business, however, we should realize that individual people frequently make equally selfish decisions. Every person who drives to work in a large city (rather than walking, riding a bike, or taking public transportation) contributes to the air pollution of that city. The reason that many people behave selfishly in this situation is obvious: The driver alone receives the benefits of convenience and comfort that come from driving one's own car. If the driver chose to walk, the reduction in air pollution would be so slight as to be undetectable.

Another instance of the commons tragedy can be seen in the annual trade deficit of the United States, a consequence of the large amounts of foreign products that Americans buy. Most people know that the trade deficit hurts the economy, and that it would be eliminated if people bought fewer foreign goods. Nevertheless, when an individual consumer is deciding which product to purchase, alleviating the trade deficit usually seems far less important than getting the best buy, regardless of whether the product is domestic or foreign.

Rather than end on this pessimistic note, let us examine how it might be possible to rewrite the ending to the tragedy of the commons. Hardin (1968) and Platt (1973) have suggested several ways in which the tragedy can be averted. These suggestions will probably sound familiar, because in recent years our society has focused a good deal of attention on the problems of pollution, the extinction of wildlife, and the like, as well as on potential solutions. What is interesting, however, is the strong resemblance these remedies bear to the strategies that individuals can use to avoid impulsiveness in a self-control situation.

We saw that one powerful technique for improving self-control is the precommitment strategy, in which an individual takes some action in advance that makes it difficult or impossible to make an impulsive choice later. Similarly, a society can decide to make it difficult or impossible for individuals to act selfishly. Thus a society can pass legislation that simply makes it illegal to dump dangerous chemicals where they might seep into the water supply, to pollute the air, or to kill a member of an endangered species. There will of course be people who complain that such laws are infringements of their freedom, but as Hardin points out, deciding what people are and are not free to do is one of the major tasks of society. Should an individual have any more right to kill another with a dangerous chemical than with a handgun?

Less coercive strategies for self-control situations are those that either attach a punisher to the small, immediate alternative or attach an additional (often immediate) reinforcer to the large, delayed alternative. These strategies do not make an impulsive choice impossible, only less likely. In a similar fashion, a city with traffic and pollution problems can punish the behavior of driving one's own car by prohibiting parking on city streets and by making it expensive to park in garages. Based on what we know about punishment, however, it would be advisable to couple such punishment with reinforcement for a desirable alternative behavior. For instance, the city should do all that it can to make public transportation convenient, reliable, safe, and inexpensive.

Finally, we should not underestimate the capacity of human beings to attend to and be influenced by the long-term consequences of their behaviors for society. Just as a picture on the refrigerator can remind a dieter of his or her long-term goal, educational programs and advertising campaigns can encourage individuals to alter their behaviors for the long-term benefits of the community. A good example is the personal sacrifices American civilians were willing to make for the war effort during World War II, not to mention the soldiers who gave their lives in the name of freedom. In some fishing communities, overfishing is avoided by informal agreements among individuals to limit their catches for the good of all (Leal, 1998). From a logical perspective, such behaviors may seem puzzling: Why should people behave in a way that is helpful to others but is harmful to them personally? One solution to this puzzle is simply to assert that, at least in certain circumstances, behaviors that benefit others can be inherently reinforcing for many people (just as eating, reading a novel, or exercising can be inherently reinforc-

If you are considering graduate school or a career in psychology, many Web sites provide useful information, including the following:

- *http://www.apa.org/students/brochure/ homepage.html*
- *http://www.psychologicalscience.org*
- *http://www.rider.edu/users/suler/ gradschl.html*

ing). This is admittedly not much of an explanation. But given the many examples of selfish behaviors we have been forced to consider, it is refreshing to remember that people will often make sacrifices when the only personal benefit from their behavior is the knowledge that they are promoting the common good.

## CHAPTER SUMMARY

The matching law states that the proportion of responses on each schedule tends to match the proportion of reinforcers delivered by that schedule. This law has been demonstrated with many different species of subjects, including people. However, three different types of deviations from exact matching are often found—undermatching, overmatching, and bias. The matching law has also been applied to other variables, such as reinforcer quality and amount. It has also been applied to response rates on single reinforcement schedules by assuming that the subject must choose between the reinforcers delivered by the schedule and other, extraneous reinforcers.

Herrnstein proposed that matching is a fundamental property of behavior, and later he developed a related theory called melioration. A very different theory, optimization theory, states that individuals will distribute their responses in whatever way will maximize the reinforcement they receive. Some studies that compared the predictions of the matching law and optimization theory have favored the matching law—subjects exhibited approximate matching even when this behavior decreased the overall amount of reinforcement. Momentary maximization theory states that, at each moment, an individual chooses whatever behavior has the highest value at that moment. Some experiments have found such moment-to-moment patterns in choice behavior that are predicted by this theory, but others have not.

In a self-control choice situation, an individual must choose between a small, fairly immediate reinforcer and a larger, more delayed reinforcer. Individuals frequently choose the small immediate reinforcer, even though the larger reinforcer would be better in the long run. Studies with animals and children have demonstrated several factors that can affect choice in these situations. Making a precommitment to choose the larger, delayed reinforcer is an effective self-control strategy, as is adding additional reinforcers to the long-term alternative, adding punishers to the short-term alternative, or using cognitive strategies to focus attention on the long-term consequences of one's choices.

The effects of delay can also be seen in other choice situations, such as in preference for variable over fixed reinforcement schedules and in risk-prone behavior (such as gambling when the odds are against winning). The tragedy of the commons occurs when individuals make decisions that benefit them in the short run but are harmful to society as a whole in the long run. Strategies similar to those used to improve self-control may also be helpful in such cases.

## REVIEW QUESTIONS

1. What is the matching law? Describe Herrnstein's experiment on matching, and discuss three ways that behavior can deviate from perfect matching.

2. Summarize the main differences between the matching law, optimization theory, and momentary maximizing theory. What has research found about the strengths and weaknesses of these competing theories?

3. How does the Ainslie-Rachlin theory account for the reversals in preference that occur in self-control choices? What factors can affect the behavior of animals, and of children, in these choice situations?

4. What is the tragedy of the commons? Give a few modern-day examples of this problem, and describe some strategies that can be used to overcome the problem.

# Glossary

**a-process** In the opponent-process theory, an initial fast-acting emotional response to a stimulus, which is later followed by the b-process, leading to the opposite emotion.

**ABAB design** A design for behavioral treatment, where each "A" phase is a baseline phase in which the patient's behavior is recorded but no treatment is given, and each "B" phase is a treatment phase.

**absolute theory of stimulus control** A theory about how animals learn about reinforced and nonreinforced stimuli. The theory states that animals simply learn about the two stimuli separately but learn nothing about the relation between the two.

**abstract code** According to David Premack, a mental ability that is acquired by chimpanzees who receive language training, which allows them to learn about relations among objects, not just about the physical properties of the objects.

**acquisition phase** The period in the learning process when an individual is learning a new behavior.

**Adams's two-stage theory** A theory of motor-skill learning that consists of a verbal-motor stage in which improvement depends on the delivery of feedback from the teacher, followed by a motor stage in which the learner can continue to improve without the teacher's feedback.

**additivity theory of behavioral contrast** A theory that states that behavioral contrast occurs when autoshaped or classically conditioned responses are added to the subject's normal operant responses.

**adjunctive behaviors** Stereotyped behaviors that arise when food or some other reinforcer is delivered at regular intervals.

**AESOP (affective extension of SOP)** An extension of the sometimes opponent process theory that states that a single unconditioned stimulus can have two brain centers, one related to its sensory properties and the other to its emotional properties. These two centers activate two different types of unconditioned responses.

**Ainslie-Rachlin theory** A theory of self-control choices that explains why an individual's preference can shift from a larger, delayed reinforcer to a smaller, more immediate reinforcer as the time of reinforcer delivery approaches.

**analogy** A statement in the form "A is to B as C is to D." To test the ability to understand analogies, the subject is given two or more choices for D and asked which is correct.

**arborization** The branching of the dendrites of neurons, a process that occurs especially rapidly before birth and during the first year of a child's life.

**assertiveness training** A form of therapy for people who are overly submissive in certain situations and want to develop the ability to stand up for their rights. It frequently consists of a combination of modeling, role playing, and behavioral rehearsal.

**Associationists** Philosophers who developed early theories about how people learn to associate separate thoughts or ideas as a result of their experiences.

**associative rehearsal** A type of rehearsal that strengthens the information in long-term memory.

**autism** A severe disorder that affects about 2 to 4 of every 10,000 children, usually appearing when a child is a few years old. Major symptoms are extreme social withdrawal and failure to learn language.

**automatic reinforcement** Reinforcement of a behavior derived from the sensory stimulation that occurs as a result of performing the behavior itself.

**aversive counterconditioning** A treatment for alcoholism and other addictions in which the addictive substance is paired with an aversive stimulus, such as an illness-inducing drug, designed to condition an aversive response to the addictive substance.

**avoidance** A type of negative reinforcement in which performing a response prevents an aversive stimulus from occurring in the first place.

**avoidance paradox** The puzzle about how the nonoccurrence of an aversive event can serve as a reinforcer for an avoidance response.

**axon** A long, branch-like part of a neuron that transmits electrical pulses, or action potentials, when the neuron is stimulated. Enlarged structures at the ends of the axons, the axon terminals, release chemical transmitters that stimulate the dendrites of other neurons.

**b-process** In the opponent-process theory, an emotional response that is the opposite of the a-process. The b-process is supposedly activated only in response to the activity of the a-process, and it is more sluggish both to rise and to decay.

**backward chaining** A strategy, used for teaching response chains, in which the teacher starts with the last response in the chain and works backward.

**backward conditioning** A classical conditioning procedure in which the conditioned stimulus is presented after the unconditioned stimulus.

**Bandura's theory of imitation** A theory that four factors are needed for imitation to occur: attentional processes, retentional processes, motor reproductive processes, and incentive and motivational processes.

**behavior decelerator** Any procedure that leads to a slowing, reduction, or elimination of an unwanted behavior.

**behavior-systems analysis** The view that different reinforcers evoke different systems or collections of species-typical behaviors, which can account for the types of behaviors seen in autoshaping, classical conditioning, and some operant conditioning situations.

**behavioral contrast** A phenomenon in which responding in the presence of one stimulus changes as a result of a change in the reinforcement conditions during another stimulus.

**behavioral economics** A field that uses principles from both behavioral psychology and economics to predict people's choices and behaviors.

**behavioral momentum** An operant behavior's resistance to change when the reinforcement conditions change (such as when free reinforcers are delivered or when the schedule changes to extinction).

**behavioral theory of timing** A theory of animal timing proposed by Killeen and Fetterman that states that animals use their own behaviors to measure durations. The theory states that the rate of reinforcement controls the rate of the internal clock, which in turn controls the rate of the animal's behaviors, and the animal uses these behaviors to measure the passage of time.

**behaviorism** An approach to psychology and the field of learning that emphasizes the study of external events (observable stimuli and responses) and avoids speculation about processes inside the organism.

**bias** In choice behavior, a deviation from matching in which a subject consistently allocates more time or responding to one alternative than predicted by the matching equation.

**biased sample** In psychological research, a sample of subjects who do not accurately reflect the characteristics of the whole population.

**biofeedback** A procedure that provides a person with amplified feedback about some bodily function, usually presented with the intention of increasing the individual's control over that bodily function to treat some medical problem.

**blocking** In classical conditioning, the finding that there is little or no conditioning to a stimulus if it is presented along with a previously conditioned stimulus on conditioning trials.

**British Associationists** British philosophers who proposed early theories about how the ideas in memory are formed from a person's experiences.

**case history method** A research technique that relies on the detailed analysis of one individual or on a small number of individuals.

**cell body** The part of a neuron that contains the nucleus, which regulates the basic metabolic functions of the cell.

**central instance** In research of concept formation, an example from a natural category that people tend to judge as a "good," or "typical," example.

**cerebellum** A part of the brain, located in the back of the head beneath the cerebral cortex, that is important for many skilled movements.

**chained schedule** A set of two or more reinforcement schedules that must be completed in a specific sequence before the reinforcer is delivered. Each schedule is signaled by a different stimulus.

**changeover delay** In choice behavior, a requirement that a certain amount of time must pass after a subject switches from one response to another before any reinforcer can be delivered.

**chaos theory** A theory that uses mathematical techniques to analyze complex physical systems. One of the themes of chaos theory is that complex physical systems may be inherently unpredictable, because very small changes in the current conditions can snowball into much larger changes as time passes.

**chunk** A group of items that the learner combines into a single unit (such as a group of letters that form a word), which makes learning easier than if all the items had to be learned individually.

**classical conditioning** The procedure of repeatedly pairing an initially-neutral stimulus (the conditioned stimulus) and an unconditioned stimulus, through which the conditioned stimulus develops the capacity to elicit a conditioned response.

**closed-loop movement** In feedback theory, a movement during which the performer continually receives feedback about whether the movement is proceeding correctly and can adjust his or her behavior in response to this feedback.

**cognitive map** According to Tolman, a mental map of its environment that an animal develops by exploring or observing its surroundings (as when a rat learns a maze).

**cognitive psychology** An approach to psychology which, unlike behaviorism, makes use of theories about processes that take place inside the head (memory, attention, rehearsal, and so on) that cannot be observed directly.

**cognitive theory of avoidance** The theory that avoidance responses will occur when the individual has expectations that (1) an aversive event will occur if no response is made, and (2) the aversive event will be avoided if a response is made. Avoidance responding will continue until one or both of these expectations are violated.

**comparative cognition** A field of psychology that compares the cognitive processes and abilities of different species, including humans.

**comparator** In control systems theory, a device that compares its goal state (the reference input) and the current situation (the actual input), and signals that action is necessary if the two are not equal.

**comparator theory** A theory of classical conditioning that states that the strength of a conditioned response depends on a comparison of the likelihood of an unconditioned stimulus in the presence of the conditioned stimulus versus its absence.

**complex idea** A term used by James Mill, a British Associationist, to describe what happens when two or more simple ideas are combined.

**compound CS** In classical conditioning, the simultaneous presentation of two or more conditioned stimuli.

**concurrent schedule** A situation in which two or more reinforcement schedules are available at the same time, each requiring its own responses and delivering its own reinforcers.

**conditional discrimination** A discrimination task in which the subject must choose between one of two stimuli, and the correct response depends on which of two other stimuli was presented previously.

**conditioned compensatory responses** In classical conditioning, a conditioned response that is the opposite of the unconditioned response.

**conditioned emotional response (CER)** A classical conditioning procedure in which the conditioned stimulus signals that an aversive event is coming. The measure of conditioning is the suppression of ongoing behavior (such as pressing a lever to obtain food) when the conditioned stimulus is presented, so this procedure is also called **conditioned suppression.**

**conditioned inhibitor (CS⁻)** In classical conditioning, a conditioned stimulus that prevents the occurrence of a conditioned response or reduces the size of the conditioned response from what it would otherwise be. It is also called an **inhibitory CS.**

**conditioned opponent theory** A theory of classical conditioning that states that the later portions of an unconditioned response (which are often opposite in form to the early portions) become associated with the conditioned stimulus. The theory accounts for conditioned responses that appear to be the opposite of the unconditioned response.

**conditioned reflex** Another name for a conditioned response.

**conditioned reinforcer** A previously neutral stimulus that has acquired the capacity

to strengthen responses because it has been repeatedly paired with a primary reinforcer.

**conditioned response (CR)** The response that is elicited by a conditioned stimulus after classical conditioning has taken place.

**conditioned stimulus (CS)** An initially neutral stimulus that develops the capacity to elicit a conditioned response after it is paired with an unconditioned stimulus.

**confounding variable** A variable that is not of interest to the researcher but might nevertheless affect the results of an experiment, thereby making the results difficult or impossible to interpret.

**contextual stimuli** The sights, sounds, and smells of a creature's environment.

**contiguity** One of Aristotle's principle of association, which states that two ideas will be associated if they tend to occur together in space or time. In modern psychology, contiguity between stimuli is an important factor in classical conditioning, and contiguity between a response and its consequences is important in operant conditioning.

**contingency contract** A written agreement used in behavior therapy that lists the duties (behaviors) required of each party and the privileges (reinforcers) that will result if the duties are performed.

**contingency-shaped behavior** Behavior that is controlled by the schedule of reinforcement or punishment (as opposed to rule-governed behavior, which is controlled by a verbal or mental rule about how to behave).

**continuous reinforcement (CRF)** A reinforcement schedule that delivers a reinforcer after every occurrence of a specific response.

**contrast** One of Aristotle's principles of association, which states that the thought of one concept often leads to the thought of the opposite concept.

**control group** In experimental research, a group of subjects that receives no special training or treatment, and whose performance is compared to that of the experimental group.

**control systems theory** A branch of science that analyzes goal-directed behaviors in both living creatures and inanimate objects.

**CS preexposure effect** The finding that classical conditioning proceeds more slowly if the conditioned stimulus is repeatedly presented by itself before it is paired with the unconditioned stimulus.

**CS-US interval**   In classical conditioning, the amount of time between the start of the conditioned stimulus and the start of the unconditioned stimulus.

**cumulative recorder**   A simple mechanical device that records responses in a way that plots time on the horizontal axis and cumulative responses on the vertical axis. It allows the observer to see at a glance the moment-to-moment patterns of a subject's behavior.

**delayed matching to sample (DMTS)** A procedure used to measure short-term memory, or working memory. First, a sample stimulus is presented, followed by a delay with no stimuli, and then two comparison stimuli are presented, and a choice of the comparison that matches the sample is reinforced.

**dendrite**   A branch-like structure on the receptive side of a neuron that is sensitive to transmitters released by the axon terminals of other neurons.

**dependent variable**   In psychological research, the behavior of a subject that is measured by the experimenter to see how it is affected by changes in the independent variable.

**determinism**   A philosophical position that all the events of the world, including all human behaviors, are determined by physical causes that could, at least in principle, be discovered and analyzed with the techniques of science.

**differential reinforcement of high rates schedule (DRH)**   A reinforcement schedule in which a reinforcer is delivered if a certain number of responses have occurred within a fixed amount of time.

**differential reinforcement of low rates schedule (DRL)**   A reinforcement schedule in which a reinforcer is delivered if a certain amount of time has elapsed between two responses.

**directed forgetting**   A procedure for studying memory and forgetting in which the learner (either human or animal) is taught that on some trials it is important to remember a stimulus, and on other trials it is safe to forget the stimulus.

**discrimination**   In either classical or operant conditioning, learning to respond to one stimulus but not to another, similar stimulus.

**discrimination hypothesis**   An explanation of the partial reinforcement effect, which states that the rate of decrease in responding depends on how quickly the subject can discriminate the change from reinforcement to extinction.

**discriminative stimulus**   In operant conditioning, a stimulus that indicates whether or not responding will lead to reinforcement.

**disinhibition**   In classical conditioning, the reappearance of a conditioned response to a stimulus that has undergone extinction that can occur if a novel stimulus is presented shortly before the extinguished stimulus.

**distributed practice**   In motor-skill learning, a training procedure in which fairly brief practice periods alternate with rest periods.

**double-blind procedure**   In psychological research, a procedure in which neither the subject nor the researcher who interacts with the subject knows whether that subject is in the control group or the experimental group.

**drive-reduction theory**   A theory proposed by Hull that any decrease in a biological drive (the hunger drive, the sex drive, and so on) will serve as a reinforcer.

**duplex idea**   A term developed by James Mill, a British Associationist, to describe what happens when complex ideas are combined.

**elaborative rehearsal**   A type of rehearsal that strengthens associations in long-term memory.

**elastic demand**   In economics, demand for a product that exhibits large changes as the price increases or decreases.

**electrical stimulation of the brain (ESB)** A mild, pulsating electrical current which, when delivered to certain parts of the brain, acts as a powerful reinforcer.

**equipotentiality premise**   The hypothesis that a stimulus or response that is difficult to condition in one context should also be difficult to condition in all other contexts.

**errorless discrimination learning**   A procedure for teaching discriminations developed by Herbert Terrace; errorless discrimination learning begins with stimuli that are easy for the subject to discriminate and progresses to more difficult ones, so the subject makes very few errors during the course of learning.

**escape** A type of negative reinforcement in which performing a response leads to the termination of an aversive stimulus.

**evaluative conditioning** A form of second-order classical conditioning with human subjects in which neutral stimuli are paired with a positive or negative stimuli, and then the subjects are asked to rate how much they like or dislike the stimuli.

**excitatory CS (CS⁺)** In classical conditioning, a conditioned stimulus that regularly elicits a conditioned response.

**experimental group** In experimental research, a group of subjects that receives special training or treatment, and whose performance is usually compared to that of a control group.

**extinction** In classical conditioning, presenting the conditioned stimulus without the unconditioned stimulus. In operant conditioning, no longer presenting the reinforcer when the operant response is made. In both cases, responding decreases and eventually disappears.

**fading** A behavior modification procedure in which a prompt for a desired behavior is gradually withdrawn, thereby teaching the learner to produce the behavior without the prompt.

**falsifiability** The testability of a scientific theory, or the degree to which it makes unambiguous predictions that can be tested against the facts.

**field experiment** A study that is conducted in a realistic as opposed to a laboratory setting.

**first-order CS** In classical conditioning, a stimulus that has been conditioned by pairing it directly with the unconditioned stimulus.

**fixed action pattern** An innate sequence of behaviors that is elicited by a specific stimulus and, once started, continues to its end whether or not the behaviors are appropriate in the current situation.

**fixed-interval schedule (FI)** A reinforcement schedule in which the first response after a fixed amount of time has elapsed is reinforced.

**fixed-ratio schedule (FR)** A reinforcement schedule that delivers a reinforcer after a fixed number of responses.

**flooding** A treatment for phobias in which a patient is presented with a highly feared object or situation, which is not removed until the patient's fear diminishes.

**forgetting curve** A graph showing how performance on a memory task declines with the passage of time since learning.

**forward chaining** A strategy used to teach a response chain, in which the teacher starts by reinforcing the first response of the chain, and then gradually adding the second response, the third response, and so on.

**free operant procedure** A procedure developed by Skinner in which, unlike a discrete-trial procedure, the operant response can occur at any time and can occur repeatedly for as long as the subject remains in the experimental chamber.

**free-recall procedure** A procedure in which subjects are asked to remember a list of items and then recall them in any order they wish.

**free will** A philosophical position that some nonphysical entity, such as the will or the soul, can direct human behavior, and that not all behavior can be predicted or explained by a scientific analysis.

**fruitfulness** The degree to which a scientific theory stimulates further research and further thinking about a particular topic.

**functional analysis** A method in which stimuli and/or reinforcers are systematically varied so that a therapist can determine which are maintaining a patient's behavior.

**generality** The breadth of a scientific theory, or the extent to which it can be applied to many different situations and subject populations.

**generalization** The transfer of a learned response from one stimulus to another, similar stimulus.

**generalization decrement hypothesis** An explanation of the partial reinforcement effect, which states that responding during extinction will be rapid if the stimuli present during extinction are different from those that occurred during reinforcement, but slow if the stimuli are similar to those that occurred during reinforcement.

**generalization gradient** A graphic representation of generalization in which the *x*-axis plots some dimension along which the test stimuli are varied, and the *y*-axis shows the strength of conditioned responding to the different stimuli.

**generalized reinforcer** A conditioned reinforcer that has been associated with a large number of different primary reinforcers.

**graduated modeling** A type of modeling in which the model's behaviors steadily progress from simple to more difficult behaviors.

**guidance hypothesis** In motor-skill learning, a theory that if knowledge of results (KR) is given on every trial during learning, the learner becomes overly dependent on this KR and will not perform well in a later test without KR.

**habituation** A decrease in the strength of a reflexive response after repeated presentation of the stimulus that elicits the response.

**higher-order conditioning** A form of classical conditioning in which a conditioned response is transferred from one conditioned stimulus to another, rather than from an unconditioned stimulus.

**Humphrey's paradox** Another name for the partial reinforcement effect, or the seemingly paradoxical finding that a response that is only intermittently reinforced is more resistant to extinction than a response that is reinforced every time it occurs.

**imaginal code** According to Premack, a mental code related to the visual properties of objects that chimpanzees without language training use in tests of reasoning, as opposed to the abstract code used by language-trained chimpanzees.

**impulsive choice** In a self-control choice situation, choosing a smaller, more immediate reinforcer rather than a larger, more delayed reinforcer.

**independent variable** In scientific research, a variable that the experimenter manipulates to determine how this affects the dependent variable.

**inelastic demand** In economics, demand for a product that shows relatively little change as the price increases or decreases.

**inferential statistics** A type of statistics used by researchers to draw inferences or theoretical conclusions from their data.

**instinctive drift** In operant conditioning, innate behaviors that are related to the type of reinforcer being used that cause an animal's performance to drift away from the reinforced behavior and toward instinctive behaviors.

**interim behavior** A behavior pattern that occurs in the early parts of each interval when food or some other primary reinforcer is delivered at regular intervals.

**intermediate-size problem** A discrimination problem in which the subject learns to choose the middle stimulus along some dimension (such as a medium-sized circle), and is then tested when this stimulus is no longer the medium one (for instance, it is now the smallest of three circles).

**interneuron** Any neuron that occurs in a chain of synapses that begins with a sensory neuron and ends with a motor neuron.

**interoceptive conditioning** In classical conditioning, a procedure in which either the conditioned stimulus or the unconditioned stimulus is the stimulation of some internal gland or organ.

**interresponse time (IRT) reinforcement theory** The theory that responding is faster on variable-ratio schedules than on variable-interval schedules because long IRTs (long pauses between responses) are more frequently reinforced on variable-interval schedules.

**intervening variable** A theoretical concept that cannot be observed directly, but is used in science to predict the relationship between independent and dependent variables.

**intradimensional training** A type of discrimination training in which responses in the presence of one stimulus are reinforced, but responses in the presence of a different stimulus from the same physical continuum are not reinforced.

**ironic error** In motor-skill learning, a false movement that a person is trying hard to avoid but has a tendency to make, especially if attention is distracted by some competing task.

**kinesis** A tropism in which the direction of the movement is random in relation to the stimulus.

**knowledge of performance (KP)** In motor-skill learning, detailed feedback given to the learner, such as information about which parts of the movement were performed well, and how other parts of the movement could be improved.

**knowledge of results (KR)** In motor-skill learning, feedback given to the learner about how close his or her movement came to the goal.

**latent learning** Tolman's term for the hidden learning that occurs on trials when no reinforcer is delivered, but can only be seen in the subject's behavior once trials with reinforcement begin.

**Law of Effect** Thorndike's version of the principle of reinforcement, which states that responses that are followed by pleasant or satisfying stimuli will be strengthened and will occur more often in the future.

**learned helplessness** Seligman's term for the impaired ability to learn an avoidance response that occurs after a subject has been exposed to inescapable aversive stimuli.

**learning set** An improvement in the rate of learning across a series of discrimination problems, which occurs even though the positive and negative stimuli are different from one problem to the next.

**local enhancement** Thorpe's term for a type of imitation in which a model directs the learner's attention to a particular object or place in the environment, so that the learner acquires a new behavior more quickly than through trial and error.

**long-term memory** A part of memory that has a very large capacity and can retain information for months, years, or longer, although some information is lost through interference or forgetting.

**long-term potentiation** An increase in the strengths of connections between neurons caused by electrical stimulation, which can last for weeks or months.

**longitudinal study** In psychological research, a method in which the same individuals are repeatedly observed at different points in time, to look for possible changes in their behavior.

**magnetic resonance imaging (MRI)** A brain imaging technique that can show which parts of a person's brain are currently most active.

**maintenance rehearsal** A type of rehearsal that retains information in short-term memory, but does not necessarily strengthen information in long-term memory.

**massed practice** In motor-skill learning, a training procedure in which practice takes place in one continuous block, without rest periods.

**matching law** Herrnstein's general principle of choice behavior that states that in a two-choice situation, the percentage of responses directed toward one alternative will equal the percentage of reinforcers delivered by that alternative.

**matching to sample** A procedure in which reinforcement is delivered if the subject chooses the comparison stimulus that matches a sample stimulus.

**melioration** A principle proposed by Herrnstein and Vaughan that states that matching behavior in choice situations is the result of a process in which the individual invests increasing amounts of time and effort into whichever alternative delivers a higher ratio of reinforcers per response.

**molar theory** A theory of behavior that focuses on the long-term relationships between behaviors and their consequences.

**molecular theory** A theory of behavior that focuses on the moment-by-moment relationships between behaviors and their consequences.

**momentary maximization theory** A theory of choice behavior that states that at each moment, a creature will select whichever alternative has the highest value at that moment, even though it may not be the best choice in the long run.

**motor program** A brain or spinal cord mechanism, first proposed by Lashley, that controls a sequence of movements and does not rely on sensory feedback from one movement to initiate the next movement in the sequence.

**multiple schedule** A procedure in which two or more reinforcement schedules are presented one at a time in an alternating pattern, and each schedule is signaled by a different discriminative stimulus.

**nativism** The hypothesis that some ideas are innate (inborn) and do not depend on an individual's past experience.

**need reduction theory** A theory proposed by Hull that all primary reinforcers are stimuli that reduce some biological need, and all stimuli that reduce a biological need will act as reinforcers.

**negative contrast** A type of behavioral contrast in which there is a decrease in responding in the presence of one stimulus due to an increase in the reinforcement conditions for another stimulus.

**negative punishment** A behavior reduction procedure, more commonly called omission, in which a desired stimulus is removed or omitted if the behavior occurs.

**negative reinforcement** A behavior strengthening procedure in which an aversive stimulus is removed or omitted if the behavior occurs.

**negative transfer** In motor-skill learning, when practice of one task interferes with learning or performance on another task.

**neurogenesis** The growth of new neurons.

**noncontingent reinforcement** The delivery of free reinforcers at random times regardless of the subject's behavior.

**nondifferential training** A simple type of discrimination training in which the positive stimulus is presented on every trial, and there are no trials with negative stimuli.

**nonsense syllable** A meaningless syllable consisting of two consonants separated by a vowel, first used in memory experiments by Hermann Ebbinghaus.

**object permanence** An understanding that objects continue to exist even when they are not visible. Researchers have studied how and when young children develop the concept of object permanence and whether different species of animals can also develop this concept.

**omission** A behavior reduction procedure in which a desired stimulus is removed or omitted if the unwanted behavior occurs.

**one-factor theory** A theory of avoidance that states that avoidance of an aversive stimulus, such as a shock, can in itself serve as a reinforcer, and that the classical conditioning component of two-factor theory is not necessary.

**open-loop movement** In feedback theory, a movement that occurs so rapidly that there is no time to make any corrections once the movement begins.

**opponent-process theory** Solomon and Corbit's theory that states that many emotional responses include an initial emotional reaction followed by an afterreaction of the opposite emotion.

**optimization theory** A theory of choice behavior that states that people tend to make decisions that maximize their satisfaction.

**orienting response** An innate reaction to a sudden or unexpected stimulus in which an animal stops its current activity to look at or listen to the novel stimulus.

**overcorrection** A behavior reduction procedure in which the individual is required to make several repetitions of an alternate, more desirable behavior if an undesired behavior occurs.

**overexpectation effect** A decrease in the strength of responding to two conditioned stimuli that have been trained separately that occurs if they are presented as a compound CS and followed by the usual unconditioned stimulus.

**overlearning** Continuing to practice a response after performance is apparently perfect, which often results in stronger or more accurate performance in a delayed test.

**overmatching** A deviation from matching in which response percentages are consistently more extreme than reinforcement percentages in a choice situation.

**overshadowing** In classical conditioning, the finding that there is less conditioning to a weak conditioned stimulus if it is presented along with a more intense conditioned stimulus.

**pacemaker** In theories of animal timing, a hypothetical internal process that pulses at a steady rate and allows the animal to measure durations.

**partial reinforcement effect** The finding that responses are more rapidly extinguished after continuous reinforcement than after a schedule of intermittent reinforcement.

**participant modeling** A type of modeling in which the learner imitates the behavior of the model in each step of the treatment.

**peak procedure** A procedure for studying animal timing abilities in which the time of its peak response rate shows how accurately the animal can time the intervals.

**peak shift** After discrimination training with a reinforced stimulus and an unreinforced stimulus, a shift in the peak of a generalization gradient from the reinforced stimulus in a direction away from the unreinforced stimulus.

**percentile schedule** A reinforcement schedule in which a given response is reinforced if it is better than a certain percentage of the last several responses the learner has made.

**peripheral instance** In research of concept formation, an example from a natural category that people tend to judge as a "bad," or "atypical," example.

**placebo effect** The finding that when people know they are participating in an experiment, their behaviors may change or improve, even if they are in a control group and receive no special treatment.

**plasticity** The nervous system's ability to change as a result of experience or stimulation.

**positive contrast** A type of behavioral contrast in which there is an increase in responding in the presence of one stimulus due to a decrease in the reinforcement conditions for another stimulus.

**positive reinforcement** A behavior strengthening procedure in which the occurrence of a behavior is followed by a desired stimulus, or reinforcer.

**positive transfer** In motor-skill learning, when practice of one task improves learning or performance on a similar task.

**positron emission tomography (PET)** A brain imaging technique that can show which parts of a person's brain are currently most active.

**postreinforcement pause** A pause in responding that usually occurs after each reinforcer in fixed-ratio schedules.

**precommitment** A technique for improving self-control in which the individual makes a choice in advance that is difficult or impossible to change at a later time.

**Premack's principle** The theory that more probable behaviors will act as reinforcers for less probable behaviors, and that less probable behaviors will act as punishers for more probable behaviors.

**prepared association** An association between stimuli, or between stimuli and responses, that members of a particular species have an innate tendency to learn quickly and easily.

**presence-absence training** A type of discrimination training in which the presence or absence of a specific stimulus indicates whether or not responding will be reinforced.

**primary reinforcer** A stimulus that naturally strengthens any response it follows (such as food, water, sexual pleasure, and comfort).

**proactive interference** When previously learned material impairs the learning of new material.

**progressive relaxation** (or **deep muscle relaxation**) A technique for inducing a state of bodily calm and relaxation by having the person alternately tense and relax specific groups of muscles.

**prompt** In behavior modification, a stimulus that makes a desired response very likely to occur, and is gradually removed (faded out) as training proceeds.

**prospective coding** A memory strategy in which subjects remember what response needs to be made next, rather than remembering what events have occurred previously.

**punishment** A behavior reduction procedure in which the occurrence of a behavior is followed by an aversive stimulus.

**puzzle box** A type of experimental chamber used by Thorndike in which an animal had to make a certain response in order to open the door and obtain food that was available outside.

**ratio strain** A general weakening of responding that is found when a fixed-ratio schedule requires a very large number of responses.

**reaction chain** An innate sequence of behaviors in which the progression from one behavior to the next depends on the presence of the appropriate external stimulus. Portions of the sequence may be skipped or omitted depending on which stimuli are presented and which are not.

**reactive inhibition** In motor-skill learning, a phenomenon similar to fatigue, which, according to Hull, steadily builds up during massed practice and artificially depresses performance.

**receptor** A specialized neuron that responds to sensory stimulation, either from the traditional "five senses" or from internal bodily sensations such as muscle tension and balance.

**reciprocal contingency** A procedure that ensures that two behaviors occur in a fixed proportion, by requiring the individual to perform fixed amounts of the two behaviors in alternation.

**reflex** An innate movement that can be reliably elicited by presenting the appropriate stimulus.

**rehearsal** An active processing of stimuli or events after they have occurred, which can keep information active in short-term memory, and it promote its transfer into long-term memory.

**reinforcement relativity** An idea promoted by Premack that there are no absolute categories of reinforcers and reinforceable responses, but that more probably behaviors can reinforce less probable behaviors.

**reinforcement schedule** A rule that states under what conditions a reinforcer will be delivered.

**reinforcer** A stimulus that strengthens behavior if it is delivered after the behavior occurs.

**relational theory of stimulus control** The theory that animals can learn to respond to relationships between stimuli (such as larger, redder, or brighter). The opposite is the absolute theory of stimulus control, which assumes that animals cannot learn such relationships.

**Rescorla-Wagner model** A mathematical theory of classical conditioning that states that, on each trial, the amount of excitatory or inhibitory conditioning depends on the associative strengths of all the conditioned stimuli that are present and on the intensity of the unconditioned stimulus.

**resistance to extinction** The degree to which a response continues when it is no longer reinforced.

**response blocking** A behavior reduction procedure in which the individual is physically prevented from making an unwanted response. In extinction of avoidance responding, response blocking can teach the individual that the avoidance response is no longer necessary.

**response chain** A sequence of learned behaviors that must occur in a specific order, with a primary reinforcer delivered only after the final response. Each stimulus in the middle of a response chain is assumed to serve as a conditioned reinforcer for the previous response and a discriminative stimulus for the next response of the chain.

**response cost** A behavior reduction procedure in which the individual is penalized by the loss of reinforcers if an undesired behavior occurs.

**response deprivation theory** A theory of reinforcement which states that any contingency that deprives an animal of its preferred level of a behavior will cause that behavior to act as a reinforcer for less restricted behaviors.

**response-reinforcer correlation theory** The theory that responding is faster on variable-ratio schedules than on variable-interval schedules because faster responding leads to more reinforcers on variable-ratio schedules, but not on variable-interval schedules.

**retroactive interference** When the presentation of new material interferes with the memory of something that was learned earlier.

**retrospective coding** A memory strategy in which subjects choose later responses by remembering what stimuli have occurred previously.

**rule-governed behavior** Behavior that is controlled by a verbal or mental rule about how to behave (as opposed to contingency-shaped behavior, which is controlled by the schedule of reinforcement or punishment).

**S-R association** A hypothetical association between brain areas representing the conditioned stimulus and a response, which might develop during classical conditioning and thereby give the conditioned stimulus the capacity to elicit a conditioned response.

**S-S association** A hypothetical association between brain areas representing two different stimuli, which might develop if the two stimuli are paired.

**sampling error** In scientific research, an error in measurement caused by random or uncontrolled variations in the quantity being measured.

**savings** Ebbinghaus's measure of the strength of memory, which showed how much less time was required to relearn a previously learned list of nonsense syllables.

**Schmidt's schema theory** A theory of motor-skill learning that applies to open-ended classes of movements, where a person may need to make a response that has never been practiced. The theory states that as people practice a task, they acquire general rules (schemas) about how to recognize the correct response and how to produce it.

**second-order conditioning** A classical-conditioning procedure in which a conditioned response is transferred from one stimulus to another by pairing a neutral stimulus with a previously conditioned stimulus.

**self-control choice** A choice between a small, more immediate reinforcer, and a larger but more delayed reinforcer.

**self-reinforcement** A behavior modification technique in which the individual delivers his or her own reinforcers for appropriate behavior.

**sensory preconditioning** A classical conditioning procedure in which two neutral stimuli are repeatedly paired before either is paired with an unconditioned stimulus.

**shaping** (or **method of successive approximations**) A procedure for teaching a new behavior in which closer and closer approximations to the desired behavior are reinforced.

**short-delay conditioning** A classical conditioning procedure in which the conditioned stimulus begins a second or so before the unconditioned stimulus.

**short-term memory** A type of memory that can only hold information for a matter of seconds and has a very limited capacity.

**shuttle box** An experimental chamber with two rectangular compartments. An animal may be required to move from one compartment to the other in order to escape or avoid an aversive stimulus, such as shock.

**Sidman avoidance task** An avoidance procedure in which shocks occur at regular intervals if the subject does not respond, but a response postpones the next shock for a fixed period of time.

**sign stimulus** A stimulus that initiates a fixed action pattern.

**sign-tracking theory** A theory of classical conditioning that states that animals tend to orient themselves toward, approach, and explore any stimuli that are good predictors of important events, such as the delivery of food.

**similarity** One of Aristotle's principles of association, which states that the thought of one concept often leads to the thought of similar concepts.

**simple cell** A type of neuron in the visual cortex, discovered by Hubel and Wiesel, which fires most rapidly when a a line is presented at a specific angle in a specific part of the visual field.

**simple systems approach** In physiological research, the strategy of studying primitive creatures, which have smaller and less complex nervous systems.

**simultaneous conditioning** A type of classical conditioning in which the conditioned stimulus and unconditioned stimulus begin at the same moment.

**simultaneous discrimination procedure** A discrimination procedure in which the positive and negative stimuli are presented together and the subject must choose between them.

**single neuron doctrine of perception** The theory that there are individual neurons in the brain that respond to specific, complex stimuli in the individual's environment.

**skin conductance response (SCR)** A change in the electrical conductivity of the skin often caused by emotions such as fear or surprise, which can be measured by placing sensors on a person's palm.

**slow positioning task** A motor learning task in which the subject must move an object toward a target, usually out of sight, with no time limit.

**social facilitation** Thorpe's term for a type of imitation in which the behavior of one individual prompts a similar behavior from another individual, but that behavior was already in the repertoire of the imitator.

**social learning theory** A theory developed by Bandura and Walters that states that people learn both through the traditional principles of classical and operant conditioning and through observational learning.

**sometimes opponent process theory (SOP)** A general theory of classical conditioning developed by Allan Wagner, which speculates about why some conditioned responses are similar in form and others are opposite in form to the unconditioned response.

**species-specific defense reaction (SSDR)** An innate defensive reaction that occurs when an animal encounters any kind of new or sudden stimulus in the wild. SSDRs usually fall into the categories of freezing, fleeing, or fighting.

**spinal reflex arc** Neural pathways that produce the reflexive withdrawal of one's hand from a painful stimulus, consisting of pain-sensitive neurons in the hand with axons that extend into the spinal cord, interneurons, and motor neurons that activate the muscles of the arm.

**spontaneous recovery** In classical or operant conditioning, the reappearance of a response that has undergone extinction after a passage of time without further conditioning trials.

**statistically significant** A research finding that scientists accept as being accurate because statistical analysis shows that the results were unlikely to have occurred by chance. By convention, a result is usually called statistically significant if there is less than a 5 percent probability that it occurred by chance.

**stimulus control** The general topic of how behaviors can be controlled by the stimuli that precede them.

**stimulus equivalence** A situation in which an individual learns to respond to all stimuli in a category as if they are interchange-able, even though the individual has been taught only a few relations between these stimuli, not all the possible relations.

**stimulus satiation** A behavior reduction procedure in which the reinforcer is presented in such great quantities that it loses its effectiveness.

**stimulus substitution theory** Pavlov's theory of classical conditioning, which states that the conditioned stimulus becomes a substitute for the unconditioned stimulus and elicits the same response.

**stop-action principle** A principle of reinforcement that states that the precise movements being performed at the moment of reinforcer delivery will be strengthened and be more likely to occur in the future.

**successive discrimination procedure** A discrimination procedure in which the positive and negative stimuli are presented at separate times.

**superstition experiment** Skinner's classic experiment in which food was delivered to pigeons every 15 seconds no matter what they were doing, and most pigeons developed distinctive behaviors that they performed repeatedly between food presentations.

**superstitious behavior** A behavior that occurs because, by accident or coincidence, it has previously been followed by a reinforcer.

**synapse** A small gap between the axon terminal of one neuron and the dendrite of another neuron into which transmitters are released.

**syntax** The rules and definitions of a scientific theory, which state how the independent and dependent variables are to be measured and specify the relationships among independent variables, intervening variables, and dependent variables.

**systematic desensitization** A behavioral treatment for phobias that involves slowly presenting the patient with increasingly strong fear-provoking stimuli while keeping the patient in a very relaxed state.

**taxis** A tropism in which the eliciting stimulus determines the direction of the creature's movement.

**terminal behavior** A behavior pattern that occurs near the end of each interval when food or some other primary reinforcer is delivered at regular intervals.

**three-term contingency** A contingency involving a discriminative stimulus, a response, and a reinforcer or punisher. The contingency states that in the presence of a specific discriminative stimulus, a specific response will lead to specific consequences.

**time-out** A behavior reduction procedure in which one or more desirable stimuli are temporarily removed if the individual performs some unwanted behavior.

**token economy** A behavior modification system, often used with groups of people, in which each person can earn tokens by performing specific behaviors and can later exchange these tokens for a variety of primary reinforcers.

**tolerance** A decrease in the effects of a drug that is observed after repeated use of the drug.

**trace conditioning** A classical conditioning procedure in which the conditioned stimulus and the unconditioned stimulus are separated by some time interval in which neither stimulus is present.

**tragedy of the commons** A situation in which people, acting in their individual short-term interests, make choices that are detrimental to society as a whole.

**transfer of training** In motor-skill learning, how experience on one task affects performance on another task.

**transitive inference** Learning a rule about the relation between three stimuli, such as the following: "If A < B, and B < C, then A < C."

**transmitter** A chemical released into the synapse by the axon terminals of a neuron, to which cell bodies and dendrites of other neurons are sensitive.

**transposition** A case in which a subject receives reinforcers for choosing one of two stimuli in a discrimination task (such as choosing a 2-inch circle rather than a 1-inch circle), but later chooses a more extreme stimulus along the same dimension rather than the previously reinforced stimulus (such as choosing a 3-inch circle rather than the 2-inch circle).

**trans-situationality** The theory that once a stimulus is determined to be a reinforcer in one situation, it will also serve as a reinforcer in other situations.

**tropism** An innate movement of a creature's entire body in response to a specific stimulus. The two major categories of tropisms are kineses and taxes.

**true imitation** Thorpe's term for the imitation of a behavior pattern that is very unusual or improbable for the species, so that it would seldom be learned through trial and error.

**two-factor theory** (or **two-process theory**) The theory that both classical conditioning (learning to fear a stimulus) and operant conditioning (escape from the fear-eliciting stimulus) are required for avoidance responding.

**unconditioned response (UR)** In classical conditioning, an innate response that is elicited by an unconditioned stimulus.

**unconditioned stimulus (US)** In classical conditioning, a stimulus that naturally elicits a specific response (an unconditioned response).

**US preexposure effect** The finding that classical conditioning is slower if the unconditioned stimulus is repeatedly presented by itself in a particular context before it is paired with a conditioned stimulus.

**undermatching** A deviation from matching in which response percentages are consistently less extreme than reinforcement percentages in a choice situation.

**variable-interval schedule (VI)** A reinforcement schedule in which reinforcers become available after variable and unpredictable time intervals. Once a reinforcer becomes available, a single response is required to collect it.

**variable-ratio schedule (VR)** A reinforcement schedule that delivers a reinforcer after a variable and unpredictable number of responses.

**videotape self-modeling** A behavior modification technique in which clients watch videotapes of themselves correctly performing the desired behaviors.

**virtual reality therapy**  A type of systematic desensitization in which a patient wears a headset that displays realistic visual images that change with every head movement, simulating a three-dimensional environment.

**visual cortex**  An area of the cerebral cortex, located in the back of the head, just beneath the skull, which processes visual information.

**Weber's law**  A principle of perception that states that the just noticeable difference (the smallest difference between two stimuli that can be detected) is proportional to the sizes of the stimuli.

# References

Abbott, B. B., & Badia, P. (1986). Predictable versus unpredictable shock conditions and physiological measures of stress: A reply to Arthur. *Psychological Bulletin, 100,* 384–387.

Abramowitz, A. J., & O'Leary, S. G. (1990). Effectiveness of delayed punishment in an applied setting. *Behavior Therapy, 21,* 231–239.

Abramson, L. Y., Seligman, M. E. P., & Teasdale, J. D. (1978). Learned helplessness in humans: Critique and reformulation. *Journal of Abnormal Psychology, 87,* 49–74.

Adams, C. D., & Kelley, M. L. (1992). Managing sibling aggression: Overcorrection as an alternative to time-out. *Behavior Therapy, 23,* 707–717.

Adams, J. A. (1971). A closed-loop theory of motor learning. *Journal of Motor Behavior, 3,* 111–150.

Adams, J. A. (1976). *Learning and memory: An introduction.* Homewood, IL: Dorsey Press.

Adams, J. A., & Reynolds, B. (1954). Effect of shift in distribution of practice conditions following interpolated rest. *Journal of Experimental Psychology, 47,* 32–36.

Ader, R., & Cohen, N. (1975). Behaviorally conditioned immunosuppression. *Psychosomatic Medicine, 37,* 333–340.

Ader, R., & Cohen, N. (1993). Psychoneuroimmunology: Conditioning and stress. *Annual Review of Psychology, 44,* 53–85.

Ader, R., Felten, D., & Cohen, N. (1990). Interactions between the brain and the immune system. *Annual Review of Pharmacology and Toxicology, 30,* 561–602.

Ainslie, G. (1974). Impulse control in pigeons. *Journal of the Experimental Analysis of Behavior, 21,* 485–489.

Ainslie, G. (1975). Specious reward: A behavioral theory of impulsiveness and impulse control. *Psychological Bulletin, 82,* 463–496.

Albert, M., Ricker, S., Bevins, R. A., & Ayres, J. J. B. (1993). Extending continuous versus discontinuous conditioned stimuli before versus after unconditioned stimuli. *Journal of Experimental Psychology: Animal Behavior Processes, 19,* 255–264.

Alberto, P., & Andrews, D. (1991). Are moral considerations sufficient for selecting nonaversive interventions?: A review of Repp and Singh's *Perspectives on the use of nonaversive and aversive interventions for persons with developmental disabilities. The Behavior Analyst, 14,* 219–224.

Alberts, E., & Ehrenfreund, D. (1951). Transposition in children as a function of age. *Journal of Experimental Psychology, 41,* 30–38.

Allaway, T. A. (1971). *Attention, information, and autoshaping.* Ph.D. dissertation, University of Pennsylvania.

Allen, J. D., & Butler, J. A. (1990). The effect of interplay interval on adjunctive behavior in humans in a game-playing situation. *Physiology and Behavior, 47,* 719–725.

Allison, J. (1993). Response deprivation, reinforcement, and economics. *Journal of the Experimental Analysis of Behavior, 60,* 129–140.

Alvarez-Borda, B., Ramirez-Amaya, V., Perez-Montfort, R., & Bermudez-Rattoni, F. (1995).

Enhancement of antibody production by a learning paradigm. *Neurobiology of Learning and Memory, 64*, 103–105.

Amiro, T. W., & Bitterman, M. E. (1980). Second-order appetitive conditioning in goldfish. *Journal of Experimental Psychology: Animal Behavior Processes, 6*, 41–48.

Ammerman, R. T., & Hersen, M. (Eds.) (1995). *Handbook of child behavior therapy in the psychiatric setting.* New York: Wiley.

Andrews, E. A., & Braveman, N. S. (1975). The combined effects of dosage level and interstimulus interval on the formation of one-trial poison-based aversions in rats. *Animal Learning and Behavior, 3*, 287–289.

Andrews, J. A., Hops, H., & Duncan, S. C. (1997). Adolescent modeling of parent substance use: The moderating effect of the relationship with the parent. *Journal of Family Psychology, 11*, 259–270.

Anger, D. (1956). The dependence of interresponse times upon the relative reinforcement of different interresponse times. *Journal of Experimental Psychology, 52*, 145–161.

Anger, W. K., Rohlman, D. S., & Sizemore, O. J. (1994). A comparison of instruction formats for administering a computerized behavior test. *Behavior Research Methods, Instruments, and Computers, 26*, 209–212.

Anisfeld, M. (1991). Neonatal imitation. *Developmental Review, 11*, 60–97.

Antonov, I., Kandel, E. R., & Hawkins, R. D. (1999). The contribution of facilitation of monosynaptic PSPs to dishabituation and sensitization of the Aplysia siphon withdrawal reflex. *Journal of Neuroscience, 19*, 10438–10450.

Arena, J. G., Bruno, G. M., Hannah, S. L., & Meador, K. J. (1995). A comparison of frontal electromyographic biofeedback training, trapezius electromyographic biofeedback training, and progressive muscle relaxation therapy in the treatment of tension headache. *Headache, 35*, 411–419.

Aristotle. (ca. 350 B.C.). *De memoria et reminiscentia.* In J. A. Smith (trans.) and W. D. Ross (Ed.), *The Works of Aristotle* (Vol. 3). Oxford: Clarendon Press. (English translation published 1931.)

Arthur, A. Z. (1986). Stress of predictable and unpredictable shock. *Psychological Bulletin, 100*, 379–383.

Ash, D. W., & Holding, D. H. (1990). Backward versus forward chaining in the acquisition of a keyboard skill. *Human Factors, 32*, 139–146.

Averill, J. R. (1973). Personal control over aversive stimuli and its relationship to stress. *Psychological Bulletin, 80*, 286–303.

Axelrod, S. (1990). Myths that (mis)guide our profession. In A. C. Repp & N. N. Singh (Eds.), *Perspectives on the use of nonaversive and aversive interventions for persons with developmental disabilities.* Sycamore, IL: Sycamore Publishing.

Ayllon, T. (1963). Intensive treatment of psychotic behavior by stimulus satiation and food reinforcement. *Behaviour Research and Therapy, 1*, 53–62.

Ayllon, T., & Haughton, E. (1964). Modification of symptomatic verbal behavior of mental patients. *Behaviour Research and Therapy, 2*, 87–97.

Ayres, J. J. B., Bombace, J. C., Shurtleff, D., & Vigorito, M. (1985). Conditioned suppression tests of context-blocking hypothesis: Testing in the absence of the preconditioned context. *Journal of Experimental Psychology: Animal Behavior Processes, 11*, 1–14.

Ayres, J. J. B., Haddad, C., & Albert, M. (1987). One-trial excitatory backward conditioning as assessed by conditioned suppression of licking in rats: Concurrent observations of lick suppression and defensive behaviors. *Animal Learning and Behavior, 15*, 212–217.

Azrin, N. H. (1956). Effects of two intermittent schedules of immediate and nonimmediate punishment. *Journal of Psychology, 42*, 3–21.

Azrin, N. H. (1960). Effects of punishment intensity during variable–interval reinforcement. *Journal of the Experimental Analysis of Behavior, 3*, 123–142.

Azrin, N. H., & Holz, W. C. (1966). Punishment. In W. K. Honig (Ed.), *Operant behavior: Areas of research and application.* Englewood Cliffs, NJ: Prentice-Hall.

Azrin, N. H., Holz, W. C., & Hake, D. F. (1963). Fixed–ratio punishment. *Journal of the Experimental Analysis of Behavior, 6*, 141–148.

Badia, P., Culbertson, S., & Harsch, J. (1973). Choice of longer or stronger signaled shock over shorter or weaker unsignaled shock. *Journal of the Experimental Analysis of Behavior, 19*, 25–32.

Baer, D. M., Peterson, R. F., & Sherman, J. A. (1967). The development of imitation by reinforcing behavioral similarity to a model. *Journal of the Experimental Analysis of Behavior, 10*, 405–416.

Baeyens, F., Eelen, P., Van den Bergh, O., & Crombez, G. (1992). The content of learning in human evaluative conditioning: Acquired valence is sensitive to US revaluation. *Learning and Motivation, 23,* 200–224.

Baker, K. E., Wylie, R. C., & Gagne, R. M. (1950). Transfer of training to a motor skill as a function of variation in rate of response. *Journal of Experimental Psychology, 40,* 721–732.

Baker, T. B., & Tiffany, S. T. (1985). Morphine tolerance as habituation. *Psychological Review, 92,* 78–108.

Balaban, M. T., Rhodes, D. L, & Neuringer, A. (1990). Orienting and defense responses to punishment: Effects on learning. *Biological Psychology, 30,* 203–217.

Balaz, M. A., Kasprow, W. J., & Miller, R. R. (1982). Blocking with a single compound trial. *Animal Learning and Behavior, 10,* 271–276.

Baldwin, E. (1993). The case for animal research in psychology. *Journal of Social Issues, 49,* 121–131.

Balsam, P. D., & Gibbon, J. (1988). Formation of tone-US associations does not interfere with the formation of context-US associations in pigeons. *Journal of Experimental Psychology: Animal Behavior Processes, 14,* 401–412.

Balsam, P. D., & Tomie, A. (Eds.) (1985). *Context and learning.* Hillsdale, NJ: Erlbaum.

Bandura, A. (1965). Influence of models' reinforcement contingencies on the acquisition of imitative responses. *Journal of Personality and Social Psychology, 1,* 589–595.

Bandura, A. (1969). *Principles of behavior modification.* New York: Holt, Rinehart & Winston.

Bandura, A. (1986). *Social foundations of thought and action.* Englewood Cliffs, NJ: Prentice-Hall.

Bandura, A. (1994). *Self-efficacy: The exercise of control.* New York: Freeman.

Bandura, A., Blanchard, E. B., & Ritter, B. (1969). Relative efficacy of desensitization and modeling approaches for inducing behavioral, affective, and attitudinal changes. *Journal of Personality and Social Psychology, 13,* 173–199.

Bandura, A., Grusec, J. E., & Menlove, F. L. (1967). Vicarious extinction of avoidance behavior. *Journal of Personality and Social Psychology, 5,* 16–23.

Bandura, A., & Huston, A. C. (1961). Identification as a process of incidental learning. *Journal of Abnormal and Social Psychology, 63,* 311–318.

Bandura, A., & Kupers, C. J. (1964). The transmission of patterns of self-reinforcement through modeling. *Journal of Abnormal and Social Psychology, 69,* 1–9.

Bandura, A., & Menlove, F. L. (1968). Factors determining vicarious extinction of avoidance behavior through symbolic modeling. *Journal of Personality and Social Psychology, 8,* 99–108.

Bandura, A., Ross, D., & Ross, S. A. (1963). Imitation of film-mediated aggressive models. *Journal of Abnormal and Social Psychology, 66,* 3–11.

Bandura, A., & Walters, R. H. (1959). *Adolescent aggression.* New York: Ronald Press.

Bandura, A., & Walters, R. H. (1963). *Social learning and personality development.* New York: Holt, Rinehart & Winston.

Bao, J. X., Kandel, E. R., & Hawkins, R. D. (1998). Involvement of presynaptic and postsynaptic mechanisms in a cellular analog of classical conditioning at *Aplysia* sensory-motor neuron synapses in isolated cell culture. *Journal of Neuroscience, 18,* 458–466.

Barlow, H. B. (1972). Single units and sensation: A neural doctrine for perceptual psychology? *Perception, 1,* 371–394.

Barnes, D., & Keenan, M. (1993). Concurrent activities and instructed human fixed-interval performance. *Journal of the Experimental Analysis of Behavior, 59,* 501–520.

Baron, A., Kaufman, A., & Fazzini, D. (1969). Density and delay of punishment of free-operant avoidance. *Journal of the Experimental Analysis of Behavior, 12,* 1029–1037.

Baron, A., & Leinenweber, A. (1994). Molecular and molar analyses of fixed-interval performance. *Journal of the Experimental Analysis of Behavior, 61,* 11–18.

Bartlett, F. C. (1932). *Remembering: A study in experimental and social psychology.* Cambridge: Cambridge University Press.

Batsell, W. R., & Batson, J. D. (1999). Augmentation of taste conditioning by a preconditioned odor. *Journal of Experimental Psychology: Animal Behavior Processes, 25,* 374–388.

Battig, W. F., & Montague, W. E. (1969). Category norms for verbal items in 56 categories: A replication and extension of the Connecticut category norms. *Journal of Experimental Psychology Monograph* (No. 3 Part 2).

Baum, M. (1966). Rapid extinction of an avoidance response following a period of response prevention in the avoidance apparatus. *Psychological Reports, 18,* 59–64.

Baum, M. (1976). Instrumental learning: Comparative studies. In M. P. Feldman & A. Broadhurst (Eds.), *Theoretical and experimental bases of the behavior therapies.* New York: John Wiley.

Baum, W. M. (1973). The correlation-based law of effect. *Journal of the Experimental Analysis of Behavior, 20,* 137–153.

Baum, W. M. (1974). On two types of deviation from the matching law: Bias and undermatching. *Journal of the Experimental Analysis of Behavior, 22,* 231–242.

Baum, W. M. (1979). Matching, undermatching, and overmatching in studies of choice. *Journal of the Experimental Analysis of Behavior, 32,* 269–281.

Baum, W. M. (1982). Choice, changeover, and travel. *Journal of the Experimental Analysis of Behavior, 38,* 35–49.

Baum, W. M. (1993). Performances on ratio and interval schedules of reinforcement: Data and theory. *Journal of the Experimental Analysis of Behavior, 59,* 245–264.

Baum, W. M., & Rachlin, H. C. (1969). Choice as time allocation. *Journal of the Experimental Analysis of Behavior, 12,* 861–874.

Beardsley, S. D., & McDowell, J. J. (1992). Application of Herrnstein's hyperbola to time allocation of naturalistic human behavior maintained by naturalistic social reinforcement. *Journal of the Experimental Analysis of Behavior, 57,* 177–185.

Beatty, W. W., & Shavalia, D. A. (1980). Rat spatial memory: Resistance to retroactive interference at long retention intervals. *Animal Learning and Behavior, 8,* 550–552.

Beauchamp, A. J., Gluck, J. P., Fouty, H. E., & Lewis, M. H. (1991). Associative processes in differentially reared rhesus monkeys (*Macaca mulata*): Blocking. *Developmental Psychobiology, 24,* 175–189.

Beidleman, W. B. (1981). Group assertive training in correctional settings: A review and methodological critique. *Journal of Offender Counseling, Services & Rehabilitation, 6,* 69–87.

Bekesy, G. von. (1964). Sweetness produced electrically on the tongue and its relation to taste theories. *Journal of Applied Physiology, 19,* 1105–1113.

Bekesy, G. von. (1966). Taste theories and the chemical stimulation of single papillae. *Journal of Applied Physiology, 21,* 1–9.

Bentall, R. P., & Lowe, C. F. (1987). The role of verbal behavior in human learning: III. Instructional effects in children. *Journal of the Experimental Analysis of Behavior, 47,* 177–190.

Berger, T. W., & Weisz, D. J. (1987). Rabbit nictitating membrane responses. In I.

Gormezano, W. F. Prokasy, & R. F. Thompson (Eds.), *Classical conditioning* (3rd ed.). Hillsdale, NJ: Erlbaum.

Bernstein, I. L., Webster, M. M., & Bernstein, I. D. (1982). Food aversions in children receiving chemotherapy for cancer. *Cancer, 50,* 2961–2963.

Bersh, P. J., Notterman, J. M., & Schoenfeld, W. N. (1956). Extinction of human cardiac-response during avoidance-conditioning. *American Journal of Psychology, 69,* 244–251.

Besson, A., Privat, A. M., Eschalier, A., & Fialip, J. (1999). Dopaminergic and opioidergic mediations of tricyclic antidepressants in the learned helplessness paradigm. *Pharmacology, Biochemistry, and Behavior, 64,* 541–548.

Bevins, R. A., Jensen, H. C., Hinze, T. S., & Besheer, J. (1999). Taste quality and extinction of a conditioned taste aversion in rats. *Animal Learning and Behavior, 27,* 358–366.

Bickel, W. K., DeGrandpre, R. J., & Higgins, S. T. (1995). The behavioral economics of concurrent drug reinforcers: A review and reanalysis of drug self-administration research. *Psychopharmacology, 118,* 250–259.

Bickel, W. K., Green, L., & Vuchinich, R. E. (1995). Behavioral economics. *Journal of the Experimental Analysis of Behavior, 64,* 257–262.

Bickel, W. K., Odum, A. L., & Madden, G. J. (1999). Impulsivity and cigarette smoking: delay discounting in current, never, and ex-smokers. *Psychopharmacology, 146,* 447–454.

Bickel, W. K., & Vuchinich, R. (Eds.) (2000). *Reframing health behavior change with behavioral economics.* Mahwah, NJ: Erlbaum.

Biermann, K. (1990). Why animal experimentation should continue. *The Humanist, 50,* 8–9.

Bilodeau, E. A. (1954). Rate recovery in a repetitive motor task as a function of successive rest periods. *Journal of Experimental Psychology, 48,* 197–203.

Bilodeau, I. M. (1966). Information feedback. In E. A. Bilodeau (Ed.), *Acquisition of skill.* New York: Academic Press.

Black, A. H. (1959). Heart rate changes during avoidance learning in dogs. *Canadian Journal of Psychology, 13,* 229–242.

Black, A. H. (1965). Cardiac conditioning in curarized dogs: The relationship between heart rate and skeletal behavior. In W. F. Prokasy (Ed.), *Classical conditioning: A symposium.* New York: Appleton-Century-Crofts.

Blais, C., Kerr, R., & Hughes, K. (1993). Negative transfer or cognitive confusion. *Human Performance, 6,* 197–206.

Blaisdell, A. P., Gunther, L. M., & Miller, R. R. (1999). Recovery from blocking achieved by extinguishing the blocking CS. *Animal Learning and Behavior, 27,* 63–76.

Blaisdell, A. P., Bristol, A. S., Gunther, L. M., & Miller, R. R. (1998). Overshadowing and latent inhibition counteract each other: Support for the comparator hypothesis. *Journal of Experimental Psychology: Animal Behavior Processes, 24,* 335–351.

Blakely, E., & Schlinger, H. (1988). Determinants of pausing under variable-ratio schedules: Reinforcer magnitude, ratio size, and schedule configuration. *Journal of the Experimental Analysis of Behavior, 50,* 65–73.

Blakemore, C., & Cooper, G. F. (1970). Development of the brain depends on the visual environment. *Nature, 228,* 477–478.

Bleak, J. L., & Frederick, C. M. (1998). Superstitious behavior in sport: Levels of effectiveness and determinants of use in three collegiate sports. *Journal of Sport Behavior, 21,* 1–15.

Bliss, T. V. P., & Lomo, T. (1973). Long-lasting potentiation of synaptic transmission in the dentate area of the anaesthetized rabbit following stimulation of the perforant path. *Journal of Physiology, 232,* 331–356.

Blough, D. S. (1959). Delayed matching in the pigeon. *Journal of the Experimental Analysis of Behavior, 2,* 151–160.

Blough, D. S. (1982). Pigeon perception of letters of the alphabet. *Science, 218,* 397–398.

Boakes, R. A., & Halliday, M. S. (1975). Disinhibition and spontaneous recovery of response decrements produced by free reinforcement in rats. *Journal of Comparative and Physiological Psychology, 88,* 436–446.

Bolles, R. C. (1970). Species-specific defense reactions and avoidance learning. *Psychological Review, 77,* 32–48.

Bonardi, C., & Hall, G. (1994). A search for blocking of occasion setting using a nonexplicit training procedure. *Learning and Motivation, 25,* 105–125.

Bootzin, R. R. (1972). Stimulus control treatment for insomnia. *Proceedings of the 80th Annual Convention of the American Psychological Association, 7,* 395–396.

Bordens, K. S., & Abbott, B. B. (1998). *Research design and methods: A process approach* (4th edition). Mountain View, CA: Mayfield Publishing.

Bossom, J. (1974). Movement without proprioception. *Brain Research, 71,* 285–296.

Bottjer, S. W. (1982). Conditioned approach and withdrawal behavior in the pigeon: Effects of a novel extraneous stimulus during acquisition and extinction. *Learning and Motivation, 13,* 44–67.

Bouton, M. E. (2000). A learning theory perspective on lapse, relapse, and the maintenance of behavior change. *Health Psychology, 19,* 57–63.

Bouton, M. E., & Bolles, R. C. (1985). Contexts, event-memories, and extinction. In P. D. Balsam & A. Tomie (Eds.), *Context and learning.* Hillsdale, NJ: Erlbaum.

Bowd, A. D., & Shapiro, K. J. (1993). The case against laboratory animal research in psychology. *Journal of Social Issues, 49,* 133–142.

Bower, G. H. (1975). Cognitive psychology: An introduction. In W. K. Estes (Ed.), *Handbook of learning and cognitive processes* (Vol. 1). Hillsdale, NJ: Erlbaum.

Brakke, K. E., & Savage-Rumbaugh, E. S. (1995). The development of language skills in bonobo and chimpanzee: I. Comprehension. *Language and Communication, 15,* 121–148.

Brandon, S. E., Bombace, J. C., Falls, W. A., & Wagner, A. R. (1991). Modulation of unconditioned defensive reflexes by a putative emotive Pavlovian conditioned stimulus. *Journal of Experimental Psychology: Animal Behavior Processes, 17,* 312–322.

Brannon, E. M., & Terrace, H. S. (2000). Representation of the numerosities 1-9 by Rhesus Macaques (Macaca mulata). *Journal of Experimental Psychology: Animal Behavior Processes, 26,* 31–49.

Braveman, N. S. (1977). Visually guided avoidance of poisonous foods in mammals. In L. M. Barker, M. R. Best, & M. Domjan (Eds.), *Learning mechanisms in food selection.* Waco, TX: Baylor University Press.

Bray, M. A., & Kehle, T. J. (1998). Self-modeling as an intervention for stuttering. *School Psychology Review, 27,* 587–598.

Breland, K., & Breland, M. (1961). The misbehavior of organisms. *American Psychologist, 16,* 681–684.

Brogden, W. J. (1939). Sensory pre-conditioning. *Journal of Experimental Psychology, 25,* 323–332.

Brooks, D. C., & Bouton, M. E. (1993). A retrieval cue for extinction attenuates spontaneous recovery. *Journal of Experimental Psychology: Animal Behavior Processes, 19,* 77–89.

Brooks, D. C., Palmatier, M. I., Garcia, E. O., & Johnson, J. L. (1999). An extinction cue reduces spontaneous recovery of a conditioned taste aversion. *Animal Learning and Behavior, 27*, 77–88.

Brown, G. E., Hughes, G. D., & Jones, A. A. (1988). Effects of shock controllability on subsequent aggressive and defensive behaviors in the cockroach (*Periplaneta americana*). *Psychological Reports, 63*, 563–569.

Brown, M. F. (1992). Does a cognitive map guide choices in the radial-arm maze? *Journal of Experimental Psychology: Animal Behavior Processes, 18*, 56–66.

Brown, P. L., & Jenkins, H. M. (1968). Autoshaping of the pigeon's key-peck. *Journal of the Experimental Analysis of Behavior, 11*, 1–8.

Brown, R. (1985). *Social psychology* (2nd ed.). New York: Free Press.

Brown, R., & Herrnstein, R. J. (1975). *Psychology.* Boston: Little, Brown.

Brown, T. (1820). *Lectures on the philosophy of the human mind* (Vols. 1 and 2). Edinburgh: James Ballantyne.

Bruce, D. (1994). Lashley and the problem of serial order. *American Psychologist, 49*, 93–103.

Buchel, C., Dolan, R. J., Armony, J. L., & Friston, K. J. (1999). Amygdala-hippocampal involvement in human aversive trace conditioning revealed through event-related functional magnetic resonance imaging. *Journal of Neuroscience, 19*, 10869–10876.

Bucher, B., & Fabricatore, J. (1970). Use of patient-administered shock to suppress hallucinations. *Behavior Therapy, 1*, 382–385.

Budzynski, T. H., Stoyva, J. M., Adler, C. S., & Mullaney, M. A. (1973). EMG biofeedback and tension headache: A controlled outcome study. In L. Birk (Ed.), *Biofeedback: Behavioral medicine.* New York: Grune & Stratton.

Bullock, D., & Neuringer, A. (1977). Social learning by following: An analysis. *Journal of the Experimental Analysis of Behavior, 25*, 127–135.

Burnstein, E., Stotland, E., & Zander, A. (1961). Similarity to a model and self-evaluation. *Journal of Abnormal and Social Psychology, 62*, 257–264.

Bush, R. R., & Mosteller, F. (1955). *Stochastic models for learning.* New York: John Wiley.

Buske-Kirschbaum, A., Kirschbaum, C., Stierle, H., Jabaij, L., & Hellhammer, D. (1994). Conditioned manipulation of natural killer (NK) cells in humans using a discriminative learning protocol. *Biological Psychology, 38*, 143–155.

Butler, R. A. (1953). Discrimination learning by rhesus monkeys to visual-exploration motivation. *Journal of Comparative and Physiological Psychology, 46*, 95–98.

Byrne, R. W., & Russon, A. E. (1998). Learning by imitation: A hierarchical approach. *Behavioral and Brain Sciences, 21*, 667–721.

Canli, T., & Donegan, N. H. (1995). Conditioned diminution of the unconditioned response in rabbit eyeblink conditioning: Identifying neural substrates in the cerebellum and brainstem. *Behavioral Neuroscience, 109*, 874–892.

Capaldi, E. J. (1966). Partial reinforcement: A hypothesis of sequential effects. *Psychological Review, 73*, 459–477.

Capaldi, E. J., & Miller, D. J. (1988). Counting in rats: Its functional significance and the independent cognitive processes which comprise it. *Journal of Experimental Psychology: Animal Behavior Processes, 14*, 3–17.

Capaldi, E. J., Miller, D. J., Alptekin, S., & Barry, K. (1990). Organized responding in instrumental learning: Chunks and superchunks. *Learning and Motivation, 21*, 415–433.

Capaldi, E. J., Verry, D. R., & Davison, T. L. (1980). Memory, serial anticipation pattern learning and transfer in rats. *Animal Learning and Behavior, 8*, 575–585.

Caraco, T., Martindale, S., & Whittam, T. S. (1980). An empirical demonstration of risk-sensitive foraging preferences. *Animal Behavior, 28*, 820–830.

Carew, T. J., Hawkins, R. D., & Kandel, E. R. (1983). Differential classical conditioning of a defensive withdrawal reflex in *Aplysia californica. Science, 219*, 397–400.

Carmagnani, A., & Carmagnani, E. F. (1999). Biofeedback: Present state and future possibilities. *International Journal of Mental Health, 28*, 83–86.

Carroll, M. E. (1993). The economic context of drug and non-drug reinforcers affects acquisition and maintenance of drug-reinforced behavior and withdrawal effects. *Drug and Alcohol Dependence, 33*, 201–210.

Casaer, P. (1993). Old and new facts about perinatal brain development. *Journal of Child Psychology and Psychiatry and Allied Disciplines, 34*, 101–109.

Case, D. A., Nichols, P., & Fantino, E. (1995). Pigeons' preference for variable-interval water reinforcement under widely varied water budgets. *Journal of the Experimental Analysis of Behavior, 64*, 299–311.

Castellucci, V., Pinsker, H., Kupfermann, I., & Kandel, E. R. (1970). Neuronal mechanisms of habituation and dishabituation of the gill-withdrawal reflex in *Aplysia. Science, 167,* 1745–1748.

Castro, C. A., & Larsen, T. (1992). Primacy and recency effects in nonhuman primates. *Journal of Experimental Psychology: Animal Behavior Processes, 18,* 335–340.

Catania, A. C. (1963). Concurrent performances: A baseline for the study of reinforcement magnitude. *Journal of the Experimental Analysis of Behavior, 6,* 299–300.

Catania, A. C. (1973). Self-inhibiting effects of reinforcement. *Journal of the Experimental Analysis of Behavior, 19,* 517–526.

Catania, A. C. (1975). Freedom and knowledge: An experimental analysis of preference in pigeons. *Journal of the Experimental Analysis of Behavior, 24,* 89–106.

Catania, A. C., Matthews, B. A., & Shimoff, E. (1982). Instructed versus shaped human verbal behavior: Interactions with nonverbal responding. *Journal of the Experimental Analysis of Behavior, 38,* 233–248.

Catania, A. C., & Reynolds, G. S. (1968). A quantitative analysis of the responding maintained by interval schedules of reinforcement. *Journal of the Experimental Analysis of Behavior, 11,* 327–383.

Cavalier, A. R., Feretti, R. P., & Hodges, A. E. (1997). Self-management within a classroom token economy for students with learning disabilities. *Research in Developmental Disabilities, 18,* 167–178.

Cerella, J. (1982). Mechanisms of concept formation in the pigeon. In D. J. Ingle, M. A. Goodale, & R. J. W. Mansfield (Eds.), *Analysis of visual behavior.* Cambridge, MA: MIT Press.

Chamberlin, C. J., & Magill, R. A. (1992). The memory representation of motor skills: A test of schema theory. *Journal of Motor Behavior, 24,* 309–319.

Chambers, K. C. (1990). A neural model for conditioned taste aversions. *Annual Review of Neuroscience, 13,* 373–385.

Champion, R. A., & Jones, J. E. (1961). Forward, backward, and pseudoconditioning of the GSR. *Journal of Experimental Psychology, 62,* 58–61.

Chaney, J. M., Mulins, L. L., Uretsky, D. L., Pace, T. M., Werden, D., & Hartman, V. L. (1999). An experimental examination of learned helplessness in older adolescents and young adults with long-standing asthma. *Journal of Pediatric Psychology, 24,* 259–270.

Charnov, E. L. (1976). Optimal foraging: Attack strategy of a mantid. *American Naturalist, 110,* 141–151.

Chen, W. R., Lee, S. H., Kato, K., Spencer, D. D., Shepherd, G. M., & Williamson, A (1996). Long-term modifications of synaptic efficacy in the human inferior and middle temporal cortex. *Proceedings of the National Academy of Sciences, 93,* 8011–8015.

Chomsky, N. (1959). Review of Skinner's verbal behavior. *Language, 35,* 26–58.

Chomsky, N. (1972a). *Language and the mind.* New York: Harcourt Brace Jovanovich, Inc.

Chomsky, N. (1972b). Psychology and ideology. *Cognition, 1,* 11–46.

Christensen, A., & Jacobson, N. S. (2000). *Reconcilable differences.* New York: Guilford Press.

Church, R. M. (1978). The internal clock. In S. H. Hulse, H. Fowler, & W. K. Honig (Eds.), *Cognitive processes in animal behavior.* Hillsdale, NJ: Erlbaum.

Church, R. M. (1984). Properties of the internal clock. In J. Gibbon & L. Allen (Eds.), *Timing and time perception.* New York: Annals of the New York Academy of Sciences, Vol. 438.

Church, R. M., Getty, D. J., & Lerner, N. D. (1976). Duration discrimination by rats. *Journal of Experimental Psychology: Animal Behavior Processes, 4,* 303–312.

Church, R. M., LoLordo, V. M., Overmier, J. B., Solomon, R. L., & Turner, L. H. (1966). Cardiac responses to shock in curarized dogs. *Journal of Comparative and Physiological Psychology, 62,* 1–7.

Church, R. M., & Meck, W. H. (1984). The numerical attribute of stimuli. In H. L. Roitblat, T. G. Bever, & H.S. Terrace (Eds.), *Animal cognition.* Hillsdale, NJ: Erlbaum.

Ciborowski, T. (1997). "Superstition" in the collegiate baseball player. *Sport Psychologist, 11,* 305–317.

Cicero, S. D., & Tryon, W. W. (1989). Classical conditioning of meaning: II. A replication and triplet associative extension. *Journal of Behavior Therapy and Experimental Psychiatry, 20,* 197–202.

Cipani, E., Brendlinger, J., McDowell, L., & Usher, S. (1991). Continuous vs. intermittent punishment: A case study. *Journal of Developmental and Physical Disabilities, 3,* 147–156.

Clearfield, M. W., & Mix, K. S. (1999). Number versus countour length in infants' discrimination of small visual sets. *Psychological Science, 10,* 408–411.

Cohen, L. B., Rundell, L. J., Spellman, B. A., & Cashon, C. H. (1999). Infants' perception of causal chains. *Psychological Science, 10,* 412–418.

Cohen, P. S., & Campagnoni, F. R. (1989). The nature and determinants of spatial retreat in the pigeon between periodic grain presentations. *Animal Learning and Behavior, 17,* 39–48.

Cohen, P. S., & Looney, T. A. (1973). Schedule-induced mirror responding in the pigeon. *Journal of the Experimental Analysis of Behavior, 19,* 395–408.

Coldwells, A., & Hare, M. E. (1994). The transfer of skill from short tennis to lawn tennis. *Ergonomics, 37,* 17–21.

Cole, M. R. (1999). Molar and molecular control in variable-interval and variable-ratio schedules. *Journal of the Experimental Analysis of Behavior, 71,* 319–328.

Cole, R. P., Barnet, R. C., & Miller, R. R. (1995). Effect of relative stimulus validity: Learning or performance deficit? *Journal of Experimental Psychology: Animal Behavior Processes, 21,* 293–303.

Colwill, R. M. (1996). Detecting associations in Pavlovian conditioning and instrumental learning in vertebrates and in invertebrates. In C. F. Moss & S. J. Shettleworth (Eds.), Neuroethological studies of cognitive and perceptual processes. Boulder, CO: Westview Press.

Colwill, R. M., & Rescorla, R. A. (1985). Post-conditioning devaluation of a reinforcer affects instrumental responding. *Journal of Experimental Psychology: Animal Behavior Processes, 11,* 120–132.

Colwill, R. M., & Rescorla, R. A. (1986). Associative structures in instrumental learning. In G. H. Bower (Ed.), *The psychology of learning and motivation* (Vol. 20). New York: Academic Press.

Colwill, R. M., & Rescorla, R. A. (1988). Associations between the discriminative stimulus and the reinforcer in instrumental learning. *Journal of Experimental Psychology: Animal Behavior Processes, 14,* 155–164.

Colwill, R. M., & Rescorla, R. A. (1990). Evidence for the hierarchical structure of instrumental learning. *Animal Learning and Behavior, 18,* 71–82.

Compton, D. M., Dietrich, K. L, & Johnson, S. D. (1995). Animal rights activism and animal welfare concerns in the academic setting: Levels of activism and the perceived impor-

tance of research with animals. *Psychological Reports, 76,* 23–31.

Condon, B., McFadzean, R., Hadley, D. M., Bradnam, M. S., & Shahani, U. (1997). Habituation-like effects cause a significant decrease in response in MRI neuroactivation during visual stimulation. *Vision Research, 37,* 1243–1247.

Condon, C. D., & Weinberger, N. M. (1991). Habituation produces frequency-specific plasticity of receptive fields in the auditory cortex. *Behavioral Neuroscience, 105,* 416–430.

Conger, R., & Killeen, P. (1974). Use of concurrent operants in small group research. *Pacific Sociological Review, 17,* 399–416.

Conners, F. A. (1992). Reading instruction for students with moderate mental retardation: Review and analysis of research. *American Journal of Mental Retardation, 96,* 577–597.

Cook, R. G., Brown, M. F., & Riley, D. A. (1985). Flexible memory processing by rats: Use of prospective and retrospective information in the radial maze. *Journal of Experimental Psychology: Animal Behavior Processes, 11,* 453–469.

Cournoyer, M., & Trudel, M. (1991). Behavioral correlates of self-control at 33 months. *Infant Behavior and Development, 14,* 497–503.

Couvillon, P. A., & Bitterman, M. E. (1991). How honeybees make choices. In L. J. Goodman & R. C. Fisher (Eds.), *The behaviour and physiology of bees.* Wallingford: CAB International.

Cozby, P. C. (1997). *Methods in behavioral research* (6th edition). Mountain View, CA: Mayfield Publishing.

Creer, T. L., Chai, H., & Hoffman, A. (1977). A single application of an aversive stimulus to eliminate chronic cough. *Journal of Behavior Therapy and Experimental Psychiatry, 8,* 107–109.

Crossman, E. K. (1968). Pause relationships in multiple and chained fixed-ratio schedules. *Journal of the Experimental Analysis of Behavior, 11,* 117–126.

Crossman, E. K., Bonem, E. J., & Phelps, B. J. (1987). A comparison of response patterns on fixed-, variable-, and random-ratio schedules. *Journal of the Experimental Analysis of Behavior, 48,* 395–406.

Crowell, C. R., Hinson, R. E., & Siegel, S. (1981). The role of conditional drug responses in tolerance to the hypothermic effect of ethanol. *Psychopharmacology, 72,* 147–153.

Cunningham, C. E., & Linscheid, T. R. (1976). Elimination of chronic infant ruminating by electric shock. *Behavior Therapy, 1*, 231–234.

Dallal, N. L., & Meck, W. H. (1990). Hierarchical structures: Chunking by food type facilitates spatial memory. *Journal of Experimental Psychology: Animal Behavior Processes, 16*, 69–84.

Dallery, J., McDowell, J. J, & Lancaster, J. S. (2000). Falsification of matching theory's account of single-alternative responding: Herrnstein's *K* varies with sucrose concentration. *Journal of the Experimental Analysis of Behavior, 73*, 23–43.

D'Amato, M. R. (1973). Delayed matching and short-term memory in monkeys. In G. H. Bower (Ed.), *The psychology of learning and motivation* (Vol. 7). New York: Academic Press.

D'Amato, M. R., Salmon, D. P., & Colombo, M. (1985). Extent and limits of the matching concept in monkeys (*Cebus apella*). *Journal of Experimental Psychology: Animal Behavior Processes, 11*, 35–51.

D'Amato, M. R., & Van Sant, P. (1988). The person concept in monkeys (*Cebus apella*). *Journal of Experimental Psychology: Animal Behavior Processes, 14*, 43–55.

Daum, I., & Schugens, M. M. (1996). On the cerebellum and classical conditioning. *Current Directions in Psychological Science, 5*, 58–61.

Daum, I., Schugens, M. M., Ackermann, H., Lutzenberger, W., Dichgans, J., & Birbaumer, N. (1993). Classical conditioning after cerebellar lesions in humans. *Behavioral Neuroscience, 107*, 748–756.

Davenport, D. G., & Olson, R. D. (1968). A reinterpretation of extinction in discriminated avoidance. *Psychonomic Science, 13*, 5–6.

Davey, G. C. L. (1995). Preparedness and phobias: Specific evolved associations or a generalized expectancy bias? *Behavioral and Brain Sciences, 18*, 289–325.

Davey, G. C. L., & McKenna, I. (1983). The effect of postconditioning revaluation of CS1 and CS2 following Pavlovian second-order electrodermal conditioning in humans. *Quarterly Journal of Experimental Psychology, 35B*, 125–133.

Davidson, E. S., & Smith, W. P. (1982). Imitation, social comparison, and self-reward. *Child Development, 53*, 928–932.

Davidson, T. L., & Rescorla, R. A. (1986). Transfer of facilitation in the rat. *Animal Learning and Behavior, 14*, 380–386.

Davies, D. R. (1991). A comparison of hypnotic and non-hypnotic uses in the group therapy of insomnia. *Behavioral Psychotherapy, 19*, 193–204.

Davies, S. N., Lester, R. A. J., Reymann, K. G., & Collingridge, G. L. (1989). Temporally distinct pre- and post-synaptic mechanisms maintain long-term potentiation. *Nature, 338*, 500–503.

Davis, H. (1992). Transitive inference in rats (*Rattus norvegicus*). *Journal of Comparative Psychology, 106*, 342–349.

Davis, H., & Albert, M. (1986). Numerical discrimination by rats using sequential auditory stimuli. *Animal Learning and Behavior, 14*, 57–59.

Davis, H., & Bradford, S. A. (1991). Numerically restricted food intake in the rat in a free-feeding situation. *Animal Learning and Behavior, 19*, 215–222.

Davis, J. R., & Russell, R. H. (1990). Behavioral staff management: An analogue study of acceptability and its behavioral correlates. *Behavioral Residential Treatment, 5*, 259–270.

Davis, M. (1989). Neural systems involved in fear-potentiated startle. *Annals of the New York Academy of Sciences, 563*, 165–183.

Davis, M., Gendelman, D. S., Tischler, M. D., & Gendelman, P. M. (1982). A primary acoustic startle circuit: Lesion and stimulation studies. *Journal of Neuroscience, 2*, 791–805.

Davison, M., & Hogsden, I. (1984). Concurrent variable-interval schedule performance: Fixed versus mixed reinforcer durations. *Journal of the Experimental Analysis of Behavior, 41*, 169–182.

Davison, M., & Jenkins, P. E. (1985). Stimulus discriminability, contingency discriminability, and schedule performance. *Animal Learning and Behavior, 13*, 77–84.

Davison, M., & McCarthy, D. (1988). *The matching law*. Hillsdale, NJ: Erlbaum.

DeCarlo, L. T. (1985). Matching and maximizing with variable-time schedules. *Journal of the Experimental Analysis of Behavior, 43*, 75–81.

DeGrandpre, R. J., Bickel, W. K., Hughes, J. R., & Higgins, S. T. (1992). Behavioral economics of drug self-administration. *Psychopharmacology, 108*, 1–10.

Delius, J. D. (1992). Categorical discrimination of objects and pictures by pigeons. *Animal Learning and Behavior, 20*, 301–311.

Deluty, M. Z., Whitehouse, W. G., Mellitz, M., & Hineline, P. N. (1983). Self-control and commitment involving aversive events. *Behaviour Analysis Letters, 3,* 213–219.

den Brinker, B. P., Stabler, J. R., Whiting, H. T., & Van Wieringen, P. C. (1986). The effect of manipulating knowledge of results on the learning of slalom-type ski movements. *Ergonomics, 29,* 31–40.

Desimone, R., Albright, T. D., Gross, C. G., & Bruce, C. (1984). Stimulus-selective properties of inferior temporal neurons in the macaque. *Journal of Neuroscience, 4,* 2051–2062.

Devenport, L. D., & Devenport, J. A. (1994). Time-dependent averaging of foraging information in least chipmunks and golden-mantled ground squirrels. *Animal Behaviour, 47,* 787–802.

de Villiers, P. A. (1977). Choice in concurrent schedules and a quantitative formulation of the law of effect. In W. K. Honig & J. E. R. Staddon (Eds.), *Handbook of operant behavior.* Englewood Cliffs, NJ: Prentice-Hall.

de Villiers, P. A., & Herrnstein, R. J. (1976). Toward a law of response strength. *Psychological Bulletin, 83,* 1131–1153.

Dews, P. B. (1962). The effect of multiple SΔ periods on responding on a fixed-interval schedule. *Journal of the Experimental Analysis of Behavior, 5,* 369–374.

DiCara, L. V. (1970). Learning in the autonomic nervous system. *Scientific American, 222,* 30–39.

Dielenberg, R. A., & McGregor, I. S. (1999). Habituation of the hiding response to cat odor in rats (*Rattus norvegicus*). *Journal of Comparative Psychology, 113,* 376–387.

Dill, K. E., & Dill, J. C. (1998). Video game violence: A review of the empirical literature. *Aggression and Violent Behavior, 3,* 407–428.

Dimberg, U., & Ohman, A. (1983). The effects of directional facial cues on electrodermal conditioning to facial stimuli. *Psychophysiology, 20,* 160–167.

Dixon, M. R., Hayes, L. J., Binder, L. M., Manthey, S., Sigman, C., & Zdanowski, D. M. (1998). Using a self-control training procedure to increase appropriate behavior. *Journal of Applied Behavior Analysis, 31,* 203–210.

Dodwell, P. C., & Bessant, D. E. (1960). Learning without swimming in a water maze. *Journal of Comparative and Physiological Psychology, 53,* 422–425.

Domjan, M. (1983). Biological constraints on instrumental and classical conditioning: Implications for general process theory. In G. H. Bower (Ed.), *The psychology of learning and motivation* (Vol. 17). New York: Academic Press.

Domjan, M., & Best, M. R. (1980). Interference with ingestional aversion learning produced by preexposure to the unconditioned stimulus: Associative and nonassociative aspects. *Learning and Motivation, 11,* 522–537.

Domjan, M., & Burkhard, B. (1982). *The principles of learning and behavior.* Monterey, CA: Brooks/Cole.

Domjan, M., & Galef, B. G. (1983). Biological constraints on instrumental and classical conditioning: Retrospect and prospect. *Animal Learning and Behavior, 11,* 151–161.

Donegan, N. H., & Wagner, A. R. (1987). Conditioned diminution and facilitation of the UR: A sometimes opponent-process interpretation. In I. Gormezano, W. F. Prokasy, & R. F. Thompson (Eds.), *Classical conditioning.* Hillsdale, NJ: Erlbaum.

Dore, F. Y., & Dumas, C. (1987). Psychology of animal cognition: Piagetian studies. *Psychological Bulletin, 102,* 219–233.

Dougan, J. D., McSweeney, F. K., & Farmer-Dougan, V. A. (1986). Behavioral contrast in competitive and noncompetitive environments. *Journal of the Experimental Analysis of Behavior, 46,* 185–197.

Dowrick, P. W. (1999). A review of self modeling and related interventions. *Applied and Preventive Psychology, 8,* 23–39.

Dowrick, P. W., & Raeburn, J. M. (1995). Self-modeling: Rapid skill training for children with physical disabilities. *Journal of Developmental and Physical Disabilities, 7,* 25–37.

Dragoi, V., & Staddon, J. E. R. (1999). The dynamics of operant conditioning. *Psychological Review, 106,* 20–61.

Ducharme, J. M., & Van Houten, R. (1994). Operant extinction in the treatment of severe maladaptive behavior. *Behavior Modification, 18,* 139–170.

Duffy, L., & Wishart, J. G. (1987). A comparison of two procedures for teaching discrimination skills to Down's syndrome and non-handicapped children. *British Journal of Educational Psychology, 57,* 265–278.

Dugdale, N., & Lowe, F. C. (2000). Testing for symmetry in the conditional discriminations of language-trained chimpanzees. *Journal of the Experimental Analysis of Behavior, 73,* 5–22.

Duke, M. P. (1994). Chaos theory and psychology: Seven propositions. *Genetic, Social, and General Psychology Monographs, 120,* 267–286.

Dunn, R. M. (1982). Choice, relative reinforcer duration, and the changeover ratio. *Journal of the Experimental Analysis of Behavior*, *38*, 313–319.

Durlach, P. J. (1986). Explicitly unpaired procedure as a response elimination technique in autoshaping. *Journal of Experimental Psychology: Animal Behavior Processes*, *12*, 172–185.

Easterbrook, M. A., Kisilevsky, B. S., Muir, D. W., & Laplante, D. P. (1999). Newborns discriminate schematic faces from scrambled faces. *Canadian Journal of Experimental Psychology*, *53*, 231–241.

Ebbinghaus, H. (1885). *Memory*. Leipzig: Duncker.

Eibl-Eibesfeldt, I. (1975). *Ethology* (2nd ed.). New York: Holt, Rinehart & Winston.

Eikelboom, R., & Stewart, J. (1982). Conditioning of drug-induced physiological responses. *Psychological Review*, *89*, 507–528.

Eisenberger, R., & Adornetto, M. (1986). Generalized self-control of delay and effort. *Journal of Personality and Social Psychology*, *51*, 1020–1031.

Eisenberger, R., Karpman, M., & Trattner, J. (1967). What is the necessary and sufficient condition for reinforcement in the contingency condition? *Journal of Experimental Psychology*, *74*, 342–350.

Eiserer, L. A. (1990). Effects of environmental novelty on distress vocalizations of ducklings following withdrawal of an imprinting object. *Bulletin of the Psychonomic Society*, *28*, 225–227.

Elk, R., Schmitz, J., Spiga, R., Rhoades, H., Andres, R., & Grabowski, J. (1995). Behavioral treatment of cocaine-dependent pregnant women and TB-exposed patients. *Addictive Behaviors*, *20*, 533–542.

Ellingson, S. A., Miltenberger, R. G., Stricker, J. M., Garlinghouse, M. A., Roberts, J., Galensky, T. L., & Rapp, J. T. (2000). Analysis and treatment of finger sucking. *Journal of Applied Behavior Analysis*, *33*, 41–52.

Ellison, G. D. (1964). Differential salivary conditioning to traces. *Journal of Comparative and Physiological Psychology*, *57*, 373–380.

Elmes, D. G., Kantowitz, B. H., & Roediger, H. L. (1999). *Research methods in psychology* (6th ed.). St. Paul, MN: West Publishing.

Elsmore, T. F., Fletcher, G. V., Conrad, D. G., & Sodetz, F. J. (1980). Reduction of heroin intake in baboons by an economic constraint. *Pharmacology, Biochemistry and Behavior*, *13*, 729–731.

Ennet, S. T., Bauman, K. E., & Koch, G. G. (1994). Variability in cigarette smoking within and between adolescent friendship cliques. *Addictive Behaviors*, *19*, 295–305.

Epstein, S. M. (1967). Toward a unified theory of anxiety. In B. A. Maher (Ed.), *Progress in experimental personality research* (Vol. 4). New York: Academic Press.

Eron, L. D. (1987). The development of aggressive behavior from the perspective of developing behaviorism. *American Psychologist*, *42*, 435–442.

Eron, L. D., Huesmann, L. R., Lefkowitz, M. M., & Walder, L. O. (1972). Does television violence cause aggression? *American Psychologist*, *27*, 253–263.

Estes, W. K. (1944). An experimental study of punishment. *Psychological Monographs*, *57* (3, Whole No. 263).

Estes, W. K. (1950). Toward a statistical theory of learning. *Psychological Review*, *57*, 94–107.

Estes, W. K. (1955). Statistical theory of spontaneous recovery and regression. *Psychological Review*, *62*, 145–154.

Etscorn, F., & Stephens, R. (1973). Establishment of conditioned taste aversions with a 24-hour CS-US interval. *Physiological Psychology*, *1*, 251–253.

Ettinger, R. H., Reid, A. K., & Staddon, J. E. R. (1987). Sensitivity to molar feedback functions: A test of molar optimality theory. *Journal of Experimental Psychology: Animal Behavior Processes*, *13*, 366–375.

Ettinger, R. H., & Staddon, J. E. R. (1982). Behavioral competition, component duration and multiple-schedule contrast. *Behavioural Analysis Letters*, *2*, 31–38.

Fagan, A., Eichenbaum, H., & Cohen, N. (1985). Normal learning set and facilitation of reversal learning in rats with combined fornix-amygdala lesions: Implications for preserved learning abilities in amnesia. *Annals of the New York Academy of Sciences*, *444*, 510–512.

Falk, J. L. (1961). Production of polydipsia in normal rats by an intermittent food schedule. *Science*, *133*, 195–196.

Fanselow, M. S. (1980). Conditional and unconditional components of post-shock freezing. *Pavlovian Journal of Biological Science*, *15*, 177–182.

Fanselow, M. S. (1997). Species-specific defense reactions: Retrospect and prospect. In M. E. Bouton & M. S. Fanselow (Eds.), *Learning, motivation, and cognition: The functional behaviorism of Robert C. Bolles.* Washington, DC: American Psychological Association.

Fanselow, M. S., DeCola, J. P., & Young, S. L. (1993). Mechanisms responsible for reduced contextual conditioning with massed unsignaled unconditional stimuli. *Journal of Experimental Psychology: Animal Behavior Processes, 19,* 121–137.

Fantino, E. (1967). Preference for mixed- versus fixed-ratios. *Journal of the Experimental Analysis of Behavior, 10,* 35–43.

Fantino, E. (1969). Choice and rate of reinforcement. *Journal of the Experimental Analysis of Behavior, 12,* 723–730.

Fantino, E., Preston, R. A., & Dunn, R. (1993). Delay reduction: Current status. *Journal of the Experimental Analysis of Behavior, 60,* 159–169.

Farley, J., Richards, W. G., & Grover, L. M. (1990). Associative learning changes intrinsic to *Hermissenda* Type A photoreceptors. *Behavioral Neuroscience, 104,* 135–152.

Fehr, A., & Beckwith, B. E. (1989). Water misting: Treating self-injurious behavior in a multiply handicapped, visually impaired child. *Journal of Visual Impairment and Blindness, 83,* 245–248.

Ferchmin, P. A., & Eterovic, V. A. (1980). Four hours of enriched experience are sufficient to increase cortical weight of rats. *Society for Neuroscience Abstracts, 6,* 857.

Ferster, C. B. (1958). Control of behavior in chimpanzees and pigeons by time-out from positive reinforcement. *Psychological Monographs, 72,* 461.

Ferster, C. B., & Skinner, B. F. (1957). *Schedules of reinforcement.* New York: Appleton-Century-Crofts.

Fetterman, J. G., & Killeen, P. R. (1991). Adjusting the pacemaker. *Learning and Motivation, 22,* 226–252.

Fetterman, J. G., & Killeen, P. R. (1992). Time discrimination in *Columba livia* and Homo sapiens. *Journal of Experimental Psychology: Animal Behavior Processes, 18,* 80–94.

Field, T. M., Woodson, R., Greenberg, R., & Cohen, D. (1982). Discrimination and imitation of facial expressions by neonates. *Science, 218,* 179–181.

Finfgeld, D. L. (1999). Computer-assisted therapy: Harbinger of the 21st century? *Archives of Psychiatric Nursing, 13,* 303–310.

Fischer, S. M., Iwata, B. A., & Worsdell, A. S. (1997). Attention as an establishing operation and as reinforcement during functional analyses. *Journal of Applied Behavior Analysis, 30,* 335–338.

Fischman, M. G., & Lim, C. H. (1991). Influence of extended practice on programming time, movement time, and transfer in simple target-striking responses. *Journal of Motor Behavior, 23,* 39–50.

Fisher, J., & Hinde, C. A. (1949). The opening of milk bottles by birds. *British Birds, 42,* 347–357.

Fisher, W. W., Adelinis, J. D., Thompson, R. H., Worsdell, A. S., & Zarcone, J. R. (1998). Functional analysis and treatment of destructive behavior maintained by termination of "don't" (and symmetrical "do") requests. *Journal of Applied Behavior Analysis, 31,* 339–356.

Fisher, W. W., Lindauer, S. E., Alterson, C. J., & Thompson, R. H. (1998). Assessment and treatment of destructive behavior maintained by stereotypic object manipulation. *Journal of Applied Behavior Analysis, 31,* 513–527.

Foster, T. M., Temple, W., Robertson, B., Nair, V., & Poling, A. (1996). Concurrent-schedule performance in dairy cows: Persistent undermatching. *Journal of the Experimental Analysis of Behavior, 65,* 57–80.

Fouts, R., Fouts, D., & Schoenfield, D. (1984). Sign language conversation interaction between chimpanzees. *Sign Language Studies, 42,* 1–12.

Fox, D. K., Hopkins, B. L., & Anger, W. K. (1987). The long-term effects of a token economy on safety performance in open-pit mining. *Journal of Applied Behavior Analysis, 20,* 215–224.

Fox, L. (1962). Effecting the use of efficient study habits. *Journal of Mathetics, 1,* 75–86.

Fraenkel, G. S., & Gunn, D. L. (1940). *The orientation of animals: Kineses, taxes, and compass reactions.* Oxford: Oxford University Press.

Franks, J. J., & Bransford, J. D. (1971). Abstraction of visual patterns. *Journal of Experimental Psychology, 90,* 65–74.

Freagon, S. (1990). One educator's perspective on the use of punishment or aversives: Advocating for supportive and protective systems. In A. C. Repp & N. N. Singh (Eds.), *Perspectives on the use of nonaversive and aversive interventions for persons with developmental disabilities.* Sycamore, IL: Sycamore Publishing.

Freeman, T. J., & Lattal, K. A. (1992). Stimulus control of behavioral history. *Journal of the Experimental Analysis of Behavior, 57,* 5–15.

Friedrich-Cofer, L., & Huston, A. C. (1986). Television violence and aggression: The debate continues. *Psychological Bulletin, 100,* 364–371.

Funahashi, S., Bruce, C. J., & Goldman-Rakic, P. S. (1989). Mnemonic coding of visual space in the monkey's dorsolateral prefrontal cortex. *Journal of Neurophysiology, 61,* 331–349.

Galbicka, G. (1994). Shaping in the 21st century: Moving percentile schedules into applied settings. *Journal of Applied Behavior Analysis, 27,* 739–760.

Galbicka, G., & Branch, M. N. (1981). Selective punishment of interresponse times. *Journal of the Experimental Analysis of Behavior, 35,* 311–322.

Galbicka, G., & Platt, J. R. (1984). Interresponse-time punishment: A basis for shock-maintained behavior. *Journal of the Experimental Analysis of Behavior, 41,* 291–308.

Gao, L. G., & Zelaznik, H. N. (1991). The modification of an already-programmed response: A new interpretation of Henry and Harrison (1961). *Journal of Motor Behavior, 23,* 221–223.

Garcia, J., Ervin, F. R., & Koelling R. A. (1966). Learning with prolonged delay of reinforcement. *Psychonomic Science, 5,* 121–122.

Garcia, J., & Koelling, R. (1966). Relation of cue to consequence in avoidance learning. *Psychonomic Science, 4,* 123–124.

Garcia, J., McGowan, B. K., & Green, K. F. (1972). Biological constraints on conditioning. In A. H. Black and W. F. Prokasy (Eds.), *Classical conditioning II: Current theory and research.* New York: Appleton-Century-Crofts.

Garcia-Colera, A., & Semjen, A. (1988). Distributed planning of movement sequences. *Journal of Motor Behavior, 20,* 341–367.

Gardner, R. A., & Gardner, B. T. (1969). Teaching sign language to a chimpanzee. *Science, 165,* 664–672.

Gardner, R. A., & Gardner, B. T. (1975). Early signs of language in child and chimpanzee. *Science, 187,* 752–753.

Geinisman, Y. (1999). Restructuring of synapses on hippocampal dendritic spines associated with hippocampal LTP. *Developmental Neuropsychology, 16,* 325–328.

Gerbner, G., Gross, L., Eleey, M. F., Jackson-Beeck, M., Jeffries-Fox, S., & Signorielli, N. (1977). TV violence profile No. 8: The highlights. *Journal of Communication, 27,* 171–180.

Gibbon, J., & Balsam, P. (1981). Spreading association in time. In C. M. Locurto, H. S. Terrace, & J. Gibbons (Eds.), *Autoshaping and conditioning theory.* New York: Academic Press.

Gillan, D. J. (1981). Reasoning in the chimpanzee: II. Transitive inference. *Journal of Experimental Psychology: Animal Behavior Processes, 7,* 150–164.

Gillan, D. J., Premack, D., & Woodruff, G. (1981). Reasoning in the chimpanzee: I. Analogical Reasoning. *Journal of Experimental Psychology: Animal Behavior Processes, 7,* 1–17.

Gittelson, B. (1977). *Biorhythm: A personal science.* New York: Warner Books.

Gittelson, B. (1996). *Biorhythm: A personal science, 1997–1999.* New York: Warner Books.

Glaister, B. (1985). A case of auditory hallucination treated by satiation. *Behaviour Research and Therapy, 23,* 213–215.

Glanzman, D. L. (1995). The cellular basis of classical conditioning in *Aplysia californica*—it's less simple than you think. *Trends in Neuroscience, 18,* 30–36.

Glasscock, S. G., Friman, P. C., O'Brien, S., & Christopherson, E. R. (1986). Varied citrus treatment of ruminant gagging in a teenager with Batten's disease. *Journal of Behavior Therapy and Experimental Psychiatry, 17,* 129–133.

Gleeson, S., Lattal, K. A., & Williams, K. S. (1989). Superstitious conditioning: A replication and extension of Neuringer (1970). *Psychological Record, 39,* 563–571.

Gleitman, H. (1971). Forgetting of long-term memories in animals. In W. K. Honig & P. H. R. James (Eds.), *Animal memory.* New York: Academic Press.

Glencross, D. J. (1977). Control of skilled movements. *Psychological Bulletin, 84,* 14–29.

Glover, H. (1992). Emotional numbing: A possible endorphin-mediated phenomenon associated with post-traumatic stress disorders and other allied psychopathologic states. *Journal of Traumatic Stress, 5,* 643–675.

Gluck, M. A. (1991). Stimulus generalization and representation in adaptive network models of category learning. *Psychological Science, 2,* 50–55.

Glueck, S., & Glueck, E. (1950). *Unravelling juvenile delinquency.* Cambridge, MA: Harvard University Press.

Glynn, S. M. (1990). Token economy approaches for psychiatric patients: Progress and pitfalls over 25 years. *Behavior Modification, 14,* 383–407.

Goddard, M. J., & Jenkins, H. M. (1988). Blocking of a CS-US association by a US-US association. *Journal of Experimental Psychology: Animal Behavior Processes, 14,* 177–186.

Goh, H. L., Iwata, B. A., Shore, B. A., DeLeon, I. G., Lerman, D. C., Ulrich, S. M., & Smith, R. G. (1995). An analysis of the reinforcing properties of hand mouthing. *Journal of Applied Behavior Analysis, 28,* 269–283.

Goldiamond, I., Atkinson, C. J., & Bilger, R. C. (1962). Stabilization of behavior and prolonged exposure to delayed auditory feedback. *Science, 135,* 437–438.

Goldsmith, J. B., & McFall, R. M. (1975). Development and evaluation of an interpersonal skill-training program for psychiatric inpatients. *Journal of Abnormal Psychology, 84,* 51–58.

Gonzalez, R. C., Gentry, G. V., & Bitterman, M. E. (1954). Relational discrimination of intermediate size in the chimpanzee. *Journal of Comparative and Physiological Psychology, 47,* 385–388.

Good, M. (1998). Biofeedback. In M. Snider & R. Lindquist (Eds.), *Complementary/alternative therapies in nursing* (3rd edition). New York: Springer Publishing.

Good, M., & Macphail, E. M. (1994). Hippocampal lesions in pigeons (*Columba livia*) disrupt reinforced preexposure but not overshadowing or blocking. *Quarterly Journal of Experimental Psychology, 47B,* 263–291.

Gorczynski, R. M. (1990). Conditioned enhancement of skin allografts in mice. *Brain, Behavior, and Immunity, 4,* 85–92.

Gordon, W. C. (1983). The malleability of memory in animals. In R. L. Mellgren (Ed.), *Animal cognition and behavior.* Amsterdam: North-Holland Publishing.

Gordon, W. C., McGinnis, C. M., & Weaver, M. S. (1985). The effect of cuing after backward conditioning trials. *Learning and Motivation, 16,* 444–463.

Gordon, W. C., Smith, G. J., & Katz, D. S. (1979). Dual effects of response blocking following avoidance learning. *Behavior Research and Therapy, 17,* 479–487.

Gormezano, I., & Coleman, S. R. (1973). The law of effect and CR contingent modification of the UCS. *Conditional Reflex, 8,* 41–56.

Gottfried, A. E., Fleming, J. S., & Gottfried, A. W. (1998). Role of cognitively stimulating home environment in children's academic intrinsic motivation: A longitudinal study. *Child Development, 69,* 1448–1460.

Gould, E., Beylin, A., Tanapat, P., Reeves, A., & Shors, T. J. (1999). Learning enhances adult neurogenesis in the hippocampal formation. *Nature Neuroscience, 2,* 260–265.

Gould, E., Reeves, A. J., Graziano, M. S., & Gross, C. G. (1999). Neurogenesis in the neocortex of adult primates. *Science, 286,* 548–552.

Grace, R. C. (1994). A contextual choice model of concurrent-chains choice. *Journal of the Experimental Analysis of Behavior, 61,* 113–129.

Grant, D. S. (1975). Proactive interference in pigeon short-term memory. *Journal of Experimental Psychology: Animal Behavior Processes, 1,* 207–220.

Grant, D. S. (1981). Short-term memory in the pigeon. In N. E. Spear & R. R. Miller (Eds.), *Information processing in animals: Memory mechanisms.* Hillsdale, NJ: Erlbaum.

Grant, D. S. (1982). Stimulus control of information processing in rat short-term memory. *Journal of Experimental Psychology: Animal Behavior Processes, 8,* 154–164.

Grant, D. S. (1984). Rehearsal in pigeon short-term memory. In H. L. Roitblat, T. L. Bever, & H. S. Terrace (Eds.), *Animal behavior.* Hillsdale, NJ: Erlbaum.

Green, L., Fischer, E. B., Perlow, S., & Sherman, L. (1981). Preference reversal and self control: Choice as a function of reward amount and delay. *Behavior Analysis Letters, 1,* 43–51.

Green, L., Fry, A. F., & Myerson, J. (1994). Discounting of delayed rewards: A life-span comparison. *Psychological Science, 5,* 33–36.

Green, L., & Freed, D. E. (1993). The substitutability of reinforcers. *Journal of the Experimental Analysis of Behavior, 60,* 141–158.

Green, L., & Kagel, J. H. (Eds.). (1996). *Advances in behavioral economics. Vol 3: Substance use and abuse.* Norwood, NJ: Ablex.

Green, L., Kagel, J. H., & Battalio, R. C. (1987). Consumption-leisure tradeoffs in pigeons: Effects of changing marginal rates by varying amount of reinforcement. *Journal of the Experimental Analysis of Behavior, 47,* 17–28.

Greenfield, P. M., & Savage-Rumbaugh, E. S. (1993). Comparing communicative competence in child and chimp: The pragmatics of repetition. *Journal of Child Language, 20,* 1–26.

Grinker, R., & Spiegel, J. (1945). *Men under stress.* London: Churchill.

Groome, L. J., Watson, J. E., & Dykman, R. A. (1994). Heart rate changes following habituation testing of the motor response in normal human fetuses. *Early Human Development, 36,* 69–77.

Grosch, J., & Neuringer, A. (1981). Self-control in pigeons under the Mischel paradigm. *Journal of the Experimental Analysis of Behavior, 35,* 3–21.

Guess, D., & Sailor, W. (1993). Chaos theory and the study of human behavior: Implications for special education and developmental disabilities. *Journal of Special Education, 27,* 16–34.

Gulliksen, H. (1932). Studies of transfer of response: I. Relative versus absolute factors in the discrimination of size by the white rat. *Journal of Genetic Psychology, 40,* 37–51.

Guthrie, E. R., & Horton, G. P. (1946). *Cats in a puzzle box.* New York: Holt, Rinehart and Winston.

Gutman, A. (1977). Positive contrast, negative induction, and inhibitory stimulus control in the rat. *Journal of the Experimental Analysis of Behavior, 27,* 219–233.

Guttman, N., & Kalish, H. I. (1956). Discriminability and stimulus generalization. *Journal of Experimental Psychology, 51,* 79–88.

Hake, D. F., Donaldson, T., & Hyten, C. (1983). Analysis of discriminative control by social behavioral stimuli. *Journal of the Experimental Analysis of Behavior, 39,* 7–23.

Hall, G., Kaye, H., & Pearce, J. M. (1985). Attention and conditioned inhibition. In R. R. Miller & N. E. Spear (Eds.), *Information processing in animals: Conditioned inhibition.* Hillsdale, NJ: Erlbaum.

Hall, G., & Pearce, J. M. (1983). Changes in stimulus associability during acquisition: Implications for theories of acquisition. In M. L. Commons, R. J. Herrnstein, & A. R. Wagner (Eds.), *Quantitative analyses of behavior* (Vol. 3): *Acquisition.* Cambridge, MA: Ballinger.

Halliday, M. S., & Boakes, R. A. (1971). Behavioral contrast and response independent reinforcement. *Journal of the Experimental Analysis of Behavior, 16,* 429–434.

Halweg, K., & Markman, H. J. (1988). The effectiveness of behavioral marriage therapy: Empirical status of behavioral techniques in preventing and alleviating marital distress. *Journal of Consulting and Clinical Psychology, 56,* 440–447.

Hanson, H. M. (1959). Effects of discrimination training on stimulus generalization. *Journal of Experimental Psychology, 58,* 321–334.

Hardin, G. (1968). The tragedy of the commons. *Science, 162,* 1243–1248.

Harlow, H. F. (1949). The formation of learning sets. *Psychological Review, 56,* 51–65.

Hart, J., Berndt, R. S., & Caramazza, A. (1985). Category-specific naming deficit following cerebral infarction. *Nature, 316,* 439–440.

Hatze, H. (1976). Biomechanical aspects of a successful motion optimization. In P. V. Komi (Ed.), *Biomechanics V-B.* Baltimore: University Park Press.

Hawkins, R. D., Carew, T. J., & Kandel, E. R. (1983). Effects of interstimulus interval and contingency on classical conditioning in *Aplysia. Society for Neuroscience Abstracts, 9,* 168.

Hawkins, R. D., Greene, W., & Kandel, E. R. (1998). Classical conditioning, differential conditioning, and second-order conditioning of the *Aplysia* gill-withdrawal reflex in a simplified mantle organ preparation. *Behavioral Neuroscience, 112,* 636–645.

Hayes, C. (1951). *The ape in our house.* New York: Harper.

Hayes, S. C. (1989). Nonhumans have not yet shown stimulus equivalence. *Journal of the Experimental Analysis of Behavior, 51,* 385–392.

Hearst, E., & Jenkins, H. M. (1974). Sign tracking: The stimulus-reinforcer relation and directed action. *Monograph of the Psychonomic Society.* Austin, TX.

Hebb, D. O. (1956). The distinction between "classical" and "instrumental." *Canadian Journal of Psychology, 10,* 165–166.

Hekimian, L. J., & Gershon, S. (1968). Characteristics of drug abusers admitted to a psychiatric hospital. *Journal of the American Medical Association, 205,* 125–130.

Heller, R. F., & Strang, H.R. (1973). Controlling bruxism through automated aversive conditioning. *Behavior Research and Therapy, 11,* 327–329.

Hendry, D. P., & Van-Toller, C. (1964). Fixed-ratio punishment with continuous reinforcement. *Journal of the Experimental Analysis of Behavior, 7,* 293–300.

Herman, L. M., & Forestell, P. H. (1985). Reporting presence or absence of named objects by a language-trained dolphin. *Neuroscience & Biobehavioral Reviews, 9,* 667–681.

Herman, L. M., Richards, D. G., & Wolz, J. P. (1984). Comprehension of sentences by bottlenosed dolphins. *Cognition, 16,* 1–90.

Herman, L. M., & Uyeyama, R. K. (1999). The dolphin's grammatical competency: Comments on Kako (1999). *Animal Learning and Behavior, 27,* 18–23.

Heron, W. T., & Skinner, B. F. (1940). The rate of extinction in maze-bright and maze-dull rats. *Psychological Record, 4,* 11–18.

Herrnstein, R. J. (1961). Relative and absolute strength of response as a function of frequency of reinforcement. *Journal of the Experimental Analysis of Behavior, 4,* 267–272.

Herrnstein, R. J. (1964). Aperiodicity as a factor in choice. *Journal of the Experimental Analysis of Behavior, 7,* 179–182.

Herrnstein, R. J. (1966). Superstition: A corollary of the principles of operant conditioning. In W. K. Honig (Ed.), *Operant behavior: Areas of research and application.* New York: Appleton-Century-Crofts.

Herrnstein, R. J. (1970). On the law of effect. *Journal of the Experimental Analysis of Behavior, 13,* 243–266.

Herrnstein, R. J. (1974). Formal properties of the matching law. *Journal of the Experimental Analysis of Behavior, 21,* 159–164.

Herrnstein, R. J. (1977). The evolution of behaviorism. *American Psychologist, 32,* 593–603.

Herrnstein, R. J. (1979). Acquisition, generalization, and reversal of a natural concept. *Journal of Experimental Psychology: Animal Behavior Processes, 5,* 116–129.

Herrnstein, R. J. (1990). Rational choice theory: Necessary but not sufficient. *American Psychologist, 45,* 356–367.

Herrnstein, R. J., & de Villiers, P. A. (1980). Fish as a natural category for people and pigeons. In G. H. Bower (Ed.), *The psychology of learning and motivation* (Vol. 14). New York: Academic Press.

Herrnstein, R. J., & Hineline, P. N. (1966). Negative reinforcement as shock-frequency reduction. *Journal of the Experimental Analysis of Behavior, 9,* 421–430.

Herrnstein, R. J., & Loveland, D. H. (1964). Complex visual concept in the pigeon. *Science, 146,* 549–551.

Herrnstein, R. J., & Loveland, D. H. (1974). Hunger and contrast in a multiple schedule. *Journal of the Experimental Analysis of Behavior, 21,* 511–517.

Herrnstein, R. J., Loveland, D. H., & Cable, C. (1976). Natural concepts in pigeons. *Journal of Experimental Psychology: Animal Behavior Processes, 2,* 285–302.

Herrnstein, R. J., & Mazur, J. E. (1987). Making up our minds: A new model of economic behavior. *The Sciences, 27,* 40–47.

Herrnstein, R. J., & Prelec, D. (1991). Melioration: A theory of distributed choice. *Journal of Economic Perspectives, 5,* 137–156.

Herrnstein, R. J., & Vaughan, W. (1980). Melioration and behavioral allocation. In J. E. R. Staddon (Ed.), *Limits to action: The allocation of individual behavior.* New York: Academic Press.

Hersen, M., Eisler, R. M. & Miller, P. M. (Eds.). (1994). *Progress in behavior modification* (Vol. 29). Pacific Grove, CA: Brooks/Cole.

Herzog, M., & Hopf, S. (1986). Recognition of visual pattern components in squirrel monkeys. *European Archives of Psychiatry and Neurological Science, 236,* 10–16.

Heth, C. D. (1985). Within-compound associations of taste and temperature. *Learning and Motivation, 16,* 413–422.

Heyes, C. M., Jaldown, E., & Dawson, G. R. (1994). Imitation in rats: Conditions of occurrence in a bidirectional control procedure. *Learning and Motivation, 25,* 276–287.

Heyman, G. M. (1979). A Markov model description of changeover probabilities on concurrent variable-interval schedules. *Journal of the Experimental Analysis of Behavior, 31,* 41–51.

Heyman, G. M., & Herrnstein, R. J. (1986). More on concurrent interval-ratio schedules: A replication and review. *Journal of the Experimental Analysis of Behavior, 46,* 331–351.

Higgins, S. T., Morris, E. K., & Johnson, L. M. (1989). Social transmission of superstitious behavior in preschool children. *Psychological Record, 39,* 307–323.

Hilgard, E. R. (1936). The nature of the conditioned response: I. The case for and against stimulus-substitution. *Psychological Review, 43,* 366–385.

Hilliard, S., & Domjan, M. (1995). Effects on sexual conditioning of devaluing the US through satiation. *Quarterly Journal of Experimental Psychology, 48B,* 84–92.

Hines, T. M. (1998). Comprehensive review of biorhythm theory. *Psychological Reports, 83,* 19–64.

Hinson, J. M., & Staddon, J. E. R. (1983). Hill-climbing by pigeons. *Journal of the Experimental Analysis of Behavior, 39,* 25–47.

Hiroto, D. S., & Seligman, M. E. P. (1975). Generality of learned helplessness in man. *Journal of Personality and Social Psychology, 31,* 311–327.

Hobbes, T. (1651). *Leviathan, or the matter, forme and power of a commonwealth ecclesiasticall and civill.* London: Andrew Crooke.

Hoberman, H. M. (1990). Study group report on the impact of television violence on adolescents. *Journal of Adolescent Health Care, 11,* 45–49.

Hobson, S. L., & Newman, F. (1981). Fixed-ratio-counting schedules: Response and time measures considered. In M. L. Commons & J. A. Nevin (Eds.), *Quantitative analyses of behavior* (Vol. 1): *Discriminative properties of reinforcement schedules.* Cambridge, MA: Ballinger.

Hoehler, F. K., Kirschenbaum, D. S., & Leonard, D. W. (1973). The effects of overtraining and successive extinctions upon nictitating membrane conditioning in the rabbit. *Learning and Motivation, 4,* 91–101.

Hoffman, M. L. (1960). Power assertion by the parent and its impact on the child. *Child Development, 31,* 129–143.

Hogben, M. (1998). Factors moderating the effect of televised aggression on viewer behavior. *Communication Research, 25,* 220–247.

Holland, P. C. (1985). Element pretraining influences the content of appetitive serial compound conditioning in rats. *Journal of Experimental Psychology: Animal Behavior Processes, 11,* 367–387.

Holland, P. C. (1986). Temporal determinants of occasion setting in feature-positive discriminations. *Animal Learning and Behavior, 14,* 111–120.

Holland, P. C. (1991). Transfer of control in ambiguous discriminations. *Journal of Experimental Psychology: Animal Behavior Processes, 17,* 231–248.

Holland, P. C., & Rescorla, R. A. (1975). The effect of two ways of devaluing the unconditioned stimulus after first- and second-order appetitive conditioning. *Journal of Experimental Psychology: Animal Behavior Processes, 1,* 355–363.

Hollister, J. M. Mednick, S. A., Brennan, P. A., & Cannon, T. D. (1994). Impaired autonomic nervous system habituation in those at genetic risk for schizophrenia. *Archives of General Psychiatry, 51,* 552–558.

Holman, T. B., Jensen, L., & Capell, M. (1993). Predicting alcohol use among young adults. *Addictive Behaviors, 18,* 41–49.

Holz, W. C., & Azrin, N. H. (1961). Discriminative properties of punishment. *Journal of the Experimental Analysis of Behavior, 4,* 225–232.

Homans, G. C. (1961). *Social behavior: Its elementary forms.* New York: Harcourt, Brace & World.

Homme, L. E., deBaca, P. C., Devine, J. V., Steinhorst, R., & Rickert, E. J. (1963). Use of the Premack principle in controlling the behavior of nursery school children. *Journal of the Experimental Analysis of Behavior, 6,* 544.

Honig, W. K. (1974). Effects of extradimensional discrimination training upon previously acquired stimulus control. *Learning and Motivation, 5,* 1–15.

Honig, W. K. (1984). Contributions of animal memory to the interpretation of animal learning. In H. L. Roitblat, T. G. Bever, & H. S.

Terrace (Eds.), *Animal cognition.* Hillsdale, NJ: Erlbaum.

Honig, W. K., Boneau, C. A., Burstein, K. R., & Pennypacker, H. S. (1963). Positive and negative generalization gradients obtained after equivalent training conditions. *Journal of Comparative and Physiological Psychology, 56,* 111–116.

Honig, W. K., & Dodd, P. W. D. (1983). Delayed discriminations in the pigeon: The role of within-trial location of conditional cues. *Animal Learning and Behavior, 11,* 1–9.

Honig, W. K., & Stewart, K. E. (1988). Pigeons can discriminate locations presented in pictures. *Journal of the Experimental Analysis of Behavior, 50,* 541–551.

Honig, W. K., & Stewart, K. E. (1993). Relative numerosity as a dimension of stimulus control: The peak shift. *Animal Learning and Behavior, 21,* 346–354.

Hopfield, J. F., & Gelperin, A. (1989). Differential conditioning to a compound stimulus and its components in the terrestrial mollusc *Limax maximus. Behavioral Neuroscience, 103,* 329–333.

Horne, P. J., & Lowe, C. F. (1993). Determinants of human performance on concurrent schedules. *Journal of the Experimental Analysis of Behavior, 59,* 29–60.

Howell, D. C. (1999). *Fundamental statistics for the behavioral sciences* (4th edition). Pacific Grove, CA: Brooks/Cole.

Hryshko-Mullen, A. S., Broeckl, L. S., Haddock, C. K., & Peterson, A. L. (2000). Behavioral treatment of insomnia: The Wilford Hall Insomnia Program. *Military Medicine, 165,* 200–207.

Hubel, D. H., & Wiesel, T. N. (1963). Receptive fields of cells in striate cortex of very young, visually inexperienced kittens. *Journal of Neurophysiology, 26,* 994–1002.

Hubel, D. H., & Wiesel, T. N. (1965). Binocular interaction in striate cortex of kittens reared with artificial squint. *Journal of Neurophysiology, 28,* 1041–1059.

Hubel, D. H., & Wiesel, T. N. (1970). The period of susceptibility to the physiological effects of unilateral eye closure in kittens. *Journal of Physiology, 206,* 419–436.

Hubel, D. H., & Wiesel, T. N. (1979). Brain mechanisms in vision. *Scientific American, 241,* 150–162.

Huesmann, L. R., Lagerspetz, K., & Eron, L. D. (1984). Intervening variables in the TV violence-aggression relation: Evidence from two countries. *Developmental Psychology, 20,* 746–775.

Hugdahl, K. (1998). Cortical control of human classical conditioning: Autonomic and positron emission tomography data. *Psychophysiology, 35,* 170–178.

Hugdahl, K., & Ohman, A. (1977). Effects of instruction on acquisition and extinction of electrodermal responses to fear-relevant stimuli. *Journal of Experimental Psychology: Human Learning and Memory, 3,* 608–618.

Hull, C. L. (1934). Learning II: The factor of the conditioned reflex. In C. Murchison (Ed.), *A handbook of general experimental psychology.* Worcester, MA: Clark University Press.

Hull, C. L. (1943). *Principles of behavior.* New York: Appleton-Century-Crofts.

Hulse, S. H., & Campbell, C. E. (1975). "Thinking ahead" in rat discrimination learning. *Animal Learning and Behavior, 3,* 305–311.

Hulse, S. H., & Dorsky, N. P. (1979). Serial pattern learning by rats: Transfer of a formally defined stimulus relationship and the significance of nonreinforcement. *Animal Learning and Behavior, 7,* 211–220.

Hunter, S. M., Vizelberg, I. A., & Berenson, G. S. (1991). Identifying mechanisms of adoption of tobacco and alcohol use among youth: The Bogalusa heart study. *Social Networks, 13,* 91–104.

Hunter, W. S. (1920). The temporal maze and kinaesthetic sensory processes in the white rat. *Psychobiology, 2,* 1–18.

Hur, J., & Osborne, S. (1993). A comparison of forward and backward chaining methods used in teaching corsage making skills to mentally retarded adults. *British Journal of Developmental Disabilities, 39,* 108–117.

Hursh, S. R. (1991). Behavioral economics of drug self-administration and drug abuse policy. *Journal of the Experimental Analysis of Behavior, 56,* 377–393.

Hursh, S. R., & Bauman, R. A. (1987). The behavioral analysis of demand. In L. Green & J. H. Kagel (Eds.), *Behavioral economics.* Norwood, NJ: Ablex.

Huttenlocher, P. R. (1990). Morphometric study of human cerebral cortex development. *Neuropsychologia, 28,* 517–527.

Isaacs, W., Thomas, J., & Goldiamond, I. (1960). Application of operant conditioning to reinstate verbal behavior in psychotics. *Journal of Speech and Hearing Disorders, 25,* 8–12.

Israely, Y., & Guttman, J. (1983). Children's sharing behavior as a function of exposure to

puppet-show and story models. *Journal of Genetic Psychology, 142,* 311–312.

Ito, M., Takatsuru, S., & Saeki, D. (2000). Choice between constant and variable alternatives by rats: Effects of different reinforcer amounts and energy budgets. *Journal of the Experimental Analysis of Behavior, 73,* 79–92.

Iverson, I. H., Sidman, M., & Carrigan, P. (1986). Stimulus definition in conditional discriminations. *Journal of the Experimental Analysis of Behavior, 45,* 297–304.

Jackson, R. L., Alexander, J. H., & Maier, S. F. (1980). Learned helplessness, inactivity, and associative deficits: Effects of inescapable shock on response choice escape learning. *Journal of Experimental Psychology: Animal Behavior Processes, 6,* 1–20.

Jackson, T. (1999). Dyspraxia: Guidelines for intervention. *British Journal of Occupational Therapy, 62,* 321–326.

Jacob-Timm, S. (1996). Ethical and legal issues associated with the use of aversives in the public schools: The SIBIS controversy. *School Psychology Review, 25,* 184–199.

Jacobs, E. A., & Hackenberg, T. D. (1996). Humans' choices in situations of time-based diminishing returns: Effects of fixed-interval duration and progressive-interval step size. *Journal of the Experimental Analysis of Behavior, 65,* 5–19.

Jacobs, E. A., & Hackenberg, T. D. (2000). Human performance on negative slope schedules of points exchangeable for money: A failure of molar maximization. *Journal of the Experimental Analysis of Behavior, 73,* 241–260.

Jacobson, N. S. (1977). Problem solving and contingency contracting in the treatment of marital discord. *Journal of Consulting and Clinical Psychology, 45,* 92–100.

Jacobson, N. S., & Addis, M. E. (1993). Research on couples and couple therapy: What do we know? Where are we going? *Journal of Consulting and Clinical Psychology, 61,* 85–93.

Jacobson, N. S., Christensen, A., Prince, S. E., Cordova, J., & Eldridge, K. (2000). Integrative behavioral couple therapy: An acceptance-based, promising new treatment for couple discord. *Journal of Consulting and Clinical Psychology, 68,* 351–355.

Jacobson, N. S., & Dallas, M. (1981). Helping married couples improve their relationships. In W. E. Craighead, A. E. Kazdin, & M. J. Mahoney (Eds.), *Behavior modification: Principles, issues and applications.* Boston: Houghton Mifflin.

James, J. E. (1986). Review of the relative efficacy of imaginal and in vivo flooding in the treatment of clinical fear. *Behavioral Psychotherapy, 14*, 183–191.

James, W. (1890). *The principles of psychology.* New York: Holt, Rinehart & Winston.

Janelle, C. M. (1999). Ironic mental processes in sport: Implications for sport psychologists. *Sport Psychologist, 13*, 201–220.

Jarvik, M. E., Goldfarb, T. L., & Carley, J. L. (1969). Influence of interference on delayed matching in monkeys. *Journal of Experimental Psychology, 81*, 1–6.

Jenkins, H. M., & Harrison, R. H. (1960). Effects of discrimination training on auditory generalization. *Journal of Experimental Psychology, 59*, 246–253.

Jenkins, H. M., & Harrison, R. H. (1962). Generalization gradients of inhibition following auditory discrimination learning. *Journal of the Experimental Analysis of Behavior, 5*, 435–441.

Jenkins, H. M., & Moore, B. R. (1973). The form of the autoshaped response with food or water reinforcers. *Journal of the Experimental Analysis of Behavior, 20*, 163–181.

Jennings, P. J. (1995). Evidence of incomplete motor programming in Parkinson's disease. *Journal of Motor Behavior, 27*, 310–324.

John, E. R. (1967). *Mechanisms of memory.* New York: Academic Press.

John, E. R., Tang, Y., Brill, A. B., Young, R., & Ono, K. (1986). Double-labeled metabolic maps of memory. *Science, 233*, 1167–1175.

Johnson, H. E., & Garton, W. H. (1973). Muscle re-education in hemiplegia by use of electromyographic device. *Archives of Physiological and Medical Rehabilitation, 54*, 320–325.

Johnson, S. B. (1981). Enuresis. In D. Reid (Ed.), *Clinical behavior therapy and behavior modification* (Vol. 1). New York: Garland Publications.

Johnson, S. B., Hamm, R. J., & Leahey, T. H. (1986). Observational learning in *Gallus gallus domesticus* with and without a conspecific model. *Bulletin of the Psychonomic Society, 24*, 237–239.

Johnson, S. P., & Aslin, R. N. (1995). Perception of object unity in 2-month-old infants. *Developmental Psychology, 31*, 739–745.

Johnson, S. P., Welsh, T. M., Miller, L. K., & Altus, D. E. (1991). Participatory management: Maintaining staff performance in a university housing cooperative. *Journal of Applied Behavior Analysis, 24*, 119–127.

Joiner, T. E. (1999). The clustering and contagion of suicide. *Current Directions in Psychological Science, 8*, 89–92.

Jones, R. S. (1992). The use of errorless learning procedures in teaching people with a learning disability: A critical review. *Mental Handicap Research, 5*, 204–214.

Jones, T. A., & Schallert, T. (1994). Use-dependent growth of pyramidal neurons after neocortical damage. *Journal of Neuroscience, 14*, 2140–2152.

Junginger, J. (1997). Fetishism: Assessment and treatment. In D. R. Laws & W. T. O'Donohue (Eds.), *Sexual deviance: Theory, assessment, and treatment.* New York: Guilford Press.

Justice, T. C., & Looney, T. A. (1990). Another look at "superstitions" in pigeons. *Bulletin of the Psychonomic Society, 28*, 64–66.

Kako, E. (1999). Elements of syntax in the systems of three language-trained animals. *Animal Learning and Behavior, 27*, 1–14.

Kamil, A. C., & Balda, R. P. (1985). Cache recovery and spatial memory in Clark's nutcrackers. *Journal of Experimental Psychology: Animal Behavior Processes, 11*, 95–111.

Kamin, L. J. (1968). Attention-like processes in classical conditioning. In M. R. Jones (Ed.), *Miami symposium on the prediction of behavior: Aversive stimulation.* Miami, FL: University of Miami Press.

Kandel, E. R. (1979). Small systems of neurons. *Scientific American, 241*, 66–76.

Kandel, E. R., & Schwartz, J. H. (1982). Molecular biology of learning: Modulation of transmitter release. *Science, 218*, 433–443.

Kandel, E. R., & Tauc, L. (1964). Mechanism of prolonged heterosynaptic facilitation. *Nature, 202*, 145–147.

Kandel, E. R., & Tauc, L. (1965). Heterosynaptic facilitation in neurons of the abdominal ganglion of *Aplysia depilans*. *Journal of Physiology, 181*, 1–27.

Kanner, L., Rodriguez, A., & Ashenden, B. (1972). How far can autistic children go in matters of social adaptation? *Journal of Autism and Childhood Schizophrenia, 2*, 9–33.

Kant, I. (1781). *Kritik der reinen Vernunft.* Riga. Max Muller (trans.) (1881). [*Critique of pure reason*]. London: Henry G. Bohn.

Katzmann, S., & Mix, C. (1994). Improving functional independence in a patient with encephalitis through behavior modification shaping techniques. *American Journal of Occupational Therapy, 48*, 259–262.

Kawai, M. (1965). Newly acquired pre-cultural behavior of the natural troop of Japanese monkeys on Koshima Islet. *Primates, 6,* 1–30.

Kazdin, A. E. (1977). *The token economy: A review and evaluation.* New York: Plenum.

Kazdin, A. E. (1980). *Behavior modification in applied settings* (Rev. ed.). Homewood, IL: Dorsey Press.

Kazdin, A. E. (1983). The token economy: A decade later. *Journal of Applied Behavior Analysis, 15,* 431–445.

Keele, S. W. (1973). *Attention and human performance.* Pacific Palisades, CA: Goodyear Publishing Co.

Keith, J. R., & McVety, K. M. (1988). Latent place learning in a novel environment and the influences of prior training in rats. *Psychobiology, 16,* 146–151.

Kellogg, W. N., & Kellogg, L. A. (1933). *The ape and the child: A study of environmental influence upon early behavior.* New York: McGraw-Hill.

Kendler, H. H., & Underwood, B. J. (1948). The role of reward in conditioning theory. *Psychological Review, 55,* 209–215.

Kendrick, D. F., & Rilling, M. (1984). The role of interpolated stimuli in the retroactive interference of pigeon short-term memory. *Animal Learning and Behavior, 12,* 391–401.

Kendrick, D. F., Wright, A. A., & Cook, R. G. (1990). On the role of memory in concept learning by pigeons. *Psychological Record, 40,* 359–371.

Keppel, G. (1968). Retroactive and proactive inhibition. In T. R. Dixon & O. L. Horton (Eds.), *Verbal behavior and general behavior theory.* Englewood Cliffs, NJ: Prentice Hall.

Kernodle, M. W., & Carlton, L. G. (1992). Information feedback and the learning of multiple-degree-of-freedom activities. *Journal of Motor Behavior, 24,* 187–196.

Kerr, R., & Booth, B. (1978). Specific and varied practice of motor skill. *Perceptual and Motor Skills, 46,* 395–401.

Kesner, R. P., & Olton, D. S. (1990). *Neurobiology of comparative cognition.* Hillsdale, NJ: Erlbaum.

Khallad, Y., & Moore, J. (1996). Blocking, unblocking, and overexpectation in autoshaping with pigeons. *Journal of the Experimental Analysis of Behavior, 65,* 575–591.

Killeen, P. (1972). The matching law. *Journal of the Experimental Analysis of Behavior, 17,* 489–495.

Killeen, P. R. (1982). Incentive theory: II. Models for choice. *Journal of the Experimental Analysis of Behavior, 38,* 217–232.

Killeen, P. R. (1991). Behavior's time. *The Psychology of Learning and Motivation, 27,* 295–334.

Killeen, P. R., & Fetterman, J. G. (1988). A behavioral theory of timing. *Psychological Review, 95,* 274–295.

Kimble, G. A. (1961). *Hilgard and Marquis' conditioning and learning* (2nd ed.). New York: Appleton-Century-Crofts.

King, G. D. (1974). Wheel running in the rat induced by a fixed-time presentation of water. *Animal Learning and Behavior, 2,* 325–328.

Kintsch, W. (1965). Frequency distribution of interresponse times during VI and VR reinforcement. *Journal of the Experimental Analysis of Behavior, 8,* 347–352.

Kirkland, K., & Caughlin-Carvar, J. (1982). Maintenance and generalization of assertive skills. *Education & Training of the Mentally Retarded, 17,* 313–318.

Kirkpatrick-Steger, K., Wasserman, E. A., & Biederman, I. (1996). Effects of spatial rearrangement of object components on picture recognition in pigeons. *Journal of the Experimental Analysis of Behavior, 65,* 465–475.

Klass, E. T. (1979). Relative influence of sincere, insincere, and neutral symbolic models. *Journal of Experimental Child Psychology, 27,* 48–59.

Klein, M., Shapiro, E., & Kandel, E. R. (1980). Synaptic plasticity and the modulation of the calcium current. *Journal of Experimental Biology, 89,* 117–157.

Knowlton, B. J., & Thompson, R. F. (1992). Conditioning using a cerebral cortical conditioned stimulus is dependent on the cerebellum and brain stem circuitry. *Behavioral Neuroscience, 106,* 509–517.

Kohler, W. (1939). Simple structural function in the chimpanzee and the chicken. In W. D. Ellis (Ed.), *A source book of gestalt psychology.* New York: Harcourt Brace.

Kolb, B., Gibb, R., Gorny, G., & Whishaw, I. Q. (1998). Possible regeneration of rat medial frontal cortex following neonatal frontal lesions. *Behavioural Brain Research, 91,* 127–141.

Kolb, B., & Whishaw, I. Q. (1998). Brain plasticity and behavior. *Annual Review of Psychology, 49,* 43–64.

Konarski, E. A. (1987). Effects of response deprivation on the instrumental performance of mentally retarded persons. *American Journal of Mental Deficiency, 91,* 537–542.

Konorski, J. (1948). *Conditioned reflexes and neuron organization.* New York: Cambridge University Press.

Konorski, J. (1967). *Integrative activity of the brain: An interdisciplinary approach*. Chicago: University of Chicago Press.

Konorski, J., & Miller, S. (1937). On two types of conditioned reflex. *Journal of Genetic Psychology, 16,* 264–272.

Koob, G. F., Caine, S. B., Parsons, L., Markou, A, & Weiss, F. (1997). Opponent process model and psychostimulant addiction. *Pharmacology, Biochemistry & Behavior, 57,* 513–521.

Krebs, J. R., & Davies, N. B. (Eds.). (1978). *Behavioral ecology: An evolutionary approach*. Sunderland, MA: Sinauer.

Kremer, E. F. (1978). The Rescorla-Wagner model: Losses in associative strength in compound conditioned stimuli. *Journal of Experimental Psychology: Animal Behavior Processes, 4,* 22–36.

Kuo, Z. Y. (1921). Giving up instincts in psychology. *Journal of Philosophy, 18,* 645–664.

Kushner, M. (1965). Desensitization of a posttraumatic phobia. In L. P. Ullman & L. Krasner (Eds.), *Case studies in behavior modification*. New York: Holt, Rinehart & Winston.

Kushner, M. (1968). The operant control of intractable sneezing. In C. D. Spielberger, R. Fox, & D. Masterson (Eds.), *Contributions to general psychology*. New York: Ronald Press.

Kymissis, E., & Poulson, C. L. (1990). The history of imitation in learning theory: The language acquisition process. *Journal of the Experimental Analysis of Behavior, 54,* 113–127.

Kymissis, E., & Poulson, C. L. (1994). Generalized imitation in preschool boys. *Journal of Experimental Child Psychology, 58,* 389–404.

Lai, Q., & Shea, C. H. (1998). Generalized motor program (GMP) learning: Effects of reduced frequency of knowledge of results and practice variability. *Journal of Motor Behavior, 30,* 51–59.

Lalli, J. S., Livezey, K., & Kates, K. (1996). Functional analysis and treatment of eye poking with response blocking. *Journal of Applied Behavior Analysis, 29,* 129–132.

Lane, I. M., Wesolowski, M.D., & Burke, W. H. (1989). Teaching socially appropriate behavior to eliminate hoarding in a brain-injured adult. *Journal of Behavior Therapy and Experimental Psychiatry, 20,* 79–82.

Lane, S. D., & Critchfield, T. S. (1998). Classification of vowels and consonants by individuals with moderate mental retardation: Development of arbitrary relations via match-to-sample training with compound stimuli. *Journal of Applied Behavior Analysis, 31,* 21–41.

Lashley, K. S. (1917). The accuracy of movement in the absence of excitation from the moving organ. *American Journal of Physiology, 43,* 169–194.

Lashley, K. S. (1924). Studies of the cerebral function in learning: V. The retention of motor habits after destruction of the so-called motor areas in primates. *Archives of Neurology and Psychiatry, 12,* 249–276.

Lashley, K. S. (1929). *Brain mechanisms and intelligence: A quantitative study of injuries to the brain*. Chicago: University of Chicago Press.

Lashley, K. S. (1950). In search of the engram: Physiological mechanisms in animal behavior. In J. F. Danielli and R. Brown (Eds.), *Symposium of the Society for Experimental Biology*. Cambridge: Cambridge University Press.

Lashley, K. S. (1951). The problem of serial order in behavior. In L. A. Jeffress (Ed.), *Cerebral mechanisms in behavior*. New York: John Wiley.

Lashley, K. S., & Wade, M. (1946). The Pavlovian theory of generalization. *Psychological Review, 53,* 72–87.

Latash, M. L. (1999). Mirror writing: Learning, transfer, and implications for internal inverse models. *Journal of Motor Behavior, 31,* 107–111.

Laucht, M., Esser, G., & Schmidt, M. H. (1994). Contrasting infant predictors of later cognitive functioning. *Journal of Child Psychology and Psychiatry and Allied Disciplines, 35,* 649–662.

La Vigna, G. W., & Donnellan, A. M. (1986). *Alternatives to punishment: Solving behavior problems with nonaversive strategies*. New York: Irvington.

Lavond, D. G., Hembree, T. L., & Thompson, R. F. (1985). Effects of kainic acid lesions of the cerebellar interpositus nucleus on eyelid conditioning in the rabbit. *Brain Research, 326,* 179–182.

Lawrence, D. H., & DeRivera, J. (1954). Evidence for relational transposition. *Journal of Comparative and Physiological Psychology, 47,* 465–471.

Lea, S. E. G. (1978). The psychology and economics of demand. *Psychological Bulletin, 85,* 441–466.

Lea, S. E. G., & Roper, T. J. (1977). Demand for food on fixed-ratio schedules as a function of the quality of concurrently available reinforcement. *Journal of the Experimental Analysis of Behavior, 27,* 371–380.

Leal, D. R. (1998). Community-run fisheries: Avoiding the "tragedy of the commons."

*Population and Environment: A Journal of Interdisciplinary Studies, 19,* 225–245.

Leander, J. D., Lippman, L. G., & Meyer, M. E. (1968). Fixed interval performance as related to subject's verbalization of the reinforcement contingency. *Psychological Record, 18,* 469–474.

Lee, B. S. (1950). Effects of delayed speech feedback. *Journal of the Acoustical Society of America, 22,* 824–826.

Lee, T. D., Magill, R. A., & Weeks, D. J. (1985). Influence of practice schedule on testing schema theory predictions in adults. *Journal of Motor Behavior, 17,* 238–299.

Lee, T. D., White, M. A., & Carnahan, H. (1990). On the role of knowledge of results in motor learning: Exploring the guidance hypothesis. *Journal of Motor Behavior, 22,* 191–208.

Lee, V. L. (1996). Superstitious location changes by human beings. *Psychological Record, 46,* 71–86.

Lefkowitz, M., Blake, R. R., & Mouton, J. S. (1955). Status factors in pedestrian violation of traffic signals. *Journal of Abnormal and Social Psychology, 51,* 704–706.

Lefkowitz, M. M., Huesmann, L. R., & Eron, L. D. (1978). Parental punishment: A longitudinal analysis of effect. *Archives of General Psychiatry, 35,* 186–191.

LeFrancois, J. R., & Metzger, B. (1993). Low-response-rate conditioning history and fixed-interval responding in rats. *Journal of the Experimental Analysis of Behavior, 59,* 543–549.

Lemere, F., & Voegtlin, W. L. (1950). An evaluation of the aversion treatment of alcoholism. *Quarterly Journal of Studies on Alcohol, 11,* 199–204.

Lemere, F., Voegtlin, W. L., Broz, W. R., O'Hallaren, P., & Tupper, W. E. (1942). The conditioned reflex treatment of chronic alcoholism. VIII. A review of six years' experience with this treatment of 1526 patients. *Journal of the American Medical Association, 120,* 269–270.

LePage, J. P. (1999). The impact of a token economy on injuries and negative events on an acute psychiatric unit. *Psychiatric Services, 50,* 941–944.

Lerman, D. C., Iwata, B. A., Shore, B. A., & DeLeon, I. G. (1997). Effects of intermittent punishment on self-injurious behavior: An evaluation of schedule thinning. *Journal of Applied Behavior Analysis, 30,* 198–201.

Lett, B. T. (1973). Delayed reward learning: Disproof of the traditional theory. *Learning and Motivation, 4,* 237–246.

Lett, B. T. (1975). Long delay learning in the T-maze. *Learning and Motivation, 6,* 80–90.

Lett, B. T. (1979). Long-delay learning: Implications for learning and memory theory. In N. S. Sutherland (Ed.), *Tutorial essays in psychology* (Vol. 2). Hillsdale, NJ: Erlbaum.

Leung, L. S., & Shen, B. (1995). Long-term potentiation at the apical and basal and dendritic synapses of CA1 after local stimulation in behaving rats. *Journal of Neurophysiology, 73,* 1938–1946.

Levis, D. J. (1989). The case for a return to a two-factor theory of avoidance: The failure of non-fear interpretations. In S. B. Klein & R. R. Mowrer (Eds.), *Contemporary learning theories: Pavlovian conditioning and the status of traditional learning theory.* Hillsdale, NJ: Erlbaum.

Lewis, D., McAllister, D. E., & Adams, J. A. (1951). Facilitation and interference in performance on the modified Mashburn apparatus: I. The effects of varying the amount of original learning. *Journal of Experimental Psychology, 41,* 247–260.

Ley, R. (1994). An opponent-process interpretation of the anxiolytic effects of single inhalations of large concentrations of carbon dioxide. *Journal of Behavior Therapy and Experimental Psychiatry, 25,* 301–309.

Linden, M., Habib, T., & Radojevic, V. (1996). A controlled study of the effects of EEG biofeedback on cognition and behavior of children with attention deficit disorder and learning disabilities. *Biofeedback and Self-Regulation, 21,* 35–49.

Lipp, O. V., Siddle, D. A. T., & Vaitl, D. (1992). Latent inhibition in humans: Single-cue conditioning revisited. *Journal of Experimental Psychology: Animal Behavior Processes, 18,* 115–125.

Lochbaum, M. R. (1999). Affective and cognitive performance due to exercise training: An examination of individual difference variables. *Dissertation Abstracts International: Section B: The Sciences and Engineering, 59(10-B),* 5611.

Lockard, R. B. (1971). Reflections on the fall of comparative psychology: Is there a message for us all? *American Psychologist, 26,* 168–179.

Locke, J. (1690). *An essay concerning humane understanding: In four books.* London: Thomas Bassett.

Locurto, C. M., Terrace, H. S., & Gibbon, J. (Eds.). (1981). *Autoshaping and conditioning theory.* New York: Academic Press.

Loeb, J. (1900). *Comparative physiology of the brain and comparative psychology.* New York: Putnam's.

Logue, A. W. (1979). Taste aversion and the generality of the laws of learning. *Psychological Bulletin, 86,* 276–296.

Logue, A. W. (1988). A comparison of taste-aversion learning in humans and other vertebrates: Evolutionary pressures in common. In R. C. Bolles & M.D. Beecher (Eds.), *Evolution and learning.* Hillsdale, NJ: Erlbaum.

Logue, A. W., & Chavarro, A. (1987). Effect on choice of absolute and relative values of reinforcer delay, amount, and frequency. *Journal of Experimental Psychology: Animal Behavior Processes, 13,* 280–291.

Logue, A. W., Logue, K. R., & Strauss, K. E. (1983). The acquisition of taste aversions in humans with eating and drinking disorders. *Behavior Research and Therapy, 21,* 275–289.

Logue, A. W., Ophir, I., & Strauss, K. E. (1981). The acquisition of taste aversions in humans. *Behavior Research and Therapy, 19,* 319–333.

Lohrman-O'Rourke, S., & Zirkel, P. A. (1998). The case law on aversive interventions for students with disabilities. *Exceptional Children, 65,* 101–123.

Lovaas, O. I. (1967). A behavior therapy approach to the treatment of childhood schizophrenia. In J. P. Hill (Ed.), *Minnesota symposium on child psychology.* Minneapolis: University of Minnesota Press.

Lovaas, O. I. (1977). *The autistic child.* New York: John Wiley.

Lovaas, O. I. (1987). Behavioral treatment and normal educational and intellectual functioning in young autistic children. *Journal of Consulting and Clinical Psychology, 55,* 3–9.

Lovaas, O. I., Freitag, L., Nelson, K., & Whalen, C. (1967). The establishment of imitation and its use for the development of complex behavior in schizophrenic children. *Behavior Research and Therapy, 5,* 171–181.

Lowe, C. F. (1979). Determinants of human operant behaviour. In M.D. Zeiler & P. Harzem (Eds.), *Advances in the analysis of behaviour:* Vol. 1. *Reinforcement and the organization of behaviour.* Chichester, England: John Wiley.

Lowe, C. F., Beasty, A., & Bentall, R. P. (1983). The role of verbal behavior in human learning: Infant performance on fixed-interval schedules. *Journal of the Experimental Analysis of Behavior, 39,* 157–164.

Lowe, C. F., Harzem, P., & Bagshaw, M. (1978). Species differences in the temporal control of behavior: Human performance. *Journal of the Experimental Analysis of Behavior, 29,* 351–361.

Lubow, R. E. (1974). High-order concept formation in the pigeon. *Journal of the Experimental Analysis of Behavior, 21,* 475–483.

Lubow, R. E., & Gewirtz, J. C. (1995). Latent inhibition in humans: Data, theory, and implications for schizophrenia. *Psychological Bulletin, 117,* 87–103.

Lubow, R. E., & Moore, A. U. (1959). Latent inhibition: The effect of nonreinforced preexposure to the conditional stimulus. *Journal of Comparative and Physiological Psychology, 52,* 415–419.

Lucas, G. A., Deich, J. D., & Wasserman, E. A. (1981). Trace autoshaping: Acquisition, maintenance, and path dependence at long trace intervals. *Journal of the Experimental Analysis of Behavior, 36,* 61–74.

Lucchelli, F., Muggia, S., & Spinnler, H. (1997). Selective proper name anomia: A case involving only contemporary celebrities. *Cognitive Neuropsychology, 14,* 881–900.

MacCorquodale, K., & Meehl, P. E. (1954). Edward C. Tolman. In W. K. Estes, S. Koch, K. MacCorquodale, P. Meehl, C. G. Mueller, Jr., W. N. Schoenfeld, & W. S. Verplanck (Eds.), *Modern learning theory.* New York: Appleton-Century-Crofts.

Mackintosh, N. J. (1975). A theory of attention: Variations in the associability of stimuli with reinforcement. *Psychological Review, 82,* 276–298.

Mackintosh, N. J., & Dickinson, A. (1979). Instrumental (Type II) conditioning. In A. Dickinson & R. A. Boakes (Eds.), *Mechanisms of learning and motivation.* Hillsdale, NJ: Erlbaum.

Macuda, T., & Roberts, W. A. (1995). Further evidence for hierarchical chunking in rat spatial memory. *Journal of Experimental Psychology: Animal Behavior Processes, 21,* 20–32.

Madison, D. V., Malenka, R. C., & Nicoll, R. A. (1991). Mechanisms underlying long-term potentiation of synaptic transmission. *Annual Review of Neuroscience, 14,* 379–397.

Maes, J. R., & Vossen, J. M. (1993). Competition between contextual and punctate stimuli for inhibitory control in a Pavlovian discrimination procedure. *Learning and Motivation, 24,* 194–218.

Maier, S. F., & Seligman, M. E. P. (1976). Learned helplessness: Theory and evidence. *Journal of Experimental Psychology: General, 105,* 3–46.

Maier, S. F., & Warren, D. A. (1988). Controllability and safety signals exert dissimilar proactive effects on nociception and escape performance. *Journal of Experimental Psychology: Animal Behavior Processes, 14,* 18–25.

Maki, W. S. (1981). Directed forgetting in animals. In N. E. Spear & R. R. Miller (Eds.), *Information processing in animals: Memory mechanisms.* Hillsdale, NJ: Erlbaum.

Maki, W. S., & Hegvik, D. K. (1980). Directed forgetting in pigeons. *Animal Learning and Behavior, 8,* 567–574.

Malott, M. K. (1968). Stimulus control in stimulus-deprived chickens. *Journal of Comparative and Physiological Psychology, 66,* 276–282.

March, J. G., & Shapira, Z. (1992). Variable risk preferences and the focus of attention. *Psychological Review, 99,* 172–183.

Marcus, B. A., & Vollmer, T. R. (1996). Combining noncontingent reinforcement and differential reinforcement schedules as treatment for aberrant behavior. *Journal of Applied Behavior Analysis, 29,* 43–51.

Maren, S., & Baudry, M. (1995). Properties and mechanisms of long-term synaptic plasticity in the mammalian brain: Relationships to learning and memory. *Neurobiology of Learning and Memory, 63,* 1–18.

Marks, I. M., & Gelder, M. (1967). Transvestism and fetishism: Clinical and psychological changes during faradic aversion. *British Journal of Psychiatry, 113,* 711–739.

Marsden, C. D., Merton, P. A., & Morton, H. B. (1972). Servo action in human voluntary movement. *Nature, 238,* 140–143.

Martens, B. K., & Houk, J. L. (1989). The application of Herrnstein's law of effect to disruptive and on-task behavior of a retarded adolescent girl. *Journal of the Experimental Analysis of Behavior, 51,* 17–27.

Martin, G. (1998). Media influence to suicide: The search for solutions. *Archives of Suicide Research, 4,* 51–66.

Martin, G., & Pear, J. (1999). *Behavior modification: What it is and how to do it.* Upper Saddle River, NJ: Prentice Hall.

Martin, I., & Levey, A. B. (1991). Blocking observed in human eyelid conditioning. *Integrative Physiological and Behavioral Science, 26,* 127–131.

Matson, J. L., & Duncan, D. (1997). Aggression. In N. N. Singh (Ed.), *Prevention and treatment of severe behavior problems: Models and methods in developmental disabilities.* Pacific Grove, CA: Brooks/Cole.

Matsuzawa, T. (1985). Use of numbers by a chimpanzee. *Nature, 315,* 57–59.

Matthews, B. A., Catania, A. C., & Shimoff, E. (1985). Effects of uninstructed verbal responding on nonverbal responding: Contingency descriptions versus performance descriptions. *Journal of the Experimental Analysis of Behavior, 43,* 155–164.

Matthews, B. A., Shimoff, E., Catania, A. C., & Sagvolden, T. (1977). Uninstructed human responding: Sensitivity to ratio and interval contingencies. *Journal of the Experimental Analysis of Behavior, 27,* 453–467.

Matute, H. (1994). Learned helplessness and superstitious behavior as opposite effects of uncontrollable reinforcement in humans. *Learning and Motivation, 25,* 216–232.

Matute, H. (1995). Human reactions to uncontrollable outcomes: Further evidence for superstitions rather than helplessness. *Quarterly Journal of Experimental Psychology. B, Comparative and Physiological Psychology, 48B,* 142–157.

Matzel, L. D., Brown, A. M., & Miller, R. R. (1987). Associative effects of US preexposure: Modulation of conditioned responding by an excitatory training context. *Journal of Experimental Psychology: Animal Behavior Processes, 13,* 65–72.

Mawhinney, T. C., & Gowen, C. R. (1990). Gainsharing and the law of effect as the matching law: A theoretical framework. *Journal of Organizational Behavior Management, 11,* 61–75.

Mawhinney, V. T., Bostow, D. E., Laws, D. R., Blumenfeld, G. J., & Hopkins, B. L. (1971). A comparison of students studying-behavior produced by daily, weekly, and three-week testing schedules. *Journal of Applied Behavior Analysis, 4,* 257–264.

May, R. (1950). *The meaning of anxiety.* New York: Ronald Press.

Mazmanian, D. S., & Roberts, W. A. (1983). Spatial memory in rats under restricted viewing conditions. *Learning and Motivation, 14,* 123–139.

Mazur, J. E. (1975). The matching law and quantifications related to Premack's principle. *Journal of Experimental Psychology: Animal Behavior Processes, 1,* 374–386.

Mazur, J. E. (1981). Optimization theory fails to predict performance of pigeons in a two-response situation. *Science, 214,* 823–825.

Mazur, J. E. (1983). Steady-state performance on fixed-, mixed-, and random-ratio schedules.

*Journal of the Experimental Analysis of Behavior, 39*, 293–307.

Mazur, J. E. (1984). Tests of an equivalence rule for fixed and variable reinforcer delays. *Journal of Experimental Psychology: Animal Behavior Processes, 10*, 426–436.

Mazur, J. E. (1986). Fixed and variable ratios and delays: Further tests of an equivalence rule. *Journal of Experimental Psychology: Animal Behavior Processes, 12*, 116–124.

Mazur, J. E. (1991). Choice with probabilistic reinforcement: Effects of delay and conditioned reinforcers. *Journal of the Experimental Analysis of Behavior, 55*, 63–77.

Mazur, J. E. (2000). Two- versus three-alternative concurrent-chain schedules: A test of three models. *Journal of Experimental Psychology: Animal Behavior Processes, 26*, 286–293.

Mazur, J. E., & Wagner, A. R. (1982). An episodic model of associative learning. In M. L. Commons, R. J. Herrnstein, & A. R. Wagner (Eds.), *Quantitative analyses of behavior*: Vol. 3. *Acquisition*. Cambridge, MA: Ballinger.

McAfee, R. B., & Winn, A. R. (1989). The use of incentives/feedback to enhance workplace safety: A critique of the literature. *Journal of Safety Research, 20*, 7–19.

McBurney, D. H. (2000). *Research methods* (5th edition). Belmont, MA: Wadsworth Publishing.

McClelland, D.C. (1961). *The achieving society*. Princeton, NJ: Van Nostrand.

McCormick, D. A., & Thompson, R. F. (1984). Neuronal responses of the rabbit cerebellum during acquisition and performance of a classically conditioned nictitating membrane-eyelid response. *Journal of Neuroscience, 4*, 2811–2822.

McDonnell, J., & McFarland, S. (1988). A comparison of forward and concurrent chaining strategies in teaching laundromat skills to students with severe handicaps. *Research in Developmental Disabilities, 9*, 177–194.

McDougall, W. (1908). *An introduction to social psychology*. London: Methuen.

McDowell, J. J. (1988). Matching theory in natural human environments. *The Behavior Analyst, 11*, 95–109.

McEachin, J. J., Smith, T., & Lovaas, O. I. (1993). Long-term outcome for children with autism who received early intensive behavioral treatment. *American Journal of Mental Retardation, 97*, 359–372.

McFarland, D. S. (1971). *Feedback mechanisms in animal behavior*. New York: Academic Press.

McIlvane, W. J., Kledaras, J. B., Iennaco, F. M., McDonald, S. J., & Stoddard, L. T. (1995). Some possible limits on errorless discrimination reversals in individuals with severe mental retardation. *American Journal of Mental Retardation, 99*, 430–436.

McKean, K. J. (1994). Academic helplessness: Applying learned helplessness theory to undergraduates who give up when faced with academic setbacks. *College Student Journal, 28*, 456–462.

McLaren, I. P. L., Bennet, C. H., Guttman-Nahir, T., Kim, K., & Mackintosh, N. J. (1995). Prototype effects and peak shift in categorization. *Journal of Experimental Psychology: Learning, Memory, and Cognition, 21*, 662–673.

McNally, R. J. (1987). Preparedness and phobias: A review. *Psychological Bulletin, 101*, 283–303.

McNamara, H. J., Long, J. B., & Wike, E. L. (1956). Learning without response under two conditions of external cues. *Journal of Comparative and Physiological Psychology, 49*, 477–480.

McNish, K. A., Betts, S. L., Brandon, S. E., & Wagner, A. R. (1997). Divergence of conditioned eyeblink and conditioned fear in backward Pavlovian training. *Animal Learning and Behavior, 25*, 43–52.

McSweeney, F. K., & Melville, C. L. (1991). Positive behavioral contrast as a function of time-out duration when pigeons peck keys on a within-session procedure. *Animal Learning and Behavior, 19*, 249–256.

Mechner, F. (1958). Probability relations within response sequences under ratio reinforcement. *Journal of the Experimental Analysis of Behavior, 1*, 109–121.

Meck, W. H., & Church, R. M. (1983). A mode control model of counting and timing processes. *Journal of Experimental Psychology: Animal Behavior Processes, 9*, 320–334.

Meehl, P. E. (1950). On the circularity of the law of effect. *Psychological Bulletin, 47*, 52–75.

Meichenbaum, D. H., & Goodman, J. (1971). Training impulsive children to talk to themselves: A means of developing self-control. *Journal of Abnormal Psychology, 77*, 115–126.

Melchiori, L. E., de Souza, D. G., & de Rose, J. C. (2000). Reading, equivalence, and recombination of units: A replication with students with different learning histories. *Journal of Applied Behavior Analysis, 33*, 97–100.

Meltzoff, A. N., & Moore, M. K. (1977). Imitation of facial and manual gestures by human neonates. *Science, 198*, 75–78.

Meltzoff, A. N., & Moore, M. K. (1983). Newborn infants imitate adult facial gestures. *Child Development, 54,* 702–709.

Meltzoff, A. N., & Moore, M. K. (1989). Imitation in newborn infants: Exploring the range of gestures imitated and the underlying mechanisms. *Developmental Psychology, 25,* 954–962.

Merckelbach, H., Arntz, A., & de Jong, P. (1991). Conditioning experiences in spider phobics. *Behavioral Research and Therapy, 29,* 333–335.

Meyer, E. A., Hagopian, L. P., & Paclawskyj, T. R. (1999). A function-based treatment for school refusal behavior using shaping and fading. *Research in Developmental Disabilities, 20,* 401–410.

Middleton, M. B. & Cartledge, G. (1995). The effects of social skills instruction and parental involvement on the aggressive behaviors of African American males. *Behavior Modification, 19,* 192–210.

Milavsky, J. R., Stipp, H. H., Kessler, R. C., & Rubens, W. S. (1982). *Television and aggression: A panel study.* New York: Academic Press.

Miles, H. L. (1983). Apes and language: The search for communicative competence. In J. de Luce & H. T. Wilder (Eds.), *Language in primates: Perspectives and implications.* New York: Springer-Verlag.

Milgrom, P., Mancl, L., King, B., & Weinstein, P. (1995). Origins of childhood dental fear. *Behavior Research and Therapy, 33,* 313–319.

Mill, J. (1829). *Analysis of the phenomena of the human mind.* London: Baldwin & Cradock.

Mill, J. S. (1843). *A system of logic, ratiocinative and inductive, being a connected view of the principles of evidence, and the methods of scientific investigation.* London: J. W. Parker.

Miller, G. A. (1956). The magical number seven, plus or minus two. *Psychological Review, 63,* 81–97.

Miller, H. L. (1976). Matching-based hedonic scaling in the pigeon. *Journal of the Experimental Analysis of Behavior, 26,* 335–347.

Miller, J. S., Jagielo, J. A., & Spear, N. E. (1993). The influence of retention interval on the US preexposure effect: Changes in contextual blocking over time. *Learning and Motivation, 24,* 376–394.

Miller, N. E. (1948). Studies of fear as an acquirable drive: I. Fear as motivation and fear-reduction as reinforcement in the learning of new responses. *Journal of Experimental Psychology, 38,* 89–101.

Miller, N. E. (1951a). Comments on multiple-process conceptions of learning. *Psychological Review, 58,* 375–381.

Miller, N. E. (1951b). Learnable drives and rewards. In S. S. Stevens (Ed.), *Handbook of experimental psychology.* New York: John Wiley.

Miller, N. E. (1959). Liberalization of basic S-R concepts: Extensions to conflict behavior, motivation, and social learning. In S. Koch (Ed.), *Psychology: A study of a science* (Vol. 2). New York: McGraw-Hill.

Miller, N. E. (1985). The value of behavioral research with animals. *American Psychologist, 40,* 423–440.

Miller, N. E., & DiCara, L. (1967). Instrumental learning of heart rate changes in curarized rats: Shaping, and specificity to discriminative stimulus. *Journal of Comparative and Physiological Psychology, 63,* 12–19.

Miller, N. E., & Dollard, J. (1941). *Social learning and imitation.* New Haven: Yale University Press.

Miller, N. E., & Dworkin, B. R. (1974). Visceral learning: Recent difficulties with curarized rats and significant problems for human research. In P. A. Obrist, A. H. Black, J. Brener, & L. V. DiCara (Eds.), *Cardiovascular psychophysiology.* Chicago: Aldine.

Miller, R. R., & Schachtman, T. R. (1985). The several roles of context at the time of retrieval. In P. D. Balsam & A. Tomie (Eds.), *Context and learning.* Hillsdale, NJ: Erlbaum.

Miller, R. R., & Spear, N. E. (Eds.) (1985). *Information processing in animals: Conditioned inhibition.* Hillsdale, NJ: Erlbaum.

Miller, S., & Konorski, J. (1928). Sur une forme particuliere des reflexes conditionnels. *Compte Rendu Hebdomadaire des Seances et Memoires de la Societe de Biologie, 99,* 1151–1157.

Miltenberger, R. G. (1997). *Behavior modification: Principles and procedures.* Pacific Grove, CA: Brooks/Cole.

Mineka, S. (1985). The frightful complexity of the origins of fears. In F. R. Brush & J. B. Overmier (Eds.), *Affect, conditioning, and cognition.* Hillsdale, NJ: Erlbaum.

Mineka, S., Davidson, M., Cook, M., & Kerr, R. (1984). Observational conditioning of snake fear in rhesus monkeys. *Journal of Abnormal Psychology, 93,* 355–372.

Mineka, S., Mystkowski, J. L., Hladek, D., & Rodriguez, B. I. (1999). The effects of changing contexts on return of fear following exposure therapy for spider fear. *Journal of Consulting and Clinical Psychology, 67,* 599–604.

Mintz, D. E., Mourer, D. J., & Gofseyeff, M. (1967). Sequential effects in fixed-ratio postreinforcement pause duration. *Psychonomic Science, 9,* 387–388.

Miranda, A., & Presentacion, M. J. (2000). Efficacy of cognitive-behavioral therapy in the treatment of children with ADHD, with and without aggressiveness. *Psychology in the Schools, 37,* 169–182.

Mischel, W. (1961). Father-absence and delay of gratification: Cross-cultural comparisons. *Journal of Abnormal and Social Psychology, 63,* 116–124.

Mischel, W. (1966). Theory and research on the antecedents of self-imposed delay of reward. *Progress in Experimental Personality Research, 3,* 85–132.

Mischel, W. (1971). *Introduction to personality.* New York: Holt, Rinehart & Winston.

Mischel, W. (1974). Processes in delay of gratification. In L. Berkowitz (Ed.), *Advances in experimental social psychology* (Vol. 7). New York: Academic Press.

Mischel, W. (1981). Objective and subjective rules for delay of gratification. In G. d'Ydewalle & W. Lens (Eds.), *Cognition in human motivation and learning.* Hillsdale, NJ: Erlbaum.

Mischel, W. (1983). Delay of gratification as process and as person variable in development. In D. Magnusson & V. L. Allen (Eds.), *Human development.* New York: Academic Press.

Mischel, W., & Ebbesen, E. B. (1970). Attention in delay of gratification. *Journal of Personality and Social Psychology, 16,* 329–337.

Mischel, W., Ebbesen, E. B., & Zeiss, A. R. (1972). Cognitive and attentional mechanisms in delay of gratification. *Journal of Personality and Social Psychology, 21,* 204–218.

Mischel, W., & Grusec, J. (1966). Determinants of the rehearsal and transmission of neutral and aversive behaviors. *Journal of Personality and Social Psychology, 3,* 197–205.

Mischel, W., Shoda, Y., & Rodriguez, M. L. (1989). Delay of gratification in children. *Science, 244,* 933–938.

Mitchell, S. H. (1999). Measures of impulsivity in cigarette smokers and non-smokers. *Psychopharmacology, 146,* 455–464.

Mitchell, W. S., & Stoffelmayr, B. E. (1973). Application of the Premack principle to the behavioral control of extremely inactive schizophrenics. *Journal of Applied Behavior Analysis, 6,* 419–423.

Modaresi, H. A. (1990). The avoidance barpress problem: Effects of enhanced reinforcement and an SSDR-congruent lever. *Learning and Motivation, 21,* 199–220.

Molchan, S. E., Sunderland, T., McIntosh, A. R., Herscovitch, P., & Schreurs, B. G. (1994). A functional anatomical study of associative learning in humans. *Proceedings of the National Academy of Sciences USA, 91,* 8122–8126.

Moore, B. R. (1973). The role of directed Pavlovian reactions in simple instrumental learning in the pigeon. In R. A. Hinde & J. Stevenson-Hinde (Eds.), *Constraints on learning.* New York: Academic Press.

Moore, J. W. (1972). Stimulus control: Studies of auditory generalization in rabbits. In A. H. Black & W. F. Prokasy (Eds.), *Classical conditioning II: Current research and theory.* New York: Appleton-Century-Crofts.

Morgan, C. L. (1894). *An introduction to comparative psychology.* London: W. Scott.

Morgan, C. L. (1896). *Habit and instinct.* London: E. Arnold.

Morganstern, K. P. (1973). Implosive therapy and flooding procedures: A critical review. *Psychological Bulletin, 79,* 318–334.

Morin, C. M., Culbert, J. P., & Schwartz, S. M. (1994). Nonpharmacological interventions for insomnia: A meta-analysis of treatment efficacy. *American Journal of Psychiatry, 151,* 1172–1180.

Morris, R. J., & Kratochwill, T. R. (1983). *Treating children's fears and phobias: A behavioral approach.* New York: Pergamon Press.

Mowrer, O. H. (1947). On the dual nature of learning—a reinterpretation of "conditioning" and "problem solving." *Harvard Educational Review, 17,* 102–148.

Mowrer, O. H., & Jones, H. (1945). Habit strength as a function of the pattern of reinforcement. *Journal of Experimental Psychology, 35,* 293–311.

Mowrer, O. H., & Mowrer, W. M. (1938). Enuresis: A method for its study and treatment. *American Journal of Orthopsychiatry, 8,* 436–459.

Mucha, R. F., Volkovskis, C., & Kalant, H. (1981). Conditioned increase in locomotor activity produced with morphine as an unconditioned stimulus, and the relation of conditioning to acute morphine effect and tolerance. *Journal of Comparative and Physiological Psychology, 96,* 351–362.

Muenzinger, K. F. (1928). Plasticity and mechanization of the problem box habit in guinea pigs. *Journal of Comparative Psychology, 8,* 45–69.

Mueser, K. T., & Liberman, R. P. (1995). *Behavior therapy in practice.* New York: Oxford University Press.

Mulder, T., & Hulstijn, W. (1985a). Delayed sensory feedback in the learning of a novel motor task. *Psychological Research, 47,* 203–209.

Mulder, T., & Hulstijn, W. (1985b). Sensory feedback in the learning of a novel motor task. *Journal of Motor Behavior, 17,* 110–128.

Mustaca, A. E., Gabelli, F., Papini, M. R., & Balsam, P. (1991). The effects of varying the interreinforcement interval on appetitive contextual conditioning. *Animal Learning and Behavior, 19,* 125–138.

Myers, A. K., & Miller, N. E. (1954). Failure to find a learned drive based on hunger; evidence for learning motivated by "exploration." *Journal of Comparative and Physiological Psychology, 47,* 428–436.

Myers, D. L., & Myers, L. E. (1977). Undermatching: A reappraisal of performance on concurrent variable-interval schedules of reinforcement. *Journal of the Experimental Analysis of Behavior, 27,* 203–214.

Nakagawa, E. (1999). Acquired equivalence of discriminative stimuli following two concurrent discrimination learning tasks as a function of overtraining in rats. *Psychological Record, 49,* 327–348.

Nakajima, S. (2000). Putative inhibitory training of a stimulus makes it a facilitator: A within-subject comparison of visual and auditory stimuli in autoshaping. *Behavioural Processes, 48,* 129–136.

Nakao, M., Nomura, S., Shimosawa, T., Fujita, T, & Kuboki, T. (2000). Blood pressure biofeedback treatment of white-coat hypertension. *Journal of Psychosomatic Research, 48,* 161–169.

Napier, R. M., Macrae, M., & Kehoe, E. J. (1992). Rapid reacquisition in conditioning of the rabbit's nictitating membrane response. *Journal of Experimental Psychology: Animal Behavior Processes, 18,* 182–192.

Neef, N. A., Bill-Harvey, D., Shade, D, Iezzi, M., & DeLorenzo, T. (1995). Exercise participation with videotaped modeling: Effects on balance and gait in elderly residents of care facilities. *Behavior Therapy, 26,* 135–151.

Neef, N. A., Mace, F. C., Shea, M. C., & Shade, D. (1992). Effects of reinforcer rate and reinforcer quality on time allocation: Extensions of matching theory to educational settings. *Journal of Applied Behavior Analysis, 25,* 691–699.

Neef, N. A., Shade, D., & Miller, M. S. (1994). Assessing influential dimensions of reinforcers on choice in students with serious emotional disturbances. *Journal of Applied Behavior Analysis, 27,* 575–583.

Neuman, S. B. (1988). The displacement effect: Assessing the relation between television viewing and reading performance. *Reading Research Quarterly, 23,* 414–440.

Neuringer, A. J. (1970). Superstitious key pecking after three peck-produced reinforcements. *Journal of the Experimental Analysis of Behavior, 13,* 127–134.

Nevin, J. A. (1969). Interval reinforcement of choice behavior in discrete trials. *Journal of the Experimental Analysis of Behavior, 12,* 875–885.

Nevin, J. A. (1974). Response strength in multiple schedules. *Journal of the Experimental Analysis of Behavior, 21,* 389–408.

Nevin, J. A. (1979). Overall matching versus momentary maximizing: Nevin (1969) revisited. *Journal of Experimental Psychology: Animal Behavior Processes, 5,* 300–306.

Nevin, J. A. (1992). An integrative model for the study of behavioral momentum. *Journal of the Experimental Analysis of Behavior, 57,* 301–316.

Nevin, J. A. (1998). Choice and momentum. In W. O'Donohue (Ed.), *Learning and behavior therapy.* New York: Allyn & Bacon.

Nevin, J. A., & Grace, R. C. (2000). Behavioral momentum and the law of effect. *Behavioral and Brain Sciences, 23,* 73–130.

Newell, K. M. (1974). Knowledge of results and motor learning. *Journal of Motor Behavior, 6,* 235–244.

Newell, K. M. (1976). Motor learning without knowledge of results through the development of a response–recognition mechanism. *Journal of Motor Behavior, 8,* 209–217.

Nicholas, J. M. (1984). Lessons from the history of science? *Behavioral and Brain Sciences, 7,* 530–531.

North, M. M., North, S. M., & Coble, J. R. (1998). Virtual reality therapy: An effective treatment for phobias. In G. Riva, B. K. Wiederhold, & E. Molinari (Eds.), *Virtual environments in clinical psychology and neuroscience: Methods and techniques in advanced patient-therapist interaction.* Amsterdam, Netherlands Antilles: IOS Press.

Nottebohm, F. (1970). The ontogeny of birdsong. *Science, 167,* 950–956.

Novak, M. A., Suomi, S. J., Bowman, R. E., & Mohr, D. (1991). Problem solving in elderly sophisticated and naive monkeys. *Journals of Gerontology, 46,* P102–P108.

O'Connor, R. D. (1969). Modification of social withdrawal through symbolic modeling. *Journal of Applied Behavior Analysis, 2,* 15–22.

Ogden, J. A. (2000). Neurorehabilitation in the new millennium: New roles for our environment, behaviors, and mind in brain damage and recovery? *Brain and Cognition, 42,* 110–112.

Ohman, A., Dimberg, U., & Ost, L. G. (1985). Animal and social phobias: Biological constraints on learned fear responses. In S. Reiss & R. R. Bootzin (Eds.), *Theoretical issues in behavior therapy.* New York: Academic Press.

Olds, J., & Milner, P. (1954). Positive reinforcement produced by electrical stimulation of septal area and other regions of rat brain. *Journal of Comparative and Physiological Psychology, 47,* 419–427.

O'Leary, K. D., Kaufman, K. F., Kass, R. E., & Drabman, R. S. (1970). The effects of loud and soft reprimands on the behavior of disruptive students. *Exceptional Children, 37,* 145–155.

Ollendick, T. H., & King, N. J. (1998). Empirically supported treatments for children with phobic and anxiety disorders: Current status. *Journal of Clinical Child Psychology, 27,* 156–167.

Olness, K. (1999). Contemporary context: Psychoneuroimmunology. In R. Temes, (Ed.), *Medical hypnosis: An introduction and clinical guide.* New York: Churchill Livingstone, Inc.

Olson, S. L., Bates, J. E., & Bayles, K. (1990). Early antecedents of childhood impulsivity: The role of parent-child interaction, cognitive competence, and temperament. *Journal of Abnormal Child Psychology, 18,* 317–334.

Olton, D. S. (1978). Characteristics of spatial memory. In S. H. Hulse, H. Fowler, & W. K. Honig (Eds.), *Cognitive processes in animal behavior.* Hillsdale, NJ: Erlbaum.

Olton, D. S., Collison, C., & Werz, W. A. (1977). Spatial memory and radial arm maze performance by rats. *Learning and Motivation, 8,* 289–314.

Olton, D. S., & Samuelson, R. J. (1976). Remembrance of places past: Spatial memory in rats. *Journal of Experimental Psychology: Animal Behavior Processes, 2,* 97–116.

O'Mara, H. (1991). Quantitative and methodological aspects of stimulus equivalence. *Journal of the Experimental Analysis of Behavior, 55,* 125–132.

Ono, K. (1987). Superstitious behavior in humans. *Journal of the Experimental Analysis of Behavior, 47,* 261–271.

Osgood, C. E. (1949). The similarity paradox in human learning: A resolution. *Psychological Review, 56,* 132–143.

Ost, L. G. (1989). One-session treatment for specific phobias. *Behavior Research and Therapy, 27,* 1–7.

Overmier, J. B., & Seligman, M. E. P. (1967). Effects of inescapable shock upon subsequent escape and avoidance responding. *Journal of Comparative and Physiological Psychology, 63,* 28–33.

Overmier, J. B., & Wielkiewicz, R. M. (1983). On unpredictability as a causal factor in "learned helplessness." *Learning and Motivation, 14,* 324–337.

Pace, G. M., Iwata, B. A., Cowdery, G. E., Andree, P. J., & McIntyre, T. (1993). Stimulus (instructional) fading during extinction of self-injurious escape behavior. *Journal of Applied Behavior Analysis, 26,* 205–212.

Packer, J. S., Clark, B. M., Bond, N. W., & Siddle, D. A. (1991). Conditioning with facial expression of emotion: A comparison of aversive and non-aversive unconditioned stimuli. *Journal of Psychophysiology, 5,* 79–88.

Page, H. A., & Hall, J. F. (1953). Experimental extinction as a function of the prevention of a response. *Journal of Comparative and Physiological Psychology, 46,* 33–34.

Paletta, M. S., & Wagner, A. R. (1986). Development of context-specific tolerance to morphine: Support for a dual-process interpretation. *Behavioral Neuroscience, 100,* 611–623.

Palmer, C., & Meyer, R. K. (2000). Conceptual and motor learning in music performance. *Psychological Science, 11,* 63–68.

Pardes, H., West, A., & Pincus, H. A. (1991). Physicians and the animal-rights movement. *New England Journal of Medicine, 324,* 1640–1643.

Parker, G. A. (1978). Searching for mates. In J. R. Krebs & N. B. Davies (Eds.), *Behavioral ecology: An evolutionary approach.* Sunderland, MA: Sinauer.

Patterson, F. G. (1978). The gestures of a gorilla: Language acquisition in another pongid. *Brain and Language, 5,* 72–97.

Patterson, F. G., & Linden, E. (1981). *The education of Koko.* New York: Holt, Rinehart & Winston.

Patterson, G. R., Chamberlain, P., & Reid, J. B. (1982). A comparative evaluation of a parent-training program. *Behavior Therapy, 13,* 638–650.

Patterson, G. R., & Reid, J. B. (1973). Intervention for families of aggressive boys: A replication study. *Behavior Research and Therapy, 11,* 383–394.

Paul, G. L. (1969). Outcome of systematic desensitization: II. Controlled investigations of individual treatment, technique variations, and current status. In C. M. Franks (Ed.), *Behavior therapy: Appraisal and status.* New York: McGraw-Hill.

Paul, G. L., & Lentz, R. J. (1977). *Psychosocial treatment of chronic mental patients: Milieu versus social-learning programs.* Cambridge, MA: Harvard University Press.

Paulsen, K., Rimm, D. C., Woodburn, L. T., & Rimm, S. (1977). A self-control approach to inefficient spending. *Journal of Consulting and Clinical Psychology, 45,* 433–435.

Pavlov, I. P. (1927). *Conditioned reflexes.* Oxford: Oxford University Press.

Pavlov, I. P. (1928). *Lectures on conditioned reflexes.* New York: International Publishers.

Pearce, J. M., & Hall, G. (1980). A model for Pavlovian learning: Variations in the effectiveness of conditioned but not unconditioned stimuli. *Psychological Review, 87,* 532–552.

Penfield, W. (1959). The interpretive cortex. *Science, 129,* 1719–1725.

Pepperberg, I. M. (1981). Functional vocalizations of an African Grey parrot (*Psitticus erithacus*). *Zeitschrift für Tierpsychologie, 55,* 139–151.

Pepperberg, I. M. (1983). Cognition in the African Grey parrot: Preliminary evidence for auditory/vocal comprehension of a class concept. *Animal Learning and Behavior, 11,* 179–185.

Pepperberg, I. M. (1987). Evidence for conceptual quantitative abilities in the African parrot: Labeling of cardinal sets. *Ethology, 75,* 37–61.

Pepperberg, I. M. (1999). *The Alex studies: Cognitive and communicative abilities of Grey parrots.* Cambridge, MA: Harvard University Press.

Pepperberg, I. M., & Funk, M. S. (1990). Object permanence in four species of psittacine birds: An African Grey parrot (*Psittacus erithacus*), an Illiger mini macaw (*Ara maracana*), a parakeet (*Melopsittacus undulatus*), and a cockatiel (*Nymphicus hollandicus*). *Animal Learning and Behavior, 18,* 97–108.

Perrett, S. P., & Mauk, M. D. (1995). Extinction of conditioned eyelid responses requires the anterior lobe of cerebellar cortex. *Journal of Neuroscience, 15,* 2074–2080.

Perrins, R., & Weiss, K. R. (1996). A cerebral central pattern generation in Aplysia and its connections with buccal feeding circuitry. *Journal of Neuroscience, 16,* 7030–7045.

Peterson, G. B., Ackil, J. E., Frommer, G. P., & Hearst, E. S. (1972). Conditioned approach and contact behavior towards signals for food or brain-stimulation reinforcement. *Science, 177,* 1009–1011.

Peterson, L. R., & Peterson, M. J. (1959). Short-term retention of individual verbal items. *Journal of Experimental Psychology, 58,* 193–198.

Peterson, N. (1962). Effect of monochromatic rearing on the control of responding by wavelength. *Science, 136,* 774–775.

Petrinovich, L. F. (1999). *Darwinian dominion: Animal welfare and human interests.* Cambridge, MA: The MIT Press.

Pfautz, P. L., Donegan, N. H., & Wagner, A. R. (1978). Sensory preconditioning versus protection from habituation. *Journal of Experimental Psychology: Animal Behavior Processes, 4,* 286–295.

Phillips, D. P. (1982). The impact of fictional television stories on U.S. adult fatalities: New evidence on the effect of the mass media on violence. *American Journal of Sociology, 87,* 1340–1359.

Phillips, E. L. (1968). Achievement place: Token reinforcement procedures in a home-style rehabilitation setting for "pre-delinquent" boys. *Journal of Applied Behavior Analysis, 1,* 213–223.

Phillips, R. G., & LeDoux, J. E. (1992). Differential contribution of amygdala and hippocampus to cued and contextual fear conditioning. *Behavioral Neuroscience, 106,* 274–285.

Piaget, J. (1926). *The language and thought of the child* (M. Gabain, Trans.). London: Routledge & Kegan Paul.

Piaget, J. (1929). *The child's conception of the world.* New York: Harcourt, Brace.

Pitariu, H., Bostenaru, N., Lucaciu, L., & Oachis, A. (1984). The theory and practice of biorhythms are not confirmed. *Revista de Psichologie, 30,* 166–171.

Platt, J. (1973). Social traps. *American Psychologist, 28,* 641–651.

Platt, J. R. (1973). Percentile reinforcement: Paradigms for experimental analysis of response shaping. In G. H. Bower (Ed.), *The psychology of learning and motivation*: Vol 7. *Advances in theory and research*. New York: Academic Press.

Platt, J. R. (1979). Interresponse-time shaping by variable-interval-like interresponse-time reinforcement contingencies. *Journal of the Experimental Analysis of Behavior, 31*, 3–14.

Polka, L., & Werker, J. F. (1994). Developmental changes in perception of nonnative vowel contrasts. *Journal of Experimental Psychology: Human Perception and Performance, 20*, 421–435.

Popper, K. (1959). *The logic of scientific discovery*. New York: Harper.

Portier, S. J., Van Galen, G. P., & Meulenbroek, R. G. (1990). Practice and the dynamics of handwriting performance: Evidence for a shift of motor programming load. *Journal of Motor Behavior, 22*, 474–492.

Postman, L. (1947). The history and present status of the law of effect. *Psychological Review, 44*, 489–563.

Poulson, C. L., Kymissis, E., Reeve, K. F., Andreatos, M., & Reeve, L. (1991). Generalized vocal imitation in infants. *Journal of Experimental Child Psychology, 51*, 267–279.

Pouthas, V., Droit, S., Jacquet, A. Y., & Wearden, J. H. (1990). Temporal differentiation of response duration in children of different ages: Developmental changes in relations between verbal and nonverbal behavior. *Journal of the Experimental Analysis of Behavior, 53*, 21–31.

Powell, R. W. (1969). The effect of reinforcement magnitude upon responding under fixed-ratio schedules. *Journal of the Experimental Analysis of Behavior, 12*, 605–608.

Premack, D. (1959). Toward empirical behavioral laws: I. Positive reinforcement. *Psychological Review, 66*, 219–233.

Premack, D. (1963). Rate differential reinforcement in monkey manipulation. *Journal of the Experimental Analysis of Behavior, 6*, 81–89.

Premack, D. (1965). Reinforcement theory. In D. Levine (Ed.), *Nebraska symposium on motivation*. Lincoln: University of Nebraska Press.

Premack, D. (1971a). Catching up with common sense or two sides of a generalization: Reinforcement and punishment. In R. Glaser (Ed.), *The nature of reinforcement*. New York: Academic Press.

Premack, D. (1971b). Language in chimpanzee? *Science, 172*, 808–822.

Premack, D. (1983). The codes of man and beasts. *Behavioral and Brain Sciences, 6*, 125–167.

Premack, D. (1986). *Gavagai!* Cambridge, MA: MIT Press.

Premack, D. (1988). Minds with and without language. In L. Weiskrantz (Ed.), *Thought without language*. Oxford: Clarendon Press.

Pribram, K. H. (1966). Some dimensions of remembering: Steps toward a neuropsychological model of memory. In J. Gaito (Ed.), *Macromolecules and behavior*. New York: Appleton-Century-Crofts.

Prochaska, J., Smith, N., Marzilli, R., Colby, J., & Donovan, W. (1974). Remote-control aversive stimulation in the treatment of head-banging in a retarded child. *Journal of Behavior Therapy and Experimental Psychiatry, 5*, 285–289.

Provine, R. R. (1989). Faces as releasers of contagious yawning: An approach to face detection using normal human subjects. *Bulletin of the Psychonomic Society, 27*, 211–214.

Rachlin, H. (1966). Recovery of responses during mild punishment. *Journal of the Experimental Analysis of Behavior, 9*, 251–263.

Rachlin, H. (1969). Autoshaping of key pecking in pigeons with negative reinforcement. *Journal of the Experimental Analysis of Behavior, 12*, 521–531.

Rachlin, H. (1970). *Introduction to modern behaviorism*. San Francisco: W. H. Freeman & Company Publishers.

Rachlin, H. (1974). Self–control. *Behaviorism, 2*, 94–107.

Rachlin, H. (1978). A molar theory of reinforcement schedules. *Journal of the Experimental Analysis of Behavior, 30*, 345–360.

Rachlin, H. (1990). Why do people gamble and keep gambling despite heavy losses? *Psychological Science, 1*, 294–297.

Rachlin, H., & Green, L. (1972). Commitment, choice, and self-control. *Journal of the Experimental Analysis of Behavior, 17*, 15–22.

Rachlin, H., Green, L., Kagel, J. H., & Battalio, R. C. (1976). Economic demand theory and psychological studies of choice. In G. H. Bower (Ed.), *The psychology of learning and motivation, 10*, 129–154.

Rachlin, H., Raineri, A., & Cross, D. (1991). Subjective probability and delay. *Journal of the Experimental Analysis of Behavior, 55*, 233–244.

Rachman, S. (1977). The conditioning theory of fear-acquisition: A critical examination. *Brain Research and Therapy, 15*, 375–387.

Rachman, S. (1991). Neo-conditioning and the classical theory of fear acquisition. *Clinical Psychology Review, 11*, 155–173.

Rajigah, L. S. (1996). Treatment of choice for nocturnal enuresis: Review and recommendations. *Journal of Psychological Practice, 2,* 33–42.

Rashotte, M. E., Griffin, R. W., & Sisk, C. L. (1977). Second-order conditioning of the pigeon's keypeck. *Animal Learning and Behavior, 5,* 25–38.

Rauhut, A. S., McPhee, J., DiPietro, N. T., & Ayres, J. J. B. (2000). Conditioned inhibition training of the competing cue after compound conditioning does not reduce cue competition. *Animal Learning and Behavior, 28,* 92–108.

Razran, G. (1949). Semantic and phonetographic generalizations of salivary conditioning to verbal stimuli. *Journal of Experimental Psychology, 39,* 642–652.

Redmon, W. K., & Lockwood, K. (1986). The matching law and organizational behavior. *Journal of Organizational Behavior Management, 8,* 57–72.

Reese, E. S. (1963). The behavioral mechanisms underlying shell selection by hermit crabs. *Behaviour, 21,* 78–126.

Regan, T. (1983). *The case for animal rights.* Berkeley: University of California Press.

Reisel, W. D., & Kopelman, R. E. (1995). The effects of failure on subsequent group performance in a professional sports setting. *Journal of Psychology, 129,* 103–113.

Rescorla, R. A. (1966). Predictability and number of pairings in Pavlovian fear conditioning. *Psychonomic Science, 4,* 383–384.

Rescorla, R. A. (1968). Probability of shock in the presence and absence of CS in fear conditioning. *Journal of Comparative and Physiological Psychology, 66,* 1–5.

Rescorla, R. A. (1969). Pavlovian conditioned inhibition. *Psychological Bulletin, 72,* 77–94.

Rescorla, R. A. (1973). Second order conditioning: Implications for theories of learning. In F. J. McGuigan and D. B. Lumsden (Eds.), *Contemporary approaches to conditioning and learning.* New York: John Wiley.

Rescorla, R. A. (1982). Simultaneous second-order conditioning produces S-S learning in conditioned suppression. *Journal of Experimental Psychology: Animal Behavior Processes, 8,* 23–32.

Rescorla, R. A. (1984). Associations between Pavlovian CSs and context. *Journal of Experimental Psychology: Animal Behavior Processes, 10,* 195–204.

Rescorla, R. A. (1985). Inhibition and facilitation. In R. R. Miller & N. E. Spear (Eds.), *Informa-tion processing in animals: Conditioned inhibition.* Hillsdale, NJ: Erlbaum.

Rescorla, R. A. (1986). Two perceptual variables in within–event learning. *Animal Learning and Behavior, 14,* 387–392.

Rescorla, R. A. (1998). Instrumental learning: Nature and persistence. In M. Sabourin, F. Craik, & R. Michele (Eds.), *Advances in psychological science,* Vol. 2: *Biological and cognitive aspects.* Hove, England: Psychology Press/Erlbaum.

Rescorla, R. A. (1999). Partial reinforcement reduces the associative change produced by nonreinforcement. *Journal of Experimental Psychology: Animal Behavior Processes, 25,* 403–414.

Rescorla, R. A., & Cunningham, C. L. (1978). Within-compound flavor associations. *Journal of Experimental Psychology: Animal Behavior Processes, 4,* 267–275.

Rescorla, R. A., Durlach, P. J., & Grau, J. W. (1985). Contextual learning in Pavlovian conditioning. In P. D. Balsam & A. Tomie (Eds.), *Context and learning.* Hillsdale, NJ: Erlbaum.

Rescorla, R. A., & LoLordo, V. M. (1965). Inhibition of avoidance behavior. *Journal of Comparative and Physiological Psychology, 59,* 406–412.

Rescorla, R. A., & Wagner, A. R. (1972). A theory of Pavlovian conditioning: Variations in the effectiveness of reinforcement and nonreinforcement. In A. H. Black and W. F. Prokasy (Eds.), *Classical conditioning II: Current research and theory.* New York: Appleton-Century-Crofts.

Revusky, S. H. (1977). Learning as a general process with an emphasis on data from feeding experiments. In N. W. Milgram, L. Krames, & T. M. Alloway, (Eds.), *Food aversion learning.* New York: Plenum.

Reynolds, G. S. (1961). An analysis of interactions in a multiple schedule. *Journal of the Experimental Analysis of Behavior, 4,* 107–117.

Rice, M. L., Huston, A. C., Truglio, R., & Wright, J. (1990). Words from "Sesame Street": Learning vocabulary while viewing. *Developmental Psychology, 26,* 421–428.

Richards, C. S. (1981). Improving college students' study behaviors through self-control techniques: A brief review. *Behavioral Counseling Quarterly, 1,* 159–175.

Richards, J. B. Sabol, K. E., & Seiden, L. S. (1993). DRL interresponse-time distributions: Quantification by peak deviation analysis.

*Journal of the Experimental Analysis of Behavior, 60*, 361–385.

Rider, R. A., & Abdulahad, D. T. (1991). Effects of massed versus distributed practice on gross and fine motor proficiency of educable mentally handicapped adolescents. *Perceptual and Motor Skills, 73*, 219–224.

Rilling, M. (1977). Stimulus control and inhibitory processes. In W. K. Honig & J. E. R. Staddon (Eds.), *Handbook of operant behavior*. Englewood Cliffs, NJ: Prentice-Hall.

Rilling, M. E., & Neiworth, J. J. (1986). Comparative cognition: A general process approach. In D. F. Kendrick, M. E. Rilling, & M. R. Denny (Eds.), *Theories of animal memory*. Hillsdale, NJ: Erlbaum.

Rivera, D. M., & Smith, D. D. (1987). Influence of modeling on acquisition and generalization of computational skills: A summary of research findings from three sites. *Learning Disability Quarterly, 10*, 69–80.

Robbins, S. J. (1990). Mechanisms underlying spontaneous recovery in autoshaping. *Journal of Experimental Psychology: Animal Behavior Processes, 16*, 235–249.

Robert, M. (1990). Observational learning in fish, birds, and mammals: A classified bibliography spanning over 100 years of research. *Psychological Record, 40*, 289–311.

Roberts, S. (1981). Isolation of an internal clock. *Journal of Experimental Psychology: Animal Behavior Processes, 7*, 242–268.

Roberts, S. (1982). Cross modal use of an internal clock. *Journal of Experimental Psychology: Animal Behavior Processes, 8*, 2–22.

Roberts, S. (1983). Properties and function of an internal clock. In R. L. Mellgren (Ed.), *Animal cognition and behavior*. Amsterdam: North-Holland Publishing.

Roberts, W. A. (1998). *Principles of animal cognition*. Boston, MA: McGraw-Hill.

Roberts, W. A., Coughlin, R., & Roberts, S. (2000). Pigeons flexibly time or count on cue. *Psychological Science, 11*, 218–222.

Roberts, W. A., & Grant, D. S. (1978). An analysis of light-induced retroactive inhibition in pigeon short-term memory. *Journal of Experimental Psychology: Animal Behavior Processes, 4*, 219–236.

Roberts, W. A., Mazmanian, D. S., & Kraemer, P. J. (1984). Directed forgetting in monkeys. *Animal Learning and Behavior, 12*, 29–40.

Roberts, W. A., & Phelps, M. T. (1994). Transitive inference in rats: A test of the spatial coding hypothesis. *Psychological Science, 5*, 368–374.

Rodgers, W., & Rozin, P. (1966). Novel food preferences in thiamine-deficient rats. *Journal of Comparative and Physiological Psychology, 61*, 1–4.

Roitblat, H. L. (1980). Codes and coding processes in pigeon short–term memory. *Animal Learning and Behavior, 8*, 341–351.

Roitblat, H. L. (1987). *Introduction to comparative cognition*. New York: W. H. Freeman & Company Publishers.

Roitblat, H. L., Pologe, B., & Scopatz, R. A. (1983). The representation of items in serial position. *Animal Learning and Behavior, 11*, 489–498.

Roitblat, H. L., Scopatz, R. A., & Bever, T. G. (1987). The hierarchical representation of three-item sequences. *Animal Learning and Behavior, 15*, 179–192.

Roper, K. L., Kaiser, D. H., & Zentall, T. R. (1995). True directed forgetting in pigeons may occur only when alternative working memory is required on forget-cue trials. *Animal Learning and Behavior, 23*, 280–285.

Roper, K. L., & Zentall, T. R. (1993). Directed forgetting in animals. *Psychological Bulletin, 113*, 513–532.

Rosch, E. (1973). On the internal structure of perceptual and semantic categories. In T. E. Moore (Ed.), *Cognitive development and the acquisition of language*. New York: Academic Press.

Rosch, E. (1975). Cognitive representations of semantic categories. *Journal of Experimental Psychology: General, 104*, 192–233.

Rosch, E. (1977). Human categorization. In N. Warren (Ed.), *Advances in cross-cultural psychology* (Vol. 1). London: Academic Press.

Rosellini, R. A., Warren, D. A., & DeCola, J. P. (1987). Predictability and controllability: Differential effects upon contextual fear. *Learning and Motivation, 18*, 392–420.

Rosen, B., & D'Andrade, R. (1959). The psychosocial origins of achievement motivation. *Sociometry, 22*, 185–218.

Rosenthal, R. (1966). *Experimenter effects in behavioral research*. New York: Appleton-Century-Crofts.

Rosenthal, T. L., & Zimmerman, B. J. (1972). Modeling by exemplification and instruction in training conservation. *Developmental Psychology, 6*, 392–401.

Rosenthal, T. L., & Zimmerman, B. J. (1978). *Social learning and cognition*. New York: Academic Press.

Rosenzweig, M. R. (1966). Environmental complexity, cerebral change, and behavior. *American Psychologist, 21*, 321–332.

Rosenzweig, M. R. (1984). Experience and the brain. *American Psychologist, 39*, 365–376.

Rosenzweig, M. R., Mollgaard, K., Diamond, M. C., & Bennet, T. E. L. (1972). Negative as well as positive synaptic changes may store memory. *Psychological Review, 79*, 93–96.

Ross, J. A. (1974). The use of contingency contracting in controlling adult nailbiting. *Journal of Behavior Therapy and Experimental Psychiatry, 5*, 105–106.

Ross, R. T., & Holland, P. C. (1981). Conditioning of simultaneous and serial feature-positive discriminations. *Animal Learning and Behavior, 9*, 293–303.

Rowland, W. J. (1989). Mate choice and the supernormality effect in female sticklebacks (*Gasterosteus aculeatus*). *Behavioral Ecology and Sociobiology, 24*, 433–438.

Rozin, P., & Kalat, J. W. (1971). Specific hungers and poison avoidance as adaptive specializations of learning. *Psychological Review, 78*, 459–486.

Rozin, P., Reff, D., Mack, M., & Schull, J. (1984). Conditioned opponent responses in human tolerance to caffeine. *Bulletin of the Psychonomic Society, 22*, 117–120.

Rudolph, R. L., Honig, W. K., & Gerry, J. E. (1969). Effects of monochromatic rearing on the acquisition of stimulus control. *Journal of Comparative and Physiological Psychology, 67*, 50–57.

Rumbaugh, D. M. (Ed.). (1977). *Language learning by a chimpanzee: The Lana project.* New York: Academic Press.

Rumbaugh, D. M., Savage-Rumbaugh, E. S., & Sevcik, R. A. (1994). Biobehavioral roots of language: A comparative perspective of chimpanzee, child, and culture. In R. W. Wrangham, W. C. McGrew, F. B. M. de Waal, & P. G. Heltne (Eds.), *Chimpanzee cultures.* Cambridge, MA: Harvard University Press.

Runyon, R. P., Coleman, K. A., & Pittenger, D. J. (2000). *Fundamentals of behavioral statistics* (9th edition). New York: McGraw-Hill.

Rushford, N. B., Burnett, A., & Maynard, R. (1963). Behavior in Hydra: Contraction responses of *Hydra pirardi* to mechanical and light stimuli. *Science, 139*, 760–761.

Rusiniak, K. W., Hankins, W. G., Garcia, J., & Brett, C. P. (1979). Flavor-illness aversions: Potentiation of odor by taste in rats. *Behavioral and Neural Biology, 25*, 1–17.

Russek, M., & Pina, S. (1962). Conditioning of adrenalin anorexia. *Nature, 193*, 1296–1297.

Russon, A. E., & Galdikas, B. M. F. (1995). Constraints on great apes' imitation: Model and action selectivity in rehabilitant orangutan (*Pongo pygmaeus*) imitation. *Journal of Comparative Psychology, 109*, 5–17.

Russon, A. E., & Waite, B. E. (1991). Patterns of dominance and imitation in an infant peer group. *Ethology and Sociobiology, 12*, 55–73.

Sachs, D. A., & Mayhall, B. (1971). Behavioral control of spasms using aversive conditioning with a cerebral palsied adult. *Journal of Nervous and Mental Disorders, 152*, 362–363.

Sahoo, F. M., & Tripathy, S. (1990). Learned helplessness in industrial employees: A study on non-contingency, satisfaction and motivational deficits. *Psychological Studies, 35*, 79–87.

Sakagami, T., Hursh, S. R., Christensen, J., & Silberberg, A. (1989). Income maximizing in concurrent interval-ratio schedules. *Journal of the Experimental Analysis of Behavior, 52*, 41–46.

Salmoni, A. W., Schmidt, R. A., & Walter, C. B. (1984). Knowledge of results and motor learning: A review and critical reappraisal. *Psychological Bulletin, 95*, 355–386.

Savage, T. (1998). Shaping: The link between rats and robots. *Connection Science: Journal of Neural Computing, Artificial Intelligence and Cognitive Research, 10*, 321–340.

Savage-Rumbaugh, E. S. (1984). Acquisition of functional symbol usage in apes and children. In H. L. Roitblat, T. G. Bever, & H. S. Terrace (Eds.), *Animal cognition.* Hillsdale, NJ: Erlbaum.

Savage-Rumbaugh, S., McDonald, K., Sevcik, R. A., Hopkins, W. D., & Rubert, E. (1986). Spontaneous symbol acquisition and communicative use by pygmy chimpanzees (*Pan paniscus*). *Journal of Experimental Psychology: General, 115*, 211–235.

Savastano, H. I., & Fantino, E. (1994). Human choice in concurrent ratio-interval schedules of reinforcement. *Journal of the Experimental Analysis of Behavior, 61*, 453–463.

Schaefer, H. H., & Martin, P. L. (1966). Behavioral therapy for "apathy" of schizophrenics. *Psychological Reports, 19*, 1147–1158.

Schell, A. M., Dawson, M. E., & Marinkovic, K. (1991). Effects of potentially phobic conditioned stimuli on retention, reconditioning, and extinction of the conditioned skin conductance response. *Psychophysiology, 28*, 140–153.

Schlosberg, H. (1928). A study of the conditioned patellar reflex. *Journal of Experimental Psychology, 11*, 468–494.

Schlosberg, H. (1937). The relationship between success and the laws of conditioning. *Psychological Review, 44*, 379–394.

Schlosberg, H., & Katz, A. (1943). Double alternation lever–pressing in the white rat. *American Journal of Psychology, 56*, 274–282.

Schmidt, R. A. (1975). A schema theory of discrete motor skill learning. *Psychological Review, 82*, 225–260.

Schmidt, R. A. (1988). *Motor control and learning: A behavioral emphasis* (2nd ed.). Champagne, IL: Human Kinetics Publishers.

Schmidt, R. A., & Wulf, G. (1997). Continuous concurrent feedback degrades skill learning: Implications for training and simulation. *Human Factors, 39*, 509–525.

Schmidt, R. A., & Young, D. E. (1991). Methodology for motor learning: A paradigm for kinematic feedback. *Journal of Motor Behavior, 23*, 13–24.

Schmidt, R. A., Young, D. E., Swinnen, S., & Shapiro, D. C. (1989). Summary knowledge of results for skill acquisition: Support for the guidance hypothesis. *Journal of Experimental Psychology: Learning, Memory, and Cognition, 15*, 352–359.

Schneider, J. W. (1973). Reinforcer effectiveness as a function of reinforcer rate and magnitude: A comparison of concurrent performances. *Journal of the Experimental Analysis of Behavior, 20*, 461–471.

Schneiderman, N. (1966). Interstimulus interval function of the nictitating membrane response of the rabbit under delay versus trace conditioning. *Journal of Comparative and Physiological Psychology, 62*, 397–402.

Schneiderman, N., McCabe, P. M., Haselton, J. R., Ellenberger, H. H., Jarrell, T. W., & Gentile, C. G. (1987). Neurobiological bases of conditioned bradycardia in rabbits. In I. Gormezano, W. F. Prokasy, & R. F. Thompson (Eds.), *Classical conditioning* (3rd ed.). Hillsdale, NJ: Erlbaum.

Schneirla, T. C. (1933). Some important features of ant learning. *Zeitschrift für Vergleichenden Physiologie, 19*, 439–452.

Schoener, T. W. (1971). Theory of feeding strategies. *Annual Review of Ecology and Systematics, 2*, 27–39.

Schoenfeld, W. N. (1950). An experimental approach to anxiety, escape, and avoidance behavior. In P. H. Hoch & J. Zubin (Eds.), *Anxiety*. New York: Grune and Stratton.

Schrier, A. M., & Brady, P. M. (1987). Categorization of natural stimuli by monkeys (*Macaca mulatta*): Effects of stimulus set size and modification of exemplars. *Journal of Experimental Psychology: Animal Behavior Processes, 13*, 136–143.

Schull, J. (1979). A conditioned opponent theory of Pavlovian conditioning and habituation. In G. H. Bower (Ed.), *The psychology of learning and motivation* (Vol. 13). New York: Academic Press.

Schuster, R., & Rachlin, H. (1968). Indifference between punishment and free shock: Evidence for the negative law of effect. *Journal of the Experimental Analysis of Behavior, 11*, 777–786.

Schusterman, R. J., & Krieger, K. (1984). California sea lions are capable of semantic comprehension. *Psychological Record, 34*, 3–23.

Schwartz, M. S. (1995). *Biofeedback: A practitioner's guide* (2nd edition). New York: Guilford Press.

Schwartz, S. P., Taylor, A. E., Scharff, L., & Blanchard, E. B. (1990). Behaviorally treated irritable bowel syndrome patients: A four-year follow-up. *Behavioral Research and Therapy, 28*, 331–335.

Schweitzer, J. B., & Sulzer-Azaroff, B. (1988). Self-control: Teaching tolerance for delay in impulsive children. *Journal of the Experimental Analysis of Behavior, 50*, 173–186.

Sears, R. R., Maccoby, E. E., & Levin, H. (1957). *Patterns of child rearing*. New York: Harper.

Seligman, M. E. P. (1970). On the generality of the laws of learning. *Psychological Review, 77*, 406–418.

Seligman, M. E. P. (1975). *Helplessness: On depression, development, and death*. San Francisco: W. H. Freeman & Company Publishers.

Seligman, M. E. P., & Campbell, B. A. (1965). Effects of intensity and duration of punishment on extinction of an avoidance response. *Journal of Comparative and Physiological Psychology, 59*, 295–297.

Seligman, M. E. P., & Hager, J. L. (1972). *Biological boundaries of learning*. New York: Appleton-Century-Crofts.

Seligman, M. E. P., & Johnston, J. C. (1973). A cognitive theory of avoidance learning. In F. J. McGuigan and D. B. Lumsden (Eds.), *Contemporary approaches to conditioning and learning*. Washington, DC: Winston-Wiley.

Shaffer, L. H. (1978). Timing in the motor programming of typing. *Quarterly Journal of Experimental Psychology, 30*, 333–345.

Shah, K., Bradshaw, C. M., & Szabadi, E. (1989). Performance of humans in concurrent variable-ratio variable-ratio schedules of monetary reinforcement. *Psychological Reports, 65,* 515–520.

Shapiro, D. C., & Schmidt, R. A. (1982). The schema theory: Recent evidence and developmental implications. In J. A. S. Kelso and J. E. Clark (Eds.), *The development of movement control and coordination.* New York: John Wiley.

Shea, C. H., Wright, D. L., Wulf, G., & Whitacre, C. (2000). Physical and observational practice afford unique learning opportunities. *Journal of Motor Behavior, 32,* 27–36.

Shea, C. H., Wulf, G., & Whitacre, C. (1999). Enhancing training efficiency and effectiveness through the use of dyad training. *Journal of Motor Behavior, 31,* 119–125.

Sheffield, F. D. (1948). Avoidance training and the contiguity principle. *Journal of Comparative and Physiological Psychology, 41,* 165–177.

Sheffield, F. D., Wulff, J. J., & Backer, R. (1951). Reward value of copulation without sex drive reduction. *Journal of Comparative and Physiological Psychology, 44,* 3–8.

Shepard, R. N. (1967). Recognition memory for words, sentences, and pictures. *Journal of Verbal Learning and Verbal Behavior, 6,* 156–163.

Sherman, R. A. (1991). Aversives, fundamental rights, and the courts. *The Behavior Analyst, 14,* 197–206.

Sherry, D. (1984). Food storage by black-capped chickadees: Memory for the location and contents of caches. *Animal Behaviour, 32,* 451–464.

Shettleworth, S. J. (1983). Function and mechanism in learning. In M. D. Zeiler & P. Harzem (Eds.), *Advances in analysis of behavior:* (Vol. 3). *Biological factors in learning.* New York: John Wiley.

Shettleworth, S. J., & Krebs, J. R. (1982). How marsh tits find their hoards: The role of site preference and spatial memory. *Journal of Experimental Psychology: Animal Behavior Processes, 8,* 354–375.

Shettleworth, S. J., & Krebs, J. R. (1986). Stored and encountered seeds: A comparison of two spatial memory tasks in marsh tits and chickadees. *Journal of Experimental Psychology: Animal Behavior Processes, 12,* 248–257.

Shimp, C. P. (1966). Probabilistically reinforced choice behavior in pigeons. *Journal of the Experimental Analysis of Behavior, 9,* 443–455.

Shimp, C. P. (1968). Magnitude and frequency of reinforcement and frequencies of interresponse times. *Journal of the Experimental Analysis of Behavior, 11,* 525–535.

Shimp, C. P. (1969). Optimal behavior in free-operant experiments. *Psychological Review, 76,* 97–112.

Shimp, C. P. (1973). Synthetic variable-interval schedules of reinforcement. *Journal of the Experimental Analysis of Behavior, 19,* 311–330.

Sidman, M. (1953). Two temporal parameters of the maintenance of avoidance behavior by the white rat. *Journal of Comparative and Physiological Psychology, 46,* 253–261.

Sidman, M., Rauzin, R., Lazar, R., Cunningham, S., Tailby, W., & Carrigan, P. (1982). A search for symmetry in the conditional discriminations of rhesus monkeys, baboons and children. *Journal of the Experimental Analysis of Behavior, 43,* 21–42.

Sidman, M., & Tailby, W. (1982). Conditional discrimination versus matching to sample: An extension of the testing paradigm. *Journal of the Experimental Analysis of Behavior, 37,* 5–22.

Siegel, S. (1975). Evidence from rats that morphine tolerance is a learned response. *Journal of Comparative and Physiological Psychology, 89,* 498–506.

Siegel, S. (1982). Pharmacological habituation and learning. In M. L. Commons, R. J. Herrnstein, & A. R. Wagner (Eds.), *Quantitative analyses of behavior:* (Vol. 3). *Acquisition.* Cambridge, MA: Ballinger.

Siegel, S. (1999). Drug anticipation and drug addiction: The 1998 H. David Archibald lecture. *Addiction, 94,* 1113–1124.

Siegel, S., & Domjan, M. (1971). Backward conditioning as an inhibitory procedure. *Learning and Motivation, 2,* 1–11.

Siegel, S., Hinson, R. E., Krank, M. D., & McCully, J. (1982). Heroin "overdose" death: The contribution of drug-associated environmental cues. *Science, 216,* 436–437.

Siegel S., Sherman, J. E., & Mitchell, D. (1980). Extinction of morphine analgesic tolerance. *Learning and Motivation, 11,* 289–301.

Silberberg, A., Bauman, R., & Hursh, S. (1993). Stock optimizing: Maximizing reinforcers per session on a variable-interval schedule. *Journal of the Experimental Analysis of Behavior, 59,* 389–399.

Silberberg, A., Hamilton, B., Ziriax, J. M., & Casey, J. (1978). The structure of choice. *Journal of Experimental Psychology: Animal Behavior Processes, 4,* 368–398.

Silberberg, A., Thomas, J. R., & Berendzen, N. (1991). Human choice on concurrent variable-interval, variable-ratio schedules. *Journal of the Experimental Analysis of Behavior, 56,* 575–584.

Silberberg, A., Warren-Boulton, F. R., & Asano, T. (1988). Maximizing present value: A model to explain why moderate response rates obtain on variable-interval schedules. *Journal of the Experimental Analysis of Behavior, 49*, 331–338.

Silva, K. M., & Timberlake, W. (1997). A behavior systems view of conditioned states during long and short CS-US intervals. *Learning and Motivation, 28*, 465–490.

Silva, K. M., & Timberlake, W. (2000). A clarification of the nature of backward excitatory conditioning. *Learning and Motivation, 31*, 67–80.

Silverman, I. W., & Ragusa, D. M. (1990). Child and maternal correlates of impulse control in 24-month-old children. *Genetic, Social, and General Psychology Monographs, 116*, 435–473.

Sisson, L. A., Hersen, M., & Van Hasselt, V. B. (1993). Improving the performance of youth with dual sensory impairment: Analyses and social validation of procedures to reduce maladaptive responding in vocational and leisure settings. *Behavior Therapy, 24*, 553–571.

Siuciak, J. A., Lewis, D. R., Wiegand, S. J., & Lindsay, R. M. (1997). Antidepressant-like effect of brain-derived neurotrophic factor (BDNF). *Pharmacology, Biochemistry, and Behavior, 56*, 131-137.

Skinner, B. F. (1935). The generic nature of the concepts of stimulus and response. *Journal of General Psychology, 12*, 40–65.

Skinner, B. F. (1938). *The behavior of organisms.* New York: Appleton-Century-Crofts.

Skinner, B. F. (1948). "Superstition" in the pigeon. *Journal of Experimental Psychology, 38*, 168–172.

Skinner, B. F. (1950). Are theories of learning necessary? *Psychological Review, 57*, 193–216.

Skinner, B. F. (1953). *Science and human behavior.* New York: Macmillan.

Skinner, B. F. (1956a). What is psychotic behavior? In F. Gildea (Ed.), *Theory and treatment of the psychoses: Some newer aspects.* St. Louis, MO: Washington University Press.

Skinner, B. F. (1956b). A case history in scientific method. *American Psychologist, 11*, 221–233.

Skinner, B. F. (1966). The phylogeny and ontogeny of behavior. *Science, 11*, 159–166.

Skinner, B. F. (1969). *Contingencies of reinforcement: A theoretical analysis.* Englewood Cliffs, NJ: Prentice Hall.

Skinner, B. F. (1977). Herrnstein and the evolution of behaviorism. *American Psychologist, 32*, 1006–1012.

Skinner, B. F. (1985). Cognitive science and behaviourism. *British Journal of Psychology, 76*, 291–301.

Smith, E. E. (2000). Neural bases of human working memory. *Current Directions in Psychological Science, 9*, 45–49.

Smith, J. E., & Levis, D. J. (1991). Is fear present following sustained asymptotic avoidance responding? *Behavioural Processes, 24*, 37–47.

Smith, J. W., & Frawley, P. J. (1990). Long-term abstinence from alcohol in patients receiving aversion therapy as part of a multimodal inpatient program. *Journal of Substance Abuse Treatment, 7*, 77–82.

Smith, K. (1954). Conditioning as an artifact. *Psychological Review, 61*, 217–225.

Smith, K. U. (1962). *Delayed sensory feedback and behavior.* Philadelphia: Saunders.

Smith, M. C., & Gormezano, I. (1965). Conditioning of the nictitating membrane response of the rabbit as a function of backward, simultaneous and forward CS–UCS intervals. Paper presented at the meeting of the Psychonomic Society, Chicago.

Smith, O. A., Astley, C. A., DeVito, J. L., Stein, J. M., & Walsh, K. E. (1980). Functional analysis of hypothalamic control of the cardiovascular responses accompanying emotional behavior. *Federation Proceedings, 39*, 2487–2494.

Smith, R. G., Russo, L., & Le, D. D. (1999). Distinguishing between extinction and punishment effects of response blocking: A replication. *Journal of Applied Behavior Analysis, 32*, 367-370.

Solomon, K. (1990). Learned helplessness in the elderly: Theoretic and clinical considerations. *Occupational Therapy in Mental Health, 10*, 31–51.

Solomon, P. R. (1977). Role of the hippocampus in blocking and conditioned inhibition of the rabbit's nictitating membrane response. *Journal of Comparative and Physiological Psychology, 91*, 407–417.

Solomon, P. R., Blanchard, S., Levine, E., Velazquez, E., & Groccia-Ellison, M. (1991). Attenuation of age-related conditioning deficits in humans by extension of the interstimulus interval. *Psychology and Aging, 6*, 36–42.

Solomon, R. L. (1980). The opponent process theory of acquired motivation. *American Psychologist, 35*, 691–712.

Solomon, R. L., & Corbit, J. D. (1974). An opponent-process theory of motivation: I. Temporal dynamics of affect. *Psychological Review, 81*, 119–145.

Solomon, R. L., Kamin, L. J., & Wynne, L. C. (1953). Traumatic avoidance learning: The outcomes of several extinction procedures with dogs. *Journal of Abnormal and Social Psychology*, *48*, 291–302.

Solomon, R. L., & Wynne, L. C. (1953). Traumatic avoidance learning: Acquisition in normal dogs. *Psychological Monographs*, *67*, 354.

Solomon, R. L., & Wynne, L. C. (1954). Traumatic avoidance learning: The principles of anxiety conservation and partial irreversibility. *Psychological Review*, *61*, 353–385.

Soltysik, S. (1960). Studies on the avoidance conditioning: II. Differentiation and extinction of avoidance responses. *Acta Biologiae Experimentalis*, *20*, 171–182.

Solvason, H. B., Ghanata, V., & Hiramoto, R. H. (1988). Conditioned augmentation of natural killer cell activity: Independence from nociceptive effects and dependence on interferon-B. *Journal of Immunology*, *140*, 661–665.

Sparrow, W. A., & Summers, J. J. (1992). Performance on trials without knowledge of results (KR) in reduced relative frequency presentations of KR. *Journal of Motor Behavior*, *24*, 197–209.

Spear, N. E. (1971). Forgetting as retrieval failure. In W. K. Honig & P. H. R. James (Eds.), *Animal memory*. New York: Academic Press.

Spence, K. W. (1937). The differential response in animals to stimuli varying within a single dimension. *Psychological Review*, *44*, 430–444.

Spetch, M. L. (1995). Overshadowing in landmark learning: Touch-screen studies with pigeons and humans. *Journal of Experimental Psychology: Animal Behavior Processes*, *21*, 166–181.

Spetch, M. L., & Cheng, K. (1998). A step function in pigeons' temporal generalization in the peak shift task. *Animal Learning and Behavior*, *26*, 103–118.

Spinelli, D. H., Jensen, F. E., & DiPrisco, G. V. (1980). Early experience effect on dendritic branching in normally reared kittens. *Experimental Neurology*, *62*, 1–11.

Staddon, J. E. R., & Simmelhag, V. L. (1971). The "superstition" experiment: A reexamination of its implications for the principles of adaptive behavior. *Psychological Review*, *78*, 3–43.

Starr, M. D., & Mineka, S. (1977). Determinants of fear over the cause of avoidance learning. *Learning and Motivation*, *8*, 332–350.

Stasiewicz, P. R., & Maisto, S. A. (1993). Two-factor theory: The role of negative affect in the maintenance of substance use and substance use disorder. *Behavior Therapy*, *24*, 337–356.

Staub, E. (1968). Duration of stimulus-exposure as determinant of the efficacy of flooding procedures in the elimination of fear. *Behavior Research and Therapy*, *6*, 131–132.

Stefan, K., Kunesch, E., Cohen, L. G., Benecke, R., & Classen, J. (2000). Induction of plasticity in the human motor cortex by paired associative stimulation. *Brain*, *123*, 572–584.

Steinmetz, J. E. (1999). A renewed interest in human classical eyeblink conditioning. *Psychological Science*, *10*, 24–25.

Stempowski, N. K., Carman, H. M., & Fountain, S. B. (1999). Temporal phrasing and overshadowing in rat serial-pattern learning. *Learning and Motivation*, *30*, 74–100.

Stuart, R. B. (1967). Behavioral control over eating. *Behavior Research and Therapy*, *5*, 357–365.

Stuart, R. B. (1971). A three-dimensional program for the treatment of obesity. *Behaviour Research and Therapy*, *9*, 177–186.

Stubbs, A. (1968). The discrimination of stimulus duration by pigeons. *Journal of the Experimental Analysis of Behavior*, *11*, 223–238.

Sturges, J. W., & Sturges, L. V. (1998). In vivo systematic desensitization in a single-session treatment of an 11-year-old girl's elevator phobia. *Child & Family Behavior Therapy*, *20*, 55–62.

Sulzer-Azaroff, B., Loafman, B., Merante, R. J., & Hlavacek, A. C. (1990). Improving occupational safety in a large industrial plant: A systematic replication. *Journal of Organizational Behavior Management*, *11*, 99–120.

Summers, J. J. (1981). Motor programs. In D. Holding (Ed.), *Human skills*. New York: John Wiley.

Swain, J. C., & McLaughlin, T. F. (1998). The effects of bonus contingencies in a classwide token program on math accuracy with middle-school students with behavioral disorders. *Behavioral Interventions*, *13*, 11–19.

Swan, J. A., & Pearce, J. M. (1987). The influence of predictive accuracy on serial autoshaping: Evidence of orienting responses. *Journal of Experimental Psychology: Animal Behavior Processes*, *13*, 407–417.

Swinnen, S. P. (1990). Interpolated activities during the knowledge-of-results delay and post-knowledge-of-results interval: Effects on performance and learning. *Journal of Experimental Psychology: Learning, Memory, and Cognition*, *16*, 692–705.

Swinnen, S. P., Schmidt, R. A., Nicholson, D. E., & Shapiro, D. C. (1990). Information feedback for skill acquisition: Instantaneous knowledge of results degrades learning. *Journal of Experimental Psychology: Learning, Memory, and Cognition, 16,* 706–716.

Tait, R. W., & Saladin, M. E. (1986). Concurrent development of excitatory and inhibitory associations during backward conditioning. *Animal Learning and Behavior, 14,* 133–137.

Taub, E., & Berman, A. J. (1968). Movement and learning in the absence of sensory feedback. In S. J. Freedman (Ed.), *The neuro-psychology of spatially oriented behavior.* Homewood, IL: Dorsey Press.

Taylor, B. A., & Harris, S. L. (1995). Teaching children with autism to seek information: Acquisition of novel information and generalization of responding. *Journal of Applied Behavior Analysis, 28,* 3–14.

Taylor, I., & O'Reilly, M. F. (2000). Generalization of supermarket shopping skills for individuals with mild intellectual disabilities using stimulus equivalence training. *Psychological Record, 50,* 49–62.

Terhune, J. G., & Premack, D. (1970). On the proportionality between the probability of not-running and the punishment effect of being forced to run. *Learning and Motivation, 1,* 141–147.

Terrace, H. S. (1963). Errorless transfer of a discrimination across two continua. *Journal of the Experimental Analysis of Behavior, 6,* 223–232.

Terrace, H. S. (1966). Stimulus control. In W. K. Honig (Ed.), *Operant conditioning: Areas of research and application.* Englewood Cliffs, NJ: Prentice Hall.

Terrace, H. S. (1972). By-products of discrimination learning. In G. H. Bower (Ed.), *The psychology of learning and motivation* (Vol. 5). New York: Academic Press.

Terrace, H. S. (1979). *Nim.* New York: Knopf.

Terrace, H. S. (1985). On the nature of animal thinking. *Neuroscience & Biobehavioral Reviews, 9,* 643–652.

Terrace, H. S. (1991). Chunking during serial learning by a pigeon: I. Basic evidence. *Journal of Experimental Psychology: Animal Behavior Processes, 17,* 81–93.

Terrace, H. S., & Chen, S. (1991). Chunking during serial learning by a pigeon: II. Integrity of a chunk on a new list. *Journal of Experimental Psychology: Animal Behavior Processes, 17,* 94–106.

Terrace, H. S., Petitto, L. A., Sanders, R. J., & Bever, T. G. (1979). Can an ape create a sentence? *Science, 206,* 891–902.

Terry, W. S., & Wagner, A. R. (1975). Short-term memory for "surprising" versus "expected" unconditioned stimuli in Pavlovian conditioning. *Journal of Experimental Psychology: Animal Behavior Processes, 1,* 122–133.

Thomas, D. R. (1981). Studies of long-term memory in the pigeon. In N. E. Spear & R. R. Miller (Eds.), *Information processing in animals: Memory mechanisms.* Hillsdale, NJ: Erlbaum.

Thomas, D. R. (1993). A model for adaptation-level effects on stimulus generalization. *Psychological Review, 100,* 658–673.

Thomas, D. R., & Lopez, L. J. (1962). The effect of delayed testing on generalization slope. *Journal of Comparative and Physiological Psychology, 44,* 541–544.

Thomas, D. R., Mood, K., Morrison, S., & Wiertelak, E. (1991). Peak shift revisited: A test of alternative interpretations. *Journal of Experimental Psychology: Animal Behavior Processes, 17,* 130–140.

Thompson, R. F. (1986). The neurobiology of learning and memory. *Science, 233,* 941–947.

Thompson, R. F. (1991). Are memory traces localized or distributed? *Neuropsychologia, 29,* 571–582.

Thompson, R. F., Donegan, N. H., & Lavond, D. G. (1988). The psychobiology of learning and memory. In R. C. Atkinson, R. J. Herrnstein, G. Lindzey, & R. D. Luce, (Eds.), *Stevens' handbook of experimental psychology* (2nd ed.): (Vol. 2). *Learning and cognition.* New York: John Wiley.

Thompson, R. F., & Krupa, D. J. (1994). Organization of memory traces in the mammalian brain. *Annual Review of Neuroscience, 17,* 519–549.

Thompson, R. F., McCormick, D. A., & Lavond, D. G. (1986). Localization of the essential memory-trace system for a basic form of associative learning in the mammalian brain. In S. H. Hulse & B. F. Green, Jr., (Eds.), *One hundred years of psychological research in America.* Baltimore: Johns Hopkins University Press.

Thompson, R. F., & Spencer, W. A. (1966). Habituation: A model phenomenon for the study of neuronal substrates of behavior. *Psychological Review, 73,* 16–43.

Thompson, R. K. R., Oden, D. L., & Boysen, S. T. (1997). Language-naive chimpanzees (*Pan torglodytes*) judge relations between relations in a conceptual matching-to-sample task. *Journal of Experimental Psychology: Animal Behavior Processes, 23,* 31–43.

Thorndike, E. L. (1898). Animal intelligence: An experimental study of the associative processes in animals. *Psychological Review Monograph Supplement, 2,* 8.

Thorndike, E. L. (1911). *Animal intelligence.* New York: Macmillan.

Thorndike, E. L. (1927). The law of effect. *American Journal of Psychology, 39,* 212–222.

Thorndike, E. L. (1946). Expectation. *Psychological Review, 53,* 277–281.

Thorne, B. M., & Giesen, J. M. (2000). *Statistics for the behavioral sciences* (3rd edition). Mountain View, CA: Mayfield Publishing.

Thorpe, W. H. (1963). *Learning and instinct in animals* (2nd ed.). London: Methuen.

Thurstone, L. L. (1919). The learning curve equation. *Psychological Monographs, 26,* 114.

Timberlake, W. (1983). Rats' responses to a moving object related to food or water: A behavior-systems analysis. *Animal Learning and Behavior, 11,* 309–320.

Timberlake, W. (1993). Behavior systems and reinforcement: An integrative approach. *Journal of the Experimental Analysis of Behavior, 60,* 105–128.

Timberlake, W., & Allison, J. (1974). Response deprivation: An empirical approach to instrumental performance. *Psychological Review, 81,* 146–164.

Timberlake, W., & Farmer-Dougan, V. A. (1991). Reinforcement in applied settings: Figuring out ahead of time what will work. *Psychological Bulletin, 110,* 379–391.

Timberlake, W., & Grant, D. L. (1975). Autoshaping in rats to the presentation of another rat predicting food. *Science, 190,* 690–692.

Timberlake, W., & Lucas, G. A. (1985). The basis of superstitious behavior: Chance contingency, stimulus substitution, or appetitive behavior. *Journal of the Experimental Analysis of Behavior, 44,* 279–299.

Timberlake, W., & Lucas, G. A. (1989). Behavior systems and learning: From misbehavior to general principles. In S. B. Klein & R. R. Mowrer (Eds.), *Contemporary learning theories: Instrumental conditioning theories and the impact of biological constraints on learning.* Hillsdale, NJ: Erlbaum.

Timmann, D., and others. (1998). Involvement of the human cerebellum during habituation of the acoustic startle response: A PET study. *Journal of Neurology, Neurosurgery & Psychiatry, 65,* 771–773.

Tinbergen, N. (1951). *The study of instinct.* Oxford: Oxford University Press.

Tinbergen, N., & Perdeck, A. C. (1950). On the stimulus situation releasing the begging response in the newly hatched herring gull chick (*Larus argentatus argentatus Pont*). *Behaviour, 3,* 1–39.

Tinklepaugh, O. L. (1928). An experimental study of representative factors in monkeys. *Journal of Comparative Psychology, 8,* 197–236.

Todrank, J., Byrnes, D., Wrzesniewski, A., & Rozin, P. (1995). Odors can change preferences for people in photographs: A cross-modal evaluative conditioning study with olfactory USs and visual CSs. *Learning and Motivation, 26,* 116–140.

Tolman, E. C. (1932). *Purposive behavior in animals and men.* New York: Appleton-Century-Crofts.

Tolman, E. C. (1951). *Collected papers in psychology.* Berkeley: University of California Press.

Tolman, E. C. (1959). Principles of purposive behavior. In S. Koch (Ed.), *Psychology: A study of a science* (Vol. 2). New York: McGraw-Hill.

Tolman, E. C., & Honzik, C. H. (1930). Introduction and removal of reward, and maze performance in rats. *University of California Publications in Psychology, 4,* 257–275.

Tomie, A., Brooks, W., & Zito, B. (1989). Sign-tracking: The search for reward. In S. B. Klein & R. R. Mowrer (Eds.), *Contemporary learning theories: Pavlovian conditioning and the status of traditional learning theory.* Hillsdale, NJ: Erlbaum.

Towe, A. L. (1954). A study of figural equivalence in the pigeon. *Journal of Comparative and Physiological Psychology, 47,* 283–287.

Tracy, W. K. (1970). Wavelength generalization and preference in monochromatically reared ducklings. *Journal of the Experimental Analysis of Behavior, 13,* 163–178.

Trapold, M. A., & Spence, K. W. (1960). Performance changes in eyelid conditioning as related to the motivational and reinforcing properties of the UCS. *Journal of Experimental Psychology, 59,* 209–213.

Trinkaus, J. W., & Booke, A. L. (1982). Biorhythms: Another look. *Psychological Reports, 50,* 396–398.

Trowbridge, M. H., & Cason, H. (1932). An experimental test of Thorndike's theory of learning. *Journal of General Psychology, 7,* 245–260.

Turner, E. R. A. (1964). Social feeding in birds. *Behaviour, 24,* 1–46.

Turney, T. H. (1982). The association of visual concepts and imitative vocalization in the mynah (*Gracula religiosa*). *Bulletin of the Psychonomic Society, 19,* 59–62.

Tzetzis, G., Kioumourtzoglou, E., & Mavromatis, G. (1997). Goal setting and feedback for the development of instructional strategies. *Perceptual and Motor Skills, 84,* 1411–1427.

Ulrich, R., Giray, M., & Schaffer, R. (1990). Is it possible to prepare the second component of a movement before the first one? *Journal of Motor Behavior, 22,* 125–148.

Ulrich, R. E., & Azrin, N. H. (1962). Reflexive fighting in response to aversive stimulation. *Journal of the Experimental Analysis of Behavior, 5,* 511–520.

Urcuioli, P. J., & Zentall, T. R. (1986). Retrospective coding in pigeons' delayed matching-to-sample. *Journal of Experimental Psychology: Animal Behavior Processes, 12,* 69–77.

Urcuioli, P. J., & Zentall, T. R. (1992). Transfer across delayed discriminations: Evidence regarding the nature of prospective working memory. *Journal of Experimental Psychology: Animal Behavior Processes, 18,* 154–173.

Usherwood, P. N. R. (1993). 'Memories are made of this.' *Trends in Neuroscience, 16,* 427–429.

Vander Wall, S. B. (1982). An experimental analysis of cache recovery by Clark's nutcracker. *Animal Behaviour, 30,* 84–94.

Vauclair, J. (1996). *Animal cognition: An introduction to modern comparative psychology.* Cambridge, MA: Harvard University Press.

Vaughan, W. (1981). Melioration, matching, and maximization. *Journal of the Experimental Analysis of Behavior, 36,* 141–149.

Vaughan, W. (1985). Choice: A local analysis. *Journal of the Experimental Analysis of Behavior, 43,* 383–405.

Vaughan, W. (1987). Dissociation of value and response strength. *Journal of the Experimental Analysis of Behavior, 48,* 367–381.

Vaughan, W. (1988). Formation of equivalence sets in pigeons. *Journal of Experimental Psychology: Animal Behavior Processes, 14,* 36–42.

Vaughan, W., & Greene, S. L. (1983). Acquisition of absolute discriminations in pigeons. In M. L. Commons, A. R. Wagner, & R. J. Herrnstein (Eds.), *Quantitative analyses of behavior:* (Vol. 4). *Discrimination processes.* Cambridge, MA: Ballinger.

Vaughan, W., & Greene, S. L. (1984). Pigeon visual memory capacity. *Journal of Experimental Psychology: Animal Behavior Processes, 10,* 256–271.

Vaughan, W., & Miller, H. L. (1984). Optimization versus response-strength accounts of behavior. *Journal of the Experimental Analysis of Behavior, 42,* 337–348.

Verwey, W. B., & Dronkert, Y. (1996). Practicing a structured continuous key-pressing task: Motor chunking or rhythm consolidation? *Journal of Motor Behavior, 28,* 71–79.

Vienero, V., & Lagerspetz, K. (1984). The relation of parent background and TV-viewing habits to child aggression in six different countries. *Psykologia (Finland), 19,* 414–419.

Voegtlin, W. L. (1940). The treatment of alcoholism by establishing a conditioned reflex. *American Journal of Medical Science, 199,* 802–810.

Vogel, W., Young, M., & Primack, W. (1996). A survey of physician use of treatment methods for functional enuresis. *Journal of Developmental & Behavioral Pediatrics, 17,* 90–93.

Volpicelli, J. R., Ulm, R. R., & Altenor, A. (1984). Feedback during exposure to inescapable shocks and subsequent shock-escape performance. *Learning and Motivation, 15,* 279–286.

von Fersen, L., Wynne, C. D., Delius, J. D., & Staddon, J. E. R. (1991). Transitive inference formation in pigeons. *Journal of Experimental Psychology: Animal Behavior Processes, 17,* 334–341.

von Holst, E. (1935). Über den Lichtruckenreflex bei Fischen. *Publicazioni della Stazione zoologica di Napoli, 15,* 143–158.

Vuchinich, R. E. (1999). Behavioral economics as a framework for organizing the expanded range of substance abuse interventions. In J. A. Tucker, D. M. Donovan, & G. A. Marlatt (Eds.), *Changing addictive behavior: Bridging clinical and public health strategies.* New York: Guilford Press.

Vyse, S. A., & Belke, T. W. (1992). Maximizing versus matching on concurrent variable-interval schedules. *Journal of the Experimental Analysis of Behavior, 58,* 325–334.

Wagner, A. R. (1978). Expectancies and the priming of STM. In S. H. Hulse, H. Fowler, & W. K. Honig (Eds.), *Cognitive aspects of animal behavior.* Hillsdale, NJ: Erlbaum.

Wagner, A. R. (1981). SOP: A model of automatic memory processing in animal behavior. In N. E. Spear & R. R. Miller (Eds.), *Information processing in animals: Memory mechanisms.* Hillsdale, NJ: Erlbaum.

Wagner, A. R., & Brandon, S. E. (1989). Evolution of a structured connectionist model of

Pavlovian conditioning (AESOP). In S. B. Klein and R. R. Mowrer (Eds.), *Contemporary learning theories: Pavlovian conditioning and the status of traditional learning theory.* Hillsdale, NJ: Erlbaum.

Wagner, A. R., & Donegan, N. H. (1989). Some relationships between a computational model (SOP) and a neural circuit for Pavlovian (rabbit eyeblink) conditioning. In R. D. Hawkins & G. H. Bower (Eds.), *The psychology of learning and motivation*: (Vol. 22). *Computational models of learning in simple neural systems.* Orlando, FL: Academic Press.

Wagner, A. R., & Larew, M. B. (1985). Opponent processes and Pavlovian inhibition. In R. R. Miller & N. E. Spear (Eds.), *Information processing in animals: Conditioned inhibition.* Hillsdale, NJ: Erlbaum.

Wagner, A. R., Rudy, J. W., & Whitlow, J. W. (1973). Rehearsal in animal conditioning. *Journal of Experimental Psychology, 97,* 407–426.

Wagner, G. A., & Morris, E. K. (1987). "Superstitious" behavior in children. *Psychological Record, 37,* 471–488.

Wallin, J. A., & Johnson, R. D. (1976). The positive reinforcement approach to controlling employee absenteeism. *Personnel Journal, 55,* 390–392.

Walters, R. H., Leat, M., & Mezei, L. (1963). Inhibition and disinhibition of responses through empathetic learning. *Canadian Journal of Psychology, 17,* 235–243.

Walton, D. (1960). The application of learning theory to the treatment of a case of neurodermatitis. In H. J. Eysenck (Ed.), *Behavior therapy and the neuroses.* Oxford: Pergamon Press.

Wanchisen, B. A., Tatham, T. A., & Mooney, S. E. (1989). Variable-ratio conditioning history produces high-and low-rate fixed-interval performance in rats. *Journal of the Experimental Analysis of Behavior, 52,* 167–179.

Warden, C. J., Fjeld, H. A., & Koch, A. M. (1940). Imitative behavior in cebus and rhesus monkeys. *Journal of Genetic Psychology, 56,* 311–322.

Warren, J. M. (1965). Primate learning in comparative perspective. In A. M. Schrier, H. F. Harlow, & F. Stollnitz (Eds.), *Behavior of nonhuman primates* (Vol. 1). New York: Academic Press.

Wasserman, E. A. (1973). Pavlovian conditioning with heat reinforcement produces stimulus-directed pecking in chicks. *Science, 81,* 875–877.

Watanabe, S., Sakamoto, J., & Wakita, M. (1995). Pigeons' discrimination of paintings by Monet and Picasso. *Journal of the Experimental Analysis of Behavior, 63,* 165–174.

Watson, D. L., & Tharp, R. G. (1985). *Self-directed behavior: Self–modification for personal adjustment* (4th ed.). Monterey, CA: Brooks/Cole.

Watson, J. B. (1919). *Psychology from the standpoint of a behaviorist.* Philadelphia: Lippincott.

Watson, J. B., & Rayner, R. (1921). Studies in infant psychology. *Scientific Monthly, 13,* 493–515.

Watson, T. S. (1993). Effectiveness of arousal and arousal plus overcorrection to reduce nocturnal bruxism. *Journal of Behavior Therapy and Experimental Psychiatry, 24,* 181–185.

Watson, T. S., Ray, K. P., Turner, H. S., & Logan, P. (1999). Teacher-implemented functional analysis and treatment: A method for linking assessment to intervention. *School Psychology Review, 28,* 292–302.

Wearden, J. H. (1988). Some neglected problems in the analysis of human behavior. In G. Davey & C. Cullen (Eds.), *Human operant conditioning and behavior modification.* Chichester, UK: John Wiley.

Weaver, M. T., & McGrady, A. (1995). A provisional model to predict blood pressure response to biofeedback-assisted relaxation. *Biofeedback and Self-Regulation, 20,* 229–239.

Wegner, D. M. (1997). When the antidote is the poison: Ironic mental control processes. *Psychological Science, 8,* 148–150.

Wegner, D. M., Ansfield, M., & Pilloff, D. (1998). The putt and the pendulum: Ironic effects of the mental control of action. *Psychological Science, 9,* 196–199.

Weiner, H. (1964). Conditioning history and human fixed-interval performance. *Journal of the Experimental Analysis of Behavior, 7,* 383–385.

Weisberg, P., Stout, R., & Hendler, M. (1986). Training and generalization of a "yes-no" discrimination with a developmentally delayed child. *Child and Family Behavior Therapy, 8,* 49–64.

Weisman, R. G., & Litner, J. S. (1969). Positive conditioned reinforcement of Sidman avoidance in rats. *Journal of Comparative and Physiological Psychology, 68,* 597–603.

Werner, G. A. (1992). Employee recognition: A procedure to reinforce work attendance. *Behavioral Residential Treatment, 7,* 199–204.

Werner, G. E., & Hall, D. J. (1974). Optimal foraging and size selection of prey by the bluegill sunfish (*Lepomis macrochirus*). *Ecology, 55*, 1042–1052.

Whitacre, C. A., & Shea, C. H. (2000). Performance and learning of generalized motor programs: Relative (GMP) and absolute (parameter) errors. *Journal of Motor Behavior, 32*, 163–175.

White, A. G., & Bailey, J. S. (1990). Reducing disruptive behaviors of elementary physical education students with Sit and Wait. *Journal of Applied Behavior Analysis, 23*, 353–359.

White, K., & Davey, G. C. L. (1989). Sensory preconditioning and UCS inflation in human "fear" conditioning. *Behaviour Research and Therapy, 27*, 161–166.

Whiten, A., & Ham, R. (1992). On the nature and evolution of imitation in the animal kingdom: Reappraisal of a century of research. In P. J. B. Slater, J. S. Rosenblatt, C. Beer, & M. Milinski (Eds.), *Advances in the study of behavior* (Vol. 21). New York: Academic Press.

Wickelgren, W. A. (1979). Chunking and consolidation: A theoretical synthesis of semantic networks, configuring in conditioning, S-R versus cognitive learning, normal forgetting, the amnesiac syndrome, and the hippocampal arousal system. *Psychological Review, 86*, 44–60.

Wilcoxon, H. C., Dragoin, W. B., & Kral, P. A. (1971). Illness-induced aversions in rat and quail: Relative salience of visual and gustatory cues. *Science, 171*, 826–828.

Wilkie, D. M. (1983). Pigeons' spatial memory: II. Acquisition of delayed matching of key location and transfer to new locations. *Journal of the Experimental Analysis of Behavior, 39*, 69–76.

Wilkie, D. M., & Slobin, P. (1983). Gerbils in space: Performance on the 17-arm radial maze. *Journal of the Experimental Analysis of Behavior, 40*, 301–312.

Williams, B. A. (1983). Another look at contrast in multiple schedules. *Journal of the Experimental Analysis of Behavior, 39*, 345–384.

Williams, B. A. (1991). Behavioral contrast and reinforcement value. *Animal Learning and Behavior, 19*, 337–344.

Williams, D. R., & Williams, H. (1969). Automaintenance in the pigeon: Sustained pecking despite contingent non-reinforcement. *Journal of the Experimental Analysis of Behavior, 12*, 511–520.

Williams, H., & Staples, K. (1992). Syllable chunking in zebra finch (*Taeniopygia guttata*) song. *Journal of Comparative Psychology, 106*, 278–286.

Williams, J. L., & Lierle, D. M. (1986). Effects of stress controllability, immunization, and therapy on the subsequent defeat of colony intruders. *Animal Learning and Behavior, 14*, 305–314.

Wilson, A., Brooks, D. C., & Bouton, M. E. (1995). The role of the rat hippocampal system in several effects of context in extinction. *Behavioral Neuroscience, 109*, 828–836.

Wilson, D. M. (1961). The central nervous control of flight in a locust. *Journal of Experimental Biology, 38*, 471–490.

Wilson, F. A., O'Scalaidhe, S. P., & Goldman-Rakic, P. S. (1993). Dissociation of object and spatial processing domains in primate prefrontal cortex. *Science, 260*, 1955–1958.

Windle, M. (2000). Parental, sibling, and peer influences on adolescent substance use and alcohol problems. *Applied Developmental Science, 4*, 98–110.

Wing, L. (1972). *Autistic children: A guide for parents and professionals*. New York: Brunner/Mazel.

Winnick, W. A., & Hunt, J. McV. (1951). The effect of an extra stimulus upon strength of response during acquisition and extinction. *Journal of Experimental Psychology, 41*, 205–215.

Winstein, C. J., & Schmidt, R. A. (1990). Reduced frequency of knowledge of results enhances motor skill learning. *Journal of Experimental Psychology: Learning, Memory, and Cognition, 16*, 677–691.

Winter, J., & Hunkin, N. M. (1999). Re-learning in Alzheimer's disease. *International Journal of Geriatric Psychiatry, 14*, 987–990.

Wolpe, J. (1958). *Psychotherapy by reciprocal inhibition*. Stanford, CA: Stanford University Press.

Wolpe, J., & Lazarus, A. A. (1966). *Behavior therapy techniques: A guide to the treatment of neurosis*. Oxford: Pergamon Press.

Woltersdorf, M. A. (1992). Videotape self-modeling in the treatment of attention-deficit hyperactivity disorder. *Child and Family Behavior Therapy, 14*, 53–73.

Wood, D.C. (1973). Stimulus specific habituation in a protozoan. *Physiology and Behavior, 11*, 349–354.

Wood, W., Wong, F. Y., & Chachere, G. (1991). Effects of media violence on viewers' aggression in unconstrained social interaction. *Psychological Bulletin, 109*, 371–383.

Woodruff-Pak, D. S. (1999). New directions for a classical paradigm: Human eyeblink conditioning. *Psychological Science, 10,* 1–3.

Wright, A. A. (1994). Primacy effects in animal memory and human nonverbal memory. *Animal Learning and Behavior, 22,* 219–223.

Wright, A. A., Santiago, H. C., Sands, S. F., Kendrick, D. F., & Cook, R. G. (1985). Memory processing of serial lists by pigeons, monkeys, and people. *Science, 229,* 287–289.

Wulf, G., & Schmidt, R. A. (1989). The learning of generalized motor programs: Reducing the relative frequency of knowledge of results enhances memory. *Journal of Experimental Psychology: Learning, Memory, and Cognition, 15,* 748–757.

Wynne, C. D. L. (1995). Reinforcement accounts for transitive inference performance. *Animal Learning and Behavior, 23,* 207–217.

Wyrwicka, W. (1978). Imitation of mother's inappropriate food preference in weanling kittens. *Pavlovian Journal of Biological Science, 13,* 55–72.

Yamadori, A., & Albert, M. L. (1973). Word category aphasia. *Cortex, 9,* 112–125.

Yamamoto, J., & Asano, T. (1995). Stimulus equivalence in a chimpanzee (*Pan troglodytes*). *Psychological Record, 45,* 3–21.

Yates, C. M. (1991). A response to nonaversive behavior management and "default" technologies. *The Behavior Analyst, 14,* 217–218.

Yell, M. L. (1994). Timeout and students with behavior disorders: A legal analysis. *Education and Treatment of Children, 17,* 293–301.

Yerkes, R. M., & Morgulis, S. (1909). The method of Pavlov in animal psychology. *Psychological Bulletin, 6,* 257–273.

Yin, H., Barnet, R. C., & Miller, R. R. (1994). Trial spacing and trial distribution effects in Pavlovian conditioning: Contributions of a comparator mechanism. *Journal of Experimental Psychology: Animal Behavior Processes, 20,* 123–134.

Yoshikubo, S. (1985). Species discrimination and concept formation by rhesus monkeys (*Macaca mulatta*). *Primates, 26,* 285–299.

Young, G. C., & Morgan, R. T. (1972). Overlearning in the conditioning treatment of enuresis: A long term follow-up study. *Behavior Research and Therapy, 10,* 419–420.

Yule, W., Sacks, B., & Hersov, L. (1974). Successful flooding treatment of a noise phobia in an eleven-year-old. *Journal of Behavior Therapy and Experimental Psychiatry, 5,* 209–211.

Zalstein-Orda, N., & Lubow, R. E. (1995). Context control of negative transfer induced by preexposure to irrelevant stimuli: Latent inhibition in humans. *Learning and Motivation, 26,* 11–28.

Zamble, E., Hadad, G. M., Mitchell, J. B., & Cutmore, T. R. H. (1985). Pavlovian conditioning of sexual arousal: First-and second-order effects. *Journal of Experimental Psychology: Animal Behavior Processes, 11,* 598–610.

Zeldin, R. K., & Olton, D. S. (1986). Rats acquire spatial learning sets. *Journal of Experimental Psychology: Animal Behavior Processes, 12,* 412–419.

Zellner, D. A. (1991). How foods get to be liked: Some general mechanisms and some special cases. In R. C. Bolles (Ed.), *The hedonics of taste.* Hillsdale, NJ: Erlbaum.

Zener, K. (1937). The significance of behavior accompanying conditioned salivary secretion for theories of the conditioned response. *American Journal of Psychology, 50,* 384–403.

Zentall, T. R. (1998). Symbolic representation in animals: Emergent stimulus relations in conditional discrimination learning. *Animal Learning and Behavior, 26,* 363–377.

Zentall, T. R., & Hogan, D. E. (1978). Same/different concept learning in the pigeon: The effect of negative instances and prior adaptation to the transfer stimuli. *Journal of the Experimental Analysis of Behavior, 30,* 177–186.

Zentall, T. R., Roper, K. L., & Sherburne, L. M. (1995). Most directed forgetting in pigeons can be attributed to the absence of reinforcement on forget trials during training or to other procedural artifacts. *Journal of the Experimental Analysis of Behavior, 36,* 127–137.

Zentall, T. R., & Sherburne, L. M. (1994). Transfer of value from S+ to S- in a simultaneous discrimination. *Journal of Experimental Psychology: Animal Behavior Processes, 20,* 176–183.

Zentall, T. R., Steirn, J. N., & Jackson-Smith, P. (1990). Memory strategies in pigeons' performance of a radial-arm-maze analog task. *Journal of Experimental Psychology: Animal Behavior Processes, 16,* 358–371.

Zentall, T. R., Urcuioli, P. J., Jagielo, J. A., & Jackson-Smith, P. (1989). Interaction of sample dimension and sample-comparison mapping on pigeons' performance of delayed conditional discriminations. *Animal Learning and Behavior, 17,* 172–178.

Zhuikov, A. Y., Couvillon, P. A., & Bitterman, M. E. (1994). Quantitative two-process analysis of avoidance conditioning in goldfish. *Journal of Experimental Psychology: Animal Behavior Processes, 20,* 32–43.

Zimmerman, B. J., & Blom, D. E. (1983). Toward an empirical test of the role of cognitive conflict in learning. *Developmental Review, 3,* 18–38.

Zubiaur, M., Ona, A., & Delgado, J. (1999). Learning volleyball serves: A preliminary study of the effects of knowledge of performance and of results. *Perceptual and Motor Skills, 89,* 223–232.

Zygmont, D. M., Lazar, R. M., Dube, W. V., & McIlvane, W. J. (1992). Teaching arbitrary matching via sample stimulus-control shaping to young children and mentally retarded individuals: A methodological note. *Journal of the Experimental Analysis of Behavior, 57,* 109–117.

# Acknowledgments

**FIGURE 1-3:** An adaptation of Figure 11 on page 276 from Miller, N. E., Liberalization of basic S-R concepts: Extensions to conflict behavior, motivation, and social learning. In S. Koch (Ed.), *Psychology: A study of a science* (Vol. 2). New York: McGraw-Hill, 1959. Copyright 1959 by McGraw-Hill Book Company, Inc.

**FIGURE 1-4:** An adaptation of Figure 13 on page 278 from Miller, N. E., Liberalization of basic S-R concepts: Extensions to conflict behavior, motivation, and social learning. In S. Koch (Ed.), *Psychology: A study of a science* (Vol. 2). New York: McGraw-Hill, 1959. Copyright 1959 by McGraw-Hill Book Company, Inc.

**FIGURE 3-3:** An adaptation of Figure 3 on page 150 from von Holst, E., Über den Lichtruckenreflex bei Fischen. *Pubblicazioni della Stazione zoologica de Napoli, 15,* 143–158. Copyright 1935 by Francesco Giannini & Figli.

**FIGURE 3-6:** Adapted from Dielenberg, R. A. and McGregor, I. S., Habituation of the hiding response to cat odor in rats (*Rattus norvegicus*). *Journal of Comparative Psychology, 113,* 376–387. Figure 2, p. 379. Copyright 1999 by the American Psychological Association. Adapted with permission.

**FIGURE 3-8:** From Kandel, E. R., Small systems of neurons. *Scientific American,* September 1979, 68 and 75. Copyright 1979 by Scientific American, Inc. All rights reserved.

**FIGURE 3-9:** From Solomon, R. L. and Corbit, J. D., An opponent-process theory of motivation: I. Temporal dynamics of affect. *Psychological Review, 81,* 119–145. Figure 1, page 120. Copyright 1974 by the American Psychological Association. Reprinted by permission.

**FIGURE 3-10:** From Solomon, R. L. and Corbit, J. D., An opponent-process theory of motivation: I. Temporal dynamics of affect. *Psychological Review, 81,* 119–145. Figure 4, page 128. Copyright 1974 by the American Psychological Association. Reprinted by permission.

**FIGURE 4-3:** From Figure 4.2 on page 59 from Domjan, M. and Burkhard, B. *The principles of learning and behavior.* Copyright 1982 by Wadsworth, Inc. Reprinted by permission of Brooks/Cole Publishing Company, Monterey, CA 93940.

**FIGURE 4-5:** An adaptation of Figure 1 on page 212 from Trapold, M. A. and Spence,

K. W., Performance changes in eyelid conditioning as related to the motivational and reinforcing properties of the UCS. *Journal of Experimental Psychology, 59,* 209-213. Copyright 1960 by the American Psychological Association. Reprinted by permission of the publisher.

**FIGURE 4-7:** From Moore, J., Stimulus control: Studies of auditory generalization in rabbits. In Black and Prokasy (Eds.), *Classical conditioning II: Current theory and research.* 1972, page 214. Reprinted by permission of Prentice Hall, Inc., Englewood Cliffs, NJ 07632.

**FIGURE 5-6:** An adaptation of Figure 1 on page 124 from Garcia, J., Ervin, F. R., and Koelling, R. A., Learning with prolonged delay of reinforcement. *Psychonomic Science, 5,* 121–122. Copyright 1966 by the Psychonomic Society.

**FIGURE 5-7A:** An adaptation of Figure 3 on page 1034 from Baron, A., Kaufman, A., and Fazzini, D., Density and delay of punishment of free-operant avoidance. *Journal of the Experimental Analysis of Behavior, 12,* 1029–1037. Copyright 1969 by the Society for the Experimental Analysis of Behavior, Inc. Reprinted by permission of the publisher.

**FIGURE 5-7B:** An adaptation of Figure 1 on page 288 from Andrews, E. A. and Braveman, N. S., The combined effects of dosage level and interstimulus interval on the formation of one-trial poison-based aversions in rats. *Animal Learning & Behavior, 3,* 287–289. Copyright 1975 by the Psychonomic Society.

**FIGURE 5-9:** Adapted from Hughdahl, K., et al., Brain mechanisms in human classical conditioning: A PET blood flow study. *Neuroreport, 6,* 1723–1728. Figure 2, p. 1727. Copyright 1995 by Lippincott, Williams & Wilkins. Adapted by permission of the publisher and author.

**FIGURE 6-3:** Record of cat B on page 46 from Guthrie, E. R. and Horton, G. P., *Cats in a puzzle box.* New York: Rinehart & Company, 1946. Copyright 1946 by Edwin R. Guthrie and George P. Horton.

**FIGURE 6-4:** Record of cat G on page 52 from Guthrie, E. R. and Horton, G. P., *Cats in a puzzle box.* New York: Rinehart & Company, 1946. Copyright 1946 by Edwin R. Guthrie and George P. Horton.

**FIGURE 6-6:** From Jenkins, H. M. and Moore, B. R., The form of the auto-shaped response with food or water reinforcers. *Journal of the Experimental Analysis of Behavior, 20,* 163–181. Figure 2, page 175. Copyright 1973 by the Society for the Experimental Analysis of Behavior, Inc. Reprinted by permission of the publisher.

**FIGURE 7-3:** From Mawhinney, V. T., Bostow, D. E., Laws, D. R., Blumenfeld, G. J., and Hopkins, B. L., A comparison of students' studying behavior produced by daily, weekly, and three-week testing schedules. *Journal of Applied Behavior Analysis, 4,* 257–264. Figure 3, page 262. Copyright 1971 by the Society for the Experimental Analysis of Behavior. Reprinted by permission of the publisher.

**FIGURE 7-5:** From Baum, W. M., Performance on ratio and interval schedules of reinforcement: Data and theory. *Journal of the Experimental Analysis of Behavior, 59,* 245–264. Figure 4, page 251. Copyright 1993 by the Society for the Experimental Analysis of Behavior, Inc. Reprinted by permission of the publisher and author.

**FIGURE 7-7:** From Pear, J. J., Spatiotemporal patterns of behavior produced by variable-interval schedules of reinforcement. *Journal of the Experimental Analysis of Behavior, 44,* 217–231. Portions of Figures 1 and 2. Copyright 1985 by the Society for the Experimental Analysis of Behavior.

**FIGURE 7-8:** From Johnson, S. P., Welsh, T. M., Miller, L. K., & Altus, D. E., Participatory management: Maintaining staff performance in a university housing cooperative. *Journal of Applied Behavior Analysis, 24,* 119–127. Figure 1, page 124. Copyright 1991 by the Society for the Experimental Analysis of Behavior.

**FIGURE 8-4:** From Skinner, B. F., *The behavior of organisms.* Figure 47, page 154. Copyright 1938 by D. Appleton-Century Co., Inc.

**FIGURE 8-5:** From Lane, I. M., Wesolowski, M. D., and Burke, W. H., Teaching socially appropriate behavior to eliminate hoarding in a brain injured adult. *Journal of Behavior Therapy and Experimental Psychiatry, 20,* 79–82. Copyright 1989 by Pergamon Press and the Behavior and Research Society.

**FIGURE 8-6:** From Aylon, T. and Haughton, E., Modification of symptomatic verbal behavior of mental patients. *Behaviour Research and Therapy, 2,* 87–97. Figure 1, page 91. Reprinted with kind permission from Elsevier Science Ltd, The Boulevard, Langford Lane, Kidlington 0X5 1GB, UK.

**FIGURE 9-1:** An adaptation of Figure 4 on page 267 from Tolman, E. C. and Honzik, C. H., Introduction and removal of reward, and maze performance in rats. *University of California Publications in Psychology, 4,* 257–275. Copyright 1930 by the University of California Press.

**FIGURE 9-2:** From Dicara, L. V., Learning in the autonomic nervous system. *Scientific American,* January 1970, page 33. Copyright 1970 by Scientific American, Inc. All rights reserved.

**FIGURE 9-4:** An adaptation of Figure 2 on page 381 from Mazur, J. E., The matching law and quantifications related to Premack's principle. *Journal of Experimental Psychology: Animal Behavior Processes, 1,* 374–386. Adapted by permission.

**FIGURE 10-1:** An adaptation of Figure 1 on page 81 from Guttman, N. and Kalish, H. I., Discriminability and stimulus generalization. *Journal of Experimental Psychology, 51,* 79–88. Copyright 1956 by the American Psychological Association. Reprinted by permission of the publisher.

**FIGURE 10-3:** An adaptation of Figure 1 on page 324 from Hanson, H. M., Effects of discrimination training on stimulus generalization. *Journal of Experimental Psychology, 58,* 321–334. Copyright 1959 by the American Psychological Association. Reprinted by permission of the publisher.

**FIGURE 10-6:** An adaptation of Figure 1 on page 112 from Honig, W. K., Boneau, C. A., Burstein, K. R., and Pennypacker, H. S., Positive and negative generalization gradients obtained after equivalent training conditions. *Journal of Comparative and Physiological Psychology, 56,* 111–116. Copyright 1963 by the American Psychological Association. Reprinted by permission of the publisher.

**FIGURE 10-7:** An adaptation from Table 1 on page 222 from Gutman, A., Positive contrast, negative induction, and inhibitory stimulus control in the rat. *Journal of the Experimental Analysis of Behavior, 27,* 219–233. Copyright 1972 by the Society for the Experimental Analysis of Behavior, Inc. Reprinted by permission of the publisher.

**FIGURE 10-9:** From Warren, J. M., Primate learning in comparative perspective. In A. M. Schrier, H. F. Harlow, and F. Stollnitz (Eds.), *Behavior of nonhuman primates* (Vol. 1). New York: Academic Press, 1965. Figure 4, page 262. Copyright 1965 by the Academic Press.

**FIGURE 11-2A:** An adaptation of Figure 1 on page 210 from Grant, D. S., Proactive interference in pigeon short-term memory. *Journal of Experimental Psychology: Animal Behavior Processes, 1,* 207–220. Copyright 1975 by the American Psychological Association. Reprinted by permission of the publisher.

**FIGURE 11-2B:** An adaptation of Figure 1 on page 329 from D'Amato, M. R. and O'Neill, W., Effect of delay-interval illumination on matching behavior in the capuchin monkey. *Journal of the Experimental Analysis of Behavior, 15,* 327–333. Copyright 1971 by the Society for the Experimental Analysis of Behavior, Inc. Reprinted by permission of the publisher.

**FIGURE 11-5:** From Wagner, A. R., Rudy, J. W., and Whitlow, J. W., Rehearsal in animal conditioning. *Journal of Experimental Psychology, 97,* 407–426. Figure 11, page 421. Copyright 1973 by the American Psychological Association. Reprinted by permission of the publisher.

**FIGURE 11-6:** An adaptation of Figure 2 in Roberts, S., Isolation of an internal clock. *Journal of Experimental Psychology: Animal Behavior Processes, 7,* 242–268. Copyright 1981 by the American Psychological Association. Reprinted by permission of the publisher and author.

**FIGURE 11-7:** From Figure 2 in Mechner, F., Probability relations within response sequences under ratio reinforcement. *Journal of the Experimental Analysis of Behavior*, *1*, 109–121. Copyright 1958 by the Society for the Experimental Analysis of Behavior, Inc. Reprinted by permission of the publisher.

**FIGURE 11-9:** From Figure 2 in Gillan, D. J., Premack, D., and Woodruff, G., Reasoning in the chimpanzee: I. Analogical reasoning. *Journal of Experimental Psychology: Animal Behavior Processes*, *7*, 1–7. Copyright 1981 by the American Psychological Association. Reprinted by permission of the publisher.

**FIGURE 12-1:** From Bandura, A., Ross, D. and Ross, S. A., Imitation of film-mediated aggressive models. *Journal of Abnormal and Social Psychology*, *66*, 3–11. Figure 1, page 8. Copyright 1963 by the American Psychological Association. Reprinted by permission.

**FIGURE 12-3:** An adaptation of Figure 1 on page 21 from Bandura, A., Grusec, J. E., and Menlove, F. L., Vicarious extinction of avoidance behavior. *Journal of Personality and Social Psychology*, *5*, 16–23. Copyright 1967 by the American Psychological Association. Reprinted by permission of the publisher and authors.

**FIGURE 13-1:** An adaptation from Table 2 on page 253 from Trowbridge, M. H. and Cason, H., An experimental study of Thorndike's theory of learning. *Journal of General Psychology*, *7*, 245–260. Copyright 1932 by the Helen Dwight Reid Educational Foundation.

**FIGURE 13-2:** An adaptation of Figure 4 on page 11 from Hatze, H., Biomechanical aspects of a successful motion optimization. In P. V. Komi (Ed.), *Biomechanics V-B*. Copyright 1976 by University Park Press.

**FIGURE 13-3:** From Schmidt, R. A. and Young, D. E., Methodology for motor learning: A paradigm for kinematic feedback. *Journal of Motor Behavior*, *23*, 13–24. Reprinted with permission of the Helen Dwight Reid Educational Foundation. Published by Heldref Publications, 1319 Eighteenth St., N.W., Washington, D.C. 20036-1802. Copyright 1991.

**FIGURE 13-4:** An adaptation of Figure 2 on page 240 from Newell, K. M., Knowledge of results and motor learning. *Journal of Motor Behavior*, *6*, 234–244. Copyright by Heldref Publications.

**FIGURE 13-6:** From Portier, S. J., van Galen, G. P., and Meulenbroek, R. G., Practice and the dynamics of handwriting performance: Evidence for a shift of motor programming load. *Journal of Motor Behavior*, *22*, 474–492. Reprinted with permission of the Helen Dwight Reid Educational Foundation. Published by Heldref Publications, 1319 Eighteenth St., N.W., Washington, D.C. 20036-1802. Copyright 1990.

**FIGURE 14-1:** An adaptation of Figure 1 on page 268 from Herrnstein, R. J., Relative and absolute strength of response as a function of frequency of reinforcement. *Journal of the Experimental Analysis of Behavior*, *4*, 267–272. Copyright 1961 by the Society for the Experimental Analysis of Behavior. Reprinted by permission of the publisher and author.

**FIGURE 14-4:** From Herrnstein, R. J., On the law of effect. *Journal of the Experimental Analysis of Behavior*, *13*, 243–266. Figure 8, page 255. Copyright 1970 by the Society for the Experimental Analysis of Behavior. Reprinted by permission of the publisher and author.

**FIGURE 14-5:** An adaptation of Table 1 on page 147 from Rachlin, H., Green, L., Kagel, J. H., and Battalio, R. C., Economic demand theory and psychological studies of choice. In G. Bower (Ed.), *The psychology of learning and motivation* (Vol. 10). Copyright 1976 by Academic Press Inc., 111 Fifth Avenue, New York, NY 10003.

**FIGURE 14-9:** An adaptation of Figure 1 on page 486 from Ainslie, G. W., Impulse control in pigeons. *Journal of the Experimental Analysis of Behavior*, *21*, 485–489. Copyright 1974 by the Society for the Experimental Analysis of Behavior, Inc. Reprinted by permission of the publisher and author.

# Author Index

Abbot, B. B., 7
Abdulah, D. T., 312
Abramovitch, R., 290
Abramowitz, A. J., 189, 290
Abramson, L. Y., 185
Ackermann, H., 118
Ackil, J. E., 143
Adams, C. D., 196
Adams, J. A., 312–315
Addis, M. E., 170
Adelinis, J. D., 219
Ader, D. N., 80
Adler, C. S., 210
Adornetto, M., 350
Ainslie, G., 345, 347, 351
Albert, M., 75, 113, 269
Albert, M. L., 35
Alberto, P., 200
Alberts, E., 233
Albright, T. D., 31
Alexander, J. H., 185
Allaway, T. A., 142
Allen, J. D., 146
Allison, J., 218
Alptekin, S., 272
Alterson, C. J., 197
Altus, D. E., 168–169
Alvarez-Borda, B., 80
Amiro, T. W., 100
Ammerman, R. T., 165
Andreatos, M., 286
Andree, P. J., 197
Andres, R., 132
Andrews, D., 200
Andrews, E. A., 109

Andrews, J. A., 296
Anger, D., 162
Anger, W. K., 132, 169
Anisfeld, M., 283, 314
Antonov, I., 49
Arena, J. G., 210
Aristotle, 19–20
Armony, J. L., 117
Arntz, A., 295
Asano, T., 249, 343
Ash, D. W., 139
Ashenden, B., 165
Aslin, R. N., 48–49
Astley, C. A., 116
Atkinson, C. J., 308
Axelrod, S., 200
Ayllon, T., 196–199
Ayres, J. J. B., 75, 99, 113
Azrin, N. H., 187–191

Backer, R., 213–214
Baer, D. M., 286
Baeyens, F., 77
Bagshaw, M., 158
Bailey, J. S., 195
Baker, K. E., 313
Baker, T. B., 55, 112
Balaban, M.T., 190
Balaz, M. A., 98
Balda, R. P., 264
Baldwin, E., 12
Balsam, P. D., 98, 100–101
Bandura, A., 282, 285–293,
    299–301

Bao, J. X., 116
Barlow, H. B., 32
Barnes, D., 153
Barnet, R. C., 99
Baron, A., 109, 153, 188
Barry, K., 272
Bartlett, F. C., 317
Bates, J. E., 349
Batsell, W. R., 110
Batson, J. D., 110
Battalio, R. C., 163, 337–338
Battig, W. F., 245
Baudry, M., 34
Baum, M., 180
Baum, W. M., 161–163,
    330–332
Bauman, K. E., 296
Bauman, R., 223
Bauman, R. A., 224
Bayles, K., 349
Beardsley, S. D., 334
Beasty, A., 159
Beatty, W. W., 259
Beauchamp, A. J., 102
Beckwith, B. E., 193
Beidleman, W. B., 298
Bekesy, G. von, 30
Belke, T. W., 340
Benecke, R., 34
Bennet, T. E. L., 32
Bennett, C. H., 234
Bentall, R. P., 158–159
Berendzen, N., 337
Berenson, G. S., 296
Berger, T. W., 117

Berman, A. J., 322
Bermudez-Rattoni, F., 45
Berndt, R. S., 35
Bernstein, I. D., 108
Bernstein, I. L., 108
Bersh, P. J., 176
Besheer, J., 110
Bessant, D. E., 203
Besson, A., 186
Best, M. R., 101
Betts, S. L., 114
Bever, T. G., 277
Bevins, R. A., 110, 113
Beylin, A., 34
Bickel, W. K., 221, 224–225,
   345
Biederman, I., 247
Biermann, K., 12
Bilger, R. C., 308
Bill-Harvey, D., 301
Bilodeau, I. M., 308
Binder, L. M., 350
Birbaumer, N., 118
Bitterman, M. E., 100, 183,
   235–236, 344
Black, A. H., 64, 113, 176
Blais, C., 313
Blake, R. R., 297
Blakemore, C., 32
Blakely, E., 151, 211
Blanchard, E. B., 299
Blanchard, S., 73
Bleak, J. L., 126
Bliss, T. V. P., 34
Blom, D. E., 297
Blough, D. S., 25, 246, 255
Blumenfeld, G. J., 152
Boakes, R. A., 69, 239
Bolles, R. C., 101, 181
Bombace, J. C., 99, 114
Bonardi, C., 103
Bond, N. W., 108
Bonem, E. J., 150
Booke, A. L., 8
Booth, B., 319
Bootzin, R. R., 251
Bordens, K. S., 7
Bossom, J., 322
Bostenaru, N., 8
Bostow, D. E., 152
Bottjer, S. W., 70
Bouton, M. E., 69–70, 101, 117
Bowd, A. D., 12
Bower, G. H., 254

Bowman, R. E., 280
Boysen, S. T., 280
Bradnam, M. S., 51
Bradford, S. A., 269
Bradshaw, C. M., 336
Brady, P.M., 246
Brakke, K. E., 275
Branch, M. N., 189
Brandon, S. E., 113–114
Brannon, E. M., 269
Bransford, J. D., 245
Braveman, N. S., 107, 109
Bray, M. A., 301
Breland, K., 140
Breland, M., 140
Brendlinger, J., 189
Brennan, P. A., 47
Brill, A. B., 35
Broeckl, L. S., 251
Brogden, W. J., 78
Brooks, D. C., 69–70, 117
Brooks, W., 64
Brown, A. M., 99
Brown, G. E., 184
Brown, M. F., 258–259
Brown, P. L., 141–142, 239
Brown, R., 123, 276
Brown, T., 22, 88
Broz, W. R., 83
Bruce, C., 31
Bruce, C. J., 254
Bruce, D., 322
Bruno, G. M., 210
Bucher, B., 194
Büchel, C., 117
Budzynski, T. H., 210
Bullock, D., 284
Burke, W. H., 194–195
Burkhard, B., 61
Burnett, A., 47
Burnstein, E., 290
Burstein, K. R., 236
Bush, R. R., 88
Buske-Kirschbaum, A., 80
Butler, J. A., 146
Butler, R. A., 214
Byrne, R. W., 284
Byrnes, D., 79


Cable, C., 246–247
Caine, S. B., 56
Campagnoni, F. R., 146
Campbell, B. A., 181
Campbell, C. E., 270

Canli, T., 116
Cannon, T. D., 47
Capaldi, E. J., 70, 109, 155,
   269–270, 272
Capell, M., 296
Caraco, T., 353
Caramazza, A., 35
Carew, T. J., 115
Carley, J. L., 256
Carlton, L. G., 309
Carmagnani, A., 211
Carmagnani, E. F., 211
Carman, H. M., 272
Carnahan, H., 307
Carrigan, P., 249, 257
Carroll, M. E., 224
Cartledge, G., 300
Casaer, P., 33
Case, D. A., 353
Casey, J., 342
Cashon, C. H., 49
Cason, H., 306–307
Castellucci, V., 49
Castro, C. A., 265
Catania, A. C., 158–159, 161,
   332–335, 352
Caughlin-Carvar, J., 298
Cavalier, A. R., 168
Cerella, J., 247
Chachere, G., 294
Chai, H., 194
Chamberlain, P., 293
Chamberlin, C. J., 319
Chambers, K. C., 110
Champion, R. A., 75
Chaney, J. M., 185
Charnov, E. L., 223
Chavarro, A., 332
Chen, S., 271–272
Chen, W. R., 34
Cheng, K., 234
Chomsky, N., 212, 273
Christopherson, E. R., 194
Christensen, A., 171
Christensen, J., 341
Church, R. M., 52, 55, 266–269
Ciborowski, T., 126
Cicero, S. D., 77
Cipani, E., 189
Clark, B. M., 108
Classen, J., 34
Clearfield, M. W., 49
Coble, J. R., 83
Cohen, D., 80, 283
Cohen, L. B., 49

Cohen, L. G., 34
Cohen, N., 244
Cohen, P. S., 146
Colby, J., 193
Coldwells, A., 314
Cole, M. R., 164
Cole, R. P., 99
Coleman, K. A., 10
Coleman, S. R., 207
Collingridge, G. L., 34
Collison, C., 258
Colombo, M., 257
Colwill, R. M., 205–206
Compton, D. M., 12
Condon, B., 51
Condon, C. D., 51
Conger, R., 329
Conners, F. A., 242
Conrad, D. G., 224
Cook, M., 259, 295
Cook, R. G., 247, 265
Cooper, G. F., 32
Corbit, J. D., 52–56
Cordova, J., 171
Coughlin, R., 268
Cournoyer, M., 349
Couvillon, P. A., 183, 344
Cowdery, G. E., 197
Cozby, P. C., 7
Creer, T. L., 194
Critchfield, T. S., 250
Crombez, G., 77
Cross, D., 354
Crossman, E. K., 150, 161
Crowell, C. R., 112
Culbert, J. P., 251
Cunningham, C. E., 194
Cunningham, C. L., 101
Cunningham, S., 249
Cutmore, T. R. H., 100

Dallal, N. L., 272
Dallas, M., 170
Dallery, J., 334
D'Amato, M. R., 247, 255, 257
D'Andrade, R., 291–292
Daum, I., 117–118
Davenport, D. G., 181
Davey, G. C. L., 66, 108
Davidson, E. S., 290
Davidson, M., 295
Davidson, T. L., 102
Davies, D. R., 251
Davies, N. B., 222

Davies, S. N., 34
Davis, H., 269, 279
Davis, J. R., 191
Davis, M., 51
Davison, M., 329, 331–332
Davison, T. L., 270
Dawson, G. R., 285
Dawson, M. E., 108
deBaca, P. C., 217
DeCarlo, L. T., 340
DeCola, J. P., 56
DeGrandpre, R. J., 224
Deich, J. D., 74
de Jong, P., 295
DeLeon, I. G., 192
Delgado, J., 309
Delius, J. D., 247, 279
DeLorenzo, T., 301
Deluty, M. Z., 348
den Brinker, B. P., 309
DeRivera, J., 233
Desimone, R., 31
de Rose, J. C., 250
de Souza, D. G., 250
Devenport, J. A., 344
Devenport, L. D., 344
de Villiers, P. A., 246, 332–333
Devine, J. V., 217
DeVito, J. L., 116
Dews, P. B., 265
Diamond, M. C., 32
DiCara, L. V., 208–209
Dichgens, J., 118
Dickinson, A., 205
Dielenberg, R. A., 46–47
Dietrich, K. L., 12
Dill, J. C., 294
Dill, K. E., 294
Dimberg, U., 108
DiPietro, N. T., 99
DiPrisco, G. V., 33
Dixon, M. R., 350
Dodd, P. W. D., 257
Dodwell, P. C., 203
Dolan, R. J., 117
Dollard, J., 285
Domjan, M., 61, 66, 75, 101, 110, 146
Donaldson, T., 285
Donegan, N. H., 78, 113, 116
Donnellan, A. M., 200
Donovan, W., 193
Dore, F. Y., 278
Dorsky, N. P., 270
Dougan, J. D., 239

Dowrick, P. W., 301
Drabman, R. S., 192
Dragoi, V., 344
Dragoin, W. B., 107
Droit, S., 159
Dronkert, Y., 324
Dube, W. V., 242
Ducharme, J. M., 197
Duffy, L., 241–242
Dugdale, N., 249
Duke, M. P., 17
Dumas, C., 278
Duncan, D., 193
Duncan, S. C., 296
Dunn, R. M., 332, 343
Durlach, P. J., 101, 142
Dworkin, B. R., 209
Dykman, R. A., 47

Easterbrook, M. A., 49
Eayrs, 242
Ebbesen, E. B., 349
Ebbinghaus, H., 23–24, 311
Eelen, P., 77
Ehrenfreund, D., 233
Eibl-Eibesfeldt, I., 42
Eichenbaum, H., 243
Eikelboom, R., 64
Eisenberger, R., 218, 350
Eiserer, L. A., 56
Eisler, R. M., 165
Eldridge, K., 171
Eleey, M. F., 293
Elk, R., 132
Ellenberger, H. H., 117
Ellingson, S. A., 220
Ellison, G. D., 74
Elmes, D. G., 7
Elsmore, T. F., 224
Ennet, S. T., 296
Epstein, S. M., 55
Eron, L. D., 292–293
Ervin, F. R., 104
Eschalier, A., 186
Esser, G., 46
Estes, W. K., 69, 88, 187
Eterovic, V. A., 33
Etscorn, F., 104
Ettinger, R. H., 239, 341

Fabricatore, J., 194
Fagan, A., 243
Falk, J. L., 146
Falls, W. A., 114

Fanselow, M. S., 56, 113, 182
Fantino, E., 341, 343, 352–353
Farley, J., 116
Farmer-Dougan, V. A., 219, 239
Fazzini, D., 109, 188
Fehr, A., 193
Felten, D., 80
Ferchmin, P. A., 33
Ferretti, R. P., 168
Ferster, C. B., 148, 158, 192
Fetterman, J. G., 267
Fialip, J., 186
Field, T. M., 283
Finfgeld, D. L., 83
Fischer, E. B., 347
Fischer, S. M., 220
Fischman, M. G., 323
Fisher, J., 219, 284
Fisher, W. W., 197
Fjeld, H. A., 284
Fleming, J. S., 292
Fletcher, G. V., 224
Forestell, P. H., 275
Foster, T. M., 332
Fountain, S. B., 272
Fouts, D. H., 277
Fouts, R. S., 277
Fouty, H. E., 102
Fox, D. K., 169
Fox, L., 250
Fraenkel, G. S., 40
Franks, J. J., 245
Frawley, P. J., 84
Freagon, S., 200
Frederick, C. M., 126
Freed, D. E., 224
Freeman, T. J., 159
Freitag, L., 299
Friedrich-Cofer, L., 294
Friman, P. C., 194
Friston, K. J., 117
Frommer, G. P., 143
Fry, A. F., 345
Fujita, T., 211
Funahashi, S., 254
Funk, M. S., 278

Gabelli, F., 101
Gagne, R. M., 313
Galbicka, G., 133, 189
Galdikas, B. M. F., 290
Galef, B. G., 146
Galensky, T. L., 220
Gamzu, E. R., 239

Gao, L. G., 322
Garcia, J., 70, 104–105
Garcia-Colera, A., 324
Gardner, B. T., 273
Gardner, R. A., 273
Garlinghouse, M. A., 220
Garton, W. H., 210
Geinisman, Y., 34
Gelder, M., 84
Gelperin, A., 116
Gendelman, D. S., 51
Gendelman, P. M., 51
Gentile, C. G., 117
Gentry, G. V., 235–236
Gerbner, G., 293
Gerry, J. E., 232
Gershon, S., 296
Getty, D. J., 266
Gewirtz, J. C., 101
Ghanata, V., 80
Gibb, R., 34
Gibbon, J., 98, 145
Giesen, J. M., 10
Gillan, D. J., 278–279
Giray, M., 323
Gittelson, B., 4–5, 7–8
Glanzman, D. L., 115
Glaister, B., 199
Glasscock, S. G., 194
Gleeson, S., 126
Gleitman, H., 264
Glencross, D. J., 322
Glover, H., 56
Gluck, J. P., 102
Gluck, M. A., 229
Glueck, E., 292
Glueck, S., 292
Glynn, S. M., 168
Goddard, M. J., 89
Gofseyeff, M., 161
Goldfarb, T. L., 256
Goldiamond, I., 131, 308
Goldman-Rakic, P. S., 254
Goldsmith, J. B., 298
Gonzalez, R. C., 235–236
Good, M., 117, 211
Goodman, J., 300–301
Gorczynski, R. M., 80
Gordon, W. C., 264–265
Gormezano, I., 73, 207
Gorny, G., 34
Gottfried, A. E., 292
Gottfried, A. W., 292
Gould, E., 33–34
Gowen, C. R., 330

Grabowski, J., 132
Grace, R. C., 157, 344
Grant, D. L., 144
Grant, D. S., 255–256, 260, 262
Grau, J. W., 101
Graziano, M. S., 33
Green, K. F., 104
Green, L., 163, 221, 224,
    337–338, 345, 347–348
Greenberg, R., 283
Greene, S. L., 263
Greene, W., 115
Greenfield, P. M., 277
Griffin, R. W., 100
Grinker, R., 295
Groccia-Ellison, M., 73
Groome, L. J., 47
Grosch, J., 348
Gross, C. G., 31, 33
Gross, L., 293
Grover, L. M., 116
Grusec, J. E., 290, 299–300
Guess, D., 17
Gulliksen, H., 233
Gunn, D. L., 40
Guthrie, E. R., 123–124
Gutman, A., 238
Guttman, J., 297
Guttman, N., 228–229, 231
Guttman-Nahir, T., 234

Habib, T., 211
Hackenberg, T. D., 341
Hadad, G. M., 100
Haddad, C., 75
Haddock, C. K., 251
Hadley, D. M., 51
Hager, J. L., 105, 110
Hagopian, L. P., 132
Hake, D. F., 188–189, 285
Hall, D. J., 223
Hall, G., 98, 103
Hall, J. F., 180
Halliday, M. S., 69, 239
Halweg, K., 170
Hamilton, B., 342
Ham, R., 283
Hamm, R. J., 284
Hannah, S. L., 210
Hanson, H. M., 233–234
Hardin, G., 354–355
Harlow, H. F., 242, 244
Hare, M. E., 314
Harris, S. L., 166

Harrison, R. H., 229–231
Hart, J., 35
Hartman, V., 185
Harzem, P., 158
Haselton, J. R., 117
Hatze, H., 309–310
Haughton, E., 196–198
Hawkins, R. D., 49, 115–116
Hayes, C., 273
Hayes, L. J., 350
Hayes, S. C., 249
Hearst, E. S., 64, 143
Hebb, D. O., 207
Hegvik, D. K., 260–261
Hekimian, L. J., 296
Heller, R. F., 193
Hellhammer, D., 80
Hembree, T. L., 116
Hendler, M., 286
Hendry, D. P., 189
Herman, L. M., 275, 277
Heron, W. T., 146
Herrnstein, R. J., 123, 126, 146,
    177–179, 182, 239,
    246–247, 328–337, 339,
    344, 352
Herscovitch, P., 118
Hersen, M., 165, 196
Hersov, L., 183
Herzog, M., 247
Heth, C. D., 102
Heyes, C. M., 285
Heyman, G. M., 339, 343
Higgins, S. T., 127, 224
Hilgard, E. R., 63
Hilliard, S., 66
Hinde, C. A., 284
Hineline, P. N., 177–179, 182,
    348
Hines, T. M., 10
Hinson, J. M., 343
Hinson, R. E., 112
Hinze, T. S., 110
Hiramoto, R. H., 80
Hiroto, D. S., 184
Hladek, D., 300
Hlavacek, A. C., 170
Hobbes, T., 20
Hoberman, H. M., 294
Hobson, S. L., 268
Hodges, A. E., 168
Hoehler, F. K., 70
Hoffman, A., 194
Hoffman, M. L., 292
Hogan, D. E., 257

Hogben, M., 294
Hogsden, I., 332
Holding, D. H., 139
Holland, P. C., 66, 100, 102–103
Hollister, J. M., 47
Holman, T. B., 296
Holz, W. C., 188–190
Homans, G. C., 330
Homme, L. E., 217
Honig, W. K., 232, 234,
    236–237, 247, 257, 263–264
Honzik, C. H., 203–204,
    288–289
Hopf, S., 247
Hopfield, J. F., 116
Hopkins, B. L., 152, 169
Hopkins, W. D., 277
Hops, H., 296
Horton, G. P., 123–124
Houk, J. L., 334
Howell, D. C., 10
Hryshko-Mullen, A. S., 251
Hubel, D. H., 30, 32, 37
Huesmann, L. R., 292–293
Hugdahl, K., 108, 118–119
Hughes, G. D., 184
Hughes, J. R., 224
Hughes, K., 313
Hull, C. L., 60, 88, 203, 205,
    207, 212–213, 311
Hulse, S. H., 270
Hulstijn, W., 308–309
Hunkin, N. M., 242
Hunt, J. McV., 70
Hunter, S. M., 296
Hunter, W. S., 244
Hur, J., 139
Hursh, S. R., 223–225, 341
Huston, A. C., 290, 294
Huttenlocher, P. R., 33
Hyten, C., 285

Iennaco, F. M., 242
Iezzi, M., 301
Isaacs, W., 131
Israely, Y., 297
Ito, M., 353
Iverson, I. H., 257
Iwata, B. A., 192, 197, 220

Jabaij, L., 80
Jackson, R. L., 185
Jackson, T., 242
Jackson-Beeck, M., 293

Jackson-Smith, P., 258–259
Jacob-Timm, S., 200
Jacobs, E. A., 341
Jacobson, N. S., 170–171
Jacquet, A. Y., 159
Jagielo, J. A., 99, 258
Jaldow, E., 285
James, J. E., 184
James, W., 283
Janelle, C. M., 314
Jarrell, T. W., 117
Jarvik, M. E., 256
Jeffries-Fox, S., 293
Jenkins, H. M., 64, 89, 141–143,
    229–231, 239
Jenkins, P. E., 331
Jennings, P. J., 325
Jensen, F. E., 33
Jensen, H. C., 110
Jensen, L., 296
John, E. R., 35
Johnson, H. E., 210
Johnson, J. L., 70
Johnson, L. M., 127
Johnson, R. D., 169
Johnson, S. B., 85, 284
Johnson, S. D., 12
Johnson, S. P., 48–49, 168–169
Johnston, J. C., 179
Joiner, T. E., Jr., 297
Jones, A. A., 184
Jones, H., 154
Jones, J. E., 75
Jones, R. S., 242
Jones, T. A., 33
Junginger, J., 84
Justice, T. C., 126

Kagel, J. H., 163, 221, 337–338
Kaiser, D. H., 262
Kako, E., 277
Kalant, H., 112
Kalat, J. W., 104
Kalish, H. I., 228–229, 231
Kamil, A. C., 264
Kamin, L. J., 88, 177
Kandel, E. R., 49–50, 114–116
Kanner, L, 165
Kant, I., 20
Kantowitz, B. H., 7
Karpman, M., 218
Kasprow, W. J., 98
Kass, R. E., 192
Kates, K., 197

Kato, K., 34
Katz, A., 244
Katz, D. S., 264
Katzmann, S., 132
Kaufman, A., 109, 188
Kaufman, K. F., 192
Kawai, M., 284
Kaye, H., 98
Kazdin, A. E., 167–168, 171
Keele, S. W., 321
Keenan, M., 153
Kehle, T. J., 301
Kehoe, E. J., 70
Keith, J. R., 203
Kelley, M. L., 196
Kellogg, L. A., 273
Kellogg, W. N., 273
Kendler, H. H., 207
Kendrick, D. F., 247, 256, 265
Keppel, G., 264
Kernodle, M. W., 309
Kerr, R., 295, 313, 319
Kesner, R. P., 253
Kessler, R. C., 293
Khallad, Y., 92
Killeen, P. R., 267, 329, 332, 334, 344
Kim, K., 234
Kimble, G. A., 104, 207–208
King, B., 295
King, G. D., 146
King, N. J., 300
Kintsch, W., 151
Kioumourtzoglou, E., 310
Kirkland, K. D., 298
Kirkpatrick-Steger, K., 247
Kirschbaum, C., 80
Kirschenbaum, D. S., 70
Kisilevsky, B. S., 49
Klass, E. T., 290
Kledaras, J. B., 242
Klein, M., 50
Knowlton, B. J., 116
Koch, A. M., 284
Koch, G. G., 296
Koelling, R. A., 104–106
Kohler, W., 233
Kolb, B., 33–34
Konarski, E. A., 219
Konorski, J., 35, 69, 207–208
Koob, G. F., 56
Kopelman, R. E., 185
Kraemer, P. J., 262
Kral, P. A., 107

Krank, M. D., 112
Kratochwill, T. R., 184
Krebs, J. R., 222, 264
Kremer, E. F., 92
Krieger, K., 275
Krupa, D. J., 116
Kuboki, T., 211
Kunesch, E., 34
Kuo, Z. Y., 146
Kupers, C. J., 291
Kupfermann, I., 49
Kushner, M., 82, 194
Kymissis, E., 286, 289

Lagerspetz, K., 292–293
Lai, Q., 325
Lalli, J. S., 197
Lancaster, J. S., 334
Lane, I. M., 194–195
Lane, S. D., 250
Laplante, D. P., 49
Larew, M. B., 75
Larsen, T., 265
Lashley, K. S., 32, 35, 128, 229, 286, 322
Latash, M. L., 313
Lattal, K. A., 126, 159
Laucht, M., 46
LaVigna, G. W., 200
Lavond, D. G., 116
Lawrence, D. H., 233
Laws, D. R., 152
Lazar, R. M., 242, 249
Lazarus, A. A., 298
Le, D. D., 197
Lea, S. E. G., 221, 223
Leahey, T. H., 284
Leal, D. R., 356
Leander, J. D., 158
Leat, M., 297
LeDoux, J. E., 117
Lee, B. S., 308
Lee, S. H., 34
Lee, T. D., 307, 320
Lee, V. L., 126
Lefkowitz, M. M., 292–293, 297
LeFrancois, J. R., 159
Leinenweber, A., 153
Lemere, F., 83–84
Lentz, R. J., 167
Leonard, D. W., 70
LePage, J. P., 168
Lerman, D. C., 192

Lerner, N. D., 266
Lester, R. A. J., 34
Lett, B. T., 108
Leung, L. S., 34
Levin, H., 292
Levine, E., 73
Levis, D. J., 182
Levey, A. B., 89
Lewis, D., 313
Lewis, D. R., 186
Lewis, M. H., 102
Ley, R., 56
Lierle, D. M., 186
Lim, C. H., 323
Lindauer, S. E., 197
Linden, E., 275
Linden, M., 211
Lindsay, R. M., 186
Linscheid, T. R., 194
Lipp, O. V., 96
Lippman, L. G., 158
Litner, J. S., 176
Livezy, K., 197
Loafman, B., 170
Lochbaum, M. R., 56
Lockard, R. B., 104
Locke, J., 20
Lockwood, K., 330
Locurto, C. M., 145
Loeb, J., 40
Logan, P., 219–220
Logue, A. W., 62, 107–108, 110, 146, 332
Logue, K. R., 108
Lohrmann-O'Rourke, S., 200
LoLordo, V. M., 52, 176, 182
Lomo, T., 34
Long, J. B., 203
Looney, T. A., 126, 146
Lopez, L. J., 264
Lovaas, O. I., 165–166, 298–299
Loveland, D. H., 246–247, 336
Lowe, C. F., 158–159, 249
Lubow, R. E., 96, 101, 246
Lucaciu, L., 8
Lucas, G. A., 74, 127, 145
Lucchelli, F., 35
Lutzenberger, W., 118

Maccoby, E. E., 292
MacCorquodale, K., 205
Mace, F. C., 332
Machado, A., 292

Mack, M., 112
Mackintosh, N.J., 97, 101, 205, 234
Macrae, M., 70
Macphail, E. M., 117
Macuda, T., 272
Madden, G. J., 345
Madison, D. V., 34
Maes, J. R., 103
Magill, R. A., 319–320
Maier, S. F., 184–186
Maisto, S. A., 183
Maki, W. S., 260–261
Malenka, R. C., 34
Malott, M. K., 232
Mancl, L., 295
Manthey, S., 350
March, J. G., 354
Marcus, B. A., 198
Maren, S., 34
Marinkovic, K., 108
Markman, H. J., 170
Markou, A., 56
Marks, I. M., 84
Marsden, C. D., 324
Martens, B. K., 334
Martin, G., 165, 297
Martin, I., 89
Martin, P. L., 167
Martindale, S., 353
Marzilli, R., 193
Matson, J. L., 193
Matsuzawa, T., 269
Matthews, B. A., 158–159, 161
Matute, H., 126
Matzel, L. D., 99
Mauk, M. D., 116
Mavromatis, G., 310
Mawhinney, T. C., 330
Mawhinney, V. T., 152, 154
May, R., 295
Mayhall, B., 194
Maynard, R., 47
Mazmanian, D. S., 258, 262
Mazur, J. E., 113, 151, 216–218, 339–340, 344, 352, 354
McAfee, R. B., 170
McAllister, D. E., 313
McBurney, P. H., 7
McCabe, P. M., 117
McCarthy, D., 329
McClelland, D.C., 292
McCormick, D. A., 116–117
McCully, J., 112

McDonald, K., 277
McDonald, S. J., 242
McDonnell, J., 138
McDougall, W., 283
McDowell, J. J., 334
McDowell, L., 189
McEachin, J. J., 166
McFadzean, R., 51
McFall, R. M., 298
McFarland, D. S., 38
McFarland, S., 138
McGinnis, C. M., 265
McGowan, B. K., 104
McGrady, A., 211
McGregor, I. S., 46–47
McIlvane, W. J., 242
McIntosh, A. R., 118
McIntyre, T., 197
McKean, K. J., 186
McKenna, I., 66
McLaren, I. P. L., 234
McLaughlin, T. F., 168
McNally, R. J., 108
McNamara, H. J., 203
McNish, K. A., 114
McPhee, J., 99
McSweeney, F. K., 239
McVety, K. M., 203
Meador, K. J., 210
Mechner, F., 268
Meck, W. H., 268–269, 272
Mednick, S. A., 47
Meehl, P. E., 205, 214
Meichenbaum, D. H., 300–301
Melchiori, L. E., 250
Mellitz, M., 348
Meltzoff, A. N., 283
Melville, C. L., 239
Menlove, F. L., 299–300
Merante, R. J., 170
Merckelbach, H., 295
Merton, P. A., 324
Metzger, B., 159
Meulenbroek, R. G., 323
Meyer, E. A, 132
Meyer, M. E., 158
Meyer, R. K., 313
Mezei, L., 297
Middleton, M. B., 300
Milavsky, J. R., 293
Miles, H. L., 275, 277
Milgrom, P., 295
Mill, J., 20, 22
Mill, J. S., 20

Miller, D. J., 269, 272
Miller, G. A., 270
Miller, H. L., 331, 343
Miller, J. S., 99
Miller, L. K., 168–169
Miller, M. S., 156
Miller, N. E., 12, 15–16, 176, 182, 207–209, 213–214, 285
Miller, P. M., 165
Miller, R. R., 71, 98–99
Miller, S., 207
Milner, P., 208
Miltenberger, R. G., 165, 220
Mineka, S., 81, 177, 295, 300
Mintz, D. E., 161
Miranda, A., 301
Mischel, W., 290, 349–350
Mitchell, D., 111
Mitchell, S. H., 345
Mitchell, J. B., 100
Mitchell, W. S., 217
Mix, C., 132
Mix, K. S., 49
Modaresi, H. A., 182
Mohr, D., 280
Molchan, S. E., 118
Mollgaard, K., 32
Montague, W. E., 245
Mood, K., 237
Mooney, S. E., 159
Moore, A. U., 96
Moore, B. R., 142–143
Moore, J., 92
Moore, J. W., 72
Moore, M. K., 283
Morgan, C. L., 283
Morgan, R. T., 85
Morganstern, K. P., 183
Morgulis, S., 59
Morin, C. M., 251
Morris, E. K., 127–128
Morris, R. J., 184
Morrison, S., 237
Morton, H. B., 324
Mosteller, F., 88
Mourer, D. J., 161
Mouton, J. S., 297
Mowrer, O. H., 85, 154, 175, 203, 207–208
Mowrer, W. M., 85
Mucha, R. F., 112
Muenzinger, K. F., 128
Muggia, S., 35
Muir, D. W., 49

Mulder, T., 308–309
Mullaney, M. A., 210
Mullins, L. L., 185
Mustaca, A. E., 101
Myers, A. K., 214
Myers, D. L., 331
Myers, L. E., 331
Myerson, J., 345
Mystkowski, J. L., 300

Nair, V., 332
Nakagawa, E., 249
Nakajima, S., 145, 249
Nakao, M., 211
Napier, R. M., 70
Neef, N. A., 156, 301, 332
Neiworth, J. J., 253
Nelson, K., 299
Neuman, S. B., 294
Neuringer, A., 126, 190, 284, 348
Nevin, J. A., 157, 343
Newell, K. M., 316–317
Newman, F., 268
Nicholas, J. M., 16
Nichols, P., 353
Nicholson, D. E., 308
Nicoll, R. A., 34
Nomura, S., 211
North, M. M., 83
North, S. M., 83
Nottebohm, F., 322
Notterman, J. M., 176
Novak, M. A., 280

Oachis, A., 8
O'Brien, S., 194
O'Connor, R. D., 298
Oden, D. L., 280
Odum, A. L., 345
Ogden, J. A., 34
O'Hallaren, P., 83
Ohman, A., 108
Olds, J., 208
O'Leary, K. D., 192
O'Leary, S. G., 189
Ollendick, T. H., 300
Olness, K., 80
Olson, R. D., 181
Olson, S. L., 349
Olton, D. S., 244, 258–259
O'Mara, H., 249
Ona, A., 309
Ono, K., 35, 128

Ophir, I., 62, 107
O'Reilly, M. F., 250
Osborne, S., 139
O'Scalaidhe, S. P., 254
Osgood, C. E., 312
Ost, L. G., 108, 300
Overmier, J. B., 52, 184

Pace, G. M., 197
Pace, T. M., 185
Packer, J. S., 108
Paclawskyj, T. R., 132
Page, H. A., 180
Paletta, M. S., 112–113
Palmatier, M. I., 70
Palmer, C., 313
Papini, M. R., 101
Pardes, H., 12
Parker, G. A., 223
Parsons, L., 56
Patterson, F. G., 275
Patterson, G. R., 293
Paul, G. L., 82, 167
Paulsen, K., 350
Pavlov, I. P., 105, 229
Pear, J., 165
Pearce, J. M., 98, 145
Penfield, W., 35
Pennypacker, H. S., 236
Pepperberg, I. M., 246, 269, 275, 278
Perdeck, A. C., 43
Perez-Montfort, R., 80
Perlow, S., 347
Perret, S. P., 116
Perrins, R., 325
Peterson, A. L., 251
Peterson, G. B., 143
Peterson, L. R., 259
Peterson, M. J., 259
Peterson, N., 25, 232
Peterson, R. F., 25, 286
Petitto, L. A., 276
Petrinovich, L. F., 12
Pfautz, P. L., 78
Phelps, B. J., 150, 279
Phillips, D. P., 297
Phillips, E. L., 194
Phillips, R. G., 117
Piaget, J., 296
Pilloff, D., 314
Pina, S., 112
Pincus, H. A., 12
Pinsker, H., 49

Pitariu, H., 8
Pittenger, D. J., 10
Platt, J., 133
Platt, J. R., 162, 189, 355
Poling, A., 332
Polka, L., 46
Pologe, B., 270
Popper, K., 6
Portier, S. J., 323
Postman, L., 212
Poulson, C. L., 286, 289
Pouthas, V., 159
Powell, R. W., 150
Prelec, D., 337
Preston, R. A., 343
Premack, D., 215–216, 274, 276–278
Presentacion, M. J., 301
Pribram, K. H., 32
Primack, W., 86
Prince, S. E., 171
Privat, A. M., 186
Prochaska, J., 193
Provine, R. R., 43

Rachlin, H. C., 131, 141, 182, 187–188, 332, 337–338, 345, 348, 354
Rachman, S., 81, 295
Radojevic, V., 211
Raeburn, J. M., 301
Ragusa, D. M., 349
Raineri, A., 354
Rajigah, L. S., 86
Ramirez-Amaya, V., 80
Rapp, J. T., 220
Rashotte, M. E., 100
Rauhut, A. S., 99
Rauzin, R., 249
Ray, K. P., 219
Rayner, R., 81
Razran, G., 72
Redmon, W. K., 330
Reese, E. S., 44–45
Reeve, K. F., 286
Reeve, L., 286
Reeves, A., 34
Reeves, A. J., 33
Reff, D., 111
Regan, T., 12
Reid, A. K., 341
Reid, J. B., 293
Reisel, W. D., 185

Rescorla, R. A., 65–66, 72, 75, 98, 100–103, 142, 145, 176, 182, 205–206
Revusky, S. H., 110
Reymann, K. G., 34
Reynolds, B., 312
Reynolds, G. S., 238, 333, 335
Rhoades, H., 132
Rhodes, D. L., 190
Rice, M. L., 294
Richards, J. B., 155
Richards, C. S., 251
Richards, D. G., 275
Richards, W. G., 116
Ricker, S., 113
Rickert, E. J., 217
Rider, R. A., 312
Riley, D. A., 259
Rilling, M., 236, 241, 253, 256
Rimm, D.C., 350
Rimm, S., 350
Ritter, B., 299
Rivera, D. M., 297
Robbins, S. J., 69
Robert, M., 283
Roberts, J., 220
Roberts, S., 266–268
Roberts, W. A., 253, 255, 258, 262, 268, 272, 279
Robertson, B., 332
Rodgers, W., 213
Rodriguez, A., 165
Rodriguez, B. I., 300
Rodriguez, M. L., 350
Roediger, H. L., 7
Rohlman, D. S., 132
Roitblat, H. L., 253, 257, 263, 270
Roper, T. J., 223, 262
Rosch, E., 245
Rosen, B., 291–292
Rosenthal, R., 9
Rosenthal, T. L., 296
Rosenzweig, M. R., 32–33
Ross, D., 287, 293
Ross, J. A., 351
Ross, R. T., 102–103
Ross, S. A., 287, 293
Rowland, W. J., 44
Rozin, P., 79, 104, 111, 213
Rubens, W. S., 293
Rubert, E., 277
Rudolph, R. L., 232
Rudy, J. W., 262–263

Rumbaugh, D. M., 275–276
Rundell, L. J., 49
Runyon, R. P., 10
Rushford, N. B., 47
Russek, M., 112
Russell, R. H., 191
Russo, L., 197
Russon, A. E., 284, 290

Sabol, K. E., 155
Sachs, D. A., 194
Sacks, B., 183, 194
Saeki, D., 353
Sagvolden, T., 161
Sakagami, T., 341
Sakamoto, J., 247
Sahoo, F. M., 185
Sailor, W., 17
Saladin, M. E., 75
Salmon, D. P., 257
Salmoni, A. W., 307
Samuelson, R. J., 259
Sanders, R. J., 276
Sands, S. F., 265
Santiago, H. C., 265
Saunders, S. S., 276
Savage, T., 132
Savage-Rumbaugh, E. S., 275–277
Savastano, H. I., 341
Schachtman, T. R., 98
Schaffer, R., 323
Schaefer, H. H., 167
Scharff, L., 211
Schallert, T., 33
Schell, A. M., 108
Schlinger, H., 151
Schlosberg, H., 60, 207, 244
Schmidt, M. H., 46
Schmidt, R. A., 307–311, 313, 317, 319, 324–325
Schmitz, J., 132
Schneider, J. W., 332
Schneiderman, N., 74, 117
Schneirla, T. C., 41
Schoener, T. W., 223
Schoenfeld, W. N., 175–176
Schoenfield, D., 277
Schreurs, B. G., 118
Schrier, A. M., 246
Schugens, M. M., 117–118
Schull, J., 112
Schuster, R., 188
Schusterman, R. J., 275

Schwartz, B., 239
Schwartz, J. H., 49
Schwartz, M. S., 211
Schwartz, S. M., 251
Schwartz, S. P., 211
Schweitzer, J. B., 350
Scopatz, R. A., 270
Sears, R. R., 292
Seiden, L. S., 155
Seligman, M. E. P., 104–106, 110, 179, 181, 184–186
Semjen, A., 324
Sevcik, R. A., 276–277
Shade, D., 156, 301, 332
Shaffer, L. H., 322
Shah, K., 336
Shahani, U., 51
Shapira, Z., 354
Shapiro, D. C., 308–309, 319
Shapiro, E., 50
Shapiro, K. J., 12
Shavalia, D. A., 259
Shea, C. H., 312, 325
Shea, M. C., 332
Sheffield, F. D., 213–214
Shen, B., 34
Shepard, R. N., 110, 264
Shepherd, G. M., 34
Sherburne, L. M., 262, 279
Sherman, J. A., 286
Sherman, J. E., 111
Sherman, L., 347
Sherman, R. A., 200
Sherry, D. F., 264
Shettleworth, S. J., 110, 264
Shimoff, E., 158–159, 161
Shimosawa, T., 211
Shimp, C. P., 162–163, 342
Shoda, Y., 350
Shore, B. A., 192
Shors, T. J., 34
Shurtleff, D., 99
Siddle, D. A. T., 96, 108
Sidman, M., 177, 248–249, 257
Siegel, S., 64, 75, 110–112
Sigman, C., 350
Signorielli, N., 293
Silberberg, A., 223, 337, 341–343
Silva, F. J., 145
Silva, K. M., 145
Silverman, I. W., 349
Simmelhag, V. L., 127, 146
Sisk, C. L., 100
Sisson, L. A., 196

Siuciak, J. A., 186
Sizemore, O. J., 132
Skinner, B. F., 2, 14–16, 69,
    125–126, 136, 146, 148,
    158, 162–163, 186–187, 207
Slobin, P., 258
Smith, D. D., 297
Smith, E. E., 254
Smith, G. J., 264
Smith, J. E., 182
Smith, J. W., 84
Smith, K., 207
Smith, K. U., 308
Smith, M. C., 73
Smith, N., 193
Smith, O. A., 116
Smith, R. G., 197
Smith, T., 166
Smith, W. P., 290
Sodetz, F. J., 224
Solomon, K., 185
Solomon, P. R., 73, 117
Solomon, R. L., 52–56, 174,
    177, 184
Soltysik, S., 176
Solvason, H. B., 80
Sparrow, W. A., 316
Spear, N. E., 71, 99, 264
Spellman, B. A., 49
Spence, K. W., 67, 234–236
Spencer, D. D., 34
Spencer, W. A., 47
Spetch, M. L., 91, 234
Spiegel, J., 295
Spiga, R., 132
Spinelli, D. H., 33
Spinnler, H., 35
Stabler, J. R., 309
Staddon, J. E. R., 127, 146, 239,
    279, 341, 343–344
Staples, K., 272
Starr, M. D., 177
Stasiewicz, P. R., 183
Staub, E., 184
Stefan, K., 34
Stein, J. M., 116
Steinhorst, R., 217
Steinmetz, J. W., 61
Steirn, J. N., 259
Stempowski, N. K., 272
Stephens, R., 104
Stewart, J., 64
Stewart, K. E., 234, 247
Stierle, H., 80

Stipp, H. H., 293
Stoddard, S. J., 242
Stoffelmayr, B. E., 217
Stotland, E., 290
Stout, R., 286
Stoyva, J. M., 210
Strang, H. R., 193
Strauss, K. E., 62, 107–108
Stricker, J. M., 220
Stuart, R. B., 170, 350
Stubbs, A., 266
Sturges, J. W., 83
Sturges, L. V., 83
Sulzer-Azaroff, B., 170, 350
Summers, J. J., 316, 324
Sunderland, T., 118
Suomi, S. J., 280
Swain, J. C., 168
Swan, J. A., 145
Swinnen, S. P., 308–309
Szabadi, E., 336

Tailby, W., 248–249
Tait, R. W., 75
Takatsuru, S., 353
Tanapat, P., 34
Tang, Y., 35
Tatham, T. A., 159
Taub, E., 322
Tauc, L., 114–115
Taylor, A. E., 211
Taylor, B. A., 166
Taylor, I., 250
Teasdale, J. D., 185
Temple, W., 332
Terhune, J. G., 216
Terrace, H. S., 145, 240–241,
    269, 271–272, 275–277
Terry, W. S., 260
Tharp, R. G., 351
Thomas, D. R., 237, 264
Thomas, J., 131
Thomas, J. R., 337
Thompson, R. F., 35, 47,
    116–117
Thompson, R. H., 197, 219
Thompson, R. K. R., 280
Thorndike, E. L., 121–122, 202,
    205, 306
Thorne, B. M., 10
Thorpe, W. H., 283, 298
Thurstone, L. L., 320
Tiffany, S. T., 55, 112

Timberlake, W., 127, 144–145,
    218–219
Timmann, D., 51
Tinbergen, N., 43–44
Tinklepaugh, O. L., 205
Tischler, M. D., 51
Todrank, J., 79
Tolman, E. C., 203–205,
    288–289
Tomie, A., 64, 100
Towe, A. L., 246
Tracy, W. K., 232
Trapold, M. A., 67
Trattner, J., 218
Trinkaus, J. W., 8
Tripathy, S., 185
Trowbridge, M. H., 306–307
Trudel, M., 349
Truglio, R., 294
Tryon, W. W., 77
Tupper, W. E., 83
Turner, E. R. A., 283–284
Turner, H. S., 219–220
Turner, L. H., 52
Turney, T. H., 246
Tzetzis, G., 310

Ulrich, R., 323
Ulrich, R. E., 191
Underwood, B. J., 207
Urcuioli, P. J., 257–258
Uretsky, D. L., 185
Usher, S., 189
Usherwood, P. N. R., 116
Uyeyama, R. K., 277

Vaitl, D., 96
Van den Bergh, O., 77
Vander Wall, S. B., 264
Van Galen, G. P., 323
Van Hasselt, V. B., 196
Van Houten, R., 197
Van Sant, P., 247
Van-Toller, C., 189
Van Wieringen, P., 309
Vauclair, J., 253
Vaughan, W., 164, 249, 263,
    336, 339, 343
Velazquez, E., 73
Verry, D. R., 270
Verwey, W. B., 324
Vienero, V., 292
Vigorito, M., 99

Vizelberg, I. A., 296
Voegtlin, W. L., 83–84
Vogel, W., 86
Volkovskis, C., 112
Vollmer, T. R., 198
von Fersen, L., 279
von Holst, E., 41–42
Vossen, J. M., 103
Vuchinich, R. E., 221, 225
Vyse, S. A., 340

Wade, M., 229
Wagner, A. R., 75, 78, 101,
   112–114, 116, 260, 262–262
Wagner, G. A., 128
Waite, B. E., 290, 297
Wakita, M., 247
Walder, L. O., 293
Wallin, J. A., 169
Walsh, K. E., 116
Walter, C. B., 307
Walters, R. H., 282, 291–292
Walton, D., 197
Wanchisen, B. A., 159
Warden, C. J., 284
Warren, J. M., 243
Warren-Boulton, F. R., 343
Wasserman, E. A., 74, 142–143,
   145, 247
Watanabe, S., 247
Watson, D. L., 351
Watson, J. B., 13, 81
Watson, J. E., 47
Watson, T. S., 196, 219–220
Wearden, J. H., 159
Weaver, M. S., 265
Weaver, M. T., 211
Webster, M. M., 108
Weeks, D. J., 320
Wegner, D. M., 314
Weinberger, N. M., 51
Weiner, H., 159
Weinstein, P., 295
Weisberg, P., 286
Weisman, R. G., 176
Weiss, F., 56
Weiss, K. R., 325
Weisz, D. J., 117
Welsh, T. M., 168–169

Werden, D., 185
Werker, J. F., 46
Werner, G. A., 169
Werner, G. E., 223
Werz, W. A., 258
Wesolowski, M.D., 194–195
West, A., 12
Whalen, C., 299
Whishaw, I. Q., 33–34
Whitacre, C., 312
White, A. G., 195, 325
White, K., 66
White, M. A., 307
Whitehouse, W. G., 348
Whiten, A., 283
Whiting, H. T., 309
Whitlow, J. W., 262–263
Whittam, T. S., 353
Wickelgren, W. A., 35
Wiegand, S. J., 186
Wiertelak, E., 237
Wiesel, T. N., 30, 32, 37
Wike, E. L., 203
Wilcoxon, H. C., 107
Wilkie, D. M., 257–258
Williams, B. A., 239
Williams, D. R., 141
Williams, H., 141, 272
Williams, J. L., 186
Williams, K. S., 126
Williamson, A., 34
Wilson, A., 117
Wilson, D. M., 322
Wilson, F. A., 254
Windle, M., 296
Wing, L., 165
Winn, A. R., 170
Winnick, W. A., 70
Winstein, C. J., 307
Winter, J., 242
Wishart, J. G., 241–242
Wolpe, J., 82, 298
Woltersdorf, M. A., 301
Wolz, J. P., 275
Wong, F. Y., 294
Wood, D. C., 47
Wood, W., 294
Woodburn, L. T., 350
Woodruff, G., 278
Woodruff-Pak, D. S., 61

Woodson, R., 283
Worsdell, A. S., 219–220
Wright, A. A., 247, 265
Wright, D. L., 312
Wright, J., 294
Wrzesniewski, A., 79
Wulf, G., 307, 312, 325
Wulff, J. J., 213–214
Wylie, R. C., 313
Wynne, C. D., 279
Wynne, C. D. L., 279
Wynne, L. C., 174, 177, 184
Wyrwicka, W., 284

Yamadori, A., 35
Yamamoto, J., 249
Yates, C. M., 200
Yell, M. L., 195
Yerkes, R. M., 59
Yin, H., 99
Yoshikubo, S., 246
Young, D. E., 309–311
Young, G. C., 85
Young, M., 86
Young, R., 35
Young, S. L., 56
Yule, W., 183

Zalstein-Orda, N., 96
Zamble, E., 100
Zander, A., 290
Zarcone, J. R., 219
Zdanowski, D. M., 350
Zeiss, A. R., 349
Zelaznik, H. N., 322
Zeldin, R. K., 244
Zellner, D. A., 56
Zener, K., 63
Zentall, T. R., 249, 257–259,
   262, 279
Zhuikov, A. Y., 183
Zimmerman, B. J., 296–297
Ziriax, J. M., 342
Zirkel, P. A., 200
Zito, B., 64
Zubiaur, M., 309
Zygmont, D. M., 242

# Subject Index

ABAB design, 194–195
Absenteeism, 168–169
Absolute theory of stimulus control, 232–237
Accidents, avoiding, 169–170
Achievement motivation, 291–292
Achievement Place, 194
Acquisition:
  in classical conditioning, 67–68, 103–110
  definition, 2
  of motor skills, 306–326
  in operant conditioning, 136, 139–146
  in Rescorla-Wagner model, 90, 93
  of taste aversions, 104–110
  without reinforcement, 203–205, 288–289
  without response, 202–203, 288–289
Action system, 38–39 (*see also* Control systems theory)
  in motor skills, 315–320
Actual input, 38–39 (*see also* Control systems theory)
  in motor skills, 315–320
Adam's two-stage theory of motor learning, 314–317
Adaptation-level theory of peak shift, 237
Addiction, 55–56, 110–113, 224–225, 295–296

Additivity theory of behavioral contrast, 239
Aggression:
  and discrimination learning, 240–241
  and observational learning, 286–288, 292–293
  and punishment, 191
  and television viewing, 293–295
Ainslie-Rachlin theory of self-control, 345–351
Alcoholism, 83–84, 295–296
Alternation task, 244
Alternative behaviors:
  and matching law, 332–335
  and punishment effectiveness, 190, 197–199
  and self-control, 349
  and stimulus control, 250–252
Amount of reinforcement, 156
  and matching law, 331–332
  and self-control choice, 344–351
Analgesia, as a UR, 110–112
Analogies, 278–279
Anecdotes, as data in science, 7–8
Animal cognition (*see* Cognition)
Animal language (*see* Language)
Animal subjects:
  advantages and disadvantages of, 11–12
  ethical issues, 12–13
Ant, 41

Anticipation, errors of, 322–323
Aplysia:
  classical conditioning in, 114–116
  habituation in, 49–51
A-process (*see* Opponent-process theory)
Arborization, 33
Assertiveness training, 298
Associationism, 19–23
  Aristotle's principles, 19–20
  Brown's secondary principles, 22–23
  contiguity principle, 19–20
  contrast principle, 20
  similarity principle, 20
Associations:
  and contextual stimuli, 100–101
  CS-CS, 101–102
  in first-order conditioning, 64–66, 99–100
  and occasion setting, 102–103
  in operant conditioning, 205–206
  in second-order conditioning, 100
  S-S, 64–66, 99–103
  S-R, 64–66, 99–103
  within-compound, 101–102
Associative strength:
  in Rescorla-Wagner model, 89–96
  and Spence's theory of generalization, 234–237

Asymptote:
   in Rescorla-Wagner model,
      89–96
   and US intensity, 67–68
Attention (*see also* Orienting
      response)
   and CS preexposure effect,
      96–97
   Mackintosh's theory, 97–98
   and observational learning,
      287–288
   as reinforcer, 171, 192,
      197–198
Autism, 165–167, 298–299
Automatic reinforcement,
      219–220
Autoshaping, 141–146
Aversive counterconditioning,
      83–85
Aversive events (*see* Avoidance;
      Learned helplessness;
      Punishment)
Aversives controversy,
      199–200
Avoidance, 174–184
   cognitive theory, 179–183
   definition, 173
   one-factor theory, 177–179,
      182–183
   preparedness in, 181–182
   Sidman task, 177–178
   species-specific defense
      reactions, 181–182
   two-factor theory, 175–177,
      182–183
Avoidance paradox, 175, 179
Axon, 27–28
Axon terminal, 27–28


Backward associations, 26
Backward chaining, 137–138
Backward conditioning, 74–75
Behavior decelerators,
      192–199
Behavioral approach, compared
      to cognitive, 11–16, 26–27,
      267, 288–289
Behavioral contrast, 238–239
Behavioral ecology, 222–223
Behavioral economics,
      221–225
Behavioral theory of timing, 267
Behaviorism (*see* Behavioral
      approach)

Behavior modification:
   with autistic children,
      165–167
   aversive counterconditioning,
      83–85
   biofeedback, 209–211
   in business, 168–170
   in classroom, 192
   contingency contracts, 170
   definition, 4
   and errorless learning,
      241–242
   flooding, 183–184
   with married couples,
      170–171
   in mental institutions,
      131–132, 167–168
   modeling, 297–302
   for nocturnal enuresis,
      85–86
   Premack's principle,
      216–218
   punishment, 192–194
   for self-control, 350–351
   shaping, 131–132, 165–167
   and stimulus control,
      249–252
   systematic desensitization,
      80–83
   token economy, 167–168
Behavioral marriage therapy,
      170–171
Behavioral momentum, 157
Behaviors as reinforcers,
      214–220
Behavior-systems analysis of
      autoshaping, 144–145
Behavior therapy (*see* Behavior
      modification)
Beta waves, 211
Bias, in choice behavior,
      330–331
Biased sample, 8
Biofeedback, 209–211
Biological constraints on
      learning:
   in avoidance, 181–182
   in human learning, 107–108
   in operant conditioning,
      139–146
   in taste-aversion learning,
      104–110
Biorhythm theory, 4–11
Birdsong, 322
Blocking effect, 88–89, 95, 98

Blood pressure, 211
B-process (see Opponent-
      process theory)
British Associationists,
      20–23, 26 (*see also*
      Associationism)
Bruxism, 193–194
Butterfly effect, 17


Cache, 264
Calcium current, 50
Case histories, as data in science,
      7–8
Categorization, 35, 244–249
Cats, 30–32, 121–125, 243,
      284
Central category members,
      245
CER (*see* Conditioned
      suppression)
Cerebellum, 116–118
Cerebral cortex:
   growth of, 32–33
   and memory, 34–35
   and vision, 30–32
Chain (*see* Chained schedules,
      Chaining, Reaction chain,
      Response chain)
Chained schedules, 156
Chaining:
   backward, 137–138
   forward, 138–139
Changeover delay, 331
Chaos theory, 16–17
Chickens, 121, 233
Chicks, 143–144, 232, 284
Child abuse, 292
Chimpanzees, 233, 235–236,
      273–280
Choice,
   and matching law, 328–343
   and melioration theory,
      336–337
   and momentary maximization
      theory, 341–343
   and optimization theory,
      221–225, 337–341
   and preference for variability,
      352–353
   between punished and
      unpunished responses,
      187–188, 351
   self-control, 344–351
Chunking, 270–273

Classical conditioning,
58–120
acquisition, 67–68, 90, 93–94,
104–110
and autoshaping, 142–146
blocking, 88–89, 95, 97–98
comparator theories, 98–99
conditioned inhibition, 71–72,
90–91, 95–96
extinction, 68–69, 90–91
generalization, 72–73
and immune system, 79–80
Mackintosh's theory, 97–98
opponent-process theories,
112–114
paradigm, 59–60
physiological research,
114–119
preparedness in, 103–110
rehearsal in, 262–263
Rescorla-Wagner model,
89–99
role of reinforcement,
206–207
spontaneous recovery,
69–70
temporal relationships,
73–76
therapies based on, 80–86
Clock (*see* Timing)
Closed-loop movements, 305
Closed-loop system, 38–39 (*see
also* Control systems theory)
Cocktail party phenomenon, 97
Code:
abstract, 277–280
imaginal, 277–280
Coding:
prospective, 257–259
retrospective, 257–259
Cognition, 253–280
Cognitive approach:
in animal learning, 253–280
and avoidance, 179–183
compared to behavioral approach, 11–16, 26–27, 267,
288–289
and learned helplessness,
184–186
and observational learning,
286–290
Color:
and generalization gradients,
227–228, 231–232
sensory receptors for, 29

Commons tragedy, 354–356
Comparative cognition (*see*
Cognition)
Comparator, 38–39 (*see also*
Control systems theory)
Comparator theories, 98–99
Comparison stimulus, 255
Compensatory CR, 110–114
Complex idea, 21–22, 30–32,
34–36
Compound CS:
definition, 71
procedures employing, 88–99,
102–103
in Rescorla-Wagner model,
89–96
Concept formation, 244–249
Concurrent schedules, 156,
326–332, 335–343
Concurrent VI VI, 328–332,
335–343
Concurrent VI VR, 340–341
Concurrent VR VR, 336–337
Conditioned compensatory
response, 64, 110–114
Conditioned emotional response
(*see* Conditioned
suppression; Emotions)
Conditioned inhibition, 71–72
(*see also* Inhibition)
in avoidance, 176
and backward conditioning,
75
with negative CS-US
correlation, 75–76
physiological mechanisms,
117
in Rescorla-Wagner model,
90–91, 95–96
Conditioned opponent theories,
112–114
Conditioned reinforcers:
definition, 130
and real-world behaviors,
137
in a response chain, 137–139
compared to second-order
conditioning, 136
in a token economy, 167–168
Conditioned response (*see also*
Classical conditioning)
common examples of, 60–63
definition, 59
topography, compared to UR,
63–64, 110–114, 142–145

Conditioned stimulus (*see also*
Classical conditioning)
in avoidance, 175–179
definition, 59
interaction with US,
105–110
representation in brain,
Pavlov's theory, 63–65
salience of, 90, 95
second-order, 76–78, 100
Conditioned suppression:
compared to punishment,
187–188
description, 61–62
experiments employing,
75–76, 88–89
Cone, 29
Confounding variable, 9
Conservation task, 296–297
Constraints on learning (*see*
Biological constraints on
learning)
Contextual stimuli:
and comparator theories,
98–99
and CS preexposure, 101
and drug tolerance,
110–112
and US preexposure, 101
Contiguity (*see also* Delay)
in Associationism, 19–20
in classical conditioning,
73–76
versus correlation, 75–76
in list learning, 25–26
in operant conditioning,
122–128, 129–130
in punishment, 109,
192
and taste-aversion learning,
104–105, 108–110
Contingency:
four types, operant conditioning, 173–174
in punishment, 187–188
reciprocal, 216–219
three-term, 135–136
Contingency contract, 170
Contingency-shaped behaviors,
156–159
Continuous movements, 305
Continuous reinforcement, 148,
154–155
Contraprepared associations,
106–110

Contrast:
  behavioral, 238–239
  in classical conditioning, 73
  as a principle of Association-
    ism, 20
Control systems theory, 38–39
  applied to flexion reflex, 40
  applied to kinesis, 41
  and motor learning, 314–320
Correlation:
  in autoshaping, 142
  versus causation, 293
  versus contiguity, in classical
    conditioning, 75–76
  response-reinforcer, 163–165
Counterconditioning, aversive,
  83–85
Counting (*see also* Serial pattern
    learning)
  by chimpanzee, 269
  and conditional discrimina-
    tion, 269
  by parrot, 269
  by rats, 268–269
CR (*see* Conditioned response)
Crab, 44
CRF (see Continuous
    reinforcement)
Critical period, 32
CS (*see* Conditioned stimulus)
CS effectiveness, theories of,
  96–98
CS preexposure effect, 96–98,
  101 (*see also* Habituation)
Cumulative recorder, 148–149
Curare, 208–209
Cyclophosphamide, 80

Decelerators, behavior,
  192–199
Decisions (*see* Choice; Risk
    taking)
Deep-muscle relaxation, 82
Deer, 77
Delay (*see also* Contiguity; Self-
    control)
  in classical conditioning,
    73–75
  of feedback, in motor
    learning, 308–309
  in list learning, 24–25
  in maze learning, 108–109
  in operant conditioning,
    129–130

preference for variability,
    352–353
  in punishment, 109, 188–189
  of reinforcement, 130, 156,
    344–353
  in taste-aversion learning,
    104–105, 108–110
  in variable-interval schedules,
    341–343
Delay of gratification (*see* Self-
    control)
Delayed matching to sample,
  255–257
  symbolic, 257
Delay reduction theory, 343–344
Demand, 223–225
Dendrites, 27–28
  growth of, 32–33
Dependent variable:
  definition, 5
  in psychological theories,
    14–16
Depression, 185–186
Deprivation:
  food, 189, 212–213
  response, 218–219
  sensory, 32, 232
  water, 14–16, 142–143, 213
Deprivation experiment, 43
Desensitization (*see* Systematic
    desensitization)
Determinism, 16–17
Devaluation:
  of reinforcer, 205–206
  of US, 65–66, 100
Deviations from matching,
  330–331
Differential reinforcement of
    alternative behaviors, 190,
    197–199
Differential reinforcement of
    high rates, 155–156
Differential reinforcement of
    low rates, 155
Discrete movements, 305
Discrimination (*see* Concept
    formation; Discriminative
    stimulus; Generalization;
    Generalization gradients)
  in classical conditioning,
    72–73
  conditional, 257
  errorless learning, 240–242
  intradimensional training, 231
  in operant conditioning, 136

presence-absence training,
    229–231
  reversal, 244
  simultaneous, 233–238
  successive, 233–234, 236–238
  temporal, in FI schedule,
    265–267
Discrimination hypothesis of
    extinction, 154–155
Discriminative stimulus (*see also*
    Discrimination; Generaliza-
    tion; Generalization
    gradients)
  in behavior modification,
    249–252
  definition, 135
  expectations involving,
    205–206
  extinction as, 154–155, 179
  flooding procedure as, 180
  FR postreinforcement pause
    as, 160
  and observational learning,
    285
  punishment as, 190
  in response chains, 137–139
  in three-term contingency,
    135
  time as, in FI schedule,
    265–267
Disinhibition, 70
Disturbance, 39 (*see also* Control
    systems theory)
Double alternation task, 244
Double-blind procedure, 10
Drive reduction, 213–214
Drug tolerance, 110–113 (*see also*
    Addiction)
Ducklings, 232
Dung fly, 223
Duplex idea, 22

Echolalia, 165
Economics, behavioral, 221–225
Effort, 156
Elasticity:
  of demand, 223–224
  of drug use, 224–225
Electrical stimulation of the
    brain, 143, 208–209
Emetic, 83 (*see also* Taste
    aversion)
Emotions (*see also* Conditioned
    suppression; Fear; Phobias)

and classical conditioning, 78–79
and opponent-process theory, 52–56
during punishment, 190–191
Enhancement, local, 284
Enuresis, nocturnal, 85–86
Equipotentiality premise, 105–110 (*see also* Biological constraints on learning; Preparedness)
Equivalence, stimulus, 248–250
Errorless discrimination learning, 240–242
ESB, 143, 208–209
Escape, 173–175 (*see also* Avoidance)
from punishment, 191
Ethical issues:
    and animal research, 12–13
    and aversive stimuli, 199–200
Evaluative conditioning, 77–78
Excitatory CS (*see also* Classical conditioning; Conditioned stimulus)
    and CS-US relationships, 73–76
    definition, 71
    and Rescorla-Wagner model, 89–90, 93–96
Expectation:
    in avoidance, 179–181
    and imitation, 288–289
    in learned helplessness, 184–186
    and learning, memory, 260–263
    about reinforcer, 205–206
    in Rescorla-Wagner model, 89–93
Expectation effect, 9
Expected post-trial episode, 262–263
Experimental techniques, 9–10
Extinction:
    of avoidance behavior, 177, 180–181
    and behavior modification, 196–197
    and behavioral contrast, 238–239
    in classical conditioning, 68–69, 90–91
    of drug tolerance, 111
    generalization tests in, 228

in operant conditioning, 136, 154–155
of phobias, 81–83, 183–184, 299–300
and reinforcement schedules, 154–155
Eyeblink conditioning:
    description, 60–61
    experiments employing, 66–68, 72–75, 262–263
    physiological research on, 116–119
    possible reinforcement in, 207
    theoretical analyses, 63, 113, 207

Facilitation:
    and occasion setting, 102–103
    social, 283–284
Fading, 166, 240
Falsifiability, 6
Fatigue:
    and FR postreinforcement pause, 160–161
    and motor learning, 311–312
Fear (*see also* Conditioned suppression; Fear; Phobias)
    and avoidance responses, 175–183
    and higher-order conditioning, 77
    and punishment, 190
Fear hierarchy, 82
Feature detectors:
    in hearing, taste, and touch, 29–30
    in vision, 30–32
Feedback (*see also* Control systems theory; Knowledge of results)
    sensory, removal of, 322
Fetish, 84–85
FI (*see* Fixed interval)
First-order conditioning, associations in, 64–66, 99–100
Fish:
    orientation by, 41–42
    prey selection by, 223
    territorial defense, 43
Fixed action pattern, 42–44
Fixed interval, 152–154
    extinction, 154–155
    human performance, 158–159
    punishment schedule, 189

Fixed ratio, 149–150
    compared to variable ratio, 352
    with drugs, 224
    extinction, 154–155
    punishment schedule, 189
    theories of postreinforcement pause, 160–161
Flooding, 180, 183–184
Food aversion (*see* Taste aversion)
Forgetting:
    in classical conditioning, 68
    directed, 260–261
    of habituation, 48
    of lists of nonsense syllables, 24–25
    in motor learning, 308–309, 315–320
Forward chaining, 138–139
FR (*see* Fixed ratio)
Free association, 19–20
Free operant, 134–135
Free-operant avoidance, 177–178
Free will, 16–17
Frequency principle (*see also* Practice)
    in Associationism, 23
    limitations, 88–89, 91–92
    in list learning, 24
Fruitfulness of a scientific theory, 7
Functional analysis, 219–220

Gagging, 194
Galvanic skin response (*see* Skin conductance response)
Gambling, 354
Generality of a scientific theory, 7
Generalization (*see also* Concept formation; Discrimination; Generalization gradients; Transfer of learning)
    in classical conditioning, 72–73
    in extinction after partial reinforcement, 155
    of habituation, 48
    and imitation, 285–286, 288–289
    in learned helplessness, 184–186
    in modeling, 299–301

Generalization (*cont.*)
in motor learning, 312–314,
317–320
in operant conditioning, 136
Generalization decrement hypothesis of extinction, 155
Generalization gradients:
in classical conditioning, 72
inhibitory, 236–237
after intradimensional
training, 231–232
Lashley and Wade theory,
229–232
measurement of, 227–228
after nondifferential training,
229–232
Pavlov's theory, 229–232
peak shift in, 233–236
after presence-absence
training, 229–231
after sensory deprivation, 232
Generalized reinforcer, 136–137
(*see also* Conditioned
reinforcers)
General principles of learning:
challenges to, 103–110,
139–146, 181–182
defense of, 108–110,
145–146
rationale for, 2–4, 103–104
GSR (*see* Skin conductance
response)
Guidance hypothesis of KR,
307–308
Guinea pigs, 128
Gull (*see* Herring gull)

Habituation, 47–56, 66
CS preexposure effect, 96–97,
101
general principles of, 47–49
in infants, 48–49
in opponent-process theory,
52–56
physiological mechanisms,
49–51
in primitive organisms,
49–51
of startle reaction, 51
of an unconditioned response,
101
Headaches, 210
Heart rate:
and avoidance learning,
176–177

as a conditioned response, 64
controlled by reinforcement,
208–209
and opponent-process theory,
53–55
and shock, 53–55, 176–177
Helplessness, learned,
184–186
Hemiplegia, 210–211
Heredity (*see also* Fixed action
pattern; Reaction chain;
Reflex; Tropism)
and imitation, 283–285
influence on avoidance
learning, 181–182
influence on human learning,
107–108
influence on operant
conditioning, 139–146
influence on taste-aversion
learning, 104–110
Hermissenda, 116
Hermit crab, 44–45
Heroin, 113, 224–225, 296
Herring gull, 43
Higher-order conditioning,
76–78, 100
Hippocampus, 117
Hoarding behavior, 199
Humphrey's paradox,
154–155
Hydra, 47
Hyperactivity, 211, 300–301
Hyperalgesia as a CR, 111
Hypothalamus, 117

IACUC, 13
Imitation, (*see also* Modeling;
Observational learning)
of aggressive behavior,
286–288, 292–293
by animals, 283–285
Bandura's theory, 286–289
factors affecting, 290–291
as a generalized operant
response, 285–286
by infants, 283
as an instinct, 283–285
as an operant response, 285
Immediacy (*see* Contiguity;
Delay; Self-control)
Immune system, 79–80
Impulsiveness, 300–301 (*see also*
Self-control)

Independent variable:
definition, 5
in psychological theories,
14–16
Inelasticity (*see* Elasticity)
Inferential statistics, 10–11
Inhibition (*see also* Conditioned
inhibition)
and disinhibition, 70
during extinction, 69
and generalization gradients,
234–237
reactive, 311–312
in Rescorla-Wagner model,
90–91, 95–96
and spontaneous recovery, 69
Inhibitory CS (*see* Conditioned
inhibition)
Insomnia, 251–252
Instinct (*see* Fixed action pattern;
Heredity; Reaction chain;
Reflex; Tropism)
Instinctive drift, 139–141
Instrumental learning (*see*
Operant conditioning)
Intensity, stimulus:
and acquisition of a conditioned response, 67–68,
89–96
and asymptote of conditioned
response, 67–68, 89–96
and habituation, 48
and punishment, 188
Interference (*see also*
Overshadowing)
and memory, 255–256,
264–265
in motor learning, 312–314
proactive, 255–256,
264–265
retroactive, 255–256,
264–265
Interferon, 80
Interim behaviors, 127
Intermediate size problem,
235–237
Internal clock (*see* Timing)
Interresponse times:
definition, 162
punishment of, 189
reinforcement of, 162–165
and VI/VR difference,
162–165
Interval schedules (*see* Fixed
interval; Variable interval)

Intervening variables:
  arguments over the use of,
    14–16
  definition, 5
  in opponent-process theory,
    53–55
  in Rescorla-Wagner model,
    93
Intestinal activity, 209–211
Intradimensional training,
  231–232
Introspection, 13–14
Ironic errors, 314
Irritable bowel syndrome, 211
IRT (*see* Interresponse times)

Kinesis, 40–41
Knowledge of performance,
  309–311 (*see also* Knowledge
  of results)
Knowledge of results (*see also*
  Knowledge of performance)
  compared to reinforcement,
    306–307
  delayed, 308–309
  guidance hypothesis of, 307
  intermittent, 307–308,
    315–316
  quantitative versus qualitative,
    306–308
  withdrawal of, 307–308,
    315–317
KP (*see* Knowledge of
  performance)
KR (*see* Knowledge of results)

Language:
  in animals, 273–277
  in chimpanzees, 273–277
  in dolphins, 275
  and reinforcement schedules,
    158–159
  restored through shaping
    procedure, 131–132
  and stimulus equivalence,
    249–250
  training with autistic children,
    165–167
Latency, response, 111–112,
  122–123 (*see also* Reaction
  time)
Latent learning, 203–205
Law of Effect, 121–129, 306
Law of Practice, 306

Learned helplessness,
  184–186 (*see also* Aversive
  events)
Learning/performance
  distinction, 1–2, 203–205,
  288–290
Learning set, 242–244
Learning to learn, 243
Limax, 116
Line-drawing task, 306–307
List length and memory, 24
Local enhancement, 284
Long-delay conditioning, 74–75,
  104–105, 108–109
Longitudinal studies, 293
Long-term memory, 34–36,
  263–265 (*see also*
  Memory)
Long-term potentiation, 34

Magnetic Resonance Imaging,
  51
Marriage therapy, 170–171
Masochism, 190
Matching law, 328–343
  and amount of reinforcement,
    331–332
  deviations from, 330–331
  and quality of reinforcement,
    331–332
  and single VI schedules,
    332–335
  theories related to, 335–343
Matching to sample, 255
Maximization (*see* Momentary
  maximizing theory;
  Optimization theory)
Maze learning, 108–109,
  206–208
Mean length of utterance, 276
Melioration, 336–337
Memory:
  and chunking, 27–273
  for lists of nonsense syllables,
    23–27
  location in brain, 34–36
  long-term, 263–265
  and observational learning,
    288
  reference, 263–265
  short-term, 254–259
  working, 254–259
Methadone, 225
Microeconomics, 221–225

Model, in observational
  learning, 290–291 (*see also*
  Imitation; Modeling;
  Observational learning)
Modeling (*see also* Imitation;
  Model; Observational
  learning)
  and assertiveness training, 298
  and autistic children,
    298–299
  graduated, 298
  and hyperactive children,
    300–301
  motor skills, 312
  participant, 299–300
  and phobias, 299–300
  and socially withdrawn
    children, 298
  videotaped, 301–302
Molar theories, 162–165,
  335–341
Molecular theories, 161–165,
  341–343
Momentary maximizing theory,
  341–343
Momentum, behavioral, 157
Monkeys:
  imitation by, 284
  learning sets, 242–244
  movement without sensory
    feedback, 322
  and Premack's principle,
    214–216
  short-term memory, 255–256
  visual system, 30–31
Moral standards, 297
Morphine, 64, 110–113
Motor program, 321–326
Motor skills:
  Adams's two-stage theory,
    314–317
  classification of, 304–305
  distribution of practice and,
    311–312
  and imitation, 288
  ironic errors, 314
  knowledge of performance
    and, 309–311
  knowledge of results and,
    306–309
  movement sequences in,
    320–326
  observational learning of, 312
  reinforcement and,
    306–307

Motor skills: (*cont.*)
  Schmidt's schema theory, 317–320, 324–326
  transfer in, 312–314
Motor schema, 317–320
Motor stage, 315–317
Motor trace, 315
Movement sequences, 320–326 (*see also* Reaction chain; Response chain)
MRI (*see* Magnetic Resonance Imaging)
Multiple schedule, 160–161, 238–239

Nativism, 20
Natural categories, 245–248
Natural killer cells, 80
Need reduction, 212–213
Negative contrast, 238
Negative punishment, 173–174, 192, 194–196
Negative reinforcement, 173–184 (*see also* Avoidance; Escape)
Negative transfer, 312–314
Neurogenesis, 33–34
Neurons (*see also* Physiological mechanisms)
  basic characteristics, 27–28
  changes during classical conditioning, 114–119
  changes during habituation, 49–51
  growth of, 33–34
Nocturnal enuresis, 85–86
Noise:
  as a punisher, 193–194
  as an unconditioned stimulus, 65–66
Noncontingent reinforcement, 198
Nondifferential training and generalization gradients, 229–232
Nonsense syllable, 23–27
Number (*see* Counting)
Nutcracker, Clark's, 264

Object permanence, 278
Observational learning, 282–303 (*see also* Imitation; Modeling)

and achievement motivation, 291–292
and addictions, 295–296
and aggression, 286–288, 292–293
and cognitive development, 296–297
compared to operant conditioning, 285–286, 302
interaction with operant conditioning, 291–293
and moral standards, 297
and motor skills, 312
and phobias, 295
and self-control, 291, 349–350
and suicide, 297
and television, 293–295
Observational techniques, 8
Occasion setting, 102–103
Omission (*see also* Negative punishment)
  in autoshaping procedure, 141
  definition, 173
  effects of, 192
  in therapy, 194–196
  of US in classical conditioning, 207
One-factor theory:
  of avoidance, 177–179, 182–183
  and classical/operant distinction, 206–207
Open-loop movements, 305
Operant conditioning, 121–172, 202–225 (*see also* Reinforcement; Reinforcement schedules)
  applications of, 165–171
  definition, 134
  Guthrie and Horton's experiments, 123–124
  shaping, 129–134
  Skinner's approach, 134–139
  superstitious behaviors, 124–128
  Thorndike's research, 121–123
Operant response (*see also* Free operant; Operant conditioning)
  learning without, 202–203
  in three-term contingency, 135
  variability in, 129–134
Opiates, 55–56 (*see also* Heroin)

Opponent-process theory, 52–56, 110–114
Optimization theory, 221–223 (*see also* Momentary maximizing theory)
  and behavioral ecology, 222–223
  as an explanation of matching, 337–341
  and microeconomics, 221–223
  tests of, 222–223, 339–341
Orientation, 41–42
Orienting response:
  as component of a CR, 63
  habituation of, 46
Overcorrection, 196
Overexpectation effect, 91–92
Overlearning:
  in habituation, 48
  in memory for nonsense syllables, 24
  in treatment for nocturnal enuresis, 85–86
Overmatching, 330–331
Overshadowing:
  in classical conditioning, 91, 93–95
  and generalization gradients, 230–231
Oyster catcher, 43–44

Pacemaker, 267
Paradoxical conditioning (*see* Conditioned compensatory response)
Parkinson's disease, 325
Partial reinforcement effect, 154–155
Participant modeling, 299–300
Pavlovian conditioning (*see* Classical conditioning)
Peak shift, 233–237, 241
Percentile schedule, 132–133
Perceptual schema, 317–320
Perceptual trace, 314–317
Performance:
  distinguished from learning, 2, 203–205, 287–289
Peripheral category members, 245
PET (*see* Positron Emission Tomography)

Phobias:
   acquisition through classical
      conditioning, 80–81
   flooding as treatment for,
      183–184
   modeling as treatment for,
      299–300
   observational learning of, 295
   systematic desensitization as
      treatment for, 82–83
Physiological mechanisms:
   of association formation,
      32–36
   of classical conditioning,
      114–119
   of habituation, 49–51
   of spinal withdrawal reflex,
      39–40
   of vision and other senses,
      28–32
Pigs, 140
Placebo, 9
Poison (*see* Aversive countercon-
      ditioning; Taste aversions)
Pollution, 355
Positioning tasks:
   rapid, 316–317
   slow, 308–309, 314
Positive contrast, 238–239
Positive punishment, 173 (*see
      also* Punishment)
Positive reinforcement (*see*
      Reinforcement)
Positive transfer, 312–314
Positron Emission Tomography,
      51, 118–119
Postreinforcement pause:
   on fixed interval schedules,
      152
   on fixed ratio schedules,
      149–150, 160–161
   on variable ratio schedules,
      151
Postsynaptic neuron, 28
   possible changes during
      learning, 34
Post-trial episode, 262–263
Potentiation, long-term, 34
Practice (*see also* Acquisition;
      Frequency principle)
   fixed versus variable, 319–320
   law of, 306
   massed versus distributed,
      311–312
Precommitment, 347–350

Predelinquent boys, 194
Preexposure, stimulus, 96–97,
      101
Preference (*see* Choice)
Preference reversal, 344–346
Preference for variability,
      352–353
Premack's principle, 214–218
Preparedness:
   in avoidance learning,
      181–182
   definition, 106
   and generalization gradients,
      232
   in human learning, 107–108
   in taste-aversion learning,
      105–110
Presence-absence training and
      generalization gradients,
      229–231
Presynaptic neuron, 28
   changes during learning, 34,
      49–50, 115–116
Primary reinforcer:
   definition, 130
   in response chain, 137–139
   in token economy, 167
Probability, behavior (*see also*
      Time allocation)
   and Law of Effect,
      121–126
   and Premack's principle,
      214–218
Probability of reinforcement,
      151, 341–343, 353–354
Probe trials, 228
Progressive relaxation,
      82, 210
Prompt, 166
Punishment, 186–196 (*see also*
      Negative punishment)
   compared to conditioned
      suppression, 187–188
   contingency, importance of,
      187–188
   definition, 173
   delay in, 188–189
   disadvantages, 190–191
   ethical issues, 199–200
   factors influencing
      effectiveness, 188–190
   and imitation, 286–287,
      292–293
   permanence of effects,
      187–188

and Premack's principle,
      216–217
   schedules, 189
   and self-control choices, 351
   in therapy, 192–196
Puzzle box:
   Guthrie and Horton's
      experiments, 123–124
   Thorndike's experiments,
      121–123

Quail, 107, 232
Quality of reinforcement:
   and matching law, 331–332
   and self-control, 348–350

Raccoon, 140–141
Radial-arm maze, 258–259, 272
Random ratio, 151, 169
Rapid positioning task, 316–317
Rate of reinforcement:
   and matching law, 328–335
   optimization of, 337–341
   on variable interval schedules,
      161–165, 332–335
   on variable ratio schedules,
      161–165, 340
Ratio schedules (*see* Fixed ratio;
      Random ratio; Variable
      ratio)
Ratio strain, 150
Reacquisition, 70–71
Reaction chain, 44–45 (*see also*
      Response chain)
Reaction time, 322–324 (*see also*
      Latency, response)
Reactive inhibition, 311–312
Reasoning, 277–280
   analogies, 278–279
   and language training,
      277–280
   and object permanence,
      278
   transitive inference, 279
Recency (*see also* Forgetting)
   and memory for nonsense
      syllables, 24–25
   as a principle of
      Associationism, 23
Reciprocal contingency,
      216–218
Reference input (*see* Control
      systems theory)
   in motor skills, 314–317

Reflex, 39–40
  conditioned (*see* Classical
    conditioning)
  feedback in, 40
  spinal reflex arc, 39
Rehearsal, 259–263
  associative, 260, 262–263
  maintenance, 260–263
Reinforcement (*see also*
    Reinforcement, negative;
    Reinforcement schedules)
  automatic, 219–220
  in classical conditioning,
    possible role, 206–207
  definition, 123
  drive reduction theory,
    213–214
  functional analysis, 219–220
  of imitation, 285–289
  influence of heredity on,
    139–146
  learning without, 203–205
  and motor learning, 306–307
  need reduction theory,
    212–213
  and observational learning,
    291–293
  Premack's principle, 214–218
  response deprivation theory,
    218–219
  and shaping, 129–134
  trans-situationality, 214
Reinforcement history, 159
Reinforcement, negative,
    173–184 (*see also* Escape;
    Avoidance)
  definition, 173
Reinforcement relativity:
  and matching law, 334–335
  and Premack's principle,
    215–218
Reinforcement schedules,
    148–165
  chained, 156
  concurrent, 156, 328–332,
    335–343
  continuous reinforcement,
    148, 154–155
  differential reinforcement of
    high rates, 155–156
  differential reinforcement of
    low rates, 155–156, 159
  extinction after, 154–155
  fixed interval, 152–153,
    157–159

fixed ratio, 149–150, 160–161
  human performance, 159–159
  multiple, 160–161, 238–239
  percentile schedules, 132–133
  and reinforcement history,
    159
  and rule-governed behavior,
    157–159
  variable interval, 153–154,
    161–165, 332–335
  variable ratio, 150–152,
    161–165
Reinforcer (*see also* Conditioned
    reinforcers; Reinforcement;
    Primary reinforcer)
  definition, 123
  devaluation, 205–206
  expectations about, 205–206
  in response chain, 137–139
  in three-term contingency,
    135
Relational theory of stimulus
    control, 232–237
Relaxation, 82, 210
Remaining responses hypothesis
    of FR postreinforcement
    pause, 160–161
Repetition, 24 (*see also* Fre-
    quency principle; Practice)
Rescorla-Wagner model, 89–99
  and acquisition, 90, 93–94
  and blocking, 90, 95
  and conditioned inhibition,
    90–91, 95–96
  and CS preexposure, 96–97
  equations, 92–96
  and extinction, 90–91
  and overexpectation effect,
    91–92
  and overshadowing, 91, 93–95
  weaknesses, 96–97
Response (*see* Conditioned
    response; Operant response;
    Reflex; Unconditioned
    response)
Response blocking, 197 (*see also*
    Flooding)
Response chain, 137–139 (*see also*
    Reaction chain)
  and skilled movements,
    320–326
Response cost, 194–196
Response deprivation theory,
    218–219
Response effort, 156

Response-reinforcer correlation
    in VI and VR, 163–165
Retardation test for conditioned
    inhibition, 71–72
Retina, 29–31
Revaluation, US, 66
Reversal, discrimination, 244
Risk taking, 353–354
RR (*see* Random ratio)
RT (*see* Random time)
Rule-governed behavior,
    158–159

Saccharine, 104–106, 212
Salience, stimulus, 67–68, 90–91,
    93–95 (*see also* Intensity,
    stimulus)
  of absolute versus relational
    cues, 237
  and generalization gradients,
    230–232
Salivary conditioning:
  description, 58–60
  procedures employing,
    68–77
  theoretical analyses of, 63–64,
    207
Sample stimulus, 255
Sampling error, 8, 10
Satiation hypothesis of FR
    postreinforcement pause,
    160–161
Satiation, stimulus, 199
Savings:
  in habituation, 48
  in list learning, 23–26
  in motor learning, 311–314
Scallop, fixed-interval, 152
Schedules of punishment, 189
Schedules of reinforcement
    (*see* Reinforcement
    schedules)
Schmidt's schema theory,
    317–320, 324–326
Scientific theories:
  components of, 5–6
  standards for, 6–7
Secondary reinforcer (*see*
    Conditioned reinforcers)
Second-order conditioning,
    76–78
  associations in, 100
  compared to conditioned
    reinforcement, 136

Self-control, 344–351
   Ainslie-Rachlin theory, 345–346
   in animals, 346–349
   in children, 349–350
   and punishment, 351
   techniques for improving, 350–351
Self-injurious behavior (SIB), 219–220
Self-modeling, videotape, 301–302
Self-reinforcement, 351
Sensations, simple:
   in Associationism, 21–22
   in vision, 28–30
Sensitization, 105
Sensory deprivation, 32, 232
Sensory preconditioning, 78
Sequences, movement, 320–326
   (*see also* Reaction chain; Response chain)
Serial pattern learning, 244, 270, 320–326 (*see also* Chunking)
Sesame Street, 294
Sex drive, 213–214
Shaping, 129–134
   with adults, 131–132
   with autistic children, 165–167
   in autoshaping procedure, 141
   and percentile schedules, 132–133
   and preparedness of response, 182
   with rats, lever pressing, 129–131
Short-delay conditioning, 73–74, 115
Short-term memory, 253–259
Shuttle box, 174–175, 184–186
Sidman avoidance task, 177–178
Significance tests, 11–12
Sign stimulus, 43–44
Sign-tracking, 142–143
Similarity:
   in classical conditioning, 72–73 (*see also* Generalization)
   as a principle of Associationism, 20
   and transfer in motor learning, 312–314
Simple cell in vision, 30–31

Simple idea, 21–22
Simplicity of a scientific theory, 6–7, 14–16
Simultaneous conditioning, 73–74
Single neuron doctrine, 32
Skin conductance response, 62, 108, 207
Slow positioning task, 308–309, 314
S⁻:
   definition, 231
   in errorless discrimination learning, 240–242
   in simultaneous discrimination, 231–237
   in successive discrimination, 231–232, 233–237
   in transfer procedures, 242–244
Smoking:
   aversive counterconditioning as treatment for, 84
   and observational learning, 295–296
Social facilitation, 283–284
Social learning theory, 282–293
   (*see also* Imitation; Observational learning)
Sometimes opponent process theory, 113–114, 116–117
Species-specific defense reactions, 181–182
Speech (*see* Language)
Spinal reflex arc, 39–40 (*see also* Reflex)
S⁺:
   definition, 231
   in errorless discrimination learning, 240–242
   in simultaneous discrimination, 231–237
   in successive discrimination, 231–232, 233–237
   in transfer procedures, 242–244
Spontaneous recovery:
   in classical conditioning, 69–70
   in operant conditioning, 136
Squirrel, 42–43
S-R associations, 64–66, 99–100, 122, 205–206
S-S associations, 64–66, 99–102, 205–206

SSDRs, 181–182
Startle reaction, 46, 51
Stickleback, 43
Stimulus control (*see* Concept formation; Discrimination; Generalization)
Stimulus equivalence, 248–250
Stimulus preexposure, 96–97, 101
Stimulus satiation, 199
Stimulus substitution theory, 63–65
   and autoshaped behaviors, 142–145
Stop-action principle, 123–129
Stretch receptor, 40
Studying, 250–251
Subjective value, 221–222
Substitutability, 220–225
Successive approximations (*see* Shaping)
Suicide, 297
Summation test for conditioned inhibition, 71
Supernormal stimulus, 44
Superstitious behaviors, 124–128
   and autoshaping, 141
Suppression, response, 187–188, 190 (*see also* Conditioned suppression)
Surprise (*see also* Expectation)
   and learning, memory, 262–263
   and Rescorla-Wagner model, 89–90
Surprising post-trial episode, 262–263
Symptom substitution, 83
Synapse, 28
   changes during classical conditioning, 115–116
   changes during habituation, 49–51
   growth of, 32–33
Syntax of a scientific theory, 6
Systematic desensitization, 81–83
   compared to flooding, 183
   compared to modeling, 299


Tabula rasa, 20
Taste aversions, 62–63, 104–110
   (*see also* Aversive counter-conditioning)

Taxis, 41–42
Television viewing:
  and aggression, 293–295
  and reading comprehension, 294
  and suicide, 297
Temperature, body:
  as a conditioned response, 64
  controlled by biofeedback, 211
Terminal behaviors, 127
Testability of a scientific theory, 6
Therapy (*see* Behavior modification)
Thiamine, 212–213
Third-order conditioning, 77
Three-term contingency, 135 205–206
Time (*see also* Contiguity; Delay)
  discrimination of, 265–267
Time allocation:
  and matching law, 333–335
  and momentary maximizing theory, 341–343
  and optimization theory, 222–223, 337–341
  and Premack's principle, 214–218
  and response deprivation theory, 218–219
Time-out, 192, 194–196
Timing (*see also* Contiguity; Delay)
  behavioral theory, 267
  in conditional discrimination, 266–267
  in fixed-interval schedules, 265–267
  in peak procedure, 265–266
  and Weber's law, 266–267
Token economy, 167–168
Tolerance, drug, 55, 110–112
  (*see also* Addiction)

Tone frequency, and generalization gradients, 229–232
Total task method, 138–139
Trace conditioning, 74
Tragedy of the commons, 354–356
Transfer of learning, 242–244, 312–314 (*see also* Generalization)
Transitive inference, 279
Transmitter, chemical, 27–28
  changes during learning, 34, 50–51, 115–116
Transposition, 233–234
Trans-situationality, 214
Tropism, 40–42
Two-factor theory:
  of avoidance, 175–183
  and classical/operant distinction, 206–209
Two-process theory (*see* Two-factor theory)
Two-stage theory of motor learning, Adams's, 314–317
Typing, 322–323, 325

Unconditioned response:
  definition, 59
  topography, compared to CR, 63–64, 110–114, 142–145
Unconditioned stimulus:
  definition, 59
  devaluation, 65–66, 100
  effects of intensity, 67–68
  representation in brain, Pavlov's theory, 64–65
  revaluation, 66
Undermatching, 330–331
Unprepared associations, 106–107
UR (*see* Unconditioned response)
US (*see* Unconditioned stimulus)
US preexposure effect, 101

Value:
  and matching law, 333–335
  and optimization theory, 221–222
Variable interval, 153–154 (*see also* Concurrent VI VI)
  as baseline, 187, 192, 227–231, 238–239
  compared to variable ratio, 161–165, 340–341
  extinction, 154–155
  and matching law, 332–335
Variable ratio, 150–152 (*see also* Concurrent VR VR)
  compared to fixed ratio, 352
  compared to variable interval, 161–165, 340–341
  extinction, 154–155
Verbal-motor stage, 315
VI (*see* Variable interval)
Videotape self-modeling, 301–302
Violence (*see* Aggression)
Virtual reality therapy, 83
Visceral responses:
  control by operant conditioning, 208–211
Vision, 29–32
Visual cortex, 30–32
VR (*see* Variable ratio)

Warmth as a reinforcer, 143–145, 212–214
Water as a reinforcer, 14–16, 142–143
Wavelength of light (*see* Color)
Weber's law, 266–267
Wood louse, 40–41
Working memory, 253–259 (*see also* Memory; Short-term memory)